Restoration
and
Renewal

The Church in the Third Millennium

Joseph F. Eagan, S.J.

D1507671

Sheed & Ward
Kansas City

Sheed & Ward™ is a service of The National Catholic Reporter Publishing Company.

Imprimi potest: Bert Thelen, S.J., Wisconsin Provincial

◆

Library of Congress Cataloguing-in-Publication Data

Eagan, Joseph F., S.J.
    Restoration and renewal : the Church in the third millennium / Joseph F. Eagan.
        p.   cm.
    Includes bibliographical references and index.
    ISBN 1-55612-763-4 (pbk. : alk. paper)
    1. Church. 2. Vatican Council (2nd : 1962-1965) 3. Catholic Church
—Doctrines. 4. Church renewal—Catholic Church. 5. Christianity—
Forecasting. I. Title.
BX1746.E14 1995
282'.09'045—dc20   95-14282
                                               CIP

◆

Published by: Sheed & Ward
                 115 E. Armour Blvd.
                 P.O. Box 419492
                 Kansas City, MO 64141-6492

To order, call: (800) 333-7373

Cover design by Emil Antonucci.

Contents

Part V
Major Issues in Today's Church

Part VI
Toward the Third Millennium

Dedication

Dr. Joseph Vercruysse: scholar-ecumenist, my dissertation director and friend.

Fr. Frank Buckley: theologian, esteemed colleague and Jesuit, valued friend.

Fr. John Eagan: priest, teacher, inspirer of young people, who taught his many friends and admirers how to live fully and die confidently.

Acknowledgments

THIS BOOK IS THE HAPPY RESULT OF A FORTUITOUS EVENT, THE SUPPORT OF some wonderful people, and generous "angels" unexpectedly appearing "out of the sky" as befits such creatures. To all I am immensely grateful, more than these few words can convey.

The joy of teaching University of San Francisco students Theology 305, "Today's Church: Problems and Values," two sections every semester for over a decade, qualifies as our fortuitous event. One day four years ago, Jim Matthews and Lisa Damberger blurted out: "Instead of all those great handouts you give us, why don't you write your own book!" It hit a chord: thanks, Jim and Lisa. I'm indebted to the 140 students who evaluated the result in considerable written specificity at the end of the Fall 1992 and Spring 1993 semesters.

I owe so much to truly wonderful persons, valued colleagues and friends, who supported me throughout: Stanley Nel, USF dean extraordinaire, who encouraged me to keep writing and generously provided student help and a Macintosh computer; colleague Frank Buckley, Jesuit brother, good friend, accomplished theologian, whose constant encouragement and insights were most helpful; esteemed colleagues in the USF theology department, Dr. Ray Noll and Fr. Frank Buckley, plus graduate student Peter Millington, who read the entire work, offering valuable suggestions, and Doctors Hamilton Hess, Jack Elliott, James Counelis, who contributed their expertise to individual sections; highly respected scholars and Jesuit friends, ecclesiologist Avery Dulles, moralists William Spohn and Richard McCormick, liberation theologian Arthur McGovern, and Harvey Egan, spirituality expert, whose detailed comments on individual chapters were enormously valuable.

I feel a special kind of gratitude for these "angels" who happened along the way: Megeen Egan, who so efficiently deciphered and typed my initial patchwork chapters; affable student Alexandra Leonardini, who painstakingly produced computer printouts for the campus print shop and student consumption; the ever-available USF computer analysts Eric Scheide and Clint Powell, who patiently nurtured my stumbling skills; Pat Langley, St. Anselm's smiling secretary, who more than once rescued my computer miscues; Frs. Joe O'Connell and Peter McDonald, friendly Irish pastors of Mt. Carmel and St. Anselm parishes in beautiful Marin County, who welcomed me with open arms as "resident scholar" while I struggled through the revision phase; Fr. Joe Downey, Loyola University Press editor, whose invaluable advice, experience, and encouragement are much appreciated; my Jesuit superior, Fr. Bert Thelen, whose understanding and support provided necessary sabbatical time; finally, an angel deserving of upgrade to archangel rank, computer consultant Gail Ward (who adopted this project after answering an emergency call to extricate me from one of my computer foul-ups), whose expertise, given with unfailing generosity and ever-radiant smile, helped me prepare the final manuscript for the publisher.

To all the above, my profound thanks.

Abbreviations

QUOTATIONS FROM THE 10 VATICAN II DOCUMENTS USED IN THIS BOOK ARE identified by the following two letters — abbreviations of their Latin title — in parentheses with their section number. A few other abbreviations often used are also given.

AA   *Apostolicam actuositatem*: Decree on the Apostolate of the Laity

AG   *Ad gentes:* Decree on the Church's Missionary Activity

DH   *Dignitatis humanae*: Declaration on Religious Freedom

DV   *Dei Verbum*: Dogmatic Constitution on Divine Revelation

GS   *Gaudium et spes*: Pastoral Constitution on the Church in the Modern World

LG   *Lumen gentium*: Dogmatic Constitution on the Church

NA   *Nostra aetate*: Declaration on the Relationship of the Church to the Non-Christian Religions

PC   *Perfectae caritatis*: Decree on the Appropriate Renewal of Religious Life

SC   *Sacrosanctum concilium*: Constitution on the Sacred Liturgy

UR   *Unitatis redintegratio*: Decree on Ecumenism

Other Abbreviations:

BEM   Baptism, Eucharist and Ministry (Faith and Order Commission)

CDF   Congregation for the Doctrine of the Faith (Roman curia)

WCC   World Council of Churches (Geneva, Switzerland)

Preface

"I haven't lost my faith in God but my faith in the church."

"I sometimes feel that what the church is saying is not at all what God is saying."

"I don't feel committed to the institution; I do to Christ."

"Since I was a child I have had nothing but fear when it came to thinking about the church."

"The church has the negative mother syndrome — gave birth to us, then doesn't want to give us freedom."

At the beginning of each course on "The Church Today," I ask my students to write in one page what they honestly feel about the church. No grade will be assigned. The above represent only a few of their comments.

In a second page, I ask them to respond to a forthright question: "What would you like to see changed in the church today and why?" Their answers covered a wide range of concerns.

"The church must be more of a prophet in first-world countries where poverty and ignorance abound amid outrageous wealth."

"There must be much more open-mindedness and toleration for diversity within the church."

"The church's position on sexual matters needs to be inclusive and flexible so the faithful can feel comfortable in a church that is serving the authentic aspirations of young people in sexual matters."

"The world in which we live is now ripe for a renewal of missionary activity."

"With the world population reaching critical numbers and the world's resources dwindling, the church must reflect more seriously about the use of contraceptives."

"Rome must become less authoritarian and live more fully in accord with the collegiality of bishops." (a graduate student)

"I resent the church saying everything about everything."

I then asked them to finish this sentence: "If I were pope, the first thing I'd do is. . . " This provoked both predictable and surprising responses.

> ". . . allow priests to marry. The church is starving for priests. The Eucharist is central to the Catholic Church."

> ". . . lighten the church's stand on divorced and remarried Catholics."

> ". . . move out of the Vatican palace into an ordinary household."

> ". . . call a meeting with the bishops and make it clear I don't think it's wrong to use contraceptives in marriage."

> ". . . listen more to the people and to my theologians."

> ". . . totally reorganize the Vatican Curia."

> ". . . ordain women.

> ". . . call another Vatican Council."

> ". . . well, I'd be a woman."

Their sincere, often insightful responses showed me today's students genuinely care about the church, even though often negative toward it. It also became clear that many lacked basic knowledge about the contemporary church. Those with Catholic elementary and high school religion classes too often exhibited memorized answers rather than integrated knowledge and personally appropriated understanding. And most had never even heard of Vatican Council II! Their spontaneous attitudes and concerns semester after semester focused issues for me and in no small measure inspired me to write this book.

There was another motive. More than a few friends, concerned Catholics, felt the Catholic Church is in a crisis today. Several even wondered if there was danger of schism between the American church and "Rome." As a theologian with special interest in the contemporary church, I am acutely aware of what some term the struggle for control of the Catholic Church today: between those convinced the church is in bad shape, even out of control, and work for a return to traditional values and practices and those who see the church differently and desire further renewal according to the Second Vatican Council.

I have written this book with four groups especially in mind. One, university students and young couples who in their search for meaning desire to learn about the church as it exists today, but who often have difficulties with the church either out of ignorance or negative adolescent experiences; two, educated older Catholics often confused by the seeming contradiction between the changes inaugurated by Vatican II and what they learned in Catholic schools or bewildered, even scandalized, by the much-publicized tensions and divisions within the church; three, parish study and discussion groups eager to better understand their contemporary church and its Vatican II renewal; four, our sisters and brothers in other Christian churches and in the great world religions who might find this approach informative and helpful in understanding the Catholic Church and their Catholic friends. For these groups, this book may serve as a unique introduction to the contemporary Catholic Church.

Accordingly, I established a five-fold goal or purpose that would hopefully constitute this book's special contribution. One, to present as faithfully as possible the complex Catholic Church *as it actually exists today:* its strengths and limitations, its magnificent values as well as its current problems, its attractive beauty yet sometimes repelling features. This necessarily involved treating controversial topics and differing theological positions, including the reality of dissent. Two, to comment on the extent of the church's renewal 30 years after the Council. This, too, involved an honest, realistic acknowledgement of problems as well as accomplishments. For the church's herculean effort to incarnate Vatican II's theological insights into its life is a veritable "reshaping of Catholicism," in Avery Dulles' striking phrase. Three, to look to the future to consider crucial challenges and consequent opportunities for the church and to suggest decisions a renewed church may need to take.

My final two goals I see as particularly important and valuable in a book of this kind. Four, I sought to emphasize "doing theology" in almost every chapter by explaining the theological bases behind "the changes" begun by the Council, by pointing out the theological positions often at the center of divisive issues and tensions in today's church, and by indicating theological insights that offer possiblities for further church development. Five, I endeavored to keep a constant ecumenical sensitivity and appreciation for other Christian churches and their rich traditions and contributions, including also the great world religions that testify to God's presence and activity in all peoples.

This five-fold focus will, I hope, provide answers to these important questions: What does it mean to be a Vatican II church today? A Vatican II Catholic? Is the church moving forward, stalling, or retrogressing in the vision and direction offered it by the Second Vatican Council? How are we to judge the tensions and divisions within the church? What steps might — should — the church take to enter its 21st century?

Some key themes run throughout *Restoration and Renewal: The Church in the Third Millennium* serving to unite and focus the book. A controlling theme is that of *renewal*, both in theology and Christian life, inspired by the Council. Closely related is the current *struggle* between the forces for further renewal and those for "the restoration" with the underlying *ecclesiological* issue of two competing theologies or understandings of church. These involve the theme of *pluralism* or *diversity in unity*, which likewise involves the ever-prevalent theme of *change* by a church in transition today. The above themes point to and call for *conversion*, both personal and institutional. Pervading all is the positive theme of *optimism* concerning the present and future church, thanks to the risen Christ present in the church and to his Spirit ever guiding the church, members and leaders alike.

These themes point to urgent questions today. How far can the church change and remain faithful to the tradition? Though we must be wary of facile dichotomies, we may still ask what the appropriate emphasis is today: a more spiritualized, internal looking church or one continuing to address the needs of the world? Authority centralized in the Holy See or dispersed and shared in the local churches of the Catholic world? A prophetic church of pastoral service and practical love or one emphasizing authority and obedience? To what extent is today's church responding to John XXIII's "signs of the times"? Does the Catholic Church actually need a conversion, a letting go of historical accretions so that gospel values might shine through more clearly? What changes must occur for the church to be more transparently the sacrament of Christ to its own members and the world at large?

But why another book on the Catholic Church? From my contacts with university students, younger couples and older Catholics, parish groups through lectures and discussions, and ecumenical leaders from other Christian churches, it seemed there was need for a book that treated the contemporary Catholic Church somewhere between traditional church textbooks and specialized works on church history, spirituality, sacraments, doctrine, or Scripture; and a book that endeavored to treat objectively the church as it actually exists today with its problems and challenges as well as its wonderful values. With this niche in mind, I settled on the five-fold focus and the various themes mentioned above.

The contents of the book are organized to move from Vatican II's vision of the church's nature, purpose, leadership and religious life to current major issues and tensions, climaxing in the church's values, challenges and opportunities as it moves into its third millennium. Part I opens with two introductory chapters: the first to spark interest in the broader Christian Church and provide the necessary theological "tools" for the chapters ahead; the second to present the event of Vatican II as foundation for the subsequent chapters. The next three chapters explain the Council's new vision of the nature of the church. Part II treats the mission Vatican II emphasized for the church. Part III considers how the Council endeavored to reaffirm and renew the leadership structures in the church. Part IV shows how through renewed sacraments this human-divine church helps its members relate to God and each other. Part V attempts to deal frankly with the major issues and tensions confronting a church in renewal as it seeks to fulfill its lofty mission today. Part VI looks hopefully to the church on the threshhold of its third millennium.This section gathers together 20 special gifts the church offers its members and the human family today and reflects on 12 challenges that constitute rich opportunities for the Catholic Church moving toward the 21st century. An epilogue reflects optimistically on the church and its future.

The book offers special features for its varied audiences. Each chapter provides aids both for students, parish study groups and interested individuals: introductory quotations to highlight the topic and create interest; preview of purpose and major content; technical terms in bold in the text and defined in a glossary; capsule summary of most important points; discussion questions to stimulate thought; topics for personal action; suggestions for further reading or for reports. I have deliberately provided a broad spectrum of information on today's church not available elsewhere in one place, and quotations from the documents of Vatican II and other sources so the reader may directly and personally experience the contemporary church "in action." Though my text employs inclusive language and a minimum of capitalization, I retained the noninclusive language and capitalization of ecclesial terms used in the original documents. Scripture quotes are from *The New American Bible*, Confraternity of Christian Doctrine 1970 copyright, Catholic Bible Publishers, Wichita, KS, 1983.

Today's Vatican II Catholic Church is dynamic, complex, fascinating, often frustrating. Its unresolved issues, inner tensions, and painful divisions are the vital signs of a living organism that grows and develops as it adapts to changing environments. It is a church of modern holiness; a heroic church of martyrs in its struggle for justice and human rights; a genuinely respected Church yet burdened by a credibility problem. It seeks, despite its sinfulness and contemporary problems, to be the sacrament or sign to the world of the risen Christ and his salvation. Its deepest reality is mystery. To know more fully this human-divine church can be an enriching, exciting experience. May this book provide such an experience for all who read or study or discuss its contents!

Part I

Vatican II's
New Vision of Church

CHAPTER 1

Introducing the Christian Church and "Doing" Theology

"Go therefore and make disciples of all nations . . . and know that I will be with you always until the end of the world."
—Matthew 28:18-20

"Father, all powerful and living God, when your children sinned and wandered far from your friendship, you reunited them with yourself through the blood of your Son and the power of the Holy Spirit. You gather them into your Church, to be one as you, Father, are one with your Son and the Holy Spirit. . . . You make them the body of Christ and the dwelling place of the Holy Spirit."   —Preface for Sunday Masses

"Faith seeking understanding."
—St. Anselm's definition of 'theology'

Introduction

A Unique Phenomenon

Of all the great institutions and empires and religions in the history of the world, the Christian Church is utterly unique. Only the Christian Church claims as its founder a person who she believes is both God and man, the historical Jesus of Nazareth. Only the Christian Church makes the seemingly incredible claim that this Jesus' death by crucifixion brought salvation to the human family and that the crucified one was resurrected by the power of God and lives today as Jesus the Christ. Only the Christian Church claims that the risen Christ and the Spirit he promised to send his followers are present day-by-day to church members, guiding and helping them in manifold ways, most dramatically in the seven ecclesial sacraments. Only the Christian Church offers a theology of hope for humankind in this world and in the next because of Jesus' **Resurrection**.

We can describe the church as a human-divine reality, that is, a church made up of women and men, sinners and saints, yet one in which God is present and active in manifold ways. As such it has inspired millions of people through almost 2000 years to have **faith** in a transcendent God whom no one has seen and to believe in the extraordinary event of the **Incarnation,** that God entered our history by taking on human flesh in the God-man, Jesus of Nazareth. As a human-divine reality, it has inspired millions to cling to the Christian virtue of **hope** that after this earthly pilgrimage, their high vocation and destiny is an eternity of happiness and peace with God and their loved ones. Finally, as a human-divine reality the church has helped millions to **love** God and each other according to the example and teaching of Jesus. It has thus produced countless saints and **martyrs** who have lived lives of extraordinary, heroic goodness or suffered torture and death as witness to Jesus Christ.

Moreover, the Christian Church is remarkable in its *humble beginnings* and *extraordinary growth.* It began with a handful of unlearned fishermen, the 12 Apostles, in an obscure part of the Roman world called Palestine. From there it spread throughout the Mediterranean world in a remarkably short time. By the end of the Middle Ages, the Christian Church was strongly established in Europe. Centuries later it spread to South America, Asia and Australia, and this past century to Africa. Today, the Christian Church numbers over 1.8 billion people, one-quarter of the human race.

The Christian Church is also notable in its *ability to survive.* There were many times when, naturally speaking, the church should have been destroyed. Yet it survived the fierce Roman persecutions, when Emperors like Nero and Diocletian tortured and killed tens of thousands of Christians. It survived two cataclysmic ruptures in its own body: in the 11th century, when it split into the western Roman and eastern **Orthodox** sections, and in the 16th century, when the Protestant **Reformation** claimed almost half of the Roman Catholic membership. Moreover, the western church managed to survive a major leadership crisis of the 70-year-long Western Schism, when three men claimed to be pope, to the confusion of the Christian world. It also survived periods of especially corrupt leadership, in the 10th and 12th centuries and in the 15th and 16th when popes and bishops were unworthy men. It survived the attack on the possibility of faith and belief in God and transcendent realities in the **Age of Enlightenment** in 18th-century Europe. In our own times, both the eastern Orthodox and western Catholic and Protestant churches survived devastating persecution under communist regimes in Russia, China, and Eastern Europe and under Nazi "cleansing" in western Europe. Christians believe the church has survived because its founder, the risen Christ, promised to protect it down through the centuries.

Though the nearly 2000-year history of the Christian Church is beyond the scope of these pages, nevertheless knowledge of church history is not only personally rewarding but indispensable to understand the church of today. For the contemporary church has been far more conditioned by its history than has previously been realized. Several readable recent church histories are mentioned at the end of this chapter, which both students and older Catholics, as well as our sister and brother Christians, may find stimulating and helpful for a better understanding of the contemporary church.

An Important Clarification

Up to this point we have often used the expression "the Christian Church." There is an important theological, rather **ecclesiological** principle behind this usage, as will become evident in subsequent chapters. For the present, it is sufficient to stress that the church is entered through baptism and therefore is primarily and most essentially made up of all *baptized, believing* Christian people, whether Catholic or Orthodox or Anglican or Protestant. We can accordingly say that the Christian Church is a broader reality than any one existing church, in fact is more than 1.8 billion Christian people, despite its unfortunate division into many individual churches. Throughout these pages, we will not lose sight of this ecclesiological fact: that all the baptized are truly members of the Christian Church. We will treat the various Christian churches with ecumenical appreciation and sensitivity.

We must point out, however, that this book will deal primarily with the Roman Catholic Church. There are several reasons for this. First, the Catholic Church makes the claim, along with the Orthodox churches, of being an Apostolic church, that is, a church reaching back to the time of the 12 Apostles and Christ. Second, we see still preserved and emphasized in the Catholic Church, as in the Orthodox churches, such structured elements as bishops and the sacramental system, especially the Eucharist, as well as the complete Christian beliefs. Third, the Catholic Church makes the serious claim to be the unique and fullest expression of the church Jesus established on the 12 Apostles and gave to Peter to shepherd. Fourth, a major reason for this claim is the office of the pope as the successor of Peter the Apostle, chosen by Jesus to be the church's foundation of unity. Fifth, a pragmatic reason, the Catholic Church is by far the largest of all the Christian churches, with over one billion members, and has the greatest visibility and influence in today's world, especially in the person of its vigorous, world-traveling Pope John Paul II. Finally, thanks to the ecumenical movement, many Protestant churches have a new attitude toward the Catholic Church and realize that in the future united Church of Christ, the **"Catholic substance,"** including in some way even the pope, needs to be present!

◆

Preview: The two-fold purpose of this first chapter is to introduce readers to this unique 2000-year Christian Church in the hope of stimulating interest to learn more about it; and secondly to provide the theological skills to understand the contemporary church and appreciate the remarkable changes the Second Vatican Council brought to it. Accordingly we treat four topics: characteristics of today's Christian Church, theology and "doing" theology, the Second Vatican Council and its traumatic effects, and a concluding reflection on the Catholic Church.

◆

Characteristics of the Contemporary Christian Church

The most obvious characteristic is its *size*. Baptized, believing Christians number more than 1.8 billion people, or about one-third of the world population of 5,423,000,000.

Another obvious but painful characteristic is the Christian Church's *division* into many different groupings or churches, perhaps over 1000 if small churches and sects are considered. Most visibly it is divided into the Roman Catholic, Orthodox, Anglican, and Protestant.

Such continuing division is clearly contrary to the wishes and designs of its founder, who prayed at his last supper on earth with his Apostles before his death "that all may be one as thou, Father, and I are one." The modern ecumenical movement seeks to make this prayer of Jesus a reality.

An all-too-obvious characteristic but one too frequently overlooked is the fact that Christians constitute a *sinful Church* in constant need of renewal and reform. As a human-*divine* reality, the church, as the creed announces, is holy because Christ is holy, because he has given it the rich means to holiness, and because of the holiness of its vast number of saints and martyrs. But as *human*-divine reality, the church will in its members, including its leaders, always manifest the pettiness and selfishness and pride and greed and sinfulness of the world about them. So treatment of the church today will be abundantly aware of this fact of life and will not shirk from treating it where necessary.

The *extraordinary vitality* of the Christian Church today (despite major problems individual churches experience) is another characteristic of the contemporary church. The church is growing by leaps and bounds in Africa and some parts of Asia. With the new freedom for religion in Russia and Eastern Europe, large numbers are returning to the **Russian Orthodox** Church and in Eastern Europe to Catholicism and Protestantism in their search for meaning. In mainland China, with its 1.13 billion people, there is a small but fervent group of Christians, the possible harbinger of a future great harvest. In South America, the once slumbering Catholic Church has

Christians	1,833,022,000
Muslim	971,328,700
Hindus	732,812,000
Buddhists	314,939,000
Chinese Folk Religionists	187,107,000
New Religionists	143,415,000
Tribal Religionists	96,581,000
Sikhs	18,800,500
Jews	17,822,000
Others (Shamanists, Confucians, Baha'is, Jains, Shintoists, Other Religionists)	47,640,800
Source: 1993 *Encyclopedia Brittanica Book of the Year*. Figures are for mid-1992	

been awakened by liberation theology, with its tens of thousands of "base Christian communities" whose members fervently live the gospel message of love and liberation and have died by the thousands as martyrs for justice. In many countries, especially Poland, Eastern Europe, the Philippines, Central and South America, the Catholic Church has been in the forefront of the fight for freedom and human rights.

A somewhat ambiguous characteristic of the Christian Church today is the *recent challenge* of **Pentecostal** and **evangelistic** churches to the older and more established churches: Catholic, Orthodox, **Anglican,** and the mainline Protestant churches (**Lutheran, Reformed, Methodist, Baptist**) which came directly out of the Reformation. These youthful pentecostal churches preach the "born-again" religious experience; for them one is not a

Roman Catholics	1,025,585,000
Protestants	373,698,000
Orthodox	170,422,000
Anglicans	74,883,400
Other Christians	188,433,600

true Christian, a previous baptism and present belief notwithstanding, until one has had this conversion experience given by the **Holy Spirit** and then makes an adult total commitment to Jesus Christ and is thus "saved." This evangelical theology of a "true Christian" is a direct challenge to the traditional Christian churches that perform infant baptism. The pentecostal churches are strongly missionary and are accused of "stealing sheep," that is, making converts out of people who already are Christian. Americans are familiar with some of these churches through the popular TV evangelists.

A recent characteristic of most churches, but especially of the Roman Catholic Church today, is the struggle to *adapt to modernity and to change*. This should not come as a surprise since the church, as a living organism, must confront its environment and change when necessary. Throughout its history, but especially today, all Christian churches have two very difficult, closely interrelated challenges: to remain true to their ancient tradition founded on the teachings of Christ and the Apostles and contained in the four Gospels and the letters of **St. Paul** and, at the same time, to present these teachings and the Christian life in such a way as to be intelligible to the scientific, secularistic 20th-century world and capable of answering the deepest yearnings of the human heart for meaning and transcendence. Indeed, a great challenge!

The Role of Theology and Professional Theologians

To accomplish such a formidable task is the work of theology and professional theologians. Theology has always been necessary and at the center of the church's life throughout its long history. Indeed, in its beginning years different theologies were present in each of the four Gospel writers and in St. Paul as they endeavored to explain the mystery of the God-man Jesus and of his teaching and the great saving actions of his crucifixion, resurrection, ascension, and sending the Spirit at **Pentecost**. So it should not surprise us that throughout the church's history, various theologies or theological explanations emerged. Since we will be "doing theology" frequently throughout these pages, it will be helpful, indeed necessary, to understand what theology is and how it works.

Broadly speaking, theology, or more exactly, theologizing, is simply faith seeking understanding. It is thus critical, rational reflection on any religious tradition and the resulting systematic expression of that reflection. Theology thus has two elements[1]: the *process* of reflection and the *product* of that reflection in statements of belief (creeds), in worship (cult), and in moral behavior (code). We can speak of Islamic theology, Jewish theology, and, within Christian theology, Protestant or Catholic or Orthodox theology.

---

1. For this material, I am indebted to Brennan Hill, Paul Knitter, and William Madges, *Faith, Religion and Theology* (Mystic, CT: Twenty-Third Publications, 1990), 251-61.

We can further specify within Protestant theology Lutheran theology, Baptist theology, Pentecostal theology, and within Catholicism we can distinguish Augustinian, Thomistic, Rahnerian, theologies following St. Augustine, St. Thomas Aquinas, and Karl Rahner, to mention only a few.

Christian theology then is the process of critical reflection on what Christians believe about God, Jesus Christ, the Holy Spirit, the church, the sacraments, and so forth, as found in the Christian **Scriptures** and in the Christian **tradition**. Such theologizing obviously entails serious study and careful thinking and the asking of questions. Most persons of mature faith engage in theological reflection at some time in their lives. For example, Anne, a freshman at a Midwestern university during a Welcome Week tug-of-war was injured and became permanently paralyzed. She and her friends asked these theological questions: "Why Anne? How could a good and loving God permit such a tragedy? What of the Christian belief of divine providence? Why do such evils happen to good young people?" To theologize is to ask serious adult faith-questions in order to come to a deeper understanding of what one believes. This is the first aspect.

Its second aspect is the attempt to *express* what one believes, the *content* of Christian faith, in a way that people in any given period of history can understand and make sense of. In the 4th century, the great theologian-bishops of the church wrestled with the mystery of Jesus Christ as both God and man; their resulting explanation was expressed in the **Nicene Constantinopolitan creed**, which almost all Christian churches accept and which Catholics recite every Sunday at worship. Theology is thus the science of finding adequate descriptive language to speak about the things of God.

Another way of expressing this second aspect is that theology attempts to explain the significance and meaning of these beliefs for human living today, that is, for the questions and problems people meet in daily life. Two examples illustrate this second aspect of theology. First, the environment. By reflecting on the Christian belief of a creator God who gave us a good world as gift for us to use responsibly, we realize better today that a Christian has a two-fold responsibility to make land and food available to all people and to protect the environment. From this has developed a new appreciation for human rights and planet earth. Second, **liberation theology**. **Gustavo Gutiérrez** of Peru and other Latin American liberation theologians reflected on the words of Jesus in Luke 4:18: "The spirit of the Lord has been given me for he has anointed me. He has sent me to bring the good news to the poor, to proclaim liberty to captives and to the blind new sight, to set the downtrodden free, to proclaim the Lord's year of favor." These theologians applied Jesus' words to the situation of massive poverty, oppression, denial of the most basic human rights to the majority of Latin Americans. Liberation theology was born!

It is obvious then that Christian theology cannot be done in the abstract, divorced from the real world. It must take into account human experience and our growth in knowledge. Accordingly, the critical reflection of Christian theology has two focal points: the Christian **Tradition**, that is, Christian belief as expressed in the Hebrew and Christian Scriptures and in the practices, **doctrine**, and code of behavior of the church; and two, human life as we experience it today. These two focal points bring us to an important aspect of modern theology, the reality of change or **"development of doctrine,"** to use the technical term. Since our understanding of the Christian Tradition has developed and deepened over the centuries and since our own self-understanding and experiences of life have matured and changed us, both the *process* of theologizing as well as the *product* of theology have undergone change throughout the history of the church and continue to do so today. One example: before Vatican Council II, an older theology held that the primary purpose of marriage is children and the secondary purpose is the sexual love of the spouses. A more fully developed understanding of the human person and of the nature and place of sexual love in marriage caused the Catholic Church during the Second Vatican Council to develop a more complete theology of marriage, which stated that both children and the spouses' sexual love are equally the primary purpose of the sacrament of marriage. This newer theology of marriage has profound consequences, as we shall see later.

We can draw conclusions from our treatment of theology and theologizing:

- Christian faith is the necessary starting point for doing Christian theology;

- most mature, thoughtful Christians are capable of doing theology and, in fact, have often done so without realizing it;

- theology can and must change in the course of time since our understanding of Christian doctrine "develops" and since the world and our experience of it changes;

- there can be different theologies for there are different legitimate explanations of the same basic Christian beliefs and practices;

- theology, then, is of great importance and indeed is absolutely necessary for the church and its members, for without it there would be no adult coherent understanding of the Christian faith and no growth and development to meet changing historical situations.

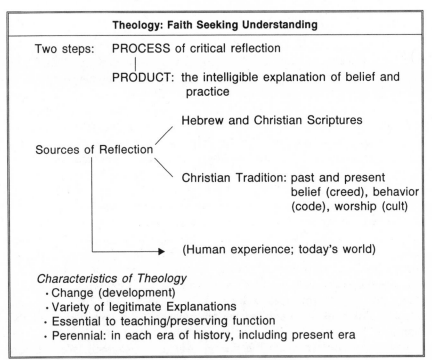

Theology: Faith Seeking Understanding

Two steps: PROCESS of critical reflection

PRODUCT: the intelligible explanation of belief and
practice

Hebrew and Christian Scriptures

Sources of Reflection

Christian Tradition: past and present
belief (creed), behavior
(code), worship (cult)

(Human experience; today's world)

Characteristics of Theology
- Change (development)
- Variety of legitimate Explanations
- Essential to teaching/preserving function
- Perennial: in each era of history, including present era

The specially trained women and men who carry out the important role of theology are known as professional theologians. Their double responsibility is to express the Christian beliefs accurately and responsibly to render them understandable and credible to contemporary persons and to propose fresh interpretations and insights where these are needed (as in the case of the newer insights on the purposes of marriage). On the other hand, the bishops of the world, as successors of the 12 Apostles, have the responsibility of teaching the Christian Tradition and of preserving it from error. This teaching-preserving office in the Catholic Church is called the **magisterium** and is held by all the bishops in union with the pope as successor of Peter. Because not all bishops are specialists in theology and since their duties are so all-embracing, they need the help of professional theologians in their teaching-preserving function.

Ideally, bishops and theologians will work together, respecting each others' roles in the church. But inevitably tensions will arise when, for example, theologians advance new understandings of the Christian Tradition which bishops and the pope are not yet ready or able to accept. This tension is particularly acute in some areas of the Catholic Church today, though it has always been present throughout the church's history. In later chapters we shall treat some of these areas of tension; for the present, it is sufficient to realize that professional theologians are the indispensable helpers of the bishops in their teaching-preserving responsibility.

Vatican Council II, 1962-1965

Today's Catholic Church is the result of a momentous event that took place in Rome from 1962 to 1965, called the Second Vatican Council. This meeting of all the bishops of the Roman Catholic church was the brain-child — inspiration of the Holy Spirit, he called it — of the 78-year-old pope, the much beloved John XXIII. His purpose was for the church to examine itself to see how it could better carry out its mission of proclaiming the good news of Christ to the 20th-century world and to try to heal the tragic division between Catholics, Orthodox, Anglicans and Protestants. Pope John had in mind a profound renewal of the church and its updating to meet the challenges of the modern world; his favorite term for the guiding spirit behind the Council was *aggiornamento*, updating or bringing the church up to the present day, *giorno* being the Italian word for day. The 2500 Catholic bishops (with Orthodox, Anglican, Protestant and Jewish observers) present produced over the four-year period 16 documents that set the Roman Catholic Church on a brand new course. Thus the contemporary Catholic Church is the Vatican II church and cannot be understood apart from the teaching and spirit of Vatican II. A major purpose of this book is to explain the teaching and to interpret the authentic spirit of Vatican II, while assessing to what extent the Catholic Church today has incarnated in its life the renewal of the Council. We will refer constantly throughout these pages to the Second Vatican Council.

Though many Catholics welcomed the renewal ushered in by the Council and the "fresh air" that John XXIII let into the church, others were confused and resisted "the changes." Part of the confusion and resistance was the normal reluctance to change and the challenge to think and act in new ways. But perhaps the major cause was the fact that the reasons for the changes and the theological principles behind them were not sufficiently explained to the average Catholic. The changes were thus thrust on a membership psychologically and theologically unprepared to accept them.

The resistance was particularly acute when it came to religious practices and the devotional life of Catholics. "Many Catholics had been deeply devoted to . . . benediction and adoration of the Blessed Sacrament, private confession, the cult of the saints, and popular novenas. When all these treasures were suddenly swept away . . . they felt cheated, bewildered and distressed."[2]

A second result of the Council was the heightening of division within the church between progressive and traditionalist Catholics who understood its directives and spirit in different ways. One cause was that some bishops, priests, and lay Catholics did not understand and accept the full implications of the theological principles expressed in the documents and the depth of renewal they called for. Tension also developed between pro-

---

2. Avery Dulles, *The Reshaping of Catholicism* (San Francisco: Harper & Row, 1988), 11.

gressive theologians, priests, sisters and lay Catholics who wanted the church to move more swiftly on the path to renewal and those who felt the church was changing too fast and losing valuable parts of its tradition.

Another cause of the tension between progressives and traditionalists lay in the difficulty of interpreting the documents themselves. For the 16 documents were the work of a large number of bishops desirous of obtaining a consensus; thus the final wording was often a compromise. Because the progressives more and more dominated the Council, **Avery Dulles** commented that "in every decree of Vatican II the conservatives had succeeded in safeguarding their own special concerns . . . For example, the *Constitution on the Church*, while encouraging the participation of the laity, kept all real power in the hands of the clergy."[3] The result was the phenomenon of parallel texts in the documents where old teaching is put alongside the new.

Thus, in reading the documents of Vatican II, the principle of interpretation becomes critical. To discover the "larger" teaching and spirit of the Council bishops, one must avoid the "text approach" of choosing, as Bible fundamentalists do, individual texts to prove one's point. Rather, the following **hermeneutical** principles are essential: John XXIII's intention in calling the Council and the goals he set for it; the thinking of the majority of the Council bishops; and the overall thrust of each document and the context of its individual chapters. The five-volume[4] *Commentary on the Documents of Vatican II*, which gives the preliminary argumentation and the intended meaning of various passages and texts, is indispensable for correct interpretation of the documents.

Yet a further cause of the tension and division within the Catholic Church today between progressives and traditionalists is the concept and practice of **"the restoration,"** a term first used by Cardinal Joseph Ratzinger, head of the Roman curia's Congregation for the Doctrine of the Faith, in an interview given to an Italian journalist in 1984 and published in English in 1985 as *The Ratzinger Report: An Exclusive Interview on the State of the Church*. Because of its considerable influence in today's church, we must treat this "restoration."

The cardinal believes that Vatican II, though good in itself, has not been correctly understood and interpreted according to its "true spirit." This has led after the Council to errors and excesses in theology and Catholic practice and been "disastrous" for the church. The cardinal uses such expressions as: "progressive process of decadence," "erroneous paths whose catastrophic consequences are already incontestable."[5] Those particularly guilty were progressive theologians, priests, sisters, lay Catholics, and even

---

3. *Ibid.*, 12.
4. Herbert Vorgrimler, ed., *Commentary on the Documents of Vatican II*, vol.'s 1-5. (New York: Herder and Herder, 1967).
5. Joseph Cardinal Ratzinger with Vittorio Messori, *The Ratzinger Report: An Exclusive Interview on the State of the Church* (San Francisco: Ignatius Press, 1985), 30.

some bishops. The solution is the two-fold return (restoration) to the Council's letter and true spirit and to an earlier vision of the faith before the Council. The cardinal defines restoration as "the search for a new balance after all the exaggerations of an indiscriminate opening to the world, after the overly positive interpretations of an agnostic and atheistic world . . . ."[6] He stated that "a restoration understood in this sense . . . is altogether desirable and . . . is already in operation in the church," signaling that "the first phase after Vatican II has come to a close." Thus "the recovery of lost values . . . is precisely the task . . . in the second phase of the postconciliar period."[7] The effort of his congregation has been to restore order and discipline to the church by various means we shall discuss in subsequent chapters.

Progressive Catholics — theologians, priests, laity, and more than a few bishops — disagree with the cardinal's interpretation of the "true spirit" of the Council and his negative assessment of the postconciliar period in the church. Archbishop Weakland of Milwaukee for example, states that "this attempt seems to be inspired by the desire to turn back the clock, not to the pre-Vatican II period, but to the texts themselves, as if there had been no development since then, to interpret them in the light of only one side of the debate during the council itself, and to begin the implementation all over again, but in a controlled and highly centralized way."[8] The cardinal's ultimate solution and concern appears to be obedience to the authority of the church's hierarchy: "Only if this perspective [the church based on the authority of Christ passed on to the hierarchy] is acquired

Contrasting Values / Characteristics	
Restoration	*Renewal*
Looking backward	Looking forward
Central Control	Local Church
Stability	Flexibility, risk
Certitude	Ambiguity
Authority, obedience	Collegiality, service
Letter of law, rule	Spirit, pastoral

6. *Ibid.*, 37.

7. *Ibid.*, 37-38.

8. Archbishop Rembert Weakland, *Faith and the Human Enterprise: A Post-Vatican II Appraisal* (Maryknoll, New York: Orbis Books, 1992), 13.

anew will it be possible to rediscover the necessity and fruitfulness of obedience to the legitimate ecclesiastical hierarchies."[9]

As we read and discuss the following chapters, it will help to keep in mind the restoration mentality within the Catholic Church today and CDF's efforts to accomplish this restoration-reform. It will also help to realize that both progressives and traditionalists (sometimes termed liberals and conservatives) are generally intelligent, sincere Catholics devoted to Christ and his church; but since their values and convictions are strongly held, tensions are severe, and cause much strain and harm. One unhappy result is that some traditionalists have adopted the restoration as their "battle cry" and become confrontational, petitioning Rome to restore the church to a kind of pre-Vatican II mentality and practice and to discipline progressive bishops and theologians, while some progressives make premature demands for change and are unduly critical of church leadership. So the Catholic Church today finds itself in need of inner healing. To accomplish this, Catholics need to better understand their ancient tradition, the theology behind the "new" teaching of Vatican II, the reasons as well as the permissible and appropriate limits of change, and the challenges facing the church today which themselves point to the need for change and renewal. This book will attempt to deal with this interesting and formidable agenda.

Caricature or Reality?

Too often the Catholic Church today has appeared to both its own members and other Christians as an impersonal, aloof, even arrogant bureaucracy that makes rules for people to obey and threatens punishment and hellfire to rule-breakers. Is this an accurate picture or a caricature?

The fact is that despite its human limitations and even sinfulness, the Catholic Church has been throughout its long history a *caring* church and is so today in many ways. First and foremost, it cares about Jesus Christ. It aims to *be* Jesus Christ in the world, to mirror him and his love and forgiveness. The theological statement for this high purpose is that the church is meant to be a sacrament or sign to the world of the risen Christ and his values. We shall consider this in a later chapter. The church cares about Christ's teachings, especially those about his Father, about the kingdom of God which he constantly preached, about salvation. The church cares deeply about the good news as written down in the four Gospels and the letters of St. Paul. It values the Christian tradition handed down to Christians through the centuries. It cares about the unity of its members in one faith. It cares about its members today, like a mother for her children. It cares deeply about their happiness in this life and above all their eternal happiness in the next life. It has a special love for sinners — all of us —

---

9. *The Ratzinger Report*, 49.

and longs to bring Christ's healing and mercy and forgiveness to us. It cares about the sick. It cares especially about the poor in the world: the hungry, the homeless, the deprived. Today it cares greatly about human rights and justice so that all people, but especially the poor and and the victims of injustice, can enjoy God's gifts meant for all. It cares about world peace, since war is the ultimate destruction of life and global resources. It cares about life in all its manifestations. It cares especially about the young because it understands their struggle to become mature amid contemporary allurements and because they are its future.

Is this too idealistic? Is the Catholic Church today really this way? Or, as some maintain, does it rather care about itself: its own preservation, its power, its many buildings and property holdings, its authority over its members, its ability to influence society, in a word, its institutional interests? Truth demands we state that at certain times in its history individual church leaders were guilty of these very things. What then is the picture of the Catholic Church today? Does she, for example, truly care about the divorced and remarried, gay people, women in their struggle for a greater role in the church? Throughout these pages, we shall attempt to deal frankly and objectively with these and other issues.

Summary

We have attempted to introduce the Christian Church as an utterly unique human-divine reality. We made an important distinction between the Christian Church made up of all believing, baptized Christians and the many separated Christian churches, including the Roman Catholic. We pointed out that while this book will deal primarily with the Roman Catholic Church, other Christian churches will receive prominent and appreciative treatment. In this context, we considered various characteristics of the broader Christian Church, explained the important role of theology with a view to doing theology in subsequent chapters, identified the momentous event of the Second Vatican Council, and closed with a reflection on the Catholic Church as a genuinely caring church. We are now ready to turn to that totally unexpected and exciting event which defines the Catholic Church today and without which it cannot be understood: Vatican Council II.

For Discussion

1. Why is the chapter entitled the "Christian Church" rather than the "Catholic Church"?

2. How does one theologize or "do theology"? Can you give an example of yourself "doing theology," even if you may not have realized it?

3. Why are theology and theologizing absolutely necessary for the Christian Church?

4. How would you account for the fact there are progressives (liberals) and traditionalists (conservatives) in the Catholic Church today?

5. What do you see as the major concern of the Catholic Church today: caring for the spiritual and human needs of its members or preserving itself as a strong institution? Give examples.

For Action

1. Find out why the Christian Church formally split into the eastern Orthodox and western Roman Catholic churches in 1054.

2. Discover what were the most important reasons for the Protestant Reformation led by Martin Luther in the early decades of the 16th century.

3. Do you know what the 70-year Western Schism within the Roman Catholic Church was? How was it resolved? What formidable ecclesiological issues did this situation raise?

4. "Do theology" on attending Mass on Sunday; on drinking; on a problem that bothers you.

5. Go to the library and page through these magazines: *The Catholic World* and *U.S. Catholic;* these weekly newspapers: *National Catholic Reporter* and *The Wanderer*. What did you discover?

6. Before your next birthday, treat yourself to reading a brief history of the Catholic Church! Of Christianity!

Further Reading[10]

Bokenkotter, Thomas. *A Concise History of the Catholic Church*. Garden City, NY: Doubleday, 1977.

Dwyer, John. *Church History, Twenty Centuries of Catholic Christianity*. New York: Paulist Press, 1985.

Ratzinger, Joseph. *The Ratzinger Report: An Exclusive Interview on the State of the Church*. San Francisco: Ignatius Press, 1985.

---

10. To know and experience today's church throughout these pages, it will be very interesting and educational to become acquainted with *periodicals* and *magazines* and *newspapers* that report ongoing events and struggles of the contemporary church. See the conclusion of the bibliography section at the end of this book for a selection of the most informative publications, with brief identifying description of each.

Weakland, Rembert. *All God's People, Catholic Identity After the Second Vatican Council.* New York: Paulist Press, 1985, and *Faith and the Human Enterprise: A Post-Vatican II Vision.* Maryknoll, New York: Orbis Books, 1992.

CHAPTER 2

A Revolutionary[1] Event

"... a major turning point in the history of Catholicism."[2]

"... conversion experience for the Roman Catholic Church."[3]

"... perhaps the most profound religious event of the twentieth century."[4]

"... the church's first official actualization as a world church."[5]

"... the fundamental event in the life of the contemporary church."[6]

---

1. A theological debate exists on whether the Council as a whole merely made adaptations in Catholic teaching and further developed teaching already present or was in fact a revolution involving a paradigm shift, that is, the deliberate substitution of one model or vision of church for another. John O'Malley sees Vatican II as "constituting" a new ecclesiological or theological paradigm, whereas T. Howland Sanks nuances Vatican II not as a paradigm shift in itself but an example of "an institution in the process of a paradigm shift." I incline to the paradigm shift position, but often use revolutionary as a more popular term for totally unexpected and sweeping change.

2. John W. O'Malley, *Tradition and Transition: Historical Perspectives on Vatican II* (Wilmington: Michael Glazier, Inc., 1989), 24.

3. Franz Jozef van Beeck, *Catholic Identity after Vatican II* (Chicago: Loyola University Press, 1985), 19.

4. Timothy E. O'Connell, ed., *Vatican II and Its Documents: An American Reappraisal* (Wilmington: Michael Glazier, Inc., 1986), 7.

5. Karl Rahner, "Toward a Fundamental Theological Interpretation of Vatican II," *Theological Studies* 40 (Dec., 1979): 717. Rahner defines world church as "for the first time a world-wide Council with a world-wide episcopate came into existence and functioned independently."

6. Pope John Paul II, from address announcing the Extraordinary Synod of 1985, quoted in Peter Hebblethwaite, *Synod Extraordinary* (Garden City, NY: Doubleday and Co., 1986), 1.

Introduction

These comments attempt to capture the profound meaning of the Second Vatican Council. For Vatican II has rightly been called the greatest event in the Catholic Church since the Protestant Reformation 475 years ago. The Council put an end to the **Counter Reformation** period in the Catholic Church, during which the church had overreacted to Protestantism, developed a "fortress or ghetto" mentality against the world, and too often spent its energies in condemnations of "errors and false teachings," both outside and within the Catholic Church.

Moreover, the Council set the Catholic Church in an entirely new direction. Armed with a fresh theology of itself as church, the bishops of Vatican II gave the Catholic Church a new attitude toward other Christian churches, world religions and the modern world; at the same time it made startling changes in official Catholic worship, gave bishops and their local churches a new importance, extolled the role of nonordained persons in the church, encouraged Catholics to discover the riches of the Bible, and inspired a new spirituality. This constituted "a new paradigm of religious consciousness and church order."[7] Pope John Paul II stated that "for me the Second Vatican Council has always been . . . the constant reference point of every pastoral action."[8]

It is thus clear we are dealing with an extraordinary, even revolutionary, event in the Catholic Church. Yet most of my students had not even heard of Vatican II, let alone known its accomplishments. Even older Catholics and Protestant and Orthodox friends have scant acquaintance with the specific teachings of Vatican II and its influence on the Catholic Church today and on other Christian churches as well. This chapter, then, is pivotal. It forms the theological foundation for the entire book. It reveals the Catholic Church today: its tensions and divisions and its remarkable development in the 30 years since the Council ended. It helps us envision the future, still unknown, enfolding for the church. Furthermore, the Council was seen as the work of the Holy Spirit and a dramatic verification of Catholic belief, referred to in the previous chapter, that the Spirit is present and active in the church.

Vatican II was the 21st ecumenical council of the Catholic Church. An ecumenical or universal council is understood today as a meeting of all Catholic bishops and archbishops in the world and convoked by the pope.[9] Councils were summoned to meet a crisis in the church, generally of a doctrinal or teaching nature, to clarify and express Christian teaching or to con-

---

7. *Tradition and Transition*, 120.

8. Pope John Paul II address in *Synod Extraordinary*, 1.

9. The first seven ecumenical councils, covering the years 325-787, were called by the emperors of the time and were attended mainly by eastern bishops; today, only these seven councils are recognized by Orthodox churches. Succeeding councils were called by the popes and were attended by western or Roman Catholic bishops.

demn a major error or **heresy** in Christian belief. For example, the first ecumenical council in 325 in the city of Nicaea near Constantinople (modern Istanbul, Turkey) condemned Arianism, the heresy that Jesus is not equal to the Father in the trinity of persons, and therefore is not God. The second council in Constantinople in 381 formulated the teaching on the trinity of persons in one God expressed in the Nicene-Constantinopolitan creed recited during each Sunday Mass. However, a council can also deal with disciplinary matters, as in the Counter-Reformation **Council of Trent,** named after the northern Italian city of Trent where it was held from 1545-1563. Here the bishops reformed church life and corrected abuses, in addition to clarifying Catholic teaching challenged by Martin Luther and John Calvin and to condemning some of their teachings. The last council was Vatican I in Rome, from 1869 to 1870.

◆

Preview: To help us appreciate the revolutionary nature and extraordinary achievement of the Second Vatican Council, this chapter treats six topics essential to understanding and evaluating the Council: the remarkable person who summoned the Council, Pope John XXIII, and his worldwide vision; the Council itself and the great debate that reversed the influence of the Roman Curia and the traditionalist group of bishops, thus setting a new direction for the Council; the seven most important documents the Council produced, with an analysis of the theology they express; 10 major theological achievements of the Council; and an official evaluation of Vatican II made 20 years later by the bishops of the world meeting in an Extraordinary Synod.

◆

John XXIII

What kind of pope was responsible for convening Vatican II? Angelo Roncalli, Cardinal Archbishop of Venice, was a grandfatherly man of 79, deliberately elected pope so that, as it was facetiously said, he would not be able "to rock the boat" (the barque of Peter, the church) by being pope for a long period! The much-loved Pope John XXIII was a man unashamed of his peasant origin, a humble man blessed with a sense of humor and the common touch, a wise man of broad vision, owing to his sense of history and his experience as **nuncio** (ambassador) in countries as diverse as Bulgaria and Turkey after World War I and France after World War II; above all, he was a prayerful, saintly man.

His biographer said of Pope John:

Instead of maintaining the remote aristocratic presence of Pius XII [his predecessor as pope] on public occasions, he was fraternal and friendly. One of his favorite texts was from Genesis: "I am Joseph, your brother." He meant it. He used it to welcome Socialists to Venice and the American Jews that came to visit him in Rome. . . . People were amazed and delighted by Pope John because previous office-holders led them to expect to meet an autocrat inbred with a sense of his own dignity, and instead they met a brother.[10]

And so it was that this elderly pope of youthful spirit "by means of an impulse of Divine Providence felt the urgency of the duty to call our sons together" and ". . . welcoming as from above the intimate voice of our Spirit, we consider that the times now were right to offer to the Catholic Church and to the world the gift of a new ecumenical Council."[11] In another speech, he later seemed to say that the idea of calling the Council came to him while in prayer after celebrating Mass.

What were John's reasons for calling a Council? The Catholic Church appeared to be in excellent shape, with Catholic life prospering. In the United States, for example, city churches were full for as many as seven Sunday masses, the seminaries and convents were bulging with young men and women studying for the priesthood and to be religious sisters, prominent figures as well as ordinary people became converts to Catholicism at the rate of 150,000 a year, with the stories of their conversions often becoming best-sellers. The Catholic grade and high school and university system was the marvel of the Catholic world, educating millions each year; Catholic people flocked to the churches on weekdays for novenas and Forty Hours and Stations of the Cross and other devotional services; priests and sisters enjoyed high esteem, and the pope's statements were the "final word," as if from God. Catholics "prayed, obeyed, and paid"!

But John XXIII took a broader view. In his official document[12] of December 25, 1961, convening the Council, John looked toward the modern world. He optimistically felt that "humanity is on the edge of a new era." Yet he realistically saw "a crisis is under way within society," "a weakening . . . toward the values of the spirit," a world which reveals a grave state of spiritual poverty," and the "completely new and disconcerting fact [of] the existence of a militant atheism." He looked also at the division within the Christian Church and praised the "generous and growing efforts" for "rebuilding that visible unity of all Christians" which Christ desires; thus the Council can provide "doctrinal clarity and mutual

---

10. Peter Hebblethwaite, *In the Vatican* (London: Sidgwick & Jackson, 1986), 34.

11. John XXIII, *Humanae Salutis* convoking the Council, in Walter Abbott, ed., *The Documents of Vatican II* (New York: Guild Press, 1966), 705.

12. *Ibid.*, 703-4, 706.

charity" that will inspire even more in our "separated brothers the wish for the return to unity and will smooth the way to it." To refer to Protestants as "our separated brothers" was a positive first for a pope. Pope John also had in mind "all men of good will," that the Council might "turn their thoughts and their intentions toward peace" in a world "under the constant threat of new, frightful conflicts." John closed his words with a beautiful ecumenical prayer that the Council would be for all Christians a new outpouring of the Spirit on earth.

> Renew Your wonders in our time, as though for a new **Pentecost**, and grant that the holy Church, preserving unanimous and continuous prayer, together with Mary, the mother of Jesus, and also under the guidance of St. Peter, may increase the reign of the Divine Savior, the reign of truth and justice, the reign of love and peace. Amen.[13]

John's positive, optimistic, world-embracing vision shone even more in the stirring address he gave to the 2540 bishops assembled in St. Peter's basilica for the opening session of Vatican II on October 11, 1962. Several passages are particularly significant.

> In the daily exercise of our pastoral office, we sometimes have to listen, much to our regret, to voices of persons who, though burning with zeal, are not endowed with too much sense of discretion or measure. In these modern times they can see nothing but prevarication and ruin. They say that our era, in comparison with past eras, is getting worse, and they behave as though they had learned nothing from history, which is, nonetheless, the teacher of life. They behave as though at the time of former Councils everything was a full triumph for the Christian idea and life and for proper religious liberty.

> We feel we must disagree with those prophets of gloom, who are always forecasting disaster, as though the end of the world were at hand. In the present order of things, Divine providence is leading us to a new order of human relations which, by men's own efforts and even beyond their very expectations, are directed toward the fulfillment of God's superior and inscrutable designs. And everything, even human differences, leads to the greater good of the Church.

> [The church] must ever look to the present, to the new conditions and new forms of life introduced into the modern world which have opened new avenues to the Catholic apostolate.[14]

---

13. *Ibid.,* 709.
14. *Ibid.,* 712-13.

The "prophets of gloom" to whom John refers are officials in the **Roman curia** who opposed the ecumenical council and constantly put obstacles in its way. Never before had a pope spoken so bluntly.

Two phrases stand out in John's opening remarks: "signs of the times" and "*aggiornamento.*" John had a strong conviction that God spoke to the church and people of good will everywhere by the events and movements in history, which were "signs" pointing to God's activity and concerns. John thus urged the bishops to consider deeply what was happening in the world so that the church could respond. Obviously this was a new idea that the church had something to learn from the world; the pre-Vatican II church had seen the world as evil and a threat to be avoided. *Aggiornamento,* or updating, expressed John's desire to modernize the church to make it a more effective voice in the modern world. This spirit fired the imagination of the bishops and became a pervasive theme during the four years of the Council. In the context of reading the signs of the times and updating the church to respond to the events and needs of both the church and the contemporary world, we can distinguish four specific purposes of the Council:

- to *renew* the Catholic Church so that it will more faithfully reflect the gospel of Jesus;
- to *reunite* the divided church of Christ;
- to *apply the gospel of Christ* to the great problems of the world so that the human family might live in peace and justice;
- to *modernize* or update the church.

Thus did Pope John XXIII challenge the assembled bishops and give a new spirit and direction to the Catholic Church.

A New Kind of Council and the Great Debate

Vatican Council II differed dramatically from the previous 22 ecumenical councils in many ways. First, in sheer numbers. Trent at best had 200 members; Vatican I some 700, whereas 2540 bishops attended the opening session of Vatican II. Secondly, Vatican II was representative of the whole world; bishops from Africa and Asia came, as well as large numbers from Latin America. Previous councils had been predominantly European in makeup. Third, with his ecumenical sensitivity, John invited Orthodox and Protestant churches to send observers, who attended all the sessions but did not vote; the many informal conversations between the bishops and these non-Catholic observers added a rich dimension to the Council. It allowed the Council deliberations to be reviewed by scholars and churchmen with different viewpoints from those of Catholic theology and discipline. Fourth, journalists and radio and television followed the

Council closely, publicizing its debates and rousing the interest and expectations of the Christian world. Fifth, many of the bishops brought theologians along as their *periti* or experts to advise them; these theological experts, especially the European ones, employed a historical approach that made change possible.

> This mentality was a result of the revival of historical studies in the nineteenth century and the consequent application of historical methods to sacred subjects, particularly to the history of doctrine, discipline and liturgy. Theologians were thus much more aware of the profound changes that had taken place in the long history of the Church . . . [and which] could be adequately explained in merely human terms as expressions of a given culture and that they were therefore not necessarily irreversible.[15]

Sixth, the Council was positive in tone and pastoral in purpose. That is, its goal was not to condemn heresies or alleged aberrations in the church but to renew the church in its teaching and practices so that the gospel values of Jesus would shine forth more clearly for Catholics and all people. Seventh, its major topic and concern was the church: to achieve greater understanding of the church in its inner nature and to discover how it might better achieve its mission to its own members and to the world at large. This open-ended purpose allowed the bishops to examine all aspects of church life. Indeed, Vatican II is preeminently the Council of the church.

So the bishops set to work. A split soon developed between traditional bishops resistant to change, who understood the church according to the Council of Trent and its counter-Reformation theology and practices, and progressive bishops, who took *aggiornamento* according to the signs of the times seriously and wanted the church to change in its worship, its disciplinary practices, and even in its doctrinal formulations. This, of course, was seen by the traditionalists as disloyalty to the great Tradition of the Church and an embarassing admission that the church could change and in fact needed to change. However, Bishop DeSmedt from Bruges, Belgium, had the audacity to stand up and criticize the traditionalists' first draft on the church as being *triumphalistic* (a superiority attitude), *clericalistic* (bishops and priests dominating the laity in all phases of church life) and *legalistic* (too law-centered, thus failing to emphasize the larger "law of love" that is the gospel of Jesus). This three-fold critique aptly expressed progressives' thinking on the pre-Vatican II, Counter-Reformation church.

The great debate between these two groups took up much of the first session in 1962 and extended into the second session the following year. This debate makes interesting, even fascinating reading; one is privileged

---

15. *Tradition and Transition*, 14.

to see the inner workings of a so-called monolithic church as revered, famous cardinals and bishops rose to argue their convictions with force and emotion, disagreeing among themselves and sometimes verbally attacking their "esteemed confreres." The debate also helps us understand the church's need for change and why that change would be so difficult to achieve, for the issues were serious and the supporters of each side were intelligent, dedicated churchmen.

The leaders of the two groups soon became household names, thanks to international press coverage. The conservatives were led by the venerable Cardinal Alfredo Ottaviani, the most powerful man in the Roman Curia and the "watchdog of orthodoxy," as head of the much-feared **"Holy Office"**; Archbishop Pericle Felici, secretary-general of the Council, whose wit and Latin verses enlivened the general assembly; Archbishop Guiseppi Siri of Genoa, Italy; the Curia's Cardinal Michael Browne of Ireland; Archbishop Sigaud of Brazil, and lesser lights. The progressives were led by the indefatigable Cardinal Josef Frings of Cologne, who was responsible for getting most of the legislation passed; the stately, charismatic Cardinal Josef Suenens of Belgium, who suggested the Council should treat the church both "from within and looking outside," an insight that led to the document on the church in the modern world; Cardinal Franciscus Koenig of Vienna, who relied heavily on Karl Rahner, the German Jesuit theologian; Cardinals Lienart of France and Julius Doepfner of Munich; Cardinal Augustine Bea, the Jesuit scripture scholar who became head of the newly constituted Secretariate for Christian Unity; Cardinals Meyer of Chicago, Paul Leger of Montreal and Bernard Alfrink of Holland. They were aided by theologian-experts who have been called the intellectual architects of the Council: Rahner, Holland's Edward Schillebeeckx, the Dominican Yves Congar of France, Joseph Ratzinger of Germany and Hans Küng of Switzerland. In the confrontations between these two groups, several decisive moments in the first session of the Council occurred when the progressives mentioned above succeeded in having the much-criticized preliminary drafts on the liturgy and revelation prepared by the Curia and their conservative Roman theologians sent back to newly constituted commissions for rewriting.

Between the first and second sessions, John XXIII died after a long, painful illness and final agony, which he offered to God for the success of the Council. With typical humor and peacefulness, he told his doctors, "Don't be too worried. My bags are packed and I'm ready to go." Cardinal Giovanni-Battista Montini of Milan was elected on the first ballot and took the name Paul VI. It was Pope Paul VI, a brilliant, cautious progressive with much Vatican experience under Pope Pius XII, who successfully steered the Council through the next three years.

Two turning points came in the second session in 1963 that cemented the progressives' control of the Council. In a key vote on October 30, the conservative draft of the emotionally charged and theologically complex issue of episcopal **collegiality** was decisively repudiated. On November 8, called by Michael Novak "The Most Dramatic Day"[16] dealing with Cardinal Ottaviani's Holy Office, Cardinal Frings expressed amazement at Cardinal Browne's remarks against collegiality, and severely criticized the Roman curia and especially the procedures of the Holy Office as being "out of harmony with modern times" and "a source of harm to the faithful and of scandal to those outside the Church."[17] Cardinal Ottaviani rose to "protest most vigorously against the condemnation of the Holy Office" and to argue against the collegiality of bishops. Then in a powerful talk, Archbishop D'Souza of India said the Roman curia "must be thoroughly reformed," and concerning collegiality of bishops asked rhetorically: "We 20th-century bishops, are we so dangerous after all? Have we no sense of responsibility for the Church? Are we really incapable of deciding what is good for the churches entrusted to our care?"[18]

We have treated this debate at length for three reasons: to recreate in a small way the exciting dynamics of the Council and its giant personalities debating complex issues of great importance for the church; two, to show that Vatican II was a deliberate break with the church's dominant pre-Vatican II theology and practice; and three, to indicate that, despite progressive theology prevailing at the Council, the concerns of the traditionalist minority are very much alive in the church today

The Council's 16 Documents

The Council's final documents are the result of a complete revision of the original traditional drafts produced by the **Vatican curia** and their Roman theologians, of seemingly endless "interventions" or speeches by the bishops, of extensive work in multiple drafting commissions, of chapter-by-chapter and even article-by-article discussions and votes by the entire Council, and through it all of considerable compromise by both traditionalists and progressives to assure a consensus vote on each document. Nine documents are decrees, three are declarations, and four are termed constitutions to signify their importance and close relationship to the nature of the church. Of these constitutions, two are called dogmatic to stress their doctrinal or teaching content, and one pastoral to highlight how the church as pastor or shepherd cares for the needs of people and of the world. Because of the debate we have just considered, the first session produced no documents and the second only two; the last two sessions

---

16. Michael Novak, *The Open Church, Vatican II, Act II* (New York: The Macmillan Co., 1964), 223-41.
17. *Ibid.*, 224.
18. *Ibid.*, 228.

1963:

Constitution on the Sacred Liturgy
Decree on the Means of Social Communication

1964:

Dogmatic Constitution on the Church
Decree on the Catholic Eastern Churches
Decree on Ecumenism

1965:

Decree on the Pastoral Office of Bishops
Decree on the Up-to-Date Renewal of Religious Life
Decree on the Training of Priests
Declaration on Christian Education
Declaration on the Relation of the Church to Non-Christian Religions
Dogmatic Constitution on Divine Revelation
Decree on the Apostolate of Lay People
Declaration on Religious Liberty
Decree on the Church's Missionary Activity
Decree on the Ministry and Life of Priests
Pastoral Constitution on the Church in the Modern World

---

issued three and eleven documents respectively. The following list indicates the variety of important topics the Council dealt with.

Since these documents are of varying quality and importance, we shall introduce the seven most significant ones, reserving a fuller treatment for subsequent chapters. It is only honest to say that the documents make difficult, often boring reading, since they are lengthy, wordy, repetitious, technical, full of scriptural references, "churchy," and attempt to say almost everything about each topic. Yet perhaps it could not be otherwise, considering they break such new ground and are the work of so many bishops representing worldwide backgrounds and concerns, divergent theological positions, and varied experiences of Catholic and church life. Considering everything, their very existence is almost miraculous.

The Seven Most Influential Council Documents

1. Dogmatic Constitution on the Church (*Lumen Gentium*, Light of Nations), *Nov. 21, 1964.*

To appreciate why this document has been called "the centerpiece of the Council" or "perhaps the greatest achievement of the Council," we need to understand how the church viewed herself before the Council. Prior to the Protestant Reformation, the Catholic Church gave little explicit theological thought to her own nature as church. Since the office of pope and bishop were attacked by Luther, Calvin and other reformers, the Catholic Church emphasized structure, authority, the power of the pope and of bishops and clergy. The church became defensive and focused on hierarchical and institutional aspects. For the next 400 years, this theology of church dominated Roman Catholic thinking, climaxing in the definition of Vatican Council I in 1870 on the primacy and infallibility of the pope.

In the 19th century, certain movements in and outside the church caused Catholic theologians to challenge the predominant juridical and institutional approach to the church. For example: Bible scholarship challenged church assumptions about the origin of ecclesial institutions, drew attention to the role of Jesus and the Spirit in the life of the church, and made untenable an absolute identification of the historical church with the kingdom of God; the recovery of the teaching of the great bishop-theologians of the 4th to 7th centuries called attention to the historical character of the church as a developing and changing reality; the liturgical movement recovered the sense of the church as the primordial sacrament of Christ and shifted the focus from the universal church to the local worshipping community; the ecumenical movement begun by Protestants forced the Roman Catholic Church to reconsider its negative assessment of other Christian churches and even of other religions; and the philosophical shift from classical metaphysics to post-Kantian critical philosophies led to more emphasis on experience and existence and changed the method of theological reflection.

Thus was born a "new" ecclesiology or theology of church as mystery, as the people of God, as sacrament of the risen Christ and of our salvation. It was new in the sense that it recovered older understandings "lost" in the growth and centralization of papal power through the centuries and in Rome's defensive reaction to Protestantism before and during the Council of Trent. This newer ecclesiology embraced by the progressive bishops and their theologians clashed with the classical Roman theology centered in pope, hierarchy, and church as institution. The two theologies of church have been popularly visualized as a pyramid with pope, bishops, priests on top and the nonordained lay Christians below (traditional Roman ecclesiology) or as a large circle made up of all the baptized with the hierarchy in the center serving rather than dominating the people (newer ecclesiology). The confrontation of these two ecclesiologies resulted in a long battle over this document, lasting into the third session of the Council: the sharply criticized first draft of the church document was sent back for a complete rewriting; the second draft received 4000 amendments; a thoroughly revised third draft was voted on chapter-by-chapter, with the third chapter on "The Hierarchical Structure of the Church" voted on article by article. Finally on November 21, 1964, the *Dogmatic Constitution on the Church* of eight chapters[19] was approved by a vote of 2151 positive, 5 negative.

---

19. 1. The Mystery of the Church. 2. The People of God. 3. The Hierarchic Structure of the Church with Special Reference to the Episcopate. 4. The Laity. 5. The Call of the Whole Church to

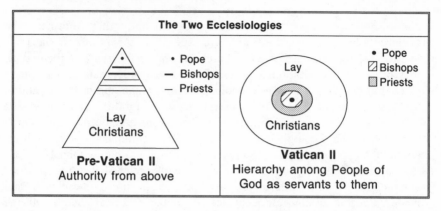

We have described the genesis of this document in order to highlight its great importance. We now have the official teaching of the Roman Catholic Church on its own nature; in a certain sense, the other documents depend on this teaching and are a further development of it. With a newer understanding of itself, the church embarks on a new direction for the decades ahead.

◆

Key Theological Foundations of *Lumen Gentium's* New Ecclesiology

1. The church in its deepest nature is a participation in the communitarian life of the trinity of persons in one God. This establishes the theology of the *church as communion*, a central insight of the Council. For the church is Christ-centered (the sacrament of Christ) and Spirit-oriented (the Spirit is the life of the church, its guide, source of its gifts, principle of its inner unity). This emphasis on church as mystery puts its institutional, hierarchic structure in perspective.

2. The church is described as the *people of God*. This stresses the church primarily as a community of persons, thus shifting the emphasis from the institutional aspect of the church.

3. The *office of bishops* is significantly upgraded when the Council teaches that the pope and bishops constitute a "college" or group which has supreme authority in the universal church when in communion, with the pope as its head. This restores a needed balance, for Vatican I treated only the powers of the pope. Moreover, *Lumen Gentium* solemnly teaches that the office of bishop is of divine institution, that is, created

Holiness. 6. Religious. 7. The Eschatological Nature of the Pilgrim Church and her Union with the Heavenly Church. 8. The Role of the Blessed Virgin Mary, Mother of God, in the Mystery of Christ and the Church.

by Christ the God-man and conferred by episcopal ordination. Thus bishops are essential to the church.

4. *Local churches,* the individual dioceses headed by a bishop, truly constitute the church of Christ and are not simply a subdivision of the *universal church.* This is important because Catholics had habitually thought in terms of the universal church to the neglect of the *local church.* Emphasis on local churches helps counteract the tendency to centralize all power and authority and decision-making in Rome, often to the grave harm of local churches. This recovery of an older emphasis on the local church has important implications for the church today.

5. The constitution emphasized the *dignity, equality, and mission of the nonordained* in the church. It stressed that they too are called by God to the fullness of Christian life and love.

6. The church is *not identical with the kingdom of God.* This makes it possible to appreciate other religions and all people of good will.

7. The Roman Catholic Church is *not identified exclusively* with the church founded by Christ. This opens the door for recognition of other Christian churches and participation in the ecumenical movement, and radically changes the notion that "outside the church there is no salvation."

8. By refusing to have a special document on Mary, as many bishops desired, and by inserting a chapter on Mary, the bishops moderated excessive Marian devotions and articulated a *more balanced theology of Mary* by emphasizing her role in the mystery of salvation and in the life of the church. The Vatican II title for Mary is "Mother of the Church."

However, *Lumen Gentium* left important ecclesiological issues unresolved that need further discussion by theologians.

2. The Pastoral Constitution on the Church in the Modern World (*Gaudium et Spes,* Joy and Hope), Dec. 7, 1965.

No other document shows so dramatically the contrast between how the pre-Vatican II church viewed itself in relation to the world and how the bishops at Vatican II envisioned the role of the church in the modern world. It was the first time in the long history of the Catholic Church that a document related the church so directly to the contemporary world.

This document has great significance for the Catholic Church because it redefined the church's mission and work and what it means to be a Catholic in today's world. We shall treat this document in detail in Chapter 9 when we consider the church's social teaching and its commitment to social justice.

3. The Constitution on the Sacred Liturgy (*Sacrosanctum Concilium,* The Most Holy Council), Dec. 4, 1963.

This document, more than all the others, brought home immediately and concretely to Catholics the changes made by the Council. For in the past, Catholic **liturgy** or worship, especially the Sunday Mass or Eucharist, was fixed, **rubrical**, clergy-oriented, and unintelligible. That is, liturgy never changed, it stressed external ritual actions, it was what priests with their back to the people did "up there" while the people were passive viewers, and it was in Latin. To the joy of most Catholics and the consternation of some, the bishops at Vatican II changed all this. It is important to understand their thinking and the ecclesiological and liturgical principles behind the changes.

This document was truly revolutionary. In calling for a complete revision of all the liturgical rites then in use, the bishops provided Catholics with a new experience of worship and of a spirituality based on the Bible. The effects soon became apparent in those parishes that carried out liturgical renewal. Good liturgy, especially in the Sunday Eucharist, creates a community who experience and share their Christian faith and love with each other and who develop a social consciousness that moves out in works of justice and love for others, thus overcoming excessive individualism and the devotionalism of a "me and God" spirituality.

Chapter 5 is devoted to liturgy and sacraments.

4. Decree on Ecumenism (*Unitatis redintegratio,* The Restoration of Unity), Nov. 21, 1964.

This decree constituted one of the great "breakthroughs" of Vatican II and is directly traceable to Pope John XXIII's goal for the Council of restoring unity among the separated Christian churches. With this decree, the Roman Catholic Church entered enthusiastically into the ecumenical movement which had been led by the predominantly Protestant World Council of Churches.

The magnitude of this breakthrough can only be appreciated if one contrasts the attitude of Catholics toward Protestants before and after the Council. Before Vatican II, Catholics were deliberately isolated from Protestants, were ignorant of their beliefs and practices, often were hostile and felt superior to them. What supported this situation was the Catholic conviction that "we" were the only true church of Christ, having real priests and therefore a real Eucharist because of ordinations in the apostolic succession. Thus "they" belonged to false churches and had false worship; Catholics, therefore, would sin by participating in Protestant worship. Some Catholics even held that Protestants could not be saved!

But thanks to the new theology of the Church of Christ, extending beyond the Roman Catholic Church enunciated in the *Dogmatic Constitu-*

tion on the Church and to the recommendations of this decree, Catholic theologians began to enter into serious theological dialogue with their Protestant counterparts, and rank-and-file Catholics began to pray with their newly termed "separated brothers and sisters in Christ." This remarkable about-face on the part of the Catholic Church delighted most Catholics, who saw it as reasonable and long overdue, for they had recognized the goodness and holiness and Christian commitment of their Protestant acquaintances and friends; but it distressed other Catholics, who felt the church was guilty of compromise and of becoming Protestant; for some, ecumenism became a "dirty word," ecclesially speaking!

We shall analyze this document in Chapter 8.

5. Dogmatic Constitution on Divine Revelation (Dei Verbum, Word of God), Nov. 18, 1965.

". . . this document represents an incredible achievement; it is a genuine watershed in the history of Roman Catholicism." So speaks Scripture scholar Fr. Donald Senior. He goes on to say:

> One has only to remember how some things were before the Council: the style of manual theology, the virtual absence of the Bible from Catholic devotional life, the rationalist approach to our catechisms, the muffling of the Word within our liturgical life, the ridicule directed towards Protestants because of their clinging to the Bible, the pale diet of historical minutiae and archaeological questions considered the only legitimate interest of Catholic biblical studies. Such memories help us realize the extraordinary change in consciousness that has come over Roman Catholicism since the time of the Council.[20]

In the light of this pre-Vatican II situation, it is not surprising that momentous battles between traditionalists and progressives occurred throughout all four years of the Council over this document. For "nothing is more fundamental and nothing so exposes one's theological worldview as this topic" of **revelation.**[21] That is, did God reveal or speak to us *exclusively* in the Bible, as Protestants held, or *primarily* through Tradition, as Catholics emphasized against the Protestant Reformers? It took the initiatives by Pope John XXIII in 1962 and Pope Paul VI in 1963 to send the highly traditional draft back to committee for revision and then to move the more progressive statement to completion. Yet the final document evidences an "uneasy compromise between opposing worldviews: one, more traditional, essentialist, heavily supernaturalist and static; the other more historically sensitive, immanentist, dialectical and process-oriented."[22]

---

20. *An American Reappraisal,* 139.
21. *Ibid.,* 123.
22. *Ibid.*

◆

Theological Achievements of *Dei Verbum* (DV)

1. A dynamic view of revelation as *God's ongoing self-communication* to humans in a myriad of ways, including the circumstances of daily life. This opened up rich possibilities of appreciation for contact with God through human experience, created realities, and other religious traditions. (DV 2 and 3)

2. On the issues of the inspiration and inerrancy of the Bible, it *avoided* the worst traps of *fundamentalism*, that is, literal interpretation of the Bible on the supposition that *everything* is *directly* inspired by God and thus free of *all* error. (DV 11 and 12)

3. It stressed the role of the *human authors* of the Bible, so that to understand the Bible one must consider the time-conditioned circumstances of their writing. (DV 11-13)

4. It admits that both "sacred Tradition and sacred Scripture make up a *single deposit of the Word of God* which is entrusted to the Church." (DV 10) This avoids affirming two separate sources of revelation: tradition and Scripture. The inevitable historical effect of holding the two-source theory was that for 400 years after the Council of Trent, the Roman Catholic Church emphasized Tradition to such an extent that the Bible played a minor role in theologizing and in the spiritual life of Catholic people and failed to prophetically challenge the hierarchical church.

5. "One of the most significant achievements of the Council, and one whose impact is just being felt, is its unabashed endorsement of the *historical-critical method* of **biblical criticism.**"[23] In thus encouraging biblical scholarship, Catholic scripture scholars have now taken their place alongside Protestant, Orthodox and Anglican biblical scholars.

6. Finally, a valuable practical effect has been Catholics' *"rediscovery" of the Bible:* Catholics read and pray the Bible, join Bible study-prayer groups with their Protestant sisters and brothers, experience how the Hebrew and Christian scriptures inspire them to a deeper love of God and Jesus and the Spirit, and challenge them to a practical love of others based on justice. This new biblical spirituality has greatly enriched the Catholic Church.

◆

We shall not devote a separate chapter to this important document; however, its influence pervades today's church.

---

23. *Ibid.,* 127.

6. Declaration on Religious Liberty (*Dignitatis Humanae,* Of Human Dignity), Dec. 7, 1965.

Pope Paul VI called this declaration "one of the major texts of the Council." The American Jesuit John Courtney Murray, the architect of this document, termed it "a significant event in the history of the Church" and "the most controversial document of the whole Council."[24]

Approval of *Dignitatis Humanae* did not come easily in the Council. Catholic teaching for at least a thousand years on religious tolerance of **"heretics"** with its impact on the relation of church and state, went like this: all must embrace the true faith; civil society (the state) must promote that true faith; but if in the state some do not accept the true faith, the state may for the sake of the common good and peace "tolerate" their profession of a false religion; but these people do not have a *right* to profess another religion because error has no rights.[25] Thus in the Catholic countries of Europe and of South America, Protestants who were considered heretics had a hard time. Recall also the institution of the much-feared **Inquisition.**

According to John Courtney Murray, "the notion of development, not of religious freedom, was the real sticking point for many of those who opposed *Dignitatis Humanae* even to the end . . . because it raised with sharp emphasis the issue that lay continually below the surface of the conciliar debates . . . the development of doctrine."[26] Because the Catholic Church in the 1864 **Syllabus of Errors** had condemned religious freedom, many bishops saw this document as reversing long-held Catholic teaching by embracing a new doctrine. But progressive bishops, following their theological experts, accepted the thesis of John Henry Newman's groundbreaking scholarly work, *The Development of Doctrine,* which argued that Christian teaching had indeed "developed" in the history of the church.

Against this background it is not surprising that *Dignitatis Humanae* went through six drafts before it was finally approved 2308 for, 7 against. The major objections were these:

- the above reasoning on the tolerance of error and especially the concept of "development," that a new doctrine had come to the fore;
- fear that the church would lose status and its privileged position in society;
- the lack of clear evidence that Scripture supported the declaration;
- fear that it promoted religious indifference, that is, that one church or religion is as good as another;
- concern that it would give the state power over the church, a concern not unfounded in communist countries or totally secularist states.

---

24. John Courtney Murray, quoted in Abbott, *Documents of Vatican II,* 673.
25. *Ibid.*
26. *Ibid.*

The basis of this revolutionary declaration on religious liberty can be summarized in the following important statement:

> . . . the right to freedom in religious matters, freedom from psychological and external coercion, and freedom to seek truth, embrace it, adhere to it, and act on it inheres in each man and woman by reason of his/her dignity as a person endowed with reason and free will and therefore endowed with conscience and personal responsibility.[27]

Each person "is bound to follow his conscience faithfully in all his activity so that he may come to God who is his last end." (DH 3) Consequently, no one can be forced to act contrary to conscience nor prevented from acting according to conscience. The reason for this is that "the exercise of religion of its very nature consists primarily of those voluntary and free acts by which a man directs himself to God."(DH 3) Civil authority must protect these basic rights of each person.

◆

Immense Importance of *Dignitatis Humanae*

1. The Catholic Church formally recognizes that "the human person has a *right to religious freedom*" (emphasis added) which means that "in matters religious no one is to be forced to act in a manner contrary to his own beliefs" (DH 2). The church thus repudiates the double standard of "freedom for the church when Catholics are a minority and intolerance for others when Catholics are a majority."[28] This principle has strong implications for relations with other Christian churches and the world religions.

2. The Council has officially approved the theological principle of the *"development of doctrine."* This refers to the fact that Catholic teaching has changed by being further "developed" by theologians over the centuries, under the guidance of the Spirit and in response to changing historical conditions. It can therefore continue to do so in the future. This principle has far-reaching implications for serious church issues today, as we shall consider in future chapters.

3. The Council affirmed the *primacy of individual conscience.* This too has had important application, especially in contemporary moral questions and the relationship of Catholics to church authority.

4. The Council made a strong case for the right of the church and its members to enjoy *free exercise of religion,* especially in totalitarian states. That Pope John Paul II has so strongly insisted on this principle

---

27. *An American Reappraisal,* 168.
28. Murray in *Documents of Vatican II,* 673.

in his world travels has in no small measure contributed to the recent events in Eastern Europe and Soviet Russia.

◆

Before we leave this remarkable document, three significant points are of interest. First, the Council bishops admitted that the church in the past had failed in regard to religious freedom, a welcome but long-overdue action. (DH 12) Second, what softened the opposition to Dignitatis Humanae was the theological distinction championed by Murray between error, which has no rights, and the erring person, who has rights despite his error. Third, the document is a concrete example of Pope John XXIII's exhortation to look at the "signs of the times" to find God at work in the world. The bishops express this in their eloquent opening lines of *Dignitatis Humanae:*

> Contemporary man is becoming increasingly conscious of the dignity of the human person; more and more people are demanding that men should exercise fully their own judgment and a responsible freedom in their actions . . . at the same time they are demanding constitutional limitation of the powers of government to prevent excessive restriction of the rightful freedom of individuals and associations. This demand for freedom . . . is concerned chiefly with . . . the free practice of religion in society. This Vatican Council pays careful attention to these spiritual aspirations. (DH 1)

We think of the extraordinary transformation of Soviet society, and realize how prophetic and in tune with modern hopes and aspirations the bishops of Vatican II were.

The principles enunciated in this document pervade our entire book, having major implications for the inner life of the Catholic Church and for topics and issues to be treated in many of the chapters.

7. Decree on the Church's Missionary Activity (*Ad Gentes,* To the Nations), Dec. 7, 1965.

Though not as "revolutionary" as the previous six documents, this decree has become increasingly important and of much interest today because of Pope John Paul II's challenge of the "new evangelization" and the consequent urgency of **inculturation**. For **evangelization**, bringing the good news of Christ to all peoples and planting the church where it has not existed before, and inculturation, adapting the Christian message to the different cultures of the world, are major goals of the contemporary church. Evangelization through inculturation involves insights and new direction enunciated in the Council's key documents on liturgy, ecumenism, revelation, religious liberty, and especially the two constitutions on the church[29] and on the church in the modern world.[30]

Thus the significant contribution of *Ad Gentes* is the principles and inspiration it established for the church's evangelization and inculturation in the period after the Council. In its most memorable sentence, the decree states that "The Church on earth is by its very nature missionary" (AG 2). Its urgency is the fact that "there are two billion people . . . who have never or barely heard the Gospel message" (AG 10).

In its final chapter, *Ad Gentes* stresses that evangelization is "the fundamental task" of the whole people of God (AG 35) — of local bishops, their priests, and the nonordained laity — and not as in the past almost exclusively of religious orders and congregations.

This decree has special importance for our chapter 6, where we consider evangelization and inculturation as part of the mission of the church, and in chapters 19 and 21, when we discuss the church's unresolved issues and challenges/opportunities.

Achievements: Ten Basic Principles

What has the Council accomplished for the church? We shall follow the formulation of Avery Dulles, a leading American ecclesiologist.[31] In setting forth "the basic vision of the Church as understood by Vatican II," his contention is that these 10 principles are "unquestionably endorsed by the Council" and "whoever does not accept all ten of these principles, I contend, cannot honestly claim to have accepted the results of Vatican II."[32] These principles, which provide a succinct overview of the major achievements of the Council, will appear often throughout subsequent chapters as essential to the continuing renewal of the Catholic Church and its promise for the future.

1. *Aggiornamento.* As we have seen, John XXIII "made this concept fundamental to his own program for the coming Council. . . . The Church, glorying in its magnificent heritage, should not allow itself to become a museum piece."[33]

---

29. The theological basis for the church sending missionaries to preach the gospel and plant the church is found in the following emphases in *Lumen Gentium*: the mystery of the Father sending his Son to save all peoples and of Jesus establishing God's kingdom and sending his Spirit into the world; the importance of local churches; the mission and ministry of all the people of God.

30. *Gaudium et Spes* committed the church to dialogue with the modern world and all cultures, devoting an entire section (Part II, ch. 2, #'s 53-62) to culture. It recognized the positive values of various cultures and called attention to how "the Gospel of Christ constantly renews the life and culture of fallen humanity . . . ," works to "purify and elevate the morality of peoples . . . makes fruitful the spiritual qualities and traditions of every people." (#58)

31. Avery Dulles, *The Reshaping of Catholicism: Current Challenges in the Theology of Church* (San Francisco: Harper & Row, 1988), 19-33.

32. *Ibid.*, 20.

33. *Ibid.*, 20-21.

2. *The Reformability of the Church.* Catholics had regarded the church as pure and holy. But Vatican II called it the people of God, a pilgrim people, capable of sin, and in need of continual reformation. "Thanks to Vatican II, however, we are relieved of the burden of having to defend the whole record of the past. We can freely admit that not only individual Catholics, but the church itself in its official actions has committed errors and sins, such as the burning of heretics, the persecution of Jews, and the excesses of Holy Wars. We can admit that Catholics had a large share of responsibility in bringing on the divisions among Christians that so weaken the Christian witness in our time."[34]

3. *Renewed Attention to the Word of God.* Since the Middle Ages, "Catholicism tended to become the church of law and sacraments rather than the Church of the gospel and the word. Catholics too often neglected the spiritual riches contained in the Bible. . . . In Catholic theology, the Bible was viewed as a remote source of doctrine, hardly used except to find proof texts for later church doctrines."[35] Vatican II changed this. The *Decree on Revelation* has this eloquent sentence. "For in the sacred books the Father who is in heaven meets his children with great love and speaks with them; and the force and power of the word of God is so great that it remains the support and energy of the Church, the strength of faith for her children, the food of the soul, and a pure and perennial source of spiritual life" (DV, 21).

4. *Collegiality.* Father Dulles asserts that "the principle of collegiality runs through the documents of Vatican II like a golden thread."[36] This principle, the sharing of decision-making and collaboration at all levels of the life of the church, pope and bishops, local bishop and his priests, parish priests and people, is one of the most important aspects of the renewal of the church envisioned by the Council. It will reappear often throughout these pages.

5. *Religious Freedom.* As we have seen in speaking of *Dignitatis Humanae,* this truly was a momentous step for the church.

6. *Active Role of the Laity.* Prior to Vatican II, Catholic laity were rather passive. Vatican II sought to change this. The *Decree on the Apostolate of the Laity* exhorted laypersons "to exercise their apostolate both in the Church and in the world, in both the spiritual and temporal orders."[37] *Gaudium et Spes* insisted that "all the faithful, clerical and lay, possess a lawful freedom of inquiry and of thought, and the freedom to express their minds humbly and courageously. . ."[38] The great in-

---

34. *Ibid.,* 22.
35. *Ibid.,* 23.
36. *Ibid.,* 25.
37. *AA,* 5.

crease in lay ministries since the Council has become one of the most important developments of the Vatican II church and will continue even more so.

7. *Regional and Local Variety.* This emphasis on the local church or diocese is another one of those major emphases of Vatican II. This offsets the centralization of power and decision-making in Rome that had been increasing ever since the Council of Trent, but especially since Vatican I with its strong emphasis on the pope and his powers. Dulles characterized it thus:

From the late Middle Ages until Vatican II, the characteristic emphasis of Catholicism had been on the universal church, commonly depicted as an almost monolithic society. Vatican II, by contrast, emphasized the local churches, each of them under direction of a bishop. . . . The local bishop, on the ground of his ordination and appointment, is given authority to be a true pastor of his own community, making responsible decisions rather than simply carrying out Roman directives. [39]

8. *Ecumenism.* We have seen how Pope John XXIII and Vatican II have effected a major change in regard to accepting other Christian churches and to working for the full unity of Christ's one church. We shall devote the entire chapter 8 to this subject and to the progress made since the Council.

9. *Dialogue with Other Religions.* Though Vatican II continued to "insist on the God-given uniqueness of the Church of Christ and consequently on the abiding necessity of missionary labor,"[40] nonetheless the Council moved the church into respectful dialogue with the great world religions, especially with Judaism.

10. *The Social Mission of the Church.* This commitment of the church to working for the kingdom of God on earth precisely as part of its gospel mission is another one of the great insights and revolutionary principles of Vatican II and the result of John XXIII's openness to the world. Dulles points out that since the Reformation, the Catholic Church has tended to regard its mission as an exclusively religious one, aimed at preparing individuals through faith, worship, and right behavior to attain eternal life. Gradually, with the social encyclicals of popes such as Leo XIII and Pius XI, the church began to assume responsibility to teach the principles of a just social order, but this order was viewed in terms of conformity to the natural law rather than as an implementation of the Gospel.[41] This principle will be treated in Chapters 9 and 18.

---

38. *GS*, 62.
39. *Reshaping of Catholicism*, 28.
40. *Ibid.*, 31.
41. *Ibid.*, 31-2.

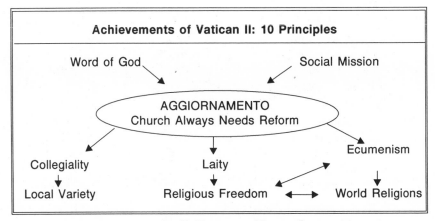

Evaluation of the Council Twenty Years Later

Having analyzed the purposes, documents and theological achievements of Vatican II, we ask: was Vatican II good for the Catholic Church? has the church understood and carried out the teaching and renewal of the Council? It would appear not from the evaluation made by Cardinal Josef Ratzinger in 1985, referred to in the previous chapter as *The Ratzinger Report.*[42] The cardinal presented a pessimistic view of the Catholic Church, which he felt had opened itself indiscriminately to an atheistic and agnostic world. "He portrayed the post-conciliar period as largely a time of dissent, discouragement, decadence and self-destruction on the part of large groups of Catholics who, in their endeavor to put the Council into practice, were guilty of 'every kind of heretical deviation.'"[43]

However, another evaluation of the Council is possible. To celebrate the 20th anniversary of the completion of Vatican II, Pope John Paul II called the Extraordinary **Synod** of bishops to meet in Rome from November 25 to December 8, 1985. His three-fold purpose was to revive the "extraordinary atmosphere of ecclesial communion" which characterized the Council, to examine how Vatican II has been carried out in the various regions of the world, and to decide how better to apply the Council to the life of the church. Thirteen questions[44] to evaluate how well the church has promoted, interpreted, and applied Vatican II were sent to 104 national bishops' con-

---

42. *The Ratzinger Report* (San Francisco: Ignatius Press, 1985).

43. Xavier Rynne, *John Paul's Extraordinary Synod: A Collegial Achievement* (Wilmington: Michael Glazier, 1986), 25.

44. The first four questions were sent out first: "1. What has been done to make the Council known, faithfully accepted, and put into practice? 2. What benefits have followed from the Council in the actual life of your church? 3. Are there any errors or abuses in the interpretation and application of Vatican II . . . ? 4. What have been the difficulties in putting the Council into practice . . . ? What should be laid down . . . to encourage further progress according to the letter and spirit of Vatican II?" The later additional nine questions dealt with the 16 Council documents. See Peter Hebblethwaite, *Synod Extraordinary* (Garden City, NY: Doubleday & Co., 1986), 29-32.

ferences. Their reports were summarized by Cardinal Godfried Danneels at the opening of the Synod.

The cardinal gave a positive assessment. He summarized the achievements of the four constitutions[45] he termed the *Magna Carta* of the church today: Liturgy, Revelation, Church as Light of Nations, Church in Modern World. He mentioned other positive points concerning bishops and priests, vowed religious life, ecumenism, missionary spirit, concluding that:

> all of this constitutes a great motive for joy and gratitude throughout the Church. An objective vision, not to mention a vision of faith, authorizes neither pessimism nor resignation nor discouragement. The post-conciliar church is alive and lives with intensity.[46]

As to "negative elements" and "difficulties" in applying the renewal of the Council, Cardinal Danneels appeared to disagree with Cardinal Ratzinger's judgment. The remedies "cannot be reduced to disciplinary or administrative measures. Postconciliar weaknesses cannot be put right by preconciliar measures."[47] What was needed, he believed, was not a repudiation of the Council or even a revision of its teachings but a deeper knowledge and understanding of them.

According to Avery Dulles, the Synod and the reports of its various discussion groups reflected two schools of thought among the bishops. The first group, led by Cardinals Ratzinger and Josef Hoeffner of Germany, had in Dulles' view "a markedly supernaturalistic point of view, tending to depict the church as an island of grace in a world given over to sin." Since "the world is falling into misery, division and violence" and since "Catholics who seek friendship with the world easily fall into materialism, consumerism and religious indifference . . . the church today must take a sharper stance against the world and seek to arouse a sense of God's holy mystery."[48] The second group, represented by Cardinal Hume of England and Bishops James Malone and Bernard Hubert, presidents of the U.S.A. and Canadian bishops' conferences, took a "more humanistic and communitarian view." Dulles summarized the views of the second group:

> Convinced that great progress had been made as a result of the Council, they attributed the main difficulties to the failure of conservative prelates [bishops] to carry through the reforms of Vatican II. If there is disenchantment among youth, it is . . . because the necessary reforms have been resisted and partly blocked. The Catholic Church has not yet succeeded in giving its laity an adequate sense of participation in and coresponsibility for the mission of the church. The urgent need today is for a further development of collegial and synodal structures so that the church may become

---

45. *Ibid.*, 111.
46. *Ibid.*, 112.
47. *Ibid.*, 115.
48. *Reshaping Catholicism*, 191.

a free and progressive society, a sign of unity in diversity, at home in every nation and every sociological group.[49]

Incorporating the concerns of both schools of thought, the Synod's brief *Message to the People of God* and the longer *Final Report*[50] present a balanced picture of the church's renewal today and a positive affirmation of Vatican II. The *Message* calls the Council "a gift of God to the church and to the world," "a source of light and strength," "the great grace of this century." The more restrained *Final Report* saw Vatican II as "a lawful and valid expression and interpretation of the deposit of faith (I 1), as being "in continuity with the great tradition of the church" (I 5), and "the greatest grace of this century." (IID 7) Thus "the message of the Council, already received with great agreement by the whole church, is and remains the [church's] *Magna Carta* for future times." (IID 7)

The *Final Report* affirmed major themes of the Council, though with cautions: unity and pluriformity, collegiality, bishops' conferences, participation and coresponsibility, ecumenism, *aggiornamento*, inculturation, interfaith dialogue, and preferential option for the poor. Noteworthy was the Final Report's stress that "the ecclesiology of communion is a central and fundamental idea in the documents of Vatican II" (IIC) and the Message's reaffirmation of the Council's call for the full participation of Christians in the struggle to build "a civilization of love."

We have treated this Extraordinary Synod in detail to make two important points for the rest of the book: one, the Catholic Church through its bishops and Pope John Paul II has officially reaffirmed Vatican II and given a positive assessment to the renewal taking place throughout the Catholic Church worldwide; and two, serious reservations by dedicated bishops about the renewal of the church since the Council and even about Vatican II itself exist in the Catholic Church as a continuing source of division and tension. Taking a hopeful view, Dulles judged that the Synod's *Final Report* as a compromise/consensus statement can "become a unifying and stabilizing factor in a divided and turbulent church" and "in effecting reconciliation between two groups that would otherwise clash."[51]

Summary

The Second Vatican Council was a revolutionary event for the Catholic Church because it overturned four centuries of the defensive and unchanging counter-Reformation Church of the Council of Trent, moved the church into the modern world and into the ecumenical movement with other Christian churches, changed its worship dramatically, and provided

---

49. *Ibid.*, 192.
50. These are printed in full in Rynne's *John Paul's Extraordinary Synod*, 107-132.
51. *Reshaping Catholicism*, 195.

new theological principles for present and future change and development. The Council must be understood in relation to John XXIII, who called it. Change did not come easily, as the great debate in the first two sessions demonstrated. Seven of the 16 documents produced by the Council are singled out for explanation and theological analysis since they constitute the theological heart of the Council and have most changed the Catholic Church. To help pinpoint the work of the Council, Avery Dulles' formulation of 10 principles express and summarize the theological accomplishments of Vatican II. Because Catholics today are either ignorant of Vatican II or divided in their reaction to it, an evaluation is necessary. In 1985, 20 years after the Council, Vatican II received a positive official evaluation from the Extraordinary Synod of bishops called by Pope Paul II "to celebrate, reaffirm, and carry forward the work of the Second Vatican Council."

For Discussion

1. Why is the kind of person Pope John XXIII was essential to understanding Vatican II?

2. For Christians today, what are some of the "signs of the times" both in the world and within the church? To what might the signs be pointing?

3. What do you think are the most important reasons why the *Dogmatic Constitution on the Church* is "the greatest achievement of the Council"?

4. Why basically is the *Dogmatic Constitution on Divine Revelation* "a genuine watershed in the history of Roman Catholicism"? Stress its *practical* results in the life of Catholics.

5. Why is the *Declaration on Religious Liberty* a truly revolutionary change in the Catholic Church? In what ways has it affected Catholics today?

6. Do you agree with Cardinal Ratzinger's judgement about the effects of the Council? What is the evidence on which you base your opinion?

For Action

1. To capture one of the most dramatic moments of the Council, read Michael Novak's account of "The Most Dramatic Day" in his book *The Open Church*.

2. Get acquainted with the much loved and admired Pope John XXIII by reading a brief account of his life in an encyclopedia.

Further Reading

Abbott, Walter, ed. *The Documents of Vatican II.* New York: Guild Press, 1966.

Dulles, Avery. *The Craft of Theology: From Symbol to System.* New York: Crossroad, 1992.

_____. *The Reshaping of Catholicism: Current Challenges in the Theology of the Church.* San Francisco: Harper and Row, 1988.

Hebblethwaite, Peter. *Synod Extraordinary: the Inside Story of the Rome Synod.* Garden City, NY: Doubleday & Co., 1986.

Novak, Michael. *The Open Church: Vatican II, Act II.* New York: The Macmillan Company, 1964.

O'Connell, Timothy, ed. *Vatican II and Its Documents, An American Reappraisal.* Wilmington, DE: Michael Glazier, 1986.

O'Malley, John. *Tradition and Transition: Historical Perspectives on Vatican II.* Wilmington, DE: Michael Glazier, 1989.

Rynne, Xavier. *John Paul's Extraordinary Synod, A Collegial Achievement.* Wilmington, DE: Michael Glazier, 1986.

Sanks, T. Howland. *Salt, Leaven, and Light: the Community Called Church.* New York: Crossroad Publishing Co., 1992.

Wiltgen, Ralph. *The Rhine Flows into the Tiber.* New York: Hawthorne Books, Inc., 1967.

CHAPTER 3

Church as Mystery

"The Church is a mystery, that is, it is a reality imbued with the hidden presence of God."   —Pope Paul VI

"The Church . . . the Kingdom of Christ now present in mystery, grows visibly through the power of God in the world."
—Lumen Gentium, 8

"Christ . . . established and ceaselessly sustains here on earth His holy Church, the community of faith, hope and charity as a visible structure. . . . This is the unique Church of Christ which in the Creed we avow as one, holy, catholic and apostolic. . . . By the power of the risen Lord, she is given strength . . . to show forth in the world the mystery of the Lord."
—Lumen Gentium, 8

Introduction

Each semester in my church course more than a few students write that they have either left the church or no longer are practicing Catholics. Their reasons are varied, but they often mention unhappy experiences with priests or nuns, disagreement with church teachings they consider unreasonable or even oppressive, or "hypocritical" Catholics. A recent informative book, *Once a Catholic,*[1] contains interesting and nuanced interviews with 25 prominent former or "lapsed" Catholics and current Catholics who are outspoken critics of aspects of the church. Their accounts, personal and specific, are instructive. Both my students and those interviewed appeared

---

1. Peter Occhiogrosso, *Once a Catholic* (New York: Ballantine Books, 1987).

to have become disillusioned with the church or even left it for sincere but seemingly inadequate reasons: the church's human and sinful and institutional aspects.

There is also an opposite reality. Some Catholics are overly impressed with the grand aspects of church: magnificent cathedrals and church buildings, the pageantry of popes and bishops, inspiring choir music, and the law and order aspects of discipline, rigid orthodoxy, the certitude of truth. This too easily leads to triumphalism and pride, the temptation of all religion.

Common to both groups is the tendency to focus on externals, on the human and sinful side of church leaders and members, on the church as institution or large organization. In so doing they overlook or do not take seriously enough the deeper reality of church as the special domain of the Triune God.

Vatican II sought to describe and emphasize this profound reality by using the word "mystery" to name the church.

"Mystery" is a difficult term for moderns to understand and accept for it connotes different things. It can mean something I don't understand, as in "It's a mystery to me." It can signify something above and beyond the ordinary and normal, as "It's a miracle." Or it can hint at the ghostly, with overtones of superstition, as "That's mysterious." By mystery, Vatican II meant something vastly different. Mystery refers to a reality beyond our senses, the divine dimension and nature of the church. Mystery points to the transcendent God, the risen Christ and his Spirit; to their presence and activity in the church; to the divine realities of grace and salvation and God's design for the human family.

Naming the church a mystery was another one of those great achievements of Vatican II. Prior to the Council, the church was presented almost exclusively as a visible organization and in terms of its leaders. For example, the juridical definition by Cardinal Bellarmine in the 17th century: The one and true church is "the assembly of humans, bound together by the profession of the same faith, and the communion of the same sacraments, under the governance of legitimate pastors and especially under the one vicar of Christ on earth, the Roman Pontiff."[2] At first reading this seems to be an excellent definition; it enumerates the visible, external qualities of the Catholic Church and provides clear norms for recognizing and distinguishing that church from the Reformation churches of Bellarmine's time.

---

2. Cardinal Robert Bellarmine, *Controversies*, quoted in T. Howland Sanks, *Salt, Leaven and Light* (New York: Crossroad, 1992), 90.

But Vatican II refused to define the church in this fashion. By calling the church "mystery," the bishops chose to emphasize the most profound aspect of the church, that which makes it utterly unique: not a mere human organization but a human-divine reality, a mystery. For in its deepest nature the triune God is present to and active in the church. The Christian Church on earth is thus the realization of God's plan to unify all things in Christ. To emphasize this vision of the church, the bishops deliberately changed the order of chapters in the *Dogmatic Constitution on the Church.* They made "the Church as Mystery" the first chapter, moving the original first chapter on "The Hierarchical Church" to Chapter 3. This seemingly insignificant change served to highlight the divine nature of the church and returned the emphasis on church from its external to its internal reality, from its human, institutional aspects to its divine elements. The passage from *Lumen Gentium,* 8, quoted above, describes this reality.

◆

Preview: Since we too often focus on the visible, human, and sinful aspects of the church and because the pre-Vatican II church had emphasized its institutional dimensions, the Council bishops wanted to stress that in its most profound nature the church is a human-divine reality, a mystery. In our theological reflection on the Church as mystery, we shall for the most part follow the order of chapter 1 in *Lumen Gentium.* We reflect theologically on four aspects of the church: as sacrament of the risen Christ, as God's incredible plan for the human family, as founded by Jesus the God-man, and as the body of Christ according to St. Paul's vivid metaphor. We then consider in what ways the risen Christ and his Holy Spirit are present and active in the church. From the previous considerations we reflect on how the church as mystery can only be understood and accepted by God's gift of Christian faith. We close by showing the practical results for the life of the church today when one emphasizes the church as mystery.

◆

Theological Reflection on the Christian Church as Mystery

Our reflection on the Christian Church in this chapter is largely theological. That is, by reflecting on what God has revealed to us in the Christian Scriptures, we draw theological conclusions and offer theological explanations on the divine-transcendent nature of the Christian Church. We should note that, even though our reflections present *Catholic* theology on the nature of the church, this theology nonetheless applies to other Christian churches and is accepted by most of them as their understanding and belief also.

The Church as Sacrament of the Risen Christ

What does it mean to call the church **sacrament**? For example, why can we say the following are "sacraments"? Ocean waves crashing white against a rocky coast? The delicate beauty of an orchid? An athlete's grace and the "moves" of a Michael Jordan? A loving, selfless parent or grandparent? A treasured friend?

Each of these somehow point to something beyond themselves. To persons sensitive to the transcendent dimension of nature and human life, the ocean speaks eloquently of the power and immensity of God, the flower of God's beauty, the athlete's ballet agility of God's creative gifts, loving relatives and friends of God's enduring love and attractiveness. Nature and people are like mirrors reflecting the divine. They make God real and present in human life. In fact, the whole universe is the sacrament of God — of his love and creative power. The poet Gerard Manley Hopkins captured the sacramental reality in his poem *God's Grandeur,* whose opening line proclaims "The world is charged with the grandeur of God."[3] Malcolm Muggeridge in his brief gem of a book, *Something Beautiful for God,*[4] saw in Mother Teresa of Calcutta the face of a loving God. At the funeral in St. Patrick's cathedral in New York of Dorothy Day, who dedicated her long life to helping the extreme poor and fighting for social justice, a street person with tears streaming down his face said "This dear lady is the closest thing to God I will ever see!"

The above examples express the first aspect of sacrament: a *sign* pointing to something beyond itself, to a more profound reality, ultimately to the transcendent reality pervading the universe, to God. The second aspect of a sacrament is its ability to accomplish or effect the spiritual reality it points to. It is thus an *instrument* used by God. *Lumen Gentium* explains this dual aspect of sacrament in its eloquent opening statement:

> Christ is the light of all nations. . . . By her relationship with
> Christ, the Church is a kind of sacrament or sign of intimate union
> with God and the unity of all mankind. She is also the instrument
> for the achievement of such union and unity. (LG 1)

The church is a sacrament of Christ "by her relationship with Christ." Jesus Christ is called the first or basic sacrament of God because as God-man he revealed in his lifetime the invisible God to all who heard his teachings and experienced his miracles and healings; he "incarnated" in his

---

3. "The world is charged with the grandeur of God. It will flame out, like shining from shook foil; It gathers to a greatness, like the ooze of oil Crushed . . . nature is never spent; There lives the dearest freshness deep down things; And though the last lights off the black West went Oh, morning, at the brown brink eastward, springs—Because the Holy Ghost over the bent World broods with warm breast and with ah! bright wings." Norman Mackenzie, ed., *The Poetical Works of Gerard Manley Hopkins* (New York: Oxford University Press, 1990), 131.

4. Malcolm Muggeridge, *Something Beautiful for God* (New York: Harper and Row, 1971).

human flesh God's compassion and love for the Jews of his day. Moreover, he not only revealed God but *brought about* God's plan on earth through his powerful teaching and healings.

Thus, as Christ is the visible sacrament of God on earth, so the church is the visible sacrament of Christ to the human family. For the church not only *reveals* or *manifests* the risen Christ but actually *carries out* and *accomplishes* Christ's saving work. The church does today what Jesus did in his lifetime: the church forgives sins, heals people's hurts, establishes God's kingdom of justice and peace and love in our world, leads people to know and love God, helps Christians in countless ways in their pilgrimage to heaven. Especially through its seven sacraments, Christ acts through the church's ministers whenever the church baptizes, confirms, celebrates Eucharist, reconciles sinners with God, blesses married love, ordains bishops and priests and deacons, and anoints the sick.

This theological understanding of the Christian Church as sacrament of the risen Christ is a major insight and contribution of the Second Vatican Council. The renewal of the Catholic Church envisioned by the Council is for the church to manifest more fully and authentically to the world the person of Jesus, his values and compassionate love, and to bring more effectively Jesus' healing and salvation to the human family. The church must truly be good news for all people.

◆

This insight of the church as sacrament of Christ provides a norm to judge the contemporary church. Does the church mirror Christ in what it says and does today? Can people see in the lives of Christian people and in the words and actions of its leaders the humble, loving, selfless Christ? Is the church in some real way "Christ alive in the world today"? Are we Christians "sacraments" of Christ to our friends and others today?

◆

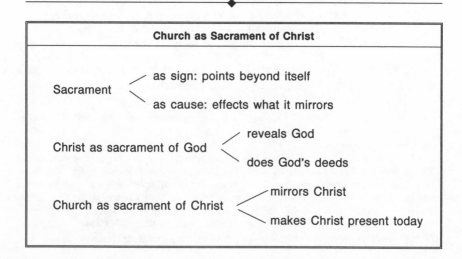

Church as Sacrament of Christ
Sacrament — as sign: points beyond itself / as cause: effects what it mirrors
Christ as sacrament of God — reveals God / does God's deeds
Church as sacrament of Christ — mirrors Christ / makes Christ present today

God's Plan or Purpose for the Human Family

From all eternity God had a grand design for the human family. The Triune God, Father, Son, and Holy Spirit, desire that every human person be saved, that is, share in their own trinitarian life in an eternity of joy, glory, and peace. The theological term is God's "salvific will." To accomplish this plan, at a certain point in history the Father sent the Son to become a human like ourselves. This enfleshment of a divine person is the mystery of the Incarnation. The Father gave Jesus, the "Word made flesh," the mission of revealing to the world God's grand design and of accomplishing it. So Jesus, the God-man, announced God's kingdom, healed people, forgave sins, sent his Apostles to announce to all peoples the good news of God's grand design, thus establishing his church, and then died to destroy our sins and bring us eternal salvation. The Father raised Jesus from the dead to risen life to guarantee that we too would rise from death to be with God forever in the glory of heaven.

St. Paul, the great apostle to the **Gentiles** and a "Johnny-come-lately" to the other Apostles, was so excited by "God's secret plan" (Ephesians 3:3) and "that mystery hidden from ages and generations past" and now revealed in and through Jesus (Colossians 1:26) that he wrote about it again and again in the stirring words of his letters to the churches he founded.

> To me, the least of all believers, was given the grace to preach to the Gentiles the unfathomable riches of Christ and to enlighten all men on the mysterious design which for ages was hidden in God, the Creator of all. Now, therefore, through the Church, God's manifold wisdom is made known . . . in accord with his age-old purpose, carried out in Christ Jesus Our Lord. In Christ and through faith in Him we can speak freely to God, drawing near Him with confidence. (Ephesians 3:8-12)

For Paul, God's plan is Jesus Christ. God's grand design is the mystery of Christ in us, sharing God's life and salvation.

> Of this Church I have been made a minister in virtue of the commission given me by God for our benefit, to proclaim without ceasing the word of God, the mystery hidden for ages and generations, but now clearly shown to his saints. To them God willed to make known how rich in glory is this mystery . . . Christ in you, your hope of glory." (Colossians 1:25-27)

We can distinguish four stages in God's plan.

- The starting point is God's tremendous love that moved God to create the human family and thus to share God's divine life with us.

- God sent the Son, the Eternal Word, to become man. As God-man, Jesus revealed his Father's personal love for each person and both revealed and carried out God's plan of the kingdom.

• The kingdom of God embraces both this life and the next: that people acknowledge God and live in love, justice and peace with each other on this earth and enjoy an eternity of happiness with God in heaven.

• The Christian church is the instrument to carry out God's plan of the kingdom through the centuries. For the Christian church is where people come to know God and experience God's love; where the kingdom is preached and lived, where we share the very life of the risen Christ, where we as pilgrims move toward the grand climax of God's plan: eternal joy with God forever.

For these reasons, the Christian church as the realization of God's grand design is rightly called "mystery," a unique human-*divine* reality.

Is it possible for us today to appreciate and realize the extraordinary excitement and enthusiasm of Paul and the early Christians when they realized the enormity of God's plan for them? Perhaps we have heard it too often. But for Paul's Gentile listeners who had known nothing of God's plan and of Jesus Christ, it came as great good news that God loved them passionately, that God's plan for them was to share God's own life in the community of love called the church, that God's Son had become man to reveal this plan and to share his own risen life with them in this life and to enjoy it fully in the next world.

It was indeed startling good news for them.

Lumen Gentium summarizes how the church as mystery is the culmination of God's plan.

> By an utterly free and mysterious decree of his own wisdom and goodness, the eternal Father created the whole world. His plan was to dignify men with participation in his own divine life. He planned to assemble in the holy Church all those who would believe in Christ. She [the Church] was prepared for in a remarkable way throughout the history of the people of Israel and by means of the old Covenant. Established in the present era of time, the Church was made manifest by the outpouring of the Spirit. At the end of time she will achieve her glorious fulfillment. (LG 2)

The Church's Founder and Founding

The Church is mystery, a human-*divine* reality, because its founder, Jesus of Nazareth, is himself the eternal Son, the God-man, and because the church was established through the powerful action of God in Jesus' preaching, death and resurrection, sending of his Spirit and in the preaching and witness of the Apostles.

> The mystery of the holy Church is manifest in her very foundation, for the Lord Jesus inaugurated her by preaching the Good News, that is, the coming of God's Kingdom, which for centuries had been promised in the Scriptures. . . . In Christ's word,

---

God's "Secret" or Grand Design

LOVE of Father, Son, and Holy Spirit for Us
↓
Creates the Human Family
↓
Eternal Son Becomes a Man
↓
Jesus Establishes God's Kingdom
↓
Christian Church Builds the Kingdom

---

in his works, and in his presence this Kingdom reveals itself to men. . . . the Kingdom is clearly visible in the person of Christ. . . . When Jesus rose up again after suffering death on the cross for mankind . . . he poured out on his disciples the Spirit promised by the Father. The Church consequently . . . receives the mission to proclaim and to establish among all peoples the kingdom of Christ and of God. (LG 5)

"Body of Christ"

By communicating His Spirit to His brothers, called together from all peoples, Christ made them mystically into his own body. In that body the life of Christ is poured into the believers who through the sacraments are united in a hidden and real way to Christ. . . . as all the members of the human body, though they are many, form one body, so also are the faithful in Christ   . . . (LG 6)

All baptized believers are incorporated into the body of Christ, the church. St. Paul refers to this as being "in Christ Jesus," a favorite phrase he used 164 times in his letters, especially to the Galatians, first letter to the Corinthians, to the Colossians and to the Ephesians. In these letters Paul insists that through baptism Christians are so completely united to Christ that they form one body, a single supernatural organism, with Christ as their head. This living organism is the church, the "mystical" body of Christ, the extension of Christ in space and time. In this living organism Christ is the source of the supernatural life of each member; the baptized live the risen life of Christ and receive from Christ all the graces or gifts they need to live the Christian way of life. Since they form one body in Christ, Christians then are profoundly united with each other "in Christ Jesus." This mystical body of Christ includes all baptized Christians: Anglicans, Orthodox, Protestants and Roman Catholics, since baptism is incorporation (*corpus*, body) into the body of Christ, the church.

Obviously we should not imagine all Christians as some huge physical body like our material body and Christ as a physical head like ours. It is better to take our understanding from Paul's own way of expressing this mystery-reality of being "IN CHRIST JESUS."

Do you not know that your bodies are members of Christ? (1 Corinthians 6:15)

The body is one and has many members, but all the members, many though they are, are one body; and so it is with Christ. It was in one Spirit that all of us, whether Jew or Greek, slave or free, were baptized into one body. . . . You then are the body of Christ. Every one of you is a member of it. (1 Cor 12:12-13, 27).

Just as each of us has one body with many members, and not all the members have the same function, so too we, though many, are one body in Christ and individually members one of another. (Romans 12:4-5)

It is he [Christ] who gave apostles, prophets, evangelists, pastors and teachers in roles of service for the faithful to build up the body of Christ, till we become one in faith and in the knowledge of God's Son, and form that perfect man who is Christ come to full stature. Let us then be children no longer. . . . Rather, let us profess the truth in love and grow to the full maturity of Christ the head. Through him the whole body grows, and with the proper functioning of the members joined firmly together by each supporting ligament, builds itself up in love. (Ephesians 4:11-16)

Husbands, love your wives as Christ loved the church. . . . No one ever hates his own flesh; no, he nourishes it and takes care of it as Christ cares for the church, for we are members of His Body. (Ephesians: 5:25-32)

Number 7 of chapter 1 in *Lumen Gentium* is a beautiful development of the body of Christ reality based on St. Paul.

The Risen Christ and His Spirit are Present and Active in the Church

The church is mystery because its Lord and founder, the risen Christ, is present and active in his church. We encounter him in the word of God whenever we read or hear the Scriptures; we meet him in each of the seven sacraments, especially in the Eucharist, where we receive his body and blood. We meet him in the worshipping community each Sunday for "whenever two or three are gathered together in my name, there I am in your midst." Catholics make much of his presence in the tabernacle of Catholic churches, and come often to pray and experience his presence symbolized by the red sanctuary lamp. Moreover, the risen Christ promised his special presence and protection to the church before he visibly left this earth: "Know that I am with you always until the end of the world." (Mt. 28:20)

> By the power of the risen Lord, it [the church] is given strength so that it might . . . overcome its sorrows and challenges, both within itself and from without, and that it might reveal to the world, faithfully though darkly, the mystery of its Lord until, in the end, it will be manifested in full light. (LG 8)

Yet another aspect of the church as mystery is that the third person of the Trinity, the Holy Spirit, is ever present in the church, guiding its leaders and members alike in faith, hope and love toward eternal salvation. Though we cannot see or feel the Holy Spirit, we are often aware of being strengthened in our faith, of receiving light and help to make right decisions, of hoping when all looks bleak, of being able to love God and our neighbor. The Holy Spirit is the dynamic presence in Christians, making it possible for them to accept in faith the total Christ event. In addition, every good act we do is inspired and helped by the Spirit. Jesus, at the Last Supper, promised to send his Spirit on the disciples so that they could understand Jesus. The *Constitution of the Church* expresses this reality in the following way.

> ". . . He has shared with us His Spirit . . . [who] vivifies, unites, and moves the whole body." (LG 7)

> "The Spirit dwells in the Church and in the hearts of the faithful as in a temple. . . . The Spirit guides the Church into the fullness of truth and gives her a unity of fellowship and service." (LG 4)

The Spirit's presence to and guidance of all Christians gives rise to the theological reality of the **sensus fidei** or that instinctive awareness that believers have, thanks to the Spirit, of Christian Catholic faith and teaching.

> The body of the faithful as a whole . . . cannot err in matters of faith. Thanks to a supernatural sense of the faith which characterizes the people as a whole, it manifests this unerring quality when "from bishops down to the last member of the laity" it shows universal agreement in matters of faith and morals. For by this sense of faith which is aroused and sustained by the Spirit of truth, God's people accepts not the word of men but the very Word of God. (LG 12)

It should be evident that another aspect of the church as mystery is *Christian faith.* For the church, as human-divine reality, can only be accepted by the gift of faith. It takes faith to believe that we encounter Christ in the seven sacraments. It takes faith to believe in an after-life of eternal happiness with God. It takes faith to believe that God has a grand design for humankind. It takes faith to believe that Jesus is both man and God, that his suffering and death truly saved us from sin, that he actually rose from the dead and lives now in a risen body, that he sent his Spirit at Pentecost. It takes faith to believe that the risen Christ is present in the Church and that his Spirit is active in the depth personalities of each Christian, helping the pilgrim people live Christian life now and reach eternal joy in heaven.

Christian faith itself is a human-*divine* reality, part of the mystery of the church. It is a gift given by the risen Christ and his Spirit. Thus a beautiful name that Vatican II gave the church is "community of faith." We are indeed on the threshold of mystery.

Practical Significance of Vatican II Describing the Church as Mystery

- Church as mystery shifted the emphasis from the institutional, human aspect of the church to its deeper, inner nature. Too often Christians have focused on the human, sinful side of the church, missing its full reality and profound reason for existing.

- Church as mystery broadens and enriches our understanding of church, opening the way for ecumenical activity with other Christian churches.

- Church as mystery sharpens faith, putting the gift of faith in clearer focus. We more fully appreciate the church when we recognize its transcendent, divine nature.

- Church as mystery is a major corrective for those who say, "Jesus yes, church no!" We cannot separate Jesus and his Spirit from the existing, visible Church, with its human failings.

- Mystery helps us understand why Catholics through the centuries have been so fiercely loyal to the church, even to shedding their blood as martyrs. The generosity and courage of countless men and women from so many countries and cultures who gave their lives as martyrs to faith, and the heroic holiness of the vast number of canonized saints witness to the church as mystery.

- The church as mystery helps us understand why so many young men and women sacrifice the goods of this world to enter religious orders and congregations, taking the three vows of poverty, chastity and obedience.

- Mystery helps us put into perspective difficult claims and challenges the church often makes on its members. A realization of the transcendent, divine nature of the church can at least in some cases help Christians understand and accept humanly debatable decisions and actions of church leaders.

• The church as mystery can make more intelligible and put in perspective the complex issues we will treat in subsequent chapters. In dealing with these issues, understanding the church as mystery casts light on why the church is often a stumbling block and scandal to those immersed in worldly values and goals.

Summary

One cannot fully understand and appreciate the Christian Church until one recognizes its transcendent divine nature. To facilitate this understanding is the task of theology. Vatican II emphasized that the church's high vocation is to be a sacrament-sign manifesting Christ to the world and doing his work. People must be able to recognize Christ in what the church is and does. Theological reflection highlights how the Christian Church is God's plan for the human family, "the mystery hidden for ages," according to St. Paul. The church is mystery in its divine founder and in the nature of its founding. In many of his letters St. Paul developed an extensive theology of Christians forming the body of Christ, thus establishing a profound relationship to Christ and each other. A further aspect of the church as mystery is the fact that the risen Christ is present and active in many ways in his church and that his Spirit guides, inspires, and helps the church, members and leaders alike. The church can thus be understood and accepted only with the Spirit's gift of Christian faith. That the Second Vatican Council emphasized the church as mystery has had and will continue to have important practical consequences for the Catholic Church, for individual Catholics, and for other Christian churches.

For Discussion

1. Explain how theological reflection has given us a more profound understanding of the church.

2. Do you think the Christian Church today is a credible sacrament/sign of Christ to the world? to its members? Give specific examples. Is the Catholic Church "good news" for people today?

3. Is Paul's theology of the church as the "body of Christ" reality or merely a nice poetic metaphor?

4. In what ways have you experienced the risen Christ present and active in the church? the Holy Spirit inspiring and strengthening you?

5. How does a person without Christian faith acquire it? with weak faith increase it?

6. What difference does it make to view the church as mystery?

For Action

1. Visit your parish, talk to the pastor or a staff member to discover in what specific ways the parish is a genuine "sacrament of Christ."
2. A Christian's vocation or call is to "be Christ" in the world today. List the specific, down-to-earth ways a Christian is called to be Christ today.
3. St. Paul challenged his Christians to build the body of Christ to its full stature. Make a list of the practical ways this needs to be done in your neighborhood. In the United States. In the world at large.

Further Reading

Abbot, Walter. *The Documents of Vatican II*. New York: Guild Press, 1966. *Dogmatic Constitution on the Church*, Chapter 1, "The Mystery of the Church," 14-24.

Powell, John. *The Mystery of the Church*. New York: Bruce Publishing Company, 1967.

C H A P T E R 4

Pilgrim People of God

"The days are coming, says the Lord, when I will make a new covenant with the house of Israel, and with the house of Judah. . . . I will place my law within them and write it upon their hearts; I will be their God, and they shall be my people."

—Jeremiah 31: 31-33

"You however are a chosen race, a royal priesthood, a holy nation, a people he claims for his own. . . . Once you were no people, but now you are God's people."

—1st Letter of St. Peter 2: 9-10

"The church is an organization of lay people served by the hierarchy."   —Archbishop Daniel Pilarczyk of Cincinnati

Introduction

When you think of church, what first comes to mind? A building like St. Ignatius church or St. Mary's cathedral? The Lutheran Church or Catholic Church or Baptist Church? The pope and bishops and priests: the hierarchical church? A big, structured organization like the communist party once was in Russia: the church as institution? Or do you think of yourself, your friends and family, men, women and children, Catholics, Orthodox and Protestants, sinners and saints? If you think of church as *people*, you are in tune with Vatican II's new model or image of church as the "people of God."

The word "church" comes from the Greek *ekklesia*, which simply means a "gathering" or assembly of people. It was used to describe the Sunday gatherings of the new Christians in Palestine, who came together in the homes of Christians to have a meal, to hear the teachings and stories of Jesus read aloud, to offer prayers and petitions, and then to receive Jesus' body and blood as their spiritual food and drink. *Ekklesia* thus meant the assembly gathered in fellowship to pray, to hear the good news, and to share the Lord's supper. Only later did "church" take on the meanings we think of today; originally it simply meant these gatherings of Christians in each city — the local church.

The church can be conceived according to different models. A model is a particular way of thinking about the nature and purpose of the church; it thus expresses that aspect of the church one chooses to emphasize. In his famous book, *The Models of the Church,* Avery Dulles formulated five models or ways of considering the church: as institution, as communion, as sacrament, as herald, as servant. The *institutional* model emphasizes the organizational elements of leaders, laws, rituals, and teachings; the *communion* model stresses the members joined in a community and united by a common belief and spirituality; the *sacrament* model focuses on how the church makes the risen Christ present and active in the world; the *herald* model emphasizes the mission of the church to preach the good news of Christ to all nations and to establish the kingdom of God; the *servant* model calls attention to the church's role in helping its members and in transforming society through service rather than domination.

Though Vatican II supported all five of these models of church, one of the Council's major accomplishments was to shift the emphasis from the hierarchical, institutional model to the communion model of the church as people forming a community in Christ. This was a momentous move. For the institutional model had prevailed in the church for over four-and-a-half centuries since the Council of Trent (1545 to 1563), which inaugurated the counter-Reformation Catholic Church. Because the Protestant Reformers had attacked the authority of pope and bishops, the priesthood, and five of the seven sacraments, the counter-Reformation church reacted

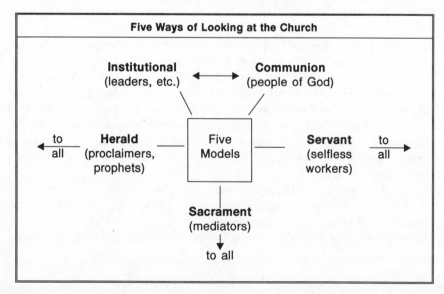

Five Ways of Looking at the Church

Institutional (leaders, etc.) ⟷ Communion (people of God)

to all ⟵ Herald (proclaimers, prophets) — Five Models — Servant (selfless workers) to all ⟶

Sacrament (mediators)

to all

by emphasizing the hierarchical, institutional nature of the church and stressing its authority.

It was a momentous move in another way, the future ramifications of which perhaps not all the bishops foresaw. Once Catholics become convinced that "*We* are the church," they seek a larger role in their church, they ask for a voice in the decisions that affect them, they recognize their rights as baptized members. Many of the tensions in the Catholic Church today, such as women's role and the so-called "people's church" in Latin America, are related to the shift in consciousness from institution to people as church. Because of this consciousness-raising on the part of Catholics and the resulting tensions between Church authorities and large numbers of Catholics, there has been a subtle movement to tone down this new vision of church as the people of God. It is significant that the Extraordinary Synod of bishops in 1985 failed even to mention the people-of-God model in its final report. This distancing from the ecclesiology of the church as people of God is a characteristic of "the restoration" mentality prevalent today. In Chapter 18 on liberation theology, we shall see how part of the Vatican's opposition to liberation theology was its perceived threat of the people's church to the Vatican's authority and control over the local churches of Latin America.

This conviction, "We are the church," has also given rise to the new emphasis in the Catholic Church on lay *ministry.* Catholic laity no longer look on themselves as second-class Christians, somehow inferior to the ordained clergy. They realize they have a genuine ministry from Christ through their baptism and confirmation to further God's kingdom in their day-to-day lives. The *Decree on the Apostolate of the Laity* describes this ministry of the Christian faithful as sharing "in the role of Christ, the Priest, the Prophet, and the King." (AA 10) As sharing in the *priesthood* of Christ, Christian laypersons offer themselves to God and bring holiness to the world in their daily lives; as *prophet* they witness Jesus' values by the way they live; as *king* they work for justice, peace and love, knowledge and respect for God and God's plan among the people with whom they live and work.

We have reflected at some length on this shift from institutional model to people model of church to highlight its major importance. Far from being a mere change of name, this new emphasis has had and will continue to have a major impact on the life of the Catholic Church and is an example of how a change in theological understanding has momentous practical consequences.

There was another shift of emphasis that deserves our reflection. In 1943, Pope Pius XII had written an impressive letter to Catholics called *Mystici Corporis*, the Mystical Body. Following St. Paul's dramatic image in his first letter to his Christians at Corinth (1 Cor 12: 12-27) of Christians forming the body of Christ, Pius XII developed in detail the analogy of Catholics forming Christ's body, with Christ as head and the Holy Spirit as soul of the body. This image was proposed to the Council bishops as the most prominent image to explain the nature of the church. It had, however, several limitations. Pius XII identified the body of Christ exclusively with the Catholic Church. But restricting membership in the body of Christ to Catholics failed to recognize that the sacrament of baptism incorporates those baptized into Christ's body, the Christian Church. Furthermore, it was difficult to view the church as sinful and in need of renewal and reformation when its body is so closely identified with its head, the sinless Christ. Likewise, the word mystical tended to overspiritualize the church and to confuse people. Consequently, though the Council retained the body of Christ image in treating the church as mystery, it chose to give greater emphasis to the people-of-God model.

◆

Preview: This chapter has a two-fold purpose: to present the Vatican II vision of the church as a community of people on pilgrimage and to call attention to the major consequences for the Catholic Church today of this model of church as pilgrim people of God. We begin with a reflection on the rich theological meaning of the people-of-God and pilgrim images. We then consider six theological and practical consequences for the life of the Catholic Church in emphasizing the pilgrim people-of-God model. We reflect on Christian laypersons' vocation to Christian ministry and their rights as members of the church. Next, we highlight the community-fellowship aspect of the church as constituting perhaps the major benefit of envisioning church as a pilgrim people. This reflection leads naturally to describing what a Vatican II parish would be like today. Our source throughout these reflections is chapters two, four and seven of the *Dogmatic Constitution on the Church*.

◆

Two Images of Church: People of God and Pilgrim

The title of Chapter 2 in *Lumen Gentium* is "The People of God." We must keep in mind both "people" and "God" because it is God who, by his special call, makes separated individuals into "a people." Some commentators have tended to emphasize the people aspect to the extent that God almost disappeared.

1. People of God

The people-of-God image comes from the Hebrew Scriptures where God chose Israel from among all the pagan tribes and made a **covenant** or solemn agreement with them. Through their hardships in the Sinai desert, God fashioned them into a unified group, "a people." Athletes know well how through painful hours of tough conditioning, fatiguing practice, and many sacrifices a group of independent individuals become "a team."

> God, however, does not make man holy and save them merely as individuals without bond or link between them. Rather it has pleased him to bring men together as one people, a people who might acknowledge him and serve him in holiness. He therefore chose the Israelite race to be his own people and established a covenant with it. Step by step he instructed this people, making known in its history both himself and the decree of his will and by making it holy unto himself. (LG 9)

However, God's plan reached beyond the Jewish people of God. For God would send his Son into the world, Jesus the Christ, who would make a new covenant with women and men in his own blood. This new people of God is the Christian Church.

> All these things, however, were done by way of preparation and as a figure of that new and perfect covenant which was to be ratified in Christ, and of the fuller revelation which was to be given through the Word made flesh. "Behold, the days are coming, says the Lord, when I will make a new covenant with the house of Israel and the house of Judah. . . . I will put my law within them, and I will write it upon their hearts, and they shall be my people. . . . For they shall all know me from the least of them to the greatest, says the Lord." (Jer. 31:31-4) Christ instituted this new covenant, namely the new covenant in his blood (Cf. 1 Cor 11:25); he called a race made up of Jews and Gentiles which would be one, not according to the flesh, but in the Spirit, and this race would be the new People of God. (LG 9)

This new people of God are those who believe in Christ and who have been baptized into Christ. Because they share in Christ's priesthood through baptism, they are called a royal priesthood. Because they believe Jesus is the promised Messiah, they are a messianic people.

> For those who believe in Christ, who are reborn . . . not from flesh, but from water and the Holy Spirit, are finally established as "a chosen race, a royal priesthood, a holy nation . . . who in times past were not a people, but now are the People of God." (1 Peter 2:9-10)
> That Messianic people has as its head Christ. (LG 9)

2. Pilgrim People

Chapter 7 adds a further dimension to the new people of God. Its full title is "The Eschatological Nature of the Pilgrim Church and Her Union with the Heavenly Church." This pretentious title means that the final goal of the pilgrim people of God at the end of the world, from *eschaton*, the end time, is the complete and perfect fulfillment of the church in union with Christ in heaven; nonetheless, we pilgrims here on earth are united in the communion of saints with all those who have gone ahead of us and are in heaven, making up a kind of "heavenly church."

> The Church, . . . will receive its perfection only in the glory of heaven when will come the time of renewal of all things (Acts 3:21). At that time, together with the human race, the universe itself . . . will be perfectly reestablished in Christ. (LG 9)

> When the Lord will come in glory and all his angels with him, death will be no more and all things will be subject to him. But at the present time . . . his disciples are pilgrims on earth. (LG 48)

Christians are called pilgrims because this earth and this life are not their final home. They are people on the move, not totally at home on this earth, journeyers seeking a better life in their permanent home. Pilgrims also tend to lose their way on their pilgrimage to God; they need the help of fellow pilgrims, of the church.

Another dimension of people on pilgrimage is that they are united with those who have gone ahead in death. The term to describe this Christian belief is "the **communion of saints**." Numbers 49 and 50 of chapter 7 speak eloquently about the union of the church on earth, with "the church suffering" in purgatory and "the church triumphant" in heaven. Pilgrim Christians can proclaim in the Apostles' Creed, "I believe in . . . the communion of saints, the resurrection of the body, and life everlasting." St. Paul describes the glorious destiny of Christian pilgrims in his letter to the church at Corinth. "We believe and so we speak, knowing that he who raised up the Lord Jesus will raise us up along with Jesus and place both us and you in his presence. . . . Indeed, we know that when the earthly tent in which we dwell is destroyed we have a dwelling provided for us by God, a dwelling in the heavens, not made by hands, but to last forever." (2 Cor 4:13-5:1)

This pilgrim title of the church brings out in a magnificent way the utter uniqueness of the Christian church; for it is a church that bursts the bonds of time and this cosmos to encompass eternity itself: the heavenly church made up of those who have passed through the barrier of death to life eternal, the church as communion of saints.

Combining these two images of a people and of pilgrimage gives us Vatican II's primary image and name of the church: the pilgrim people of God.

Practical Consequences of the Pilgrim People of God Image

One may ask what difference does it make to describe the church as pilgrim people. Does it really matter whether one emphasizes the people-of-God aspect of the church over the hierarchical and Mystical Body images? Actually, this seemingly unimportant change of emphasis has immense consequences, both theological and practical, for the church today. Let us try to appreciate this idea.

1. First, to stress God's role in calling a people together and establishing the Christian Church is to emphasize a fundamental fact of great importance: *the church exists*, not for itself or its institutional interests, but *to carry out God's plan* to establish the kingdom on this earth and to lead the whole human race to the glorious heavenly kingdom. This plan broadens immensely our vision of the church's purpose. It means that the church should rejoice whenever and wherever God's kingdom is being planted and is making progress, even if not accomplished directly by the Catholic Church. This vision leads to new respect for those great world religions who take God and God's will seriously and who labor, each in its own way, to found God's kingdom on earth and to lead their members to the heavenly kingdom.

2. As we stressed in Chapter 1, the church of Christ as baptized and believing people is a broader reality than any one Christian Church. This is the theological basis, as we shall see, for the modern ecumenical movement. The fact that all Christians in the world, numbering 1.8 billion, are still tragically divided should be a source of deep shame to Christian churches. Practical consequences should be the end of lingering triumphalism, the "we're better than you" syndrome among the churches, and the determination to work more wholeheartedly in the ecumenical movement to recover the broken unity of Christ's Church.

3. A balance is restored for understanding the composition of the church. Before Vatican II, in Avery Dulles' strong words:

> In the minds of most Americans, Catholic and non-Catholic, the prevailing image of the Catholic Church is highly institutional. The church is understood in terms of dogmas, laws, and hierarchical agencies which impose heavy demands of conformity. . . . At the risk of caricature, one may say that many think of the church as a huge, impersonal machine set over its own members.[1]

The key "hierarchical agencies" in this institutional model are bishops and their diocesan structures, the pope and the Vatican curia that help the pope govern the universal church. This hierarchy is not exclusively

---

1. Avery Dulles, *A Church to Believe In: Discipleship and the Dynamics of Freedom* (New York: Crossroad, 1982), 3.

the church. Not even the pope is the church. The people-of-God image restores the proper emphasis: *baptized believers are the church. We* are the church. Correlatively, this highlights the role of the hierarchy as serving rather than dominating the people-of-God. Furthermore, the people-of-God image is a more realistic and attractive view of the church. But the other side of the coin is that it puts much greater responsibility on the members to truly *be* the church.

4. Pilgrim people of God form a church *immersed in history* and constitute a *sinful church always in need of reform*. By calling the church a pilgrim, Vatican II wanted to emphasize first, that the church has been profoundly influenced in its leadership structures, its laws and disciplinary decrees, its worship, and even its doctrinal formulations by the historical era and place in which it has existed. Examples are its government structures from the Roman Empire; terms like curia, pontiff, province; the Latin language in its worship and prayer; Greek philosophical categories of person and nature to explain the mystery of the Trinity and of Christ; its past negative approach to sex; the role of women, and so forth.

Second, Vatican II wanted to emphasize the human, limited, sinful nature of the church, a church always in need of renewal-reformation, thus laying to rest past triumphalism. A pilgrim church is a humble church, aware of its proneness to losing its way, of its great need for healing and help to continue its pilgrim journey to the Lord. Moreover, a pilgrim church is a confident and trusting church because of Christ's promise: "I will be with you all days until the end of the world." (Mt. 28:20)

Practical consequences of being a pilgrim church include humbly admitting past inadequacies, rededication to the work of renewal/reform, and the attempt to divest itself of "baggage" accumulated through the centuries, such as now-meaningless practices, laws, terms, and even theological formulations.

5. The people-of-God image, by stressing the dignity and role of the laity in the church and by promoting the conviction that "We are the Church," has inspired the dramatic rise in *Christian lay ministry*. It has also contributed to the decline of clericalism in the church, that tendency to give too much influence and power to the clergy, thus keeping the laity passive and "obedient."

6. Another benefit of the pilgrim people-of-God image is that it reveals and emphasizes that the church in its best moments is *a community*, a loving fellowship called together by God in Jesus Christ.

Because these last two consequences are of such practical importance for the Catholic Church today, we shall devote separate sections to each.

We are the Church: Vocation and Rights of the Laity

Chapter 4 of *Lumen Gentium* is titled "The Laity." Recognizing laypersons in the church represents another "first" by Vatican II and was long overdue, since the **laity**, from *laos*, Greek for people, constitute by far the majority in the church. The following statements summarize the Council's tribute to the nonordained Christian faithful. The numbers in parentheses refer to the numbered sections of chapter 4 in *Lumen Gentium*.

The laity are defined first of all as "all the faithful except those in Holy Orders and who belong to a religious state [congregation]." This negative description is immediately corrected: " . . . that is, the faithful who by baptism are incorporated into Christ are placed in the People of God." (31) The rest of the chapter speaks of their special vocation: "to seek the kingdom of God by engaging in temporal affairs and directing them according to God's will" (31); their equality in the church (32); their apostolate "a sharing in the salvific mission of the church . . . through baptism and confirmation" (33); their high role as sharing in Christ's priestly and prophetic roles (34-6); and their rights in the church (37). The chapter closes with this eloquent sentence.

◆

"Each individual layman must be a witness before the world to the resurrection and life of the Lord Jesus and a sign of the living God." (38).

◆

No longer, therefore, can the description of the laity's vocation as "pray, pay, obey" be considered a harmless bit of humor.

Christian Ministry, Vocation of Laity

The word ministry means service. Christian lay ministry refers to the vocation or call to service which Catholic lay women and men have from Christ. Their ministry of service is primarily to the world but is also, in rapidly increasing ways since Vatican II, in and to the church.

The Council insisted that the primary ministry of the lay faithful is a *ministry in and to the world*. This secular ministry is proper to them as living and working in the world; they are the church, the people of God in the world. Through them, in Michael Lawler's graphic statement, "the church is incarnate in the world to be leaven-symbol of love, hope, reconciliation, forgiveness, peace, justice, transformation, grace, presence, mystery."[2] That is, to establish and build the kingdom of God in our world.

Since Vatican II, more and more Catholics have come to realize and appreciate that their roles as fathers and mothers, husbands and wives, and

---

2. Michael Lawler, *A Theology of Ministry* (Kansas City: Sheed & Ward, 1990), 49.

their daily work are their Christian ministry, their noble vocation for God's kingdom. In growing numbers they consciously choose careers in politics, foreign service, healing professions, teaching, social work. Likewise young people are increasingly joining the Peace Corps, Jesuit Volunteers, Maryknoll Associates and similar groups from a motive of Christian ministry. As Catholics deepen their conviction that they are the church and have a ministry in and to the world, we will begin to recover the situation of the church of the first few centuries, when every Christian was a deliberate witness to Christ in daily life.

Lumen Gentium expresses this vocation of the laity to the world in many eloquent passages. The laity:

". . . share the priestly, prophetic and kingly office of Christ and to the best of their ability carry on the mission of the whole Christian people in the Church and in the world" (31).

"They are called by God that . . . they may contribute to the sanctification of the world from within like a leaven . . ." (31).

"The laity are . . . to make the Church present and fruitful in those places and circumstances where it is only through them that she can become the salt of the earth" (33).

". . . the laity consecrate the world itself to God" (34).

By spreading

". . . the kingdom of truth and life, the kingdom of holiness and grace, the kingdom of justice, love and peace . . . they will impregnate culture and human works with a moral value" (36).

Another ministry that is attracting growing numbers of Catholics, especially women, young adults, and married couples, is *church ministry*. Catholic laypeople are full-time teachers in Catholic schools, parish youth ministers, spiritual directors, retreat givers, directors of CCD (Confraternity of Christian Doctine), members of parish pastoral teams, eucharistic ministers. In a growing number of European and North American parishes, religious women — technically considered among the laity because nonordained — and lay people have been appointed parish administrators, ministering to the people in everything except conducting the Eucharist and the sacrament of reconciliation. Such opportunities, expanding at a fast pace, are changing the face of the church. The 21st century will see a far different church than we know today.

Rights of Laity

After the *vocation* of the laity, Chapter 4 takes up the *rights* of the laity as members of the church, a topic that perhaps appeared obvious and innocuous to many of the Council bishops but which has considerable practical relevance today.

Like all Christians the laity have the right to receive in abundance the help of the spiritual goods of the Church, especially that of the word of God and the sacraments from the pastors. To the latter the laity should disclose their needs and desires with that liberty and confidence which befits children of God and brothers of Christ. By reason of the knowledge, competence or preeminence which they have the laity are empowered — indeed sometimes obliged — to manifest their opinion on those things that pertain to the good of the Church. (37)

Some pertinent phrases bear repeating: "have the right to receive . . . the sacraments"; "should disclose their needs and desires . . . "; "are empowered — indeed sometimes obliged . . . to manifest their opinion . . . [for] the good of the Church."

Only now is the church beginning to realize the far-reaching practical consequences of these brave words. One such immediate application is the situation in entire continents where the sacraments, especially the Eucharist, are denied Catholics because there simply are not enough priests available. This is especially true in Latin America, where city parishes often number 50,000 Catholics or more, and where countryside chapels are visited by a priest only two or three times a year. In the United States and Europe the number of priestless parishes is rapidly increasing. A pressing question then is whether Catholics do not in fact have a right to hear the word of God and to have access to regular celebration of the sacraments, even if this means a married priesthood. For Vatican II stated in its *Decree on the Ministry and Life of Priests* that "No Christian community, however, can be built up unless it has its basis and center in the celebration of the most Holy Eucharist" (PO 6).

The post-Vatican II period in the church has been termed "the age of the laity." One of the results of Vatican II's emphasis on the laity in the context of the diminishing numbers of priests and sisters has been the phenomenal growth in lay ministry in Catholic parishes across the United States and Europe, wherein men and women are engaging in new and creative forms of ministry. Theologians are attempting to formulate a theology of lay ministry in order to respond to Vatican II's new emphasis on the laity.

The Church as Communion or *Koinonia*

This Greek word *koinonia* means community or fellowship and is used to describe the church as made up of persons bonded together by common convictions, goals and shared ideals, who take responsibility for each other. The church as community then is a fellowship of believers in Jesus Christ who desire to live the Christian life more fully. Realizing that "no man is an island," they come together to support each other in their life of faith and hope in Jesus and their love of God and of each other. Their peak experience of being a community in Christ is the Sunday Eucharist, when they come together to experience the presence of the crucified, risen Christ in their midst, to recall the Christ event of his life-death-resurrection-ascension-glorification in order to renew their faith and hope in him and their love of God and of each other.

Andrew Greeley describes the origin and nature of community in terms of *encounter and response:*

> . . . fundamentally an encounter with the Christ event . . . the place where both the Christ event is brought to its fullness and where we respond to that event. The original Christian community emerged as an inevitable result of the tremendous surge of religious energies that Easter unleashed. The followers of Jesus had an overpowering experience of being released from a trap and an incredible joy of reconciliation between God and their fellows. It was that experience and in their common effort to respond to that experience that the community of the faithful came into being.[3]

Jesus Christ is thus the basic experience of the community. The Spirit he sent on the Apostles at Pentecost is the vivifying life of the community. For the risen Christ and his Spirit are present in the church because present in each member of the community. The Spirit gives each member certain gifts for the building-up of the church community.

Vatican II's vision of the church as community or fellowship of believers in Jesus Christ is one of the most important and fundamental insights and emphases of the Council. It has important practical applications; four are especially noteworthy.

Practical Effects of Church as Communion or Community

First, this vision highlights our need for the church as *our link with Jesus Christ* and his saving death, resurrection, and glorification. Without today's living church, none of us would be Christians. Andrew Greeley explains why:

> I have encountered Jesus only through the community. As a child, those members of the community who were my parents disclosed him to me; as a student, the sisters and priests who functioned in the community revealed Jesus to me; and then the great theologians of the past and present deepened and enriched my knowledge of him; and finally other human beings, also members of the community of the faithful, have strengthened, reinforced, challenged, and reassured me as I have tried, however ineptly, to grow in my knowledge of Jesus as a person, in my faith in him as the Lord, and in my loving service in imitation of him as savior.[4]

---

3. Andrew Greeley, *A New Agenda* (Garden City, NY: Doubleday, 1973), 252-53.

The Christian community is thus not a conglomeration of individuals that approach God isolated from each other; rather, they attain salvation together.

Second, community answers a *deep-felt need of people today*. As modern life becomes more urbanized and impersonal, people instinctively feel the need for identity, to relate to others on deeper levels, to belong. A living, loving Christian community where people truly care about each other and move out to help others is a necessary support today.

Third, the Church as community is therefore *good news for people* in a way the institutional church alone cannot be. Christians whose lives radiate the enthusiasm and joy of the love of Christ and their neighbor are powerful attractive examples to others, becoming "good news" for them. Mother Teresa of Calcutta is one such. An example I personally was privileged to experience is the community of St. Egidius in Rome. This group of young Christians, single and married, ages 17 to 30 or 40, have taken seriously the gospel of Christ to love others, especially those in need. They distribute clothes to the poor of Rome; serve a substantial hot meal daily to 500 hungry men and women, young and old; provide counseling to the mentally disturbed of the streets who otherwise have no care; tutor poor students and immigrants; and do other works of Christian love. Their spiritual energy comes from their nightly half-hour community prayer, based on the Scriptures, and their weekly Eucharist together. Other young people see their dedication to Christ's poor and their joy and love in action and ask to join the community, which now numbers over 500 and has spread to other cities in Italy and even Latin America.

Fourth, to view the church as community is to *emphasize the local church*. Pre-Vatican II Catholics were rightly conscious of being members of a worldwide church; but in emphasizing the universal church, the values and importance of the local diocesan church were often minimized and overlooked. The *Constitution on the Church* declared that the whole church is present in each local church. This is why the Apostle Paul, in his letters to the Christians of Asia Minor, addressed them as "the church of Corinth," "the church at Ephesus," "the church at Rome," and so forth.

> This Church of Christ is truly present in all legitimate local congregations of the faithful which, united with their pastors, are themselves called churches in the New Testament. For in their own locality these are the new people called by God. . . . In them the faithful are gathered together by the preaching of the Gospel of Christ and the mystery of the Lord's Supper is celebrated. . . . Christ is present. By virtue of him the one, holy, catholic and apostolic Church gathers together. (LG 26)

---

4. *Ibid.*, 253.

Recovery of the importance of the local church has vast implications for the Catholic Church today, especially in regards to the principle of collegiality within the church, to the ecumenical movement, and to the priority of the kingdom of God in the mission of the church. We shall discuss these themes in future chapters.

Descriptions of Church as Community

Lumen Gentium calls the church "a communion of life, love and truth." Greeley likes "community of the faithful." Others like "eucharistic fellowship," to emphasize the role of the Eucharist in creating and maintaining the bond of community.

Drawing on these descriptions, we may define the Christian Church as God's pilgrim people, consisting of baptized believing Christians who, as a faith community, accept the total Christ event as described in the Gospels and expressed in the Apostles' Creed, and who celebrate their belief and fellowship through Eucharist together. This description emphasizes that God takes the initiative in forming individuals into a faith community; that one enters the community through baptism; and that faith in the life, teaching, sacrificial death, resurrection and glorification of Christ and his sending the Spirit celebrated weekly in the Eucharist is the bond of the community.

A Vatican II Parish — What Would It Look Like?

Most basic of all, a Vatican II **parish** will be a Christian community, a fellowship where the members know and care for each other and are united around the risen Christ and his Spirit. Such a parish will manifest the following characteristics:

- Since the risen Christ and his Spirit are the uniting forces of the parish community in the weekly celebration of the Eucharist, a Vatican II parish makes its *highest priority an outstanding liturgy* that stresses the people's full participation. A liturgy team plans each Sunday Mass: it trains lay readers who do not merely recite but clearly proclaim the word of God in the readings from the Hebrew Scriptures and the letters of St. Paul; it sees that the music is of high quality, is expressive of the word of God for that Sunday, and is both a prayer and a celebration of the two-fold nature of the Eucharist as Christ's sacrifice and meal; it assigns lay eucharistic ministers to give communion under both species of bread and wine; it makes much of the prayers of the faithful and of the greeting of peace, for here fellowship is especially experienced and deepened.

- In a Vatican II parish, the people *genuinely care about each other* in two ways: their faith life and their human needs. To support the faith life of the parishioners, there is an active religious education committee which oversees the Christian education of the young people and provides ongoing religious education for adults. Another group plans retreats and prayer days or evenings so that prayer becomes a natural part of the community. Clergy and parishioners lead marriage preparation programs and **RCIA** classes (the Rite of Christian Initiation for Adults) to prepare them for baptism, confirmation and Eucharist. There will also be programs for the parents of infants to be baptized. To support the various human needs of the parish community, groups visit the elderly and sick, organize youth programs, reach out to the poor and to ethnic groups within and outside the parish. A Vatican II parish will in some way address the various spiritual and human needs of its members.

- The Vatican II parish is a community that *reaches beyond itself* to the world and to the broader church. Since needs are so varied and complex, the parish council or a special outreach committee prioritizes needs and makes proposals to the parishioners for their decision. A Vatican II parish will be particularly solicitous for justice and poverty and peace issues. Various volunteer groups will emerge to do what is possible in these pressing areas. If the parish is financially well-off, it may decide to "twin" with a poor inner-city parish to assist it to each other's mutual growth.

- A Vatican II parish is an *evangelizing parish.* Its members are so convinced that Jesus Christ and the Christian Church are such good news that they want to share it with others and discover ways to do so.

- Finally, the pastor of a Vatican II parish will be *a shepherd who truly serves his people.* He sees his goal as building a dynamic faith community around the risen Christ, rather than merely dispensing sacraments. He puts the highest priority on the Sunday worship: this means carefully-prepared homilies and presiding at the Eucharist in a way that creates Christian community and aids the spiritual growth of his people. He sees himself as a facilitator, one who recognizes and respects the gifts of his people and thus empowers them in their various ministries. He promotes an active parish council with real authority, whose counsel he follows gratefully.

Summary

In reflecting on the nature of the church, Vatican II deliberately shifted the emphasis from the hierarchical, institutional model to that of communion to emphasize that the church is all baptized, believing Christian persons. Accordingly, its new name is pilgrim people of God: "people" emphasizes that God in Jesus creates the church as Yahweh formed the Hebrews into a covenant people; "pilgrim" stresses the eternal, heavenly destination of this new people of God. This change in theological understanding has six very practical consequences for today's Catholic Church: the church exists not for itself but for God's kingdom; the end of triumphalism toward other Christian churches; the people *are* the church, signalling the end of clericalism; as immersed in history, the church needs constant reform; the dignity and role of the laity; and the church as communion. Because of their special importance, the final two consequences are developed in detail. Being the church, Catholic laity have a specific ministry through their work and life to witness Christ's values and build God's kingdom in the world; moreover, their rights as baptized Christians must be respected. Vatican II's vision of the church as a community-fellowship in Jesus Christ has important practical applications. We close by describing the local Vatican II parish as a community in Christ.

For Discussion

1. Is the contemporary Catholic Church sufficiently conscious of itself as the pilgrim people of God?

2. What practical steps could/should lay Catholics take in the church today to fulfill their high calling, to express their dignity, and to realize their rights?

3. Can you think of examples of "excess baggage" accumulated in the church through the centuries that could or even should be discarded today?

4. Has the Catholic Church succeeded in creating genuine Christian community-fellowship-in-Christ in its members today? If yes, how? If no, what would you suggest be done?

5. What needs to be done in your parish or other parishes you are acquainted with so to become genuine Vatican II parishes?

For Action

1. Talk to your parish priest, to a member of the parish council, to several active members of the parish to discover: to what extent they carry out their vocation, dignity, and rights as Catholic laity; to what degree they think their parish is a Vatican II parish.

2. Attend a Sunday eucharistic celebration at a parish church known for its sense of community and vibrant liturgy.

3. Attend a Sunday worship service at a Protestant church that is a real community. (Baptist and Pentecostal services often are good examples of community.)

Further Reading

Bausch, William. *Traditions, Tensions, Transitions in Ministry*. Mystic, CT: Twenty-Third Publications, 1982.

Dolan, Jay, et al. *Transforming Parish Ministry: The Changing Roles of Catholic Clergy, Laity, and Women Religious*. New York: Crossroad, 1990.

Dulles, Avery. M*odels of the Church*. Garden City, NY: Image Books, 1987. (original 1974)

Abbott, Walter. "The Dogmatic Constitution on the Church," chapters 2,4,7; "Decree on the Apostolate of the Laity," chapters 1,2,3 in *The Documents of Vatican II*. New York: Guild Press, 1966.

John Paul II. *Christifideles Laici (The Vocation and Mission of the Lay Faithful in the Church and in the World)*, Washington, DC: United States Catholic Conference, 1989.

CHAPTER 5

A Liturgical-Sacramental Church

... the liturgy is the summit toward which the activity of the Church is directed; it is also the fount from which all her power flows.   *—Sacrosanctum concilium* 10

... every liturgical celebration, because it is an action of Christ the Priest and of his body which is the Church, is a sacred action surpassing all others.   *—Sacrosanctum concilium* 7

It is the liturgy through which ... the work of our redemption is accomplished ... and [by which] the faithful are enabled to express in their lives and manifest to others the mystery of Christ and the real nature of the true Church.
                                        —Sacrosanctum concilium 14

In the restoration and promotion of the sacred liturgy, the full and active participation by all the people is the aim to be considered above all else.   *—Sacrosanctum concilium* 14

"Whatever was visible in our Redeemer has passed over into the sacraments."   —Pope St. Leo the Great

"A sacrament is when God reaches out a hand to you. It's not with a fist or a pointed finger. It's to walk with you. ... But sacraments are not zaps of lightning. They're not like booster shots to make you feel good. We have to grab hold of God's hand. Confession, for example. It's not a car wash. The idea is that you change a little. Grow."[1]

---

1. Fr. Marty of Good Counsel Catholic Church, southside Chicago, quoted in *Life* magazine, August, 1991, page 50.

Introduction

The Constitution on the Sacred Liturgy was the first document produced by the bishops of Vatican II in 1963. They chose the word liturgy to stress how the Church *celebrates* what she *is* and what she *does*. For liturgy is the *public* worship and prayer Catholics do together to celebrate their relationship to God, to the risen Christ, to the Holy Spirit and to each other. As the above passages from the *Constitution* state, liturgy is the high point, "summit," of the church's religious actions and the source, "fount," of her spiritual power; the shared action of Christ and Christians; the way Christians are saved, "redeemed," and the way they live and witness to the mystery of Christ and of the church. Liturgical celebrations dramatically reveal the church as mystery because they involve God in Christ present and active in the Christian community. In celebrating liturgy, the church celebrates ever anew her inner divine nature.

The bishops intended to renew the liturgical practices of the Catholic Church by restoring the way the church worshipped in its early centuries. They first set principles for this renewal-restoration, then mandated specific changes in the way Catholics worship. This renewal meant dramatic change because Catholic worship had been the same everywhere in the world for over 450 years, since the Council of Trent had "frozen" the liturgy. The **Mass,** for example, was in unintelligible Latin, and the priest "up there" with his back to the people was the main actor, while the people were passive spectators filling their time saying the rosary or reading their prayer books or, on great feast days, being entertained by large choirs.

Then almost out of the blue came Vatican II's revolutionary change of the liturgy. Not understanding the reasons behind liturgical renewal, older Catholics felt cheated of their beautiful "high masses" and of the sense of mystery and the sacred created by Latin and stately **Gregorian** chant; they missed the silent, impersonal "low" masses where one could commune with God privately and could find respite from the harsh realities of the world. Some even felt "the changes" had Protestantized the Catholic Church!

Why such dramatic changes in a highly successful 450-year style of worship that had nourished the faith life of Catholics so well? In the United States, for example, Catholic churches in urban areas had been packed for five or more masses each Sunday.

Painstaking scholarly research, like the Austrian Jesuit Josef Jungmann's monumental book, *The Mass of the Roman Rite: Its Origins and Development,*[2] revealed that over the centuries many practices and prayers and pageantry had crept into the liturgy, obscuring the fundamental com-

---

2. Josef Jungmann, *The Mass of the Roman Rite: Its Origins and Development* (New York: Benziger, 1951).

munity-oriented worship in the early centuries of the church. In their effort
to recover and restore the earlier form of worship, the bishops at Vatican
II were guided by the following liturgical principles:

- foundational principle: "Liturgical services are not private functions but
  are celebrations of the Church" (SC 26) since the church is a community, the pilgrim people of God.

- people's participation: "In the restoration and promotion of the sacred
  liturgy, the full and active participation by all the people is the aim to
  be considered above all else" (SC 14).

- intelligibility of the texts and rituals: They should "express more clearly
  the holy things they signify" so that "the faithful understand them with
  ease" (SC 21).

- Scriptural: "Sacred Scripture is of paramount importance in the celebration of the liturgy" (SC 24); therefore, "the treasures of the Bible are to
  be opened up more lavishly" (SC 51).

- cultural adaptation: The rituals used must have meaning for all cultures,
  not just Mediterreanean or European or white Anglo-Saxon cultures (SC
  37-41). An example is the use of drums and the dance in African worship.

The liturgical renewal of Vatican II was thus to be marked by community, participation, intelligibility, the word of God, and cultural adaptation.

◆

Preview: We begin by stressing that liturgy is the official public, not
private, worship and prayer of the church. We call attention to the
liturgical year as the highly effective way Christians celebrate and
relive the saving life, death and resurrection of Jesus Christ. We then
identify the seven sacraments as the major liturgical actions of the
Christian Church. There follows an analysis of sacraments as symbolic ritual actions: we explain symbol and ritual, how sacraments
achieve their spiritual effects, and identify those spiritual realities the
risen Christ and his Spirit cause through each sacrament. We close
by explaining the rich theological meaning of the seven sacraments.

◆

Liturgy Is the Church's Official Public Worship of God

Liturgy is public, not private, worship of God. It is what baptized,
believing Christians do as a community when they come together in the
"liturgical assembly." They come to *praise* God, to *thank* God, to *beg forgiveness* for their sins and selfishness, and to *bring their needs* to their

loving Father through Jesus, their Savior. In liturgy, Christians relive and reenact the extraordinary life, saving death, victorious resurrection and glorification of Jesus the Christ. Through liturgy, faith-filled Christians celebrate the Triune God's presence in their midst: the Father, the risen Christ, his Holy Spirit.

The church's official worship is carefully organized throughout an entire year, known as the **liturgical year**, and is celebrated by means of the Mass or Eucharist. Thus her liturgical calendar is made up primarily of the Sunday and great "feast day" Masses celebrating the life and saving actions of Christ, and secondarily of weekday Masses which often commemorate the church's canonized saints. For example, to celebrate the great events of Christ's life, like Christmas, Easter and the 52 Sundays of the year, three Bible readings are chosen, one each from the Hebrew Scriptures, the letters of Paul, and one of the four Gospels.

The liturgical year begins in late November or early December with the four Sundays of **Advent**, whose three readings prepare us for the coming of Jesus, our Savior. Christmas Day celebrates his humble birth, with succeeding Sundays dedicated to his hidden life at Nazareth. The six Sundays of **Lent**, the traditional period of doing penance for sin and the time in the early church when the catechumens began their final preparation for baptism, prepares Christians for "the great week," the holiest of the liturgical year. On Thursday of **Holy Week**, Christians recall the Lord's Supper, when Jesus' gift of the Eucharist is celebrated; on Good Friday, Christians enter into the sufferings of Jesus leading to his cruel crucifixion that saved humanity from sin.

Easter Sunday, the greatest feast of the liturgical calendar, celebrates the resurrection of Christ the Lord, his victory over death, and the guarantee of our own ultimate resurrection. Forty days follow to commemorate the period of Jesus' visible risen life on earth, climaxed by the two great feasts of Ascension Thursday, celebrating Jesus' glorification in heaven and, nine days later, of Pentecost Sunday to commemorate Jesus' sending his Holy Spirit on the Apostles and the beginning of the Christian Church. The following Sundays until Advent recall the public life of Jesus, his teaching, miracles and healings.

The lesser but popular liturgical cycle called the *Proper of the Saints* occurs on weekdays throughout the year. Priests celebrate a special Mass for that saint with selected readings and three personalized prayers, called the opening prayer, the prayer over the gifts, and the prayer after communion. It is interesting that this calendar of canonized saints covers almost 2000 years and includes both men and women, young and old, martyrs and "confessors," founders and members of religious orders, and persons from every continent and most countries of the world. It should be noted that this represents only a small fraction of the canonized saints and is a calendar for the universal church; individual countries and each religious order and congregation may celebrate their own saints on special days set aside for them: for example, Mexico and the United States celebrate Our Lady of Guadalupe on December 12.

The Liturgical Actions Called Sacraments

The contribution of Vatican II was to "rediscover" and emphasize that sacraments are not individual, private religious events but rather *liturgical* acts, that is, what the Christian community does together in its public worship and prayer. As liturgical actions, sacraments are the lifestyle of Christians, the way they approach God and express their Christian faith. Thus sacraments are as important for Catholics as the Bible is for Protestants, since the whole of Catholic life revolves around the seven sacraments, especially the Eucharist. As liturgical acts, sacraments "belong" to the church as its official public worship and as the major means of Christian life for its members.

The Roman Catholic and Orthodox and Anglican churches are *sacramental* churches in that their official public worship consists of the seven sacraments, based on a carefully articulated sacramental theology. This theology holds that one *meets God* in these seven ritual actions, that the risen Christ and his Spirit *use these ritual actions* to give spiritual helps (grace), that these ritual actions are not only enormously helpful but *necessary* in Christians' pilgrimage-journey toward heaven. In general, Protestants, especially evangelical Protestants, do not accept this theology of sacraments, seeing no need for such "mediators" between God and humans, indeed alleging in the heated controversies of the 16th-century Reformation that Catholics "deify" sacraments by attaching "magic" powers to purely human ritual actions.

The seven official church sacraments are baptism (entrance into the church), confirmation (completion of baptism), eucharist (memorial meal of Christ's death and resurrection), marriage (union of man and woman in permanent love bond), reconciliation (forgiveness of sin), ordination (of bishops, priests and deacons to serve the Christian community), anointing of the sick (healing of mind and soul and often the body).

Since sacraments are at the heart of church life, it is essential to understand what they are, how they "work," and what they accomplish. In centuries past and still today, there is much misunderstanding and ignorance about sacraments on the part of both Catholics and Protestants. We shall then be in a position to appreciate the theological meaning of sacraments.

Sacraments are Symbolic Ritual Actions

Most fundamentally sacraments are *rituals*, that is, *symbolic actions* using *words* and primordial *material elements* like water, bread and wine, oil. The actions are symbolic because the visible ritual action *points to* and *makes real* (symbolizes) invisible spiritual realities. For example, total immersion of one's body in the water of baptism is a powerful symbol of death (of Christ's death and the baptized person's death to sin), and rising up out of the waters of death an equally powerful symbol of new life (of Christ rising from the tomb and of the baptized person's new life in Jesus Christ).

To be human is to use rituals. Every primitive society has used powerful religious rituals to express its relationship to its gods. Favorite American rituals are Thanksgiving Day meals, Halloween costumes, Fourth of July celebrations, senior proms, the World Series and the Super Bowl. In the Catholic and Orthodox churches and the Anglican communion, the seven sacraments, especially the Eucharist, are the most important rituals. Lesser rituals, called "sacramentals," are the rosary, benediction of the Blessed Sacrament, way of the cross, novenas, and numerous "devotions." In addition, popular Christian family rituals are Advent wreaths and candles to prepare for the coming of Jesus at Christmas, saying the blessing (grace) over the food at the family meal, and the beautiful custom of parents blessing their children by tracing the sign of the cross on their foreheads.

I remember vividly the first time I saw such a parental blessing. It was in the crowded Budapest, Hungary, railway station a few minutes before the train was to depart. A father was saying an emotional goodbye to his teenaged daughter. They embraced, then slowly, reverently, his fingers traced the sign of Jesus' cross on her forehead. Through tears she smiled and boarded the train. It was a sacred moment.

How Sacraments Achieve Their Spiritual Effects

As symbolic rituals, sacraments achieve their effects *by signifying*; that is, the *visible* ritual action using elemental material objects like water, oil, bread and wine, combined with the words of the minister of the sacrament, expresses or signifies the *invisible* spiritual reality effected by the risen Christ and the Holy Spirit. As we have just explained, in baptism the ritual action of plunging a person three times in water (immersion) or pouring water over the person's forehead, while saying "I baptize you in the name of the Father and of the Son and of the Holy Spirit," *signifies* the total destruction and cleansing of sin and the gift of the risen life of Christ.

Catholic sacramental theology adds a further dynamic dimension. It holds that these seven rituals are efficacious, that is, the symbolic action not only signifies the invisible spiritual reality, but actually is involved in *bringing about* or *effecting* that reality through the action of the risen Christ and the Holy Spirit. It is important to emphasize that only the risen Christ and his Spirit can and do cause the spiritual realities of each sacrament. However, without the ritual action done by a human minister there would be no sacrament and no spiritual effect. We can thus say that the human minister of each sacrament acts "in the person of Christ."

We should note an important point. Sacraments cause or achieve their spiritual effects *by signifying* or *symbolizing*. This means the rituals must be intelligible, effective symbols that move heart and mind; otherwise, the spiritual effect or grace will be minimized or even nonexistent. This explains why Vatican II's renewal of the sacramental rituals should "express more clearly the holy things they signify" (SC 21). This also avoids the charge that sacraments are magic, producing their effects independently from the quality of the ritual and the receptiveness of the individual. Thus the Council states:

> The purpose of sacraments is to sanctify men, to build up the body of Christ, and to give worship to God. Because they are signs, they also instruct. They not only presuppose faith but . . . also nourish, strengthen and express it. They do indeed confer grace. . . . It is therefore of the greatest importance that the faithful should clearly understand the sacramental signs. (SC 59)

To summarize: sacraments as sacred symbolic rituals both signify and effect the invisible spiritual reality conferred by the risen Christ and his Spirit and symbolized by the ritual itself; or simply, the ritual signifies and through Christ and the Spirit brings about what it signifies.

The Spiritual Realities the Risen Christ and His Spirit Cause

• in *Baptism:* total forgiveness of sin and the life of Christ so that the newly baptized becomes a new person in Christ ("christened") and a member of Christ's body, the church.

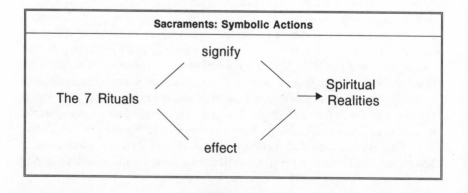

- in *Confirmation:* the Holy Spirit, through the Spirit's seven fold gifts, strengthens Christians in their struggle to witness to Christ in their daily lives.

- in *Eucharist:* as memorial meal of the life, death, resurrection and glorification of Jesus, the risen Christ becomes truly and really present, under the signs of bread and wine, to be our spiritual food and drink.

- in *Reconciliation:* the risen Christ forgives sins committed after baptism and helps us in our lifelong effort toward interior conversion from selfishness to generous living, from pride to humility, from lust to control over sexual drives.

- in *Marriage:* the risen Christ bonds the love of husband and wife in a permanent love relationship based on Christ's own, never-failing, totally unselfish, covenantal love for his body, the church.

- in *Orders:* Christ, through bishops in the apostolic succession, ordains priests to minister to his Christian people by giving them the high privilege and ability to celebrate his presence in Eucharist and to forgive sins in his name; ordains deacons to celebrate other sacraments; consecrates bishops to ordain priests and other bishops.

- in *Anointing the Sick:* Christ heals soul and mind (and sometimes the body) by strengthening the sick person with faith, hope and love, peace of mind, acceptance of sickness and of the approach of death as he or she prepares for the final journey to the side of the Lord.

Sacraments are thus Christ's love and power made visible and effective in our lives.

Sacraments are Celebrations

To fully appreciate the role sacraments as liturgical actions play in our Christian lives, it is helpful to see them as real-life celebrations. For celebration lifts our spirits, refreshes and revives us, restores self-confidence, bonds us to our fellow celebrators. Good liturgical celebration does the same: revives our faith, restores our hope, inspires us to love God and our sisters and brothers in the Christian community, gives a foretaste of what God's kingdom on earth is meant to be and what it will be in heaven.

Sacraments are celebrations of what God in Christ is doing in the midst of the Christian community right now. For example:

- in baptism we celebrate the risen Christ welcoming a new member into the Christian community with his gift of new life;

- in confirmation we celebrate the Spirit's gifts to Christians to witness to Christ in their daily lives;

- in Eucharist we celebrate the community meal in which Christ gives us his strengthening body and blood as food and drink on our pilgrimage through life;

- in reconciliation we celebrate Christ freeing us from sin and aiding us on our way to interior conversion;

- in marriage we celebrate the risen Christ uniting two persons in a permanent love bond that symbolizes his own unselfish love;

- in ordination we celebrate God calling and empowering Christians to minister to and lead the Christian community;

- in anointing the sick we celebrate the merciful, healing Christ strengthening and consoling the sick to accept sickness and death's approach with peace and faith.

Sacraments thus celebrate *peak moments* in the lives of Christians. Baptism, first communion, confirmation and marriage are joyful family celebrations. Eucharist and ordination are festive celebrations of the entire Christian community. Reconciliation and anointing the sick are celebrations of God's loving care and solicitude.

Sacraments are peak moments in another sense. They bring to heightened awareness through sacred rituals what God is constantly doing in our daily "secular" lives and in our own experiences and actions. A few examples illustrate this valuable dimension of sacraments. We forgive others and receive their forgiveness; God forgives us the moment we express sincere sorrow. The sacrament of reconciliation focuses these daily experiences of forgiving and being forgiven in the special ritual of reconciliation so we can experience and celebrate it. In the sacramental moment of conferring the Spirit in a special way, confirmation focuses our experiences of being guided and helped by the Spirit's daily inspirations and gifts. The many meals we have taken with family and dear friends take on profound meaning in the eucharistic meal the risen Christ shares with us.

Sacramental celebrations transcend time. Sacraments celebrate what God has done for us in the *past:* God becoming man in Jesus of Nazareth; Jesus' teaching and healing and forgiving; Jesus' suffering, death, resurrection and glorification; Jesus' sending his Spirit to establish his church and be with us on our journey — in a word, sacraments celebrate the mystery of God's salvific plan. And sacraments celebrate what God has in store for us in the *future*: our growth and inner conversion as Christian women and men; the deepening of our love relationship with God and the God-man, Christ; our increased service in love to others; and finally, the triune God as our eternal reward in heaven, the fulfillment of all our longings and desires and dreams.

Further, since sacraments celebrate what God is doing in the midst of the Christian community in the *present*, it is highly important we know the great realities we are celebrating. Every sacrament, especially Eucharist, celebrates the great unfailing love of Jesus for us here and now. In a word, the center of every sacramental celebration is Jesus Christ: we celebrate God's plan, the mystery of salvation in Christ Jesus.

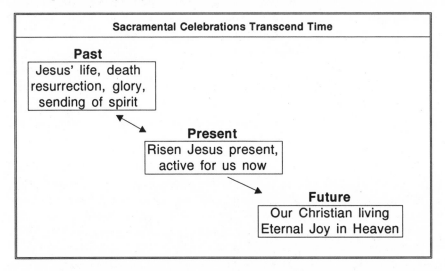

Young people often complain "The Mass is boring. I get nothing out of it. I get more from communing with nature or being with a friend who inspires me." My response invariably is: "Yes, some Masses are poor liturgy, hardly celebrations, uninspiring and boring! But if you come with faith and realize the great person and events being celebrated, and you participate actively, then everything changes!"

I often make another suggestion. As the success of our human celebrations depends on the people who celebrate, so also with religious celebrations. Their quality depends to a great extent on the quality of Christian life Christians bring to the sacramental celebration. If we are not making a sincere effort, despite failures, to develop a personal relationship with God and Jesus Christ, to love and minister to the people around us, to struggle with temptations and sin, to grow in faith, then we have little to celebrate when we come to the Sunday Eucharist or to any sacramental celebration. We can't expect God to water a dry stick!

A final thought on celebration. People rarely celebrate alone but with friends. Sacraments are the ritual celebrations of the Christian community. Faith-filled Christians who love and care for each other and whose lives are Christ-centered and God-directed will create and experience quality liturgical celebrations.

Rich Theological Meaning of Sacraments as *Liturgical Actions*

- Most simply put, sacraments are *God's actions and ours.* As *signs* they reveal to us or signify what God is doing for us and how God is challenging us. Our part is to respond to God in prayer and action, personal and social. Sacraments set up a *call-response* relationship.

- Sacraments are *actions of the whole Christ,* of Christ, the head, and of us, the members of his body. For the risen Christ acts in each sacrament to bring us the special spiritual effects of that sacrament, and we Christians cooperate in faith to receive Christ's gifts.

- Sacraments are *"encounters"* with Christ. The Dutch theologian Edward Schillebeeckx proposed this fresh theological insight in his 1960 book, *Christ, the Sacrament of the Encounter with God.* Jesus is the the *primordial* sacrament, the visible manifestation on earth of God and of God's redeeming love for us. Jesus' miracles and the mysteries of his life, suffering, death, and resurrection both *reveal* and *bring* God's compassionate love and saving power to us. Today, we encounter the risen and glorified Christ in his historical, visible body, the church, and in its visible, symbolic rituals we call sacraments. When the church baptizes or confirms or forgives sins, the risen Christ baptizes, confirms, forgives. The church can thus rightly be called the sacrament of Christ on earth: Christ's powerful love for us becomes visible in sacraments.

- Each sacrament *celebrates the saving life, death and resurrection of Jesus* and draws its spiritual power from the paschal mystery of Jesus' death and resurrection.

- Sacraments are high points in the Christian's *pilgrimage journey* to God in this life and to his or her eternal home with God in heaven. The baby or adult receives *baptism* to begin the Christian journey in the church; the late adolescent receives the strengthening Holy Spirit in *confirmation* for a new phase of the journey; young men and women unite in a *marriage* "in Christ," who helps them love unselfishly and faithfully in their journey of love; sinners receive forgiveness in the sacrament of *reconciliation* and spiritual food and drink in the *Eucharist; ordination* provides the Christian community with leaders for the journey; when old age and death approach, the church is present in the *anointing of the sick* to offer healing and consolation for the final stages of the journey. Thus do the church and Christ accompany Christians throughout their pilgrimage to God.

- In this way, sacraments are the *bond* holding the Christian community together. When the community comes together to celebrate sacraments, each Christian is strengthened in his or her faith and hope and love through each other's support and example and through the presence of Christ and his Spirit acting in each sacrament.

• Sacraments are *transformative.* The goal of sacraments is to transform us into Christ, to effect conversion, that is, a profound change in our attitudes, our values, our way of thinking and living. Obviously, this transformation is not automatic; we who participate in sacraments must come with faith, with understanding, and with the sincere desire to receive the graces Christ offers us. Otherwise, sacraments would be mere magic and superstition.

• Sacraments are *affirmations of Christian faith, hope, and love* in the face of a world of disbelief, skepticism, hopelessness, hatred and greed. For sacraments are where people find God, experience the support of Christian community, and joyously celebrate their identity as the Christian people of God.

It is evident why liturgy and sacraments are such a major part of the life of the Christian Church and are so valued by Catholics, Orthodox, and Anglicans, and to an increasing degree by the mainline Protestant churches, especially Lutherans. As a result of the World Council of Churches' Lima document, *Baptism, Eucharist and Ministry*, the WCC Faith and Order Commission has urged its member churches to recover the riches of sacraments and of sacramental theology.[3] Through theological dialogues, the ecumenical challenge for the churches is to reach agreement on the theology of sacraments.

A Reflection and Evaluation

Older Catholics value and love their sacraments. They flock to Sunday Masses in large numbers, singing enthusiastically, answering prayers in unison, happily serving as eucharistic ministers, lectors, greeters. Many attend daily Mass. Yet many young adult Catholics and even more teenagers do not share this enthusiasm and faithful attendance. Has the liturgy failed them? Or is something missing in today's younger Catholics?

Despite the visible success of Vatican II's liturgical renewal in dynamic parishes, professional liturgists believe our liturgy falls far short of achieving the full potential envisioned by Vatican II. They give various reasons: failure in theological understanding and in spirituality so that liturgy becomes a conscious encounter with the risen Christ as he gives himself totally to the Father; a sense of mystery is absent; liturgy fails to emphasize and create Christian community and social consciousness; liturgical inculturation — integrating cultural values and symbols like food and

---

3. *Baptism, Eucharist and Ministry 1982-1990: Report on the Process and Responses,* (Geneva: WCC Publications, 1990), 143-47.

drink, God's word, music, color, physical setting, etc. — is not sufficiently encouraged by Rome; liturgy is still too clerical.

Thus experimentation, liturgical education of priests and people, and skillful creative planning by parish liturgical teams are needed. A crying need remains for attractive, meaningful young people's liturgies geared to their needs and interests in a conducive setting by sensitive and creative celebrants.

How can liturgy be revitalized? One author puts it this way:

> Liturgy is an art. The Mass is a ritual, a dramatic symbolic action of Christ's death and resurrection specified by words. This ritual should be an aesthetic creation designed to set up the conditions for the possibility of religious experience. God is present in and through the people and materials. . . . Christians are present at liturgy to encounter God through his Son and in the power of the Spirit. In the Eucharist God heals, teaches, and empowers, sending Christians back to their everyday life to transform the world into the kingdom of God. The Sunday Eucharist should not be an isolated entity, but a bridge to Christian worship and service throughout the week.[4]

Summary

The Christian Church is a church that continuously celebrates the extraordinary life, crucifixion, and resurrection of its Lord Jesus Christ. The church effectively does this by means of liturgy or its official public worship and prayer celebrated throughout its liturgical year. Vatican II reemphasized that the seven sacraments are *liturgical* actions which the Christian community celebrates together publicly. These sacraments are basically visible, symbolic, ritual actions that both *point to* or *express* and, by the action of the risen Christ and his Spirit, *bring about* or *effect* the invisible spiritual realities conferred by each sacrament. As liturgical actions, sacraments are multifaceted celebrations. They also contain profound theological meaning. Sacraments are thus a dramatic example of the church as mystery or human-divine reality, for through these seven human rituals the church reveals and expresses her inner divine nature and life. Yet the liturgical reforms of Vatican II have still to reach their full potential in the life of the Catholic Church.

---

4. Timothy McCarthy, *The Catholic Tradition, Before and After Vatican II 1878-1993*. (Chicago: Loyola University Press, 1994).

For Discussion

1. Why do you think Vatican II titled its first document "sacred liturgy" rather than simply "sacraments" or "sacramental life"? What does liturgy add? connote?

2. Why did Vatican II need to recover an older practice of liturgy and sacraments? Give examples.

3. What is the importance of "official" and "public" before "liturgy"? of liturgy as prayer?

4. How can a mere ritual performed by a human priest mediate or accomplish spiritual realities?

5. What keeps sacraments from being magic rituals? superstitions?

6. Do you really believe that you can meet God, "encounter" Christ in the sacraments? Why?

For Action

1. Research the fascinating historical "development" of sacraments, especially confirmation, reconciliation, the Eucharist. Might sacramental rituals "develop" further? Which ones? In what ways?

2. Attend Sunday Mass in a parish known for successful liturgy that attracts large numbers.

3. Speak to several older Catholics who attend Mass regularly. Find out why they do this. Ask what it means to them.

4. Ask your teenage friends what they like and need in a good youth liturgy.

5. Analyze the Sunday liturgy in your parish. If good, what makes it so? If not, what is needed?

Further Reading

Bausch, William. *A New Look at Sacraments*. Mystic, CT: Twenty-Third Publications, 1983.

Cooke, Bernard. *Sacraments and Sacramentality*. Mystic, CT: Twenty-Third Publications, 1983.

Duffy, Regis, O.F.M., ed. *Alternative Futures for Worship, Vol. I: General Introduction*. Collegeville, MN: Liturgical Press, 1987.

Guzie, Tad. *The Book of Sacramental Basics*. New York: Paulist Press, 1981.

Hellwig, Monica. *The Meaning of Sacraments*. Dayton: Pflaum-Standard, 1972.

Jungmann, Josef. *The Mass of the Roman Rite: Its Origins and Development.* New York: Benziger, 1951.

Martos, Joseph. *The Catholic Sacraments.* Wilmington, DE: Michael Glazier, 1983.

Mitchell, Leonel. *The Meaning of Ritual.* New York: Paulist Press, 1977.

Osborne, Kenan. *Sacramental Theology, A General Introduction.* New York: Paulist Press, 1988.

Vorgrimler, Herbert. *Sacramental Theology.* Linda A. Maloney, trans., Collegeville, MN: Liturgical Press, 1992.

Part II

Vatican II
and the Church's Mission

CHAPTER 6

Why Church?

"Go, therefore, and make disciples of all the nations . . . "
—Matthew 28:18

The Lord Jesus, the divine Teacher and Model of all perfection, preached holiness of life to each and every one of His disciples. . . . All the faithful of Christ . . . are called to the fullness of the Christian life and to the perfection of love.
—*Lumen Gentium* 40

The Church seeks but a solitary goal: to carry forward the work of Christ under the lead of the befriending Spirit.
—*Gaudium et Spes* 3

The Lord . . . founded his Church as the sacrament of salvation.
—*Ad Gentes* 5

Introduction

Why the church? For what purpose did Christ establish the church? What task or mission did he give it? What should the church be doing today? Where should its emphasis be? Has the church gotten sidetracked from its main purpose?

Various answers have been given by theologians: "To produce saints and make holiness possible" (Jean Daniélou); "to offer worship to God for all humanity" (Jan Groot); "to be present in the world as a living witness to the love of the Trinity" (Robert Sears); "to proclaim the Gospel to the poor by word and deed" (Jon Sobrino); "to bring about the gospel values of Jesus Christ: freedom, justice, peace, charity, compassion, reconciliation" (Richard McBrien); "to be the visible sign of the Lord's presence in the struggle for a more human and just society" (Gustavo Gutiérrez); "to be a leaven amid humanity" (Juan Segundo); "to set a new worldview before our eyes, to transform and Christianize the world," to be "salt of the earth, light of the world" (Walter Bühlmann).

The question of the mission of the church is important today. Catholics who were brought up with the conviction that the church exists exclusively to "save souls" are sometimes confused and even threatened by the church's involvement today in social problems like racism, human rights, war and peace, the economy. Some feel that the church does not sufficiently emphasize or satisfy their personal religious needs. Others are puzzled by the success of the fast-growing pentecostal groups and wonder if the church has lost its missionary and religious thrust.

The question has many facets today. Should the American bishops issue documents on war and peace and the economy? Should priests be lawyers, psychiatrists, university presidents, members of Congress, like Jesuit Fr. Drinan from Massachusetts, peace activists and writers, like Fr. Dan Berrigan? Should Catholic nuns be doctors and nurses, lobbyists in Washington for justice and human rights, sanctuary advocates for refugees from Central America? Has the church become too political, too secular? Why are many Catholics disaffected toward the church? Why has Sunday Mass attendance fallen off and why is there a growing shortage of priests and sisters? Has the Catholic Church lost its identity?

What is Vatican II's position on these questions? Did the bishops at the Council give a clear direction for the church to follow?

◆

Preview: This chapter considers five aspects of the church's mission or purpose as given by Jesus and explained by Vatican II. The all-embracing mission of the church is the *salvation* of the human family. Thus one of the favorite titles the Council bishops gave the Catholic Church is "the universal sacrament of salvation." Three aspects of this mission of salvation are *sanctification* or helping its members grow in holiness, building *God's kingdom* on earth and *evangelization* through inculturation. Vatican II gave the church a fifth mission of repairing the broken unity of Christ's Church (*ecumenism*). These five lead us to a reflection on modern issues involving the church's mission.

◆

Salvation, Ultimate Mission of the Church

A favorite title given the church by the bishops at the Second Vatican Council was "the universal sacrament of salvation." This title occurs frequently, especially in the *Constitution on the Church* (*LG*), the

Church's Missionary Activity (*AG*), and the *Church in the Modern World* (*GS*).

In God's great love for the human family, God desires that every human person be saved, that is, to spend an eternity of happiness with God in heaven. Theologians call this truth "God's salvific will." To accomplish this salvific will, God "missioned" his Son to take on human flesh and become man. Jesus missioned his 12 Apostles and through them the church to be the means of bringing salvation to the human family. For as *sacrament* of salvation the church both *manifests* God's salvific love for all people and *accomplishes* that salvation.

> The Church has but one sole purpose — that the kingdom of God may come and that salvation of the human race may be accomplished. Every benefit the people of God [the Church] can confer on mankind during its earthly pilgrimage is rooted in the Church's being the "universal sacrament of salvation" at once manifesting and actualizing the mystery of God's love for men. (GS 45)

The church, as Christ's body on earth, was sent by Jesus and his Spirit to preach to all people the good news about God's salvific love for all. The church is thus by nature missionary.

> Rising from the dead he [Jesus] sent his lifegiving spirit upon his disciples and through them set up his Body which is the Church as the universal sacrament of salvation. (LG 48)

> Having been divinely sent to the nations that she might be "the universal sacrament of salvation," the Church . . . strives to preach the Gospel to all men. (AG 1)

> The Church on earth is by its very nature missionary since, according to the plan of the Father, it has its origin in the mission of the Son and the Holy Spirit. This plan flows from . . . the love of God the Father. . . . God in his great and merciful kindness freely creates us and graciously calls us to share in his life and glory. (AG 2)

The church carries out its mission of bringing salvation to all persons in a variety of ways. Three are paramount: bringing the good news about Jesus Christ to all cultures (evangelization), helping its members grow into an ever-closer love relationship with God and the risen Christ (sanctification), working to establish God's plan for the human family (the kingdom of God).

Evangelization

> The pilgrim Church is missionary by its very nature. (AG 2)

> The special end of this missionary activity is the evangelization and implanting the Church among peoples or groups in which it has not yet taken root. (AG 6)

Evangelium is the Latin word for good news; the English equivalent is gospel. The four Gospels by Matthew, Mark, Luke and John are accounts of the good news about Jesus Christ. As we have seen, Jesus came to this earth to announce astounding good news: that his Father was a God of love and mercy who had a compassionate, personal love for each woman and man, and whose eternal plan was for the divine Word or Son to enter planet earth by becoming human, and for people to worship, love and obey God and to live in love, justice and peace toward each other. This plan constitutes God's kingdom, which Jesus proclaimed unceasingly and sought to establish. Evangelization, then, is the church proclaiming this message of good news about God's love and his plan of salvation in the person of Jesus Christ. The result of evangelization is planting the church where it had not existed before. In its strict meaning, evangelization is proclaiming this good news to persons who are *not Christian* or who have *not yet heard* Jesus' message of salvation. Accordingly, the Catholic Church does not evangelize fellow Christians, for example the Orthodox, Anglicans, Lutherans and so forth; nor should they evangelize Catholics.

Evangelization is a major purpose of the Christian Church because Jesus himself gave the Apostles and, through them, the church "the great commission," as Baptists like to call it. The scene of Jesus "commissioning the Apostles," as Matthew presents it at the close of his Gospel, is impressive. It was after Jesus' resurrection, and the 11 disciples, minus Judas, had walked from Jerusalem to Galilee to a certain mountain to which Jesus had expressly invited them. Anticipation must have been keen on the journey. When they arrived at the mountain and saw Jesus, some fell down on their knees out of respect. Jesus stepped forward and gave them their mission. It was a solemn moment.

> Full authority has been given to me both in heaven and on earth; go, therefore, and make disciples of all nations. Baptize them in the name of the Father, and of the Son, and of the Holy Spirit. Teach them to carry out everything I have commanded you. And know that I am with you always until the end of the world. (Mt 28:18-20)

As Jesus was missioned by the Father with complete authority to make disciples and teach, so Jesus missions his Apostles. His final promise assures them that he, the risen Christ, will support them — and the church after them — in their great mission till the end of the world.

The author of the **Acts of the Apostles** implies this commissioning in terms of the Apostles being authoritative witnesses: "You will receive power when the Holy Spirit comes down on you; then you are to be my witnesses in Jerusalem, throughout Judea and Samaria, yes, even to the ends of the earth." (Acts 1:8)

In these accounts we see that the mission is universal, that is, to the whole world and every person, and that as proclaimers the Apostles are witnesses of Christ himself. The risen Christ's promise of support in Matthew becomes the power of the Holy Spirit in them. The *Acts of the Apostles* gives eloquent testimony to how the Apostles, especially Peter, and in the second half of *Acts,* Paul, preached with power the good news about Jesus Christ crucified, risen, and glorified.

One of the most impressive accomplishments of the Catholic Church has been its missionary work throughout the centuries. We think of St. Paul, the great Apostle to the Gentiles and to all the "churches" he established throughout Asia Minor of his day; we think of the brother monks, Cyril and Methodius, who brought Christ to the Slavic people 1000 years ago; of St. Francis Xavier, the great Jesuit apostle of the Indies, who is said to have baptized over one-half million people; of the North American martyrs, those heroic French Jesuits who brought Christ to the Iroquois, Mohawk and Huron indigenous peoples of New York state and Canada, finally to suffer extremely cruel martyrdoms; of the zealous Franciscan friars who evangelized the Indians of South and Central America; of Maryknoll priests and sisters who labored so hard to bring Christ to China and who, after their expulsion by the Communists, now labor heroically in Latin America; of the thousands of priests and sisters who have lived under great hardships and dangers to proclaim Christ in Africa, Alaska in the dogsled days, and the South Pacific Islands.

We think too of the thousands of Protestant pastors who labor strenuously to proclaim Christ on foreign shores. We recall too that the "great commission" is perhaps taken more seriously by Baptist churches and various Pentecostal groups today than by the mainline churches. Finally, we call attention to the modern missionary movement involving laypeople and young people. Examples are the Maryknoll program, where individuals and married couples give two or more years to live and work as foreign missionaries and the Jesuit Volunteer groups of college graduates who work as missionaries in the United States and in foreign countries for one or more years.

The term evangelization to describe the church's missionary activity in proclaiming the Christian message was not part of the vocabulary of the Catholic Church before Vatican II. However, the Council, in its special document *Decree on the Church's Missionary Activity* and in *Lumen Gentium*, spoke of the reality of evangelization, insisting it is the duty of every Christian (*AG,* 23, 25; *LG,* 16, 17). To stress the importance of evangelization, Pope Paul VI, just two years after the Council renamed the Vatican Curia's Congregation for the Propagation of the Faith the Congregation for the Evangelization of Peoples to emphasize its object and worldwide scope. Then in 1974 he chose evangelization as the theme of that year's Synod of Bishops. This Synod inspired Paul VI's apostolic exhortation *On*

Evangelization in the Modern World,[1] published Dec. 8, 1975, which has become the classic treatment of evangelization. As an in-depth, comprehensive, and forward-thinking presentation, this remarkable document deserves our attention.

Pope Paul VI begins by calling Jesus the first evangelizer who proclaimed the kingdom of God and the good news of salvation. The church, "born of the evangelizing activity of Jesus and the Twelve [Apostles]" (No. 15), receives from Jesus the mission of evangelizing all peoples. In a memorable sentence, Paul VI stated that "evangelizing is in fact the grace and vocation proper to the Church, her deepest identity. She exists in order to evangelize. . . " (14). This means "bringing the Good News into all the strata of humanity and through its influence transforming humanity from within and making it new" (18).

The *content* of evangelization is the "clear proclamation that in Jesus Christ, the Son of God made man who died and rose from the dead, salvation is offered to all men as a gift of God's grace and mercy" (27). Paul VI expanded the content of evangelization to include human development and liberation for the "millions of human beings" condemned "to remain on the margin of life: famine, chronic disease, illiteracy, poverty, injustices in international relations and especially in commercial exchanges, situations of economic and cultural neocolonialism sometimes as cruel as the old political colonialism" (30). Evangelization thus demands "conversion of heart and of outlook" (36).

The pope identified two groups of "beneficiaries of evangelization": "the immense section of mankind who practice non-Christian religions" and nonbelievers immersed in secularization and modern atheism (52, 53, 55); second, the "dechristianized world," that "very large number of baptized people who for the most part have not formally renounced their baptism but who are entirely indifferent to it" (56). Without using the actual

---

Who Are to be Evangelized?

YES: Individuals — nonbelievers in Christ
— nonpracticing Christians

YES: Cultures

No: Non-Catholic, practicing Christians

---

1. See Further Reading, this chapter.

term, Paul VI encouraged the new theology of inculturation. "What matters is to evangelize man's culture and cultures . . . in depth and right to their roots" (20). He thus broadened the scope of evangelization from individuals to cultures.

Inculturation

Effective evangelization demands inculturation! Vatican II broke new ground by speaking of culture in relation to faith and the gospel (GS, 57, 58) and encouraging the principle of adaptation:

> The faith should be taught by a well-adapted catechesis and celebrated in a liturgy in harmony with the character of the people . . . and embodied . . . in the healthy institutions and customs of the locality. (AG 19) . . . the young churches . . . borrow from the customs, traditions, wisdom, teaching, arts and sciences of their people. . . . Thus, the Christian life will be adapted to the mentality and character of each culture and local traditions together with the special qualities of each national family. (AG 22)

Since the Council, a specific theology of inculturation has developed in the Catholic Church. Inculturation has assumed great importance, particularly among the young churches of Africa and Asia which increasingly demand that distinctive elements of their culture be incorporated into their worship, theology, teaching of doctrine, and church practices and law.

In simplest terms, inculturation means that the Christian message and way of life become part of a particular culture so that the church is "planted" and grows in this culture. Inculturation is a complex process involving the following aspects:

1. Since the church with its message and life cannot exist in the abstract as a disembodied spirit, it always lives in a particular culture and is influenced by elements of that culture: people's customs, attitude toward life, beliefs, laws, norms of conduct, symbols and myths, art, family traditions. For example: Catholic Christianity early took on the cultural elements of Greek philosophy and Roman law, then later of European society. In its past missionary activity, it tended to bring a Europeanized, Mediterranean, Latin Catholicism to foreign countries. Obvious examples are the Latin language in the Mass, Roman theology and canon law, celibacy of priests, and so forth. Today, missionaries, respecting local cultures, seek to *avoid* exporting a Europeanized cultural Catholicism and to *present* the Christian message and life *in terms of the people's culture* so they can understand and accept it.

2. The church seeks to *transform* the non-Christian culture into a Christian one. This often involves purifying that culture of beliefs and practices opposed to essential Christian teaching and life. Examples are the human sacrifices of the Aztecs in Mexico, worship of many gods or the

multiple spirits of animism, plurality of wives according to African tribal customs. Yet the church must not be too quick to condemn all elements of a native culture, as happened in the famous Chinese rites controversy of the 17th century when the Vatican condemned as idolatrous the Chinese rituals honoring ancestors and Confucius. Inculturation means that all good and legitimate elements of the culture be preserved and find a place in the church, thus enriching it.

3. The local church *accepts* the Christian message and life and *expresses* it according to its own culture, developing its own style of worship, its own theology and law, its own symbols and art. Thus is born a "new creation,"[2] a truly inculturated African church, for example, in which Africans can be at home and call their own. The ultimate goal of inculturation is such an inculturated church.

4. To achieve true inculturation, the Catholic Church encourages the local church to develop according to its own cultural insights and gifts. This means giving its bishops and people the freedom to experiment, to make their own decisions, to create their own liturgical worship and theology and church law, for in the last analysis genuine inculturation is *the work of the local church*. For its part, the newly inculturated local church must remain in communion with the universal church in essential beliefs and practices. Inculturation is thus an ongoing process between the older evangelizing church and the newer local church in which both are changed.[3]

The happy results of such inculturation are many. The Catholic Church will not be perceived and experienced as a foreign import, as in China and Japan and much of Asia today; such a church, in times of persecution, may be expelled or merely wither and die. Second, Christianity will more easily be understood and more fruitfully and joyously lived in an inculturated local church which meets the religious needs of its people and attracts "converts." Anyone who has attended a Sunday Mass in a packed African church marvels at the exuberant singing, the whole congregation clapping to the rhythmic drumbeats, graceful dancing by young girls as they bring the bread and wine to the altar, the colorful priest's vestments of African designs. Finally, the universal church is enriched by gifts of the various inculturated local churches of the world; the church thus becomes in fact a global church, multi-cultural and truly catholic.

---

2. Term of Fr. Pedro Arrupé, former charismatic general of the Society of Jesus, who championed inculturation for Jesuits. ". . . the incarnation of Christian life and of the Christian message in a particular cultural context, in such a way that this experience . . . becomes a principle that animates, directs and unifies the culture, transforming it and remaking it so as to bring about a 'new creation.'" Quoted in T. Howland Sanks, *Salt, Leaven, and Light. The Community Called Church* (New York: Crossroad, 1992), 194.

3. *Ibid.*

Sanctification or Holiness

This abstract noun is made up of two Latin words: *sanctus* holy, and *facio* make. Sanctification is the process by which a person becomes holy and pleasing to God, a saint with a small "s." Vatican II's Constitution on the Church devoted its entire Chapter 5 to "The Call of the Whole Church to Holiness." Prior to the Council, the average Catholic did not realize that God seriously called him or her to holiness, to be a saint. "That's for priests and nuns, not me." Such thinking was understandable when the majority of canonized saints are priests or nuns, generally from religious orders, or popes. The only laypeople canonized were martyrs or kings and queens. Vatican II wanted to change this minimalist thinking. "All in the Church, whether they belong to the hierarchy or are cared for by it, are called to holiness, according to the Apostles' saying 'For this is the will of God, your sanctification'" (LG 39). And again lest the message be missed, "It is therefore quite clear that all Christians in any state or walk of life are called to the fullness of the Christian life and to the perfection of love . . . " (LG 40). This means bartenders, bank presidents, married couples, pop stars, professional athletes, business men, politicians, even teenagers and students!

The Council spelled out what this holiness involves: imitation of Christ, doing God's will, seeking God's glory, caring for others. "In this way they can follow in His footsteps and mold themselves in all their being to the glory of God and the service of their neighbor" (LG 40). Holiness involves the daily effort to "advance along the way of a living *faith* which arouses *hope* and works through *love*" (LG 41) (emphasis added). The Council obviously believes that this high vocation is, with the indispensable help of the Holy Spirit, within the reach of all Christians. This means to live the Christian life fully, which ultimately is a life of love: love of God and of our fellow sisters and brothers. Jesus said, "By this will all men know that you are my disciples, if you love one another."

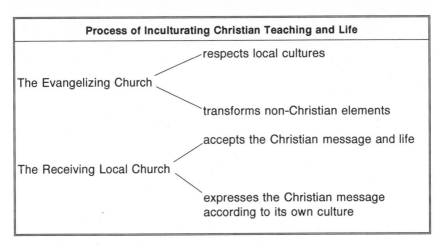

Process of Inculturating Christian Teaching and Life

The Evangelizing Church
- respects local cultures
- transforms non-Christian elements

The Receiving Local Church
- accepts the Christian message and life
- expresses the Christian message according to its own culture

Christianity is a religion of love.

How does the church help us achieve our vocation to live our Christian life more completely and to love more purely and strongly? We shall list only the most important helps, omitting many, and content ourselves with brief explanations and comments.

1. The church gives us *examples* of holiness. The second preface from the Mass for "Holy Men and Women" calls attention to this gift: "You renew the Church in every age by raising up men and women outstanding in holiness, living witnesses of your unchanging love. They inspire us by their heroic lives, and help us by their constant prayers to be the living sign of your saving power." The church offers its canonized saints as heroic examples of how to live Christianity fully and to love passionately: saints like Francis of Assisi, Ignatius of Loyola, Teresa of Avila, the Little Flower, Thérèse of Lisieux, Thomas More, patron of lawyers, and recently, Maximilian Kolbe, the Franciscan priest who died a martyr of love by volunteering to take the place of a man marked for death by the Nazis in Auschwitz. The greatest of all the saints is Mary, the Virgin Mother of Christ, who has inspired Catholics and Orthodox down through the ages as the wealth of paintings and icons testify. Of course, our best example by far is Jesus himself, the God-man: his love of his Father and his heroic obedience to his Father's wishes, his love and care and compassion for all people, especially the suffering and sick and sinners; his extraordinary courage to face his cruel passion and death. These heroic women and men have shown Christians down through the centuries how to imitate and follow Christ. (See next chapter for other saints.)

2. The church provides us with powerful *means* of holiness. Here we come upon an embarrassment of riches which the church has developed over almost 2000 years; they constitute an extraordinary array of helps to live the Christian life more fully and to love God and neighbor more generously.

   a) Most important are the *seven sacraments,* those ritual contacts with the divine in which Christians in a community setting meet Christ, are strengthened by his Spirit, grow in the God-connecting virtues of faith-hope-love, and constantly rediscover their identity as followers of Christ. The seven official sacraments of the church carry a Christian throughout life, especially at peak moments. (See chapter 5 and chapters 13-16.)

   b) Equally important is *the word of God* in the Hebrew and Christian Scriptures. We think of the power and beauty of the Psalms, of Isaiah, of the Prophets for giving us a sense of the majesty yet tenderness of God; of the four Gospels for their portraits of Jesus; of the eloquent, passionate, theological letters of Paul interpreting the meaning of the crucified and risen Christ for us.

c) Greatly helpful is *the liturgical year* in which throughout the course of a year the great events in the life of Christ are celebrated. (See chapter 5.) By living again these Christian mysteries, the Christian deepens his faith and hope and love thus growing in personal friendship with the risen Christ and in gratitude to God.

d) *Prayer.* The Church offers us countless opportunities for prayer: the sacraments, especially the Eucharist; the Bible; the liturgical year; a variety of devotions; retreats, and many more. In fact a major effort of the church is to teach and encourage us to pray. For in her 2000-year experience the church knows that prayer, like oxygen for our physical life, is essential to our spiritual life. Through prayer God and the risen Christ become real to us, our faith and hope and love develop and grow. Like human friendship and love, there can be no personal relationship with God or Jesus Christ without frequent contact and sharing through prayer.

Prayer is "lifting one's mind and heart to God," "loving intimate conversation with God or the God-man, Jesus Christ." In prayer we turn to God and become aware of God's presence; we speak to God and listen while God speaks to us. Prayer is thus a two-way loving conversation between two friends, one of whom is intensely interested in us. As weak, limited creatures we need God's help, as sinners we need to express our sorrow, as recipients of God's goodness and his many gifts to us personally we should praise and thank God. So the traditional purposes of prayer are *petition, adoration, contrition, thanksgiving* (PACT).

We can pray in many different ways. *Mental* prayer is our own spontaneous conversation with God, letting our mind and heart speak out our own thoughts and feelings. *Vocal* prayer is reciting privately or aloud with others set prayers like the Our Father or Lord's Prayer, the Hail Mary, the Angelus, the Apostles' Creed, the Act of Contrition, the Glory Be . . . , Come Holy Spirit, Prayer of St. Francis, and many others.

The church teaches various methods or types of prayer. *Meditation* is thinking about God or Christ or the truths of faith and making applications to our own life; the emphasis is on our mind and imagination. **Contemplation** is more passive than meditation; one does not use words or images but simply comes before God to enjoy God's loving company and to be open to God. The popular "Jesus Prayer" consists of phrases like "Lord Jesus Christ, Son of God, have mercy on me, a sinner" or "Jesus, have mercy on me" or simply "Jesus"; or "Come, Lord Jesus, come." Such prayer is easy, able to be made any time, anywhere and is very calming.

A somewhat similar form recently popularized by Thomas Keating and Basil Pennington is *"centering prayer"* in which a person focuses or

centers on God present in the center of one's being: a person sits re-
laxed and quiet, following three rules or guides: 1. Be in faith and love
to God who dwells in the center of your being; 2. Take up a love word
(God, Jesus, Lord, Spirit, love, Friend, etc.) and let it be gently present,
supporting your being to God in faith-filled love; 3. Whenever you become aware of anything, simply gently return to the Lord with the use
of your prayer word.

Still another popular form of prayer is *lectio divina*, the prayerful reading of Scripture. You read the sacred text with reverence, acknowledging God's presence and calling upon the Holy Spirit; then for ten
minutes you listen to the Lord and respond to him; you finish by thank-
ing the Lord and taking a "word" suggested by the prayerful reading
with you as a mantra for the day.

    e) *Spiritual direction,* in which adults and increasingly today young
       people seek a priest or sister or layperson experienced and wise "in
       the ways of the Lord" for guidance and counseling to develop a
       deeper religious life.

    f) *Spiritual reading*: here the wealth is seemingly boundless! Each
       year hundreds of new books on every aspect of Christian living are
       published to add to the rich heritage of the church's spiritual litera-
       ture: lives of the saints, lives of Christ, the writings of mystics like
       St. Teresa of Avila and John of the Cross. A walk through a Catho-
       lic or Christian book store to look at titles and authors is an as-
       tounding experience of the immense scope of present literature and
       past spiritual classics.

3. Throughout its history the church has developed other helps.

    a) A great variety of religious practices and prayers known as *devo-
       tions* by which Catholics express their love and devotion to God,
       Christ, Mary and the saints. (See the next chapter, "Devotions"
       Spirituality.)

    b) The immense richness of *religious art* in churches and museums,
       especially in Europe and South America: statues of Christ and
       Mary and Michelangelo's *Pietà* and the saints (Bernini's ecstasy of
       St. Teresa); the brilliant mosaics of churches in Ravenna, Monre-
       ale, Rome, Venice; the dazzling stained glass windows of Chartres
       and Paris; the masterpieces of painters like Michelangelo in the
       Sistine Chapel, of El Greco, Raphael; the countless madonnas of
       Mary and child; the rich icons of Christ and of Mary and child and
       the eastern Saints; the elaborate Christmas cribs of Naples and
       Rome; in South America, the realistic statues of the suffering and
       dead Christ and the richly clothed statues of Mary and the saints.

    c) *Christian symbols*: the cross on church steeples and the crucifix in
       a prominent position in every Catholic church, in Catholic schools

and in many Catholic homes. The cross is the identifying symbol of Christianity, of God's all-out love for us, and of our redemption and salvation. Less-well-known symbols are the dove (Spirit), fish[4] (Christ), boat (the church), anchor (hope), water (life), oil (healing).

d) Christian *movements* and groups that spring up spontaneously, thanks to charismatic priests or sisters or laypeople, to meet the special spiritual needs of people at certain eras of history: the *retreat movement* in which tens of thousands of men and women leave home for a weekend of talks, prayer, and sharing, such as the *Spiritual Exercises of St. Ignatius*; the *cursillo* or short course in Christianity of four intense days given predominantly by laypeople to rediscover Christ and Christianity; *Marriage Encounter* for married couples to learn to communicate with each other on deeper levels as a way of loving each other more profoundly; *Search* weekends where young people through much interaction and sharing discover an enthusiasm for God and Christ and to be Christian; the *Charismatic or Pentecostal movement* in which over a million USA Catholics have experienced deeply the love of God and the joy of prayer and of being Christian, and have sometimes received the gift of tongues and of healing; *St. Vincent de Paul Society* that cares for the poor, and many others.

4. We should not overlook the *human agents* of this wealth of means and helps toward holiness and full Christian living: those parish priests and religious order priests and teaching sisters who have dedicated their whole lives to giving us Christ in the sacraments and Christian knowledge through catechism and religion classes. Without them we would be spiritually poor indeed. Today we must include the growing number of laypeople who in exercising a variety of ministries like teaching, song directors, eucharistic ministers, social workers, members of parish teams, youth ministers and retreat givers are helping Catholics live their Christian lives more fully.

Nor can we overlook those first teachers, *our parents;* on them rest the joyful opportunity and awesome responsibility of introducing their children to the experience of God and Jesus and of thus laying the foundation for a satisfying Christian life. Godparents, too, deserve mention.

As we conclude this section, it is good to emphasize where all these good things happen: primarily and most effectively in the local *parish* where the Christian community is gathered Sunday after Sunday around Christ and his minister to celebrate Eucharist, to hear the word of God

---

4. The Greek word for fish is *ichthus:* i for Jesus, *chi* for Christ, *th* for God, *u* for son, *s* for savior, forming the phrase "Jesus Christ, son of God, savior." Christian tombstones often bore scratched outlines of a fish as symbol of Christ to identify the deceased as a Christian.

and partake in the Lord's Supper, to "remember" the Lord until he comes. Thus Vatican II could say that the universal Catholic Church is fully contained in each local church, be it the diocese around the bishop or the parish around its pastor.

The Kingdom of God on Earth

During his life on this earth, Jesus tirelessly preached and worked to establish God's kingdom on earth; many of his parables were told to illustrate the nature of this kingdom. By healing people's physical, emotional and spiritual hurts, he was establishing the kingdom. Jesus' first recorded words in the Gospel of Mark as he begins his public ministry are: "This is the time of fulfillment. The **kingdom of God** is at hand" (Mark 1:15). Luke in his Gospel also reports the beginning of Jesus' public life in the incident at the synagogue in Nazareth. Jesus reads a passage from Isaiah:

"The spirit of the Lord is upon me; therefore he has anointed me.
He has sent me to bring glad tidings to the poor, to proclaim liberty to captives, recovery of sight to the blind and release to prisoners, to announce a year of favor from the Lord." (Luke 4:18-19)

Then he states solemnly: "Today this Scripture passage is fulfilled in your hearing" (Luke 4:21), meaning that he has come and is here to establish God's kingdom on earth by doing what Isaiah had prophesied about the Messiah.

The church, in imitation of Jesus its Lord, puts high value on establishing God's kingdom on earth. In its official eucharistic liturgy, the church prays daily in the Our Father ". . . thy kingdom come, thy will be done on earth . . . give us this day our daily bread, forgive us our sins as we forgive those who sin against us. . . ." Vatican II stated that "the Church has but one sole purpose—that the Kingdom of God may come and the salvation of the human race be accomplished" (GS 45).

What then is the kingdom of God on earth?

Jesus expressed the kingdom in terms of the two great commandments: ". . . you shall love the Lord your God with all your heart, with all your soul, with all your mind, and with all your strength. This is the second, You shall love your neighbor as yourself" (Mark 12:30-31). The kingdom therefore has three realities: God, other people and ourselves.

God. To establish God's kingdom on earth means to establish *belief* in the existence of a creator God who is a God of love and *knowledge* of his plan for us. It means that people *love* God above all else, *obey* his commandments, *respect* and *worship* him above all created things.

Other People. To establish God's kingdom on earth also means to *love* our fellow sisters and brothers in the human family. We cannot effectively love them when they are denied sufficient food and housing, when their basic human rights are violated through injustice, and when millions suffer and die in war or are refugees. This situation is not God's plan or wish for humans. Jesus graphically illustrated this truth when he spoke his famous eight Beatitudes (Mt. 5:3-12) and when he identified himself with the hungry, the naked, the sick, the strangers, and the imprisoned, and promised eternal life to those who helped them (Mt. 25:31-46).

Ourselves. God's kingdom must first be established in ourselves; Jesus insisted that the kingdom of God is "within you." Moreover, we cannot love God and others unless we first genuinely love ourselves.

By way of conclusion: to found the kingdom of God on earth is to *establish a situation* where people know and love, worship and obey God and where they truly love others by respecting their basic human dignity and rights, treat them justly and thus live at peace with all. The kingdom of God is thus the expression of God's loving plan for our happiness on this earth as well as in the next life. This plan is good news indeed. Jesus came to announce this plan and accomplish it on earth. Through his Apostles he gave the church the mission of establishing the kingdom in the hearts of all people and in the structures of society. We shall study this mission more fully in chapters 9 and 18.

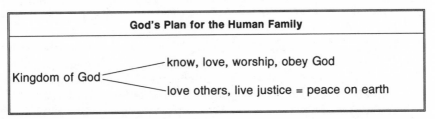

Establishing God's kingdom on earth is involved with all aspects of the church's mission: for it is an essential part of our salvation and sanctification and is the work of evangelization and ecumenism.

Ecumenism

Vatican II, following Pope John XXIII, officially established the restoration of ecclesial union as part of the mission of the church. Christ himself had given his disciples this mission when at the Last Supper he solemnly prayed, "That all may be one, as you Father, are in me and I in you; I pray that they may be one in us, that the world may believe that you sent me." (John 17:21) This prayer of Christ before his saving suffering, death and resurrection has become the motive force and rallying point of the ecumenical movement. It's important to note that Jesus' motive for his

Apostles and their followers down through the ages to be one is precisely evangelization, "that the world may believe."

The modern ecumenical movement with its remarkable accomplishments between the separated Christian churches is the topic of chapter 8.

Contemporary Issues involving the Church's Mission

1. Is the Catholic Church today a *credible sacrament of salvation* to its own members, to other Christians, and to the world at large? Many Catholics, especially women, feel alienated from the institutional church. Other Christians, after the initial enthusiasm for church unity following the Council, sense a rigidity and authoritarianism that makes the Catholic Church unattractive. Many would frame the question this way: does the Catholic Church as sacrament mirror and incarnate the humble, loving Christ who came to serve and not to dominate and who washed the feet of his disciples at the Last Supper?

2. Is the Catholic Church today *too involved in socioeconomic and political matters*? Many Catholics feel that it is. Other Catholics respond that justice and human rights' issues are essential to gospel values and the kingdom Jesus came to establish. The issue appears to be what is the most prudent, effective program of involvement, one that preserves the prophetic voice of church leaders and members, yet does not embroil them in partisan politics.

3. Has the Catholic Church *lost its missionary zeal?* Have Catholics failed in their baptismal vocation to evangelize? On the surface it appears they have since Catholics as a whole do not match the evangelizing zeal of both clergy and laity in evangelical, pentecostal groups. Mormon, Seventh-Day Adventist, Jehovah's Witnesses, Assembly of God and Church of Christ youth and clergy are flooding Russia, Eastern Europe, and Latin American to evangelize the peoples there. Avery Dulles comments that American Catholics are "wary of evangelization for a variety of reasons. They distrust the biblicism, the individualism, the emotionalism, and the aggressive proselytism of certain Protestant evangelistic preachers"; since faith is a free, personal, private response to God, they are reluctant to appear to pressure anyone; too often Catholics have believed "simply on the authority of the Church" rather than experiencing the gospel as an "extraordinary piece of good news" to be shared with others; "too many Catholics of our day seem never to have encountered Christ" in a personal, familiar way.[5]

Yet there are encouraging signs. A growing number of lay Catholics, married couples and young people volunteer for ministry in the United

---

5. Avery Dulles, "John Paul II and the New Evangelization," *America* 166 (Feb. 1, 1992): 71.

States, in Latin America, and elsewhere. Priests and sisters continue to labor heroically in missionary countries, often giving their lives as martyrs of charity. And countries with many vocations, like India, send priests and sisters as missionaries to other areas.

4. Should missionaries seek to *convert* indigenous peoples and members of the great world religions? At periods in the church's history and almost up to the present, missionaries to foreign continents like Latin America, Asia and Africa considered the "natives" pagans, totally without God and damned to hell unless they had the waters of baptism poured over them. A better theology realizes that the Holy Spirit enlightens everyone and that God's salvific will includes all persons. Thus missionaries going to other cultures and to "pagan" tribes realize that God has been present to them for centuries. So the missionary recognizes what God has already done and is presently doing among the people and builds the Christian message on that.

A modern issue is the suggestion that if this is the case should we destroy a rich native culture by conversion? There is the sad story of the missionary priest in Paraguay who destroyed the sacred books of the Indians; in his later years he realized the enormity of what he had done and spent the rest of his life trying to collect what remained. Pope John Paul II in his address to the indigenous peoples of the Americas in the Yucatan, Mexico, August 1993, recognized the abuses of Spanish evangelization and conversion methods "in the destruction of many of your artistic and cultural creations and in the violence to which you were often subjected."[6]

This issue has particular relevance today for evangelizing religious Jews, Hindus, Buddhists, Muslims and native Americans. Clearly the church must proclaim the good news about God's plan in Jesus Christ to all peoples of the world. Yet it must not force conversion on anyone and must respect the culture and religion of indigenous peoples. Missionaries today need to exercise respect, prudence, patience, and spiritual insight. In some cases their evangelization will consist in being a witness of God's love and of Christian virtues and in laboring for the physical and mental well-being of the people they serve. Thus is the seed of faith planted, with God giving the increase in God's good time!

5. What has the church's record regarding *inculturation* been since Vatican II? After judging progress in the areas of liturgy, canon law, doctrine and regional episcopal conferences to be ambiguous, T. Howland Sanks draws this conclusion:

---

6. Pope John Paul II, "The Church is Committed to Cultural Diversity," *The Pope Speaks: The Church Documents Monthly* 39, No. 2 (March/April, 1994): 81.

In summary, the experience of inculturating the faith since Vatican II has reflected the ongoing tension between a conception of the church as a highly centralized and rather uniform organization and the conception of the church as a more diffuse communion of diverse local or particular churches, between the substance of the faith and the forms of its expression, between a desire for unity and a stifling uniformity. Such tensions pose both challenges and possibilities for the future.[7]

Summary

Mission refers to a great enterprise one is sent to accomplish. The origin of the church's mission is God the Father sending his Son into our world to become a man in order to carry out God's plan for the human family, and Jesus and his Spirit sending the Apostles and, through them, the church. The great enterprise that constitutes the church's mission is no less than the salvation of the entire human family. Thus Vatican II gave the Catholic Church the cosmic title "the universal sacrament of salvation." The church carries out its mission of salvation through answering Jesus' command to bring the good news of salvation to all peoples of all times (evangelization through inculturation); through bringing its members into ever-closer love relationship with God and Jesus Christ (sanctification); and through accomplishing Jesus' life work of establishing God's kingdom in the hearts and lives of all people. Following Jesus' prayer that "all may be one," the bishops at Vatican II gave the Catholic Church the mission of uniting the separated Christian churches. The church's mission in the post-Vatican II church involves complex issues; we call attention to five.

For Discussion

1. If the Christian Church is God's plan for the human family, in what sense is the church *necessary* for their salvation?

2. Is the Catholic Church today a convincing *sacrament* or example of salvation?

3. Considering the mission of evangelization Jesus gave the church, why after 2000 years is only about 20% of the human family Christian?

4. To what extent *can* the American Catholic Church inculturate American customs and values? What elements *should* it inculturate to be more authentically American, yet Catholic?

5. Do you seriously consider holiness a worthy ideal? Why or why not?

---

7. Sanks, *Salt, Leaven and Light*, 201.

6. What means of achieving sanctification are most appealing to you?

For Action

1. Next Sunday attend a black Baptist Church. Experience how their service is a good example of inculturation by incorporating and expressing black culture.

2. Read up on how native Americans, especially the Sioux, are inculturating the "peace pipe," the sweat lodge, and other practices into Catholic worship and life.

3. During the 500th anniversary of Colombus "discovering America," much attention was focused on the Spanish evangelization and conquest of Latin America when "the cross and sword" were joined. Check out Cortez in Mexico and Pizarro in Peru for starters. Don't neglect Bishop Bartolomé de las Casas who fought tirelessly for fair treatment of the indigenous peoples (Indians) there.

4. Rent the spectacular video *The Mission* to experience another side of "evangelization through inculturation" in the famous Jesuit Reductions of Paraguay from 1607 to 1767.

Further Reading

Buhlmann, Walbert. *The Coming of the Third Church.* Maryknoll, NY: Orbis Books, 1978.

Donovan, Vincent. *Christianity Rediscovered.* Maryknoll, NY: Orbis Books, 1982.

Flendora, Carol Lee. *Enduring Grace: Living Portraits of Seven Women Mystics.* San Francisco: Harper, 1993.

Hillman, Eugene., *Toward an African Christianity, Inculturation Applied.* New York/ Mahweh: Paulist Press, 1993.

National Conference of Catholic Bishops, *Heritage and Hope, Evangelization in the United States.* Washington, D.C.: U.S. Catholic Conference, 1991.

_____ "Go and Make Disciples: A National Plan and Strategy for Catholic Evangelization." *Origins* 22 (Dec. 3, 1992): 423-32.

Pennington, Basil, O.C.S.O. *Centering Prayer.* Garden City, New York: Doubleday, 1980.

Schineller, Peter. *A Handbook on Inculturation.* New York/Mahweh: Paulist Press, 1990.

Shorter, Aylward. *Toward a Theology of Inculturation.* London: Geoffrey Chapman, 1988.

CHAPTER 7

Spirituality

> All Christians . . . are called to the fullness of Christian life and to the perfection of love.   —Constitution on the Church 40

Introduction

The lofty mission of the Church is to lead all persons, especially its own members, to union with God and a personal relationship with Jesus Christ. Traditional terms for this goal are holiness, the interior life, sanctity, spiritual life, or simply Christian life. Contemporary usage is **spirituality.** Spirituality refers to the particular way one lives the Christian life, the specific approach a person uses to achieve union with God and a personal relationship with Jesus Christ.

> That process of saying 'yes' to God is called spirituality. . . . [It is] that complex of beliefs, attitudes, and practices by which the presence of Christ is made more manifest in the lives of believers and by which we are led more fully and openly to say 'yes' to the gift of God.[1]

Throughout the history of the church, Christians have discovered and developed different paths to holiness, different ways to live the Christian life and to imitate Christ, various approaches to achieve union with God and friendship with Christ. We can thus speak of Catholic or Orthodox or Protestant spiritualities; Lutheran or Methodist or Baptist spiritualities; medieval and contemporary spiritualities; and within Catholicism Franciscan or Carmelite or Ignatian spiritualities, to mention but a few. In reading the lives of the saints, it is interesting to see the variety of ways these great

---

1. Lawrence Cunningham, *The Catholic Faith: An Introduction* (New York/Mahwah, NJ: Paulist Press, 1987), 130.

men and women expressed their unique spirituality. Moreover, beyond Christianity we can speak of Jewish or Muslim spiritualities as ways of expressing devotion to Yahweh or Allah.

In its comprehensive renewal of Catholic life, Vatican II laid the basis for a rich new spirituality for Catholics. In so doing, there emerged new approaches to living the Christian life, new ways to be Catholic. However these "new" spiritualities are new only in the sense of giving *fresh emphases*. The foundation and basis of all Christian spirituality remains the person of the risen Christ as we come to know him in the Christian Scriptures and encounter him in the liturgical and sacramental life of the church, especially in the eucharistic celebration. The constants in Christian spirituality remain *faith*, *hope* and *love* of God and others, *prayer*, *avoidance of sin*, *asceticism*. The Council Fathers were careful to guard against superstition and to correct past exaggerations in spiritual practices.

To help younger Catholics understand and appreciate the extent of the Vatican II renewal of Catholic spirituality and to remind older Catholics of how pre-Vatican II spirituality was dominated by a multiplicity of **devotions**, the following description of Catholic piety comes from an analysis made of 5000 Roman Catholic devotional pamphlets, prayer books, sacred music, catechisms and holy cards covering the years 1925-1975.

> Generally speaking . . . I remarked the virtual absence of any mention of God the Father, of Trinitarian spirituality, of the paschal mystery, of the Resurrection, of the church, of Scripture . . . There was a heavy emphasis on petition and contrition, a minimal suggestion of any other themes for prayer. Our Lady and the saints were so constantly invoked as to create the impression that Our Lord had yielded up his office as mediator. Except on All Souls Day there seemed to be small awareness of a corporate union of the faithful. The Mass was the atoning sacrifice, but not the means or the expression of the community, and the priest, to judge by the ordination cards, was regarded rather as an ambassador from heaven to the community than its servant. Holy Communion, at least on the older cards, was something added to the Mass on special occasions. Devotions abounded, subjective and individualistic in tone, with little reference to the liturgical year. It was clear that the common piety had never been introduced to the Psalms or even to most of the classic prayers of the Christian ages, such as one might find in the breviary.[2]

---◆---

Preview: This chapter attempts to explain Catholic spirituality, while recognizing the contribution and value of Orthodox, Anglican, and Protestant spiritualities. The way Christians have responded to God

---

2. William Leonard, "Popular Devotions Remembered," *America* 145 (Sept. 12, 1981), 120.

and Jesus Christ through the centuries has a *history;* our brief survey of this history along with a look at the ancient Orthodox and more recent Anglican and Lutheran spiritualities give us a context for this chapter. We then turn to Catholic spirituality, considering first the five characteristics of the *traditional* Catholic way of approaching God: sacraments, the Eucharist, devotion to Mary, to the saints, and a multiplicity of devotional practices. This leads to a reflection on various emphases that we term the *new Vatican II* spirituality: this world, lay, liturgical, biblical, ecumenical and Holy Spirit spirituality. We conclude by calling attention to areas of spirituality that are of special interest to contemporary Catholics as well as other Christians.

◆

History of Christian Spirituality

How have Christians through the centuries responded to the triune God, to the life, crucifixion and resurrection of the God-man, Jesus of Nazareth, to the Spirit inspiring them to live the Christian life as fully as possible? The many different ways Christians have tried to respond constitute the interesting, inspiring, even fascinating story of Christian spirituality. We shall focus on those great figures whose intense Christian life created the distinctive schools of spirituality in the Church: the saints and mystics and founders and members of religious orders.

Overview

Primitive Christianity preached the Resurrection of Jesus, and baptism as assimilation to his death and resurrection. The major consideration of spirituality in the first century was to live in such a way to be ready for the imminent second coming of Christ. Owing to the persecutions, martyrdom became the privileged way to imitate Christ's sufferings and achieve perfect union with him in love. After the persecutions, fervent Christians went to the deserts of Egypt for solitude, creating a spirituality of "white" martyrdom expressed by lengthy prayer, severe penances, self-discovery, and struggle against the devil. Gradually these hermits gathered around a spiritual father. The great St. Augustine (354-430) in northern Africa organized the life of the clergy around him as a new type of **monasticism**. The mystic John Cassian passed the monastic practices of the East to western Christianity. St. Benedict, in founding the famous abbey of Monte Casino, established the practical Benedictine spirituality that has enriched the church to this day.

The spirituality of the Middle Ages came from cloistered monks with their example of prayer, bodily penance and physical labor, like draining the swamps and agriculture. The monastery of Cluny, founded in France in

909, revived the monastic spirit of St. Benedict; within 150 years 2000 communities of monks became linked to Cluny! St. Bernard (1091-1153) promoted Cistercian spirituality and developed a theology of mysticism. The two great figures of the 13th century, St. Francis of Assisi (1181-1226) and St. Dominic (1170-1221), through the religious orders they founded profoundly influenced the spirituality of Christian Europe: Francis by his poverty, preaching, service of the church and Dominic by preaching, contemplative prayer, and scholarship.

A new spirituality began in Germany, Holland, and England in the 14th century that stressed the soul's union with God through contemplation. Important influences were Meister Eckhard, Tauler, the unknown English author of *The Cloud of Unknowing*, Gerard Groote, who founded the Brethren of the Common Life and the **Devotio Moderna** which in turn influenced Thomas à Kempis' spirituality classic *The Imitation of Christ*, still popular today.

Key figures establishing Renaissance and later spirituality were St. Ignatius Loyola in his *Spiritual Exercises*; the humanist Erasmus (1476-1536); the great mystical writers representing the Carmelite school of spirituality: St. Teresa of Avila (1515-1582), who stressed prayer as the exchange of love with God, and St. John of the Cross (1542-1591), whose *Dark Night of the Soul* and *Ascent of Mt. Carmel* still profoundly influence Catholic spirituality; St. Francis de Sales (1567-1622), in his *An Introduction to the Devout Life,* brought the piety of the cloister to Christians living in the world; St. Alphonsus Liguori (1696-1787), founder of the Redemptorists; and St. Margaret Mary Alacoque (1647-1690), whose revelations from Christ resulted in the worldwide devotion to the Sacred Heart of Jesus, symbol of God's love for us.

Our modern period has witnessed a complex variety of spiritualities: prodigious apostolic activity as the way to follow Christ; recovery of liturgical spirituality; emphasis on the God-man Christ, especially on his humanity, rather than on the saints; continuing filial devotion to Mary but in her relation to the mystery of Christ; revival of devotion to the Holy Spirit as the source and vivifier of spiritual living and a consequent trinitarian spirituality; emphasis on the Resurrection of Jesus as the foundation of Christianity, to name only the most prominent emphases. A phenomenon of the 20th century is the near-deluge of popular books on spirituality for religious and lay Christians alike, indicating the modern interest in and hunger for more intense Christian living. "The spiritual biography[3] that surpassed all others in popularity" was the "little way of spiritual childhood" by the extraordinary French Carmelite nun, St. Thérèse of Lisieux (1873-1897), "the Little Flower," who died at the early age of 24 after

---

3. *The Autobiography of St. Thérèse of Lisieux: The Story of a Soul* (Garden City, NY: Doubleday, 1957)

great suffering offered joyously to God for the world and for missionaries to foreign lands.

Orthodox, Anglican, Lutheran Spiritualities

Other Christian families than the Roman Catholic possess rich spiritual traditions that deserve our attention. We have chosen only three, realizing we are omitting others of merit, like Quaker and Pentecostal spirituality.

1. Orthodox Spirituality is a rich mix of the sublime and the down-to-earth. Orthodox have great devotion to the Holy Trinity, who divinize the Christian in the mutual cooperation between the triune God, offering participation in the divine nature and human persons freely willing and acting to be with God; to the Holy Spirit who dwells in each baptized person; to Mary as *Theotokos*, the Mother of God; to Jesus, the eternal Word, as redeemer and creator, who is pictured in majesty from the apse of Byzantine cathedrals as the bearded Christ holding the book of the Gospels, his right hand raised in blessing; to the Gospel, whose book always lies open on the altar for veneration as an icon of the living Word in the midst of the people; to the Divine Liturgy, whose public worship has been the main strength and unifying force of Orthodox Christians through centuries of persecution; to the sacraments, especially baptism, Eucharist, and confession, as the way to deification and union with God.

Orthodoxy expresses such sublime spirituality in a profusion of colorful, down-to-earth ways. The Divine Liturgy, often two hours or more, is celebrated with much chanting and singing, lengthy prayers, clouds of incense by bearded priests in colorful rich vestments reaching to the ankles. Orthodox Christians kiss the many two-dimensional painted **icons** or images of Christ, of Mary and of the saints, venerating them as windows or ways into the eternal and as divine images of heaven on earth. Venerating icons, many of which are art treasures, is the most visible characteristic of Orthodox spirituality. Vividly aware of the communion of saints, Orthodox Christians honor their saints and martyrs and speak of departed Christians not as dead but "sleeping." All these elements of Orthodox Christian piety are means toward the ultimate end of divinization and salvation.

The tragic schism between Eastern and Western Christianity finalized in 1054 deprived Roman Catholicism of this rich Orthodox spirituality. In referring to the hoped-for reunion of Orthodoxy and Roman Catholicism, Pope John Paul II prayed for the day when the Christian Church can breathe once again with both lungs!

2. Anglican Spirituality. Anglicanism and the many national churches that make up the Anglican communion have been called the bridge between Catholicism and Protestantism. Thus Anglican spirituality manifests both Catholic and Protestant elements. Major Catholic elements are the "apostolic ministry" of bishops, priests and deacons, the theology of the early creeds and councils, and sacramental worship, emphasizing especially the Eucharist. Protestant elements are emphasis on biblical teaching and democratic church governance. Anglican spirituality has been influenced by major historical movements within the Church of England: stern Puritanism, with insistence on morality and the individual's responsibility before God; Methodist spirituality inspired by John and Charles Wesley, who introduced a "methodical" approach to God characterized by frequent private family and public prayer and meditation on the Bible, celebrating the Lord's Supper "at every opportunity," joyous hymn singing and meditating on hymns sung and sermons heard, care of prisoners and the poor; the 19th-century Catholic Oxford Movement, led by the brilliant preacher and writer John Henry Newman, later Cardinal Newman, and other scholars who turned to the **Fathers of the Church** to study the formative years of the church and to reinforce in the church this early Catholic heritage.

The inspirational King James translation of the Bible, the muchloved Book of Common Prayer, the eucharistic liturgy called the Holy Communion or the Holy Eucharist (and by some, the Mass), the Sunday services of Morning Prayer and Evening Prayer (or "Evensong") have formed the spiritual lives of generations of Anglicans. Anglican spirituality is characterized by solemn, joyous liturgical worship and stately hymns and is nourished by a rich tradition of devotional books and theological and historical scholarship.

Anglican spirituality reflects a Catholic appeal to tradition along with the Protestant spirit of independence, freedom of the individual, and reliance on the Bible and on conciliar rather than hierachical authority.

3. Lutheran Spirituality has been formed and is still influenced by the intense spiritual struggles and prodigious scriptural and theological contributions of Martin Luther and his experience of the grace of God. Lutheran spirituality stresses the sinfulness of the human condition and the all-enduring mercy of God through Jesus Christ, whose suffering and death saved weak, helpless sinners who, through the Holy Spirit, are gathered and sanctified as the one, holy, catholic and apostolic church. Sinners are justified or experience God's favor, not through their own merits, but in the merciful love of God manifested in Jesus. Christ is the great mediator before God; no others are needed. All Christians share in the priesthood of Christ through their baptism, the great sacrament which begins the Christian life. Lutheran spirituality is centered on word and sacrament: the Bible that contains Christ, the living Word of God, and the two sacraments of baptism and the Lord's Supper. Luther's small catechism of three parts dealing with the Ten Commandments, the creed and the sacraments, and the Our Father is the "foundation-stone of Lutheran sprituality." Luther developed a spirituality of the freedom and responsibility of the Christian and of the triumph of the cross in Christian life. Lutheran spirituality is thus characterized by total devotion to the triune God and to the gospel that declares the pattern of Christian life in the world.

Characteristics of Catholic Spirituality

1. Sacramental Spirituality. Catholics, as well as Orthodox and Anglicans and a growing number of Protestants, believe that God comes to us through visible rituals or sacramental *signs*; that we encounter the risen Christ and his Spirit in the seven rituals of the church called sacraments. The Catholic conviction is that the risen Christ and his Spirit use water, oil, bread and wine and the words and action of the priest-minister of the sacrament to accomplish spiritual realities. Sacraments are thus the heart of Catholic life; Catholics worldwide flock in great numbers to "use them." Catholic spirituality is primarily a sacramental spirituality. Vatican II stressed the communitarian nature of sacraments and of liturgical worship.

2. Eucharistic Spirituality. Catholics build their spiritual lives around "the Mass," the ritual celebration of Christ's saving death, resurrection and glorification. The eucharistic celebration of the Lord's Supper or the "Holy Sacrifice of the Mass" has been the core of Catholic life and the most important action of the church from the time of the Apostles to the present. At all times, but especially in times of persecution, Catholics have made great sacrifices to attend Sunday and even daily Eucharists. When Catholics celebrate significant events — anniversaries, birthdays, death of a relative or friend — their first thought is "Let's have a Mass!" Wherever John Paul II travels on his worldwide pastoral visits, the high point is a public Mass, often attended by a half-million or more people; in Third World countries, *campesinos* have walked for days to attend such eucharistic celebrations. Catholic spirituality is characteristically a eucharistic spirituality. Vatican II went to great lengths to renew eucharistic theology and practice.

3. Marian Spirituality. Catholics' love and tender devotion to Mary as "their mother" has been a major characteristic of the Catholic Church since the early centuries, climaxing in the "age of Mary" in the Middle Ages. Witness thousands of madonnas by Renaissance painters and Orthodox icons of mother and child; the great European cathedrals bearing Mary's name (Notre Dame of Paris, Our Lady of Chartres, St. Mary Major in Rome); the number of Catholic churches and schools and hospitals called St. Mary's; titles given to Mary (Our Lady, Mother of God, Blessed Mother, Queen of Heaven, the Immaculate Conception, Blessed Virgin); the apparitions of Mary (Guadalupe, Lourdes, Fatima); the extraordinary devotion of Mexican Indians to their brown-skinned virgin of Guadalupe and of the Catalans to their black virgin in Montserrat, Spain; the many feastdays of Mary in the church calendar; the countless richly dressed and bejeweled statues of Mary in Latin America and Michelangelo's revered *Pietà* in St.

Peter's, Rome; famous Marian pilgrimage shrines all over the world, and much more!

Such profusion of devotion puzzles Protestants, who object that it deters from the central role of Jesus in Christianity and sometimes verges on superstition. There are some grounds for this, not only in Catholic Europe of the past but also today in the popular religiosity of poorly educated Catholics in Latin America and the Mediterranean world. The bishops of Vatican II shared this concern. Their response was to emphasize Mary's relationship to Christ and her role in God's plan of salvation and in the church. Accordingly, they rejected the proposed separate document on Mary, instead inserting a chapter on Mary in the *Constitution on the Church* as the beautiful final chapter 8.

The Council's teaching on Mary is founded on her "function . . . in the plan of salvation." She was chosen by God through the angel Gabriel to be the mother of God (*theotokos,* according to the Council of Ephesus, 431 AD), the human mother of Jesus the God-man. This is her preeminent title and primary claim to the veneration (not adoration) and devotion of all Christians. Vatican II gave her a new title, "Mother of the Church"; for as Mary brought Christ into the world physically, so the church brings forth Christ through faith, sacraments, grace, and preaching. The Council presents Mary to us as the ideal Christian, obedient to God's will ("Be it done to me according to thy word" was her answer to Gabriel announcing to her that she had been chosen to be the mother of the Messiah), a true disciple of Jesus, a fellow sufferer in this life, a worthy friend, a model for all Christians to imitate.

The Council insisted that "there is but one Mediator: . . . the man Jesus Christ who gave himself as redemption for all" (1 Tim 2:5-6). The bishops likewise insisted that "Mary's function as Mother of [all people] in no way obscures or diminishes this unique mediation of Christ." (*LG* 60) Thus Catholics, in recognition of Jesus on the cross saying to the apostle John "This is your mother" (Jn 19:27), take Mary as their heavenly mother, asking her to intercede with her son for their needs.

Catholics honor Mary in many beautiful prayers and devotions: the *Hail Mary;* the *rosary*, consisting of five joyful, five sorrowful, and five glorious mysteries of the life of Christ and of Mary's part in his life; the *Angelus,* traditionally recited three times daily, morning, noon and evening; the *Litany of Mary,* a series of Mary's titles followed by "pray for us"; the *First Saturday* of each month devotion, resulting from Mary's appearances at Fatima in 1917. The two-part *Hail Mary* best states the reasons for Catholics' extraordinary devotion to Mary through the centuries: "Hail Mary, full of grace, the Lord is with you; blessed are you among women and blessed is the fruit of your womb, Jesus. Holy Mary, mother of God, pray for us sinners now and at the hour of our death. Amen."

Mary is truly a much-beloved and central figure in Catholic as well as Orthodox spirituality.

4. Saint-oriented Spirituality. In its devotion to the saints, Catholicism is a highly person-oriented, down-to-earth religion. The saints have great appeal to both ordinary and highly educated Catholics. This is especially the case for Mediterranean and Latin American Catholicism. In Europe each city had its saint-protector whose feast-day was celebrated in spectacular fashion after months of preparation. The "fiesta" is the major religious event in Latin America and wherever Hispanic culture is found. The early Franciscan missionaries in California gave saints' names to the string of missions from San Diego (James) to San Francisco (Francis of Assisi): San Clemente, Los Angeles (Our Lady, Queen of the Angels), Santa Monica, Santa Barbara, San Jose, Santa Clara, San Mateo.

Who are some of the better-known Saints? Besides the Blessed Virgin Mary, there are the *"confessor* saints,"* those who witnessed to Christ by their heroic lives: Saint Joseph, Mary's spouse; Augustine, Benedict, Simeon Stylites, Hilda of Whitby, Thomas Aquinas, Bonaventure, Anthony, Francis Xavier, Peter Claver, Peter Canisius, Pope Pius V, John of the Cross, Francis de Sales, Vincent de Paul, the Curé of Ars, Joan of Arc, Bernard of Clairvaux, Clare and Scholastica, Aloysius, Rose of Lima, and on and on. Then there is the long list of **martyr**-saints: the first martyr, Stephen; the apostles Peter and Paul; the virgins Agnes in 3rd-century Rome and Maria Goretti in 20th-century Italy, the deacon Lawrence, many early popes, Edmund Campion and the 43 English martyrs, Isaac Jogues and the seven North American Jesuit martyrs, the 23 Japanese martyrs, Andrew Kim and hundreds of Korean martyrs, Charles Lwanga and the Ugandan martyrs. The list or canon is in the thousands. The multitude of the heroes and heroines of Christ is the glory of Christianity and of the Catholic Church. Their lives make exciting, inspiring reading.

> Nowhere is the catholicity of the Church better measured than in its catalogue of the saints. As we browse through the many standard dictionaries of the saints, one sees peasants and kings, queens and reformed prostitutes, hermits and people of the world, monks and married folks, men and women who range from the lovable to the fanatic, the learned and the ignorant, the noble and the humble. . . . As a whole they are as varied as are all the pilgrims who make up the Church in history. What they all give witness to is the persistent desire of those who seek out Christ. Some of them are very much creatures of their own time while others, like a St. Francis or a St. Thomas More, so transcend their own time that they become permanent resources for those who are on the spiritual journey.[4]

---

4. Cunningham, 138-9.

Vatican II Renewal. In this exuberance of devotion to the saints and in colorful fiesta celebrations, the bishops of Vatican II saw the danger of saints overshadowing the centrality of Jesus Christ in Catholic life. For example, the uneducated indigenous peoples of South and Central America tended to see Jesus as a far-away figure, whereas the saints are members of the family, humans they can go to for help in sickness, with an unfaithful spouse, during a poor harvest, in times of famine and floods and volcanic eruptions. Often superstition is intermingled in this "**popular religiosity.**" Furthermore, the liturgical year seemed to have an overbalance of saints' feastdays. The bishops suppressed many Masses of lesser or local saints to be replaced by ferial or "masses of the day," thus making possible a more continuous reading from day to day of passages from the Hebrew Scriptures, the four Gospels, and the letters of St. Paul.

Catholic devotion to the saints is based on belief in the communion of saints, personal resurrection and eternal life after death. Catholics express this belief in the ancient creed: "We believe . . . in the communion of saints, resurrection of the body, and life everlasting. Amen." The communion of the saints is the entire body of Christians now on earth (pilgrim church), those in **purgatory** (church suffering) and the saints in heaven (church in glory). Catholics believe that the saints in heaven are vitally interested in their sisters and brothers still in the pilgrim church on earth, hear their prayers to them, and intercede with God for them. Catholics pray for the "souls in purgatory." Thus this vast communion of Christians are united as family in a bond of love.

Both in official Catholic teaching on the communion of saints and in her liturgical calendar, as well as in the popular religiosity and piety of Catholics, devotion to the saints is a pervasive characteristic of Catholic spirituality.

5. "Devotions" Spirituality. The Catholic faithful have over the centuries created an almost bewildering variety and richness of both private and public devotions. Many are universal throughout the church; others are local to countries and even cities. We shall simply list a few such. To *Christ:* way of the cross (the 14 stations or stages of Jesus' suffering and death); benediction of the Blessed Sacrament; holy hours before Christ in the consecrated host; prayers to the Sacred Heart of Jesus as symbol of his great love for us, and the nine First Fridays of reparation to him; the five wounds of Jesus. To *Mary:* the rosary, litany of the Blessed Virgin, the scapular, special devotions to her under her many titles like Sorrowful Mother, Our Lady of Perpetual Help, Our Lady of Guadalupe, Our Lady of Fatima, and so forth. To *Saints:* St. Jude, St. Dismas, St. Anthony for lost articles, a multitude of others. To the *souls in Purgatory.* And *objects* like the crucifix, statues, icons, holy cards, holy water, Lourdes water. Vatican II did not repudiate these; rather it cautioned against the tendency to superstition and magic, and emphasized the essential role of Christ and of his saving life, death, and resurrection and the centrality of the sacraments, especially the Eucharist, in Catholic life.

A "New Vatican II" Spirituality

As pointed out earlier in this chapter, the new Vatican II spirituality is new only in the sense of emphasizing once again certain aspects of Christian life that through the centuries had come to be deemphasized. It is also new in developing a fresh theological approach whose practical conclusions led to fruitful and dynamic changes in Catholic thinking and life. However, the bishops at Vatican II wisely did not cast aside the extraordinarily rich traditional spirituality developed through centuries in the church; rather their aim was to complement and further develop this rich tradition. For example, in liturgy Vatican II returned the church to an earlier vision and practice; in reading the "signs of the times" concerning the modern world and ecumenism, it proposed new dimensions for one's relation to God and our fellow sisters and brothers.

1. *This-World Spirituality. The Pastoral Constitution on the Church in the Modern World* committed Catholics to find God and to imitate Christ in their day-to-day life by establishing God's kingdom in this world. Catholic spirituality thus moved from an individualistic, me-and-God emphasis to a this-world spirituality in which concern for social issues of war and peace, hunger and homelessness, justice, human rights and human dignity became a part of one's relationship to God and Jesus Christ. This was a major change because before Vatican II, "the world" was considered evil and to be avoided. But a "signs of the times" theology that recognized God as present and active in the world and saw Christians' vocation as carrying out God's plan for the human family inspired Catholics to view this world in a new light. Two recently deceased modern-day "saints" exemplified to a remarkable degree this new spirituality of building the "city of God" on our earth: Dorothy Day,[5] through the houses she opened for the poor, the Catholic Worker movement she founded, and her lifelong struggle for justice; Cesar Chavez, in his tireless struggle for just wages and safe working and decent living conditions for migrant workers, and through the United Farm Workers union he founded.

2. *Lay Spirituality.* Vatican II gave a strong impetus for developing a special spirituality of nonordained Catholics. Chapter 2 of *Lumen Gentium,* called "The Pilgrim People of God," stated that lay Catholics are called by God to exercise an important role in the church and the world; chapter 5, "The Call of the Whole Church to Holiness," emphasized God's

---

5. *The Long Loneliness: the Autobiography of Dorothy Day* (San Francisco: Harper & Row, 1952).

call of the non-ordained to the same holiness to which priests and religious are called. The practical applications of this emphasis for the spiritual life of Catholics and for the health and vigor of the church are
momentous and are just now being realized.

3. *Liturgical Spirituality. The Constitution on the Sacred Liturgy* mandated
a sweeping renewal of public worship and the sacraments, with the goal
of "full active participation" of the people of God. Since the Council
this has led to a more profound understanding and appreciation of community worship, especially the Sunday eucharistic celebration. In fact,
we can say that the Eucharist has been returned to the center of Catholic
life and that the multitude of devotional practices no longer "compete"
for importance. No longer do Catholics pray the rosary or read various
prayers during "Mass" or give more practical importance to novenas,
holy hours, and benediction of the Blessed Sacrament, worthy as these
are, than to the eucharistic celebration. Thus has Catholic spirituality
moved from an individualistic to a communitarian spirituality.

4. *Biblical Spirituality.* St. Jerome, 4th-century Scripture scholar, said "ignorance of Scripture is ignorance of Christ." Protestants have long valued and used the Bible, but since Vatican II Catholics have "rediscovered" the Bible and begun to develop a "biblical spirituality," that is,
their Christian life is more and more formed and influenced by the living word of God in both the Hebrew and Christian Scriptures. Bible
study groups are springing up on college campuses, as young people
discover Christ, and in parishes where Catholics and Protestants discuss
and pray together passages from the Christian Scriptures. Private prayerful Scripture reading nourishes spirituality: one selects a passage,
chooses a quiet place, asks the Lord's help to understand and profit
from the word of God, reads slowly, pausing frequently to discover
what the Lord is saying to him or her personally and then responding in
friendship to the Lord. Christians find the Hebrew Psalms and Isaiah
and the four Christian Gospels and the letters of St. Paul particularly
rewarding. As a result of prayerful reading of the Bible, Catholics have
come to understand God's concern for justice and special love of the
poor, to realize Jesus' emphasis on love rather than law, and to rely on
the personal guidance of the Holy Spirit.

5. *Ecumenical Spirituality.* The *Decree on Ecumenism* urged Catholics to
know and appreciate their separated Christian sisters and brothers, to
pray and collaborate with them, to work for the restoration of unity
among the still-divided Christian churches. Thus was born a distinctive
ecumenical spirituality. Since the Council, Catholics have come to realize the sinfulness of Christian disunity; they have been enriched in their
contacts with other Christians. Their commitment to Christian unity has
given them a richer, broader understanding of the church of Christ and
Christ's prayer for unity. All this has resulted in a new way of relating

to Christ and other Christians. Ecumenical spirituality sees Christian disunity as a scandal that cannot be allowed to continue, and takes very seriously Christ's Last Supper prayer for unity as a personal challenge to work perseveringly, despite setbacks for Christian unity. Ecumenical spirituality is yet in its infancy.

6. *"Spirit" Spirituality.* In a sense Vatican II "rediscovered" the role of the Holy Spirit in the church by emphasizing throughout all its documents the work or inspiration of the Spirit in all aspects of the church's life. This echoes John XXIII's prayer on announcing the Council for "a new outpouring of the Spirit on the Church" like a "second Pentecost." His prayer has been abundantly answered in the lives of individual Catholics and in the official hierarchical church.

The Holy Spirit is the third person of the Trinity of Persons in God. The Spirit that Jesus promised and then sent on the Apostles at Pentecost lives in the church and in each Christian, making it possible for us to live our Christian way of life, to believe, to hope, to love. The Spirit inspires us to live for God, to make correct decisions, to fulfill our responsibilities, to grow. The Spirit accomplishes this by acting on our human mind and will and emotions, for as God, the Spirit has direct access to the depths of our personality.

The Spirit's names are Sanctifier, Comforter, Strengthener, Counselor, Paraclete. The prophet Isaiah listed the seven special graces or "gifts" of the Holy Spirit: wisdom, understanding, counsel, fortitude, knowledge, piety, and fear of the Lord. Centuries later St. Paul described the qualities a Christian living under the guidance of the Spirit would manifest in his or her life. These are termed the effects or "fruits" of the Holy Spirit: love, joy, peace, patient endurance, kindness, generosity, faith, mildness, and chastity. Protestant and Catholic **charismatics** experience in a special way the influence and gifts of the Spirit: love of prayer, new-found joy in being Christian, great profit from reading the Scriptures, and in some cases the gifts of speaking in tongues and healing others.

Of Special Interest

Canonization. Of the vast number of holy women and men, some have been officially recognized by the Church for their extraordinary love of God and people. **Canonization** literally means being put on the list (*canon*) of official church saints. Canonization is a long process in which the church studies in great detail a person's life and writings to discover whether the person lived a heroic Christian life and practiced heroic virtue, especially faith, hope, and love. If these are established, it must be proved after rigorous examination, including scientific and medical documentation, that two miracles were worked by God through the intercession of the holy person. When all is verified, the pope in a solemn ceremony, generally in St. Peter's basilica in Rome, declares the person a saint, that is, one who is now in heaven able to hear our prayers and whom the church establishes as a model to imitate in living the Christian life. Martyrs, those who gave their lives for Christ and the Christian faith, need not go through this lengthy process, for their supreme sacrifice proves their heroic love, their immediate entrance into heaven after death, and their worthiness to be imitated by all followers of Christ.

A recent example of the canonization process is the case of Fr. John Houle, S.J., of Los Angeles who was terminally ill with pulmonary fibrosis. His superior, Fr. Frank Parrish, distributed copies of a prayer to Blessed Claude La Colombière to many people, asking them to pray for a miracle. On Friday, Feb. 23, 1990, Fr. Parrish was at Fr. Houle's bedside.

> Fr. Houle was being given oxygen but it was extremely difficult for him to breathe. The nurse on duty said that he was not expected to live over the weekend. Fr. Parrish blessed Fr. Houle with a first-class relic of Blessed Claude, asking his intercession that Fr. Houle might be healed. He subsequently blessed him several times, praying that a miracle be obtained through the intercession of Blessed Claude. By the following Monday, Feb. 26, a dramatic improvement had taken place, and by Thursday, March 1, when Fr. Parrish visited him, Fr. Houle was sitting at his bedside with a big lunch before him. He was completely alert and talked very clearly. Subsequent X-rays showed that the pulmonary fibrosis had disappeared.[6]

After all the medical records were reviewed in Rome "the medical board of the Congregation for the Causes of Saints has declared unanimously that a cure effected by God through the intercession of Blessed Claude La Colombière is so extraordinary that it cannot be explained by medical science."

This miraculous cure was accepted as the necessary second miracle; Claude La Colombière was canonized a Saint in Rome on May 31, 1992. Fr. Houle attended!

Mysticism and Mystics have been an extraordinary phenomenon in Catholicism and Orthodoxy since the early centuries of the Christian Church. **Mysticism** involves the reality of God's love for us revealed in Christ and made available to us through baptism and sacramental life and the growth in faith, hope and love. **Mystics,** men and women particularly gifted with God's grace and called by God to the mystical state, pass through the stages of *purification* from sin and earthly desires, of *illumination* by which the soul understands clearly the mystery of God's love in Jesus, to the stage of inti-

---

6. *National Jesuit News* (January, 1992): 6.

mate *union* with God in love. The mystic surrenders himself or herself completely to God and God possesses the soul and transfigures it. Some mystics
experience ecstasy during which they are totally absorbed in God, often
impervious to the world and physical stimuli, and feel intense joy and love
and extraordinary clarity of vision. The great Spanish mystics, Saints Teresa
of Avila and John of the Cross, analyzed the mystical experience in their
many writings. For example, John spoke of the two stages of the dark night
of the soul: the night of the senses and the night of the spirit, in which the
soul responds to God by purifying itself and by submitting to God's purifying action. Famous female mystics such as Bridget of Sweden, Catherine of
Siena, and Julian of Norwich wrote extensively about the nature of the mystical life.

Mystics are dramatic witnesses to the reality of the spiritual world, to
God's powerful love, to the intense joy of paradise and union with God
anticipated in this life. There is considerable interest in the church today in
Christian mysticism and mystics, as well as in the mystical life found in
Oriental religions. Likewise, there is growing interest in contemplative
prayer, as evidenced by the popularity among university students in the
1960s and 1970s of the book *Seeds of Contemplation* by the Trappist monk
Thomas Merton.

The Catholic Charismatic Renewal began in 1967 during a weekend retreat
at Duquesne University, Pittsburg, when a group of students and professors
experienced the gifts of the Holy Spirit. The **charismatic renewal** spread to
the University of Notre Dame and the University of Michigan and then rapidly throughout the Catholic world. Bishops and priests were at first skepti-
cal of the traditional pentecostal practices of speaking in tongues, prophecy,
healing, deliverance, and baptism in the Spirit. The first official church approval came in 1975 when 10,000 Catholic charismatics were received by
Pope Paul VI in Rome.

The soul of the charismatic renewal is baptism in the Spirit which "is
meant to be a life-changing experience of God's presence."[7] This is not the
sacrament of baptism which occurs only once; rather it is a stirring up, "a
release of the graces already received in baptism and confirmation."[8] It
gives "an experiential knowledge of a new love, a new peace, a new joy in
the Lord. . . . Catholic Christian life is different than before."[9] Patti Gallagher Mansfield, one of the original group at Duquesne, lists the effects
of baptism in the Spirit: "a deepening awareness of the presence and love
of God and the Lordship of Jesus Christ; a growth of intimacy with God in
prayer; a hunger for God's word and the sacraments; a love for the

---

7. Patti Gallagher Mansfield, *As By a New Pentecost: The Dramatic Beginning of the Catholic
Charismatic Renewal* (Steubenville, OH: Franciscan View Press, 1992: 160.
8. *Ibid.,* 161.
9. *Ibid.,* 160.

Church; a new power and desire to witness; a growth in the fruits of the Spirit . . . peace, love, joy; manifestations of charismatic gifts such as the gift of tongues; an experience of the promptings and guidance of the Holy Spirit; an awareness of the reality of spiritual warfare; a call to purification and holiness; a desire for Christian unity; a call to serve the needs of others."[10]

Other effects of baptism in the Spirit are **glossalalia** (speaking in tongues or words/languages generally not understood by the speaker or other charismatics); mental healings of fear, guilt, anger, hurtful memories and sometimes physical healings; prophecy, not so much of the future but conveying God's messages. However, these are secondary to the extraordinary ongoing experience of God's presence and love and the enormous inspiration of the Spirit to live a profound Christian life.

In the term Catholic Charismatic Renewal, *charismatic* refers to the gifts of the Spirit St. Paul mentions in his first letter to the Corinthians, chapter 12, verses 12-14. *Renewal* indicates that the gifts of the Spirit are given for a profound renewal of the whole Catholic Church, members and leaders alike. Cardinal Suenens of Belgium, a prominent figure of Vatican II and a leader in the charismatic movement, called the Renewal a movement of the Spirit that is offered to the entire church to renew every facet of its life. In the same vein Pope Paul VI said in 1972, "The Church needs her perennial Pentecost, she needs fire in the heart, words on the lips, prophecy in the glance. . ."[11]

Marian Apparitions. What are we to make of the frequent **apparitions** or appearances of the Blessed Virgin Mary, generally to children and the poor, the profusion of "messages" from her to the world through these children, and the alleged miracles? What is the meaning of millions of pilgrims annually at Marian shrines: 5.5 million to Lourdes in France; 4.5 million to Fatima, Portugal; 5 million to the Black Madonna icon in Czestochowa, Poland; 1.5 million in Knock, Ireland; one-half million to the Grotto of Our Lady of Lourdes in Emmitsburg, Maryland; and over 10 million pilgrims since 1981 to the mountain village of Medjugorje in Bosnia-Herzogovina, where some of the original six young people claim to receive messages from Mary continuously up to the present?

Mary's message is similar in all apparitions: she asks for deeper love of her son, repentance, turning from sin, personal conversion, private penance for the sins of the world, much prayer, especially the rosary for peace, and devotion to church leaders. The children claim to hear the spoken words of Mary and to see her, whom they describe as a beautiful young woman, generally dressed in a flowing white or blue dress. Many of the pilgrims claim to see phenomena like the dancing sun at Fatima, repre-

---

10. *Ibid.,* 161.
11. Ibid., 159.

sentations of Mary in the sky, and so forth. Genuine physical healings occur regularly at Lourdes, where rigorous medical examinations of each cure are made.

Bishops and the official church have been very cautious in accepting these *private* revelations since many alleged appearances after investigation were found to be fraudulent. The Catholic Church has officially approved Catholics' devotion at Guadalupe in Mexico City, at Lourdes and Fatima but is still studying the events of Medjugorje. Approval indicates that the messages contain nothing contrary to the Christian faith and are helpful for more fervent Christian life; but approval is not meant to authenticate all the phenomena and alleged miracles associated with the appearances.

What then are we to think concerning these phenomena that so strongly move the devotion of millions of Catholics? Is Mary really physically present? Since we do not know what a risen glorified body is like, we cannot say. As far as we can judge, the children receive an authentic religious experience; however, the words and vision which profoundly change their lives need further explanation. Perhaps the real miracles are those of God's grace at the Marian shrines: the pilgrims experience a religious conversion, confess their sins, pray with fervor, accept their sickness and cross, and come away with stronger faith and love of God and the desire to live their Christian life more fully.

Feminist Spirituality. Feminist spirituality is a serious, legitimate reality in the Catholic Church today. We may distinguish a more traditional understanding and the contemporary development by Catholic feminist writers and leaders.

A more traditional approach holds that the bodily and psychological experience of a woman is intrinsic to understanding her response to God. As bearing, delivering, and nurturing human life, her spirituality is characterized by intimacy, "receptivity, affective response, waiting or attentiveness, and the acceptance of pain as intrinsic to the bringing forth of life."[12] These characteristics are suited to contemplative prayer, to a feminine response to the mystery of life out of death, and thus to the meaning of the death and resurrection of Jesus. Thus a woman is especially attuned to the many feminine images of God in the Hebrew Scriptures. The feminine experience of God ought ideally to enrich the whole church and complement the masculine experience.

Catholic feminists today are concerned to resist and unmask **patriarchy** in society and in the church by which males have all power and decision-making and control the lives of women. Women thus seek full equality with men so that their gifts are recognized and able to be used. Catholic

---

12. Gordon Wakefield, ed., *The Westminster Dictionary of Christian Spirituality* (Philadelphia: The Westminster Press, 1983), 149.

women scholars have written extensively on the feminine images of God in the Hebrew Scriptures, on Jesus' treatment of women in the Gospels, on the role of women in the early days of Christianity. They seek to reinterpret the traditional image of Mary as a passive, docile, submissive, other-worldly figure, contending that a patriarchal church reinforced this image to control women .

These concerns and writings are establishing a new spirituality for Catholic women today and a new confidence in their own gifts and role in today's church. A vibrant feminine spirituality is thus being born which many believe is, despite struggle and controversy, inspired by the Holy Spirit to enrich the church.

Creation Spirituality. Thanks to recent emphasis on ecology and the environment, to our more profound appreciation of the rich bounty of God's creation, to our discovery of native Americans' pervasive religious relationship to nature, a spirituality of creation has risen. A missionary to the Lakota native Americans in South Dakota describes creation spirituality in this way.

> Everything that exists is good. It is good because it exists. Because it is good, it is beautiful with its own unique kind of beauty. Because it is good and beautiful it is lovable: worth relating to in a positive way. Because it is all of this, it is sacred: reflecting the presence of God within it and around it. . . . In creation spirituality the earth itself is sacred . . . the earth is our mother. . . . Humans have a sacred obligation to natural creation. We are supposed to be its caretakers, not its plunderers. To treat anything in creation merely as an object to do with as we wish is a sacrilege. . . . Christian creation spirituality is inclusive and seeks a positive subject-to-subject relationship with all creation . . . Christ is the presence, the love and the power of relationship . . . all creation is saturated with the presence of the cosmic Christ who continues to work with us and with all creation.[13]

Summary

Christian spirituality is the particular approach Christians have used through the centuries to relate to God and Jesus Christ. As such, it has a history which we treat briefly as context for our study of Catholic spirituality. In its long history, the Catholic Church has developed a variety and richness of spiritual helps and practices that are characteristic of Catholic spirituality. Catholics build their religious life around the sacraments, especially the Eucharist. Catholics have a special devotion to Mary, the virgin mother of God, honoring her in song and prayer, statues and madonna

---

13. Bill Callahan, S.J. "My Experience of Creation Spirituality," Spring 1993, Milwaukee: *Companions,* 29-35, Publication of the Wisconsin Province of Jesuits.

paintings. The vast number of canonized saints are a much-loved aspect of the spirituality of Catholics, who honor and pray to the saints as mediators with God. Catholic spirituality is also marked by a rich profusion of devotional practices. The second Vatican Council profoundly influenced Catholic spirituality by emphasizing newer theological insights and recovering older aspects of the Catholic tradition. We thus speak of this-world spirituality, specific lay spirituality, liturgical and biblical spirituality, ecumenical spirituality and "Holy Spirit" spirituality. These Vatican II spiritualities offer fresh ways for Catholics to live their Christian life in the waning years of the 20th century. We conclude by providing information on five somewhat controversial areas of importance and interest to Catholics today and other Christians as well.

For Discussion

1. How would you describe the spirituality of young people today? of older people?

2. Describe your own spirituality. What further elements would you like to have in your spirituality?

3. Do you think devotion to Mary is exaggerated in the Catholic and Orthodox churches? Give reasons for and against.

4. Does Catholic devotion to the saints take something away from the central position Christ should have? What is the theological basis for honoring and praying to the saints?

5. Do you think Catholics have acquired Vatican II spirituality today? In your opinion, what elements need improvement?

For Action

1. Attend an Orthodox Divine Liturgy; afterward look at the various sacred icons. Why does the iconostasis hide the altar?

2. Get to know one of the great mystics: St. Teresa of Avila or Thomas Merton, for example.

3. Talk to someone who has been to Medjugorje. Get the video *Medjugorje: A Pilgrim's Perspective*. Then decide for yourself.

4. Try to find out why so few *lay* Catholics are canonized. Why there are so few *married* saints? Will this change in the future?

5. Discover why the rosary is still such a popular prayer after seven centuries. Read (pray?) the litany of the Blessed Virgin to see all the titles Catholic devotion has bestowed on Mary.

6. Talk to a Jesuit or a religious sister or a layperson who has made the *Spiritual Exercises of St. Ignatius.* Why are these "exercises" so popular today? Discover their unique spirit and power. Inquire how you could make these Exercises in a 19th Annotation retreat!

7. Go to the medieval and Renaissance section of your local art museum to see all the paintings and statues of Mary. What does it all mean?

8. First talk to a member of the charismatic renewal. Then ask if you might attend a charismatic meeting!

9. Make the acquaintance of a saint who has been canonized, one who interests you. Discover what made him or her tick.

10. Get to know Dorothy Day and Cesar Chavez, two modern "saints."

Further Reading

Au, Wilkie. *By Way of the Heart: Towards a Holistic Christian Spirituality.* Mahwah, NJ: Paulist Press, 1989.

Conn, Joan Wolski. *Spirituality and Personal Maturity.* Mahwah: NJ: Paulist Press, 1989.

Downey, Michael, ed. *New Dictionary of Catholic Spirituality.* Collegeville, MN: The Liturgical Press, 1993.

Merton, Thomas. *New Seeds of Contemplation.* Norfolk, CT: New Directions, 1961.

Nouwen, Henri. *Making All Things New: An Invitation to the Spiritual Life.* San Francisco: Harper & Row, 1981.

CHAPTER 8

"That All May Be One"

"That all may be one, as you Father are in me and I in you; I pray that they may be one in us, that the world may believe that you sent me."   —John 17:21

There is but one body and one Spirit, just as there is but one hope given all of you. . . . There is one Lord, one faith, one baptism; one God and Father of all . . .   —Ephesians 4:4-6

The restoration of unity among all Christians is one of the principal concerns of the Second Vatican Council. Christ the Lord founded one Church . . . division openly contradicts the will of Christ, scandalizes the world, and damages . . . the preaching of the Gospel to every creature. The Lord of Ages . . . has begun to bestow . . . upon divided Christians remorse over their divisions and longing for unity. . . . for the one visible Church of God.
                                            —*Decree on Ecumenism* 1

The Council exhorts . . . all the Catholic faithful to recognize the signs of the times and to take an active . . . part in the work of ecumenism.   —*Decree on Ecumenism* 4

Introduction

The *Decree on Ecumenism*, one of the great accomplishments of the Vatican Council, catapulted the Catholic Church into the center of the hitherto Protestant and Orthodox ecumenical movement. Events undreamed of became commonplace: Protestants, Catholics and Orthodox "discovered" each other, grew in knowledge and respect, prayed and worked together; their theologians entered into theological dialogues resulting in remarkable agreements and signed statements; church leaders, like Pope Paul VI and Michael Ramsey, the Anglican Archbishop of Canterbury, broke centuries of isolation and distrust and open hostility, visited each other, publicly prayed together, signed agreements to work for full church union. Enthusiasm for unity ran high. Spectacular ecumenical "breakthroughs" occurred. Yet in the 30 years since Vatican II, the Christian churches remain tragically separated. Why? The broken unity of the body of Christ still remains a reality. Why? Jesus' desire and prayer for Christian unity remains unanswered, despite much effort and good will by the Protestant, Orthodox, and Catholic churches. Why? Has the **kairos** opportunity for unity passed the churches by?

◆

Preview: This chapter considers the extraordinary modern phenomenon of ecumenism among the Christian churches. We begin with a brief overview of how the one Church of Christ became so tragically divided. We then look at the Anglican, Orthodox and Protestant origins of the ecumenical movement that culminated in the founding of the World Council of Churches (WCC) in 1948, and at the nonecumenical stance of the Roman Catholic Church during these pre-Vatican II years. With this background we study Vatican II's *Decree on Ecumenism* and its *practical guidelines* for Catholic participation in the ecumenical movement. This brings us to a theological analysis of the *Decree:* the *ecclesial realities* that enabled the Catholic Church to enter the ecumenical movement after decades of isolation; the new *ecclesiology* or theology of church that resulted; and a *model* for the future union of the churches. In the light of this theological foundation, we look at the impressive *theological dialogues* initiated by the Catholic Church with other Christian churches and WCC's remarkable ecumenical achievement, the *Baptism, Eucharist and Ministry* document. The dialogues lead naturally to the next stage: actual church union. So we reflect on what the *future united Church of Christ* might be like. We conclude by considering realistically the major *present obstacles* to achieving the goal of ecumenism and call attention to the present malaise in the ecumenical movement.

◆

The Scope of Christian Disunity

A quick look in the yellow pages of the phone book in any major U.S. city under churches gives a startling picture of the magnitude of Christian disunity. It is estimated there are over 400 different Christian churches in the United States alone. The following membership statistics of the major

United States Churches, Top 25 by Membership	
Roman Catholic Church	59,230,723
Southern Baptist Convention	15,358,389
United Methodist Church (1991)	8,789,101
National Baptist Convention U.S.A.	8,200,000
Church of God in Christ (Pentecostal) (1991)	5,499,875
Evangelical Lutheran Church in America	5,234,586
Church of Jesus Christ of Latter-Day Saints	4,430,000
Presbyterian Church U.S.A.	3,758,085
National Baptist Convention of America (1987)	3,500,000
African-American Methodist Episcopal Church (1991)	3,500,000
Lutheran Church—Missouri Synod	2,609,905
Progressive National Baptist Convention (1991)	2,500,000
Episcopal Church (1991)	2,471,880
Assemblies of God	2,257,846
Churches of Christ	1,684,872
United Church of Christ	1,555,382
African Methodist Episcopal Zion Church (1991)	1,200,000
Greek Orthodox Archdiocese of North America	1,200,000
Christian Church (Disciples of Christ)	1,011,552
Jehovah's Witnesses	914,079
Seventh-Day Adventist Church	748,687
Christian Methodist Episcopal Church (1983)	718,922
Church of God (Cleveland, Tenn.)	676,008
Orthodox Church in America	600,000
Church of the Nazarene (1991)	573,834

Groupings of Religious Traditions	
19 Baptist churches	35,389,811
9 Methodist churches	14,625,950
20 Pentecostal churches	10,101,003
13 Lutheran churches	7,977,945
8 Presbyterian churches	4,249,412
15 Eastern Orthodox churches	4,007,534

churches in the United States as of 1993 illustrate the great task of ecumenism.[1]

How Did It Get This Way?

The first major split in the universal Church occurred in 1054, when the Byzantine church officially broke communion with the bishop of Rome and he with them. The tragic events covering centuries that led to this split make sad reading. Political more than theological differences are to blame, plus the insensitive, often arrogant actions of both Catholic popes and their legates and Byzantine patriarchs and bishops. Both groups must share the blame. In 1964 Pope Paul VI and Athenagoras, the Ecumenical **Patriarch** of Constantinople, met in Jerusalem, prayed together, and publicly embraced each other; this historic event led in 1965 to lifting the 900-year mutual **excommunication** between the Roman and Orthodox churches.

World Orthodoxy is divided today into numerous separate *national* churches: 15 independent, self-governing (called **autocephalous**) Orthodox churches in the mid-East, Europe and America; 13 churches with a degree of self-government (referred to as autonomous) which are attached to one of the larger **patriarchates**; and 10 more recent "jurisdictions" in North America that maintain communion with world Orthodoxy. This complex variety of churches within world Orthodoxy indicates the challenge of restoring unity not only with the Catholic Church but within Orthodoxy itself:

- The four ancient patriarchates of Constantinople (modern Istanbul), Alexandria (Egypt), Antioch (Turkey), Jerusalem. These have a special place of honor in world Orthodoxy.

- The patriarchates of Bulgaria (established 917 AD), Serbia (1346), Russia (1589), Romania (1925).

---

1. Kenneth Bedell, ed., *Yearbook of American and Canadian Churches* (Nashville: Abingdon Press, 1993), 248-255.

- The catholicate of Georgia (former Soviet Union).
- The autocephalous churches of Cyprus (431), Sinai (1575), Greece (1830), Poland (1924), Albania (1937), Czechoslovakia (1951).
- Ten autonomous churches of Finland, Estonia, Latvia, Hungary, China, Japan, Macedonia, and three autonomous Russian churches outside Russia not in communion with other Orthodox churches.
- Ten "jurisdictions" in North America, the two largest being the Greek, with 1.2 million members, and the Russian, with 830,000.

Worldwide Orthodox churches according to the World Almanac for 1993 have 170,422,000 members, but this is an educated estimate since many of these churches just emerging from living under communism could not report exact figures.

The second great split in the Catholic Church was the Protestant Reformation in Europe in the 16th century. It began when an Augustinian monk and priest named Martin Luther protested against the preaching of indulgences for money and the excessive worldliness of popes and many bishops. Though his intention was to reform the Catholic Church, events moved so swiftly that a new religious family, Lutheranism, came into being. Other reformers, like John Calvin in Geneva, Switzerland and John Knox in Scotland, became the leaders of the Reformed and Presbyterian movements. The Reformation in England began with King Henry VIII's differences with the pope over his desired divorce and with payment of taxes to Rome and culminated in a formal break of communion with the pope and the formation of the Anglican Church. By 1600 northern Germany and Holland, England and Scotland, and the Scandinavian countries were Protestant.

Protestants can be grouped into five categories. Lutheran churches follow the teaching and spirit of Martin Luther. They stress the Bible as the norm of Christian belief, emphasize preaching the word of God, and retain baptism and the Lord's Supper. The second group is the Calvinists or Reformed; in the United States they are called Presbyterian and Congregationalist. Most Reformed churches do not have bishops but are governed by the presbytery, a council of ministers and laity. Methodists, a third category, arose in 17th-century England. The Wesley brothers, both Anglican priests, tried to inject life and spirituality into the Church of England by their tireless preaching and writing. Their followers were called Methodists after the small groups practicing the spiritual "methods" of the Wesleys, and in time became a separate church.

A fourth category comprises what can be termed "Free" churches because they rebelled against religion identified with the state, as in much of Europe: Anglicans were the "Church of England," Presbyterians the "Church of Scotland," Lutherans the religion of northern Germany and the state religion of Sweden and Norway. Free churches insist that one is not

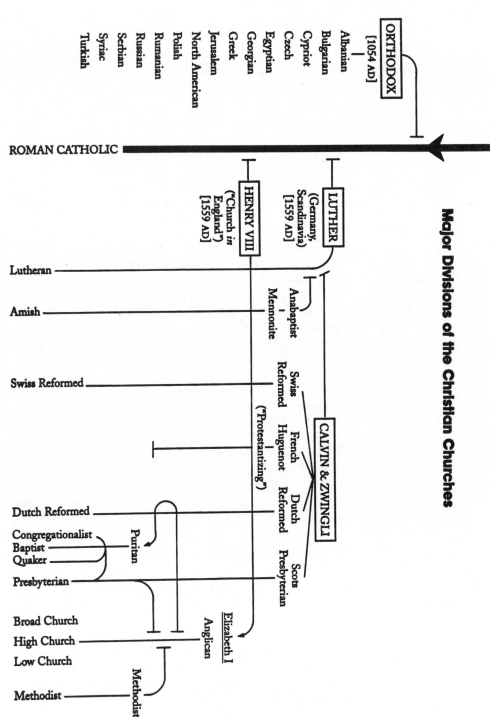

Major Divisions of the Christian Churches

ORTHODOX
[1054 AD]

Albanian
Bulgarian
Cypriot
Czech
Egyptian
Georgian
Greek
Jerusalem
North American
Polish
Rumanian
Russian
Serbian
Syriac
Turkish

ROMAN CATHOLIC

HENRY VIII
("Church *in* England")
[1559 AD]

LUTHER
(Germany, Scandinavia)
[1559 AD]

CALVIN & ZWINGLI

Lutheran

Amish

Anabaptist - Mennonite

Swiss Reformed

Swiss Reformed

French Huguenot

Dutch Reformed

("Protestantizing")

Dutch Reformed

Scots Presbyterian

Congregationalist
Baptist
Quaker

Puritan

Presbyterian

Broad Church

High Church

Low Church

Elizabeth I

Anglican

Methodist

Methodist

a Christian because born into "state" religion but because one makes a free choice of following Christ; they thus rejected infant baptism, baptizing only those who consciously commit themselves to Christ and the Christian way of life. The largest group are Baptists, founded around 1650 in England and Holland in reaction to the state churches there. Later evangelical groups sprang up in Europe and the United States.

A final group, an American invention, are the more recent Pentecostal groups. Pentecostalism began in Topeka, Kansas, in 1900 when a minister, taking the Acts of the Apostles literally, prayed for the gifts of the Spirit. He began to "speak in tongues" and started a healing apostolate. From this experience Pentecostal groups, like the Assembly of God, Church of God, Four Square Gospel and others, sprang up. These groups stress the "born again" conversion experience as necessary for baptism, the dominant role of the Holy Spirit in their lives, and the Spirit's gifts of speaking in tongues, prophecy, and healing as the visible proof that one has received "baptism in the Spirit." They generally hold to a strict literal interpretation of the Bible and so are often called fundamentalists. They are aggressively missionary, taking Christ's great commission "Go into the whole world and preach the good news to all nations. . ." very seriously. Pentecostal groups are the fastest growing churches today, especially in Latin America and the U.S. southwest, where they have massive campaigns to convert poorly instructed Hispanic Catholics. They consider such Catholics—and Protestants too—appropriate objects of conversion because, being baptized in infancy and not having had a born-again-in-the-Spirit experience, these people cannot be considered Christians. It is not surprising then that Pentecostal churches have generally not joined the ecumenical movement.

The Anglican communion does not consider itself Protestant but rather as continuing the Catholic Church in having bishops, practicing the seven sacraments and holding to the ancient Catholic faith. Anglicanism is a communion of almost 20 national churches, like the Church of England, the Church of Ireland, the Church of India, and so forth. Anglicans in the United States are called Episcopalians because they have the order of bishops. A major theological problem between Anglicans and Roman Catholics is over Anglican Orders, that is, whether Anglican bishops are within the apostolic succession and thus have validly ordained priests.

The Ecumenical Movement Prior to Vatican II

The modern ecumenical movement began with a meeting of Anglican and Protestant leaders in Edinburgh, Scotland, in 1910 to explore ways that churches competing in missionary lands could unite to effectively preach the good news of Christianity. After the interruption due to World War I, a delegation was sent to Pope Benedict XV, inviting the Catholic

Church to join the ecumenical movement. The pope received them graciously and listened carefully. But following the traditional Catholic ecclesiology at that time, Benedict told them the only way the church could be united was for Protestants to "become reunited to the visible head of the church by whom they will be received with open arms." This ecclesiology was formally stated in the 1928 encyclical *Mortalium Animos* by Pope Pius XI in terms of "the return" to the one true Church of Christ.

The World Council of Churches (WCC)

Fortunately, these rebuffs did not deter the ecumenical church leaders. They founded two groups, with headquarters in Geneva, to work for the union of the churches: Faith and Order (for questions of doctrine and church order or leadership) and Life and Work (social and charitable works). In 1948, in Amsterdam, these two groups were joined to form the **World Council of Churches.** Today the WCC has a membership of 324 Protestant and Orthodox churches with a staff of over 200 in its headquarters in Geneva. Its constitution succinctly states its nature and doctrinal basis:

> The World Council of Churches is a fellowship of churches which confess the Lord Jesus Christ as God and Savior according to the Scriptures and therefore seek to fulfill together their common calling to the glory of the one God, Father, Son and Holy Spirit.[2]

WCC's organizational structure illustrates the impressive scope of its ecumenical involvement. Unit I, *Faith and Witness,* has four commissions: Faith and Order, World Mission and Evangelism, Church and Society, and Dialogue with People of Living Faith. Unit II, *Justice and Service*, has five groups: Churches' Participation in Development; International Affairs; Inter-Church Aid, Refugee and World Service; Christian Medical Commission, and Program to Combat Racism. Unit III, *Education and Renewal* includes Education, Youth, Renewal and Congregational Life, Women in Church and Society, and Theological Education. Every seven or eight years, WCC sponsors its World Assembly, a colorful two-week meeting of more than 1000 delegates from all nations of the world. Past Assemblies were held in Amsterdam 1948; Evanston, Ill. 1954; New Delhi 1961; Uppsala, Sweden 1968; Nairobi 1975; Vancouver 1983; and Canberra, Australia, 1991.

Roman Catholic Ecumenism

Since the official Roman Catholic ecclesiology before Vatican II held that it alone is the *true* church of Jesus Christ, it was considered sinful for

---

2. *One World* 132 (Jan.-Feb., 1988): 4.

Catholics to attend "false" Protestant worship: Protestant churches did not possess real Eucharist because its ministers were not ordained by bishops in the apostolic succession. Furthermore, the Vatican had forbidden Catholic theologians to attend the WCC World Assemblies in Amsterdam and Evanston.

The average Catholic, therefore, was hardly ecumenical! He or she tended to have a superior attitude towards Protestants because "we have the Mass and the real presence of Christ in Holy Communion, we don't eat meat on Friday, we have all seven sacraments, we fill our churches for many Masses every Sunday." Catholics had to admit that many Protestants were very good people, even excellent Christians, but this was in spite of their churches! Added to this and partially responsible for it was the fact that American Catholics were largely an immigrant people and had to fight prejudice and job discrimination ("Irish need not apply"') in Protestant America; so Catholic immigrants banded together into ethnic ghettos and built their religious and social life around the parish church as their identity and protector. It is not surprising, then, that Catholics, isolated from Protestants, were ignorant of their real beliefs and religious practices. Such ignorance bred suspicion and fear as well as superiority attitudes.

Accordingly, when the Catholic Church embraced ecumenism so wholeheartedly at Vatican II, many Catholics were understandably confused and often hostile or indifferent toward it. One of the amazing surprises of Vatican II is how fast Catholics as a whole became ecumenical. This came about largely because the *Decree on Ecumenism* set a high ideal for ecumenical commitment and in its second chapter, "The Practice of Ecumenism," gave concrete guidelines for ecumenical thinking and action.

The Second Vatican Council and Ecumenism

The *Decree on Ecumenism* (*UR*) uses the phrase "the restoration of unity among all Christians" to describe the *goal* of Christian ecumenism. John XXIII's phrase "restoration of unity" rather than the traditional concept of "return"[3] to the Catholic Church was itself significant, indicating a new theological relationship between the Christian churches, including the Roman Catholic. By "ecumenical movement" the *Decree* means all the "initiatives and activities . . . organized . . . to promote Christian unity" (*UR* 4). The great *inspiration* and rallying cry of the ecumenical movement and ecumenism is Christ's solemn prayer at the Last Supper "that all may be one," that is, that his Apostles and all who would follow them as disciples of Christ down through the centuries would remain visibly united in the one Christian belief and fellowship. The compelling reason Christ gave was "that the world might believe," that is, for the sake of evangelization.

---

3. However, UR 3 and LG 14 come close to calling for a "return."

Guidelines for the Practice of Ecumenism

1. *The Decree* challenged Catholics to the lofty ideal of personal *conversion* and the practice of *spiritual ecumenism.* "There can be no ecumenism worthy of the name without interior conversion" (UR 7). "This change of heart and holiness of life, along with public and private prayer for the unity of Christians, should be regarded as the soul of the whole ecumenical movement and merits the name of 'spiritual ecumenism'" (UR 8). "They promote union among Christians better when they try to live holier lives according to the Gospel" (UR 7).

2. The Council insists that the church must first *renew* itself to be truly ecumenical. "Christ summons the Church as she goes her pilgrim way to that continual reformation of which she always has need . . ." (UR 6). This renewal must take place in all areas of the church's official life: worship, theology, preaching the word of God, biblical scholarship.

3. The first step in such renewal was for the Catholic Church to *admit* her part in the division of Christianity and to *ask for forgiveness.* She admits "deficiencies in moral conduct or in Church discipline or even in the way that Church teaching has been formulated" (UR 6) and "we beg pardon of God and of our separated brethren . . . for sins against unity" (UR 7). This represents the first time the Roman Catholic Church publicly admitted guilt for the breakup of Christianity; the pre-Vatican II approach had been to blame Protestants for the Reformation and Orthodox for the schism of 1054. A great step forward!

4. The Council urges Catholics to "become familiar with the outlook of our separated brethren . . . their respective doctrines . . . their history, their spiritual and liturgical life, their religious psychology and cultural background"(UR 9). For students preparing for the priesthood, "sacred theology and other branches of knowledge, especially those of a historical nature, must be taught with due regard to the ecumenical point of view . . . "(UR 10). *Knowledge* leads to *appreciation,* creating the climate for prayer and action together and for future union.

5. Likewise Catholics should make "every effort to *avoid* expressions, judgments and actions which do not represent the condition of our separated brethren with truth and fairness and so make mutual relations with them more difficult" (UR 4). (Emphasis added.)

6. Catholics should *cooperate* with their separated Christians in social matters.

> Cooperation among Christians vividly expresses that bond which already unites them. . . . Such cooperation . . . should contribute to a just appreciation of the dignity of the human person, the promotion of the blessings of peace, the application of gospel principles to social life, and the advancement of the arts and sciences in a Christian spirit. Christians should also

work together in the use of every possible means to relieve the afflictions of our times, such as famine and natural disasters, illiteracy and poverty, lack of housing, and the unequal distribution of wealth. Through such cooperation all believers in Christ are able to learn how to esteem each other more and how the road to the unity of Christians may be made more smooth. (UR 12)

◆

Impressive Results of the *Decree on Ecumenism*

1. It dramatically reversed the ecumenical isolation of the Catholic Church and its coldness to the ecumenical movement begun in 1910 and carried on by the largely Protestant World Council of Churches.

2. It catapulted the Catholic Church into a leadership position in the ecumenical movement, primarily through inaugurating theological dialogues between the churches.

3. The resulting unprecedented variety of theological dialogues between the Roman Catholic and Protestant and Orthodox churches both internationally and within the United States achieved remarkable agreements of faith and theological explanations of that faith.

4. The Roman Catholic entrance into the ecumenical movement is an instructive example of how a change in theology can cause a change in church discipline and practice.

5. It furnishes a striking example of the good effects strong papal leadership can have in the contemporary church.

6. It transformed to a great extent the negative, aloof, superior attitude many Catholics had toward Protestants and Orthodox and they to Catholics, resulting in new friendships, prayer together, and cooperative charitable works and social action.

7. It witnesses to the power of the Holy Spirit in guiding the Church.

◆

Thus the *Final Report* of the 1985 Extraordinary Synod of Bishops could state: "After these 20 years we can affirm that ecumenism has inscribed itself deeply and indelibly in the consciousness of the Church."[4]

Theological Reflection on the *Decree on Ecumenism*

Before a responsible church can make a major change in its teaching and practice, it must develop a theological rationale or basis which nonetheless must remain consistent with the ancient tradition. The following

---

4. Xavier Rynne, *John Paul's Extraordinary Synod, A Collegial Achievement* (Wilmington, DE: Michael Glazier, 1986), 126.

four realities form the theological basis for the new relationship between the Roman Catholic Church and other Christian churches.

1. The *Constitution of the Church* stressed in its first chapter that the church of Christ is *primarily a mystery of Christ's presence and activity;* as such, the church is too great a reality to be limited to one existing Christian church, including the Roman Catholic.

2. The Roman Catholic Church *recognized as valid* the proper baptism of other Christian churches. Since baptism is incorporation into the body of Christ, Protestant and Orthodox Christians are therefore *members of the Church of Christ:* "it remains true that all who have been justified by faith in baptism are incorporated into Christ; they therefore have a right to be honored by the title of Christian and are properly regarded as brothers in the Lord . . ." (UR 3). However, Vatican II suggests that there are degrees of incorporation and that non-Catholics are not fully incorporated into the Catholic Church (UR 3 and LG 14).

3. Because of the above two theological realities, it can no longer be held that other Christian churches are mere *sociological* groupings of Christians, but are *real churches* bringing the grace of Christ and his salvation to their members. "It follows that the separated churches and communities as such . . . have been by no means deprived of significance and importance in the mystery of salvation. For the Spirit of Christ has not refrained from using them as means of salvation. . ." (UR 3). The recognition of Orthodox, Anglican and Protestant churches as real churches and ecclesial communities is "perhaps the most significant breakthrough of the Decree" and "represents a major advance in Roman Catholic thought about ecumenism and the nature of the Church."[5]

4. The Roman Catholic Church occupies a *unique position* among the other Christian churches. In relation to Protestants it traces its lineage in an unbroken historical sequence back to the Apostles; in relation to various Orthodox churches it alone has retained the papal ministry in succession to Peter the Apostle, whom Jesus made the rock of unity and the bearer of the keys of spiritual authority. The Council expresses this uniqueness by using the language of "fullness" rather than "true-false": "It is through Christ's Catholic Church alone . . . that the fullness of the means of salvation can be obtained" (UR 3). Avery Dulles expresses this unique claim of the Catholic Church in terms of the Council's terminology of "subsist":

> The Catholic Church, while recognizing its own weakness, dares to make claim that in it the Church of Christ. . . . one, holy, catholic, and apostolic . . . continues to subsist. It is convinced that its own essential teachings, its hierarchical minis-

---

5. Lucien Richard, ed., *Vatican II, the Unfinished Agenda* (Mahwah, NJ: Paulist Press, 1987), 180.

try, and its sacraments are in conformity with Christ's will and institution.[6]

A New Ecclesiology Is Born

In the light of these four realities, the bishops of Vatican II, aided by their theologian experts, formulated a new ecclesiology in order to express the reality of a divided Christianity and to open the door for Roman Catholic participation in the ecumenical movement. The new ecclesiology is presented in two stages in the famous article 8, chapter one, of the *Constitution on the Church.*

The first stage states an important principle: the church established by Christ is *one reality.* Protestant theology, as a way of explaining its legitimacy after the Reformation, had spoken of the *visible* divided church and the *invisible* true spiritual church known to God alone. The Council firmly repudiates this duality:

> The society structured with hierarchical organs and the mystical body of Christ, the visible society and the spiritual community, the earthly Church and the Church endowed with heavenly riches, are not to be thought of as two realities. On the contrary, they form one complex reality which comes together from a human and divine element. (LG 8)

The second step is contained in the following much-discussed statement; the key words are "subsists in" and "elements." We must carefully analyze this passage.

> This is the sole Church of Christ which in the Creed we profess to be one, holy, catholic and apostolic, which our Savior, after his resurrection, entrusted to Peter's pastoral care, commissioning him and the other apostles to extend and rule it. . . . This Church, constituted and organized as a society in the present world, subsists in the Catholic Church, which is governed by the successor of Peter and by the bishops in communion with him. Nevertheless, many elements of sanctification and of truth are found outside its visible confines. Since these are gifts belonging to the Church of Christ, they are forces impelling towards Catholic unity. (LG 8)

The crucial sentence is: "This Church . . . subsists in the Catholic Church. . ." Two points must be made. First, a distinction is made between "this Church (referring to the church Jesus founded on Peter 2000 years ago) and "the Catholic Church" (referring to the Roman Catholic Church existing today). Second, the *original* draft used the verb "is" so that its sentence stated that the Church Christ founded on Peter and the Apostles is *identical* with the Roman Catholic Church today. This identification

---

6. Avery Dulles, *A Church to Believe In* (New York: Crossroad, 1982), 5.

caused spirited debate in the Council. The progressive bishops objected that such an unnuanced identification excluded not only Anglican and Protestant churches but the ancient Orthodox churches from being in some real way the Church of Christ. Therefore the Council bishops substituted "subsists in" for "is." The exact meaning of "subsists in" has often been discussed, with no fully satisfactory explanation resulting.[7] Despite this, the intention of the bishops of Vatican II is clear: to broaden the idea of the church of Christ to include at least the Orthodox and Anglican churches.

The next sentence of Article 8 refers to "elements of sanctification and truth" existing outside the Roman Catholic Church. This is the famous doctrine of "elements"; we turn to the *Decree on Ecumenism* for an explanation.

> Some, even very many, of the most significant elements and endowments which together go to build up and give life to the Church itself, can exist outside the visible boundaries of the Roman Catholic Church: the written Word of God; the life of grace; faith, hope, and charity, with the other gifts of the Holy Spirit, as well as visible elements. All of these, which come from Christ and lead back to him, belong by right to the one Church of Christ. (UR 3)

The presence in other Christian churches of elements of the one Church of Christ founded on the Apostles constitutes another reason for recognizing other Christian churches as being in some way part of the Church of Christ.

A further point remains: the Council's theology of "incorporation" into the Church of Christ and of the *fullness* of means of salvation.

> Fully incorporated into the Church are those who . . . accept all the means of salvation given to the Church together with her entire organization, and who—by the bonds constituted by the profession of faith, the sacraments, ecclesiastical government, and communion—are joined to the visible structure of the Church and through her with Christ who rules her through the Supreme Pontiff and the bishops. (LG 14)

> It is through Christ's Roman Catholic Church alone . . . that the fullness of the means of salvation can be obtained. (UR 3)

The Council establishes the principle that full membership in the church of Christ means accepting all the means of salvation given to that church: profession of faith, sacraments, episcopal structure of government, communion with the bishop of Rome. In this way one is a member of the

---

7. See Francis Sullivan, *The Church We Believe In* (Mahwah, NJ: Paulist Press, 1988), 26-29. Sullivan further clarified the phrase in a talk given in Rome, Mar. 4, 1986: "The significance of Vatican II's decision to say of the Church of Christ not that it 'is' but that it 'subsists in' the Roman Catholic Church." *Bulletin Centro Pro Unione* 29 (Spring 1986): 3-8.

visible church of Christ. The Council makes the claim that only the Roman Catholic Church contains the full means of salvation.

◆

We may now paraphrase the teaching of the Council about the relation of other churches to the Roman Catholic Church. The *one church* that Jesus founded on Peter and the 12 Apostles *subsists in* the Roman Catholic Church according to the *fullness* of that one church but truly exists in other Christian churches according to *elements* of that one church of Christ.

◆

What is the significance of this doctrinal teaching and theological reasoning? What has it accomplished? It has provided the Roman Catholic Church (RCC) one way to explain the anomalous situation of the one church of Christ being divided into many different churches today. It has permitted the RCC to recognize the ecclesial reality of other churches; no longer can they be referred to as false or heretical churches and no longer should the RCC claim to be the *exclusively true* church of Christ. It has established the principle that there are many ways and degrees in which Christians are incorporated into the one church of Christ. At the same time, it expresses the unique position of the RCC among the other churches. It has thus created the climate for ecumenical dialogue between itself and the other Christian churches. In this dialogue, the doctrine of "fullness of means" and its corelative of "full communion" present a model for the future union of the churches.

A New Model of Union between Christian Churches

With this new ecclesiology, a communion rather than a "return" model came into being for the Catholic Church. In this model the separated Christian churches seek to enter into full communion with the RCC and with each other. The Council expresses this communion model in several ways. Those "who believe in Christ and have been properly baptized are in communion with the Catholic Church even though this communion is imperfect." The differences "in doctrine and sometimes in discipline or concerning the structures of the Church . . . create many obstacles . . . to full ecclesiastical communion." It is the work of the ecumenical movement "to overcome these obstacles" (UR 3). The communion model accordingly comprises degrees: from the already-existing *imperfect* communion all the way up to the sought-after *full* communion. Full communion would involve achieving "all the means of salvation" (LG 14) or "the fullness of the means of salvation" (UR 3).

What are these means of salvation which currently are obstacles to full communion? Orthodox churches, though possessing "true sacraments, above all by apostolic succession, the priesthood and the Eucharist" (*UR*

15), do not accept the universal spiritual authority of the bishop of Rome. This prevents them from entering into full communion with the Roman Catholic Church. Protestant ecclesial communities lack "a complete profession of faith, a complete incorporation into the system of salvation such as Christ willed it . . . nor have they preserved the proper reality of the Eucharistic mystery in its fullness, especially because of the absence of the sacrament of Orders" (UR 22). The "system of salvation" means the full seven sacraments, the structure of bishops in the apostolic succession, the role of the successor of Peter as the foundation of unity/communion and his spiritual authority, the full teaching of the Catholic Church, including the papacy and the more recent dogmas of papal infallibility, the Immaculate Conception and the Assumption of Mary.

It would appear that the above lineup constitutes too great a barrier to full communion with the Catholic Church for Protestants and the Orthodox. But this is where the theological dialogues enter the ecumenical scene.

Theological Dialogues

Vatican II was responsible for the extraordinary growth of theological discussions or **dialogues** between all the major churches. These dialogues are the impressive contribution of the Catholic Church to the ecumenical movement and are the favorite official form of Catholic ecumenism.

The *Decree on Ecumenism* proposed "dialogue between competent experts from different churches and communities" in which "each explains the teaching of his communion in greater depth and brings out its distinctive features" so that "everyone gains a truer knowledge and more just appreciation of the teachings and religious life of both communions" (UR 4). In this "discussion of theological problems . . . each can treat with the other on an equal footing" (UR 9).

The goal of the dialogues then is to clarify disagreements in each church's understanding of the Christian faith and to discover both *faith* and *theological* agreement. The method employed is for theologians to research a given topic, write scholarly papers which are distributed to dialogue members in preparation for regular meetings in which the papers are thoroughly analyzed. Each church clearly explains its own teaching and theological position; questions are put to each other. A report is drawn up and published expressing agreement reached and remaining differences.

These theological dialogues beginning immediately after Vatican II represent one of the great successes of the Council. Churches grew in their understanding of each other, friendships were formed among the participating theologians, and in many cases it was discovered that the churches actually shared the same teaching and theological understanding, though often expressed in different language or terms. These surprising agreements have led some of the churches to the next stage of asking whether and how they might proceed to actual union.

The Roman Catholic Church has entered into theological dialogues on the *international* level with seven churches: Lutheran World Federation in 1965, Anglican Communion in 1966, World Methodist Council in 1966, World Alliance of Reformed Churches in 1968, some Pentecostal churches in 1970, the Disciples of Christ in 1977, and the Orthodox in 1980. In the United States the Bishops' Commission on Ecumenical and Interreligious Affairs (BCEIA) has sponsored ten dialogues: with Episcopalians, Southern Baptists, American Baptists, Disciples of Christ, Lutherans, United Methodist, Eastern Orthodox, Oriental Orthodox (Armenian, Syrian, Coptic, Ethiopian churches in USA), Presbyterian and Reformed, Assemblies of God. The reports of some of these dialogues, often termed agreed statements, are contained in two large volumes, *Building Unity, Ecumenical Documents III* (international) and *IV* (U.S.A.). Among such riches we shall consider by way of instructive example, one international and one national dialogue.

ARCIC (Anglican Roman Catholic International Commission)

The international dialogue between the Anglican and Roman Catholic churches was inaugurated in 1966 when Anglican Archbishop Ramsey and Pope Paul VI signed an agreement for their churches to work toward "full organic unity." The commission they created published its *Final Report* in 1981.[8] This report contained four documents: *Eucharistic Doctrine* in 1971 (virtual agreement); *Ministry and Ordination* in 1973 (virtual agreement); *Authority in the Church I* in 1976 and *II* in 1981 (serious differences but a "convergence" of understanding). As each document was published, critiques were invited from both churches; these were addressed in three Elucidations or further clarifications. The *Final Report* was sent to the various churches within the Anglican Communion and to the Holy See's Congregation for the Doctrine of the Faith,[9] with the recommendation that on the basis of these agreements and convergences the two communions/churches begin serious concrete steps toward union. It was agreed by church authorities on both sides that further dialogue was needed, so ARCIC II was in-

---

8. *The Final Report, Anglican-Roman Catholic International Commission* (Washington, D.C.: U.S. Catholic Conference, 1982) and Cincinnati: Forward Movement Publications, 1982).

9. CDF's response 10 years later gave a warm welcome to the Final Report, commended its achievement and drew attention to "points of convergence and even of agreement which many would not have thought possible before the Commission began its work," but noted that "there still remain between Anglicans and Catholics important differences regarding essential matters of Catholic doctrine." Full text in *Origins* 21 (Dec. 19, 1991):441-47. See also the frank, less-than-enthusiastic analysis by Francis Sullivan "The Vatican Response to ARCIC I," *Bulletin Centro Pro Unione* 40-41 (Fall-Spring 1991-92): 36-41.

augurated and is still in progress. ARCIC I is a remarkable ecumenical achievement and represents a major step toward the longed-for union of the Anglican and Roman Catholic communions.

Lutheran/Roman Catholic Dialogue, U.S.A.

Begun right after Vatican II in 1965, this is the richest dialogue theologically speaking and the one producing the most documents, both in quantity and scholarly quality. Since then theologians from each church have met for three days twice-yearly to discuss their carefully-researched papers. They have produced the following: *Status of the Nicene Creed as Dogma of the Church*, 1965; *One Baptism for the Remission of Sins*, 1966; *The Eucharist*, 1967; *Eucharist and Ministry*, 1970; *Differing Attitudes toward Papal Primacy*, 1973; *Teaching Authority and Infallibility in the Church*, 1978; *Justification by Faith*, 1983; *The One Mediator, the Saints, and Mary*, 1989.[10]

A few passages from *Differing Attitudes toward Papal Primacy* are interesting and instructive on how theologians report the results of their dialogue. In "Lutheran Perspectives," the Lutheran theologians state that:

> . . . Lutherans increasingly recognize the need for a Ministry serving the unity of the church universal. . . . [and] can also grant the beneficial role of the papacy at various periods of history. . . . they cannot deny that God may show again in the future that the papacy is his gracious gift to his people. Perhaps this might involve a primacy in which the pope's service to unity in relation to the Lutheran churches would be more pastoral than juridical. The one thing necessary, from the Lutheran point of view, is that papal primacy be so structured and interpreted that it clearly serve the gospel and the unity of the Church of Christ, and that its exercise of power not subvert Christian freedom.[11]

The Lutheran participants propose a remarkable challenge. They ask Lutheran churches to consider seriously:

- if they are prepared to affirm with us that papal primacy, renewed in the light of the gospel, need not be a barrier to reconciliation.
- if they are able to acknowledge not only the legitimacy of the papal Ministry in the service of the Roman Catholic communion but even the possibility and desirability of the papal Ministry, renewed under the gospel and committed to Christian freedom, in a larger communion which would include the Lutheran churches.[12]

---

10. Joseph Burgess and Jeffrey Gros, eds., *Building Unity, Ecumenical Documents I* (New York/Mahwah, NJ: Paulist Press, 1989), 88-290. All the documents except *The One Mediator, the Saints, and Mary* are included.

11. *Ibid.*, 136, No. 28.

12. *Ibid.*, 137, No. 32.

Thus has dialogue brought Lutherans from Martin Luther's rejection of the papacy as anti-Christ to serious consideration of its role in a future united church of Lutherans and Roman Catholics!

The Lutheran theologians then ask the Roman Catholic Church "if it is willing to open discussions on possible structures for reconciliation which would protect the legitimate traditions of the Lutheran communities and respect their spiritual heritage; if it is prepared to envisage the possibility of a reconciliation between the two churches which would recognize the self-government of Lutheran churches within a communion."[13] The communion model here suggested means the Lutheran churches would enter into communion with the Catholic Church by recognizing the role of the successor of Peter in the church, but they would continue to have their own identity and traditions (emphasis on preaching the Word of God, their own bishops and pastors and parishes, their married clergy, and so forth), much like the Eastern churches in communion with the pope.

The Lutheran theologians conclude with this appeal to their "church bodies":

> Our Lutheran teaching about the Church and the Ministry constrains us to believe that recognition of papal primacy is possible to the degree that a renewed papacy would in fact foster faithfulness to the gospel and truly exercise a Petrine function within the church. If this is indeed what Lutherans hold, ought they not be willing to say so clearly and publicly?[14]

In the light of these discussions on the role of the pope and of Lutheran willingness to recognize a "renewed papacy" in a future communion of Lutheran churches and the Catholic Church, the Catholic theologians made this petition to Catholic authorities.

> We suggest . . . that a distinct canonical status may be worked out by which Lutherans could be in official communion with the church of Rome. Such a restoration of communion, we believe, would be of great benefit to Roman Catholics, and to Lutherans, enabling them both to share in a broader Christian heritage. In such a wider communion of churches the papacy would be able to serve as a sign and instrument of unity, not simply for Roman Catholics, but for others who have never ceased to pray and labor for the manifest unity of the whole church of Christ.[15]

Before leaving these dialogues, it will be helpful to consider the existence of a **"hierarchy of truth"** within Catholic belief. "When comparing doctrines one with another, they [Catholic theologians] should remember that in Catholic doctrine, there exists an order or 'hierarchy' of truths,

---

13. *Ibid.*, 138, No. 33.
14. *Ibid.*, 147, No. 41.
15. *Ibid.*, 151.

since they vary in their relation to the foundation of Christian faith" (UR 11). The doctrines dealing with the mystery of Christ and of the Trinity are at the core of the Christian faith, whereas teachings on indulgences would be far down the list. Before Vatican II, Catholic apologists tended to make all doctrines equal, so that to call in question a less-important teaching was to destroy the entire belief system.

The Jesuit theologian Karl Rahner has suggested that agreement on the fundamental truths of the ancient creeds might constitute a sufficient basis for the unity and communion of the churches. Avery Dulles has suggested that in a union of Lutheran and Roman Catholics, acceptance of the Marian dogmas of the Immaculate Conception and the Assumption, which have "scant basis in Scripture" and are foreign to Lutheran tradition, might not be demanded as a condition for union; others, however, would see this as a dangerous compromise. Nonetheless, the ecumenical potential of this principle for the theological dialogues between the churches is enormous.

Baptism, Eucharist and Ministry (BEM)[16]

This remarkable document, over 30 years in the making, is the product of the **Faith and Order Commission** of the WCC. Its uniqueness and importance can be gathered from the following.

> This fruit of many years of ecumenical discussion has become the most widely distributed, translated, and discussed ecumenical text in modern times. Some 450,000 copies translated into 31 languages have been studied in a huge variety of situations around the world. Over a thousand written reactions have so far been published. Never before have more than 180 churches reached out to each other by responding officially to an ecumenical document. Never before have so many theological faculties, confessional families, ecumenical groups, local congregations and discussion groups of lay and ordained persons joined together in studying the same modern ecumenical document.[17]

It is important to stress two things: one, BEM is called a *convergence* rather than an agreed statement since it represents a converging of different viewpoints that are not yet fully agreed upon; two, since *BEM* is the work of *theologians* from many churches (including Roman Catholic who made important contributions), it does not represent *official* church positions. Accordingly, when BEM was completed at the Faith and Order meeting in Lima, Peru, in 1982, it was sent to the 311 member churches of the WCC and to the various national conferences of Catholic bishops, asking them to report whether BEM expresses "the faith of the Church

---

16. *Baptism, Eucharist and Ministry* (Geneva: World Council of Churches, 1982).

17. *Baptism, Eucharist and Ministry 1982-1990: Report on the Process and Responses* (Geneva: WCC Publications, 1990), 155-56.

through the ages" and provides a basis for your church's "relations and dialogues with other churches."

◆

The churches discussed BEM over a four-year period; their reports fill six volumes and can be summarized in this way. The sacramental, episcopal churches (Anglican, Catholic, Orthodox) were pleased with the sacramental emphasis, the suggestion to recover the triple ministry of bishops-priests-deacons, Eucharist as both memorial and containing the real presence of Christ, and the importance of bishops in the apostolic succession. The Reformation and Free churches had difficulty with these points. Those churches that baptize only "believers" disagreed with the endorsement of infant baptism, but appreciated its link with the faith of the infant's sponsors and its completion in confirmation.

◆

After reviewing the six volumes of the churches' responses to BEM, WCC's Faith and Order Commission singled out three areas for further serious study and discussion: the relation between *Scripture* as norm of faith and *Tradition* as both containing the apostolic faith and passing it on through the centuries; the reality and understanding of *sacraments;* the churches' different understanding of the *essential nature of church.* The ecumenical agenda for the immediate future!

BEM is a major step on the long journey to the restoration of unity between the separated Christian churches. But for union to occur, the churches must agree on these three fundamental realities of the Christian faith: baptism as entrance into the church, Eucharist as the church's act of worship, and ordained ministry as the church's leadership structure. BEM urged the churches to recover the faith and practice of baptism, Eucharist, and ministry of the undivided Church of Christ during its first thousand years. Once agreement on these three ecclesiological realities is reached, the churches will be in a position to recognize each other's ordained ministers and the Eucharists they celebrate. This is the goal envisioned by the *Decree on Ecumenism* when it looked forward to the day when "all Christians will be gathered in a common celebration of the Eucharist, into the unity . . . which Christ bestowed on his Church from the beginning" (UR 4).

The Future United Church of Christ

What might the future united "great church" of Christ look like? Is it a realistic possibility? Are we any closer to unity thirty years after Pope John XXIII convened Vatican II? What is the state of Christian ecumenism today?

Thanks to those who inaugurated the modern ecumenical movement in 1910, to the early Faith and Order work from 1920 on, and to Vatican Council II that brought the Catholic Church into the ecumenical movement, ecumenism has made extraordinary progress. The churches know and respect each other at all levels: the pope and church leaders, like the Archbishop of Canterbury and Patriarch of Constantinople, meet and pray together; some U.S. Roman Catholic and Lutheran bishops make annual retreats together; priests and ministers meet regularly for theological discussion and social gatherings; Protestant and Catholic parishes exchange pulpits at non-Eucharistic services, pray for each other, enter into covenant relationships, and cooperate in social justice work; individual Protestants and Catholics meet in bible studies and prayer groups and have come to like and respect each other. Like the Berlin Wall, the barriers of suspicion and prejudice and isolation have been torn down. And through the many theological dialogues, the churches have discovered a stunning amount of faith and even theological agreement and have come to understand more clearly and sympathetically the remaining differences.

But are we at all close to the "restoration of unity" by the year 2000, the third millennium of Christianity?

"Models" of Future Church Union

Various models exist among ecumenical theologians and church leaders. The "return-to-the-Catholic-Church" model is rejected by all Protestant and most Catholic ecumenists. The "merger" model, like the recent merger of three United States Lutheran churches into the Evangelical Lutheran Church of America (ELCA), is more suitable for Protestant churches within the same or similar traditions but would not be acceptable in a union that included Catholic and Orthodox churches. The WCC has championed a "conciliar" model defined as "the coming together of Christians—locally, regionally or globally—for common prayer, counsel and decision." What is envisaged is "a truly universal ecumenical conciliar form of life" expressed "in councils of churches at the local, national, regional and world levels." The most dramatic conciliarity would be "a genuinely universal council" that would "once more speak for all Christians and lead the way into the future," a kind of Vatican III including Catholic, Orthodox, Anglican and Protestant churches.[18] This democratic model stressing fellowship is attractive and has many advantages; however in not adequately providing for the role of the papacy, unity of faith and doctrine, and sacramental life, it would exclude Catholic and Orthodox participation. This leaves the "communion" model, which the 1985 Extraordinary Synod

---

18. *Faith and Order Louvain 1971* (Geneva: WCC, 1971), 225-229, committee report on "conciliarity and the future of the ecumenical movement."

of Bishops termed "the central and fundamental idea" pervading the second Vatican Council documents.

The goal of the **communion model** is for churches already in partial communion with each other through baptism, agreement on Christian belief as expresssed in the ancient creeds, and social action to move to full communion. This means that Protestant churches, which "have not preserved the reality of the Eucharistic mystery in its fullness, especially because of the absence of the sacrament of orders" (*UR* 22), need to recover the sacramental system, especially the sacrament of ordination, and the order of bishops ordained in the apostolic succession. Full communion also involves both Protestant and Orthodox churches recognizing the role of the pope in the church, thus to be "in communion with" Peter.

The communion model is being discussed in the theological dialogues. We have seen that the Anglican, Lutheran and Roman Catholic churches are close to full agreement on the essential beliefs of the Christian faith; that Lutherans in the U.S.A. Lutheran-Catholic dialogue proposed recognizing the role of the pope, and Anglicans in ARCIC I admit the pope's unique role in the Christian Church. Once full communion is established, Lutheran and Anglican churches could maintain their distinctive traditions: their ordained ministers, their worship and spirituality, their canon law and way of Christian life, including a married priesthood.

A similar model already exists between the Eastern Catholic churches, which have reestablished communion with the Roman Catholic Church by recognizing the spiritual authority of the bishop of Rome. They have been known as "**Uniates**" to distinguish them from Eastern Orthodox churches, though they rightly resent this term because of past Catholic insensitivity to their traditions. Each Eastern Catholic church retains its own rite, that is, its structure of bishops, priests and patriarch; its own liturgy or style of worship; its own discipline; its married clergy; its own distinctive spirituality. Examples are the Ukrainian and Ruthenian Catholics in the United States. However, what makes this model workable is that the Catholic Church already recognizes the priesthood of these churches, since their bishops are in the apostolic succession and thus ordain priests who celebrate valid Eucharists.

Contemporary Issues and Obstacles to Union

These represent some of the most pressing issues facing the Christian churches in their journey to full visible union. Since fuller treatment awaits us in chapter 21, we shall merely list these issues, with brief comments:

• That churches take meaningful, practical steps toward union on the basis of the faith agreement discovered in the theological dialogues.

- Roman Catholic-Orthodox relationships. With religious freedom now a reality in Russia and Eastern Europe, Catholics, especially in the Ukraine, ask that their churches and property given to the Russian Orthodox during the communist era be returned and the Catholic hierarchy have full freedom to minister to the large number of Catholics. The Orthodox fear Catholic proselytism of Russian Orthodox Christians.

- Official Catholic recognition of Anglican Orders. In the light of ARCIC I's *Final Report*, Catholic ecumenical theologians desire reopening the Vatican's condemnation of Anglican orders as "absolutely null and void" in 1893 under Pope Leo XIII. (See chapter 21, no. 9.)

- Catholic recognition of at least some Protestant churches' ministers and ministries.

- Eucharistic sharing between the churches.

- A new approach to apostolic succession. (See chapter 10, issue 4 and chapter 21, no. 9)

- Underlying the previous six is the issue of papal exercise of authority. Cardinal Edward Cassidy, head of the Pontifical Council for Promoting Christian Unity, commented positively on this issue when he said in a formal address to the 1993 WCC Conference on Faith and Order that it is possible for the pope to retain a juridical primacy over Catholics and a more "symbolic and honorary primacy" over other Christians.[19]

The major *doctrinal* obstacles to the union of the churches are the role of the papacy and papal infallibility, the question of apostolic succession and consequent validity of ordinations and Eucharist, the ordination of women. The major issues are thus ecclesiological, that is, what constitutes the essential nature of the church. Major divisive *moral* issues are abortion, contraceptive birth control, homosexuality, divorce and remarriage. On the grassroots level, there are still ignorance, indifference and fear toward other churches; toward ecumenism itself there is the human reluctance by all the churches but especially the smaller ones, to give up their own independence and identity.

In addition to these very real obstacles, a disturbing element has entered the ecumenical scene. After the initial enthusiasm generated by Vatican II, a sense of discouragement and frustration is noticeable among ecumenical leaders in all the churches in the past 10 years or so. This is due to the reemergence of institutional concerns and the failure of church leaders to act on the growing number of theological agreements among the churches by taking the next possible steps toward actual union. Expressions like "ecumenical malaise" or "ecumenism is dead" are heard. The

---

19. Patricia Lefevre, "Christian Unity: No Deadline, but a Boost in Spain," *National Catholic Reporter* 29 (August 27, 1993): 13.

Anglican Archbishop Desmond Tutu of Cape Town, South Africa, recently warned that if the churches do not act soon, "weariness and indifference" will continue to produce "universal ecumenical inertia."[20]

We may appropriately conclude this chapter with the realistic analysis of the WCC's Fifth World Conference on Faith and Order meeting in Santiago de Compostela, Spain, August 3-14, 1993, attended by Protestant, Orthodox and Catholic delegates, including theologians and church leaders. Its final statement on *koinonia* (defined as "the richness of our life together in Christ: community, communion, sharing, fellowship, participation, solidarity"), expressed "concern for waning commitments to ecumenism" and penitence for "our failure to do all that is ecumenically possible." The statement admits "the ecumenical goal [of visible church unity] has not yet been reached": specifically "full mutual recognition of baptism . . . the sharing together of Christians from all churches at the Lord's table . . . and a mutually recognized ministry." As to the future challenges facing the churches, "the way forward will come by new ventures and insights in the faith that unites us . . . the need for a deeper understanding of the church and its apostolic character." Thus "the churches must dare concrete steps toward fuller *koinonia*"; "the churches and the ecumenical movement itself are called to the conversion to Christ that true **koinonia** in our time demands."[21]

The ecumenical picture at present is ambiguous. Perhaps it is a question of the glass half-empty or half-full. Yet those dedicated to ecumenism, both theologians and church leaders, are convinced that unity is ultimately the work of the Holy Spirit and will come about when and how God wills it. They also recognize that the churches themselves must accept responsibility and take concrete steps toward unity.

Summary

Jesus established one Church on the Twelve Apostles. His concern was unity among those who would follow him. Yet disunity seems to be characteristic of the Christian Church through much of its history. Recognizing this scandal as a major obstacle to bringing the good news about Christ to all people, Pope John XXIII made union of the separated Christian churches one of the major purposes in calling the second Vatican Council. Our study of Christian ecumenism began by showing the great scope of disunity among the churches today, and its causes in the schism of 1054 between the Eastern and Western Churches and in the Protestant Reformation in the 16th century. The modern ecumenical movement to heal these "divorces" was begun by Anglicans and Protestants, resulting in the World

20. *Ibid.*
21. "On the Way to Fuller *Koinonia*," *Origins* 23 (Sept. 9, 1993): 231-32.

Council of Churches in 1948. The Catholic Church entered the ecumenical movement with its *Decree on Ecumenism* in 1965, urging Catholics to become ecumenical and giving guidelines for their activity.

Such a momentous change in attitude and action toward Anglican, Protestant and Orthodox churches demanded new theological insights: thus the Council bishops, aided by their theological experts, devised a new ecclesiology or theology of church that made a new relationship with other churches possible and gave a consequent new communion model for the future union of the separated churches. The Catholic Church's contribution to ecumenism became the highly successful theological dialogues between the major Christian churches. A history-making contribution of the WCC Faith and Order Commission was bringing to completion *Baptism, Eucharist and Ministry*, a document that confronted the three main obstacles to union among the churches. Agreement achieved in the dialogues led to reflection on what the future united Church of Christ might look like by considering various models of union. We concluded by listing major contemporary issues and obstacles to union.

For Discussion

1. Suppose the archbishop of Canterbury asks to reestablish communion of the Church of England with the bishop of Rome. What might the archbishop agree to do? What might the pope do? (Consider questions like women's ordination, Anglican orders, apostolic succession, papal primacy, the two Marian dogmas of the Immaculate Conception and the Assumption of Mary.)

2. Do you think the future united church of Jesus Christ has any realistic chance of coming about? What is the most promising model? What steps would Protestant churches need to take? Orthodox churches? the Roman Catholic Church?

3. Is the restoration of unity among the separated Christian churches really desirable? Might the present situation of energetic individual churches be able to accomplish more in preaching the Gospel and establishing God's kingdom on earth?

4. Considering its unique position among the other Christian churches, does the Roman Catholic Church have the principal responsibility for Christian unity? If so, what should the pope do to reunite the Orthodox? Anglicans? Lutherans? other Protestant churches? (Consider the major doctrinal and practical issues.)

5. Where does the blame for the malaise of ecumenism lie today?

6. With enthusiasm for Christian ecumenism waning today, what can and should the Catholic Church do to get ecumenism back on track? Other Christian churches do?

For Action

1. Research the complex historical problem of Anglican orders. Could the Roman Catholic Church "recognize" Anglican orders? Should it?
2. Talk to a Catholic and a Protestant ecumenist about the current ecumenical slowdown in the Catholic Church. Ask them if they think "the restoration" has anything to do with it? If the Catholic Church is currently an obstacle to unity?
3. Read up on what a "renewed papacy" might involve.
4. Research the neuralgic question of "intercommunion" (Protestants receiving Catholic eucharists and vice versa). Would it hasten or deter the union of the churches?

Further Reading

Baptism, Eucharist and Ministry. Geneva, Switzerland: WCC, 1982.

Congar, Yves. *Diversity and Communion.* Mystic, CT: Twenty-Third Publications, 1985.

Dessaux, Jacques. *Twenty Centuries of Ecumenism.* New York/Ramsey, NJ: Paulist Press, 1984.

The Final Report, Anglican-Roman Catholic International Commission. Washington, DC: U.S. Catholic Conference, 1982.

Fries, H. and Rahner, K. *Unity of the Churches, an Actual Possibility.* Philadelphia: Fortress Press, 1985.

Macquarrie, John. *Christian Unity and Christian Diversity.* London: SCM Press Ltd., 1975.

Ware, Timothy. *The Orthodox Church.* New York: Penguin Books, 1983.

CHAPTER 9

Church and World: Catholic Social Teaching

Action on behalf of justice and participation in the transformation of the world fully appear to us as a constitutive dimension of the preaching of the Gospel. —1971 Synod of Bishops

As a Church, we must be people after God's own heart, bonded by the Spirit, sustaining one another in love, setting our hearts on God's kingdom, committing ourselves to solidarity with those who suffer, working for peace and justice, acting as a sign of Christ's love and justice in the world.
—U.S. Bishops, *Economic Justice for All* 24

We need a spirituality that calls forth and supports lay initiative and witness. . . . Our faith is not just a weekend obligation. . . . It is a pervasive reality to be practiced every day in homes, offices, factories, schools and businesses across our land.
—*Economic Justice for All* 25

. . . to teach and to spread her social doctrine pertains to the Church's evangelizing mission and is an essential part of the Christian message, since this doctrine . . . situates daily work and struggles for justice in the context of bearing witness to Christ the Savior. —John Paul II, *Centesimus Annus* 5

Introduction

Recently I celebrated Sunday Mass in the home of a high school classmate. The Gospel reading spoke of Jesus' teaching on the kingdom of

God. I explained that the kingdom involved not only knowing, loving and obeying God but also God's concern for justice and equality in society. I noticed my friend was growing uneasy. He blurted out: "I disagree with all this social involvement stuff. We were taught the one important thing is to save our soul. Remember how the priests told us about St. Ignatius repeating to Francis Xavier: "Francis, what does it profit you if you gain the whole world and lose your immortal soul?" My friend, a good Catholic, did stress an important truth. But his 23-year old daughter spoke up: "There's more to being a Christian than just saving your soul." You can imagine the vigorous discussion that followed!

This incident illustrates a serious question, one that bothers some Catholics: Should the church become involved in social, economic and political affairs? Is not the goal of the church purely religious ? Should it not "stay out of politics"? Catholics before Vatican II were brought up with the conviction that the most important thing was "to save my soul"; Catholic devotional life—attendance at Mass, confession, novenas, retreats, vocal prayers—was geared toward personal salvation. It was thus no surprise that many Catholics were confused by the "new" emphasis on social action, on justice and human rights, on changing unjust structures of society, on poverty and hunger issues. Some Catholics resisted this emphasis, desiring a return to the individualist piety of their youth.

However, there is no turning back. The bishops at the Second Vatican Council clearly committed the Catholic Church to social justice and the transformation of society according to God's plan for the human family. Six years later, the Synod of Bishops meeting in Rome in 1971 made a remarkable statement, quoted above, that action for justice is a "constitutive dimension" of preaching the good news of Jesus Christ. Pope John Paul II, also quoted above, 20 years later called spreading the church's social doctrine "an essential part" of the Christian message, "essential" being much stronger than "constitutive."

Since many Catholics and other Christians are unaware of the church's **social teaching** as it has developed over the past century, we give a comprehensive overview of the most important and influential papal and episcopal letters and documents. We have purposely provided quite a few direct quotations so that our readers may personally experience the rich breadth of Catholic social teaching which the U.S. bishops, in *A Century of Social Teaching*, define as "a set of principles, a body of thought, and a call to action."

◆

Preview: This chapter has four parts: 1. We analyze in detail Vatican II's last and longest and in some ways most revolutionary document, the *Pastoral Constitution on the Church in the Modern World*. We shall consider its three theological foundations and some of its major emphases. 2. We then explain the rich but largely unknown Catholic social teaching as developed by the popes over the past 100 years, from 1891 to 1991. We will briefly summarize the teaching of four important encyclicals before Vatican II and five significant letters by Popes Paul VI and John Paul II after the Council. 3. Our next study is the three letters produced by the United States' bishops; the first two on the crucial topics of nuclear war and peace and of economic justice in the United States are noteworthy for their far-ranging consultation process. 4. We conclude with a treatment of social justice and significant results of the church's commitment to justice and the transformation of society.

◆

Pastoral Constitution on the Church in the Modern World (GS)

(The Latin title, *Gaudium et Spes*, Joy and Hope, is taken from its opening words)

No other document shows so dramatically the contrast between the pre-Vatican II church and the church envisioned by the bishops. The pre-Vatican II church was suspicious of the world and isolated itself from a world perceived as evil. It was a defensive, fortress church. But now, following the lead of John XXIII and his optimistic *aggiornamento*, guided by "the signs of the times" and recognizing that the church had something to learn from the world, the bishops opened themselves to this world and provided for the first time in the history of the church a document that related the church directly to the contemporary world. This clearly was something startlingly new and has had tremendous consequences for the church today.

The optimistic tone of the document is set from its famous opening words, in which the church identifies itself with all of humanity:

> The joy and hope, the grief and anguish of the men of this world, especially those who are poor and afflicted in any way, are the joy and hope, the grief and anguish of the followers of Christ as well. (GS 1)

This document is significant in that it redefined the church's mission and what it means to be a member of the church. It committed the church to be a moral force in the world for justice and peace, for the dignity of each person and for human rights, and to be a prophetic voice against injustice and sins against the human person. A Catholic can no longer be satisfied merely to receive the sacraments, adhere to a code of strictly personal morality, and thus earn salvation. Rather a Catholic Christian must immerse himself or herself in the world, become aware of the great issues facing humankind, and do what is possible for human needs, human rights, justice and peace.

The document is called "pastoral" in the sense of loving concern or care because the bishops, as pastors or shepherds, were acutely aware of the staggering needs and suffering of humanity and felt a personal responsibility to respond. This pastoral document has two parts: Part I. "The Church and the Human Calling" is divided into four chapters; Part II. "Some Problems of Special Urgency" comprises five chapters treating marriage and the family, development of culture, socioeconomic life, the political community, and peace and a community of nations. We shall consider mainly Part I.

Theological Bases

Underlying every major change in the church is a new theological emphasis that both explains and justifies the change. Three such theologies are operative in the document and reflect the thinking of the bishops.

1. *A theology of "the signs of the times."* The church has always had the duty of scrutinizing the signs of the times and of interpreting them in the light of the Gospel (GS 4). This is based on John XXIII's conviction that the Holy Spirit speaks to the church, leaders and members alike, through events in the world. Examples of such events are the drive for freedom in Eastern Europe and the Baltic States and the collapse of Soviet communism; the yearning for freedom and democracy throughout the world; the growing sensitivity to world poverty, homelessness, refugees, hunger; the remarkable appreciation in recent years for human dignity and human rights; the peace and ecology movements; women's issues, and so forth.

   Let us ponder the Constitution's graphic description of "signs of the times":

   > Never before has the human race enjoyed such an abundance of wealth, resources, and economic power, and yet a huge proportion of the world's citizens are still tormented by hunger and poverty while countless numbers suffer from total illiteracy. Never before has man been so understanding of freedom, yet at the same time new forms of social and psychological slavery appear. (GS 4)
   >
   > People hounded by hunger call upon those better off; women claim for themselves an equity with men, laborers and farmers seek the necessities of life . . . and to take part in regulating economic, social, political and cultural life. Now, for the first time in human history all people are convinced the benefits of culture can be for everyone. (GS 9)
   >
   > Still beneath all these demands lies a deeper and more widespread longing; persons and societies, thirst for a full and free life worthy of man. . . . Nations try harder to bring about a kind of universal community. (GS 9)

While an immense number of people still lack the absolute necessities of life, some live in luxury and squander wealth. Extravagance and wretchedness exist side by side. . . . Hence many reforms in the socioeconomic realm and a change of mentality and attitude are required of all. (GS 63)

Christ is now at work in the hearts of men through the energy of his Holy Spirit . . . animating, purifying and strengthening those noble longings by which the human family makes its life more human. (GS 38)

2. *Christian anthropology* or theology of the human person. *Gaudium et Spes* stresses the dignity of the human person as created by God: "The root reason for human dignity lies in man's call to communion with God. . . . For man would not exist were he not created by God's love" (GS 19). From this follows the basic equality of all persons. Accordingly,

Every type of discrimination, whether social or cultural, whether based on sex, race, color, social condition, language or religion, is to be overcome as contrary to God's intent. . . . The equal dignity of persons demands that a more human and just condition of life be brought about. (GS 29)

From the dignity of each person created by God comes his or her basic human rights,

There must be made available to all everything necessary for leading a life truly human, such as food, clothing and shelter; the right to choose a state of life freely and to found a family, the right to education, to employment, to a good reputation, to respect, to appropriate information, to activity in accord with the upright norm of one's own conscience, to protection of privacy and to rightful freedom even in matters religious. (GS 26)

3. *Kingdom of God theology.* God's plan for humanity is not only that all persons know, love, worship and obey God but that in this life they enjoy a life befitting their human dignity. The major preoccupation of Jesus' life was to establish the kingdom or reign of God on earth. He began his public life in the synagogue at Nazareth when he applied to himself the words of Isaiah: "The spirit of the Lord is upon me; . . . he has sent me to bring glad tidings to the poor, to proclaim liberty to captives, recovery of sight to the blind, and release to prisoners . . ." (Luke 4:18) In the *Our Father* he taught his disciples to pray "thy kingdom come, thy will be done . . . give us this day our daily bread . . ."

Kingdom of God theology permeates the entire pastoral constitution. Some examples: "to the extent that [earthly progress] can contribute to the better ordering of human society, it is of vital concern to the kingdom of God" (GS 39).

Christians who take an active part in present-day socioeconomic development and fight for justice and charity should be convinced they can make a great contribution to the prosperity of mankind and to the peace of the world. Whoever . . . seeks first the kingdom of God [is doing] the work of justice under the inspiration of charity. (GS 72)

God . . . has willed that all men should constitute one family and treat one another in a spirit of brotherhood . . . Love of God cannot be separated from love of neighbor. (GS 24)

◆

Major Emphases of *Gaudium et Spes*

1. *Individualistic morality is energetically repudiated.* "Profound and rapid changes make it particularly urgent that no one, ignoring the trend of events or drugged by laziness, content himself with a merely individualistic morality." (GS 30)

2. The *role of the church* is to be "a leaven and kind of soul for human society to be renewed in Christ and transformed into God's family." (GS 40) The church must therefore "by the Gospel committed to her proclaim the rights of man." The Council clearly affirms that "Christ gave his Church no proper mission in the political, economic, social order. The purpose he gave her is religious." (GS 42) Yet this very religious purpose, as we have seen, includes the dignity of each human person and the human rights flowing from that God-given dignity; the church will therefore of necessity become involved in the political, economic, and social order.

   The Church should have true freedom to preach the faith, to teach her social doctrine, to exercise her role freely among men and to pass moral judgment in those matters of public order when a person's fundamental rights or salvation require. (GS 76)

3. The Council defended the *"right of freely founding unions* for working people" and the consequent right to strike. (GS 68) (emphasis added)

4. The *purpose of the goods of earth.* "God intended the earth with everything in it for the use of all human beings. Thus in justice and charity created goods should be in abundance for all." (GS 69)

5. The *right to private property is not absolute.* "By its very nature private property has a social dimension based on the law of the common destination of earthly goods." (GS 71) The Council applied this principle to underdeveloped countries where large rural estates are only slightly cul-

tivated or lying completely idle for the sake of profit, while the majority are without land or have only small fields. "Insufficiently cultivated large estates should be distributed to those who can make them fruitful." (GS 71)

This forthright statement was not well accepted by wealthy landowners in many Third World countries!

6. Peace between nations is linked to a *just international order*. (GS 83-87)

7. The *vocation of Christians* in the political community is to work for a *just social order*. (GS 74)

8. The Church willingly *relinquishes special political privileges* in Catholic countries when its witness to the Gospel so demands (GS 76). Considering its past history, this is a remarkable renunciation for the Church to make, especially in Catholic Spain, Italy, and Latin America.

◆

Practical Results

Among the results of *Gaudium et Spes* committing the church to a new relationship with the world and to social justice and the transformation of society are the following:

- The three pastoral letters by the United States bishops: *Challenge to Peace (1983)*, *Economic Justice for All (1986)*, and *A Century of Social Teaching (1990)*;

- Religious priests and sisters began moving in great numbers from their traditional apostolates in schools and hospitals to live with the poor and to work for social justice and human rights, particularly in Latin America;

- Dioceses throughout the world formed Peace and Justice Commissions, while the Vatican established the Pontifical Council for Justice and Peace;

- In his world travels John Paul II constantly emphasizes justice, human rights, peace among nations, the plight of the oppressed poor of the world;

- Lay Catholics, both young and old, became "conscientized" and generously gave time and effort to a variety of social works.

100 Years of Catholic Social Teaching, 1891-1991[1]

A recent outline-summary of papal social encyclicals carried the intriguing title: *Our Best Kept Secret, the Rich Heritage of Catholic Social Teaching*. And so it is! The majority of Catholics in the United States are unaware that over a period of 100 years the church has developed a rich teaching on social, economic, political and cultural affairs. This fact was clear from the surprise and criticism by many United States Catholics at the bishops' two important letters: *Challenge to Peace* and *Economic Justice for All*. Yet, to be an educated Catholic in today's world, one needs to know his or her "rich heritage of Catholic social teaching."

Papal **encyclicals** are official letters written by popes to Catholics throughout the world. They contain the ordinary authoritative teaching of the church and are meant to educate Catholics and to serve as a guide in conscience formation. An encyclical is often known by its Latin title taken from the opening words, as *Rerum Novarum*, "of new things," in 1891. In the following survey we shall give both the English and Latin titles of each encyclical.

As we read these summaries, it will be helpful and interesting to look for two things: one, the recurring basic principles of the dignity of the human person and the human rights that flow from such dignity, the social nature of human persons, and our responsibility for all persons in the one human family; two, how social teaching "develops" from letter to letter to meet changing social, economic, and political realities.

Encyclicals That Influenced Vatican II and "Church in the Modern World"

• 1891, *"The Condition of Labor" (Rerum Novarum*, Of New Things), Pope Leo XIII.

The terrible poverty and exploitation of workers by profit-hungry employers in the Industrial Revolution in Europe prompted Pope Leo XIII to write this first-ever social justice encyclical in the history of the Catholic Church. He stressed the promotion of human dignity through just distribution of wealth. He insisted that workers have basic human rights from natural law, which recognizes that all humans are equal: the right to work, to own private property, to receive a just wage, to organize into workers' associations. Both employers and employees have rights and responsibilities. Leo stated that the church has the right to speak out on social issues, for its role is to teach social principles and to bring the social classes together. Public authority must defend the rights of workers and promote the common good of society.

---

1. See Claudia Carlen, *The Papal Encyclicals* Vol. II, 1878-1903; Vol III, 1903-1939; Vol. IV, 1939-1958; Vol. V, 1958-1981; (Wilmington, N.C.: McGrath Publishing Co., 1981).

• 1931, *"The Reconstruction of the Social Order," (Quadragesimo Anno,* "the 40th year" after Leo XIII's letter), Pope Pius XI.

This letter responded to the Great Depression beginning in 1929 that shook the economic and social foundations of society throughout the world. After calling attention to the impact *Rerum Novarum* had on society, civil authorities, and unions, Pius XI treated capital and labor as needing each other, property rights, the deteriorating condition of workers, and a just wage able to support families. He insisted that the state has the responsibility to reform the social order since the proper ordering of economic affairs cannot be left to free enterprise alone. He strongly condemned both capitalism (its free competition has destroyed itself and made the state a slave serving greed) and socialism (communism condones violence and abolishes private property). Pius introduced the new concept of **subsidiarity**, that problems should be solved on the local level first, rather than by centralized authority.

• 1961, *"Christianity and Social Progress" (Mater et Magistra,* Mother and Teacher), Pope John XXIII.

John XXIII issued his first encyclical commemorating the 70th anniversary of Leo XIII's encyclical in response to the severe imbalance between the rich and poor in the world. John's contribution was to internationalize Catholic social teaching by treating for the first time the extreme poverty of millions in the nonindustrialized nations of Asia, Africa, and Latin America, especially of the world's farmers, and the resulting disparity between rich and poor nations. He said it was the duty of wealthy, industrialized nations to help poor, nonindustrialized countries. He condemned the arms race since arms-spending contributes to poverty; peace would be possible if the economic imbalances among nations were righted. He urged a reconstruction of social relationships according to the principles of Catholic social teaching and stated the responsibility of individual Christians to work for a more just world. This letter had a great influence on Vatican II's *The Church in the Modern World.*

The effect of John's encyclical was explosive. Right-wing Catholics were outraged. Their attitude was expressed in the phrase "Mater si, Magistra no," that is, the church as mother yes, as teacher, no! Perhaps because of his peasant background, certainly because of his openness to the Spirit and his understanding of gospel values, John realized that Catholic social teaching needed a new orientation because of changed world conditions. For example, "concern for the rights of property owners had taken precedence over concern for the poor; concern for stability had taken precedence over concern for justice."[2]

---

2. Donal Dorr, *The Social Justice Agenda* (Maryknoll, NY: Orbis Books, 1991), 50.

John's new emphasis and new direction in social teaching involved distancing the church from right-wing political forces. An element of this was his strong insistence that the right to own property is subordinate to the principle that the goods of the earth are intended for the use and benefit of all. Leo XIII had minimized this principle because of his fear of socialism. Pope John was criticized for seeming to be in favor of something like a welfare state. A result was that "for the first time in at least a hundred years the Church seemed to lean more towards the left than towards the right. It was at this moment that the Church began to have new allies and new enemies." [3]

- 1963, *"Peace on Earth" (Pacem in Terris,* Peace on Earth), Pope John XXIII.

With his characteristic world vision and ecumenical spirit, John XXIII for the first time addressed this encyclical to "all people of good will" and not just to Catholics. It followed two Cold War events: the erection of the Berlin Wall in August 1961 and the Cuban missile crisis in October 1962. "Its optimistic tone and development of a philosophy of rights made a significant impression on Catholics and non-Catholics alike."[4] Pope John insisted that peace must be founded on the social order established by God, an order "founded on truth, built according to justice, vivified and integrated in charity, and put into practice in freedom." Using reason and the natural law, John listed rights and duties to be followed by individuals, public authorities, national governments, and the world community.[5] He urged that the United Nations be strengthened and insisted that justice, right reason, and human dignity demand that the arms-race cease.

Encyclicals Influenced by Vatican II

- 1967, *"The Development of Peoples,"* (*Populorum Progressio*), Pope Paul VI.

This, the first encyclical devoted to international development, is one of the most important and radical of all papal documents. Paul VI proposed a carefully thought out theology of development for the poor nations of the world. He coined the famous phrase "development is the new name for peace." For the root of world conflicts is poverty; the growing disparity between rich and poor nations tempts the poor to violence and revolution. Paul stated unambiguously that "the superfluous wealth of rich countries should be placed at the service of poor nations"

---

3. *Ibid.,* 51.
4. Michael Schultheis, ed., *Our Best Kept Secret, the Rich Heritage of Catholic Social Teaching* (Washington, D.C.: Center for Concern, 1985), 40.
5. *Ibid.*

(49). He condemned the type of capitalism that "considers profit as the key motive for economic progress, competition as the supreme law of economics, and private ownership of the means of production as an absolute right that has no limits and carries no corresponding social obligation" (26). He called for "basic reforms" and the establishment of "an international morality based on justice and equity" (81).

In this spirit, Paul VI took the remarkable stand that the poor have the right to revolution if all else fails. Paul also clarified the church's social mission. Admitting that the church was not competent to propose concrete solutions to social problems, he stressed that its mission is to be a moral critic and prophet to the world and to be an insistent voice for Catholics to make a strong commitment to the values of justice and human rights and to participate actively in the struggle for a more humane world.

• 1971, *"A Call to Action," (Octogesima Adveniens,* the "coming 80th" year commemoration of Leo XIII's *Rerum Novarum),* Pope Paul VI.

In this document, Paul introduced several important new ideas to Catholic social teaching. Since economic problems call for political solutions, he encouraged individual Christians to become involved in the political struggle for social justice. Another new concept is Paul's acknowledgement that as pope he may not be able to propose solutions that are applicable everywhere; rather each local church should judge what is necessary and act accordingly. This is an important ecclesiological principle! A pope has stated officially that the Vatican does not have all the answers for the universal church and that therefore local churches must have autonomy and freedom to act.

• 1981, *"On Human Work," (Laborem Exercens,* Doing Work), Pope John Paul II.

As a worker himself in a stone quarry in Poland before he became a priest, John Paul II speaks from personal experience. This encyclical, commemorating the 90th anniversary of Leo XIII's letter and written almost entirely by the pope himself, is a clear statement of John Paul II's thinking on the social question. He affirms the dignity of work which expresses and increases human dignity and makes life more human. Work fulfills God's command in the Hebrew book of *Genesis* to "subdue the earth" and makes family life possible. He strongly criticizes both capitalism and Marxism, which treat humans as mere instruments of production.

In his treatment of work he was concrete and specific: wages must be enough to support a family, working mothers should be given special care; workers deserve health care, right to leisure, pension, accident insurance, decent working environment; disabled people should be able to work; people have the right to leave their native countries in search of a better livelihood. John Paul strongly supported the right to unionize, and while affirming the right to private property, subordinated it to the right of common use. A major contribution was a detailed spirituality of work, which closed this remarkable encyclical.

• 1987, *"On Social Concern,"* (*Sollicitudo Rei Socialis,* Care for the Social Order), Pope John Paul II.

Written to commemorate the 20th anniversary of Paul VI's *The Development of Peoples,* John Paul II's second social encyclical calls attention to the failure of development: the widening gap between the northern and southern hemispheres, global debt that forces nations to export capital, unemployment and underemployment. Underdevelopment abounds because of East-West militarism, imperialism, neocolonialism, and exaggerated national security concerns.

John Paul II criticizes the West for its growing selfish isolation and the East for ignoring its duty to alleviate human misery. In promoting the arms-race, both East and West contribute to the millions of refugees worldwide and to increased terrorism. He singled out "super-development" in the excessive availability of goods leading to consumerism and waste. He called attention to the "structures of sin" and noted that international trade discriminates against developing countries. He stated that "the characteristic principle of Christian social doctrine" is that "the goods of this world are originally meant for all."

• 1991, *"The 100th Year,"* (*Centesimus Annus*), Pope John Paul II.

To commemorate the 100th anniversary of the Church's first social encyclical, John Paul II stated that the church's social teaching is an essential part of the Christian message. He reflected on the causes of the failure of Communism. He reaffirmed the state's responsibility to establish a framework in law to conduct its economic affairs, the decisive role of trade unions in labor negotiations, and the church's preferential option for the poor.

The U.S. Bishops' Three Letters

Inspired by Vatican II's *Church in the Modern World,* the National Conference of Catholic Bishops (NCCB) in the United States produced three significant documents. The first two featured a totally new methodology: the bishops invited experts to advise them and to criticize the various drafts of the documents.

• 1983, *"The Challenge of Peace: God's Promise and Our Response."*

This is an extraordinary document on many accounts. The bishops dealt with nuclear war which "threatens the existence of our planet . . . a more menacing threat than any the world has known" (3). Second, the document was the result of a long process of consultation with many groups, especially top U.S. administration officials and military and university experts. Third, the bishops developed a theology of peace from the Bible, from systematic and moral theology and ecclesiology, and from the experience and insight of Catholics in the peace movement. Fourth, they stated that the church's traditional "just war" theory cannot be applied to the massive destructive power of a nuclear war.

They ruled out as morally unjustifiable: the use of nuclear weapons against population centers; a retaliatory strike; a first nuclear strike. They originally condemned the possession of nuclear weapons as deterrent against a nuclear strike; but under pressure from the White House and the Vatican, which was pressured by the German bishops, they modified their position to permit possessing nuclear weapons as deterrent provided that a sincere effort is made toward full nuclear disarmament. The arms-race was condemned as ineffective for peace, as inciting to nuclear use, and as ultimately taking money from programs to help the poor.

• 1986, *Economic Justice for All: Catholic Social Teaching and the U.S. Economy.*

The document stressed that the basic norm for the health of a nation is how it treats its poor and powerless; that society has a moral obligation to ensure that no one is hungry, homeless, unemployed; that all citizens have responsibility for all members of the human family. This document was remarkable in that the bishops invited experts to advise them and held listening sessions across the country attended by economists, university professors, business executives and corporation presidents to comment on and criticize the second draft of the document. Such a process blunted the often-heard criticism that bishops have no competence to speak on economic issues. The bishops stressed that they "speak as moral teachers, not economic technicians."

The bishops laid down six moral principles for economic life:

- Every economic decision and institution must be judged on whether it protects or undermines the dignity of the human person.
- Human dignity can be realized and protected only in community.
- All people have a right to participate in the economic life of society.
- All members of society have a special obligation to the poor and vulnerable.

- Human rights are the minimum conditions for life in community.
- Society as a whole, acting through public and private institutions, has the moral responsibility to enhance human dignity and protect human rights.

To accomplish these, the bishops called for *conversion,* which they described as a profound "change of heart" (23), "to think differently and to act differently (25), "a lifelong process" (24). They asked Catholics "to join with us in service to those in need. Let us reach out personally to the hungry and homeless, to the poor and powerless, and to the troubled and the vulnerable. In serving them, we serve Christ" (26). The bishops set a noble ideal for Catholics. "As a Church, we must be people after God's own heart. . . ."(24).

The document contained memorable and eloquent passages and phrases:

> Every perspective on economic life that is human, moral, and Christian must be shaped by three questions: What does the economy do *for* people? What does it do *to* people? And how do people *participate* in it? (1)

> We are called to shape a constituency of conscience, measuring every policy by how it touches the least, the last, and the left-out among us. (Introduction 27)

> . . . the justice of a society is tested by the treatment of the poor. (Introduction 16)

- *1990, A Century of Social Teaching: A Common Heritage, a Continuing Challenge*[6]

The contribution of this brief document is its summary analysis of Catholic social teaching in terms of six basic themes that pervade all the documents we have been considering. The document's introduction to these themes highlights the nature and development of the church's social teaching over a 100-year period.

> Our Catholic social teaching is more than a set of documents. It is a living tradition of thought and action. The Church's social vision has developed and grown over time, responding to changing circumstances and emerging problems—including developments in human work, new economic questions, war and peace in a nuclear age, and poverty and development in a shrinking world. While the subjects have changed, some basic principles and themes have emerged within this tradition. (Basic Themes)

---

6. U.S. Bishops, "A Century of Social Teaching: A Common Heritage, A Continuing Challenge" in *U.S. Bishops, Contemporary Catholic Social Teaching* (Washington, DC: U.S. Catholic Conference, 1991), 1-9.

The explanatory passages after each of the following six themes are excerpts from the bishops' letter. Their clear, down-to-earth language, ethical vision, and compassionate concern merit our including these direct quotations:

- *The Life and Dignity of the Human Person*

"In the Catholic social vision, the human person is central, the clearest reflection of God among us. Each person possesses a basic dignity that comes from God. . . . The test of every institution or policy is whether it enhances or threatens human life and human dignity. We believe people are more important than things."

- *The Rights and Responsibilities of the Human Person*

"Flowing from our God-given dignity, each person has basic rights and responsibilities. These include the rights to freedom of conscience and religious liberty, to raise a family, to immigrate, to live free from unfair discrimination, and to have a share of earthly goods sufficient for oneself and one's family. People have a fundamental right to life and to those things that make life truly human: food, clothing, housing, health care, education, security, social services, and employment. Corresponding to these rights are duties and responsibilities — to one another, to our families, and to the larger society, to respect the rights of others and to work for the common good."

- *The Call to Family, Community, and Participation*

"The human person is not only sacred, but social. We realize our dignity and rights in relationship with others, in community . . . The family has major contributions to make in addressing questions of social justice. It is where we learn and act on our values. . . We also have the right and responsibility to participate in and contribute to the broader communities in society. . . A central test of political, legal, and economic institutions is what they do *to* people, what they do *for* people, and how people *participate* in them."

- *The Dignity of Work and the Rights of Workers*

"Work is more than a way to make a living; it is an expression of our dignity and a form of continuing participation in God's creation. People have the right to decent and productive work, to decent and fair wages, to private property and economic initiative. Workers have the strong support of the Church in forming and joining union and worker associations of their choosing in the exercise of their dignity and rights. . . . In Catholic teaching, the economy exists to serve people, not the other way around."

• *The Option for the Poor and Vulnerable*

"Poor and vulnerable people have a special place in Catholic social teaching. A basic moral test of a society is how its most vulnerable members are faring. . . . Our tradition calls us to put the needs of the poor and vulnerable first. As Christians, we are called to respond to the needs of all our sisters and brothers, but those with the greatest needs require the greatest response."

• *Solidarity*

"We are one human family, whatever our national, racial, ethnic, economic, and ideological difference. We are our brothers' and sisters' keepers (cf. *Genesis* 4:9). In a linked and limited world, our responsibilities to one another cross national and other boundaries. Violent conflict and the denial of dignity and rights to people anywhere on the globe diminish each of us. This emerging theme of solidarity, so strongly articulated by Pope John Paul II, expresses the core of the church's concern for world peace, global development, environment, and international human rights. . . . 'Loving our neighbor' has global dimensions in an interdependent world."

Thus Catholic social teaching, according to the bishops, offers "fundamental values that test every system, every nation, and every community. It puts the needs of the poor first. It values persons over things. It emphasizes morality over technology, asking not simply what *can* we do, but what *ought* we do. It calls us to measure our lives not by what we have, but by who we are; how we love one another; and how we contribute to the common good, to justice in our community, and to peace in our world."

The Church's Commitment to Social Justice

The preceding three sections can be summarized in the phrase "social justice." Catholic social teaching is ultimately about social justice. The most explicit statements committing the church to social justice came from the 1971 Synod of Bishops and from Pope John Paul II's *Centesimus Annus* in 1991. They deserve repeating.

◆

Action on behalf of justice and participation in the transformation of the world fully appear to us as a constitutive dimension of the preaching of the Gospel, or in other words, of the Church's mission of the redemption of the human race and its liberation from every oppressive situation.[7] . . . To teach

7. Austin Flannery, ed., *Vatican Council II, More Conciliar Documents, Vol. 2* (Northport, NY: Costello Publishing Co., 1982), 696.

and spread her social doctrine pertains to the Church's evangelizing mission and is an essential part of the Christian message, since this doctrine . . . situates daily work and struggles for justice in the context of bearing witness to Christ our Savior. (*Centesimus Annus*)

◆

Note the terms: action, justice, participation, transformation of the world, the gospel, church's mission, liberation, oppressive, social doctrine, essential, struggles for justice. The church formally commits itself to act for justice, to transform the unjust structures of society, to free humans from all forms of oppression, to teach its social doctrine. Such action is an essential part of its mission as given by Christ to preach the good news and save the human family.

What is social justice? *Justice* means giving a person what is his or her due, one's basic rights; *social* refers to the relationships between people in society. Social justice then deals with the obligations of individuals and groups (governments, nations) to apply human and gospel values to the structures and institutions of society. Donal Dorr lists 14 major issues of social justice in today's world: the gap between the rich and poor; international debt; oppression (colonialism, repressive governments) and struggles for liberation and freedom; violence or nonviolence; disarmament; justice for women; racism; human rights (economic, cultural, social, religious); the population explosion; ecology; refugees; unemployment; alternate model of development from the capitalist model; justice in the Church.[8]

The authors of *Our Best Kept Secret* list 10 major lessons or key emphases that characterize Catholic social teaching today. These highlight the broad scope of social justice and call attention to the values on which the church's social teaching is based.

- *Link of Religious and Social Dimensions of Life.* This is the basis of the now well-known expression "the faith that does justice."

- *Dignity of the Human Person.* The human person is at the center of social justice.

- *Option for the Poor.* The poor are those economically disadvantaged who suffer oppression and powerlessness; they are the special object of God's love and of the church's concern for social justice.

- *Link of Love and Justice.* It is impossible to love our neighbor without giving him or her what is their due in justice. True love demands justice.

---

8. Dorr, *The Social Justice Agenda*, 7-41.

• *Promotion of the Common Good.* Social justice promotes all those conditions of social life needed for women and men to live in a fully human way.

• *Political Participation.* Social justice demands democratic participation of all peoples in the decisions that intimately affect their lives.

• *Economic Justice.* The economy exists for people; social justice demands economic justice.

• *Stewardship.* The resources of the earth are for all people, not just rich individuals or nations. Social justice calls individuals and nations to an equal share of material goods.

• *Global Solidarity.* We belong to one human family and as such have mutual obligations to promote the development of all people on planet earth. Social justice extends to international structures and institutions.

• *Promotion of Peace.* Peace is the fruit of justice. Most wars are fought because of glaring social injustice within or between nations.

Consequences of the Catholic Church's Commitment to Social Justice

We are now in a position to evaluate the practical effects of the century-long tradition of Catholic social teaching and of Vatican II's *Gaudium et Spes* encouraging Catholics to become actively involved in the world and its needs. These consequences point to the new post-Vatican II church coming into existence and the new way to be Catholic in the 21st century.

◆

Results of Commitment to Social Justice

• Catholics became "socially aware" and began to be concerned with justice issues at home and globally. Above all they became socially sophisticated as to the causes of injustice: for example, the role of wealthy nations of the northern hemisphere through business practices of the transnational corporations, the policies of the International Monetary Fund and the World Bank, and the United States backing military dictatorships in the name of anti-Communism but in reality to protect economic interests.

• Priests and especially sisters of religious orders and congregations left their traditional institutional apostolates in schools, urban parishes, and hospitals to live and work with the poor in city barrios and in mountain villages of Latin America.

• Individual Catholics, priests and laypeople, became social activists, protesting injustices locally and nationally; they were frequently jailed for their witness.

- A noticeable shift occurred from an individualist morality and emphasis on sexual sins to a concern for justice, to recognizing injustice as gravely sinful, and to a global vision of human life.
- The Catholic Church shifted from an alliance with the state and the wealthy classes in so-called Catholic countries to a voluntary renunciation of special privileges in church-state relationships. In many countries throughout the world the church became the church of the poor.
- These shifts and the commitment to justice caused tension, misunderstanding, and division within the church and criticism from the rich and powerful and from right-wing Catholic groups.
- In becoming a force for justice throughout the world, the Catholic Church has become a church of martyrs, particularly in Latin America. Priests, nuns, even bishops, and thousands of Christian men, women, and children have been brutally murdered.

◆

The U.S. bishops, in *A Century of Social Teaching,* issued this challenge to American Catholics regarding social justice:

> Social justice is not something Catholics pursue simply through parish committees and diocesan programs, although these structures can help us to act on our faith. Our social vocation takes flesh in our homes and schools, businesses and unions, offices and factories, colleges and universities, and in community organizations and professional groups. As believers, we are called to bring our values into the marketplace and the political arena, into community and family life, using our everyday opportunities and responsibilities, our voices and votes to defend human life, human dignity, and human rights. We are called to be a leaven, applying Christian values and virtues in every aspect of our lives.
>
> We are also called to weave our social teaching into every dimension of Catholic life, especially worship, education, planning, and evangelization. The Holy Father can teach; bishops can preach; but unless our social doctrine comes alive in personal conversion and common action, it will lack real credibility and effectiveness.[9]

Summary

In the *Pastoral Constitution on the Church in the Modern World,* the Second Vatican Council gave a new direction for the church's mission by committing Catholics to become immersed in the human concerns of this world in order to build God's kingdom of justice and peace. Underlying this change from a more individualist piety was the three-fold theology of

---

9. *A Century of Social Teaching,* 10.

seeing God at work in the great social and human needs of vast numbers of people today, of recognizing the dignity of every human person created by God, and of a firmer realization that God's plan for the human family involves social justice and the transformation of society. As a consequence, we called attention to eight important emphases of *Gaudium et Spes*. Vatican II's call to justice issues did not occur in a vacuum but was prepared for by four papal encyclicals that addressed major social issues and formed a nascent body of Catholic social teaching. In turn the Second Vatican Council profoundly influenced five significant papal letters that further developed Catholic social teaching.

Following the lead of Vatican II and Popes Paul VI and John Paul II, the bishops of the United States produced, with far-reaching consultation of experts, two impressive letters challenging the richest, most powerful nation on earth to meet the nuclear threat by serious steps for peace and to do far more to bring about economic justice for all Americans. To achieve their moral principles for just economic life, the bishops called for a profound conversion of attitudes, values, and lifestyle. Their third letter was valuable in identifying basic themes at the heart of 100 years of Catholic social teaching. Catholic social teaching is best summarized and expressed in the term "social justice," to which Vatican II recommitted the church with dramatic consequences for the church in the turbulent years since the Council.

For Discussion

1. Do you think the Catholic Church's emphasis today on social justice issues is correct and necessary? Or should the church return to a greater emphasis on the personal religious life of its members?

2. Evaluate the involvement in the struggle for justice and human rights in El Salvador of the six university Jesuits murdered by government troops November 1989 in San Salvador.

3. Is the popes' criticism of the abuses of capitalism as a recurring theme in their letters justified?

4. Do the wealthy nations of the northern hemisphere have a responsibility to the underdeveloped nations of the southern hemisphere? in justice? in Christian love? in solidarity with fellow humans? in practical self-interest?

5. Do you consider the practical suggestions made by the U.S. bishops in *Economic Justice for All* doable and necessary? Or are they too idealistic and impractical?

6. Do you agree with the 14 issues of social justice today listed by Donal Dorr? What is their connection with social justice?

For Action

1. Wait on table as a volunteer at a "dining room" or soup kitchen that serves a daily hot meal to street people and the poor. Try to find out why there are so many poor persons in our society.

2. Read the U.S. Bishops' 1986 letter, *Economic Justice for All*. Evaluate their six moral principles for a just economic life.

3. Walk through a supermarket noticing row after row bulging with food. Then go to a big department store, take the escalator to the top floor and work your way down, observing the superabundance of clothes, cosmetics, luxury items, etc. Then read John Paul II's *On Social Concern*. Is there any connection?

Further Reading

Pope Paul VI. *On the Development of Peoples*, Commentary by Barbara Ward. Glen Rock, NJ: Paulist Press, 1967.

John Paul II. *On Human Work*. Washington, DC: U.S. Catholic Conference, 1982.

_____ *On Social Concern*. Washington, DC: U.S. Catholic Conference, 1988.

National Conference of Catholic Bishops. *Economic Justice for All*. Washington, DC: U.S. Catholic Conference, 1986.

Coleman, John, ed. *One Hundred Years of Catholic Social Thought, Celebration and Challenge*. Maryknoll, NY: Orbis Books, 1991.

Dorr, Donal. *The Social Justice Agenda: Justice, Ecology, Power and the Church*, Maryknoll, NY: Orbis Books, 1991.

Schultheis, Michael. *Our Best Kept Secret, the Rich Heritage of Catholic Social Teaching*, Washington, DC: Center for Concern, 1985.

Part III

Vatican II
and Church Leadership

C H A P T E R   10

The Church's VIP's

Whoever wants to be a bishop aspires to a noble task: a bishop must be irreproachable, married only once, of even temper, self-controlled, modest and hospitable. He should be a good teacher. He must not be addicted to drink. He ought not be contentious but rather gentle, a man of peace. Nor can he be someone who loves money . . . He must also be well thought of by those outside the Church. —1st Letter to Timothy, 3: 1-7

Jesus Christ, the eternal shepherd, established his holy Church by sending forth the apostles. . . . He willed that their successors, namely the bishops, should be shepherds in his Church even to the consummation of the world. —*Lumen Gentium* 18

This sacred Synod teaches that by divine institution bishops have succeeded to the place of the Apostles as shepherds of the Church. —*Lumen Gentium* 20

Introduction

Bishops are the VIP's (Very Important Persons) in the church of Christ. Throughout the long history of the church, they had much influence and power, often civil power as well as spiritual. In the great squares of European and South American cities, one sees on one side the seat of civil government and on the other the bishop's palace and his cathedral, the bishop's own church in which his chair (*cathedra*, symbol of his spiritual power), had a special place similar to the king's throne. Following this analogy, bishops came to be called "princes" of the church. In the Middle Ages bishops were men of wealth and power, often as civil rulers filling the vacuum of civil leadership owing to the barbarian invasions. This obviously led to many abuses and ultimately the Protestant Reformation. But fortunately, throughout church history many bishops were men of great learning and saintliness as well as strong leaders: St. Augustine, bishop of Hippo, North Africa; St. Ambrose, bishop of Milan, Italy; Ignatius of Antioch and Cyprian of Carthage; Charles Borromeo of Milan. Bishops have been heroic apostles in spreading the gospel of Christ and powerful defenders of the church against kings, oppressive governments and dictators out to destroy the church. Bishops by the thousands have died as martyrs in defense of the people of God.

Today we think of strong-souled bishops who have staunchly stood up against Communist oppression to defend their Christian flock: Archbishop Wyczinski of Poland, Cardinal Archbishop Mindzenty of Hungary; Bishop Walsh, martyred Maryknoll bishop in China; Archbishop Dominic Tang of Canton, China, imprisoned for 22 years by Mao's Communists; and most recently Archbishop Oscar Romero of El Salvador, who was murdered for defending the human rights of his impoverished *campesino* flock.

Bishops constitute the leadership structure of the Catholic Church; as such they are an essential part of the church established by Christ. The Roman Catholic, Orthodox, and Anglican churches have bishops. But since most Protestant groups do not have bishops ordained by the sacrament of holy orders in the apostolic succession, a two-fold major issue in the ecumenical movement is whether Protestant pastors and ministers are validly ordained to celebrate real Eucharists and whether the order of bishops is essential and necessary to the Church of Christ. The question of **episcopacy** is therefore crucial to the future union of the Christian churches and relations between **episcopal** and non-episcopal churches.

We shall attempt to answer these questions: Why did bishops have such influence throughout the history of the church? Why are they influential and important today? Are they in fact *essential* to the Church of Christ? Where did bishops come from? What is their authority and responsibility? What is their relationship to the pope within the Catholic Church?

◆

Preview: This chapter deals with a very important and complex issue for today's church. We shall treat this topic in three parts: Vatican II's extensive theological teaching on bishops and the conclusions that follow; the high responsibility bishops have in the church and the personal qualities they need to fulfill their office; and issues of considerable importance in the church today involving the office of bishops.

◆

Theological Teaching of Vatican II on Bishops

We need first to put Vatican II's teaching in historical perspective. Vatican Council I in 1869-1870 developed a rather full teaching on the bishop of Rome, the pope. But before it could take up the complementary teaching on bishops, the Council was interrupted by Garibaldi marching on Rome, forcing the bishops to flee and terminating the Council. Thus Vatican II, after considerable debate and strong opposition, restored a much-needed balance through its positive teaching on bishops. The decisive vote on four questions occurred on October 30, 1963.[1]

Several important terms will help us understand the Council's teaching. A bishop heads a geographical area called a *diocese*; an archbishop is simply a bishop of a major city who accordingly heads that *archdiocese* (Archbishop Roger Mahony heads the archdiocese of Los Angeles). The entire world is thus divided geographically into dioceses or archdioceses headed by bishops or archbishops. Some dioceses contain large numbers of Catholics, others relatively few. Some dioceses, especially in so-called missionary countries where the Catholic population is small, cover vast areas of land or sea. The United States currently has 31 archdioceses and 145 dioceses.

Vatican II's well-developed theology of the office of bishops is found in chapter 3 of the *Constitution on the Church,* entitled "The Hierarchical Structure of the Church with Special Reference to the **Episcopate**," numbers 18-27. Because of the importance of this teaching and that the reader may experience the Council "doing theology" in its carefully nuanced statements, we shall quote extensively from the document. The numbers are those of *Lumen Gentium,* chapter 3.

1. Bishops are successors of the 12 Apostles chosen by Jesus

"Jesus Christ, the eternal shepherd, established his holy church by sending forth the apostles as he himself had been sent by the Father (Cf. John 20:21). He willed that their successors, namely the bishops, should be shepherds in his church . . ." (18). The most accurate title for bishops is therefore "successors of the Apostles" (18).

But where does the Council get this title since nowhere in the Christian scriptures is found the literal words "successors of the Apostles"? The Council uses a theological reasoning process: "That divine mission

---

1. Whether episcopal consecration is the highest grade of the sacraments of orders: yes, 2,123; no, 34. 2. Whether every bishop, who is in communion with all the bishops and the pope, belongs to the body or college of bishops: yes, 2,049; no, 104. 3. Whether the college of bishops succeeds the college of the apostles and, together with the pope, has full and supreme power over the whole church: yes, 1,808; no, 336. 4. Whether the college of bishops, in union with the pope, has this power by divine right: yes, 1,710; no, 408. The sizeable "no" votes show the complexity of the issues and the opposition of traditional bishops fearful of lessening papal authority.

entrusted by Christ to the apostles will last until the end of the world (Mt. 28:20). . . . For this reason the apostles took care to appoint successors . . ." (20) The argumentation goes like this. In solemn words Jesus gave the apostles the "great mission": "Full authority has been given to me both in heaven and on earth; go, therefore, and make disciples of all nations. Baptize . . . [and] teach them. . . . And know that I am with you always until the end of the world" (Mt. 28:18-20). The mission of preaching the good news to all peoples and baptizing them is a permanent one, to last until the end of the world. Therefore, successors are needed since the apostles will die. It is thus clear that Christ intended the Apostles to have successors in fulfilling the mission until the end of time.

To stress the importance of this succession, the Council makes an official *dogmatic* teaching: "This sacred Synod teaches that *by divine institution* bishops have succeeded to the place of the apostles as shepherds of the church and that he who hears them hears Christ and he who rejects them rejects Christ and him who sent Christ" (20, emphasis added). Divine institution means that God, not humans, has set up the office of bishops in the church. Bishops are thus *essential* to the church established by Christ. This solemn teaching has important ecumenical implications, as we noted in chapter 8.

2. Apostolic Succession

From the teaching that bishops are the successors of the apostles comes the theological concept of **apostolic succession**: the office given by Christ to the 12 Apostles continues in the living church today in the persons of bishops. Or in popular terms, there exists a succession of properly ordained bishops, from the 12 Apostles to today's bishops, and conversely, from today's ordained bishops back to the Apostles. In treating this apostolic succession, *Lumen Gentium* is very careful to avoid the historical impossibility of showing there exists an *unbroken* line of ordained bishops back to one or more of the Apostles. Though the Church attaches great importance to the list of bishops in a given diocese, and in some ancient dioceses one can trace succession of bishops to the 3rd or even 2nd century (historical records are lacking for the 1st century). Nor is there evidence of whom the Apostles ordained. Accordingly, the Council refers simply to "the office of those . . . appointed to the episcopate in a sequence running back to the beginning of the church" (20). It is thus more accurate to speak of the episcopal college (group) succeeding the apostolic college (group) rather than emphasizing lines of succession for individual bishops. With this nuancing, *Lumen Gentium* concludes: "Thus, as St. Irenaeus [2nd-century bishop] testifies, through those who were appointed bishops by the Apostles and through their successors down to our own time, the apostolic tradition is manifested and preserved throughout the world" (20).

3. The Episcopal College and Collegiality

Theology has come to call the 12 Apostles viewed as a group the apostolic college, after the Latin *collegium* or group. In the words of the Council "These apostles he [the Lord Jesus] formed after the manner of a college or fixed group, over which he placed Peter. . ." (19). In turn, the bishops of the world, when united with the bishop of Rome, form an **episcopal college** (*episcopos*, meaning "one who *oversees*," is the Greek word for bishop). "Just as, by the Lord's will, St. Peter and the other apostles constituted one apostolic college, so in a similar way the Roman Pontiff [pope] as the successor of Peter, and the bishops as the successors of the apostles are joined together. The *collegial* nature and meaning of the episcopal order found expression in the very ancient practice by which bishops . . . were linked with one another and with the bishop of Rome by the bonds of unity, charity, and peace" (22, emphasis added). From this understanding of bishops, in union with the pope, comes the very important concept of collegiality.

Vatican II strongly championed collegiality. Indeed many commentators on *Lumen Gentium* say that its most important achievement for the theology of the church was to restore within the Catholic Church the doctrine of episcopal collegiality. This is reflected in the Council's statement that bishops, together with the pope, govern the worldwide church (18) and have the highest authority over it, especially in an ecumenical council. "The supreme authority with which this college is empowered over the whole church is exercised in a solemn way through an ecumenical council" (22). The teaching of Vatican II is thus authoritative for Catholics.

4. Responsibilities of Bishops

Bishops as shepherds have a three-fold responsibility: to teach, to lead worship, to govern. The Council states: ". . .bishops have therefore taken up the service of the community, presiding in place of God over the flock whose shepherds they are, as teachers of doctrine, priests of sacred worship, and officers of good order . . . the apostles' office of nurturing the church is permanent and was meant to be exercised without interruption by the sacred order of bishops" (20).

Bishops receive this three-fold office of teaching, leading worship, and governing from the Holy Spirit by episcopal ordination by means of a ritual of three bishops placing their hands on the head of the person being ordained. "This sacred Synod teaches that by episcopal consecration is conferred the *fullness* of the sacrament of orders" (20, emphasis added). This formal teaching settles a theological question about the difference in the ordinations of priests and bishops. It also emphasizes a controverted ecumenical problem: most Protestants do not accept ordination to be a sacrament and hold that a bishop's authority/office comes from the Christian congregation.

With such authority and responsibility, "bishops govern the particular churches entrusted to them as vicars and ambassadors of Christ" (27). Their power is "proper" to them, "ordinary" as coming from their ordination, and "immediate" as coming directly from Christ and his Spirit. The bishop is called "the **Ordinary**" of the diocese to distinguish him from a coadjutor or helper-bishop who has no **jurisdiction** in the diocese. Thus bishops may not interfere in the affairs of other dioceses. Even the pope is careful not to "upstage" a bishop in his own diocese. A delicate, controverted question is to what extent should the pope limit the *exercise* of a bishop's "proper, ordinary, immediate" power in his own diocese. A recent example was Rome's intervention in Archbishop Hunthausen's Seattle archdiocese, an intervention that was happily resolved several years later by Rome restoring full exercise of authority to the archbishop.

5. Teaching Authority of Bishops

Bishops have authority from Christ to preach the gospel and to teach. The Council states that the main duty of a bishop is to preach the good news of Christ. In this capacity they are "authentic teachers, that is, teachers endowed with the authority of Christ" (25). When teaching "in communion with the Roman Pontiff . . . in matters of faith and morals, the bishops speak in the name of Christ, and the faithful are to accept their teaching and adhere to it with religious assent of soul" (25). The term for this authoritative church teaching is *magisterium*.

Catholics often ask what is the exact nature of bishops' teaching authority. The Council gives a carefully stated answer. "Although individual bishops do not enjoy the prerogative of infallibility, they can nevertheless proclaim Christ's doctrine infallibly," that is, without error. "The infallibility promised to the church resides also in the body of bishops when that body exercises supreme teaching authority," that is, when bishops teach as a "college" in union with the pope (25).

It is thus abundantly clear that bishops have an extremely important, indispensable role in the church. The Council uses a striking metaphor from St. Ignatius, the 2nd-century martyr, to express how Christians should relate to their bishops. "The faithful must 'cling to their bishop' as the church does to Christ, and Jesus Christ to the Father, so that all may harmonize in unity" (27). Such was the extraordinary relationship of the poor suffering peasants of El Salvador with their Archbishop Oscar Romero, who as a true shepherd of the gospel gave his life for his flock.

6. "In Communion With"

This key phrase expresses how the worldwide Catholic Church is united: by the bishops of the world being **in communion with** the pope, the bishop of Rome. This "communion" means that each bishop representing the people of his diocese recognizes the pope as center and foundation of the church's unity. Bishops express this communion by praying for the pope by name in each Mass or Eucharist, by special love and loyalty to the "Holy Father," and by teaching in union with him. *Lumen Gentium* describes how this collegial union of bishops representing their own churches and the pope representing the universal church establishes the unity of the entire worldwide Catholic Church. The statement deserves to be quoted in full.

> The collegial union is apparent also in the mutual relations of the individual bishops with particular churches and with the universal church. The Roman Pontiff, as the successor of Peter, is the perpetual and visible source and foundation of the unity of the bishops and of the multitude of the faithful. The individual bishop, however, is the visible principle and foundation of unity in his particular church, fashioned after the model of the universal church. In and from such individual churches there comes into being the one and only Catholic church. For this reason each individual bishop represents his own church, but all of them together in union with the pope represent the entire church joined in the bond of peace, love, and unity. (23)

One billion Catholics throughout the world are thus united, forming an immense Catholic family through their own bishops, who are united with each other by being in communion with the bishop of Rome, the pope. In somewhat similar fashion, before the bishop of Rome assumed his later position of primacy among other bishops, the Christian Church of the first four centuries was united by the five major patriarchs of Alexandria (Egypt), Antioch (Syria), Constantinople, Jerusalem, and Rome being in communion with each other. The pope at that time was considered the Patriarch of the West, with jurisdiction over Italy and somewhat beyond.

The reality of collegiality and the concept of being "in communion with" took on great practical importance in mainland China when Mao and the Communists came to power. Chinese bishops and priests were given a stark choice: renounce their unity with and loyalty to the pope or go to prison. Many Chinese bishops and priests, as well as lay Catholics, chose to remain in communion with the pope and thus went to prison and suffered untold hardships for over 20 years. One such is Bishop Dominic Tang.

I was privileged to meet with Bishop Tang in Canton, China, in 1980. He had just been released from prison after 22 years, seven of which were in solitary confinement in an effort to "break" him. He was presently confined to the parish house next to the large greystone, gothic-style cathedral which ironically was "his" cathedral prior to his imprisonment. When we had a moment of relative privacy from the Communist officials, he whispered to me: "Tell the Jesuits in Hong Kong that I am still loyal to the Holy Father." He had gone to prison and suffered through those long years to remain "in communion with" the pope. His slim book, *His Inscrutable Ways*, which reports on his first years as bishop of Canton and the difficult prison years, is an eloquent witness to his love of God and the great value he put on being "in communion" with the bishop of Rome.

◆

Bishops: Important Conclusions

• Bishops are an *essential* part of the Church of Christ. Neither the Catholic Church nor the Orthodox Church could and would ever lose the order of episcopacy.

• The Church is thus **hierarchical** or priestly in nature, that is, governed by leaders ordained in the sacrament of holy orders. The Catholic Church is not a democracy, though it can and should use democratic procedures.

• Bishops receive their three-fold mission to teach, sanctify, and govern the Christian faithful and enter the apostolic succession through *sacramental ordination*. A true or valid sacrament of ordination is thus essential for a bishop to be a successor of the Apostles.

• Through the *principle of collegiality*, the Council immensely upgraded the role and authority of bishops within the Catholic Church. Bishops do not receive their authority from the pope. By placing the pope within the college of bishops, the pope is not above the episcopal college. In popular terms, collegiality means that all the bishops form a team with their brother bishop, the pope, in governing the worldwide church. And bishops are supreme in their own churches or dioceses.

• Bishops are thus the church's VIP's and constitute a great advantage for it.

◆

Awesome Responsibility of Bishops

The bishop is the leader of the local church or diocese: as such he is the ultimate person responsible as teacher for proclaiming the good news of Christ to his people and safeguarding the Catholic faith from error; the person ultimately responsible for the quality of the Christian life in all the parishes and thus the administration of the sacraments, especially the Eucharist; the ultimate overseer of the entire functioning of the diocese and of its priests and people; the one who establishes the bond of unity between his local church and the universal church; the one who, as part of the college of bishops, also has responsibility in union with the pope for the worldwide church. Since all these constitute the awesome responsibility of bishops, it is of great importance that highly qualified and worthy men be chosen as bishops. What then are the qualities bishops should have?

Personal Qualities Needed

According to the Code of Canon Law, the official law of the Catholic Church, a bishop must:

- be outstanding in strong faith, good morals, piety, zeal for souls, wisdom, prudence and human virtues and possess those gifts which equip him to fulfill the office in question;
- be held in high esteem;
- be at least 35 years old;
- be a priest ordained for at least five years;
- hold a doctorate or at least a licentiate in sacred Scripture, theology, or canon law, from an approved institute of higher studies, or at least be well-versed in these disciplines.[2]

Archbishop John Quinn of San Francisco gave a more personalized, complete list of qualities in his letter to the priests of the archdiocese of San Francisco in the context of asking them to submit to him names of suitable candidates for being bishops. It may be hard to conceive of one man possessing all these qualities; but this list forcefully illustrates the unique position bishops hold in the church and the importance the church attaches to selecting qualified persons. The following are excerpts from Archbishop Quinn's letter:

> First of all, there should be a firmness of faith. He should be a man of prayer who lives by faith and is able to teach the faith. He must be a man who loves the church and lives by her spirit and teaching. He should be one who is capable of courteous dialogue and is sensitive to the needs of the times. He should feel comfortable with the various changes of the Second Vatican Council and should be capable of growing. He should have a stability of character and, while being open to people and ideas, should not be swayed by pressure or emotion.
>
> He should have sufficient organizational and administrative qualities to be able to serve the needs of the church. He should have

2. *Code of Canon Law* (Washington, D.C.: Canon Law Society of American, 1983), 141, Canon 378, # 1.

good health and emotional stability to be able to work under pressure, while maintaining the necessary balance. He should be able to balance the demands of a positive pluralism with the demands of the necessary unity of faith and charity.

He should be able to preach effectively, and it is an advantage if he can speak more than one language. . . .

He should have some understanding of the social needs of our times and some understanding of the social teaching of the Church.

He should be a priest who is comfortable with his brother priests and shows interest in them. And he should be a man of good judgment.

Temperamentally he should be able to withstand criticism without undue stress, while at the same time being able to weigh it and where indicated, make appropriate changes.

He should relate well to the people and show evidence of priestly zeal and a spirit of service and pastoral generosity, after the example of Christ.

He should show an appreciation of the role of the laity in the Church and be encouraging to them in taking their proper role.

He should have sufficient doctrinal depth to be able to weigh ideas and trends in the light of the faith and teaching of the Church, critical judgment which will enable him to test the spirit, clinging to what is good, rejecting what is evil. He must have the courage to defend the truth and to affirm it in the face of opposition, to preach the word, welcome or unwelcome. He must not be so captured by one aspect of the Gospel as to forget the rest.

In short, he should be a man of integrity of faith, rooted and founded on faith and prayer, a man of service, of apostolic simplicity and courage, balanced and mature, capable of being a bond of unity and charity for priests and people."[3]

Archbishop Quinn is describing the ideal Vatican II bishop; the qualities he gives are those particularly needed by a leader in today's church.

Contemporary Issues Concerning Bishops

1. Choosing Bishops. At present the actual process of choosing a bishop is this. Local diocesan bishops are invited to put names on a list of candidates to be sent to the country's nuncio (pope's representative). When a vacancy in a diocese occurs, the Vatican nuncio, who is either a bishop or archbishop, "engages in wide-ranging consultations" until he comes up with

---

3. October 30, 1986 letter to "My brother Priests" from Archbishop John Quinn of San Francisco.

three names, the *terna*. He then sends these names to the Congregation of Bishops in Rome which may or may not consult further and then forwards the names to the pope, who makes the final choice. Normally the views of the Vatican nuncio or apostolic delegate in each country carry special weight; but in certain key dioceses, the pope seems to have intervened directly and chosen someone not on the *terna*.[4]

Interestingly, it was not always done this way. For the first 1000 years or so, bishops were either elected directly by the people of a given diocese or nominated by an emperor or king or even feudal lord, and then approved by the pope. The 28th canon of Ecumenical Council Lateran II in April 1139, states that bishops shall be elected by cathedral chapters. Even as late as 1829 the pope appointed bishops in only 24 dioceses outside the Papal States.

There is discussion in the Catholic Church about the local dioceses having more say in choosing the bishops they receive, especially in the light of highly unpopular appointments made by Rome in several countries.

2. National Conferences of Bishops. Vatican Council II mandated the formation of conferences of bishops in each country of the world. These conferences are made up of all the bishops in a given country; their purpose is "to foster the Church's mission to mankind by providing the bishops of this country with an opportunity to exchange views and insights of prudence and experience and to exercise in a joint manner their pastoral Office."[5] In the United States the NCCB (National Conference of Catholic Bishops) meets for three days twice a year in Washington, D.C. Besides five executive committees, it has 27 standing committees as diverse as Black Catholics, Doctrine, Ecumenical and Interreligious Affairs, Evangelization, Liturgy, Marriage and Family Life, Migration, Science and Human Values, Women in Society and Church, and 17 ad hoc committees like Aid to the Church in Central and Eastern Europe and the USSR, Catholic Charismatic Renewal, National Collections, Pastoral Response to the Challenge of Proselytism. Thus a great amount of business is discussed and voted on.

The NCCB mandates studies on various church and society issues, publishing letters or documents every year. The most famous recent ones were *The Challenge of Peace*, 1983 and *Economic Justice for All: Pastoral Letter on Catholic Social Teaching and the U.S. Economy*, 1986. Other impressive documents are: *To Teach as Jesus Did: A Pastoral Message on Catholic Education*, 1972; *The Many Faces of AIDS: A Gospel Response*, 1987; *Human Sexuality: A Catholic Perspective for Education and Lifelong Learning*, 1991; *A Pastoral Statement for Catholics on Biblical Fun-*

---

4. Peter Hebblethwaite, *In the Vatican* (London: Sidgwick and Jackson, 1986), 97-99.

5. *The Official Catholic Directory 1993* (New Providence, NJ: J.P.Kenedy and Sons, 1993), lxxviii.

damentalism, 1987; *Brothers and Sisters to Us: U.S. Bishops Pastoral Letter on Racism in Our Day*, 1979. Over the years these pastoral letters constitute a rich source of material and reflect a broad commentary on Catholic life in the United States. Most speak to concerns and challenges inspired by Vatican II.

There has been considerable recent discussion about these national bishops' conferences, owing to Rome's Cardinal Ratzinger's attempts to downgrade their authority and importance. We shall treat this effort in chapter 19.

3. The WCC 1982 Faith and Order document "Baptism, Eucharist, Ministry" (BEM). The ministry section of this document gave strong historical and theological arguments for the historic episcopacy and extended an invitation to those churches that do not have bishops to recover the historic episcopacy as a major step toward the reunion of the Christian churches. The many non-episcopal churches are in the process of discussing this issue of bishops; the outcome is far from clear.

4. Apostolic Succession. This is a very important ecumenical issue since Protestant churches (the Anglican Communion is a special situation — see Chapter 21, #9) are not considered by Catholic and Orthodox churches to be within the apostolic succession because their church leaders have not been ordained in the *Sacrament* of orders, since Protestant theology does not consider ordination to be a sacrament conferring the grace of consecrating the body and blood of Christ in the Eucharist. Thus Protestant church leaders are said to need *sacramental* ordination by bishops themselves in the apostolic succession.

The Catholic Church holds strongly to the concept of the apostolic succession as a way of determining the validity of the ordination of bishops, and consequently of priests ordained by these bishops, and therefore of the **validity** of the Masses or Eucharists celebrated by these priests. The Catholic Church recognizes the bishops-priests-Eucharists of the Orthodox and the Swedish Lutheran Church because their bishops are part of the apostolic succession. Many Anglican bishops and priests, concerned about the validity of their ordinations after Pope Leo XIII's condemnation of Anglican orders as null and void, asked Orthodox bishops to ordain them. How would Protestants, especially Lutherans and Methodists, insert themselves into the apostolic succession?

The issue is full of ambiguity and is emotionally charged. One solution proposed by *BEM* is the distinction between two ways of viewing apostolic succession.[6] One is the traditional understanding of a succession of *ordinations* stretching back to the Apostles. A second stresses a succes-

---

6. *Baptism, Eucharist and Ministry* (Geneva, Switzerland: World Council of Churches, 1982), 28-31.

sion of *apostolic teaching*; that is, the teachings of Christ and the Apostles are passed on in the local churches through their bishops. In fact, in the early centuries of the church, lists of bishops in a given diocese were kept as a guarantee that the aspostolic teaching had indeed been faithfully passed on without error. It was only later that the emphasis was shifted from succession of apostolic *teaching* to a succession of *ordinations*.

The ecumenical opening provided by this second view is obvious. If a church today can show that it faithfully holds to the essential teachings of the Apostles, an argument can be made that its leaders who guarantee this teaching are part of the apostolic succession. Thus the great importance of the theological dialogues between the churches we discussed in chapter 8.

Summary

The proper title for the bishops of the world is "successors of the Apostles." Bishops in the apostolic succession are a nearly 2000-year tradition in the Catholic and Orthodox churches. Theological questions concerning bishops are complex and very important today because they involve ecclesiology (are bishops *essential* to the Church of Christ?), *ecumenism* (must churches without bishops restore episcopacy in order to be part of the future united Church of Christ?), *sacraments* (should Protestant churches recover the sacrament of holy orders so that their ordained leaders are in the apostolic succession?), *ministry* (do Protestant clergy celebrate real Eucharists of the Body and Blood of Christ?). We stressed the extensive theological teaching of Vatican II on bishops. In essence this teaching states that God established the order of bishops in the church as successors of the Apostles to teach, sanctify and govern the faithful; bishops receive this three-fold mission and enter the apostolic succession by receiving the sacrament of holy orders. With this theological foundation, we considered the great responsibility bishops have in the church and the consequent personal qualities expected of them. We concluded by proposing four practical and theological issues that are very much in the forefront of today's church.

For Discussion

1. Why are bishops such VIP's in the Church?
2. What do you consider to be the most important theological teachings about bishops?
3. Do you think bishops of the world being "in communion with" the pope is a realistic way of reuniting the separated Christian churches? How might it work?

4. Do you think the question of apostolic succession is overemphasized today? Give reasons for either a yes or no answer.

5. Why is ordaining a bishop in the sacrament of holy orders so important, indeed essential?

6. Do you think today's bishops possess the qualities described in this chapter?

7. What would you say are the most important things bishops should be doing today? "your" bishop?

8. May a bishop disagree with an aspect of the pope's teaching and still be "in communion with" him? How might such a bishop act? Read chapter 21, verses 11-14 in St. Paul's letter to the Galatians.

For Action

1. Learn your bishop's name and where he lives. Ask for an interview with him. Find out what is involved in being shepherd of his local church. Don't be afraid to ask personal, even controversial questions!

2. Watch the video *Romero* to see how one modern bishop was a true shepherd to his people.

Further Reading

Brockman, James R. *Romero, A Life.* Maryknoll, NY: Orbis Books, 1989.

Kerrison, Raymond. *Bishop Walsh of Maryknoll.* New York: Putnam, 1962.

Reese, Thomas J. *Archbishop: Inside the Power Structure of the American Catholic Church.* San Francisco: Harper and Row, 1989.

_____. *A Flock of Shepherds: The National Conference of Catholic Bishops.* Kansas City: Sheed & Ward, 1993.

Sobrino, Jon. *Archbishop Romero: Memories and Reflections.* Maryknoll, NY: Orbis Books, 1990.

Tang, Dominic. *How Inscrutable His Ways. Memories 1951-1981.* Hong Kong: Caritas Printing Centre, 1991, 2nd edition.

Wilkes, Paul. *The Education of an Archbishop: Travels with Rembert Weakland.* Maryknoll, NY: Orbis Books, 1993.

CHAPTER 11

Peter in the Church

Peter said: You are the Christ, the Son of the living God.
Jesus answered: You are Peter, the rock on which I will build my
church. —Communion antiphon from Mass of St. Peter and Paul

"The Roman Pontiff, as the Successor of Peter, is the perpetual
and visible source and foundation of unity both of bishops and
of the whole company of the faithful." —*Lumen Gentium* 23

Introduction

Perhaps no other office has created such fascination in people's
minds than that of the papacy. No other person has caused such strong
emotions, both positive and negative, as the pope of Rome. What might be
some of the reasons for these phenomena?

First off, of all the Christian churches in the world, only the Roman
Catholic Church has the office of the papacy. Why is this the case? Then
there's the fact that the present Pope John Paul II is such a world figure:
his statements and speeches and doings are reported in the press all over
the world; heads of state sooner or later wind up in Rome to speak with
him, and in his world travels he has probably been seen in the flesh by
more people than any other human being. Why all this attention? In addition there is the reaction of Catholics to the pope: Rome and the pope are
the goals of millions of tourists every year; at the pope's weekly audience,
crowds up to 40,000 applaud him as he enters St. Peter's Square, excitedly
cry out "*Viva il papa*" ("Long live the pope"), and rush to the center aisle
to get a close look, take pictures, or grasp his hand. On his world pastoral
journeys, he attracts often over half-a-million people at his Masses. Why
all this enthusiasm for one man?

When it comes to history, the papacy as an institution is a highly emotional issue. The ancient Orthodox churches of the East accord the pope a **primacy of honor** but absolutely deny him a **primacy of jurisdiction** over all Christians. The Protestant Reformation was waged in large part over the authority of the pope; Martin Luther called him the anti-Christ. In the last century in the United States, Catholics were called papists in derision and a Catholic couldn't be elected president for fear the pope would rule America. Why such a problem? In the ecumenical movement, that effort to reunite the divided Christian churches, the office of pope is the greatest obstacle to reunion, as Pope Paul VI himself once remarked.[1] Yet Episcopal Bishop Kilmer Myers in a sermon in Grace cathedral, San Francisco, in 1967, could state "We need the pope. . . . We need a Holy Father,"[2] "we" referring to Anglicans and Protestants. Why this remarkable statement?

So a major church question today is: Why a pope? This question takes many forms. Is the pope *essential* to the church Jesus Christ established? Did Jesus establish the papacy or is it merely a *human historical* development, as many scholars maintain? Must a future united Christian Church include the pope? Can the effort to unite the separated Christian churches succeed if the pope continues to exercise his authority in the same way?

A similar question is the role of the pope within the Catholic Church today. What is the exact meaning of his prerogative of infallibility? How can a mere human be infallible? How much power does the pope have in the Roman Catholic Church? Today a rethinking is going on among some Catholic theologians as to the best way his authority should be exercised in the universal church and in regard to the bishops of the world and their local churches. How much power should the Vatican Curia have over the worldwide church? On a more personal level, what kind of person is a pope—John Paul II, for example? What does he do with his day? And how does one get to be pope?

This topic of the papacy or office of Peter is one of great importance today, both for Catholics and other Christians. Vatican II did not add new teaching on the papacy; it merely repeated that of the first Vatican Council. However, its teaching on bishops and its strong emphasis on their collegial relationship with the pope and the importance it gave to the local church put Vatican II's teaching on the papacy in an entirely new context.

---

1. "The pope, as we well know, is undoubtedly the greatest obstacle in the path of ecumenism." Patrick Granfield, *The Papacy in Transition* (Garden City, N.Y.: Doubleday and Company, 1980), 97. See also Avery Dulles, "The Papacy: Bond or Barrier," *Origins* 45 (May 2, 1974):705-12.

2. Bishop Myers' historic sermon was reported in the *San Francisco Examiner* for June 4, 1967, pages 1 and 25, under the headline "Bishop's Astounding Proposal" The bishop's words: "We should . . . acknowledge him as the Chief Pastor of the Christian family. . . . we need some one symbolically potent bishop to give expression to the Word of the Lord for our day. . . . We need a Holy Father. . . . We can no longer even think of the reunion of Christendom without the papacy."

◆

Preview: The purpose of this chapter is to show the unique role and importance of the pope in the Catholic Church and to recognize and discuss critical issues involving the office of Peter today. To answer the question "Why a pope?", we turn to the famous rock and keys metaphor in the Gospel of Matthew, where Jesus chose Peter to be the foundation of unity with spiritual authority in his future church. We establish that Jesus intended Peter to have successors since the function of unity and authority must continue in the church. We turn to history to identify the bishops of Rome as those successors of Peter that Jesus intended. We then look at the Petrine office as it exists today. We briefly examine the teaching of both Vatican I and II to see how Vatican II has put the teaching of Vatican I in an entirely new context. This leads us to reflect theologically on the three-fold role of the papal office in the light of Vatican II and the new style of papacy resulting. To understand better how the pope is able to govern the universal church, we consider briefly his "administration." We close by reflecting on five critical issues involving the exercise of the Petrine office today.

◆

Why a Pope?

The Rock and Keys Metaphor

Whenever St. Peter is pictured in mosaics high on the walls of the great European churches, he always holds a set of large keys in his hands. These are his identification. And in the largest church in the world, St. Peter's in Rome, high above the floor in four-foot golden letters in Latin and Greek, running the length and breadth of the giant basilica, are Jesus' words to Peter, beginning with: "Blessed are you, Simon. . . ." These words are taken from the famous passage in which Jesus gives Peter a new responsibility and special role among the Christian people.[3] We must analyze it carefully.

> Then Simon Peter spoke up: "You are the Messiah, the Son of the Living God." Jesus agreed and said to him: "Blessed are you Simon, son of Jonah. Flesh and blood has not revealed this to you but my Father in Heaven. And I tell you, you are Peter and on this rock I will build my Church, and the powers of death shall not

---

3. Protestant treatment of this text has generally held that the rock stands for the faith of Peter and not Peter himself. The context supports this interpretation in that Jesus praises the faith-insight given Peter to proclaim Jesus Messiah and Son of God. However, the early Church soon came to understand that the rock also refers to Peter the person. This became part of the Tradition and normative in Catholic theology.

prevail against it. I will give you the keys of the kingdom of heaven, and whatever you bind on earth shall be bound in heaven and whatever you loose on earth will be loosed in heaven." (Mt. 16:16-19)

It was evening at a little village near Caesarea Philippi. Jesus had just asked his disciples who people thought he was. All were silent, but it was Peter who made the astounding confession of faith: "You are the Messiah." Jesus tells Peter his mere human knowledge (flesh and blood) couldn't give him such insight; rather Jesus' Father, Yahweh, had given Peter this sudden revelation. Then Jesus makes a significant move: he changes Simon's name to Peter, the Greek name for rock (*petros*). In Semitic custom, to change a person's name is to give him a new vocation in life; thus God changed Abram's name to Abraham, signifying he was to be the father of the Jewish people (Gen. 17:5). Simon's, now Peter's, new vocation becomes clear in Jesus' next phrase: "On this rock," that is, on you, Peter, as rock, "I will build my church." Buildings are constructed on bedrock for firm foundation. Thus Peter is to be the strong, enduring *foundation* of Jesus' church, a foundation so strong that "the powers of death will not prevail against it." The meaning is that the church, on the foundation of Peter, will not be destroyed but will endure till the end of the world.

Jesus then moves to the second part of Peter's new vocation or responsibility, his spiritual *authority* over the Church of which he is the foundation. "I will give you the keys of the kingdom of heaven. . . ." Keys are a universal symbol of authority and stewardship. He who has the keys to a building or a warehouse controls who enters and leaves the building or what goods are dispensed from the warehouse. But this authority and stewardship is not of material things but rather "of heaven," of spiritual realities. And the authority is such that what Peter decides (bind or loose) on earth will be supported by God in heaven. An awesome authority indeed!

So from this famous text, Catholics and a growing number of Protestant scholars and ecumenists conclude that Jesus has given the Apostle Peter a unique, very special role in his church: of being the strength, firmness, stability, unity as foundation rock of his church and of having complete spiritual authority backed by God over church members.

This role of Peter in the church is further supported by the preeminence given to Peter in the four Gospels and the Acts of the Apostles. Peter is mentioned 114 times in the Gospels, far more than any other Apostle. He is presented as the spokesman of the other apostles; his name always appears first in a list of the Apostles' names; he is present at special incidents in Christ's life. In the first half of the Acts of the Apostles, Peter dominates the pages: he gives the first Christian "sermon" to the Jews, he works the first recorded miracle of the Apostles, he visits many of the newly-founded churches, and he presides over the first Council of Jerusalem. Raymond Brown, the famous American Catholic biblical scholar, has found what he calls "a trajectory of images of Peter" in the New Testament, that is, Peter grows in importance from Gospel to Gospel, indicating that the early Christian communities realized more fully as the years passed the special role Jesus had given Peter.[4]

However, up to this point we can only conclude that Jesus gave the Apostle Peter this two-fold vocation and authority. Where does the pope come in? How do we show from Scripture that Jesus intended popes in the church, because nowhere does he explicitly say this?

The reasoning process that Jesus intended Peter to have successors in this two-fold role of foundation of unity and spiritual authority is found in two statements of Jesus. In the text we have just analyzed, Matthew 16:16-19, Jesus speaks of his church against which the powers of death will not prevail. This implies he intended his church to last beyond the lifetime of Peter. If so, then the foundation rock and spiritual authority, that is, the Petrine office, must continue beyond Peter's death. We may conclude, therefore, that Jesus intended Peter to have successors in exercising this two-fold office.

A second text is Matthew 28:18-20, where Jesus sends his Apostles (including Peter) into the whole world to preach the good news to all peoples and until the end of the world. In the preceding chapter on bishops, we reasoned that since the mission of the Apostles was a permanent one, successors were needed to carry on the mission beyond the death of the Apostles. It is thus clear that Jesus, in intending his church and its mission to last till the end of the world, clearly intended Peter to have successors in the essential task of being the foundation of unity and of exercising spiritual authority in the church. These successors of Peter are the popes.

Evidence from History

However, a major question still remains. Granted that Jesus gave Peter a very special role in the church and that Jesus intended Peter to have successors in the Petrine office, how do we know that the popes *are in fact* those successors intended by Jesus? The problem is a complex historical one. During the first two centuries of the church's life, there is not clear documentary proof that the bishops of Rome claimed authority (jurisdiction) beyond Italy itself. Furthermore, there is some evidence that a group of presbyters (priests) ruled the church of Rome in its earliest years, rather than one man acting as its bishop. What appears then to have happened was a gradual *development*, under the action of the Holy Spirit, that caused

---

4. Raymond Brown, *Biblical Reflections on Crises Facing the Church* (New York: Paulist Press, 1975), 67-77.

the bishops of Rome to see themselves more clearly as the successors of Peter and accordingly to exercise their role and authority more broadly.

We can fashion our reasoning process that the bishops of Rome are in fact the successors of Peter according to these three historical facts: Peter went to Rome and was martyred there in the year 64 or 67AD; the bishops of Rome gradually claimed to be the successor of Peter and to act as foundation of unity and to exercise spiritual authority over other churches beyond Rome, and the people accepted this claim; no other bishop claimed to be Peter's successor or acted as foundation of unity with spiritual authority over other churches.

Our conclusion is that the bishops of Rome are indeed successors of Peter as intended by Christ. The most appropriate titles of the pope are therefore *successor of Peter* and *bishop of Rome*. His office is aptly called the Petrine office.

The Line of Popes

The papacy or Petrine office is thus the oldest, longest-continuing leadership institution in the world. The list of 265 Popes in a succession back to Peter is indeed impressive, even though there is some confusion owing to lack of official documents concerning the status of bishops of Rome up until about 100. Nonetheless, the ancient tradition of these names in the list carries much weight. A careful reading of the list reveals some interesting facts. Most of the popes of the first 300 years were martyrs for the Christian faith and thus were recognized as saints, for this was the period of fierce Roman persecutions of Christianity and "the shepherds died for their flocks." There are many saint-popes up until about 770, but few after that. Why?

The papacy had fallen on bad times, had become worldly and at the mercy of powerful Roman families, who engineered their relatives into the papacy because of its wealth, power, and promise of patronage. There were two periods of truly unworthy, "bad" popes: the 900s and the Renaissance, that period preceding the Reformation and the Council of Trent. The lives and exploits of some of these men make sensational but tragic reading, considering their high office.

From 1550 on, the popes were generally good, competent men, some heroic and saintly. The 20th-century popes have been outstanding men: brilliant intellectually, energetic and saintly men totally dedicated to the good of the church and to Jesus Christ. Peter Hebblethwaite, in his sometimes irreverent but always delightfully interesting and informative book, *In the Vatican,* has a fine chapter called "Twentieth-Century Popes Revisited." It is worth reading for his insights into the human side of these popes, as well as a wealth of information on the functioning of the papacy.

Catholics' Devotion to Their "Holy Father"

Jesus' promise to Peter establishing him as the rock foundation and the highest spiritual authority in his church is the ultimate reason why Catholics are so personally devoted and loyal to the pope. There are other reasons for this devotion and loyalty.

- Catholics are convinced that the papacy or office of Peter in the church can never be given up or sacrificed precisely because it constitutes an essential part of the very nature of the church as established by Jesus himself.

- Catholics see Peter in the pope, much as the bishops at the ecumenical Council of Chalcedon in 451 proclaimed "Peter has spoken through Leo," that is, through Pope Leo, who had written "Leo's tome" that broke the deadlock at the Council concerning the nature of Christ.

- Catholics sense that it is the pope who unites Catholics the world over; they realize that the office of pope as the rock of unity has kept the Catholic Church surviving through the centuries when many times, humanly speaking, it could have been destroyed.

- Catholics take one of the pope's titles, Vicar of Christ, seriously for they believe that he does visibly represent Christ, the invisible head of the church. However, theologically speaking, this title must be carefully nuanced for no mere human can take Christ's place, as the word vicar seems to imply. Vicar of Christ became the exclusive title of the pope only in the time of Pope Innocent III, 1198-1216.[5]

- Catholics see the pope truly as their Holy Father in the faith, for he is responsible for safeguarding the purity of the faith and for proclaiming it unceasingly to them.

The Papacy or Petrine Office Today

Chapter 3 of *Lumen Gentium* endorsed the teaching of Vatican Council I on the pope. "In order that the episcopate itself might be one and undivided, he [Christ] placed blessed Peter over the Apostles and instituted in him a permanent and visible source and foundation of faith and fellowship. This teaching concerning the institution, the permanence, the nature, and the import of the sacred primacy of the Roman Pontiff and his infallible teaching office, the Sacred Synod proposes anew to be firmly believed

---

5. However, in speaking of bishops' full pastoral authority in their own diocese, Vatican II comments that they are "not to be regarded as vicars of the Roman Pontiff" but rather "as the vicars and ambassadors of Christ." *Lumen Gentium*, 27.

by all the faithful" (LG 18). The reference is to the following four chapters from Vatican I on the papacy: I. The Establishment of the Apostolic Primacy in St. Peter;[6] II. The Continuation of St. Peter's Primacy in the Roman Pontiffs;[7] III. The Power and Nature of the Primacy of the Roman Pontiff;[8] and IV. The Infallible Teaching Authority of the Roman Pontiff."[9]

Significantly, Vatican II chose not to use the non-Scriptural, legalistic language of primacy and jurisdiction. Its most important statements are: "The Lord made Peter alone the rock-foundation and the holder of the keys of the Church (Mt 16:18-19) and instituted him shepherd of his whole flock (John 21:15)" (LG 22). ". . . the office which the Lord confided to Peter alone as first of the Apostles, destined to be transmitted to his successors, is a permanent one . . ." (LG 20); "The Roman Pontiff, as the successor of Peter, is the perpetual and visible source and foundation of unity both of bishops and of the whole company of the faithful" (LG 23).

However, as we considered in the previous chapter, by its teaching on bishops Vatican II completed Vatican I's exclusive emphasis on the pope. Thus Vatican II taught that bishops' authority comes directly from Christ in episcopal ordination, bishops have full authority in their own churches, and bishops as forming a "college" with the pope govern the entire church in a collegial use of authority. Vatican II's teaching on bishops has thus given a new context for interpreting the juridically-expressed teaching of Vatican I and has changed the relationship between the pope and the worldwide bishops.

Three-fold Role and Function of the Petrine Office in Light of Vatican II

Most simply put, the role of the pope is *to be Peter* in the church today. His most appropriate title is therefore successor of Peter; other titles like Roman Pontiff, Vicar of Christ, Patriarch of the West, Holy Father, and "His Holiness" accrued to him later. The title bishop of Rome, however, is appropriate because he is in fact the diocesan bishop of the city of

---

6. "We teach and declare, therefore, according to the testimony of the Gospel that the primacy of jurisdiction over the whole Church of God was immediately and directly promised to and conferred upon the blessed Apostle Peter by Christ the Lord."

7. Canon: "Therefore, if anyone says that it is not according to the institution of Christ our Lord himself, that is, by divine law, that St. Peter has perpetual successors in the primacy over the whole Church or if anyone says that the Roman Pontiff is not the successor of St. Peter in the same primacy: let him be anathema."

8. Canon: "If anyone says that the Roman Pontiff has only the office of inspection or direction, but not the full and supreme power of jurisdiction over the whole Church, not only in matters that pertain to faith and morals, but also in matters that pertain to the discipline and government of the Church throughout the whole world; . . . or if anyone says that this power is not ordinary and immediate either over each and every church or over each and every shepherd and faithful member: let him be anathema."

9. The full canon is quoted later in this chapter under Issue 3 involving the papacy.

Rome since Peter the Apostle had come to Rome, in effect making Rome the "see" of the head of the Apostles. In official documents the term **Apostolic See** means that diocese first occupied by the Apostle Peter and then by his successors; "See" comes from the Latin word *sedes* or chair, the symbol of authority for the one who "sits in the chair of Peter," since a throne is the sign of the king's authority. This idea is expressed artistically in two places in St. Peter's Basilica in Rome: the life-size black statue of St. Peter actually sitting in a chair, with his left shoe worn by the touches and kisses of millions of pilgrims; and the exuberant sunburst monument by Bernini of the chair of Peter behind the main altar of St. Peter's.

To be Peter in the Church today means the following:

1. To be the *center of unity* in the Roman Catholic Church today. For "Peter's ministry is to promote, safeguard and symbolize the unity of the Church."[10] As stated in the previous chapter, one billion Catholics in the world today are united by their individual bishops being "in communion" with the bishop of Rome. To express this unity, each Catholic bishop comes to Rome every five years for his "quinquennial visit" and to report on his own church or diocese. *Lumen Gentium* describes the universal church as a communion of local churches in union with the pope (23).

   The pope as foundation of unity has many practical applications today. One is the ecumenical movement whose goal is to reestablish unity among the separated Christian churches. In its *Decree on Ecumenism*, Vatican II inspired a rethinking of the pope's role in relation to other Christian churches. Since the Petrine office is *essential* to the church Jesus established, the pope must in some way be the unifying force in a future united church. In the ongoing Lutheran-Catholic theological dialogue, the Lutheran participants asked their churches to acknowledge "the possibility and desirability of the papal ministry, renewed under the gospel and committed to Christian freedom, in a larger communion" of the Roman Catholic and Lutheran churches.[11] (See chapter 8.)

2. To be the *universal teacher* and *protector of the Christian Tradition* coming from Christ through the Apostles and passed on by their successors through the centuries. The great Tradition with a capital "T" refers to the entire Catholic Christian life as believed and lived. It includes the truths of faith (doctrine), worship (sacraments, devotional life), and morality (right and wrong actions, law), popularly termed creed, cult, and code. The Catholic Church throughout its 1900 year history has put a high priority on unity and purity of doctrine. This emphasis on unity of

---

10. Peter Hebblethwaite, *In the Vatican* (Bethesda, MD: Adler and Adler, 1986), 25.

11. Paul Empie and T. Austin Murphy, editors, *Papal Primacy and the Universal Church* ((Minneapolis: Augsburg Publishing House, 1974), 23, No. 32.

teaching the Christian faith goes back to St. Paul who, in his letters, constantly deplored false teaching and divisions in the churches he founded and to Jesus himself, who warned against false teachers.

The Second Vatican Council taught that the pope and all the bishops have "the duty to promote and to safeguard the unity of faith" (*Lumen Gentium* 23) for they are "authentic teachers . . . endowed with the authority of Christ" (LG 25). Thus the bishops in union with the pope form the *magisterium* or teaching office of the church.

3. To be the *final decision-maker* but in a collegial fashion, consulting the bishops of the world before making a serious public teaching. Pope Pius XII acted in this way when in 1950 he proclaimed the Assumption of Mary a dogma to be believed by Catholics, the only example of a papal infallible teaching since Vatican I. Pius XII asked all the bishops of the Catholic world if they and their people believed this doctrine and whether it was appropriate to solemnly define it at this time. The response was 100% yes to the first question and overwhelmingly positive to the second. There are times, however, when the pope is the final decision-maker without collegial action. This occurred in 1968 when Pope Paul VI decided, without consulting the bishops of the world and against the majority report of his commission, to retain the church's condemnation of contraceptive use in marriage.

The New Papal "Style" of Paul VI and John Paul II

The recent biography of Pope Paul VI carries the title *Paul VI: the First Modern Pope*. Paul VI was the first pope to preside over a truly worldwide, global church; to travel extensively—to India, to Jerusalem to embrace Greek Orthodox Patriarch Athenagoras and lift the mutual 900-year excommunication, to New York to address the United Nations and plead for world peace, to Colombia for the Eucharistic Congress, to Switzerland, Turkey, Uganda, and the Philippines. He internationalized the church by creating Third-World bishops and cardinals and by putting non-Italians in charge of the Curia's congregations; he promoted evangelization by stressing respect for various cultures. He personalized the Council's commitment to ecumenism through his close relationships with the Anglican Archbishop of Canterbury and Protestant Brother Roger Schutz, founder of the **Taizé** ecumenical community. He undertook the daunting task of reforming the Roman Curia, abolished much Vatican pomp and ceremony, retiring the pope's triple **tiara**, cardinals' ermine trains, and the sedilia by which the pope was borne on the shoulders of four men into official ceremonies.

John Paul II emphasizes the pastoral role of the pope with his frequent world travels; he exhibits great skill at using television and large public gatherings to preach his message; he has become a powerful advocate for justice, human rights, and freedom for the poor of the world. He stopped using the editorial "we" in referring to himself as pope. He has canonized or beatified hundreds of holy men and women and martyrs to provide the worldwide church with heroic examples to imitate. He frequently refers to Vatican II and called an extraordinary Synod of bishops in 1985 to celebrate and apply Vatican II 20 years later. He loves people and is approachable to all, especially the young, the sick, the poor.

Both men have established a new style for being Peter in the church today.

Governing the Global Church: The Pope's "Administration"

The bishop of Rome in his capacity as successor of Peter is often called the pastor of the universal church. Such a role is obviously too much for one limited human being, however gifted. The pope is helped by the bishops of the world, the Roman curia, the cardinals dispersed throughout the world and those working in the curia. The headquarters of the pope and his curia is the Vatican situated in Vatican city in Rome.

The Vatican

The pope lives and works in the Vatican. In imperial Rome this area encompassed the Vatican hill near Nero's circus where St. Peter is said to have been crucified. Emperor Constantine, after giving Christianity freedom in 312, had the Vatican hill leveled for the foundation of the first St. Peter's church, which he had built in 324 above the tomb of the martyred Peter the Apostle. Thus the area around St. Peter's Basilica came to be called the Vatican. However, the popes lived and worked in the Lateran palace for almost 1000 years, until they moved into the present Vatican. Vatican City is the smallest state in the world occupying 108.7 acres. In this area are St. Peter's basilica and Bernini's magnificent colonnade that form the vast piazza or square in front of St. Peter's, the Vatican palace or pope's living and working quarters, the famous Vatican Museum, with the newly cleaned Sistine Chapel of Michaelangelo's famed ceiling, the beautiful Vatican Gardens, with the powerful Vatican Radio station that broadcasts daily in 40 languages all over the world, the large new Pope Paul VI Audience Hall, where the pope holds his weekly public "**audience**" during the winter, and the various administrative offices of the papal state.

Vatican City is also a separate state recognized as such by the nations of the world. The Vatican state in 1984 had political relations with 122 nations of the world, exchanging ambassadors called nuncios. In those cases where formal diplomatic relations do not exist, the pope sends an apostolic delegate instead of the nuncio to the country. As an official state, the Vatican enters into agreements with other nations, generally called **Concordats**, whose goal is to safeguard the rights of the church, like the appointing of bishops, having seminaries and schools, running publishing houses.

The pope thus has a dual role: his spiritual leadership as successor of Peter and bishop of Rome and his political role as head of Vatican state. When heads of state like Presidents Reagan, Bush and Clinton and Gorbachev of the Soviet Union visited Rome and the pope, they came to confer with him in his capacity as head of the Vatican state. However, his extraordinary world influence as spiritual leader of a billion Catholics and as world spokesman for religious and moral values, make him a doubly valuable person to talk to.

There has been suggestions on the part of Protestants and some Catholics for the pope to divest himself of the political arm of the Vatican state and to return to being a purely spiritual leader, as Peter was. There is considerable merit to this suggestion, but recent history has shown that the Vatican as a state has been able to support the cause of the church and the protection of Catholics in Communist countries in ways not otherwise possible. And it makes it easier for heads of state to visit the pope.

The Roman Curia

"The Supreme Pontiff usually conducts the business of the universal church by means of the Roman curia, which fulfills its duty in his name and by his authority for the good and for the service of the churches."[12]

Thus does the official Code of Canon Law of the Roman Catholic church describe the large bureaucracy that helps the pope run the universal Catholic Church. Jokes abound in Rome and elsewhere that "popes come and go but the curia goes on forever." It was reorganized in 1588 by Pope Sixtus V to put into effect the reforms of the Council of Trent and carry out the Counter-Reformation. It has had an ambiguous history. Staffed predominantly by cardinals, bishops, and priests, mostly career men, it has served the church with much hard work and great dedication. But like other bureaucracies, its leaders tended to entrench themselves, to lose contact with the rest of the Catholic world, to consider that they knew what is best for the church elsewhere in the world and thus to issue documents and decrees that bishops, successors of the Apostles, had to obey, often with little or no input.

At periods throughout its long history there were outcries to "reform the curia." By the time of Vatican II the chain of command seemed to be: pope—curia—bishops, rather than pope and bishops in a collegial relationship aided by the curia. In speech after speech, sometimes in unusually frank language, the bishops at Vatican II severely criticized the curia for its secretive, nondemocratic way of acting, its condemning and disciplining

---

12. *Code of Canon Law, Latin-English Edition* (Washington, D.C.: Canon Law Society of America, 1983), 131, Canon 360.

theologians without revealing their accusers, its creating a climate of fear and intimidation that brought needed theological and biblical scholarship to a standstill, thus weakening the church. (See chapter 2) The Council bishops commissioned Pope Paul VI to reform the curia.

Pope Paul VI began this reform in 1967 with his apostolic constitution *Regimini Sanctae Ecclesiae* (For the Rule of the Holy Church), which made diocesan bishops members of all curial departments (thus internationalizing what had been a predominantly Italian preserve!), required retirement at age 75 (thus striking a blow at entrenched gerontocracy), changed the names of curial offices (the once-feared Holy Office, originally the Sacred Congregation of the Universal Inquisition to defend the church against the threat of heresy, became the Congregation for the Doctrine of the Faith [CDF]), permitted modern languages to replace Latin for official documents, and so forth.

Presently the curia is made up of the Secretary of State and the Council for the Public Affairs of the Church, nine Congregations, 12 Pontifical Councils, three Tribunals, and a few offices dealing with the temporal affairs of Vatican City and the running of the "papal household." The nine congregations are the heart of the curia; in order of importance they are: Doctrine of Faith, Bishops, Divine Worship and Sacraments, Clergy, Evangelization of Peoples, Religious Orders and Secular Institutes, Catholic Education, Oriental Churches, Cause of Saints. The most important Pontifical Councils are: the Laity, Promoting Christian Unity, Justice and Peace, Interreligious Dialogue, Dialogue with non-Believers. Today, the most powerful and controversial curial office is the Congregation for the Doctrine of the Faith (CDF), headed by Joseph Cardinal Ratzinger. He and his congregation will appear again in later chapters.

Cardinals

Cardinals are bishops or archbishops who form the supreme council or "senate" of the church. They advise the pope, assist the central administration of the whole church, head the nine congregations of the Vatican curia, and since 1159 elect a new pope. It is a great honor to be chosen by the pope to be a cardinal; this privilege is generally given to archbishops (or bishops) of very large and historically important archdioceses or to high-ranking officials in the Vatican Curia or to reward outstanding service to the church. When the pope confers the honor of cardinalate on a person, it is popularly referred to as giving him "the red hat" or red birreta. Cardinals also wear red cassocks and make a colorful group at papal events in Rome. In 1990 there were 142 cardinals from most countries in the world. At present the United States has 12 cardinals: two are retired, two work in the Vatican Curia in Rome, and eight head metropolitan archdioceses (Roger Cardinal Mahony, Los Angeles; James Cardinal Hickey, Washington, D.C.; Joseph Cardinal Bernardin, Chicago; Bernard Cardinal

Law, Boston; John Cardinal O'Connor, New York; Anthony Cardinal Bevilacqua, Philadelphia; William Cardinal Keeler, Baltimore; Adam Cardinal Maida, Detroit.).

Critical Contemporary Issues Involving the Papacy Today

Catholics are sincerely devoted to the Holy Father and convinced of his necessary role in the Catholic Church. Yet many Catholics, lay and ordained, in the light of the insights of Vatican II and of their experience of church since the Council, have a growing sense there is need for change in the way the papal ministry is exercised in the Catholic Church today. Many consider authority and its exercise as the most important issue in today's church. They see it as negatively affecting important aspects of Catholic life and underlying critical issues debated today. They are aware that the exercise of authority sometimes involves putting the church's institutional interests ahead of the peoples' spiritual needs and even of important gospel values. So we consider the following interrelated issues which involve the papacy's exercise of authority today.

1. Collegiality. This refers to the effort to share authority and broaden decision-making at all levels of the church, with primary reference to the bishops of the Catholic world in relation to the pope, for the pastoral benefit of the Catholic people and contemporary needs of the church. Collegial actions and relationships were a major goal of Vatican II renewal. Collegiality has become a major issue in today's church: many church leaders, theologians, and lay Catholics feel that this goal of the Second Vatican Council has not been sufficiently implemented. We shall treat this very important issue at some length in our final chapter.

2. Primacy of Jurisdiction as it Affects Ecumenism. Jesus wills that the Christian churches recover their lost unity. Disunity must not be allowed to go on indefinitely. Vatican I's concept of absolute, unlimited power and authority centered on one man constitutes today an almost insuperable obstacle for Orthodox and Protestant churches to reestablish communion with the Roman Catholic Church. The essence of Vatican I's teaching is that since Christ gave Peter "primacy of jurisdiction over the whole church of God," the **Roman Pontiff**[13] has "full and supreme jurisdiction over the whole church . . . in matters of faith and morals . . . discipline and government of the church throughout the world . . . and over each and every shepherd and faithful member." The key words are primacy and jurisdiction

---

13. Pontiff from the Latin *pons*, bridge, and *facio*, make or build, literally means "bridge-builder" and was taken from the title *Pontifex* given to the priestly caste of the Roman Empire as mediators between the gods and the Roman populace. In present usage, pontiff indicates the pope's pastoral and teaching authority.

from Latin *primus*, first, and *jurisdictio*, meaning legal power or authority to decide cases and execute laws. These juridic terms are not found in the Christian Scriptures; Vatican II deliberately chose not to use such legalistic language in order to avoid the incongruity of expressing religious doctrine in juridic concepts and out of ecumenical sensitivity to other churches.

Thanks to the progress of ecumenism, a growing number of Protestant scholars, especially Anglican and Lutheran, accept that Jesus did confer on Peter a special role over the Apostles and that this primacy or firstness was passed to Peter's successors. However, most would have great difficulty in agreeing that the pope's primacy is willed by God (of "divine law") and that it involves such absolute supremacy in teaching and government over the whole church and all Christians. The Orthodox clearly reject a primacy of jurisdiction; they point to the undivided church of the early centuries, when the bishop of Rome as patriarch of the West was accorded a primacy of *honor* among the four other partriarchs of Antioch, Alexandria, Constantinople and Jerusalem because of Peter who was martyred in Rome.

Is there a solution to this ecumenical impasse? That the Second Vatican Council balanced Vatican I's juridic statements on papal power with its teaching on the role and authority of bishops and its strong endorsement of the principle of collegiality has put this issue in a different context. A more pressing issue today from the Orthodox and especially the Protestant viewpoint appears to be the actual, concrete exercise of authority by the pope within the Catholic Church and in its relationships with other churches. Catholic and Protestant and Orthodox theologian-ecumenists candidly admit that union is impossible in the current situation of increasing centralization and power in the Vatican and the increasing lack of collegiality between bishops and the pope.

3. Papal Infallibility. Much misunderstanding exists among Catholics as well as Protestants on this dogma. Catholics frequently manifest the phenomenon of "creeping infallibilism," mistakenly thinking that official papal documents and statements are infallible: for example, *Of Human Life* in 1968, condemning contraception in marriage. Protestants and Orthodox see papal infallibility as a serious obstacle to future union with Roman Catholics. Their opposition is two-fold: the doctrine appears to have been of human origin in order to give the pope more power and prestige; secondly, infallibility gives a mere human too much power in the church, thus opening the way to abuse. These are real concerns; it is important therefore to understand exactly what Vatican I meant by infallibility and under what conditions it exists.

The following is the technical and highly nuanced statement of Vatican I.

We teach and define that it is a divinely revealed dogma: that the Roman Pontiff, when he speaks *ex cathedra*, that is, when, acting in the office of shepherd and teacher of all Christians, he *defines*, by virtue of his supreme apostolic authority, doctrine concerning *faith or morals* to be held by the universal church, *possesses* through the *divine assistance promised to him in the person of St. Peter*, the infallibility with which the divine Redeemer *willed his Church to be endowed* in defining doctrine concerning faith or morals: and that such definitions of the Roman Pontiff are therefore *irreformable* because of their nature, but *not because of the agreement of the Church*[14] (emphases added).

It is essential to note that stringent conditions[15] must be present for an infallible statement:

- The pope must speak as official teacher as head of the church (*ex cathedra*, from the chair of Peter, that is, as Peter's successor).
- The infallible "definition" must deal with a teaching on faith and morals necessary for salvation and contained in God's revelation or a teaching necessary to explain or defend it.
- The pope must clearly state he intends this to be an infallible statement.
- The statement must be addressed to the whole church to be believed by all Catholics.

Infallibility is therefore a limited power and is given not to the pope as an individual but to his office; it is a sharing of the gift Christ gave to the whole church for the protection of Christian revelation. Such infallible statements are rare: in addition to this definition on infallibility at Vatican I in 1870, there have been only two in the past two centuries — the Immaculate Conception of Mary in 1854 and the Assumption of Mary in 1950.

Theologians questioned why the church needed this new *dogma* after 1800 years of existence without it. Church historians point out that the dogma is historically conditioned; that is, a strong movement in the church called **ultramontanism** urged the definition in order to strengthen the diminished authority of the papacy. Whatever the case, the doctrine of infallibility need not be church-dividing when properly understood. If the principle of collegiality between pope and bishops is fully observed, the likelihood of future papal infallible statements is diminished. What appears to be the greater issue in the Catholic Church today is the noninfallible exercise of teaching auithority.

4. The Roman Curia. Some bishops and many theologians object that the Roman curia is trying to reassert its pre-Vatican II power over the church at the expense of the collegiality between bishops and the pope. The Congregation for the Doctrine of the Faith (CDF) is criticized for disciplining theo-

---

14. Cuthbert Butler, *The Vatican Council,* vol. II (New York: Longmans, Green and Co., 1932), 294-5.

15. Francis Sullivan, *Magisterium* (New York: Paulist Press, 1983). Chapter 5 gives an excellent treatment of infallibility.

logians for alleged erroneous teaching without following due process norms. But others in the church applaud such moves as restoring needed discipline and clarity of doctrine and practice to the church.

Other issues within the Catholic Church involve other curial congregations. The Congregation of Bishops appears to be appointing predominantly conservative bishops, reversing the practice under Pope Paul VI of appointing pastoral and usually progressive bishops. The Congregation for Divine Worship has been critical of creative liturgical practices, particularly in Africa that incorporate African culture, and which local churches and their bishops promote. The Congregation for the Cause of Saints is beatifying and canonizing persons at a record rate, the great majority religious women and men; many Catholics think that married people and those achieving heroic holiness in the world are needed as models today.

The Congregation for the Evangelization of Peoples appears unresponsive to methods of inculturation and the appeals of local bishops, especially repeated requests of bishops' conferences to ordain married catechists. The Congregation for Religious has been criticized for its male leadership regulating insensitively the lives and apostolates of women religious. The Congregation for Catholic Education has sought to impose on seminaries and Catholic universities regulations and control strongly opposed by local bishops, university and seminary administrators, and teachers; happily, dialogue has resulted in better understanding and compromise. Finally, the Congregation for Oriental Churches, in the light of the new freedom of worship for Orthodox churches in Russia and Eastern Europe, appears to approve of Catholic proselytizing in predominantly Orthodox areas and to be resurrecting in some places the unecumenical practice of **Uniatism.**

5. Present Theological Reflection. Theologians and church historians are giving considerable attention today to the office of Peter in the Catholic Church for several reasons: the historical scholarship now available on the role of the papacy throughout the centuries; the ecumenical reality expressed by Pope Paul VI admitting that the pope is perhaps the major obstacle to church union; Vatican II's teaching on bishops and endorsement of the principle of collegiality, in contrast to the slow progress toward collegial practices since the Council; the serious diminution of respect for papal authority occasioned by the 1968 publication *Of Human Life* and the growing feeling of the irrelevancy of Rome for many Catholics; the Vatican's refusal even to discuss neuralgic issues like clerical celibacy, married priesthood, women's expanded role in the church; the restoration movement to restore some pre-Vatican II theology and practices and to centralize authority in Rome; the ongoing effort of CDF to discipline theologians and proponents of change. Because of these developments, theologians and many bishops, priests, religious sisters and brothers, and lay Catholics are reflecting on what is the most productive exercise of papal authority within the church today.

Extensive studies[16] have been made on the role of the pope in the early centuries of the church, on the exercise and claims of papal authority in subsequent centuries, and on the most fruitful exercise of the Petrine ministry in the church today. It is true that the Catholic Church is not a democracy; but with democratic principles and practices on the rise throughout the world, the church is being challenged to employ more democratic procedures' in its internal government, to listen more to its members by respecting their insights and needs, and to live more collegially. The health and growth of the Catholic Church and the future of ecumenism are at stake.

It is significant that Cardinal Joseph Ratzinger, head of the Congregation for the Doctrine of the Faith, in a recent debate on the future of ecumenism with a professor from the Waldensian Theology Faculty in Rome, recognized that "the ministry of unity entrusted to Peter and his successors can be realized in very different ways. History offers examples of different styles. . . . Today we have to respond to new situations." He declined, however, "to say what the future possible practical realizations of the papacy might be."[17]

Summary

"Peter in the Church" examines the origin, authority, and present functioning of the papacy or office of the pope in the Catholic Church. In giving the Apostle Peter the responsibility of being the rock foundation of unity of the future church and of exercising spiritual authority, Jesus established what developed into the papacy. The first Vatican Council stated Catholic teaching on its establishment in Peter, its continuance in the popes, and their authority, including infallibility. Vatican II repeated this teaching but put it in a new context through its teaching on the authority and role of bishops in the universal church and its emphasis on collegiality. The function and role of the pope is essentially "to be Peter" in the church, that is, to maintain the unity of Christian belief and life among Catholics throughout the world today. The pope lives and works in Vatican City, also a nation-state, and governs the universal church through the nine congregations and 12 lesser councils that make up the Roman Curia and with the help of cardinals worldwide. The Petrine office is the object of theological reflection today, particularly in its exercise of authority: five issues are of special importance.

16. See three excellent recent studies: Patrick Granfield, *The Limits of the Papacy* (New York: Crossroad Publishing Co., 1987); J.M.R. Tillard, *The Bishop of Rome* (Wilmington, DE: Michael Glazier, Inc., 1983); and Robert Eno, *The Rise of the Papacy* (Wilmington, DE: M. Glazier, 1990).

17. Peter Hebblethwaite, "Ratzinger comments on changing papacy," *National Catholic Reporter.* 29 (February 26, 1993): 10.

For Discussion

1. Do you find the "rock and keys" text convincing to explain the existence and function of the pope in the Catholic Church?

2. How would you answer the objection that the papacy is of human, not divine, origin since the popes appeared not to claim the rock and keys responsibility for at least the first 200 years?

3. Can you accept papal infallibility now that you understand its stringent conditions? Do you think it was good for the church that Vatican I defined papal infallibility? Does the pope really need it?

4. Should the pope voluntarily give up his political position as head of the Vatican state and become a purely spiritual leader?

5. Is Pope John Paul II a good example of Peter in the church today?

For Action

1. Talk to various people about the papacy or office of the pope today. Suggestion: a priest; a married man; a woman; a Protestant; a high school or college student. What did you learn?

2. Learn about the role of the pope in the first three or four centuries of the church. What was his relationship as Patriarch of the West to the four other patriarchs?

3. Get Peter Hebblethwaite's delightful *In the Vatican* and read his chapter on the 20th-century popes and one of his chapters on the Vatican Curia.

Further Reading

Brown, Raymond, Donfried, Karl, and Reuman, John, editors. *Peter in the New Testament.* Minneapolis: Augsburg Publishing House, 1973.

Empie, Paul and Murphy, T. Austin, editors. *Papal Primacy and the Universal Church.* Minneapolis; Augsburg Publishing House, 1974.

Eno, Robert. *The Rise of the Papacy.* Wilmington, DE: M. Glazier, 1990.

Granfield, Patrick. *The Limits of the Papacy.* New York: The Crossroad Publishing Co., 1987.

Hebblethwaite, Peter. *In the Vatican.* Bethesda, MD: Adler and Adler, 1986.

_____ *Pope John XXIII, Shepherd of the Modern World.* Garden City, NY: Doubleday, 1985.

_____ *Paul VI, the First Modern Pope.* New York: Paulist Press, 1993.

Tillard, J.M.R. *The Bishop of Rome.* Wilmington, DE: Michael Glazier, Inc., 1983.

CHAPTER   12

Phenomenon of Religious Communities

"Good teacher, what must I do to share in everlasting life?" Jesus answered, "You know the commandments." He replied: "Teacher, I have kept all these since my childhood." Then Jesus looked at him with love and told him: "There is one thing more you must do. Go and sell what you have and give to the poor; you will then have treasure in heaven. After that, come and follow me." At these words the man's face fell. He went away sad for he had many possessions.   —Mark 10:17-22

All those who are called by God to the practice of the evangelical counsels, and who make faithful profession of them, bind themselves to the Lord in a special way. They follow Christ who, virginal and poor, redeemed and sanctified men by obedience unto death on the cross. Under the impulse of love, which the Holy Spirit pours into their hearts, they live more and more for Christ and for his Body the Church.
          —Decree on the Renewal of the Religious Life 1

A life consecrated by a profession of the counsels is of surpassing value.   —Decree on the Renewal of the Religious Life 1

Introduction

Why a special chapter on the religious communities of women and men in the Catholic Church?[1] Because they:

• have shaped the history of the church in an amazing variety of ways;

---

1. Orthodox churches have a rich ancient tradition of monastic life; several churches in the Anglican communion also have religious congregations of men and women; a few religious communities of sisters remain in some Protestant churches, especially Lutheran.

- constitute a unique value in the life of the church today;
- witness to church as mystery;
- have responded so effectively to their own renewal, as inspired by the Council.

The religious orders and congregations are a remarkable multiple phenomenon in the Catholic church. Jesus did not establish them or speak directly of the "religious life." They came into existence spontaneously as God-inspired individuals sought to lead a more intense Christian life and to serve the spiritual and physical needs of people. The resulting religious communities grew by leaps and bounds, attracting tens of thousands of men and women. They assumed an amazing variety of forms: first hermits in the deserts of Egypt, then friars and monks in Europe of the Middle Ages, and currently active apostolic groups and contemplative congregations in the 16th century and up to the present.

One cannot understand the Catholic Church today unless one appreciates the awesome contribution of religious communities to the kingdom of God and to the church in the past and today. Religious women and men became preachers revivifying the Catholic faith, intrepid missionaries in far-away lands, tireless founders of schools and hospitals, creative innovators and scholars. As such they have done and are doing a multitude of apostolic works that diocesan priests with responsibility for parishes within a diocese are often unable to do. The extraordinary value of the religious orders and congregations for 1500 years in the church is evident in their most prominent works: education, scholarship, health care, foreign missions, retreats, and the prayer and penance of contemplative groups.

Vatican II devoted chapter 6 of *Lumen Gentium,* called "Religious," and a separate document, *Decree on the Up-to-Date Renewal of the Religious Life,* to these religious communities of women and men. The Council praised religious life as particularly important today and gave suggestions for its renewal.

◆

Preview: The religious communities of women and men are a great value and a remarkable phenomenon in the Catholic Church. We look first at this multiple phenomenon from four viewpoints. We then consider briefly how religious communities rose in the Catholic Church. To understand their remarkable history, we provide examples of the two largest religious orders of men: the Franciscans and Jesuits. With this background we explain three realities that constitute what is known as the "religious state" in the Catholic Church. This leads to Vatican II's renewal of religious life: the Council urged a return to the original "charism" of the founders and foundresses and involvement in the world rather than isolation from it. We conclude with the amazing success story of American "nuns."

◆

The Multiple Phenomenon of Religious Communities in the Catholic Church

The existence of religious communities throughout most of the history of the Catholic Church is a phenomenon that reveals God's active presence in the church. For each year thousands of idealistic, talented young men and women answer a special call from God, sacrificing what the world considers important and valuable — material possessions, the enjoyment of sex and family life, the freedom to do what one wishes — to enter a religious community and make a lifelong commitment to live wholeheartedly for God through the vows of poverty, chastity and obedience. In such a consecrated life they more easily develop a personal relationship with God and the risen Christ. The large number of canonized saints and martyrs among religious men and women witness to God's active presence in these religious communities.

Another aspect of this phenomenon is the large number and often confusing variety of religious communities in the Catholic Church. Of the over 120 religious groups of men[2] throughout the world, the majority are made up of priests with some non-priest "brothers." There are, however, a number of religious communities made up almost exclusively of these "lay" brothers. Examples would be the Brothers of Christian Schools (8,285 members) and Marist Brothers (5,896 members), who run high schools and colleges in many countries. Worldwide there are over 1000 religious communities of women. A common joke used to be that only God knows their exact number and only God could identify their different *habits* (the religious clothes and headdresses worn in the period before Vatican II that distinguished each group)! The following figures of men and women religious worldwide is of Dec. 31, 1990, *Annuario Pontificio*, Rome; for the United States as of 1993 in the *Catholic Almanac* of 1994.

---

2. These statistics for religious institutes of men worldwide with more than 2000 members are from the Vatican's *Annuario Pontificio*, as of Jan. 1, 1991: Jesuits 24,028; Franciscans (Friars Minor) 19,038; Salesians 17,606; Franciscans (Capuchins) 11,805; Benedictines 9,014; Brothers of Christian Schools 8,285; Dominicans 6,775; Redemptorists 6,179; Marist Brothers 5,896; Society of the Divine Word 5,707; Oblates of Mary Immaculate 5,407; Franciscans (Conventuals) 4,242; Discalced Carmelites (O.C.D.) 3,704; Vincentians 3,698; Holy Spirit Congregation 3,366; Augustinians 3,166; Claretians 2,986; Trappists 2,710; Passionists 2,694; Missionaries of Africa 2,563; Priests of the Sacred Heart 2,493; Missionaries of the Sacred Heart of Jesus 2,414; Pallottines 2,245; Christian Brothers 2,160; Carmelites (O.Carm.) 2,135.

	Worldwide	United States
Religious Sisters	882,111	92,621
Religious Priests	145,477	17,135
Religious Brothers	62,526	6,205

Yet another aspect is the extraordinary diversity of apostolic works religious men and women are involved in. They are teachers, scholars, psychiatrists, doctors, nurses, playwrights, authors, TV producers, contemplatives, parish pastors, university presidents, teachers and medics in refugee camps, retreat-givers, spiritual directors, counselors, agricultural experts, songwriters, novelists and poets, hospital chaplains, AIDS counselors, labor union specialists, and so forth.

One need only look to the amazing network of elementary and high schools, colleges and universities founded and run by religious women and men; to the impressive number and quality of scholarly books and articles, especially in philosophy, theology, and the humanities, but also in areas of science, and to the magazines, newspapers, and catechetical materials published by religious; to the large numbers of hospitals, clinics, leprosaria, orphanages founded and staffed by the nursing congregations of religious sisters; to the vast numbers of missionary priests, sisters, and brothers who journey to distant lands to preach the good news of Christ, to plant the church, and to minister to the human needs of native peoples; to the hundreds of thousands of men, women and youth who find God in annual three or eight or thirty-day retreats conducted by members of religious communities; finally, to those men and women with a special call to a life of silence and penance and prayer for the needs of the world and of the church in the contemplative communities, like the **Trappists** for men and **Carmelites** for women. The Catholic Church would be greatly impoverished without the religious communities of women and men. They are indeed the glory of the church!

Religious communities are also a phenomenon in that they do not fit neatly into the structure of the church under bishops. Religious are directly accountable to and governed by their local and regional superiors and their international leader, often called Superior General for men and Mother General for women. These international groups are called "exempt" orders in that they are outside or exempt from the direct authority of local diocesan bishops. Since they serve the universal church, they are under the Congregation for Religious in the Vatican curia and, ultimately, the pope. Nonexempt congregations are those founded by a bishop for service within his own diocese; however, these often outgrow the originating diocese and take on a national or international character.

Their Origin and Remarkable History

Neither Jesus nor probably the 12 Apostles established the religious orders. But already the Acts of the Apostles and letters of Paul to Timothy showed that religious groups had arisen in the church in response to special needs. Later, God inspired special charismatic individuals like St. Augustine in 5th-century northern Africa, St. Benedict in 6th-century Italy, St. Francis of Assisi in 13th-century Italy, St. Ignatius Loyola in 16th-century Spain, and Mother Teresa in 20th-century India to a life of extraordinary holiness and love. Such individuals attracted followers who began to live together in voluntary poverty, to practice celibacy, and to minister to people in many ways. At some point a simple rule of life or a more detailed constitution is drawn up and submitted to the pope; with his official approval, the group becomes a formal religious order or congregation within the Catholic Church.

A modern example of this process is the Missionary Sisters of Charity, founded by Mother Teresa of Calcutta. On a train to Darjeeling, India, then Loreto Sister Teresa experienced a special call from God to work for "the poorest of the poor." Her transparent love of God and her heroic love for the sick and dying outcasts of Calcutta attracted first a handful and gradually hundreds of young women to join her in her work for the poor. She drew up a plan of spiritual, ascetic and missionary work which was approved by the Vatican Congregation for Religious and by the pope. Thus was born a new religious community in the Catholic Church.

Their founding by charismatic men and women who often overcame great obstacles, their extraordinary influence on the history of Europe, their amazing adventures and accomplishments in far-away missionary lands, their contributions to education and culture, science and health care, the numerous larger-than-life saints and martyrs for Christ they produced, their prodigious labor for God and humanity—all make the history of religious communities fascinating and informative reading. To give a sense of this historical phenomenon, we consider the two largest religious orders of men: the Franciscans, founded by the gentle, much-loved Francis of Assisi and the Jesuits, founded by the soldier-saint and mystic, Ignatius of Loyola.

St. Francis of Assisi (1181-1226) and the Franciscans (1210-) or Friars Minor[3]

The founder of the religious order of Friars Minor or Franciscans was born in Assisi, Italy, about 1181, the son of a well-to-do merchant. As a young man he was irresponsible and looked forward to a life of chivalry.

---

3. Adapted from *Collier's Encyclopedia*, Vol. 10 (New York: Macmillan Educational Co., 1990), 318-19.

But a year as prisoner of war in Perugia, and the wretchedness of the beggars and lepers of his own city, led him to serious reflection and deeply roused his human sympathies.

In 1206 he left home to live as a hermit. He devoted himself to the care of lepers and to rebuilding neglected churches in and around Assisi; in one of these, the Portiuncula, his full vocation was revealed to him. On Feb. 24, 1209, he heard the 10th chapter of Matthew read as the gospel for the day, and he understood this as a call to himself to live in total poverty and to preach. Disciples quickly joined him. In 1210, when he had 11 companions, Francis wrote a short rule for a new religious order and went to Rome with his companions to ask the pope for his approval. To everyone's surprise, Innocent III did approve.

As the number of friars increased, Francis sent them out in pairs beyond the Alps and across the sea. It became necessary to establish some form of organization, and in 1217, provinces were instituted. In 1223, Pope Honorius III formally confirmed the final version of the rule.

Francis' rule of life was strikingly different from the rules of the older orders of monks and canons. The friars were new, and the novelty and originality of their profession had a special relevance in the 13th century. The church had lost touch with a large section of its members, and two different types of heretical movements were gaining recruits at her expense: the Cathars, who believed that the material world was evil, the sufferings and death of Jesus an illusion, and the hierarchy of the Roman Church false; and the Waldensians, whose leaders led a life of poverty and preaching. Francis emphasized, in opposition to the Cathars, that the world was God's world, and fundamentally good. He had a special devotion to the human Jesus—it was Francis who made popular the crib at Christmas; and he insisted that his order should be loyal and obedient to the church and her hierarchy. This loyalty and obedience enabled the Friars Minor to win many who were attracted by the idea of following the Gospel literally and in poverty.

The basic principles that Francis gave his followers were these: to help people by working in the world, preaching the gospel and caring for the sick and suffering; to obey the gospel literally; to give up everything for Christ—the rich man his wealth, the learned man his learning. They were not to handle money. If they were not paid for their work in food and clothing, they must beg for what they needed.

The order's popularity was partly due to Francis' personality, to his infectious enthusiasm, gaity, and love, but even more, to the quality of his life. He was not impressive to look at—he was short and very thin, and wore an old patched and dirty tunic. When he repudiated his father and began to serve God, he was mocked and ostracized. But when he preached, he could touch the hearts of all his audience. His sermons were extremely simple and their effectiveness lay in the burning sincerity with which they were uttered and acted. Some of his most telling effects were produced by acted parables. When preaching before the cardinals, he could not express in words his joy in Christ, but conveyed it unforgettably by dancing. He wore out his own body by penance and fasting. His sympathy toward others was unbounded. His love extended to all people, including Muslims to whom he himself preached, and beyond men to all created things. Animals trusted him and he treated them with courtesy. Everything reminded him of God; and near the end of his life, when he was sick and practically blind, he composed a song of praise and thanks to God for all created things, the "Canticle of Brother Sun."

His last years were years of mystical experience. Long meditation on the suffering of Jesus culminated in the reception of the stigmata—the marks of Jesus' wounds on his hands and feet and side—two years before his death. On Oct. 3, 1226, he died at the Portiuncula, at the height of his fame; only two years later, in 1228, his old friend and patron, the first "Cardinal Protector" of the order, now Pope Gregory IX, solemnly canonized him. The foundation of the magnificent church that was to house his relics was laid the same year, and it was in the upper church of the Basilica of St. Francis at Assisi that the Florentine painter Giotto executed his series of heroic-size frescos depicting scenes from the life of the saint.

St. Ignatius Loyola and the Society He Founded (1540-1773 and 1814-)[4]

Ignatius of Loyola, a Basque nobleman and courtier, underwent a religious conversion in 1521 while recovering from battle wounds. He spent a year as a hermit in Manresa, Spain, where he underwent a series of mystical experiences. He recorded these in a notebook that became the first draft of his *Spiritual Exercises,* which contains a systematic series of meditations and other religious practices aimed at uniting persons with God and making them more effective instruments of God's will, usually during a 30-day retreat. This great classic of Catholic spirituality has been translated into nearly 30 languages and issued in more than 5,000 editions. It contains the main lines of Ignatian spirituality and allows retreatants to share to some extent Ignatius' experiences in Manresa.

After leaving Manresa, Ignatius made a pilgrimage to Jerusalem in 1523. On returning to Spain, he realized that he would need an education if he wanted to be an effective apostle. He therefore attended a grammar school in Barcelona and then enrolled at the universities of Alcala de Henares, Salamanca, and Paris. In Paris he gathered a group of six gifted disciples that included Francis Xavier and the theological scholar Diego Lainez.

---

4. Adapted from *Encyclopedia Americana, International Edition*, Vol. 16 (Danbury, CT: Grolier Inc., 1987), 35-37.

Originally, Ignatius and his companions planned to do missionary work in the Holy Land, but in 1538, when war between Venice and the Ottoman Turks blocked their departure, they put themselves at the disposal of Pope Paul III. After lengthy discussions, they determined to give the permanent structure of a religious order to their apostolate. Ignatius drew up a statement of purpose and preliminary rules, which Paul III approved in 1540. The next year Ignatius was elected superior general of the new order, which he called the Company or Society of Jesus, whose members are known as "Jesuits." He was entrusted with writing its Constitutions, which the first General Congregation approved in 1558 and had published.

During Ignatius' 15 years as general, the order diversified its apostolate and grew to about 1,000 members. Early Jesuits gave the *Spiritual Exercises*, with many young men entering the new order as a result of experiencing the *Exercises*. Lainez, St. Peter Canisius, and Alfonso Salmeron, the best Jesuit theologians, served as papal theologians at the Council of Trent in the mid-16th century.

The first Jesuit college for lay students opened in 1548 in Messina, Sicily, and became the model for hundreds of later Jesuit colleges. During Ignatius' lifetime, the Jesuits founded 33 colleges for lay students.

Mission work is the most esteemed Jesuit apostolate. The first and greatest Jesuit missionary was Francis Xavier, who sailed from Lisbon in 1541. After several years in southern India and Indonesia, he founded a flourishing Jesuit mission in Japan. He died in 1552, after an abortive attempt to enter China. The Jesuits soon established a string of missions in the lands that Francis had visited. Other Jesuit missionary endeavors during Ignatius' lifetime were in Morocco, the Congo, Brazil, and Ethiopia.

During the century following the death of Ignatius, the Jesuits continued their rapid growth. A high point was in the early 17th century, when the order had some 15,000 members and operated more than 500 colleges and seminaries. In 1599 the Jesuits crowned many years of educational experiment by issuing the *Ratio Studiorum*, a systematic set of regulations for their schools. The majority of Jesuit colleges were financed by endowments and charged no tuition. The nobility and middle class of Catholic Europe flocked to these colleges; among their graduates were Molière, Descartes, and Voltaire. Their curriculum was based on classical languages and literature, plus some philosophy, generally Aristotelian, and religious instruction. The Jesuits adopted the theology of St. Thomas Aquinas.

The Jesuits' missionary effort increased during the century after Xavier's death. Initially, Japan was the most promising mission, but Japanese Christianity was crushed by savage persecution during the early 17th century. Matteo Ricci used Western scientific knowledge to establish a foothold at the imperial court in Peking in 1601. After him a series of Jesuit scientist-missionaries tried to adapt Christianity to Chinese traditions. Critics, however, claimed that they had gone too far, and the papacy first suppressed the Chinese rites in 1704 and finally in 1742.

More lasting success was had in the Philippines and Latin America, where traditional missionary methods were used among more primitive cultures. The Jesuit missionaries active in North America included St. Jean de Brebeuf to the Iroquois in upper New York state, the explorer Jacques Marquette in the upper midwest, and Eusebio Kino, who founded missions in northern Mexico and present-day Arizona. Hundreds of Jesuits suffered martyrdom in mission lands, of which the most dangerous was Elizabethan England. Among the many English martyrs were Sts. Edmund Campion and Robert Southwell, a poet of renown.

The literary production of the Jesuits was remarkable. Canisius and St. Robert Bellarmine wrote not only polemical works against Protestantism but also catechisms that went through hundreds of editions. Other Jesuits made important contributions to science, particularly astronomy. In addition, the Jesuits often influenced political policy as court preachers and royal confessors. The kings of France, Spain, Poland, and Portugal, as well as the Holy Roman emperor, regularly had Jesuit confessors in the 17th century.

Jesuit growth slowed and influence declined in the late 17th and early 18th centuries. The leaders of the Enlightenment considered the Jesuits a major opponent. By the mid-18th century, several kings and their ministers looked on the Jesuits as a hindrance to the increase of state control over the church. Accordingly, the monarchs of Portugal, Spain, France, and Naples first suppressed the Jesuits nationally and colonially and then, in 1773, successfully pressured Pope Clement XIV to suppress them worldwide. The disappearance of the Jesuits had an especially severe effect in mission countries.

Following the Napoleonic Wars, the conservative regimes of Europe were happy to welcome back the Jesuits, and in 1814, Pope Pius VII restored the order, which grew steadily but slowly during the 19th century, despite its continuing ban in many countries. In Latin Europe and in Latin America it was usually liberal anticlerical governments that suppressed the Jesuits, but they were also attacked and exiled by conservative, nationalistic governments—for instance, in Russia by Czar Alexander I and Germany by Chancellor Otto von Bismarck—because of their close relations with the papacy.

During the 20th century, expansion was rapid—from 15,000 in 1900 to the peak number 36,000 in 1964. Since then the number of Jesuits has declined dramatically owing to many complex causes, including the rapid secularization of society. By 1980 Jesuits were laboring in more than 100 countries worldwide. Under their charismatic Father General, the Basque Pedro Arrupe, two general congregations committed Jesuits to work for justice and the poor. This has resulted in the murder of Jesuits in many countries, climaxed by the brutal killing of six University of Central America Jesuits in San Salvador in 1989.

The most important Jesuit apostolate in the United States is education, especially higher education. Among the 27 American Jesuit universities are Fordham, Georgetown, Boston College, Marquette, St. Louis, San Franciso, Seattle, and Loyola of Chicago. The American Jesuits also conduct 42 university preparatory schools. Major American cities have Jesuit retreat houses, where men and women make a shortened version of Ignatius' *Spiritual Exercises*.

A number of 20th-century Jesuits have made major contributions to Catholic theological renewal, particularly Pierre Teilhard de Chardin of France, Bernard Lonergan of Canada, and Karl Rahner of Germany. Several Jesuits, notably Daniel Berrigan of the United States, have taken leading roles in social-protest and antiwar movements.

The "Religious State"

Three realities constitute the "religious state" in the Catholic Church: the three religious vows, life together in community, and the special spirit and apostolic work inspired by the founder.

The Three Vows

The three religious vows of poverty, chastity, and obedience are at the heart of the religious life. These vows are meant to be highly positive. They strike at the powerful human drives of greed, lust and pride, and thus free the religious to dedicate his or her energy and whole life to love Christ and other people. The vows of a religious thus express the attitude of a resurrected person, one who has made a total and free commitment to God. The vows are called *evangelical* or gospel *counsels* because Jesus, as portrayed in the four Gospels, was chaste and led a life of voluntary poverty and complete obedience to his Father, even to death on the cross; they are *counsels* because Jesus invites, not commands, this special way of life. The vows are made to God, but are publicly received by the religious superior. Let us examine each vow.

1. Poverty. Basically a person in the religious state vows to follow the poor Christ by not owning material things; his or her needs are supplied by the religious community. By taking this vow one is freed from the human drive to acquire more and more money and possessions. We all have experienced how this drive is never fully satisfied and often brings frustration and unhappiness. With the vow of poverty one doesn't have to "keep up with the Joneses" or wear the latest clothes' styles or have the newest stereo. Thus freed from the selfish compulsion to acquire more and more, the religious can give himself or herself more fully to Christ and to the people he or she serves. This freedom brings a peace of mind, making possible a more simple lifestyle. The vow is clearly countercultural, for the world of advertising promises happiness through acquiring more material possessions. Committed to poverty, one can walk past the latest car model and suits and dresses and not be constantly frustrated!

2. *Chastity*. This vow frees the human heart to love God completely. In sacrificing the great good of marriage and family, chastity makes no sense unless it leads to the "undivided heart" that loves God and other people in God. Accordingly, this vow leaves our human hearts free to be possessed by God, to choose Christ as our friend and spouse and to love Christ in all people, without the limitations of a family. Celibacy is thus a powerful witness to the secular world of the love of God and of Christ our redeemer. It is a dramatic expression of the fact that we are pilgrims on this earth moving to an eternity with God and that the love of God is the greatest of goods.

3. *Obedience*. One of the deepest drives in each of us is to follow our own will, to be free to do whatever we want without anyone else forcing his will on us. The vow of obedience puts the will of God first in the life of the religious. One is free then to make Christ's values and interest first in his or her life. Each religious order has its own rule that spells out the kind of life to be lived under obedience. This obedience makes possible the extraordinary apostolic flexibility and missionary accomplishments of the religious orders, for the superior can send his or her religious to the farthest ends of the earth to bring the good news of Christ there. One of the glories of the religious orders has been their extraordinary missionary work in foreign lands.

Each vow thus represents a specific sacrifice for a higher cause: the love of God and of our fellow persons. Is the sacrifice difficult for religious? Yes. But once the commitment is freely made and begun to be lived, God's help is very much present, bringing a sense of freedom and joy and the ability to live out the commitment gracefully and without undue strain for those truly called to this way of life.

The life of the three evangelical counsels or vows are thus another aspect of the mystery that is the church. The consecrated, committed lives of women and men religious demand the supernatural virtues of faith, hope and love and the ever-present help of the Holy Spirit. Such lives are a witness to the presence of the risen Christ in the church and to the reality of the kingdom of God on earth. They also witness to the secular world the eternal values, the existence of God, and to the fact that on this earth we do not have a lasting home.

Community Life

The second constituent of the religious state is that religious live in community. They live together, sharing all things equally. They eat together in a refectory or dining room. They worship and pray together. (The older orders that have "choir" meet several times daily to praise God in song and recitation of the divine office.) They take recreation together. This common life can at times be irksome and difficult; but in most cases community life is a great support for living the three vows, for living a vigorous apostolic life, and is a source of inspiration, joy and consolation. Today there is a movement for the larger communities to break into smaller groups of 6-10 religious, who strive in more of a family setting to live community life more personally and profitably. It is too early to judge whether this will be the style of religious life in the future.

Unique Charism

Each religious order or congregation is characterized by the unique **charism** of its founder or foundress. Charism, meaning gift of grace, refers to the special inspirations and spiritual gifts God gave the "charismatic" founder or foundress by which they felt called by God to choose special apostolic works and eventually to establish a religious community. The founder's charism is passed on to the community and becomes the unique spirit animating the members. This charism as gift to the particular religious community becomes a powerful spiritual grace from God, helping the members live the founder's vision.

The charism St. Francis of Assisi gave his friars was his extraordinary simplicity and love of "lady poverty," his love of the crucified Christ and respect for all God's creatures. St. Ignatius of Loyola's charism bequeathed to Jesuits is total service of Christ the king, everything "for the greater glory of God," special loyalty to the church in the person of Christ's vicar the pope, and the *Spiritual Exercises,* which gives each Jesuit his characteristic Ignatian spirituality.

Another aspect of this charism is the specific apostolic work which inspired founding the community. Examples are Mother Teresa giving Christ's love to the poorest of the poor; Catherine McAuley, foundress of the Sisters of Mercy, bringing Christ's merciful care to the sick and to youth needing education; Christian Brothers' founding schools for poor youth.

Vatican II Renewal of Religious Life

The *Decree on the Up-to-Date Renewal of the Religious Life (PC)* set down two significant principles and means for renewal: return "to the original inspiration of the community and adaptation to the changed conditions of the times" (PC 3). By returning to the "original inspiration of the community," Vatican II challenged today's religious to recover and live more fully the vision and charism of the founder or foundress as the best way to renew their community. For effective adaptation to modernity, the Council urged that "religious be properly instructed . . . in the behavior patterns, emotional attitudes, and thought processes of modern society." (18) Thus their "manner of living, praying and working should be suitably adapted to the physical and psychological conditions of today's religious . . . to the needs of the apostolate, the requirements of a given culture."(3)

To accomplish these two principles, the Council realistically directed that constitutions and rules, custom books and prayer books be revised, a "task that will require suppression of outmoded regulations." (3) These principles, which made possible the elimination of "excess baggage" accumulated in many congregations over the centuries and which stimulated research into historical roots and documents to recover the original charisms, were responsible for the dramatic changes in religious life since the Council.

Vatican II also made community life a priority. Any class distinctions were to be abolished. Religious were encouraged to "excel one another in showing respect," to "carry each other's burdens," to be "a true family gathered together in the Lord's name" because "brotherly [sic] unity shows that Christ has come; from it results great apostolic influence." (15)

We can summarize the renewal set in motion by the Council in three succinct phrases: return to the founder's charism, signs of the times, and needs of the members; and in two words: simplicity and adaptability.

Renewal Since the Council

What has the *Decree* accomplished in religious communities in the years since the Council? The document "opened up enormous new possibilities" for religious women and men. "For the first time in many centuries the official teaching voice of the church was actually urging religious to turn their faces *toward* the world instead of away from it."[5] The Council's principle of returning to the original inspiration and spirit and aims of each founder inspired religious orders and congregations to study in greater depth the original religious experience and charism God gave their holy founder or foundress and to appropriate it as their distinguishing charism or gift today. Thus a "dynamic model" of religious life replaced the classicist model of isolation from the world, sacredness of the religious habit, multiplicity of external regulations, elaborate ritual and a variety of traditional symbols. "A revolutionary change in the manner of exercising authority and decision-making" occurred in many congregations, resulting

---

5. Timothy O'Connell, ed., *Vatican II and Its Documents, An American Reappraisal* (Wilmington, DE: Michael Glazier, 1986), 82-83.

in a "lively sense of the importance of communal discernment and consequently of the location of authority not only in a superior but also in a community" with "a concomitant relocation of responsibility."[6]

Religious women in particular took the renewal to heart. In chapter meetings, congregations returned to their roots to rediscover the vision and energy of their foundresses, redefined their mission, changed their religious habits to a more secular dress, created Sister Formation programs, sent sisters to earn Master's and Doctoral degrees, and chose new apostolates. In a perceptive article,[7] Sister Joan Chittister, Order of St. Benedict and then-prioress of Mount St. Benedict Priory in Pennsylvania, analyzed five facets of religious life that dramatically illustrate women's religious life before and after Vatican II: modes of *spirituality* (from self-repression to self-development); *ministry* (from being the labor force of the church "to being a leaven," a Christian presence in building a Christian world); *vision of the foundress* (rediscovering the energy lost in the overinstitutionalization of congregations); *cultural needs* (addressing the signs of the times: the poor, peace and justice organization, pastoral work); and the *nature and role of women* (reestablish the personal identity of women religious as adults capable of defining and structuring their own lives).

To further these goals, American religious women formed the Leadership Conference of Women Religious (LCWR), which has become a strong force for renewal, but not without controversy. One example of an innovative, successful ministry by women religious is Network, a Washington-based group of skilled, dedicated sisters from different congregations who advocate legislation or monitor pending legislation by lobbying Congress-persons on behalf of the poor and defenceless and for peace and justice issues.

An American Success Story

This chapter would not be complete without telling the story of American religious women. We shall choose the unsung heroes of the Catholic Church in the United States, the "good sisters." They originally sailed from Europe in groups of three and four during the 18th and 19th centuries with battered suitcases and hearts full of generosity and love to a strange and difficult land. They settled in major cities or the adjoining countryside, and without money or buildings immediately set about opening schools and orphanages and hospitals. The first intrepid group were the Ursulines (founded by St. Angela Merici in 1535 in Italy), who settled in New Orleans in 1727 and soon became an integral part of the life and history of this booming Mississippi river city. They cared for Civil War

6. *Ibid.*, 89.
7. Joan Chittister, "Rome and American Religious Life," *America* 155 (Nov. 1, 1986): 258-260.

	First Foundation in USA	Foundress	Year	Country
1790	Carmelites, Maryland	St. Teresa of Avila	1562	Spain
1799	Visitation Sisters, Washington DC	St. Jane de Chantal	1610	France
1809	Sisters of Charity, Philadelphia	St. Elizabeth Seton	1809	USA
1812	Sisters of Loretto, Kentucky	Sr. Mary Rhodes	1812	USA
1813	Religious of Sacred Heart, St. Louis	St. Madeline Barat	1800	France
1822	3rd Order St. Dominic, Springfield, KY	St. Catherine of Siena	1350?	Italy
1836	Sisters of St. Joseph, St. Louis	Fr. Medaille, SJ	1650	France
1840	Sisters of Providence, Indiana	Abbe Jujarie	1806	France
1843	Sisters of Mercy, Pittsburgh	Catherine McAuley	1831	Ireland
1849	3rd Order St. Francis, Milwaukee	St. Clare of Assisi	1221	Italy
1852	Sisters of St. Benedict, St. Mary PA	St. Scholastica	6th C	Italy
1854	Presentation Nuns, San Francisco	Nan Nagle	1775	Ireland
1868	Little Sisters of the Poor, Brooklyn	Mother Marie de la Croix	1839	France
1875	The Poor Clares, Cleveland	St. Clare of Assisi	1221	Italy

soldiers and prayed for the outnumbered troops of General Stonewall Jackson, prompting him later to enter the convent walls to pay a thank-you visit to the nuns.

Other groups followed the Ursulines, settling throughout the east and midwest. The following chronological list (partial) of foundations shows graphically the extraordinary growth of religious congregations in the United States.

From such humble beginnings in the United States, these courageous dedicated women attracted scores of young American girls and women to join their communities. Soon the little wooden convents grew into large 4-5-story, multiwinged motherhouses, and one-room schools and clinics developed into large academies and hospitals. As the numbers of nuns increased, the motherhouses sent bands of two or three sisters into the frontier of ever-expanding America to found new convents and schools and hospitals and orphanages. By the early 1900s, virtually every major U.S. city had large convents full of sisters who staffed girls' high schools and women's colleges and hospitals. They built most of the Catholic hospitals, and between 1896 and 1955 they had founded more than 100 colleges for women. This remarkable growth of institutions serving the expanding Catholic immigrant population is one of the most remarkable success stories in the history of the Catholic Church.

The school system itself was an extraordinary achievement. Older Catholics today remember with a mixture of awe and affection their days in parochial schools under the stern discipline of the nuns. Poor immigrant Catholics were able to attend these schools because tuition was low, thanks to the poverty of the nuns whose salary was hardly enough to live on.

Scores of Catholic men and women owe their knowledge and practice of the Catholic faith and their strong loyalty to the church to their parochial school training—in stark contrast to large numbers of Catholic youth today.

The nuns were a visible, respected part of American life. A familiar sight was two sisters—they always went out from the convent in pairs and never at night!—riding the buses or walking downtown, their black or white habits modestly covering their bodies from wimple to black shoes. Each congregation was identified by fascinatingly different habits and wimples, the latter revealing only pinched faces; these wimples were marvelous creations of black or white headdress and white starched front covering neck and part of the chest. "God's Geese," the Sisters of Charity who displayed two-foot-long white starched wings coming to a point from their headdress, never failed to attract attention and were a definite hazard in crowded buses! Wherever nuns went, they received much respect from both Catholics and Protestants, who recognized their selfless dedication. Older Catholics view with nostalgia the absence of the sisters' immediate public identity and visible witness to their consecrated lives now that the habits and wimples have been replaced with secular dress or knee-length skirts and a simple headdress often resembling nurses' caps.

The drastic decrease in vocations to the sisterhood today and the "greying" of the sisters, whose average age is now in the 60s, is a great loss to the church. Older Catholics tend to yearn for the "old days" and feel twinges of sadness when large convent buildings are sold and girls' schools closed for lack of sisters. For "their" nuns were the glory of the Catholic Church in the United States since they, more than any other group, were responsible for the education of millions of immigrant Catholics and the enormously successful Catholic parochial system.

Yet the modern sister is an impressive person—often highly educated, possessing a doctorate, deeply apostolic, attuned to the modern world, committed to justice and human rights, especially for the poor and oppressed, profoundly spiritual withal. The modern sister is likely to be a skilled university professor or hospital administrator, medical doctor in missionary lands, member of "network sisters" lobbying in Washington for human rights and just laws, a social worker in the poorest areas of American cities or in the *favelas* of Latin America, pastor of a parish. It is said that the American sisters put into practice the renewal of Vatican II more wholeheartedly and effectively than any other group in the church.

We are witnessing a transition period in religious life of both women and men in the United States and indeed throughout the world. Will it bring a new upsurge in vocations? Will some of the traditional religious communities with their glorious history die out? Will new, different-style religious congregations be founded to replace them and to meet modern needs and life? Sister Joan Chittister believes that women religious have a future if they meet, as they did so creatively in the past, the great human, religious, and societal needs of today with their former passion and intense love.[8] The issue is not clear at present; we can only trust the Holy Spirit to continue to guide and lead the church.

Religious life was discussed at the ninth Synod of Bishops' meeting during November 1994, under the broad theme "The Consecrated Life and Its Role in the Church and the World." In its closing official "Message of the Synod,"[9] the bishops praised religious life as "indispensable" to the church in that religious women and men have a unique prophetic role as "witnesses to evangelical values." In terms of the future, the message made the following points:

- consecrated women should participate more in the church's decision-making;
- the past rich variety of consecrated life should be encouraged for the future;
- religious need sufficient autonomy to preserve their charism, but sufficient dependence to preserve the unity of the diocese;
- their consecrated lives fit them to play "a leading role in . . . the new evangelization."

It remains to be seen if the Synod and its final document will give a "new paradigm" for religious life and be a catalyst of new vitality for religious women and men in the third millennium.

Summary

The very existence in the Catholic Church of groups of women and men consecrated to God is a great value for the church and a unique expression of the church as mystery, that is, of God's active presence. We approach the topic of religious communities as a multiple phenomenon: God's special call to Christians and their response; the sheer number and variety of these religious groups; the impressive variety of their apostolic work for people; and the unique place the groups occupy in the structure of the Catholic Church. Throughout the church's history, God has inspired gifted men and women to found religious communities; the apostolic work they have done and continue to do is an immense contribution to the church's mission. The story of the founding, early years, and history up to the present of the religious communities in the Catholic Church makes informative reading, as illustrated by the Franciscan and Jesuit "orders." Re-

---

8. Joan Chittister, "Religious Orders," *National Catholic Reporter* (Feb. 18, 1994): 13-17. She asks 10 questions that she holds are at the heart of what the future might hold for religious women.

9. "Consecrated Life: Expression of Church's Spiritual Vitality," *Origins* 24 (November 10, 1994): 369-374.

ligious women and men constitute the "religious state" marked by the three religious vows, life in community, and a rule of life formulated by the foundress or founder. Vatican Council II, in urging religious communities to renewal, gave two principles for renewal that have resulted in revolutionary changes in the lives, dress, and apostolates of religious women and men. We close with the extraordinary success story of the American "nuns" and pose a difficult question: what is the future of these religious communities?

For Discussion

1. What do you think are the reasons why fewer young men and women are joining religious communities today?
2. In your opinion, what needs to be done so that the religious life would once again be an attractive, challenging, fulfilling vocation?
3. In what ways do religious communities express the nature of the church as mystery?

For Action

1. Interview a priest or sister or brother member of a religious community. Find out about their work, their motivation, their self-fulfillment, their sense of the future.
2. Read in the *New Catholic Encyclopedia* a brief life of a founder or foundress, like Benedict or Dominic or Francis de Sales or Teresa of Avila or Elizabeth Seton or Catherine McAuley.
3. See the visually beautiful movie, *Brother Son, Sister Moon*, about Francis and Clare of 13th-century Assisi.
4. Find out about the exciting missionary adventures and accomplishments of Francis Xavier in India and Japan or Mateo Ricci to the Chinese Emperor in Beijing or the heroic life and martyr deaths of Edmund Campion in England or Isaac Jogues in New York state or Miguel Pro in Mexico.
5. Make a report on the 1992 FORUS study, "The Future of Religious Orders in the United States."

Further Reading

Arbuckle, Gerald. *Out of Chaos: Refounding Religious Congregations.* Mahwah, NJ: Paulist Press, 1988.

Chittister, Joan. *Winds of Change: Women Challenge the Church.* Kansas City: Sheed & Ward, 1986.

Lernoux, Penny. *Hearts on Fire*. Maryknoll NY: Orbis Books, 1992.

Muggeridge, Malcolm. *Something Beautiful for God: Mother Teresa of Calcutta*. New York: Harper & Row, 1971.

Ware, Ann. *Midwives of the Future: American Sisters Tell Their Story*. Kansas City, MO: Leaven Press, 1985.

Part IV

Key Ecclesial Sacraments Renewed

CHAPTER 13

The Water Sacrament of Rebirth and Initiation

Man of God that you are . . . seek after integrity, piety, faith, love, steadfastness, and a gentle spirit. Fight the good fight of faith. Take firm hold on the everlasting life to which you were called when in the presence of many witnesses, you made your noble profession of faith [at baptism].

—1st Letter of Paul to Timothy 6:11-12

Baptism constitutes a sacramental bond of unity linking all who have been reborn by it. —*Unitatis Redintegratio* 22

Introduction

When I was director of Campus Ministry at a midwestern university, a sophomore young lady came to my office and asked how she, a Baptist, could become a Catholic. I asked if she was baptized. "Oh yes, when I was 13. I'll never forget it!" I invited her to explain. "My minister and I went into a tank full of water in front of all the people. He put my whole body under the water three times." With tears in her eyes, she described her experience. "I felt as if I were actually dying to my old life and my sins. Each time I came up out of the water, I felt I was rising with Christ to a new life. I felt born again. I was so happy. I'll never forget this feeling."

Christians baptized as infants did not experience their baptism. So for them baptism tends to become the forgotten sacrament, ignored and unappreciated.

Yet baptism is an extraordinary event. It starts our Christian life. So it's our second birth. It establishes our relationship to the risen Christ, to God our Father, and to the powerful Spirit. It's our "christening" by which we "put on Christ," receiving a share of God's own life. We become a new creature. Thus baptism is preeminently the sacrament of LIFE. It is our initiation rite into the Christian community; by it we enter Christ's Church. But baptism is not a one-time event of the past; our whole life is meant to be a living out of what God gave us in baptism and of our baptismal promises and commitment.

From its earliest days, Christianity chose common water to be the means of receiving all these benefits. Thus baptism is preeminently the *water*-sacrament. All peoples instinctively sense the powerful primordial cosmic symbolism of water as both life and death. Water gives life to our planet, transforming deserts into rich farm lands; water gives life and refreshment to all living creatures. Water in abundance is one of God's greatest gifts.

Water is also one of the richest symbols enjoyed by the human family. We take pleasure in rustic creeks, broad rivers, idyllic lakes, plunging waterfalls, and powerful ocean waves. We enjoy cool refreshing drinks, relaxing showers and baths, invigorating swimming. Yet water is destructive, capable of bringing death in devastating floods and raging seas. In our reflection on the sacrament of baptism, it will be rewarding to keep in mind the universal and dramatic symbolism of water.

The Second Vatican Council renewed this sacrament by restoring the ancient catechumenate for adults (SC 64), providing for revision of the rites of both adult and infant baptism (SC 66, 67), encouraging full immersion in water, and recognizing baptisms performed in other Christian churches.

◆

Preview: We shall consider these aspects of baptism: the water ritual of immersion and the complete baptism rite; a theology of baptism from New Testament images; Vatican II's recovery in the Rite of Christian Initiation for Adults of the ancient catechumenate program by which persons became Christians in the early centuries of Christianity; the ecumenical significance of baptism; and the theologically ambiguous practice of infant baptism, as well as the ecumenically-divisive practice of believers-only baptism.

◆

The Water Ritual of Immersion

The sacrament of baptism is the water ritual by which a person becomes "in Christ," hence the older term "christening." Our word baptism comes from the Greek *baptizo*, "I plunge." In baptism by immersion, the entire body is plunged into the water. Listen to St. Paul describe the dramatic symbolism of this form of baptism practiced by the early church.

> Are you not aware that we who were baptized into Christ Jesus were baptized into his death? Through baptism into his death we were buried with him, so that, just as Christ was raised from the dead by the glory of the Father, we too might live a new life. If

we have been united with him through likeness to his death, so shall we be through a like resurrection. This we know: our old self was crucified with him so that . . . we might be slaves to sin no longer. . . . You must consider yourselves dead to sin but alive for God in Christ Jesus. (Romans 6: 3-11)

The ritual of plunging or immersing a person in water symbolizes dying with Christ to all our past sins; coming out of the water symbolizes both Christ emerging from the tomb, resplendent with risen life, and our own new Christ-life. In terms of how sacraments achieve their effects, the ritual action of immersion with the words "I baptize you . . ." both *express* (symbolize) and *cause* the spiritual realities of destruction of all sin and conferral of Christ's risen life. The standard practice of pouring water on the forehead symbolizes cleansing or washing and serves to emphasize baptism as destroying original and actual sin; however, it fails to express St. Paul's powerful symbol of dying and rising with Christ and our sharing in Christ's paschal mystery. Thus the Christian Church from the very beginning made the water ritual of baptism into the death and resurrection of Jesus the means of obtaining divine life and of entering the Christian community.

The essence of baptism is the brief water ritual and the words "[Name], I baptize you in the name of the Father, and of the Son, and of the Holy Spirit." However, in order to express the full richness and power and significance of this sacrament, the church has through the centuries surrounded the basic water ritual with added symbols and a series of impressive prayers. The complete baptismal ceremony is a multiple ritual. Besides water, the complete ritual includes these down-to-earth symbols with their accompanying prayers:

- *oil,* which heals and protects.
  "We anoint you with the oil of salvation in the name of Christ our Savior. May he strengthen you with his power. . . "

- a *lighted candle,* symbolizing Christ, the light of the world.
  "You have been enlightened by Christ. Walk always as a child of the light and keep the flame of faith alive in your heart . . . "

- a *white garment,* symbolizing the newly baptized's purity of soul and being in Christ.
  "N . . ., you have become a new creation and have clothed yourself in Christ. Take this white garment and bring it unstained to the judgment seat of our Lord Jesus Christ so that you may have everlasting life."

The full rite also includes Scripture readings, prayers of those present for the one to be baptized, the priest's blessing of the baptismal water, with an eloquent prayer recalling how God used water in the history of salvation, as reported in the Hebrew and Christian scriptures, the solemn renunciation of sin and profession of faith, recitation of the Our Father, and two beautiful concluding blessing prayers for the mother and father, in the case of an infant.

Theology of Baptism

The New Testament develops a theology of baptism through various *images* that help us appreciate the privileged spiritual effects of this sacrament.

1. Cleansing and purifying from sin

"Be baptized at once and wash away your sins. . . ."   —Acts 22:16

"And such were some of you [gross sinners]; but you have been washed, consecrated, justified in the name of the Lord Jesus Christ and in the Spirit of our God."   —1 Cor 6:11

2. A new creature and a birth

"I solemnly assure you, no one can enter into God's kingdom without being begotten of water and the Holy Spirit."   —John 3:5

"But when the kindness and love of God our Savior appeared, he saved us . . . through the baptism of new birth and renewal by the Holy Spirit."   —Titus 3:4-5

3. Clothes metaphor of putting on Christ

"All you who have been baptized into Christ have clothed yourselves with him. There does not exist among you Jew or Greek, slave or free man, male or female. All are one in Christ Jesus.
                                        —Galatians 3:27-28

4. Death and life in Christ

"In baptism you were not only buried with him but also raised to life with him because you believed in the power of God who raised him from the dead. . . . God gave you new life in company with Christ."   —Colossians 2:12-13

"Our old self was crucified with him so that . . . we might be slaves to sin no longer . . . you must consider yourselves dead to sin but alive for God in Christ Jesus."   —Romans 6: 6,11

5. Members of Christ's body

"It was in one Spirit that all of us, whether Jew or Greek, slave or free, were baptized into one body."   —1 Corinthians 12:13

The Rite of Christian Initiation for Adults (RCIA)

Vatican II revived the ancient **catechumenate** in the Rite of Christian Initiation for Adults. To understand and appreciate RCIA, we shall first consider the remarkable ancient program for preparing **catechumens** for baptism.

To become a Christian and enter the Christian community was in the first centuries of Christianity a powerful and never-to-be-forgotten experience. It meant renouncing one's former sinful life and beginning a new life in Jesus Christ. Moreover, in the age of persecution, entrance into the Christian Church could mean suffering and dying as a martyr. So the church devised a lengthy period of preparation, called the catechumenate, in which the catechumens learned about Jesus and the central Christian beliefs and practiced prayer, fasting, and self-denial.

After three or more years of the catechumenate, those catechumens deemed ready were chosen by the bishop for a 40-day period of prayers, blessings and exorcisms, and formal instruction climaxing with initiation into the Christian community early on Easter Sunday.

It was an experience they would never forget! Holy Saturday night the catechumens fasted and prayed, turned to the darkened west to renounce Satan and to the east where the sun rises to commit themselves to Christ, the light of the world. Then, as dawn approached, the catechumens were stripped of their clothes, entered the sunken baptismal font, and were immersed three times; after each immersion they professed faith in the Trinity, first in the Father, then the Son, then the Holy Spirit. Coming up out of the water, their five senses were anointed with the oil of chrism and the Holy Spirit was asked to give them his power. The newly baptized in Christ then put on a long white garment and took a lighted candle. Thus attired, they left the baptistry and entered the cathedral, where the assembled Christian community welcomed them warmly with the kiss of peace. As the dawn broke, the joyful Easter eucharistic celebration began and the new Christians received the body and blood of Christ for the first time.

Thus were catechumens initiated into the Christian community by means of the three sacraments—baptism, confirmation, eucharist—that have come to be known as the "sacraments of Christian initiation."

The year-long RCIA preparation for adult catechumens has become one of the most successful renewal practices to come from Vatican II. Its success results from the dynamics of creating a prayerful sharing Christian community. Catechumens and their sponsors share their spiritual journey, discuss openly and with trust the questions they have about Catholic beliefs and practices, pray together, form friendships and experience Christian community. The pre-Vatican II "convert classes" or series of instructions by a priest tended to emphasize only information; RCIA stresses the *experience* of living the Christian way of life in a supportive community, while learning Catholic teachings and practices.

The Ecumenical Sacrament

Through baptism, Christians are brought into union with Christ, with each other, and with the Christian Church of every time and place. Our common baptism is thus a basic bond of unity.[1]

Since baptism can be received only once, other Christians who became Catholics before Vatican II were rebaptized "conditionally," that is, *under the condition* or precaution that their first baptism might have been invalid. For in the climate of suspicion and isolation toward "non-Catholics" since the Protestant Reformation, Catholic practice was to doubt the validity of Protestant baptism.

With the ecumenical spirit introduced by John XXIII and the work of theologians, especially Scripture scholar Cardinal Augustine Bea, the first head of John XXIII's newly created Secretariate for Christian Unity, the Catholic Church realized that Protestants took baptism seriously and in fact were fulfilling the conditions for valid New Testament baptism: the intention to carry out Christ's command to baptize, the use of water and the Trinitarian formula. The Catholic Church thus officially recognized Protestant baptism; the presumption became that their baptisms were valid unless it was abundantly clear that a necessary condition had been absent. Hence Catholic priests were no longer permitted to baptize converts from Protestantism conditionally. This is why there was no question of my repeating the baptism of the Baptist girl mentioned at the beginning of this chapter.

The *Decree on Ecumenism (UR)* expresses the theological basis for recognizing Protestant baptisms. "By the sacrament of baptism, whenever it is properly conferred in the way the Lord determined, and received with the appropriate dispositions of soul, a man [sic] becomes truly incorporated into the crucified and glorified Christ and is reborn to a sharing of divine life" (UR 22). Or briefly, "All those justified by faith through baptism are incorporated into Christ" (UR 3). Thus "Baptism constitutes a sacramental bond of unity linking all who have been reborn by means of it" (UR 22).

Once the Catholic Church recognized Protestant baptism, important theological conclusions followed. Because baptism is entrance into the body of Christ which is the church, Protestants are members of the Christian Church.[2] And because baptism forms a bond of unity among the bap-

---

1. *Baptism, Eucharist and Ministry* (Geneva: World Council of Churches, 1982), 3.

2. The Council was careful not to state in so many words that other Christians are members of the church, probably because Pope Pius XII, in his 1943 encyclical *The Mystical Body,* stated "Only those are to be included as real members of the Church who have been baptized and profess the true faith and have not been so unfortunate as to separate themselves from the unity of the body. . ." Pius XII thus restricted membership in the Body of Christ to Catholics, equating the Catholic Church with the Body of Christ. Cardinal Bea argued that this statement did not apply to Christians born and baptized outside the Catholic Church who had not knowingly and deliberately "separated themselves from the unity of the body." Today theologians agree that all baptized Christians, as members of the Body of Christ, are therefore members of the Christian Church; they distinguish, however, being "in partial" or "in full communion," since the separation of the

tized in Christ, Catholics began to refer to Protestants as fellow Christians, our sisters and brothers in Christ.

Catholic ecumenical theologians explored the potential of baptism for uniting the separated Christian churches. The Faith and Order commission of the World Council of Churches had already been studying baptism as a promising ecumenical sacrament for over 25 years.[3] This long study and discussion reached fruition in the baptism section of *Baptism, Eucharist and Ministry,* published in 1982.[4] Theologians of the WCC member churches, including Catholic theologians who had become members of the Faith and Order Commission, reached near-unanimous agreement on the meaning and practice of baptism; only the believer-baptist churches were unable to give complete approval.

However, the full implications of our common baptism in Christ have yet to be realized in the ecumenical relations of the churches. The intense theological reflection on baptism before and after the Council has now moved on to church-dividing issues of ministry, including episcopacy and papacy, and moral questions. The bishops at the Council voiced this caution: those "who believe in Christ and have been properly baptized are brought into a certain though imperfect communion with the Catholic Church" (UR 3) because "baptism is only a beginning . . . for it is . . . oriented toward a complete profession of faith, a complete incorporation into the system of salvation . . . and a complete participation in eucharistic communion" (UR 22).

It appears then that baptism of itself is insufficient to unite the separated Christian *churches.* Yet, the fact that today the majority of the Christian churches recognize the validity of each other's baptism has resulted in closer relationships, shared prayer and even worship services, common social action, and many other expressions of our newfound bond in Christ. Baptism can thus appropriately be called "the ecumenical sacrament."

The Question of Infant Baptism[5]

Most Christian churches practice infant baptism; Baptist churches and some others practice "believers' baptism," that is, only those believers who have made a deliberate faith commitment to Jesus Christ are baptized.

---

churches is still a fact.

3. See Joseph Eagan, S.J., *Baptism and Communion Among the Churches* (Rome: Gregorian University Press, 1975) and "A Creative Ecumenical Initiative: the World Council of Churches Challenges its Member Churches," *Mid-Stream* 17 (April, 1978): 118-134.

4. See baptism section, 2-7, in *Baptism, Eucharist and Ministry.*

5. For two divergent viewpoints, see *Review and Expositor, A Baptist Theological Journal,* 27 (Winter 1980): "The Authority and Justification for Infant Baptism" by Joseph Eagan, S.J., 47-61 and "The Authority and Justification for Believers' Baptism" by G.R. Beasley-Murray, 63-70.

This practice and the theology on which it is based diminishes the effectiveness of baptism as an ecumenical sacrament.

Some years ago I attended a weekend "retreat" dialogue with Southern Baptists. Saturday afternoon, during one of the sessions in which we shared our experiences of what it means to be Christian, one of the Baptists turned to me in seriousness and said with some surprise: "You really are a Christian!" I was not offended for I understood the theological position from which he spoke; perhaps I was a bit flattered, for he seemed to recognize that I had committed myself to "the Lord Jesus" through presumably a "conversion experience."

Believer-baptist churches argue convincingly that New Testament baptism always involves faith and commitment to live the Christian way of life. They point out that St. Paul's many references to the rich effects of baptism refer to the baptism of adults, who alone are capable of faith, and not to infants. They also make much of the fact that in some European countries infant baptism is equivalent to gaining citizenship, a practice in these national churches that invariably leads to nonpracticing baptized "unbelievers" in later years. Thus believer-baptist churches refuse to consider Christian someone baptized as an infant. Naturally, this has caused a major division within the Christian Church.

In answering these formidable arguments, the churches that baptize infants stress that infant baptism shows the power of God who causes the marvelous effects of baptism described in this chapter. They point out that infant baptism brings the infant into the church community so the child's life of faith is gradually nourished during its formative years. They also argue that faith is indeed present in infant baptism, not the infant's faith but the *vicarious* faith of parents and sponsors, who respond for the infant and accept the responsibility of rearing the child in the Christian faith until the time the child can personally complete or confirm his or her baptism in the sacrament of confirmation. And they call attention to the fact that St. Paul baptized entire households, including children presumably, and compared baptism to Jewish circumcision received eight days after birth.

It is true that adult baptism was the normal practice in the early church. At some unknown point the early church began baptizing infants, perhaps at the insistence of newly baptized Christians, who wanted their children to be part of the Christian community like themselves. Infant baptism is thus a very ancient tradition in the church. Nonetheless, these two different practices continue to divide the churches and make union between the majority of the churches that baptize infants and the believer-baptist churches very difficult. Because of the theological ambiguity of an infant receiving a sacrament that involves conscious faith commitment, Vatican II emphasized the ritual of adult baptism as normative and best expressing the full meaning of the sacrament.

Summary

Most Christians baptized as infants do not appreciate the extraordinary event of Christian baptism. With its dramatic symbolism of death and life, the water ritual of baptism is the way persons enter the Christian Church and are "reborn" into the life of Jesus Christ. The practice of baptism by immersion best brings out St. Paul's teaching on baptism as sharing in the death and resurrection of Christ. The early church developed its theology of baptism through many images expressed in the New Testament. In time, the church developed a longer ritual using symbols of oil, candles, white garments and many prayers to bring out for the Christian community the rich meaning of "the christening." In the early centuries of the Christian Church, adults underwent a lengthy preparation period for entrance into the Christian community known as "the catechumenate." Vatican II recovered this practice in a modified form, called the Rite of Christian Initiation of Adults. As entrance into the body of Christ which is the Christian Church, baptism forms a profound bond between all Christians and thus deserves to be called "the ecumenical sacrament." Baptizing infants is the practice of the majority of the Christian churches today; however it lacks the personal faith commitment of New Testament baptism of adults. Those churches that insist on personal faith refuse to accept infant baptism, thus creating an ecumenical obstacle to future church union.

For Discussion

1. What does your baptism mean to you now? How can you make it an important part of your Christian life?
2. Should the church stop baptizing babies? Do the believer-baptist churches have the better practice?
3. Does the sacrament of confirmation accomplish what infant baptism lacks?
4. Can baptism be a basis for uniting the separated Christian churches? Why or why not?
5. What about "limbo" where unbaptized babies were supposed to have gone?

For Action

1. Attend baptism by immersion in a Baptist church; talk to the baptizing minister and the person baptized.
2. Read up on the challenging ancient catechumenate practice of the early Christian Church. Imagine yourself being a catechumen then. Could you have done it?

3. Talk to someone who is leading the RCIA and someone who is making it. Find out what they experience.
4. Report on baptisms performed today in Africa by immersion in streams and rivers.

Further Reading

Baptism, Eucharist and Ministry. Geneva: World Council of Churches, 1982.

Kavanagh, Aiden. *The Shape of Baptism: The Rite of Christian Initiation.* New York: Pueblo Publishing Co., 1978.

Osborne, Kenan. *The Christian Sacraments of Initiation: Baptism, Confirmation, Eucharist.* New York/Mahwah: Paulist Press, 1987.

Searle, Mark. *Christening, the Making of Christians.* Essex, Great Britain: Devin Mayhew Ltd., 1977.

N.B.: Individual chapters on baptism are also in the books listed in chapter 5.

CHAPTER 14

Eucharist, Heart of Church

"I myself am the living bread come down from heaven . . . The bread I will give is my flesh for the life of the world." At this, the Jews quarreled among themselves saying, "How can he give us his flesh to eat?" Thereupon Jesus said to them ". . . my flesh is real food and my blood real drink. Whoever feeds on my flesh and drinks my blood remains in me and I in him."   —John 6:51-56

Before he was given up to death,
a death he freely accepted,
he took bread and gave you thanks.
He broke the bread,
gave it to his disciples and said:
Take this, all of you, and eat it:
this is my body which will be given up for you.
When the supper was ended, he took the cup.
Again he gave you thanks and praise,
gave the cup to his disciples and said:
Take this, all of you, and drink from it:
this is the cup of my blood,
the blood of the new and everlasting covenant.
It will be shed for you and for all
so that sins may be forgiven.
Do This in Memory of Me.

—Words of Institution or "the Consecration"

People's Proclamation of Eucharistic Faith
Priest: Let us proclaim the mystery of faith: People (4 options): Option 1: Christ has died, Christ is risen, Christ will come again. . . . Option 3: When we eat this bread and drink this cup, we proclaim your death, Lord Jesus, until you come in glory.

These passages describe the origin of the Eucharist and indicate why Catholics value the Eucharist as given by God to the church.

The *first passage* from John is taken from the dramatic scene in which Jesus' disciples are scandalized by his promise to give them his flesh to eat. When they realized he meant it literally, half of those who had followed him for months left him. Christians point to John's sixth chapter as evidence that Jesus' future gift of his body and blood in the Eucharist is to be taken as reality, not mere symbol. The *second passage* occurs in every Eucharist or Mass and repeats what Jesus said and did at his Last Supper with his disciples, when he formally instituted the Eucharist. It is popularly called the consecration or making sacred the elements of bread and wine. The *third passage* spoken by the people at Mass are succinct statements of what Catholics, Orthodox, Anglicans and other Christians believe about the Eucharist as mystery of faith.

It is important to understand the term Eucharist. Before Vatican II, Eucharist referred almost exclusively to the body and blood of Christ received as Holy Communion during Mass. Since Vatican II, Eucharist has come to mean the *entire* liturgical celebration, consisting of the liturgy of the word (the three Scripture readings), the brief offertory rite, and the liturgy of the Eucharist, including the words of institution and the eucharistic meal or holy communion. Thus the term Eucharist is increasingly used instead of Mass.

Why is the Eucharist or Mass the very heart of the Christian community? Why is it Jesus' greatest gift to his Christian people? Why have Catholics and Orthodox flocked to Sunday Eucharist in such large numbers for almost 2000 years? Why have so many priests throughout the centuries risked their lives in times of religious persecution to celebrate the Eucharist for their people? Why do Catholics instinctively think of "having a Eucharist" when they want to celebrate in a special way a birthday or anniversary or death of loved ones? Why does Pope John Paul II make the celebration of Eucharist the focal point of his pastoral visits across the world? In a word, why is the church a "eucharistic community"?

We are thus confronted with a phenomenon unparalleled in the history of religion: the enduring quality and fervent attachment of millions and millions of Christians in every corner of the world for almost 2000 years to this one religious ritual. All this because on the eve of his cruel suffering and death, Jesus of Nazareth asked his followers, "Do this in memory of me."

◆

Preview: We begin our reflection on why the Eucharist is the heart of Christian life by providing images of both ordinary and extraordinary eucharistic celebrations down through the centuries. We then explain 12 reasons for the great importance of the Eucharist in Christianity; this section constitutes our theological reflection that concludes with a descriptive definition of the "Mass." Since the eucharistic celebration is the Christian community's liturgical act of worship, we briefly explain Vatican II's renewal of the eucharistic liturgy. We conclude by calling attention to two important contemporary issues concerning the Eucharist.

◆

Eucharistic Celebrations through the Centuries

Graphic images leap to our minds as we visualize the amazing variety of settings of Eucharists (Masses) celebrated throughout 2000 years in response to Jesus' command, "Do this in memory of me": of an Apostle or presbyter, with a handful of followers of "the Way" (earliest name for Christians), in the simplicity of a private home, praying spontaneously, recalling stories about Jesus, repeating Jesus' words at the Last Supper, and then together joyously eating the consecrated bread and drinking from the cup, confident the risen Jesus was in their midst once again.

Of more formal Eucharists, now with set prayers and readings before large crowds in spacious Roman basilicas given to the newly freed Christian Church by the Emperor Constantine; of pageantry-filled Masses in Latin in the soaring stone cathedrals of Europe in the late Middle Ages; of nocturnal Masses said secretly in the manor houses of persecuted Catholics in Elizabethan England by "Mass priests," who hid by day in their "priest holes" behind wood paneling; of Masses said by brave Irish priests in the Irish countryside on "Mass stones" during the persecutions; of Masses hurriedly said with a few scraps of bread and drops of wine in Nazi prison camps of World War II; of chaplains' Masses in trenches or on jeep hoods or on beachheads for troops about to "move up."

Of Pope John Paul II's Eucharists celebrated on colorful raised platforms before hundreds of thousands of Catholics on his pastoral visits to all five continents; of the solemn papal Christmas Mass televised to the world in majestic St. Peter's church and of poor missionary Masses in straw-roofed, dirt-floor little chapels in Africa or the mountains of Latin

America; of the hundreds of thousands of Masses celebrated every Sunday in parish churches throughout the world.

Of deeply moving personalized Eucharists during youth retreats or Marriage Encounters or Cursillo weekends; of resurrection hope-filled funeral Masses and of joyous Eucharists of Christian marriage; of incense-filled Divine Liturgies of Orthodox Churches presided over by bearded, richly robed priests, amid chanting and lengthy prayers; of the Lord's Supper celebrated in Protestant churches in ever-increasing frequency.

Why Eucharistic Celebration is the Heart of Christian Life

Let us try to appreciate why the Eucharist is the heart of Christian life and worship, the single most important communal action Christians do Sunday after Sunday. We shall list and briefly comment on 12 important theological and practical reasons. Note that both meanings of the Eucharist—the *entire* liturgical action or Mass and the body and blood of Christ in Holy Communion—are present in these 12 reflections, though the Eucharist as Holy Communion receives emphasis in numbers 2, 4, 5 and 9.

1. *Because Jesus asked his Apostles to do this in memory of him.* Although "Do this in memory of me" meant in the context of the Last Supper "Love one another as I have loved you" or "Give your lives for one another," almost immediately after Jesus' death and resurrection and sending his Spirit on the Apostles at Pentecost the early Christians began to meet in their homes at a friendship meal to remember Jesus' saving death and resurrection. The Eucharist is thus a *memorial* meal that remembers down through the centuries Jesus' Last Supper with his Apostles and his death on the following day. It is a unique remembering because it makes the *past*—Jesus' once-for-all death on the cross—*present* to us today in each Eucharist. Vatican II used this idea of memorial as a key to describing the Eucharist (SC 47). The Anglican-Roman Catholic international theological dialogue used the theology of memorial (**anamnesis**) to reach agreement on the Eucharist.

2. *Because the risen Christ is really and truly present in each eucharistic celebration.* Catholics, Orthodox, Anglicans and most Lutherans believe that Jesus is *really*, not merely *symbolically*, present in the consecrated bread and wine as our necessary spiritual food and drink. Vatican II emphasized three other ways the risen Christ is present in each eucharistic celebration: "in the person of his minister" (the priest or bishop), in the Word of God in the three Bible readings, and in the Christian community assembled (SC 7).

3. *Because in each eucharistic celebration the risen Christ offers himself and his redemptive suffering and death to the Father.* His perfect total offering of love was for the salvation of all people. In each Eucharist

the priest-celebrant and those present *offer* Jesus' sacrifice of himself on Calvary to the Father. In fact, our great privilege and role as baptized believing Christians is to unite the offering of ourselves to the perfect offering of the risen Christ. All this is possible because each eucharistic celebration makes present sacramentally (represents, memorializes, reenacts) Jesus' perfect offering of himself to the Father centuries ago. The memorial prayer right after the words of institution bring out this offering: "In memory of his death and resurrection we offer you, Father, this life-giving bread, this saving cup," that is, Jesus' body broken on the cross and his blood poured out for us.

4. *Because the Eucharist celebrates Jesus' entire life, but especially his death and resurrection.* The Scripture readings throughout the liturgical year help us recall and relive Jesus' life. As *sacrificial* meal the Eucharist celebrates in a special way Jesus' saving death on the cross; for Jesus at the Last Supper specifically linked his body ("given for you") and his blood ("shed for you and for all") with the sacrifice of his life on the cross the following day. Before Vatican II, Catholics emphasized the *sacrifice* aspect—referring exclusively to "the Sacrifice of the Mass"; Vatican II recovered the earlier understanding of Eucharist as *meal*, albeit a *sacrificial* meal.

5. *Because the Eucharist unites the Christian community with Christ and with each other.* The eucharist is the sacrament-sign of *unity*: as the one bread comes from many grains of wheat and the wine from many clusters of grapes, so Christians of all social and economic and racial and age backgrounds become one in Christ and with each other when in Holy Communion they take the body and blood of Christ. The invocation of the Holy Spirit in the second eucharistic prayer refers to this effect of the Eucharist: "May all of us who share in the body and blood of Christ be brought together in unity by the Holy Spirit."

6. *Because each eucharistic celebration provides Christians the experience of being members* of the worldwide Christian Church and of being part of the communion of saints, those millions of Christians who have gone before us to heaven, especially the Virgin Mary and the multitude of canonized saints. The eucharistic prayer recalls this spectacular fact in the three prayers after the words of institution: "intercession for the church," "for the dead," and "in communion with the saints."

7. *Because the Eucharist celebrates and strengthens our faith in Jesus.* The focus of the three readings and the prayers proclaimed by the priest is on the risen Christ, on his life, death, resurrection and glorification. Thus the eucharistic celebration is a powerful way the gathered Christian community both expresses its Christian faith and is strengthened in that faith. The Eucharist celebrated with meaning Sunday after Sunday

truly keeps our Christian faith alive in an increasingly secularized world.

8. *Because the eucharistic celebration increases our hope in eternal life with God.* The eucharist looks to the future coming of Christ at the end of the world. St. Thomas Aquinas called it "the pledge of future glory." The community's proclamations after the words of institution in the various Eucharistic Prayers state this reality: "Christ will come again" (option A); "Lord Jesus, come in glory" (option B); "until you come in glory" (option C). Christians say in the Apostles' Creed "I believe . . . in the resurrection of the body and life everlasting." Our own resurrection, as St. Paul says in his first letter to the Corinthians, has been won for us by Jesus' saving death and resurrection. Eucharist keeps our Christian hope alive and active.

9. *Because the Eucharist as meal intensifies our love of God and of each other.* Taking a meal together is a sign of love and friendship. The Apostles remembered the many intimate friendship meals they had with Jesus; the first Christians called their eucharistic meals *agape* or love feasts. To dramatize this dynamic, Vatican II introduced the greeting of peace before taking "communion" to provide Christians the experience of being at peace in Christian love with each other. The Eucharist is preeminently the sacrament of Christian love—love of God, love of the risen Christ, love of each other.

10. *Because the eucharistic celebration is the church's way to thank God* for sending His Son Jesus to bring us his good news of salvation, to die for us, and to be raised from death by the Father. This is why most of the prayers in the Eucharist are addressed not to Jesus but to the Father. Each eucharist is also the time to *thank* God through Jesus for all the blessings of soul, mind, and body we have received and for our loved ones and friends. After all, the Greek word *eucharistia* means thanksgiving.

11. *Because the eucharistic celebration is our opportunity to praise God, to beg forgiveness* for our sins, and to *ask* our loving Creator-God through Jesus for our spiritual and material needs and those of our loved ones. The four purposes of the Eucharist—*thanks, praise, reconciliation, petition* — are spread throughout the prayers of the Mass.

12. *Because the eucharistic celebration is Christians' spiritual power-source.* Inspired and empowered by the crucified and risen Christ, supported by the faith and hope and love of the worshipping community, the Christian goes into his or her day-by-day life energized to love others, to spread the good news about Jesus Christ, to work for justice and peace in the world, to advance God's kingdom on earth. Thus, each Eucharist ends with the priest sending the Christian worshippers into the world with the challenge: "Go in peace to love and serve the Lord" (and

each other). Most dramatically today in Central and South America, Catholics have found strength and inspiration in their eucharistic celebrations to struggle for justice, to face torture, and to die by the thousands for Christ and for each other.

We may diagram the riches of each eucharistic celebration in this way.

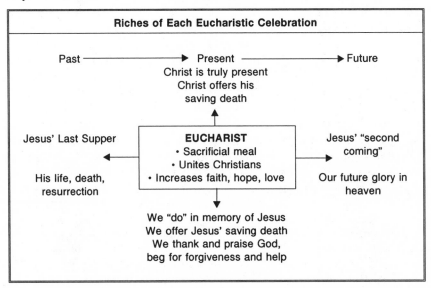

These 12 reasons are theological explanations of the great mystery of the Eucharist. As such they demand reflection and prayer. The *Constitution on the Sacred Liturgy* describes the eucharistic celebration in these words.

> At the Last Supper . . . our Savior instituted the eucharistic sacrifice of his Body and Blood. This he did in order to perpetuate the sacrifice of the Cross throughout the ages until he should come again, and so to entrust to his beloved Spouse, the Church, a memorial of his death and resurrection; a sacrament of love, a sign of unity, a bond of charity, a paschal banquet in which Christ is consumed, the mind is filled with grace, and a pledge of future glory is given to us. (SC 47)

We may thus *define* the eucharistic celebration as a ritual sacrificial meal of the real presence of the risen Christ, celebrated together as community by baptized, believing Christians in memory of Jesus' saving death and resurrection, to thank God our Father.

Vatican II Renewal of the Eucharistic Celebration

The bishops at Vatican II had three goals for the renewal of eucharistic worship: that Catholics *understand* the eucharistic ritual, actively *participate* in it, and be *nourished* by the word of God in Scripture. By upgrading the three Scripture readings, the Council stressed that the Mass as liturgical action is made up of two major parts: the **liturgy of the word** and the **liturgy of the Eucharist,** "so closely connected with each other that they form one single act of worship" (SC 56). The eucharistic celebration was no longer to be viewed as the priest's special preserve but rather the community celebration of the pilgrim people of God. Thus the bishops mandated changes like celebrating the Mass in the language of the people, giving the *altar table* and the *lectern* for the Scripture readings (SC 51) the most prominent places in the sanctuary, having the priest-celebrant face the people to better lead them in a community-oriented worship, introducing the prayers of the faithful (SC 51) and greeting of peace, and permitting the people to drink from the cup of Christ's blood (SC 51) as well as eating his body to emphasize the "meal" nature of the Mass.

> The Church earnestly desires that Christ's faithful, when present at this mystery of faith, should not be there as strangers or silent spectators. On the contrary, through a good understanding of the rites and prayers they should take part in the sacred action, conscious of what they are doing, with devotion and full collaboration. They should be instructed by God's word and be nourished at the table of the Lord's Body. They should give thanks to God. Offering the immaculate Victim, not only through the hands of the priest but also together with him, they should learn to offer themselves. (SC 48)

Two-Part Eucharistic Liturgy of the Mass	
Introductory rites:	greeting, penitential, praise, prayer of the day
Liturgy of the Word:	Three Scripture Readings Priest's Homily Creed, prayer of faithful
Liturgy of the Eucharist:	Presentation of gifts of bread, wine Preface prayer Eucharistic prayer of thanks Lord's prayer Greeting of peace Communion meal
Concluding rites:	prayer, blessing, dismissal

Contemporary Issues Concerning the Eucharist

Need for Further Renewal

Though most Catholics are pleased with the Council's renewal of eucharistic worship, one frequently hears complaints about the quality of Sunday worship by both older and younger Catholics. Many older Catholics brought up in the pre-Vatican II Mass often look nostalgically back on the Latin, on quality music by excellent choirs, the sense of mystery and the opportunities for private prayer, and the priest as central figure. They find guitar music, talking in church, the greeting of peace given to total strangers, lay readers and song directors disturbingly distracting. This group deserves to be heard for they have been faithful churchgoers all their lives, persons whose Catholic life has been nourished by a type of worship they had come to love. Young Catholics, on the other hand, tend to find the average parish Sunday liturgy repetitive, impersonal, uninspiring and therefore "boring."

What can be done so that the Sunday parish eucharistic celebration will become all that it can and should be for Catholics?

Older Catholics would be helped by an explanation of the purpose behind the "changes" in the Mass. Vatican II attempted to return to the church's worship in the early centuries, when the emphasis was on the Christian community gathered for worship rather than exclusively on what the priest did "up there" and on an individualistic "me and God" prayer. The Council bishops realized that many Catholics attended Mass primarily to fulfill their "Sunday obligation," and that a somewhat mechanistic theology of grace prevailed: one receives grace from God *merely* by being present, even if the eucharistic celebration is uninspiring and itself mechanical and even unintelligible. This is why the Council urged active participation by the people and encouraged the priest as "presider" to lead the Christian community in worship and prayer, rather than merely to perform sacred mysteries alone at the altar.

Catholic young people will be helped by clear explanation of the rich meaning of the Eucharist, of their responsibility to worship God and thank Jesus, and of their need to be strengthened in their faith life through participating as part of a faith community. It will greatly help if they come to Sunday worship with an *active faith,* realizing Christ's presence and activity in the eucharistic celebration and their own role in it; with *awareness* of their own spiritual needs; with a *positive desire* to grow in their Christian life. In this way the Mass will not be meaningless or boring!

But the pastor and presiding priests have their important part to play also. The pastor must give the Sunday "masses" the highest priority. Each eucharistic celebration should be carefully planned: this means singable hymns that express the theme of the readings and homily; lay readers who *proclaim,* not just read, clearly and with meaning the word of God; a well-prepared homily that speaks to the practical life and spiritual needs of *this*

Christian community. The priest-celebrant should be a skillful "presider," able to lead the community in prayer and worship, to create a sense of community, and to provide the encouragement and spiritual inspiration the people need for their daily struggles.

A reasonable flexibility is needed by the presiding priest and the parish liturgy group to adapt local culture and symbols and a style of worship that is meaningful to people. This means inculturation.

Eucharist and Cultural Adaptation

The Second Vatican Council endorsed, though cautiously, the principle of adapting the liturgy to various cultures. The Council stated that "the Church has no wish to impose a rigid uniformity . . ." because "she respects and fosters the spiritual . . . gifts of the various races and peoples . . . and sometimes admits such things into the liturgy itself" (SC 37). Thus ". . . the revision of liturgical books should allow for legitimate variations and adaptations to different groups, regions, and peoples, especially in mission lands" (SC 38). This obviously is a dramatic change from the 450-year practice of one unchanging form of worship throughout the Catholic world.

As a result, various cultures have introduced into eucharistic worship practices and symbols important in their culture. Some examples: African bishops have encouraged native music, clapping of hands, and joyful dance. At a recent Mass in Lusaka, Zambia, attended by an overflowing crowd in the cathedral and concelebrated by 70 bishops, a special group performed a dance at the entering procession, the *Gloria,* the offertory, and the thanksgiving, after communion. During this thanksgiving members of the congregation began to dance to express their joyous thanksgiving. Drums have also been introduced as well as the brilliant African designs for the priests' vestments and church furnishings. In India, native customs, symbols and rituals have been introduced, into the eucharistic worship: priest and worshipers sit on the floor in the lotus position, Indian music and songs are used, the priest makes solemn offerings of flowers, incense, fire and water. In the United States, in Masses for native Americans, the peace pipe ritual has been introduced.

For eucharistic worship to be an inspiring religious experience that attracts and speaks to people of various cultures, creative but sensitive adaptation is important. Liturgists recognize much remains to be done. Cultural adaptation in Africa, India, and the Philippines appears to be much further advanced than in the United States.

Summary

The phenomenon of Christians' extraordinary devotion to Jesus' gift of his body and blood as food and drink and to the eucharistic celebration in which they are contained prompts the question: why the enduring quality of this 2000-year ritual? To make this phenomenon concrete and personal, we pictured the rich variety of eucharistic celebrations from the first days of Christianity to the present. To answer the "why" question, we gave 12 reasons that are theological reflections on the nature of the eucharist and its important role for Christian living. Thoughtful, prayerful reflection is needed to appreciate the richness of the mystery of the Eucharist in Christian life. Because the eucharistic celebration or Mass is a liturgical action of the Christian community, we called attention to the changes Vatican II introduced to make the Mass a genuine community action. There is growing realization among Catholic liturgists, parish priests and both older and younger Catholics that further renewal in the eucharistic celebration is needed. Though Vatican II encouraged adapting the liturgy to various cultures, even greater liturgical inculturation is needed today.

For Discussion

1. Why isn't the Sunday Eucharist a *celebration* in many parishes today?

2. How would you overcome boredom at Sunday eucharists when the same ritual is performed Sunday after Sunday? What attitude or convictions or values might you bring to the eucharistic celebration? What might you *do* when present?

3. Do you think the bread and wine truly become the risen Christ or are mere symbols? How would you show they are more than mere symbols?

4. What is the significance of the altar becoming a "table" and the lectern or podium assuming equal importance with the altar table?

5. What is the theological and liturgical meaning of the new titles, "president" of the eucharistic assembly and "presider," given to the priest?

For Action

1. Attend a "divine liturgy" in an Orthodox church. Attend a Holy Communion liturgy in an Episcopal church. Compare them to a Catholic "Mass."

2. Find a parish known for its vibrant Vatican II liturgy. Attend a Saturday or Sunday Eucharistic celebration to experience what makes it succeed.

3. Visit a Vatican II parish church and arrange to inspect symbols important in the eucharistic celebration: priest's vestments and their liturgical

colors; candles; crucifix; altartable; president's chair; church architecture; statues; music.

4. Research how elements of African or Native American cultures have been incorporated into Catholic Eucharists in Africa and parts of the United States.

Further Reading

Cabie, Robert. *History of the Mass*. Lawrence J. Johnson, Tr. Washington, D.C.: The Pastoral Press, 1992.

Deiss, Lucien, C.S.Sp. *The Mass*. Collegeville, MN: Liturgical Press, 1989.

Foley, Edward. *From Age to Age: How Christians Celebrated the Eucharist*. Chicago: Liturgy Training Publications, 1991.

Guzie, Tad. *Jesus and the Eucharist*. New York: Paulist Press, 1974.

Hellwig, Monica. *The Eucharist and the Hunger of the World*. New York: Paulist Press, 1976.

Gospel of John, chapter 6.

Kiefer, Robert. *Blessed and Broken: An Exploration of the Contemporary Experience of God in Eucharistic Celebration*. Wilmington, DE: Michael Glazier, 1982.

CHAPTER   15

Marriage in Christ

God blessed them [Adam and Eve], saying, "Be fertile and multiply; fill the earth. . . ."   —Genesis 1:28

At the beginning of creation God made them male and female. . . . and the two shall become as one. . . . Therefore let no man separate what God has joined.   —Mark 10:6-12

Husbands, love your wives even as Christ loved the church and handed himself over for her. . . . "For this reason a man will leave father and mother and be joined to his wife and the two shall become one flesh." This a great mystery, but I speak in reference to Christ and the church.   —Ephesians 5:25-32[1]

God himself is the author of marriage. . . . The intimate union of marriage as a mutual giving of two persons, and the good of the children demand total fidelity from the spouses and require an unbreakable unity between them.   —*Gaudium et Spes* 48

Introduction

One of the most rewarding and inspiring ministries of Catholic priests is to prepare young couples for their life together in a sacramental marriage. I often use a "pre-marital inventory test" to help the couple—often present or former students—deepen their relationship and explore their readiness for marriage. Each separately writes "agree, disagree, or unsure" to 140 questions covering 10 areas crucial to a successful marriage: interests and activities, religion and philosophy, role adjustment,

1. Translation of New American Bible with revised New Testament, St. Joseph edition, 1992, Catholic Publishing Co., New York.

personal adjustment, interpersonal communication, marriage readiness, finance, in-laws, children, sexuality. The couple then compare and discuss their answers. It is not unusual for them to discover for the first time how each other thinks or feels about some of these important areas. "I didn't know you felt that way!" "Why are you unsure about that?" are remarks heard in their dialogue. I feel privileged to share their self-discovery and their trust in speaking so candidly. Invariably a high point is when the theology of Christian sacramental marriage is explained and the couple realizes, often for the first time, the rich meaning of "marriage in Christ."

◆

Preview: We look first at the two ways Vatican II changed and enriched Catholic teaching on marriage. We then turn to St. Paul's letter to the Ephesians quoted above to develop the Catholic understanding of marriage in Christ. With this theological basis, we consider the very practical questions of church requirements for a true or valid sacramental marriage and of the practice of interchurch and interfaith marriages. This leads us to the important topic of preparing for a successful sacramental marriage. We conclude by discussing what the Catholic Church does for Catholics who have experienced a breakdown of their marriage and have divorced and remarried.

◆

The Second Vatican Council's Teaching on Marriage

The Second Vatican Council significantly modified and enriched Catholic teaching on marriage in two ways. Prior to Vatican II, Christian marriage was spoken of as a legal *contract* between husband and wife. Since the language of contract was impersonal and limiting, the Council envisioned marriage as a *covenant* of love and friendship. "Just as of old God encountered his people with a covenant of love and fidelity, so our Savior . . . now encounters Christian spouses through the sacrament of marriage" (GS 48). God's covenant with the Jewish people through Moses bound God to love and protect his chosen people, and they to love, worship obey God alone. Jesus made a new covenant with his Christian people, of total unselfish love in his self-giving on the cross. To look on Christian marriage as a covenant means that the spouses are to love each other, without limits and to be utterly faithful to each other as God to the Jews and Jesus to Christians.

Secondly, Catholic teaching before Vatican II held that children or procreation was the primary purpose of marriage, with the mutual love of husband and wife a secondary purpose. This hierarchy of purposes caused many practical difficulties. Having as many children as possible came to be the Catholic ideal in marriage, with the mutual sexual love of the couple relegated to a secondary and therefore inferior position in the marriage, a stance opposed to the experience, convictions, and often capabilities of Catholic couples. Vatican II modified this position by stating that both mutual sexual love and procreation are equally primary purposes of Christian marriage.

> Marriage and married love are by nature ordered to the procreation and education of children. Indeed, children are the supreme gift of marriage and greatly contribute to the good of the parents themselves. . . . But marriage is not merely for the procreation of children; its nature as an indissoluble compact between two people and the good of the children demand that the mutual love of the partners be properly shown, that it should grow and mature. (*Gaudium et Spes* 50)

Christian Sacramental Marriage is "Marriage in Christ"

St. Paul referred to Christian marriage as mystery. "This is a great mystery but I speak in reference to Christ and the church" (Ephesians 5: 32). Recall that mystery refers to a human-*divine* reality. The mystery Paul refers to is two-fold: the total, unselfish, permanent, faithful love of Jesus for his Christian people, sealed by his sufferings and death on the cross; secondly, the love Christian spouses have for each other should mirror and imitate the quality of Christ's totally unselfish love. Their love must be permanent, faithful, generous love, as is Christ's for them.

The risen Christ is thus the third person in a Christian sacramental marriage. The marriage bond is made **indissoluble** or unbreakable by the risen Christ. As the third party in their marriage relationship, the risen Christ helps the couple love unselfishly, to be faithful "till death do us part," to care lovingly for their children, to make their marriage a success. "He abides with them in order that by their mutual self-giving the spouses will love each other with enduring fidelity as he loved the Church and delivered himself for it" (*GS* 48). This is why many Catholic couples have a crucifix in their bedroom to remind them of Christ's presence in their marriage and his example of total self-giving love.

A sacrament is a visible sign or symbol of an invisible spiritual reality. Since a Christian sacramental marriage is a symbol that points to the risen Christ's total self-giving love for his church, a Catholic couple's sacramental marriage ought to be a sign or symbol to their relatives and friends and to the larger Christian community of Christ's love for his Christian people, as mirrored and incarnated in their own unselfish, faithful, permanent love.

Let married people . . . bear witness by their faithful love in the joys and sacrifices of their calling to that mystery of love which the Lord revealed to the world by his death and resurrection. (GS 52)

[Christian marriage is] an image and a sharing in the partnership of love between Christ and the Church; it will show forth to all men Christ's living presence in the world and the authentic nature of the Church by the love and generous fruitfulness of the spouses, by their unity and fidelity . . . (GS 48)

◆

A Christian sacramental marriage comes into being when two baptized believing Christians knowingly and deliberately commit themselves by publicly giving their free consent to a lifelong, faithful covenant of love with the risen Christ as the third partner founding the marriage bond.

◆

The Council gives several brief descriptions of a sacramental marriage: in (GS 48) "the ultimate partnership of life and love," "a mutual giving of two persons," "a covenant of love and fidelity," "an image and a

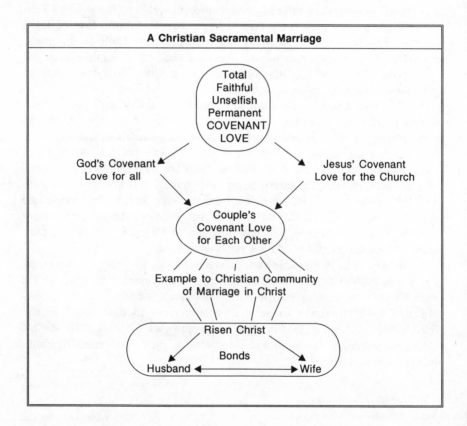

A Christian Sacramental Marriage

Total Faithful Unselfish Permanent COVENANT LOVE

God's Covenant Love for all

Jesus' Covenant Love for the Church

Couple's Covenant Love for Each Other

Example to Christian Community of Marriage in Christ

Risen Christ Bonds

Husband ◄───────► Wife

sharing in the partnership of love between Christ and the Church"' and in (GS 50) "an indissoluble compact."

Clearly, a Christian sacramental marriage in Christ is, as St. Paul teaches, a great mystery, that is, a human-*divine* reality. This is why the Catholic Church so highly values and strives to protect sacramental marriages; it is also why the church insists on careful preparation of couples for such a marriage.

Requirement for True or "Valid" Sacramental Marriage

The couple must be unmarried, not closely related by blood or marriage, seriously intend to commit themselves to a lifelong covenant of love, freely give their consent to the marriage, be capable of consummating the marriage through sexual intercourse, and be open to the possibility of having children. Furthermore, church law requires that a Catholic couple give their consent before a priest and two witnesses. If *any* of these requirements is missing, a Christian sacramental marriage does not exist according to church law, even if the couple went through with the wedding ceremony and subsequently lived together. Such a situation would be grounds for an annulment.

A marriage between a Catholic and another Christian (called a mixed marriage) or between a Catholic and a nonbaptized person, such as a Jew or Muslim or even a person with no religion (called an interfaith marriage), is a valid marriage recognized by the Catholic Church; the only condition is that the local bishop dispense the Catholic party from the church law regarding such marriages, a dispensation which is always given.

"Ecumenical" Marriages

Such mixed and interfaith marriages obviously pose a real problem for those partners who take their own religion very seriously: in which church or religion will the children be baptized and brought up? Will they go to a Catholic school? Will they worship in a Catholic or Protestant church, in a synagogue or mosque? It is preferable that both partners be deeply devoted to God and to their own religious tradition; religious indifference trivializes the sacred character of marriage.

There has developed, particularly in England where marriages between Catholics and Anglicans are increasingly common, a conviction that these "ecumenical families" are in God's plan a blessing for the Christian Church.[2] The Christian couple and their children, in experiencing keenly

---

2. See Ruth Reardon and Melanie Finch, *Sharing Communion, an Appeal to the Churches by Interchurch Families* (London: Collins Liturgical Publications, 1983). George Kilcourse in *Double Belonging, Interchurch Families and Christian Unity* treats this topic from many aspects. See further reading for this chapter.

the pain and scandal of division in Christianity for which they are not responsible, attempt to work out practical actions that respect both churches and share both religious traditions, which complement one another. Baptism, though it presently is performed in a specific church, is understood as initiation into the body of Christ, that is, into the full Church of Christ that transcends each divided church. It is important that ecumenism be lived at the grassroots family level, an experience that may greatly benefit the churches in their pilgrimage to full unity.

It is interesting to note that since Vatican II, a minister of another Christian church can, in special circumstances and with the proper dispensation, witness the marriage of a Catholic and another Christian held in the church of the Protestant pastor. The same holds for witnessing the marriage of a Catholic and a Jew. Another benefit of the Council is that, in respect for the conscience and religious convictions of the non-Catholic partner, he or she no longer must promise in writing to have the children baptized and reared as Catholics. The Catholic partner likewise need not promise in writing to convert the other partner; it is sufficient that he or she is willing to make such an effort, provided that it not endanger or put undue pressure on the harmony and success of their marriage. The reasons behind this major change from pre-Vatican II practice is the Catholic Church's new ecumenical respect for other Christian churches and its conviction concerning religious liberty and the primacy of conscience, as championed by Vatican II.

Preparation for Successful Sacramental Marriages

Prompted by the large number of failed marriages, with the consequent heartache and the harm to the children, and by the desire to bring about fulfilling and happy marriages, most dioceses in the United States have introduced marriage preparation programs. The couple are asked to see their parish priest six months before the wedding; in this initial interview the pastor verifies their freedom to marry, their understanding of the commitment they are about to make and their psychological maturity. The couple then set the date for the wedding and reserve the church. The couple signs up for a marriage instruction program, usually consisting of three or four meetings with other engaged couples, led by an experienced married couple, a priest who presents the church's teaching on marriage, and an expert on finances and legal questions. Engaged couples generally find these sessions most helpful.

The couples are encouraged to make a weekend engaged couples' retreat to deepen their relationship with each other and the risen Christ, to develop the habit of prayer, and to put their coming marriage in the hands of the Lord. Either during one of the instructions or during the retreat, couples find it very important and helpful to identify clearly the *expecta-*

tions they have of themselves, of their partners, of their marriage. These expectations are crucial to harmonious living together and should be clearly understood by each other *before* the marriage. Couples find taking a marriage expectations test separately and then discussing the results together to be very helpful for a successful and happy marriage.

A Touch of Realism

The wedding ceremony, important and beautiful as it is, is only the beginning of the marriage. The full Christian sacramental marriage is the couple's daily living their covenental love with each other; or as one couple put it, "It's in the day-to-day loving that the marriage sacrament comes alive." Couples have the assurance that the risen Lord is with them on their life journey, sanctifying their sexual love, sustaining them in the ordinary give-and-take of family life, and empowering them to be signs of love to each other, to their children, and to all their friends. To help couples grow in love and trust and communication, the Catholic Church has developed the highly successful Marriage Encounter, a weekend program facilitated by experienced married couples and a priest, in which the couple learn to shed their defenses and talk to each other on a deep level of trust. Marriage Encounter is recommended for couples "who have been married long enough to experience some disillusionment, but who are still committed and still like each other."[3]

For marriages in serious trouble, a program called *Retrouvaille* or rediscovery has been successful in "saving" couples' marriages. Founded in French Canada in the late 1970's by former Marriage Encounter couples and a priest, it is now present in many U.S. dioceses. The program, led by three couples themselves recovering from a troubled relationship and by a priest, consists of a weekend at a retreat center or hotel, followed by six sessions every other week over a 90-day period. The key to the success of *Retrouvaille* is the self-disclosure stories: the three "recovering couples" tell their own stories in a process like the Alcoholics Anonymous 12-step program.[4] The self-disclosure stories and the priest's instruction on marriage as sacrament helps "the couples to understand and more importantly to experience the way in which the saving grace of the ongoing sacramental union has its own built-in, self-healing process."[5]

---

3. *San Francisco Catholic,* February, 1993, page 22.

4. "Characteristics shared with AA . . . are listening to self-disclosure stories, recognizing the need for honesty with oneself, making a personal inventory, putting one's trust in God, acknowledging that personal selfishness is a root cause of one's problems, taking spiritual steps, granting forgiveness, aiming to change oneself rather than one's spouse, ridding oneself of resentment and finally, as a last step in recovery, participating in a ministry of helping others." Ed Gleason, "Recovery for Troubled Marriages," *America* 170 (October 10, 1992):253.

5. *Ibid.*

The Pastoral Problem of Marriage Breakdown and Divorce/Remarriage

Recently over a dinner with a Catholic couple, good friends of many years, the conversation turned to the Catholic Church's practice of forbidding remarriage after a divorce. The wife, mother of five grown children, forcefully argued that the church should change its practice. "Good people make mistakes. When love is gone, the marriage is dead. A loving God would not deny a person another chance to find happiness." With emotion she told of the mental suffering of more than a few of her friends in a failed marriage who tried to obey the church's law against remarriage.

The Catholic Church faces a difficult dilemma in regard to marriage breakdown and remarriage. On the one hand, the church desires to be faithful to Jesus' teaching in the New Testament and her own centuries-long tradition to uphold the ideal of a sacramental marriage in Christ that is faithful, permanent, and indissoluble, that is, not to be dissolved or broken except by death. On the other hand, the church in her pastoral role wants to be an understanding and compassionate "mother" to those of her members who have suffered greatly in a failed first marriage, and the subsequent divorce proceedings, and now experience serious spiritual and psychological needs in a second marriage. Can the Catholic Church do anything in this dilemma?

Marriage Annulment

The traditional and officially accepted solution is marriage **annulment**. An annulment is a statement after lengthy investigation by a diocesan marriage tribunal that the first "marriage" was not in fact a valid or real sacramental marriage because one or more requirements for validity were not present. Before the Vatican Council, conditions for an annulment were very strict, resulting in few annulments.

But the Council's teaching on marriage as covenant and partnership of love enabled the church's canon lawyers to recognize that psychological or religious immaturity could make it impossible for one or both partners to make the commitment needed for a lifelong partnership of love that constitutes a covenant marriage in Christ. Clearly in modern society, many people find it very difficult to make a personal commitment; they lack psychological maturity. If such immaturity can be shown to exist *before* the marriage, strong grounds exist for granting an annulment. However today, some tribunal officials and canon lawyers in the United States are questioning whether the cumbersome and painful, often demeaning process of annulments is the best way for the church to deal with the dilemma of divorce and remarriage.

A True Sacramental Marriage Now "Dead"

A more difficult question for the Catholic Church today is this: can the church do anything in the case of a once-truly sacramental marriage that is now dead? Can it permit Catholics to enter or remain in a second marriage and still be an active member of the church? If the answer is yes, what does this say about the Catholic ideal and teaching about the permanency and indissolubility of sacramental marriage?

Some biblical scholars, historians, and moral theologians have suggested various approaches. However, these have not been approved as official church teaching and policy.

1. The words of Jesus, "What God has joined together, let no man put asunder," can be understood as the norm and radical ideal but which in a sinful and complex world cannot always be attained. It is argued that other statements of Jesus in the Gospels have been accepted as ideal norms that do not apply to all concrete cases.

2. Historically there have been instances where some Church Fathers in the early centuries accepted divorce and remarriage, and when in some dioceses it was accepted practice for some periods.

3. The Orthodox churches' practice of **economia**, in which for pastoral reasons a second marriage is accepted but without being celebrated sacramentally in a church ceremony, is a way Orthodox discipline recognizes the indissolubility of the first marriage but shows pastoral compassion for the couple.

4. Some theologians argue that when the first marriage is irrevocably dead, that is, no longer a covenant love relationship, the church should recognize this fact and permit remarriage and full participation in the church.

Many Catholics will find these suggested approaches inadequate and unconvincing or smacking of compromise to human weakness. They argue that the church has in its long tradition been a champion of permanent, indissoluble marriage in loyalty to Jesus and should remain so, especially today when divorce-remarriage is so rampant and Christian marriage and family life itself are under attack. Other Catholics emphasize the pastoral nature of the church, the great suffering and spiritual need of thousands of divorced and remarried Catholics, the enormous stresses of modern society that put great pressures on young married couples, and finally God's mercy and love for those who have erred or sinned. These Catholics see these suggestions as having merit, for they judge the present approach cruel and unworkable. Perhaps the issue comes down to this: does the harm done to the Catholic ideal of an indissoluble sacramental marriage by the church allowing second marriages *outweigh* the harm done to persons in successful second marriages by the church forbidding such marriages?

The question of divorce and remarriage is truly a major pastoral problem for the Catholic Church today.

In the meantime, many dioceses have programs for the newly divorced, who are struggling with the pain and anger and loneliness and sense of failure and low self-esteem after divorce. These people meet regularly for mutual support and spiritual direction by a priest, pray and celebrate the Eucharist together, and often plan social events. Such groups are highly appreciated and witness to the church's pastoral understanding and compassion.

Summary

The Catholic Church takes sacramental marriage very seriously in her effort to follow Jesus' ideal of a permanent faithful union, in her theology of marriage as a sacrament, and in her discipline concerning remarriage. Vatican II modified traditional Catholic teaching by stressing that marriage is a love covenant rather than a legal contract, and that the sexual love of husband and wife, equally with procreation, is the primary purpose of marriage. The theological basis and understanding of a Christian sacramental marriage is expressed in the phrase "marriage in Christ," for the risen Christ establishes the unbreakable bond and is the couples' model for self-giving, faithful love. To safeguard this theology of marriage, the Church sets certain requirements for a true or valid sacramental marriage. When it is verified that any of these conditions was missing, the church can declare that no sacramental marriage actually took place and may grant an annulment.

Because so many marriages fail today, the Catholic Church has begun programs both to prepare couples for a successful sacramental marriage and to help them after marriage. Nevertheless, Catholic marriages do break down and Catholics do remarry, presenting the church with a difficult theological and pastoral dilemma. To help her members pastorally, the church grants annulments. Theologians are currently wrestling with the difficult question of how to deal with what was a true sacramental marriage but is now dead because of the total loss of covenantal love.

For Discussion

1. How many practical consequences can you think of that follow from the Vatican Council's stressing marriage as a covenant rather than a contract and elevating the couples' sexual love to equal importance with procreation?

2. Is the Catholic Church's prohibition of remarriage after divorce too strict? What are the pros and cons, the values involved? Which is more

important, marriage as an institution or the spiritual and psychological needs of two persons? Why?

3. Do you think that granting annulments is a good or poor practice? Is there a responsible alternative?

For Action

1. Read up on the interesting history of marriage in the Catholic Church. When and why was it considered a sacrament? When and why were the conditions for a valid marriage established?

2. Get to know the marriage preparation program in your parish or congregation. Interview one of the married couples who lead the program and one of the priests or ministers who help.

3. Do the same for the popular Marriage Encounter weekends.

Further Reading

Brunsman, Barry. *New Hope for Divorced Catholics: A Concerned Pastor Offers Alternatives to Annulment.* San Francisco: Harper and Row, 1985.

Coleman, Gerald. *Divorce and Remarriage in the Catholic Church.* New York: Paulist Press, 1988.

Hart, Kathleen and Thomas. *The First Two Years of Marriage: Foundation for Life Together.* New York: Paulist Press, 1983.

Kilcourse, George. *Double Belonging, Interchurch Families and Christian Unity.* New York/Mahwah, NJ: Paulist Press, 1992.

Lawler, Michael. *Secular Marriage, Christian Sacrament.* Mystic, CT: Twenty-Third Publications, 1985.

Reilly, Christopher. *Making Your Marriage Work, Growing in Love after Living in Love.* Mystic, CT: Twenty-Third Publications, 1989.

Roberts, William. *Marriage, Sacrament of Hope and Challenge.* Cincinnati: St. Anthony Messenger Press, 1988.

Roberts, Challon. *Partners in Intimacy: Living Christian Marriage Today.* New York: Paulist Press, 1988.

Thomas, David. *Christian Marriage, A Journey Together.* Wilmington, DE: Michael Glazier, 1983.

Young, James. *Divorcing, Believing, Belonging.* New York: Paulist Press, 1984.

CHAPTER 16

Sin and Reconciliation

Though your sins be like scarlet, they will become white as snow.   —Isaiah 1:18

"Peace be with you," he said again. "As the Father has sent me, so I send you." Then he breathed on them and said: "Receive the Holy Spirit. If you forgive men's sins, they are forgiven them; if you hold them bound, they are bound."   —John 20: 22-23

God, the Father of mercies, through the death and resurrection of his Son, has reconciled the world to himself and sent the Holy Spirit among us for the forgiveness of sins; through the ministry of the Church, may God give you pardon and peace, and I absolve you from your sins, in the name of the Father, and of the Son, and of the Holy Spirit.
    —Priest's absolution in sacrament of Reconciliation

Introduction

In his Gospel, St. John reports a beautiful meeting between Jesus and a woman taken in the act of adultery (John 8:3-11). The Pharisees had brought the woman to Jesus in order to trap him. The Jewish law for such offenders was to be "stoned" to death. So their question to Jesus was what should be done to her. If Jesus said "Obey the law," he would be labeled cruel and heartless; if he forgave her, he would sin by violating Jewish law. So Jesus merely traced with his finger something in the sand which caused the Pharisees to slink away silently! Their own secret sins?

Only Jesus and the woman remained. Jesus said to her: "Does anyone condemn you?" "No one, Lord." "Then neither will I; go, and sin no more." In this dramatic incident we see how compassionate and understanding Jesus is. His only concern is the future good of the adulteress; he desires that she change her lifestyle, that she experience conversion of heart. This intensely human scene powerfully illustrates what the sacrament of reconciliation as practiced by the church is meant to be, and which, in fact, is a personal encounter with the forgiving, merciful Christ.

In treating the sacrament of penance, the Second Vatican Council asked for a future revision of "the rite and formulas" to express better "the nature and effect of the sacrament" (SC 72). Thus in 1973 the curial Congregation for Divine Worship proposed three new rites or ways of receiving the sacrament. The first rite encouraged individual confession face-to-face with the priest, in a pleasant reconciliation room, where the penitent is invited to pray with the priest on a bible passage, to receive personalized advice and to be given a practical penance in the light of sins confessed.

The second rite involved a group reconciliation service consisting of hymns, scripture readings, prayers, and an uplifting talk to dispose the group to experience sorrow for sin, trust in God's loving mercy, and to help them examine their conscience; individual confession of sins and absolution by the priest followed.

The third ritual featured a communal reconciliation service as in the second rite, but permitted private confession to God alone, followed by *general* absolution to all present. This third rite was restricted to situations where the number of people is too large for individual confession, with the stipulation that individual confession follow at an available later time if the penitent had sinned mortally.

◆

Preview: We begin our reflection on Christ's sacrament of peace and forgiveness by acknowledging the startling fact that after Vatican II, the majority of Catholics stopped "going to confession." We naturally wonder why. To understand the church's new approach to the sacrament of reconciliation, we reflect on moral theologians' new understanding of serious sin, which involves a person's "fundamental option," and on the nature of conscience and the responsibility of each Christian to form his or her conscience. We then describe how Vatican II wishes the sacrament of reconciliation to be practiced in the church today. We close by considering everybody's question, "Why tell your sins to a man rather than to God?" and by calling attention to the extraordinary way the ritual of confession has changed down through the centuries.

◆

A Startling Development

> One of the most startling developments in the post-Vatican II Church has been the desertion by the faithful of the sacrament of penance. Until just a few years ago, regular confession was a must for any faithful Catholic. Long lines of penitents awaiting their turn in the darkened box was a common scene in most Catholic churches on Saturday afternoon and evening. . . . Within a few years after the end of the Council in 1965 this chapter of Catholic piety came to an abrupt end. Almost overnight the long lines vanished, as the great majority of Catholics simply stopped using the sacrament. It was a weird development. . . . No one publicly attacked the confessional or urged people to stay away. A silent consensus simply spread, and people abandoned this ancient and venerable means of experiencing God's forgiveness.[1]

Why? The reasons are not clear. The 1983 Bishops' Synod in Rome on Penance and Reconciliation cited as reasons: loss of sense of sin, secularism of modern life, lack of priests, and confusion over the difference between mortal and venial sin. Monica Hellwig thinks Catholics do not find the sacrament meeting their spontaneous needs to experience self-renewal and reconciliation with God and others. Others think that the exaggerated emphasis on sexual sins gave neurotic guilt feelings, making confession onerous rather than peace-giving. Still others feel the impersonality of reciting lists of faults or non-sins to an invisible priest in a dark confessional contributed to the decline.

Perhaps the new emphasis on sin as relational rather than exclusively as individual acts caused Catholics to conclude they were not committing mortal sins with such frequency. Or did Vatican II's emphasis on the inviolability of one's own conscience result in a maturity of conscience formation among Catholics? Could it be that Catholics just got tired of confession after being forced to go regularly as children by well-meaning parents and teachers in Catholic schools?

Sin: Old and New Understanding

Prompted by new insights from psychology and anthropology, and encouraged by the Council's emphasis on the primacy of individual conscience, moral theologians developed a dramatic new understanding of sin, especially of mortal sin. The traditional definition of personal sin was a free, deliberate action or word or thought or desire that violates God's commandments or those of the church. This served to emphasize sin in terms of individual acts. The new emphasis stressed *one's relationships;*

---

1. Thomas Bokenkotter, *Essential Catholicism. Dynamics of Faith and Belief* (New York: Doubleday and Company, 1986), 220.

sin came to be understood primarily as breaking our love-friendship relation with God and other people. Sin then is understood basically as a failure in love—of God, others, and myself.

This new emphasis on sin *as relationship* rather than exclusively as individual acts affects our understanding of mortal sin. In the early church, three sins were considered especially mortal (from *mors*, Latin for death), as capable of bringing death to the soul: murder, adultery, and apostasy or repudiating the Christian faith. From the Middle Ages up to Vatican II, theologians worked out lengthy lists of actions that were either mortal or venial sins. A legalistic, quantitative thinking developed.

For example, to steal up to a given amount was a venial sin, over that a mortal; to miss a portion of the Mass was venial, beyond that a mortal sin. Anything involving sex for the unmarried was mortally sinful. The result was that many Catholics became guilt-ridden and tended to see mortal sin where none existed. Yet common sense seemed to indicate that one didn't lightly break a relationship with God over and over again and thus be constantly in danger of hell. Such an approach trivialized one's friendship relation with God and the punishment of hell.

The Fundamental Option Theory

In the light of evidence from psychology, of a better understanding of human motivation and of decisions that come from one's deeper core consciousness, of the Hebrew Scriptures' idea of sin as rupture of the Jews' covenant relationship with their God, and of Jesus' emphasis on conversion and forgiveness so dramatically shown by the father's welcoming home his prodigal son (Luke 15: 11-32), moral theologians today prefer to think of mortal sin in terms of a fundamental option or choice. A **fundamental option** is the most basic decision a person can make: to *totally* reject God, however understood, from one's life and to choose a life of total selfishness, putting self before God and others; or conversely, to choose God, putting God and others before self. It is "fundamental" because the decision comes from the inner core of one's consciousness and affects the most basic values and actions of one's life.

To make such a decision against God and others would qualify as a mortal or death-dealing state of sin, for it completely destroys one's love-relationship with God. Viewed in this way, mortal sin is of rare occurrence, especially among those whose fundamental option is for God and others. Are actions important in this approach? Yes, for a series of grossly selfish actions can lead over a period of time to that definitive act that finally ruptures one's love relationship with God. The example of marriage is often used: individual acts of hurting one's partner through unkind words or flirting or fantasizing about other women or men do not themselves definitively break the love relationship; but many such acts weaken love and lead to divorce which destroys the marriage.

We should stress two points regarding the fundamental option. First, it is a theory, not a doctrine to be accepted as official Catholic teaching. Second, the fundamental option is not limited to sin. To choose habitually to live Jesus' gospel of love toward God and our fellow humans is to make a *positive* fundamental option. This involves a life-long effort of conversion, which is a major goal of the new rites of reconciliation.

Forming Conscience

Conscience is not an inner feeling but is the practical *judgment* about the rightness or wrongness of a choice that confronts me now: whether to do this or avoid that here and now. Even though the judgment may be wrong because of lack of information or differences of honest opinion or the complexity of the issues, a person must follow his or her sincere conscience because it is the final norm of conduct and the basis of God's judgment of human actions. In *Gaudium et Spes,* Vatican II has the following beautiful statement on conscience:

> Deep within his conscience man [sic] discovers a law which he has not laid on himself, but which he must obey. Its voice, even calling him to love and to do what is good and to avoid what is evil, tells him inwardly at the right moment: do this, shun that. For man has in his heart a law inscribed by God. His dignity lies in observing this law, and by it he will be judged. His conscience is man's most secret core and his sanctuary. There he is alone with God, whose voice echoes in his depths. (GS 16)

Obviously, forming one's conscience correctly and sincerely is necessary and of great importance for proper moral choices. For Christians, this involves many factors: knowing the values that Jesus preached and lived in the four Gospels, learning the church's teaching on specific points, weighing evidence from the social sciences and increasingly today from medicine and psychology, asking advice from those in a position to know, personal prayer, and listening to the Holy Spirit. After the publication in 1968 of the papal encyclical *Of Human Life* condemning contraception on the basis of argumentation from the natural law, many married Catholics followed a process of conscience-formation similar to the above to make a practical judgment on how to respond to the encyclical. Bishops and priests respected their sincere conscience judgment.

The Sacrament of Penance and Reconciliation Today

The Vatican II renewal of the ritual retained the name Penance for the sacrament, but added the dimension of *reconciliation* to stress the fact that this sacrament reconciles us not only with God but also with the community of the church. Reconciliation thus emphasizes the social dimension of sin through the harm it does to the Christian community. The early Christians were acutely aware that sinful members gave bad example, thereby weakening the community and making evangelization of the masses of non-Christians more difficult. Thus public sinners were excommunicated or expelled from the community; they could return only by being reconciled with the community, represented by the bishop.

In its renewal of the sacrament, the Council changed the ritual to allow for a dialogue between priest and penitent and their prayer on a passage of Scripture. To do this, the impersonal dark confessional "box" gave way to a "reconciliation room," with chairs and a joyful atmosphere. The priest was encouraged to be flexible and to avoid a legalistic approach. The person entering the reconciliation room is to be greeted in a friendly fashion; the priest and penitent then prayerfully reflect on a text from either the Hebrew or Christian Scriptures expressing God's mercy and call for conversion. When the person confesses his or her sins, the goal is not to mention everything but only those sins or failures that are most significant and harmful to personal character, to one's relationship with God and others. The priest may discuss these points and offer encouraging advice; he then gives a "penance" to be performed, choosing a prayer or Bible reading or a good work that are tailored to the person's individual needs. The penitent then expresses sorrow for sin and a determination to do better in the future; this expression can be memorized or spontaneous or chosen from various prayers printed on a card. At this point the priest gives absolution, placing his hand on the person's head to signify that the risen Christ's forgiveness and strong help passes through the mediation of the priest to the penitent. A brief dismissal prayer of thanks closes the ritual.

The two-fold purpose of this new ritual is personal conversion and a felt religious experience of Jesus' forgiveness and healing.

Conversion from sin and deeply imbedded attitudes and habits is a long process and does not come easily. It involves strengthening one in the fundamental option for God and others and in the lifelong struggle to overcome selfishness. In this process we need encouragement and the help of a skilled spiritual advisor. The goal then is much more than avoiding certain sinful acts, though this is important; rather the new ritual seeks to deepen one's relationship with God, to choose afresh God over self, to let love guide one's dealings with others. All this is contained in Jesus' words to the adulteress: "Go, sin no more."

Participating in the new ritual of reconciliation is meant to give the penitent the personal religious *experience* of Jesus' forgiveness and healing. This is a joyful experience resulting in deep peace of mind and soul. The priest no longer is primarily a judge but a healer, a reconciler, a source of encouragement and hope. "Neither will I condemn you."

Of Practical Interest

Why Tell Your Sins to a Priest?

Protestants and many Catholics often ask this question: "Why can't I go directly to God, say I'm sorry, and receive God's forgiveness?" The answer is "Yes, you can." The moment we turn to God in genuine sorrow and ask for forgiveness, our loving and merciful God forgives us, even before we "go to confession."

The Catholic Church offers the sacrament of reconciliation for the following reasons:

- Jesus gave the Apostles the power to forgive sins and desires that the church do this for its members;
- we need the visible proof and experience of God's forgiveness through the words of the priest, just as the prodigal son felt a strong need to return to his father and hear his words of forgiveness and receive his reassuring embrace (Luke 15:11-32);
- we need advice and human support in the difficult process of conversion;
- actually stating one's sins to another person precludes self-deception and rationalization and causes one to recognize his or her actual situation before God and others;
- we need the risen Christ's help and strength in our earthly pilgrimage to heaven.

The sacrament of penance and reconciliation is a dramatic example of the church as mystery, as *human-divine* reality. For the risen Christ comes in his power and love (*divine*) through the words of absolution and encouragement of the priest (*human*) to forgive and heal and strengthen. In this humble ritual, the drama of salvation is played again and again for our benefit.

Remarkable History[2] of this Sacramental Rite

More than the other six sacraments, the sacrament of "confession" or penance has undergone dramatic changes, an indication of the reality and legitimacy of "development" in church doctrine and discipline; moreover, this history points to the possibility of further change in the future. We can distinguish three main periods in the development of the sacrament.

1. Primitive Church: 1st to 3rd centuries. Baptism was the primary celebration of forgiveness of sin. Baptized sinners confessed sins to clergy or laity,

---

2. *Essential Catholicism*, 223-32.

especially bishops or Christians imprisoned for the faith, asking them for prayers and signs that they could be part of the Christian community.

2. *Public penance: 4th to 6th centuries.* This was the period of rigorous penances. Sinners came to the bishop, confessed their serious sins (generally public sins, like murder or adultery), were given a severe penance that often took years to perform. They were excluded from attending the Sunday Eucharist and receiving communion, had to fast, wear coarse penitential garments, abstain from sexual relations. When this severe penance was finally completed, the sinners returned to the bishop, generally on Holy Thursday, prostrated themselves before the bishop, who raised them up in an act of absolution from sin, signifying their reconciliation with the church and restoration to full communion with the Christian community. This penance was given only once; if a person slipped back into serious sin, he was left to the mercy of God.

Three things stand out in this practice: how seriously the early church took the reality of sin; its realization that sin severely damaged the Christian community; and its conviction that one of its most important ministries from Christ was not only to forgive sin but to help the sinner in the process of conversion.

3. *Private Confession: 600 AD onwards.* Such an excessively rigorous system could not last long. A new form of private confession to the abbot began in the monasteries of Ireland. In the 6th and 7th centuries, Irish missionary monks introduced this form to the European continent, where it became popular. Christians liked its privacy, its availability (the bishop was no longer needed, only an abbot or priest), its leniency (the penance assigned, generally fasting or almsgiving or certain prayers to be said, could be completed in a short period so that the penitent was soon readmitted to the Eucharist), and its consolation (the abbot or priest gave absolution or statement of forgiveness *during* the confession). It stressed healing rather than legality.

At first the Church tried to outlaw this new form, but gradually the Irish system prevailed. The Lateran Council in 1215 prescribed confession once a year for those in serious sin. The Council of Trent (1545-1564) formulated the present official teaching on the sacrament. The Reformers Luther and Calvin attacked the medieval system because of "its legalism, its lack of scriptural basis, its obligatoriness and its claims to a monopoly of forgiveness." Thus the sacrament of confession gradually disappeared in Protestant churches.

What can we say about the remarkable historical development of this sacrament? Can it provide us with insight into our present situation? Even though the church offers three new rites for the sacrament, Catholic people on the whole are not attracted to the first two. It may be that the church has not yet discovered the best way to satisfy the religious needs and cultural realities of today's Catholics. It may be that Catholics need large doses of instruction and motivation to rediscover the reality of sin and the positive benefits of the sacrament of reconciliation. It may also be that priests need to be retrained to make confession more personal and fruitful.

Or it may be that the church needs to permit and encourage the use of the third rite of general absolution without conditions attached. The church has changed the ritual dramatically over the centuries to meet the spiritual and psychological needs of her members; she can therefore do it again.

Summary

Following Jesus' forgiveness of sin and its creation of three new rites for penance and reconciliation, the church after Vatican II has introduced a new emphasis: from fear and guilt to the peace and joy of forgiveness, from a methodical recitation of sins and faults to conversion of heart, from an impersonal and private ritual to a personalized and communal experience of forgiveness and reconciliation with God and the Christian community. Past Catholic practice overemphasized the frequency of mortal sin and equated sin with individual actions. A renewed moral theology emphasized that sin is rather breaking one's relationship with God; the fundamental option theory proposed that only a definitive, very basic decision from one's deepest self rejecting God could qualify as a mortal or death-giving sin. Conscience as the practical judgment of what is right or wrong made in the inner core of one's person influences whether our fundamental option is for or against God and other people. The correct formation of conscience thus becomes important.

The goal of the more personal ritual of reconciliation is to help us in our gradual process of conversion and to give us the joyful religious experience of peace-filled forgiveness and healing. To accomplish such goals, it makes sense to receive the sacrament from an experienced compassionate minister of the church, to "tell your sins to a priest!" Since times and the needs of people change, the sacrament has dramatically developed in the course of 2000 years of Christian living. A current question is what further development is needed.

For Discussion

1. Why do you think Catholics stopped going to confession in large numbers? Why do young Catholics today rarely receive the sacrament? Is this healthy?

2. Is the fundamental option theory a good one and practical? Or is it an excuse for a lax, irresponsible conscience and for taking sin in our lives too lightly?

3. Do you think people need "conversion" today? Are they able to achieve it in their own lives? What values and convictions are necessary?

4. What do you think the church should do to attract people, including youth, to use the sacrament of peace and forgiveness?

For Action

1. Interview a parish priest on his experience of "hearing confessions" the old way and of conducting the sacrament according to the renewed ritual. What does he think of the present practice and people's spiritual needs?

2. Visit a Catholic church and compare the old "confessional box" and the new reconciliation room.

3. Experience the peace and encouragement of receiving the sacrament of reconciliation according to the new rite!

Further Reading

Bausch, William. *A New Look at the Sacraments*. Mystic, CT: Twenty-Third Publications. Chapters 11-13, pp. 153-201.

Bokenkotter, Thomas. *Essential Catholicism*. New York: Doubleday Image, 1986. Chapter 19, pp. 220-40.

Hellwig, Monica. *Sign of Reconciliation and Conversion: The Sacrament of Penance for Our Times*. Wilmington, DE: Michael Glazier, 1982.

Martos, Joseph. *Doors to the Sacred*. Garden City, NY: Doubleday Image, 1982. Chapter 9, pp. 307-63.

Part V

Major Issues
in Today's Church

CHAPTER 17

Catholic Morality

You must love the Lord your God with all your heart, with all your soul, and with all your mind. This is the greatest and first commandment. The second resembles it: You must love your neighbor as yourself. —Mathew 22:37-39

The service which moral theologians are called to provide at the present time is of the utmost importance, not only for the Church's life and mission, but also for human society and culture. —John Paul II, *Veritatis Splendor*, no. 111

[Conjugal love is] rooted in God's love for his people. . . . a gift from God which ennobles, enriches and reconciles married couples. Through sexual union couples strengthen their marital relationship and participate in a special way in God's creation of new life. From this follows the profound meaning of a life of intimacy—that communion of two persons . . . in a mutual self-donation that reaches its apex in the loving union that bears fruit in children.[1] —U.S. Bishops' 1993 Letter

Introduction

Morality deals with what is right or wrong in human actions in the concrete situations of life. Christian morality discovers what is the right or wrong thing to do by looking to Jesus Christ and to his teaching and actions. There we see that the good news Jesus brought to the world was

---

1. U.S. Bishops Conference, "Human Sexuality from God's Perspective," *Origins* 23 (Aug. 12, 1993): 164-66, summarizing Pope Paul VI's inspiring remarks on conjugal love in his 1968 encyclical *Of Human Life*.

love: to love God first and foremost above all creatures and to love our neighbor as ourselves. Love of God and of our fellow humans is thus the essence of Christian morality.

Jesus' teaching on loving our neighbor *as ourselves* is truly revolutionary. It means that the concern all of us have for our own well-being—our health and our possessions, our comfort and security—must also be the same concern for our neighbor. Who then is our neighbor? Potentially everyone, but especially those in greatest need: the poor, the oppressed, the sick and aged, victims of racism and sexism, refugees, those afflicted with AIDS. The Christian moral ethic of loving one another includes even our enemies, criminals, other perpetrators of evil. Jesus' challenge to love is without limits.

Before Vatican II, morality was too often understood as obeying or breaking a set of laws established by God and the church. The dangers of this approach is *legalism,* or an exaggerated emphasis on laws and rules rather than on our responsibility to God, to ourselves, to other people, and indeed to creation itself. Another danger is pharisaical pride and superiority attitudes: if I obey all the laws, I am better than others. This narrows and impoverishes Christian life to mere observance of law. Fr. Bernard Haring, the great Redemptorist theologian who transformed Catholic moral theology, recognized these dangers, and accordingly chose Christian love as the starting point and basis of Christian morality in his momentous work, *The Law of Christ*.

Today moral questions have become exceedingly complex. The Catholic Church, especially since the Second Vatican Council, has experienced a major shift in its approach to morality that has sometimes confused the average Catholic. Accordingly, to understand today's church we must address the important topic of Christian Catholic morality.

◆

Preview: The Catholic Church has the responsibility to teach not only in matters of Christian faith but also in the area of morality, that is, what is right or wrong in human living. The Church has developed her moral teaching with the indispensable aid of professional **moral theologians.** Since the Second Vatican Council, Catholic moral theologians have changed their methodology of "doing" **moral theology** from a predominantly natural law approach to a more contextual one that emphasizes Jesus' message of love, data and insights from various sciences, and human experience. The result has been a major debate in Catholic moral theology between those who favor the more traditional natural law approach and those who seek to revise this method of doing moral theology.

This debate is particularly acute in the complex and divisive issue of Catholic sexual morality. We first sketch a theology of human sexuality and state the Catholic vision of sexuality. We then apply both the traditional and revisionist approach to three important and controverted areas of sexual morality today. This brings us to an analysis of the major emphases Pope John Paul II makes in his recent encyclical on the foundations of Catholic moral teaching. This leads to a two-fold concluding reflection on how moral theologians and Catholics should "receive" this document, and how a Catholic might understand the current situation of disagreement between the official teaching office of the church on the one hand and professional moral theologians and many ordinary Catholics on the other. An appendix considers four crucial modern morality issues concerning the sacredness of human life.

◆

Moral Theology and Moral Theologians

Properly understood, love is the best guide to living a full Christian life and is the ultimate norm of what is right or wrong in human activity. However, life is full of complicated ethical questions and decisions which make it very difficult to decide the most loving thing to do in concrete circumstances. Hence our need for guidance and for an authentic interpreter of morality. The Catholic Church has the responsibility and spiritual authority to be a moral teacher since Christian moral living is intimately connected with a person's relationship to God and his or her eternal salvation, and because Christ commanded the Apostles to teach all persons (Mt. 28:18-20). The bishops at Vatican II stated this truth in their *Declaration on Religious Liberty*:

> The Catholic Church is by the will of Christ the teacher of truth. It is her duty to proclaim and teach with authority the truth which is Christ and at the same time to declare and confirm by her authority the principles of the moral order which spring from human nature itself. (DH 14)

The church is assisted in her responsibility to teach Christian morality through the indispensable expertise of her moral theologians. These professionally-trained persons undergo a long training in basic doctrinal theology and Scripture, plus specialized study of sociology, psychology, cultural anthropology and in some cases economics and medicine, culminating in a doctorate in moral theology or Christian ethics. This diversified study equips the moral theologian to tackle complex modern ethical questions in order to determine the morality of concrete human actions. The sophisticated study and writing of moral theologians is the necessary condition for the church to be a moral teacher.

We shall briefly consider the sources professional theologians use to arrive at moral conclusions and the two-stage process the church employs in formulating her moral teaching. Three important practical consequences follow from this process.

Moral theologians base their judgments on what is right or wrong in concrete human actions from various *sources:* what God has revealed in the Hebrew Scriptures, especially the 10 Commandments, and the life and teaching of Jesus in the Christian Scriptures; the church's teaching and its 2000-year experience of living the Christian life under the influence of the grace of the Holy Spirit, given to all Christians and moral theologians alike; the accumulated knowledge and common sense of humankind guided by the Holy Spirit, given to believers and unbelievers alike; data and insights from sciences like psychology, sociology, anthropology, medicine, biology; people's lived experience that calls for fresh approaches and responses to new technology and social movements.

The actual *two-stage process* of formulating the church's moral teaching is the work of her moral theologians achieving a consensus, which is then accepted by the bishops and pope as official church teaching. Consensus is reached through a long process of moral theologians studying complex moral questions in light of the above sources, drawing tentative conclusions published in scholarly articles and books, which in turn are critically analyzed and debated by other moral theologians until a consensus gradually emerges. In the second stage the official magisterium or teaching office of the church reviews the consensus reached, accepting or modifying or rejecting it. When accepted, it becomes official church teaching and is promulgated as such, finding its way into textbooks used in the seminary training of future priests, in Catholic university and high school theology/religion texts, and in catechetical materials. In many cases the pope or the Congregation for the Doctrine of the Faith or national bishops' conferences or individual bishops issue letters on specific moral questions, with the aid of moral theologians.

Since moral teaching is part of the church's *ordinary* magisterium and is not in all cases infallible teaching, three consequences follow: the teaching can be *incomplete* and even considered erroneous in future centuries; it can be further developed and thus *changed*; and it therefore admits of responsible **dissent** by moral theologians and knowledgeable sincere Catholics.

Major Change in Methodology of Moral Theology

Before Vatican II, Catholic moral theology used the **natural law** approach, that is, by reason reflecting on natural inclinations that embody human values and by analyzing the physical laws of nature[2] built into hu-

---

2. It should be noted that there are more forms of natural law than the narrowly physicalist approach which had flourished mostly between 1850 and 1960.

mans in God's act of creation, one deduced what was right or wrong by whether it was in accord with the human nature created by God. For example: to tell a lie or to use contraceptives were judged morally wrong because the purpose of the natural faculty or power of speech is to speak truth and of the sexual faculty to procreate human life. To thus misuse or frustrate a human faculty is to go against the Creator's purpose, and consequently is judged morally wrong. This approach tended to dominate traditional or classical Catholic morality up to Vatican II.

Before and during the Council, Catholic moral theologians began to critique the traditional natural law argument and developed what has been called "contextual ethics," "new morality," "revisionist morality." This approach holds that the *physical* laws of human nature are too narrow and limited to be an absolute, exclusive norm for morality that fits all situations. To judge the morality of human actions, one ought to consider not only the action itself and the purpose of the faculty but the person's *intention* in doing the action and all the *circumstances* surrounding the action and the *consequences* following it. An action judged morally wrong according to the physical natural law could be judged morally correct because of the circumstances/consequences and the person's intention or reason for acting. A person may speak an untruth to save his own or another's life.

The *advantage* of the traditional classical approach is that it gives clear, concise answers available to all persons through observing the purpose of our physical faculties or powers. It has God's authority since God established the laws of nature in creating us. The *disadvantage*, however, is that using our physical faculties alone is too narrow; one needs to consider *total* human nature: mind, will, emotions, including a person's reasons or intention for acting and the person's evaluation of the complex myriad of circumstances and consequences surrounding most human activity.

Conversely, the *advantages* of the contextual or revisionist approach is that it considers the person in his or her full human nature, his or her intention in acting and the attendant circumstances, including the consequences of the action. It provides reasonable, common-sense solutions to complicated moral questions and makes Catholic moral teaching credible to contemporary individuals The *disadvantages* of this approach are its openness to abuse and rationalization, and the difficulty in judging which circumstances are sufficient to justify certain actions like lying, premarital sex, taking human life. This approach is sometimes ambiguous and inconsistent, lacking the either-or clarity of the traditional approach.

Since morality profoundly touches all aspects of human life, this change from classical Catholic morality to a contextual emphasis has caused confusion for many Catholics educated in the traditional approach and has resulted in painful division within the Catholic Church today. This is so since *official* church teaching favors the natural law approach whereas the majority of today's Catholic moral theologians are convinced the newer approach better explains the reality of our moral activity and better handles complex moral questions.

The Great Debate in Catholic Moral Theology Today[3]

The major division among Catholic moral theologians today is between traditionalists and revisionists. How did this come about? We suggest four ways in which the Second Vatican Council profoundly influenced the majority of Catholic moralists.

- The Council employed a *historical* approach rather than the classical emphasis on unchangeable, eternal truths. To take history seriously and to recognize how it has shaped church teaching and discipline indicated to moral theologians how relative much church teaching is. Change is therefore possible and has occurred on major issues. Moral theologians thus challenged sacrosanct concepts, like natural law.

- The Council stressed *Scripture*. The biblical renewal within the church following the Council caused moral theologians to move from a rationalistic natural law approach to gospel values, such as love rather than law, as the source and norm for Christian morality.

- The Council downplayed *legalism*. The new emphasis on the Bible showed how Jesus was opposed to legalism and to making mere observance of law the heart of religion.

- The Council, following John XXIII's distinction between the substance of the Catholic faith and the various ways it can be presented, accepted a *pluralism* of theologies in the one church. Pluralism, now a major characteristic of Catholic moral theology, is exemplified by the two main groups among Catholic moral theologians today: the traditionalists and the revisionists

The main difference between the two groups is their approach to **moral norms**. More specifically, whether such moral rules are in fact absolute, that is, always-evil acts permitting no exceptions; or whether exceptions are possible. Because the issues debated between traditionalist and revisionist moral theologians are so important in the practical life of the church, we must understand what theologians mean by moral norms and **moral absolutes**.

A *moral norm* is a guideline, a rule, an expression of people's collective wisdom that points out values that help persons make correct moral

---

3. For fuller treatment, see Richard Gula, *What Are They Saying about Moral Norms?*(New York: Paulist Press, 1982) and Gula, *Reason Informed by Faith* (New York: Paulist Press, 1989).

decisions on what actions to do and what to avoid. Examples of moral norms are *general* statements like: do good and avoid evil, love God and your neighbor as yourself, be honest, be just, or negatively, don't be dishonest, don't act unjustly. More specific but still general statements are those expressed in the 10 Commandments: honor your father and mother; do not commit adultery, do not steal or lie. These are called *formal* norms. Both traditionalists and revisionists would agree that these formal norms are absolute, without exception. The problem arises concerning *material* norms, those that point toward *particular* actions to be performed or avoided here and now. Examples of material norms are: don't speak falsehoods, don't kill, don't take another's property. These express important values for human living.

Traditionalists hold there exist moral norms (material) that are absolute, allowing no exceptions. Such acts are therefore always wrong—"intrinsically evil." Traditionalist moral theologian Germain Grisez lists the following as examples of negative moral absolutes that permit no exceptions: masturbation, contraception, direct sterilization, artificial insemination, abortion, homosexual actions, extramarital sex.

Revisionists hold there are few *absolute* moral norms; they believe it is *theoretically* impossible in advance to foresee all the elements that enter into human moral action. They point out that the function of *negative material* norms is to express important human values: "Thou shalt not kill" shows the incomparable value of human life; "Do not speak falsehood" calls attention to the value for society in telling the truth. However, these negative material norms admit exceptions: killing in self-defense or in a "just war" is not *murder,* and speaking an untruth to preserve a greater good is not a *lie.*

Therefore, revisionist moral theologians maintain that relatively few actions are intrinsically or essentially evil *in themselves;* human actions must be judged in their context according to the reasons for acting (*intention*) and all the *circumstances* and *consequences* surrounding the action. However, revisionist theologians maintain that some material norms are *practical* absolutes or virtually exceptionless: cruel treatment of a child which is of no benefit to the child; direct killing of noncombatants in war; rape; punishing a person known to be innocent. The words "practical" and "virtually" indicate that while one cannot theoretically demonstrate their absoluteness, one should act as if they were absolute.

A key concept for revisionists is that of *proportionate reason.* To act morally, especially in "conflict" situations where several conflicting values are involved or where disvalues are present, one ought to have a proportionate reason, that is, there must be a greater reason for doing an action that preserves one or more values while sacrificing other values or involving disvalues. An example is a doctor telling a terminally-ill patient an untruth about his condition; the doctor judges the value of his patient's peace of mind to be greater than the value of telling the truth in this situation and the resulting disvalue of speaking falsely. Revisionists argue that in a sinful and imperfect world full of ambiguous situations, some disvalues may—indeed must—be permitted in order to achieve more important values.

Revisionists make an important and helpful distinction between *premoral* and *moral* evil. Only moral evil is real evil constituting sin; premoral evil is a disvalue, an action that lacks goodness that ought to be present; therefore it can be said to be evil. Examples of premoral evil are stating an untruth, contraceptive intercourse, taking food or land, even taking a person's life. Such actions do not become *moral* evil or personally sinful until the intention and circumstances, including lack of a proportionate reason, are considered. Thus premoral evil becomes moral evil and sinful when it is done *without a proportionate reason*. This distinction is helpful in complex moral questions today: removing life support systems for the terminally ill, artificial insemination, capital punishment, pre-marital sex, homosexual acts in certain circumstances, contraceptive use.

A Theology of Human Sexuality

Our reflection on this important topic is taken from *Sexual Morality: A Catholic Perspective.*[4] Two basic principles for a theology of human sexuality are established: sex is a gift of God and therefore good; sex touches human persons on all levels of their existence: the physical, psychological, spiritual and social, and therefore is "fundamental to the way we relate to ourselves, to others and to God."

By contrast, four *inadequate* theories of sexuality help us better appreciate this positive theology of sexuality: sex is evil; sex exists only for procreation or only for pleasure; sex is for my fulfillment and development as a person; society may control sexual activity by sterilization, genetic screening of undesirables, limiting number of children in a family, etc. The inadequacy of the last three lies in their overstressing the physical, romantic, and societal aspects of human sexuality.

The Christian theology of sexuality is rooted in the basic Christian doctrines of God as Trinity, the Incarnation, the Resurrection and Original Sin. That God is an eternal love relationship of three divine persons gives us a model to imitate in our own sexual relationships; Christian marriage itself is a beautiful symbol of God's trinitarian life. That God became man in taking flesh in Jesus of Nazareth shows that our human nature is good and worthy of the highest esteem. That God raised Jesus from the dead, giving him glorified risen life, dramatically tells us that our bodies also have a magnificent eternal destiny of risen life. That all of us are weak human sinners with powerful bodily desires cautions us to control our sex-

---

4. Philip Keane, *Sexual Morality: A Catholic Perspective* (New York: Paulist Press, 1977).

ual urges and to treat sex with care. Thus sexuality "contains within it profound elements of mystery, of openness to God."

With this theological basis for human sexuality, the "key question" in judging the morality of sexual acts can be formulated thus: "How I do use my God-given gift of sexuality so as to relate most responsibly to myself, to other people both individually and socially, and to the holy mystery of God." Accordingly, the basic moral criterion for sexual activity becomes "responsibility in relationships."

The Christian Catholic conviction of sexual activity and its key insight may be expressed in this way: genital sexual activity is expressed and protected in the stable, faithful permanent union of a sacramental marriage publicly witnessed between a man and woman. *Expressed*: "the conjugal love of a married couple mysteriously and wonderfully symbolizes and makes real in this world the covenantal love of God for all of us." Christ's love for his church is likewise symbolized by the sexual love of husband and wife for each other. *Protected*: only in a permanent, faithful marriage can sexual love achieve its full potential of self-giving, trust, fidelity, personal growth, loving parental care. This Catholic vision of marriage as a sacrament in Christ means that the married couples' mutual sexual activity becomes sacred, as mirroring Christ's unselfish love for the church and as a rich source of God's blessing and grace. Only in a Christian sacramental marriage can sexual love accomplish so much.

Traditionalist / Revisionist Approaches Applied to Contemporary Problems

1. Premarital Sex

Both traditionalist and revisionist moral theologians condemn *casual* premarital sex as lacking all personal commitment and self-giving love, and therefore incapable of symbolizing God's covenant love and Jesus' unselfish love for his church. A problem arises with *committed* premarital intercourse. Traditionalists see this as an intrinsically disordered action that permits no exceptions to the principle that every genital act must occur only in marriage. Many revisionists, but not all, contend that when socioeconomic or other circumstances make it impossible to marry at this particular time, the premarital sex of a truly *mature sincere* couple *genuinely committed* to each other and *seriously intending marriage* constitutes a premoral, not moral evil or sin.

However, in this case of committed premarital sexual activity, two important observations are made. First, the church's basic norm that genital sexual activity is best protected and expressed in marriage remains clearly in place since "a deep heterosexual love union between two persons needs to be publicly witnessed" and since most probably "such a union is not open . . . to the procreation of children." Second, "many of these cases of committed premarital sexual intercourse are not as good as they look at first glance" since "it can cover a fair degree of selfishness and immaturity" and since "one partner can never be sure that the other partner's words of commitment—which are not public—are genuine."[5]

With the tragic spread of AIDS and the high prevalence of sexual promiscuity extending to high school and even grade school students, a growing number of counselors, psychiatrists and psychotherapists have stressed the positive values of abstinence or celibacy. In an informative insightful article "Adolescents in a Time of AIDS: Preventive Education," Stephen Post, associate professor of bioethics at the Center of Biomedical Ethics, states:

> . . . our culture desperately needs to recover the link between sex and love, and the insight that love, to be worthy of the word, requires no sexual expression. Love also includes joy, compassion, commitment and respect, including respect for the other's freedom to refuse sexual intimacy.[6]

2. Contraception in Marriage

Pope Paul VI issued his controversial letter *Of Human Life* in 1968. Popularly known as "the birth control encyclical," it is in fact a beautiful tribute to conjugal love and contains much valuable teaching and a sensitive concern for couples. Its controversial teaching is contained in one sentence: "The Church, calling men back to the observance of the natural law . . . teaches that each and every marriage act must remain open to the transmission of life."[7] This rules out using any method inhibiting procreation. The following reason is given:

> That teaching . . . is founded upon the inseparable connection, willed by God and unable to be broken by man on his own initiative, between the two meanings of the conjugal act: the unitive meaning and the procreative meaning. . . . By safeguarding both these essential aspects . . . the conjugal act preserves in its fullness the sense of true mutual love and its ordination toward man's most high calling to parenthood.[8]

Thus "the direct interruption of the generative process already begun . . . [is] to be absolutely excluded as licit means of regulating birth."[9] Contraceptive use is thus to be considered an intrinsically evil act.

5. *Ibid.*, 105-06.

6. Stephen Post, "Adolescents in a Time of AIDS: Preventive Education," *America* 167 (Oct. 17, 1992), 279.

7. National Conference of Catholic Bishops, *Human Life in Our Day* (Washington, DC: U.S. Catholic Conference, 1968), 11.

8. *Ibid.*, 12.

9. *Ibid.*, 14.

The majority of moral theologians in the revisionist school today are unable to agree with the above reasoning. They argue that the *total married life* of a couple should be open to procreation, not *each and every act* of intercourse. Thus the couples' reason or *intention* for using contraceptives based on all the *circumstances* of their life determines the morality rather than the individual physical act. Moreover, the spouses' consciences must be respected. (See chapter 19 for the position stated in the majority report of the commission established by Popes John XXIII and Paul VI to study the question of contraceptive use in married life.)

The official Catholic teaching remains that use of contraception is morally wrong. Pope John Paul II holds strongly to this teaching and has developed a more compelling argument than natural law reasoning. He stresses the very nature of married love to be fruitful and to issue in human life.

3. Homosexual Activity

The question of the morality of homosexual acts is a profound challenge to Catholic moral theologians. Neither traditional nor revisionist theologians agree with the convictions and insistent demands of gay and lesbian persons to recognize homosexual activity as fully acceptable and on a par with heterosexual acts. For homosexual activity will never be open to the value of children and the values of man/woman relationship. Yet, moral theologians recognize that very many gay persons, are sincerely convinced in their own conscience that their love is ennobling and contributes to their growth as human persons, and that consequently their sexual activity is acceptable to God, who gave them this sexual orientation. Furthermore, the church in her pastoral life must show the understanding and compassion of Christ to homosexuals. In such a complex human situation, moral theologians are not content with either-or solutions but seek to develop a moral position that takes account of all the human, psychological, biological, and social factors, as well as data from the Scriptures.

We must insist that the Catholic Church does not condemn the homosexual as a person. Homosexual orientation is not sinful. The church condemns prejudice against homosexual persons, as well as economic and job discrimination. A clear distinction must therefore be made between homosexual orientation and homosexual activity.

The official Catholic teaching is that homosexual activity constitutes a moral evil and is sinful because it is opposed to God's plan for human sexuality. Catholic moral theologians, however, cannot evade the case of a homosexual who cannot change his or her orientation, who is unable to live a life of perfect chastity, and who is convinced in conscience that his or her stable, loving relationship with one person is acceptable to God and is not sinful. The answer traditionalist moral theologians give is easy and clear: such circumstances have no bearing because homosexual acts are against

God's plan for human sexuality and are therefore intrinsically evil and sinful.

Revisionists form a different moral judgment. Because of the *circumstances* (a gay or lesbian person not free to practice perfect chastity, possessing a clear conscience, and achieving a responsible relationship with personal human and spiritual growth) and the person's sincere *intention*, such activity should not be judged to be morally evil and sinful. However, because homosexual activity can never achieve the full potential of heterosexual sexuality, premoral evil is present. By invoking the distinction between premoral and moral evil, revisionist theologians safeguard the priority and value of heterosexual relationships in marriage, while at the same time addressing in a compassionate and understanding way the real-life situation of such homosexual relationships.

But what of homosexual marriages? Revisionist theologians would not permit such marriages on the basis that a homosexual marriage can in no way equate a Christian sacramental marriage. No proportionate reason exists to justify homosexual marriages being approved by the church.

Because of the complex issues involved and deep-seated prejudice against gay people, the above "premoral evil but not moral evil" approach will not be acceptable to either traditional Catholics or gay Catholics. Yet this moral judgment by responsible moral theologians seems to many Catholics today to best fit "the Christian tradition, contemporary understanding of moral principles, and continuing insights on homosexuality and homosexual acts."[10]

John Paul II's Teaching on Moral Theology

In *The Splendor of Truth* issued in 1993, Pope John Paul II calls attention to a "genuine crisis" in society and even within the church concerning morality and the church's moral teaching. Because dissent from the church's moral teaching is no longer "limited and occasional" but an "overall and systematic . . . questioning of traditional moral doctrine" (4),[11] the pope intends to "set forth . . . the principles of moral teaching based upon Scripture and the living apostolic tradition" and clarify the "presuppositions and consequences" of dissent (5).

The pope begins by establishing important principles as the foundation for moral theology.

---

10. Keane, *Sexual Morality*, 89.

11. Specifically, the pope refers to the rejection of "the traditional doctrine concerning the natural law, and the universality and the permanent validity of its precepts" and to the fact that "certain of the church's moral teachings are found simply unacceptable; and the magisterium itself is considered capable of intervening in matters of morality only in order to 'exhort consciences' and to 'propose values' in the light of which each individual will independently make his or her decisions and life choices." (VS 4).

• There is a close relationship between freedom and truth; obedience to the moral law is an act of true freedom.

• Christian faith, especially in the person of Jesus Christ and his death and resurrection, is the basis of Christian morality.

• The natural law as God's law written into human nature at creation is a legitimate source of morality.

• An objective morality based on God's law exists; moral relativism and subjectivism are to be rejected.

• To promote morality is to promote human persons and their freedom and to benefit society.

• The church has competency to speak on morality and to teach authoritatively.

All Catholic moral theologians would agree with these basic principles.

In the light of these principles, the following six assertions can be said to constitute the Holy Father's major emphases in the encyclical. Each deserves brief explanation.

1. The goodness or badness of a human act depends "primarily and fundamentally" on its *object*, that is, on the kind of *action* chosen and not on the person's intention in acting or on the circumstances and consequences of the act (78).[12] The pope thus rejects by name *consequentialism* and *proportionalism*[13] as theories that "cannot claim to be grounded in the Catholic moral tradition" (76).

2. This emphasis on the object of the moral act means that certain actions are intrinsically evil of themselves, which no intention or any circumstance can make good.[14] The encyclical quotes *Gaudium et Spes* 27 for "examples of such acts": those hostile to human life (homicide, genocide, abortion, euthanasia, suicide); acts violating the integrity of the human person (mutilation, physical and mental torture); acts offensive to human dignity (subhuman living conditions, arbitrary imprisonment,

---

12. "The reason why a good intention is not itself sufficient, but a correct choice of actions is also needed, is that the human act depends on its object, whether or not that object is capable of being ordered to God . . ." VS 78.

13. "The teleological ethical theories (proportionalism and consequentialism), while acknowledging that moral values are indicated by reason and by revelation, maintain that it is never possible to formulate an absolute prohibition of particular kinds of behavior which would be in conflict in every circumstance and in every culture with those values." VS 75. This section attempts a detailed presentation of the position of those who hold these two theories; it also treats the "premoral order which some term *nonmoral, physical* or *ontic* . . ."

14. Intrinsically evil acts "are such always and per se, in other words, on account of their very object and quite apart from the ulterior intentions of the one acting and the circumstances." VS 80. The encyclical quotes the new *Catechism of the Catholic Church:* "There are certain specific kinds of behavior that are always wrong to choose because choosing them involves a disorder of the will, that is, a moral evil."

slavery, prostitution, degrading conditions of work, etc.) (80). The technical term for intrinsically evil acts is "negative moral norms" or precepts. The encyclical mentions two kinds of negative norms: one, "The negative precepts of the natural law are universally valid. They oblige each and every individual, always and in every circumstance" (52); two, six of the 10 Commandments are expressed in negative norms or laws: "Thou shalt not kill . . . commit adultery . . . steal . . . bear false witness (lie) . . ." Such negative moral norms do not permit exceptions, according to the encyclical.[15]

3. The encyclical does not reduce the natural law to "bodily physical laws," "mere biological laws" which it says revisionist theologians have claimed (47).[16] Rather the natural law involves "the nature of the human person," "the unity of body and soul" (50). "Its authority therefore extends to all mankind" (51). The encyclical does, however, defend bodily functions as valid for determining morality (49).

4. The subjective conscience may not *decide* what is good or bad but first must be informed by the truth of God's revelation, as interpreted by the teaching office of the church; only such an informed conscience can then *judge* which particular acts to choose (54-64, especially 57-61). The concern of the encyclical is to reject a subjective morality and stress an objective moral order based on the "object" of human acts and the role of the church's magisterium in forming conscience.

5. While accepting the "fundamental choice or option," defined as "a decision about oneself and a setting of one's life for or against the good, for or against the truth and ultimately for or against God" (65), the encyclical rejects the "distinction" or "separation" between fundamental option and deliberate choices of concrete behavior.[17] (However, no Catholic moral theologian makes this separation.) The encyclical's purpose is to reaffirm the possibility of mortal sin in particular human acts that do not involve one's fundamental option (70).[18]

---

15. "The negative moral precepts, those prohibiting certain concrete actions or kinds of behavior as intrinsically evil, do not allow for any legitimate exception." VS 67.

16. "According to certain theologians, this kind of 'biologistic or naturalistic argumentation'" is used by the church's magisterium in "sexual and conjugal ethics." These theologians "maintain, on the basis of a naturalistic understanding of the sexual act, that contraception, direct sterilization, autoeroticism, premarital sexual relations, homosexual relations and artificial insemination were condemned as morally unacceptable." The encyclical disagrees that the church's magisterium condemns these acts on the basis of "biologistic argumentation."

17. This "separation" is "contrary to the teaching of Scripture itself which . . . links that choice profoundly to particular acts." "The fundamental option . . . is always brought into play through conscious and free decisions." VS 67.

18. In quoting the apostolic exhortation, *Reconciliation and Penance,* issued after the 1983 Synod of Bishops, the encyclical affirms that mortal sin can occur "in every act of disobedience to God's commandments in a grave matter." VS 70.

6. The role of moral theologians is to explain and support the church's magisterium in its moral teaching.[19] They are asked to give "the example of a loyal assent, both internal and external, to the magisterium's teaching in the areas of both dogma and morality" (110). They are to avoid *public* dissent as being opposed to ecclesial communion and the hierarchical nature of the church (113).[20]

It is too early at the time of this writing to report on the encyclical's long-range effect on Catholic moral theology.[21] It is clear, however, that many moral theologians have seen the encyclical as an unwelcome return to a pre-Vatican II traditional morality that may render the church's moral

---

19. "While recognizing the possible limitations of the human arguments employed by the magisterium, moral thologians are called to develop a deeper understanding of the reasons underlying its teachings and to expound the validity and obligatory nature of the precepts it proposes . . ." VS 110.

20. "Dissent, in the form of carefully orchestrated protests and polemics carried on in the media, is opposed to ecclesial communion and to a correct understanding of the hierarchical constitution of the people of God." VS 113.

21. For eight commentators, see "Veritatis Splendor," *Commonweal* 120 (Oct. 22, 1993):11-18. One, Joseph Komonchak, takes "the primary purpose of this encyclical . . . to be that of recalling certain non-negotiable aspects of Catholic teaching as the outer limits within which Catholic theological reflection ought to take place." He lists four: the Christian Gospel contains moral teaching; morality is not subjective; a sincere conscience is not sufficient in itself to judge on the goodness of a human act; one's basic life orientation or fundamental option must be reflected in particular decisions of daily life" (12). Protestant moral theologian Stanley Haueras calls the encyclical a "unique and remarkable document," "written eloquently on the nature of Christian morality," "a gold mine of insight and direction" (16-18). Moral theologian Richard McCormick praises the "beautiful Christ-centered presentation" in chapter one but calls attention to two problems. That "Actions are morally wrong from the object independently of circumstances" misses the "key issue": "what objects should be characterized as morally wrong and on what criteria?" and "what is to count as pertaining to the object?" That the "encyclical repeatedly states that proportionalism attempts to justify morally wrong action by a good intention" is a "misrepresentation." He sees "an unstated agenda item": to reject a priori "whatever does not support the moral wrongfulness of every contraceptive act." See "Veritatis Splendor and Moral Theology," *America* 169 (Oct. 30, 1993):8-11. Vatican Affairs correspondent Peter Hebblethwaite believes the encyclical's goal is disciplinary—for bishops, to whom it is addressed, to control dissenting moral theologians. *National Catholic Reporter*, (Oct. 1, 1993):9. Professors John Finnis and Germain Grisez, writing in *L'Osservatore Romano* 8 (February 23, 1994): 6-7, make these statements: "The encyclical identifies its own 'central theme' . . . : there are intrinsically evil acts prohibited always and without exception." "Certain theories . . . notably proportionalism, consequentialism or teleologism, deny that there are any intrinsically evil acts." "John Paul II makes it clear . . . that these theories are incompatible with revealed truth." Richard McCormick's lengthy article, "Some Early Reactions to Veritatis Splendor," *Theological Studies* 55, No. 3 (September, 1994): 481-506, reviews comments in the press, various symposia of scholars and individual studies by moral theologians; he then discusses three critical issues raised by the encyclical: its positive value ("strong indictment of contemporary relativism and individualism"); its central issue, the meaning of "object" (what precisely constitutes the object of moral actions); and ecclesiology, the issue behind other issues ("the Church as a pyramid where truth and authority flow uniquely from the pinnacle . . . [or] the concentric model wherein the reflections of all must flow from the periphery to the center if the wisdom resident in the Church is to be reflected persuasively and prophetically to the world.")

teaching, especially sexual morality, less credible for Catholics, thus further dividing the church, and as depriving theologians of methodology essential to deal satisfactorily with the pressing and increasingly complex moral issues today. Others have welcomed the encyclical as a much-needed, long-awaited corrective to moral relativism, to public dissent and to a vindication of the magisterium's duty to speak on morality.

Concluding Reflections

Where does *Veritatis Splendor* leave moral theologians of the revisionist school? Does it reject the dominant development in moral theology before and after the Second Vatican Council? The encyclical appears not to reject the main body of revisionist theologians. It also appears that some of their carefully expressed and nuanced positions have not been presented with sufficient accuracy in the encyclical.

Since the encyclical represents the authoritative teaching of the church's magisterium, it deserves respect. At the same time, the proper role of moral theologians in scrutinizing moral arguments and developing for the benefit of the church a coherent moral theology must be safeguarded. A hoped-for result is an open dialogue between moral theologians and the magisterium. On their part, some moral theologians may need to reevaluate some positions and refrain, as far as possible in today's open society, from public dissent. The magisterium may need to identify more clearly specific negative norms, to explain more persuasively why some acts are intrinsically evil, and to indicate more clearly those situations where intention, circumstances and consequences do in fact play a part in influencing the morality of human actions. The magisterium may need to consult more broadly and in a collegial manner with the bishops of the world and with moral theologians from a wide spectrum in reaching its moral conclusions; for the sake of its own credibility, it may also need to state its teaching in less absolute and certain assertions.

This encyclical, as an exercise of the church's ordinary magisterium about matters not directly contained in revelation, is not infallible. Because many of its assertions are the result of human reasoning, the teaching may be incomplete and open to further development. That the encyclical stated it did not intend to espouse one school of moral theology, though in fact it has done so, implies the possibility of further discussion and development.

In the last analysis, the success or failure of this teaching will depend on its **reception** by the entire Catholic Church: bishops, priests, moral theologians, lay Catholics. Historically, reception referred to local churches accepting, or in some cases rejecting, papal decisions and those of ecumenical councils.[22] This encyclical will rightfully undergo rigorous analysis by moral theologians in scholarly articles. It will inspire in-depth discussion by bishops, priests and educated lay Catholics. This activity will influence the teaching's ultimate reception or rejection.

What about "Ordinary" Catholics?

How should a sincere Catholic think and act in this period of confusion and division in the church regarding morality and sexuality? What is a Catholic to make of the situation in which the official church teaches one thing about human sexuality and a large number of reputable Catholic moral theologians disagree with this teaching? Is dissent from the authentic magisterium of the church permissible? And what does one make of the fact that over 80% of U.S. Catholics do not agree with papal teaching on contraception in marriage, yet consider themselves good Catholics and receive the sacraments regularly without confessing contraceptive use?

There are three possibilities for today's Catholic: follow official Catholic teaching fully, even if one has difficulties and misgivings; totally ignore the magisterium's teaching as irrelevant; form one's honest, sincere conscience after prayer and serious consideration of the reasons for both the official church position and that of responsible moral theologians. The first is admirable provided one is knowledgeable, understands the issues, and does not do violence to his or her conscience. Uncritical, unquestioning obedience is not the Catholic ideal. The second is immature and reprehensible and does not do justice to the competency of the church's magisterium. The third seems to be the most reasonable in today's Vatican II church, which encourages Catholics to follow their own informed conscience and which permits responsible *private* dissent from the ordinary magisterium.

An informed Catholic will understand that the role of professional moral theologians in the church is to use their expertise to deal with complex moral questions, to critique moral positions that are incomplete or no

---

22. See Thomas Rausch, *Authority and Leadership in the Church* (Wilmington, DE: Michael Glazier, 1989), 105-06 for the twofold "classical" concept of reception and two instances of rejection: the claim of Pope Boniface VIII in *Unam Sanctam* in 1302 "that it is absolutely necessary for the salvation of all men that they submit to the Roman Pontiff" and the Council of Constance decree *Haec Sancta* in 1415 on the "supremacy of a general assembly of bishops over a pope." An example of contemporary nonreception of papal and official magisterial teaching is the statement in *Of Human Life* that "Each and every marriage act must remain open to the transmission of life" so that use of a contraceptive is an intrinsically evil act. The majority of married Catholics, moral theologians, priests and many bishops did not and do not accept the teaching. Bishop Christopher Butler of England stated that the widespread and intense reaction to the encyclical constituted nonreception, "a phenomenon he viewed as 'invalidating' the teaching." See Richard McCormick, *"Humanae Vitae* 25 Years Later," *America 168* (July 17, 1993): 10 and Joseph Komonchak, "*Humanae Vitae* and Its Reception: Ecclesiological Reflections," *Theological Studies* 39 (1978): 221-57.

longer applicable, and to propose positions that best take into account comprehensive data from Scripture, church tradition, human experience, and sciences like psychology, biology, sociology, medicine. A Catholic well-versed in the history of the church will realize that the official church has on occasion taken incomplete positions it later repudiated,[23] and often been the last to respond to events, theological insights, and major cultural changes. Such a Catholic will not be scandalized or unduly perturbed because he or she is aware that necessary change in the church often came about by responsible disagreement with the ordinary magisterium. Finally, a religiously sensitive Catholic is confident that the Holy Spirit is guiding the church and is able to bring progress and much good out of apparently harmful division and confusion.

The period of transition and tension we are now living through in the church may be the harbinger of a period of vitality for the church and of growth for the kingdom of God.

Summary

Morality is what is right or wrong in specific human actions. *Christian* morality is based on Jesus' teaching on love of God and our "neighbor." Because of the difficulty in deciding right action based on love in increasingly complex moral questions, professional moral theologians are necessary for the Catholic Church to develop its moral teaching. In so doing, the church's moral theologians have moved away from the traditional act-oriented natural law methodology to a broader approach that considers not only the physical action but the person's intention in acting and all the circumstances surrounding the action. Currently the great debate among Catholic moral theologians is between the traditionalist and revisionist way of doing moral theology. Revisionists distinguish between real moral evil (sin) and premoral evil, which falls short of the full goodness desired in specific human actions but which can be permitted for a proportionately serious reason. This distinction is helpful in dealing with today's moral questions when either-or answers are insufficient and do not do justice to ambiguous human situations, where a variety of values are present.

These considerations are particularly important in the area of sexual morality. Catholic theology of sexuality affirms that sex as God's great

---

23. Examples are Pius IX's denying any truth or goodness in non-Christian religions, his condemnation of the separation of church and state and of religious freedom as an objective right and Pius XII's exclusive identification of the Roman Catholic Church with the Mystical Body of Christ. Vatican II modified or reversed these. Rausch, *Authority and Leadership in the Church*, 107. See J. Robert Dionne, *The Papacy and the Church: A Study of Praxis and Reception in Ecumenical Perspective*, (New York: Philosophical Library, 1987). See especially John Noonan "Development in Moral Doctrine," *Theological Studies* 54 (December, 1993): 662-77, for four examples of changes in the church's moral teaching: usury, marriage, slavery, religious freedom.

gift is fundamentally good, profoundly affects each of us on all levels of our existence, and partakes of the mystery of God. Accordingly, the key Christian Catholic insight and conviction about sexuality is that genital sexual activity is expressed and protected in the stable, faithful permanent union in a sacramental marriage. Casual premarital sex falls far short of this ideal. Official Catholic teaching forbids the use of contraceptives; however, Catholic couples and moral theologians find the natural law argument unconvincing. Revisionists recognize that under certain specific circumstances, sexual activity by gays and lesbians with a clear conscience is for them not a moral evil. Pope John Paul II's recent encyclical insists on an objective moral order and the existence of intrinsically evil acts, independent of circumstances and the person's reason for acting. This appears to reject the contextual ethics approach of revisionist theologians.

For Discussion

1. Evaluate the strengths and weaknesses of both the traditional natural law approach and the contextual ethics method of forming moral judgments.

2. Do you think the revisionist approach is good moral theology and realistic or do you see it as a compromise to human weakness?

3. Discuss the distinction between real evil and premoral evil. Does it make sense?

4. One frequently hears, especially from young people, that the church's teaching on sexual morality is outdated. In what areas and to what extent *can* the church change and still be faithful to Christian values and her centuries-old tradition and teaching? In what areas can it *not* change?

5. Discuss: "Intercourse ought to express the total giving of self to another, with the complete acceptance of the whole range of responsibilities that might be involved."

6. "Sexual intercourse ought to be an expression of a deep, intimate love relationship that demands permanence, fidelity, fertility. Otherwise it is either selfish pleasure, a crutch, a counterfeit act of love, or prostitution!" Comment on this.

7. Is premarital sex a good or poor way to prepare for a successful Christian marriage? Is the church's ideal of sexual love being reserved for marriage too strict for today's young people? Impractical?

8. Has our pleasure-driven society today lost the ideal and vision of human sexuality, with the consequent cheapening of sex? Discuss the benefits the church's vision of sexuality offers society today.

9. Does *Splendor of Truth* condemn revisionist moral theology? Can revisionist theologians continue to hold their position? Discuss in depth.

For Action

1. Interview a moral theologian. Prepare beforehand questions drawn from this chapter to ask him or her.
2. Talk to a gay person. Learn his or her thinking on these moral questions and on the Catholic Church's teaching on homosexuality.
3. Read up on the Billings' Method of Family Planning and talk to a Catholic couple who follow this method in their married life.

Further Reading

Avvento, Gennaro. *Sexuality, A Christian View: Toward Formation of Mature Values.* Mystic, CT: Twenty-Third Publications, 1982.

Dwyer, John. *Human Sexuality: A Christian View.* Kansas City, MO: Sheed and Ward, 1987.

Genovesi, Vincent. *In Pursuit of Love, Catholic Morality and Human Sexuality.* Wilmington, DE: Michael Glazier, 1987.

Gula, Richard. *What Are They Saying about Moral Norms?* New York: Paulist Press, 1982.

_____. *Reason Informed by Faith.* New York: Paulist Press, 1989.

Hanigan, James. *As I Have Loved You: the Challenge of Christian Ethics.* Mahwah, N.J.: Paulist Press, 1986.

_____. *Homosexuality: the Test Case for Christian Social Ethics.* New York: Paulist Press, 1988.

_____. *What Are They Saying about Sexual Morality?* New York: Paulist Press, 1982.

Keane, Philip. *Sexual Morality, A Catholic Perspective.* New York: Paulist Press, 1977.

Appendix:
Moral Questions Concerning the Sacredness of Human Life

The Catholic Church is today a strong defender of human life in all its manifestations from "womb to tomb." She insists that every human life is sacred because created by a loving God, who alone has authority over life and death. Yet a characteristic of modern society seems to be a lessening of respect for human life. It sometimes appears that the church is fighting a losing battle against the assault on human life which has reached epidemic proportions and is often carried out without remorse and guilt or with rationalization and questionable justification. The moral questions concerning human life are complex and becoming increasingly so with each new scientific, medical-biological discovery. Joseph Califano, former Secretary of Health, Education and Welfare under President Jimmy Carter and currently president of the Center on Addiction and Substance Abuse at New York's Columbia University, prophetically states that "the continuing . . . abortion debate will be remembered as a warm-up compared to what is coming over euthanasia, the use of gene research, the future of organ transplants and eugenics."[24]

We shall limit ourselves to four urgent moral issues dealing with life today.

1. Abortion

Abortion has become such a highly charged emotional question that a calm rational treatment is extremely difficult. Without attempting to deal with all the complex issues, we shall limit ourselves to three points: the contrasting views of pro-choice and pro-life advocates, four clarifying data considered by moral theologians, and a nuanced position of a growing number of Catholic moral theologians.

We must first distinguish the legal and moral questions. The *legal* question was established in January 1973, when the United States Supreme Court ruled that an anti-abortion law "that excepts from criminality only a life-saving procedure on behalf of the mother without regard to pregnancy stage and without consideration of the other interests involved" is unconstitutional. A practical effect of this ruling was abortion-on-demand up to the third trimester of pregnancy. The *moral* question for Catholic Christians is what is right or wrong according to the church's teaching and principles elaborated by its moral theologians.

We begin by considering the contrasting views of pro-choice and pro-life supporters. First, pro-choice advocates.

> In general, it is seen as a question of women's rights against a background of social problems. Anti-abortion laws are thought of as unjustifiable restriction on the personal freedom of pregnant women. Abortion itself is seen as a potential safeguard of the life, health, or convenience of pregnant women, and at the same time as easing social problems resulting from overpopulation and the birth of unwanted and defective offspring. In general, abortion is evaluated as a birth control measure, and justified on grounds similar to those applied to contraception. Abortion, like contraception, is considered a matter to be determined by private moral de-

---

24. Joseph Califano, Jr., "The Dangers of Discovery," *America* 172 (Jan. 15, 1955): 10.

cision, although it is recognized to have important consequences for society as a whole. Moreover, entrusting abortion to the mother's decision on her doctor's advice is regarded as fair to all religions and ethical differences since no one is obliged to act contrary to his own conscience or creed.[25]

Catholics in the pro-life movement take an entirely different position.

Basic to the Catholic position was the question of the rights, not of the pregnant woman, but of what Catholics generally were careful to call "the unborn child," in contrast to their opponents who were equally careful to refer to it as "the fetal tissue." For Catholics the abortion question has always been regarded primarily, and almost exclusively, as a question of the right to life [of the unborn child].[26]

Archbishop John Quinn of San Francisco called attention to the "dehumanizing effect" of abortion in a 1992 homily.

It is a shocking blow to one of the tenderest and deepest and highest of all human instincts, the love of a mother for her child. It shapes, nurtures and expresses the psychology of violence. It is one of the most violent acts imaginable: the destruction of the utterly helpless human child in the sanctuary of the mother's womb.

All science confirms the fact that the life in the womb is human life: genetics, comparative anatomy, biology, physiology. Morality and science converge in the judgment that those who exercise the choice for abortion are in fact exercising the choice to destroy innocent human life.[27]

Olivia Gans, herself a mother, looks at another aspect of abortion in American society today: its "seductive power."

The lure of abortion stems from our society's desire to avoid responsibility, collectively and individually, for our actions and attitudes. Its seductive power is its promise to eliminate a "problem" neatly and simply, as if that problem—the child—never existed.

Abortion is appealing because it allows so many to remain removed from any responsibility to this new member of the human family. It seems better to subject oneself or one's daughter to a few minutes of surgery than to a lifetime of too-soon motherhood. But such logic ignores the fact that the daughter is already the mother of a yet-unseen child.

The greatest feat of abortion on demand has been to make American society content—if uneasily so—with accepting death as a way to solve problems. All across the United States there are basi-

25. James Gaffney, *Moral Questions* (New York: Paulist Press, 1989): 30-31.
26. *Ibid.*, 31.
27. Archbishop John Quinn, homily in St. Mary's Cathedral, San Francisco.

cally good people who feel that abortion is not good but that nothing else can be done when a mother is poor or a baby is severely handicapped, or the result of rape or incest.[28]

Because the Catholic Church champions human life, it has steadfastly opposed abortion. However, complex questions are involved which defy black and white solutions. The church's moral theologians, in trying to reach a consensus on such questions, consider the following data:

1. Catholic scholastic philosophy holds that "a human *person* is constituted by the infusion of a spiritual soul into an appropriate body." It is, however, impossible to determine the exact moment when this occurs.

2. From the moment of conception when sperm and egg are united, *human life* begins with all genetic material present. For this reason Vatican II could state that "from the moment of its conception, life must be guarded with the greatest care."[29] However, over 60% of fertilized eggs are not implanted or come to term. Are these to be considered human deaths?

3. Catholic moral theology has traditionally rejected *direct* abortion (the deliberately intended destruction of the fetus) while permitting *indirect* abortion (removing a cancerous womb or an ectopic pregnancy to save the mother's life with the non-directly intended result of the death of the child). This is an application of the double-effect, that is, the good effect (mother's life) is intended while the bad effect (death of child) is reluctantly permitted.

4. The phenomenon of twinning (a fertilized egg divides into two) and recombining (two fertilized eggs become one) that can happen up to 14 or more days after conception. It is difficult philosophically to conceive of one distinct *individual* human *person* dividing into two or of two human individuals fusing into one.

Accordingly, because a human *person* may not be present, the position of a growing number of Catholic moral theologians today is to permit a *direct* abortion up to two weeks after fertilization for a proportionately serious reason, like rape or incest or the mother's life. Lesser reasons, such as economic considerations, one's reputation or convenience, the poor timing of a pregnancy, and so forth, are not proportionate reasons for terminating human life. Concerning aborting a deformed fetus or defective child, most moral theologians see no justification for aborting, for example, a fetus with Down's Syndrome.

---

28. See *Respect for Life*, 1988 publication of National Conference of Catholic Bishops.

29. *Gaudium et Spes*, 51.

2. The Terminally Ill

If human life is sacred in its beginning, it is equally so in its final stages. Today as people live longer or are kept alive by artificial means, strong emotional arguments are increasing for *active* **euthanasia** in the case of elderly and senile persons, or those in a vegetative state or those who suffer terribly and plead to be released from their misery. The church has always condemned active euthanasia, or deliberately causing death by lethal injection or excessive sleeping pills or other means. Moral theologians point to the fact that God alone has dominion over life and death; moreover, they rightly fear the abuses that would likely follow from legalizing active euthanasia, thus giving humans power over life and death. The memory of Nazi extermination camps and scientific experimentation still haunts the human family.

However, in the case of terminally ill patients kept alive by artificial life-support systems, moral theologians have permitted *passive* euthanasia, that is, allowing a person a normal death by removing life-support systems when there is no hope of recovery. They argue that there is no moral obligation to use *extraordinary* means to prolong life; only ordinary means must be used. However as medical technology has advanced so rapidly, it is increasingly difficult to distinguish between ordinary and extraordinary means, since what was once considered extraordinary has become ordinary.

Caring for seriously ill, elderly loved ones with no chance of recovery is placing increased financial and psychological burdens on families today. It is therefore sometimes tempting to consider active euthanasia. Yet a strong Christian faith in God, in God's mysterious providence in our lives, and in the role of suffering in the lives of those who follow the crucified Christ are powerful helps in such difficult periods of our faith pilgrimage. Despite the heartrending suffering of persons who plead to be assisted in terminating their own lives, the taking of one's life or the direct assistance of such suicide is contrary to Catholic moral teaching.

3. Capital Punishment

In the past there was general agreement that a murderer forfeited his right to life and that the death penalty was a necessary deterrent. Then a movement began to abolish the death penalty. Recently, however, individual states in the United States have reinstated the death penalty. In this context, the U.S. Catholic bishops issued a *Statement on Capital Punishment* in 1980 which argued that "neither the legitimate purposes of punishment nor necessity justify the imposition of the death penalty in the conditions of American society." Drawing on the argumentation of the U.S. bishops, the Catholic bishops of California issued the following statement. It illustrates how difficult it is to apply Christian values to complex concrete situations, how the teaching office of bishops provides moral guidelines rather than inflexible commands, and how moral theologians use sociological data as well as religious principles to reach moral conclusions.

. . . there are serious considerations which should prompt Christians and all Americans to support the abolition of capital punishment.

Some of these reasons have to do with problems inherent in the practice of capital punishment, such as the denial of any possibility of reform or of making compensation; the possibility of mistake by the execution of an innocent person; the long and unavoidable delays which diminish the effectiveness of capital punishment as a deterrent and can produce aimlessness, fear and despair; the extreme anguish which an execution brings, not only for the criminal, but for his family and those who perform or witness the execution; the unhealthy publicity and considerable acrimony in public discussion attracted by execution; and, finally, the not-unfounded belief that many convicted criminals are sentenced to death in an unfair and discriminatory manner; e.g., more than fifty percent of those on death row are minorities, virtually all of them are poor.

Other reasons proposed by the 1980 *Statement* have to do with important values that would be promoted by the abolition of capital punishment: 1. It would send a message that the cycle of violence can be broken, that we need not take life for life, that we can envisage more humane and more hopeful and effective responses to the growth of violent crime. 2. It would be a manifestation of our belief in the unique worth and dignity of each person from the moment of conception, a creature made in the image and likeness of God. 3. Abolition would give further testimony to our conviction that God is indeed the Lord of life, a belief we share with the Judaic and Islamic traditions. 4. It would be more consonant with the example of Jesus who both taught and practiced the forgiveness of injustice and who came "to give his life as a ransom for many." (Mark 10:45)

Not all Christians may come to this conclusion when they apply general principles and Gospel values to the concrete historical situation. . . . We dare to take this position and raise this challenge because of our commitment to a consistent ethic of life by which we wish to give unambiguous witness to the sacredness of every human life from conception through natural death, and to proclaim the good news that no person is beyond the redemptive mercy of God. [30]

4. War

The Catholic Church developed over the centuries a "just war theory" that reluctantly permitted war if *all* the following conditions were verified:

---

30. "California Bishops on Capital Punishment," *Origins* 15 (Oct. 17, 1985): 301-03.

- The decision for war must be made by a legitimate authority.
- The war can be fought only to defend against unjust aggression.
- War must be waged only as a last resort.
- There must be a reasonable chance of achieving the objective for which the war is waged.
- The good to be achieved by the war must outweigh the evil that will result from it. This is called the principle of proportionality. One cannot "destroy a city to save it."
- The war must be waged according to the principles of natural and international law. For instance, indiscriminate mass destruction of civilian populations is never justified, for whatever reason.

However, the advent of nuclear weapons has changed the picture drastically. In their 1983 pastoral statement, *The Challenge of Peace: God's Promise and Our Response*, the U.S. bishops judged that a "just" nuclear war is a contradiction in terms. Quoting the *Pastoral Constitution on the Church in the Modern World*, "any act of war aimed indiscriminately at the destruction of entire cities or of extensive areas along with their population is a crime against God and humankind [and] merits unequivocal and unhesitating condemnation" (*GS* 80), the bishops condemned the following: the intentional killing of innocent civilians or noncombatants; a "first strike" strategy; the policy of a retaliatory nuclear strike (MAD or mutually assured destruction); a so-called "limited" nuclear war.

As to the arms race, the bishops state that it "is one of the greatest curses on the human race; it is to be condemned as a danger, an act of aggression against the poor, and a folly which does not provide the security it promises."[31] We recall the statement attributed to President Eisenhower at the end of his presidency that "every dollar spent on the arms race is a dollar taken from the poor."

The U.S. bishops close with these stirring words:

Fundamentally, we are saying that the decisions about nuclear weapons are among the most pressing moral questions of our age. . . . In simple terms, we are saying that good ends (defending one's country, protecting freedom, etc.) cannot justify immoral means (the use of weapons which kill indiscriminately and threaten whole societies).

In the words of our Holy Father, we need a "moral about-face." The whole world must summon the moral courage and technical means to say "no" to nuclear conflict; "no" to weapons of mass

---

31. *The Challenge of Peace: God's Promise and Our Response* (Boston: Daughters of St. Paul, 1983), 5 (Summary, I C 1)

destruction; "no" to the moral danger of a nuclear age . . . Peace-making is . . . a requirement of our faith. We are called to be peacemakers. . . by our Lord Jesus.[32]

For Discussion

1. If abortion is the taking of human life, can it ever be justified? What are the moral principles involved? Evaluate them.

2. Is there a "proportionate reason" to justify *active* euthanasia?

3. Where do you stand on capital punishment? What principles/reasons persuade you?

4. Is the threat to use nuclear weapons if attacked (MAD) moral according to the principles of a just war and the nature of nuclear weapons?

Further Reading

MacNamara, Vincent. *Love, Law and Christian Life: Basic Attitudes of Christian Morality.* Wilmington, DE: Michael Glazier, 1988.

National Conference of Catholic Bishops. *The Challenge of Peace: God's Promise and Our Response.* Boston: Daughters of St. Paul, 1983.

Wesley, Dick. *Morality and Its Beyond.* Mystic, CT: Twenty-Third Publications, 1988. Chapter 11 "Life and Death Issues."

---

32. *Ibid.,* 8 (Summary, II C)

C H A P T E R   18

Liberation Theology

The spirit of the Lord has appointed me to proclaim good news
to the poor. He has sent me to proclaim release to captives and
recovery of sight to the blind, to set at liberty those who are
oppressed.   —Luke 4:18

What is it to be a companion of Jesus today? It is to engage in
the crucial struggle of our times: the struggle for faith and that
struggle for justice that it includes.
                                    — Jesuit General Congregation 32

U.S. foreign policy must begin to counter . . . liberation theology as it is utilized in Latin America by the "liberation theology" clergy.
                  — *A New Inter-American Policy for the Eighties,*
        the Committee of Santa Fe, May, 1980, Part Two, Proposal 3

Liberation theology is not only opportune but useful and necessary.   — Pope John Paul II

Liberation Theology is first and foremost a profoundly Christian
protest against a world in which a pampered minority condemns
the majority to a life sentence of misery and helplessness, if not
to death. . . . The issue is not socialism or capitalism, but rather
life or death for millions of human beings.[1]

---

1. Kevin O'Higgins, "Liberation Theology and the New World Order," *America* 163 (November
24, 1990): 392.

Introduction

One of the most exciting and significant results of the new spirit engendered by the Second Vatican Council was the rise of a new way to do theology, called "liberation theology." It began in Latin America as a result of the massive poverty and oppression and lack of the most basic human rights, resulting in untold suffering and early death for the majority of the people, mainly the indigenous groups made up of *campesinos* working the land or fleeing to the cities seeking work. It represented an extraordinary change in the Catholic Church from its centuries-long alliance with the state and the wealthy elite to a commitment to the poor and oppressed classes. As a result, liberation theologians and many progressive church leaders criticized the prevailing capitalist system in Latin America as unjust and oppressive. Their criticisms also threatened the privileged position of the controlling wealthy classes. Those in power viewed these new Christian views and movements as allied to Communist subversion. The military and right-wing death squads responded to this perceived threat by imprisoning and killing thousands of *campesino* leaders (catechists, delegates of the Word, teachers, health care workers, union leaders), scores of priests and nuns, culminating in the assassination of Archbishop Oscar Romero in San Salvador on March 24, 1980.

The inspiration for liberation theology can be traced back to Catholic social teaching, with its emphasis on the dignity of the human person, the basic rights of workers, and God's plan for the human family. More immediately, two documents of Vatican II had an enormous influence. The *Dogmatic Constitution on the Church* gave a new name and concept to the church: the people of God. Catholics realized for the first time that they, not exclusively bishops and priests, are in fact the church. As a result they experienced a sense of equality with the hierarchy in their mutual baptism, and of responsibility for their faith and of their newly realized role in the church. The *Church in the Modern World* encouraged and inspired Catholics to become involved in the problems of the world and to work for justice and human rights, thus to achieve God's plan for human persons.

Thanks to liberation theology, as the dramatic embodiment of Catholic social teaching and Vatican II's new theology of church, today's Catholic Church became more dynamically alive and more authentically church in Latin America. For the Latin American Church is preeminently a church of martyrs and the church of the poor. Moreover, according to Argentinian theologian Enrique Dussel, Latin America is "perhaps the continent where the Council made the most profound and far-reaching impact."[2] Knowledge of liberation theology and of recent events in Latin America is indispensable to understand today's Catholic Church.

---

2. Adrian Hastings, ed., *Modern Catholicism. Vatican II and After* (New York: Oxford University Press, 1991), 319.

◆

Preview: Liberation theology is an exciting new way of "doing theology" that began in Latin America 25 years ago. It is highly praised, strongly criticized, and often misunderstood. It can only be understood in the Latin American context of massive poverty, injustice, almost total deprivation of human rights. So we start by considering the situation in Latin America in terms of the five major realities in most Latin American countries. We then consider the two meetings of all the Catholic bishops of Latin America that set the Catholic Church on a dramatic new course. With this background, we analyze liberation theology itself: its nature, goal and three-step method; and six important factors necessary for a fuller understanding. Since there still remains considerable ignorance and confusion about liberation theology, we confront popular objections to it. We close with three dramatic examples of how both peasants and priests lived and died for their commitment to liberation theology, and with an evaluation of this new theology.

◆

Situation in Latin American out of Which Liberation Theology Emerged

> From the depths of the countries that make up Latin America a cry is rising to heaven, growing louder and more alarming all the time. It is the cry of the suffering people who demand justice, freedom, and respect for the basic rights of human beings and peoples. (Puebla 29)

> We brand the situation of inhuman poverty in which millions of Latin Americans live as the most devastating and humiliating kind of scourge. This situation finds expression in such things as a high rate of infant mortality, lack of adequate housing, health problems, starvation wages, unemployment and underemployment, malnutrition, job uncertainty, compulsory mass migrations, etc. (Puebla 29)

> . . . this poverty . . . is the product of economic, social and political situations and structures. (Puebla 30)

In virtually all Latin American countries, we can distinguish five major actors: the poor and oppressed; the oligarchy; the military; the Roman Catholic Church; the great powers of the northern hemisphere.

1. The poor and oppressed. These are predominantly **indigenous** peoples (as they prefer to be called, rather than "Indians"): *campesinos* who work tiny plots of land in hostile mountainous areas; transient laborers hired by wealthy landowners to harvest seasonal crops; the urban poor who live in shanty towns without sewage or running water, in closely packed flimsy shacks along mud "streets" or clinging to steep hillsides. The poor live on the margins of society. They are the victims of planned illiteracy, lack of health care, no access to the legal system, subsistence wages. Hunger, disease, infant deaths and early death are their lot in life. Especially in Central American countries like Guatemala and El Salvador, to be poor was to be killed — often whole villages at a time — by the military or by the infamous "death squads." To be poor, in **Jon Sobrino's** vivid expression, is to die! This oppression of the poor is no accident: the wealthy classes, aided by the military, maintain the poor in subjection in order to preserve their privileged lifestyle. Liberation theology seeks to change all this.

2. The Oligarchy (literally, rule by a few). In most Latin American countries a small very rich elite control a disproportionate amount of land, power and wealth. Behind high walls and electronic gates, these wealthy landowners and industrialists live in large mansions, waited on by their servants; they enjoy frequent vacations and shopping sprees in the United States and Europe; they send their children to prestigious universities in "the States." They often control the government and are kept in power by the military. This wedding of government, military and oligarchs constitute what liberation theologians call **"institutionalized violence"**: the very institutions and structures of society meant to help and protect all citizens are deliberately utilized to exclude the poor and oppressed, thus doing moral and physical violence to them.

3. The Military. In Latin America the military has become a privileged class, wielding great power and amassing much wealth. Generals of the army often became presidents of their countries and ruthless military dictators, like Stroessner in Paraguay, Pinochet in Chile, Somoza in Nicaragua. Alongside the military are paramilitary groups, like the National Guard and the Treasury Police. Under the guise of fighting Communism, the military and the military dictators have conned the United States into providing millions of dollars to support their "dirty little wars" to make their country "safe for democracy." The military is often guilty of gross human rights violations; innocent peasants, *campesinos,* union leaders, catechists, delegates of the Word, university students, priests and sisters — anyone guilty of "subversion" in seeking their basic rights, in educating the peasants, in organizing unions — have been tortured and murdered by the thousands. Torture and murder were commonplace in the 1960s and 1970s in Brazil, Argentina, Chile, Uruguay, Bolivia, and in the 1970s and 1980s in El Salvador, Guatemala, and Honduras.[3] In most countries of Latin America — a

---

3. See Appendix, Martyr Survey, in Penny Lernoux, *Cry of the People* (New York: Penguin Books, 1982), 463-69.

hopeful sign — military governments have now given way to civilian rule, though the military still commands great power to intervene.

4. The Catholic Church. From the forced colonization of Latin America by the Spaniards and Portuguese in the early 1500s and through most of its history, the Catholic Church has been allied with the state and the wealthy classes of Latin America. In return, the church enjoyed a privileged position in each country: for example, the exclusive right to educate the young and to have priests' salaries paid by the government. Through this alliance the church "legitimized" unjust governments and the military in the eyes of both the rich and the poor. One such example: presidents were formally inaugurated at a grand pontifical Mass celebrated in the cathedral by a cardinal or archbishop, who gave his blessing to the new president. (Archbishop Romero broke this manipulation of the church when he refused to inaugurate President Romero — no relation — with such a Mass in San Salvador in 1978.) Rather than work for the transformation of society itself, the church merely encouraged the peasants to accept their cruel class position in life as God's will, with the promise of a great reward in heaven. This attitude came to be known as **"fatalism"** and became the mind-set of the peasants for centuries.

Vatican II and the bishops of Latin America at their meetings at Medellín, Colombia, in 1968 and Puebla, Mexico, in 1979 changed this alliance. Both Medellín and Puebla admitted the church's failures of the past and committed the church to conversion and a *preferential option for the poor.* The Puebla meeting[4] referred to this dramatic change initiated at Medellín in 1968:

> We affirm the need for conversion on the part of the whole Church to a preferential option for the poor, an option aimed at integral liberation (No. 1134). Bit by bit the Church has been dissociating itself from those who hold economic and political power, freeing itself from various forms of dependence and divesting itself of privileges (No. 623).

In many countries of Latin America, the Catholic Church became a force for justice and for the human rights of the masses of the poor; national bishops' conferences produced letters strongly critical of the wealthy elites, unjust governments, and military dictatorships. A graphic example of this new prophetic role of the church was in El Salvador, where Archbishop Romero became "the voice of those who have no voice," tirelessly worked for human rights and social change, and courageously criticized the government, the military, and the wealthy class, pleading with them to be converted, to respect human rights, to "stop the killing." The result of the church's "conversion" was the killing of "Communist" priests and

---

4. John Eagleson and Phillip Scharper, *Puebla and Beyond: Documentation and Commentary* (Maryknoll, NY: Orbis, 1979).

nuns, *campesinos,* various leaders of the poor, and finally the murder of Archbishop Romero himself by an assassin's bullet while he was celebrating Mass.

Today the Catholic Church is the strongest and often only influence for social justice and human rights in Latin America, as its bishops and priests and sisters seek to defend the poor.

5. Great Powers of the Northern Hemisphere. Transnational corporations and banks, claiming to improve economic growth in Latin America, have often had a reverse effect, impeding development for the majority of Latin American peoples and increasing their dependency on foreign investment. These corporations have made enormous profits in Latin America. In decades past, transnationals often dominated the local economies, for example: Gulf and Western from sugar in the Dominican Republic, Anaconda and Kennecott Copper in Chile, United Fruit/Brands from bananas in Guatemala, and pharmaceutical companies by dumping drugs banned in the United States in various Latin American countries.[5] As condition for loans, the International Monetary Fund and the World Bank demand austerity measures that primarily hurt the poor. The already-oppressive billions of dollars' debt of most Latin American countries eat up a high percentage of their annual income just to pay the interest, thus inhibiting economic growth and social programs for the poor.

The recent role of the United States in Latin America, aside from President Kennedy's idealistic but failed Alliance for Progress, is generally not well-known in the United States. We have supported with millions of dollars of foreign aid the military dictators of Latin America, under the guise of fighting Communism, but in reality to protect our economic interests. In the School of the Americas in Panama, and later and still today at Fort Benning, Georgia, we have trained thousands of Latin American soldiers who later became their countries' officers and generals and who perpetrated terrible human rights' violations. The painstakingly researched *Cry of the People,* by Penny Lernoux, gives in great detail this sordid picture country by Latin American country.[6] That this has been a deliberate policy on the part of the United Stated is evident from the recommendation of "The Committee of Santa Fe" in its *A New Inter-American Policy for the Eighties.*[7]

---

5. See Lernoux, *Cry of the People,* Chapter 7, "U.S. Capitalism and the Multinationals," 203.

6. *Ibid.,* Chapter 6, "The Doctrine of National Security — the United States Teaches Latin America How," 155-202, especially 162-66, "Grad School for Juntas" and 181-83, the "School of the Americas."

7. Lewis Tambs, ed. Committee of Santa Fe, *A New Inter-American Policy for the Eighties,* (Washington, DC: Council for Inter-American Security, 1980).

> The United States should promote a policy conducive to private
> capitalism, free trade, and direct and local foreign investment in
> productive enterprises in Latin America.[8]

> Latin America is vital to the United States: America's global power
> projection has always rested on a *cooperative* Caribbean and a *sup-
> portive* South America . . .(emphasis added)[9]

> Reactivate as the third element of our hemispheric security system
> our traditional military training and assistance to the armed forces
> of the Americas and noncommissioned officers.[10]

The following policy was unabashedly stated in 1948 by George Kennan,
head of the State Department Planning Staff, *Policy Planning Study,* February 23, 1948:

> . . . we have about 50% of the world's wealth but only 6.3% of its
> population. . . . Our real task . . . is to devise a pattern of relation-
> ships which will help us to maintain this position of disparity. . .
> to do so, we will have to dispense with all sentimentality. . . . We
> should cease to talk about vague and unreal objectives such as
> human rights, the raising of living standards, and democratization.
> The day is not far off when we are going to have to deal in
> straight power concepts.[11]

With such arrogant and self-serving policies, it is not hard to see why a
popular expression in Latin America has been "Gringo, go home!"

The Catholic Church's Dramatic Change

Medellín, 1968

Pope Paul VI encouraged the bishops of Latin America to apply the
teaching and spirit of Vatican II to the grave situation in each of their countries.
They met in the city of Medellín, Colombia, in the late summer of 1968 and
produced a call to action that profoundly influenced the church and the political events of Latin America to this day. For never before in the history of the
church had the bishops of an entire continent spoken so forcefully and concretely about poverty, injustice, and hunger, suffering, education, and the daily
needs of their people. Nor had the causes of such massive poverty, injustice,
and deliberate oppression been so clearly stated. Medellín thus shattered the
centuries-old alliance of the church, the rich elites and the military. It committed bishops, priests, all Catholics to nothing less than the transformation of

---

8. *Ibid.,* Part Three, Economic and Social Policies, G. Economic, Trade and Investment Policies,
Proposal, 1 p. 33.

9. *Ibid.,* Summary Statement, p. 53.

10. *Ibid.,* Part One, External Military Threat, Proposal 3, p. 14.

11. U.S. Department of State, *The State Department Policy Planning Staff Papers 1947-1949, Vol.
2, 1948,* (New York: Garland Publ., 1983).

Latin American society.[12] The powerful document produced after weeks of hard analysis of the gigantic problems of Latin American society and of the church itself was aptly titled *Presence of the Church in the Present-Day Transformation of Latin America.*

The goal of the bishops' reflections was "to search for a new and dynamic presence of the Church" in this transformation (Introd. 8). Its "central theme" was "Latin American man who is living a decisive moment of his historical process" (Introd. 1). Its context was "The misery that besets large masses of human beings in all of our countries . . . [which] expresses itself as injustice that cries to the heavens" (Justice 1).

The document analyzed a broad spectrum of Latin American society. Its 16 chapters treated in order Justice, Peace, Family and Demography, Education, Youth, Pastoral Care of the Masses, Pastoral Concern for the Elites, Liturgy, Catechesis, Lay Movements, Priests, Religious, Formation of Clergy, Poverty of the Church, Joint Pastoral Planning, Mass Media. Each of these topics was considered from a three-fold perspective: "Pertinent Facts" or Analysis of the Present Situation; "Doctrinal basis" or "Reflection" from the Bible or church teaching; "Pastoral Planning" or "Guidelines" or "Recommendations" for action. This three-fold approach of "See, Judge, Act" constitutes the methodology of liberation theology and is the familiar practice of the famous base Christian communities throughout Latin America.

The bishops were unusually blunt and specific in their analysis of the problems of Latin America and in assessing the blame. "Institutionalized violence" of colonial and present structures "seeking unbounded profits foment an economic dictatorship and the international imperialism of money." Both capitalism and Communism "are affronts to the dignity of the human being" and are to be condemned, as are "developmentalists" who place "more emphasis on economic progress than on the social well-being of people." The bishops blamed social and economic injustice on those with the "greater share of wealth, culture and power [who] jealously retain their privileges and defend them through violence," thus "provoking explosive revolutions of despair."[13]

As the way out of this situation, the bishops insisted on the absolute need for conversion of heart. "For our authentic liberation, all of us need a profound conversion so that the kingdom of justice, love, and peace might come to us" (Justice 3). Earlier Pope Paul VI had described conversion in his appeal at Bogotá, Colombia, to the ruling class:

> What is required of you is generosity. This means the ability to detach yourselves from . . . a position of privilege in order to serve those who need your wealth, your culture, your author-

---

12. *The Church in the Present-Day Transformation of Latin America in the Light of the Council,* (Washington, DC: U. S. Catholic Conference, 1973).
13. See Lernoux, *Cry of the People,* 38, for this overview of the Medellin documents.

ity. . . . Your ears and hearts must be sensitive to the voices crying out for bread, concern, justice, and a more active participation
in the direction of society.[14]

Nor did the bishops spare the church itself from this urgent need for
conversion. In Chapter 14, "Poverty of the Church," the bishops stated:
"We want our Latin American Church to be free from temporal ties, from
intrigues and from a doubtful reputation; to be 'free in spirit as regards the
chains of wealth' " (18). "We wish our houses and style of life to be modest, our clothing simple, our works and institutions functional, without
show or ostentation" (12). "We the bishops wish to come closer to the
poor in sincerity and brotherhood . . ." (9).

Puebla, 1979

Eleven years later the Latin American bishops met again as a group
in Puebla, Mexico. It appeared that a group of conservative bishops, led by
Colombian Archbishop Alfonso Trujillo, secretary-general of the Latin
American Episcopal Conference, and the Roman Curia's Cardinal Se-
bastiano Baggio, president of the Pontifical Commission for Latin America, would condemn liberation theology and severely weaken the Medellín
document and the church's commitment to justice and the poor.

However, the speeches that Pope John Paul II gave during his pastoral visit to Mexico immediately before the Puebla Conference profoundly
influenced the bishop-delegates. To 40,000 Indians at Oaxaca, the pope
boldly said: "The pope wishes to be the voice of the voiceless. . . . You
have a right to be respected and not deprived of the little you have, often
by methods that amount to plunder. You have a right to throw down the
barriers of exploitation."[15] John Paul II challenged Mexico's wealthy landowners:

> For your part you have at times left the land fallow, taking bread
> from so many families who need it. Human conscience, the con-
> science of the people, the cry of the destitute, and above all, the
> voice of God and the Church repeat with me: it is not right, it is
> not human, it is not Christian to maintain such clearly unjust situ-
> ations.[16]

To the Mexican workers at Jalisco, the pope said a Christian
"must be a witness and agent of justice," and stated, "I want to tell you
with all my soul and strength that I am deeply pained by the injustices
against workers. . . ."[17]

---

14. *Cry of the People*, 37.
15. *Ibid.*, 429.
16. *Ibid.*
17. *Ibid.*

The powerful statements of the pope, the behind-the-scenes papers of liberation theologians, and the strong leadership of Brazilian Cardinal Lorscheider, president of the Latin American Bishops' Conference, of Cardinal Arns, archbishop of San Paulo, Brazil, and of Panama's Archbishop McGrath so influenced the bishops that the final document of Puebla strongly recommitted the church to the poor and to human rights. It made the phrase "preferential option for the poor" a part of liberation theology vocabulary.

What is Liberation Theology?

Having seen the tragic situation of Latin America, we are now better able to understand and appreciate the nature, goals, and three-fold methodology of **liberation theology.**

1. Nature, definitions. The Brazilian liberation theologian Leonardo Boff states that the "starting point" of liberation theology is to experience compassion for the "suffering that affects the great majority of the human race." "Liberation theology was born when faith confronted the injustice done to the poor."[18] **Gustavo Gutiérrez** defines liberation theology as "a way of speaking about God, starting from the situation of the poor in history"[19] and "a Gospel-inspired commitment to liberation of the poor and oppressed."[20]

How then does liberation theology differ from traditional theology? Christian theology is faith seeking understanding; it is the attempt to understand the mystery of God and Jesus Christ as revealed to us in the inspired Hebrew and Christian Scriptures. Traditional theology starts with God's revelation; liberation theology starts rather from the real-life situation in Latin America, and then asks how God and Jesus judge it. Liberation theology depends heavily on human experience and is meant to issue into action to confront massive poverty and injustice and to change the structures of society that perpetuate these evils. Its motivation, however, is not secular but religious: to build the kingdom of God on this earth, to live God's preferential love for the poor and oppressed. It is thus inspired by Christian faith.

◆

We can now give a fuller definition of liberation theology. As *theology* it is a reflection on the plight of the poor and oppressed in the light of the gospel of Jesus Christ; as *liberation* it is a way of freeing the poor from their poverty, oppression, injustice, and institutionalized violence, based on

---

18. L. and C. Boff, *Introducing Liberation Theology* (Maryknoll, NY: Orbis Books, 1987), 2 and 3.
19. Interview with Gustavo Gutierrez, "I am a Christian First," *Maryknoll* (November, 1986): 14.
20. *Ibid.*, 15.

God's special love for the poor in the Hebrew Scriptures and Jesus' concern for them in the four Gospels.

◆

2. Goal. Liberation theology aims at nothing less than the transformation of the present unjust society and the creation of a new society based on justice, human rights, equal opportunity, and participation of all members of society. The goal is therefore action done primarily by the poor themselves.

3. Three-step methodology. The first stage is *socioanalytic*, to analyze the causes of the real-life situation of poverty, oppression and injustice. The second stage is *prayerful reflection* on the Hebrew Scriptures and the four Gospels to see how God and Christ judge this situation, and to discover what a Christian should do about it. The third stage is *Christian action* (*praxis*) to change the unjust situation.

The same methodology of "see, judge, and act" is used by both professional liberation theologians in their writings and by uneducated peasants in the base Christian communities, but in different ways.

Liberation theologians have used the social sciences (sociology, economics, political science) in their analysis. Initially they drew heavily on two sociological and economic constructs: one, *dependency theory,* which viewed Third World underdevelopment as caused by economic policies that favor rich countries in the First World; two, *class analysis* (drawing on Marxist analysis), that focused on the domination of poorer classes by elite oligarchies within Latin America. Later analysis broadened and qualified the sometimes oversimplicity of these initial constructs.

Members of base Christian communities obviously do not use such sophisticated analysis. Rather, they recount their own experience of poverty and injustice (hunger, expropriation of land by wealthy landowners, lack of running water, open sewage ditches, low pay, lack of jobs, babies dying of dysentery and malnutrition); they discuss the Bible readings to find God's judgment of these conditions and to discover hope and inspiration; they then decide on a plan of action here and now.

Important Factors for Fuller Understanding of Liberation Theology

These constitute the "heart," the profound insights, the dynamic realities of liberation theology.

1. The poor. The poor are those specially loved by God and Jesus Christ. The poor teach liberation theologians and pastoral workers what it is to be poor and oppressed, to be loved by God, to have Christian hope in a hopeless situation, to believe wholeheartedly in God's coming kingdom, to be strengthened by the resurrection of Jesus. One learns only by living with the poor. Liberation theology therefore starts with the poor. The church's "preferential option for the poor" is the essence of liberation theology. Leonardo Boff explains that this option implies four things:

- seeing social reality and history from the point of view of the poor and their vision of the world;
- taking up the cause of the oppressed, involving such basic necessities of life as work, shelter, clothing, health, education;
- committing to the struggles of the poor for justice;
- recognizing that the poor must be the subjects of their own liberation, for only the poor can liberate the poor.

> The poor are the main protagonists of the drama being lived out in today's world because they see the problem most clearly; they feel it in their very bodies . . . The wall they must contend with, the invisible one that separates the rich "North" from the poor "South," is still intact and it grows more formidable with every passing day.[21]

2. Base Christian Communities (CEB's). Here is where liberation theology is lived and practiced. A CEB is a group of 10-15 poor persons, generally neighbors in a slum *favella* or *barrio*, who come together weekly to discuss their real life situation, read the Bible, and decide on action. Brazil alone is said to have over 100,000 such Christian communities. Though they still constitute only a small part (perhaps 2% of the overall Latin American population), these communities have been active agents for social change. Most often their actions take the form of community organizing (developing food co-ops, communal soup kitchens, cooperative farming). But at times, especially when disputes over land occur, they have been violently repressed: their leaders have often been pulled from their hovels at night, tortured, and left dead to intimidate the neighborhood; or they have simply "disappeared," never to be seen again. The CEB's are the core of the so-called "Peoples' Church" that has risen in Latin America as a result of Vatican II, Medellín and Puebla.

The bishops at their Puebla meeting highly praised the CEB's and encouraged their formation:

> . . . the CEB's . . . an important ecclesial event . . . are "the hope of the Church" (No. 629).
>
> As a community the CEB's bring together families, adults, and young people in an intimate interpersonal relationship grounded in the faith. As an ecclesial reality, it is a community of faith, hope and love. It celebrates the Word of God and takes its nourishment from the Eucharist . . . it makes present and operative the mission

---

21. O'Higgins, 393.

of the Church and its visible communion with the legitimate pastors [bishop and priests]. (No. 641).

3. Conscientization. Poor illiterate Indian *campesinos* "become aware" of the causes of their poverty and oppression and realize that God does not want this situation, but rather that they act to overcome it. **Conscientization** is thus consciousness or awareness-raising. It overcomes the centuries-old fatalism of the Indians.

4. Structural sin. Liberation theology recognizes that sin is not only personal but *social*. When the very institutions of society do violence to the poor (*institutionalized violence*) because they are essentially unjust, they are termed sinful because against God's plan for human persons. One of the major contributions of liberation theology is its emphasis on structural sin and its insistence that liberation and conversion must involve transforming the unjust institutions in a country.

5. Christian praxis. A major goal of liberation theology is *action* that transforms the unjust structures of society. It is *Christian* action because its motivation is the Christian faith: Jesus' gospel values of justice and love of neighbor, establishing the kingdom of God on earth, God's preferential love for the poor. In a broader sense, Christian praxis involves conversion of the elites and empowering the poor to be agents of their own liberation. Liberation theology stresses that *orthopractice* or correct action is, in the situation of Latin America, of greater urgency than *orthodoxy* or correct doctrinal teaching. For too long in Latin America the church's emphasis had been on doctrinal matters rather than a commitment to acting for justice.

6. Favored Model of Society. Liberation theology theoreticians criticize both the liberal capitalist system and the collectivist socialism of the Soviets, Eastern Europe and parts of Asia. Instead they favor a *participatory* democracy.

Opposition to Liberation Theology

When liberation theology broke on the world in the writings of liberation theologians, and found expression among the masses in the "peoples' church" and in popular movements for justice, it soon provoked opposition by the dominant classes of Latin America, by economic and governmental interests in the United States, and even within the Catholic Church by the Vatican. To gain a complete picture of liberation theology we must consider the following objections.

1. "Liberation theology is not a true theology." It is true that liberation theology does not follow the method of traditional theology. Contemporary theology, however, had rediscovered personal religious experience as a legitimate and valuable source of theological reflection. Starting from the experience of the majority of Latin American Catholics of what it means to be poor in an unjust society, liberation theology goes on to develop from the Scriptures a theology of God's preferential option for the poor, of Jesus' commitment in his ministry to establishing the reign of God, and of the Holy Spirit's presence in the struggle of the poor for justice and equality. Aware of the incompleteness of such a new theology, liberation theologians have produced scores of books and articles developing a fuller, systematic theology of liberation.

2. *"It's Marxist."* This has been a too-facile complaint of those who have not read liberation theologians, and was the criticism of Cardinal Ratzinger in his first "Instruction on Certain Aspects of the Theology of Liberation" in 1984. This document, while legitimately warning of the dangers of Marxism, too often equated any use of Marxist analysis as an embrace of the whole Marxist doctrine (atheism, class hatred, the necessity of violent revolution, one-party control and totalitarian rule). It is true that liberation theologians, especially at the beginning when they believed that capitalism could be replaced by a new form of democratic socialism, used Marxist analysis to criticize the prevailing system and to emphasize the role of the dominant and proletariate classes. But even then liberation theologians did not espouse the atheistic and materialistic underpinnings of Marxism or its strategies of violence. As Gustavo Gutiérrez pointed out:

> To comprehend the situation of poverty and the injustice that causes it, I need to analyze it socially, economically and politically. To do this analysis, I have to use social sciences. In contemporary social science there are some notions that come from Marxism. So it is not that the theology of liberation uses Marxism but rather social sciences. . . . In contemporary psychology, there are ideas that come from Freud. This does not mean I am Freudian; it only means I use psychology."[22]

3. *"It's Communist and subversive."* The elitist oligarchies and military of Latin American countries, elements in the United States government and the economic giants with business interests in Latin America branded liberation theologians and members of base Christian communities and of popular organizations communist and subversive. These could legitimately be termed *subversive* in that they joined in the struggle for a just society and the end to the institutionalized violence of the privileged classes and of the military. However, the *Communist* label was a momentous rationalization on the part of the elites and the military to justify massive injustices and murders by the "death squads." Certain U.S. government officials and corporation spokesmen used the Communist threat to justify frequent military and political intervention in Latin American countries.

---

22. Gutierrez Interview, 18-19.

4. "It incites class struggle, revolution, and violence." Though liberation theologians have spoken of the struggle between the dominant and the powerless classes of Latin America, they have rejected violence and revolution both as unchristian and as unworkable in the present situation of Latin America. It is interesting to note, however, that Pope Paul VI permitted insurrection as a last resort in a situation of grave injustice,[23] and that the Catholic bishops of Nicaragua supported the Sandinista revolution before the overthrow of the dictator Somoza.

5. "It was condemned by the Vatican and the Pope." Cardinal Ratzinger's first instruction on liberation theology in 1984 pointed out dangerous aspects of liberation theology, but failed to identify a single liberation theologian who held these views. His second document, "Instruction on Christian Freedom and Liberation" in 1986, was far less negative, emphasizing positive aspects of liberation theology. Pope John Paul II, in his April 9, 1986 letter to the Brazilian bishops, said that provided certain conditions are met, "we are convinced, we and you, that the theology of liberation is not only timely but useful and necessary."[24]

6. "It sets up a parallel church hostile to the official hierarchical church." The Vatican and some traditional local bishops in Latin America felt threatened by the popular or "peoples' church" of the base Christian communities and of the scores of religious order priests and nuns who worked and lived with the poor. What actually was at stake were two different ecclesiologies. Some members of the Roman Curia and some local bishops thought in terms both of rigid authoritarianism, in which Rome or the local bishop had total control and of the old alliance of church and state, in which the Catholic Church received special privileges. The newer ecclesiology of the base Christian communities, of many priests and sisters, and a large number of progressive Vatican II local bishops, favored Vatican II's "people of God" ecclesiology, in which all Catholics, including the hierarchy, are equal before God and *are* the church. Too often the real issue appeared to be one of power and control. But the reality in Latin America was that the vast majority of the poor and of the priests and sisters who worked with them remained loyal and obedient to their local bishop and to the Holy Father in Rome, despite disagreements.

---

23. "It is clear, however, that a revolutionary uprising — *save where there is manifest, longstanding tyranny which would do great damage to fundamental personal rights and dangerous harm to the common good of the country* — produces new injustices, throws more elements out of balance and brings on new disasters" (emphasis added). Paul VI, *On the Development of Peoples* (New York: Paulist Press, 1967), 31, p. 47.

24. "Pope's Letter to Brazil's Bishops," *Origins* 15 (April 9, 1986): 14.

Dramatic Examples of "Lived" Liberation Theology

Our first example is a high-ranking cleric of the Catholic Church, assassinated on March 24, 1980 in San Salvador. In his short three years as archbishop, Oscar Romero incarnated to a remarkable degree all the elements of liberation theology we have been considering: his preferential option for the poor; his untiring struggle through his Sunday homilies and in all his actions as archbishop for justice, for human rights, for the transformation of Salvadoran society; his appeals to the wealthy classes and the military to "stop the oppression" and to make a profound personal conversion; his deep faith in the God of liberation as his constant religious motivation. As the death threats intensified, he said "If they kill me, I will rise again in the Salvadoran people." Indeed he has; his picture is found in the shacks of the poor everywhere in El Salvador, and he lives in their hearts and minds as "Saint" Oscar Romero, "the voice of those who have no voice." "When I feed the hungry, they call me a saint," Archbishop Romero once said; "When I ask why the poor have no bread, they call me a communist."

Five Catholic *campesino* catechists of Santa Cruz, El Quiché: Lucas, Justo, Angel, Domingo, and Juan, are the second dramatic example. In 1982, the army took over the small market town in the mountains of Guatemala. The army assembled the villagers, accused the five catechists of being "subversives," and demanded that their relatives kill them that night; otherwise the army would destroy Santa Cruz and neighboring villages, killing all inhabitants. After discussing their brutal choice, the villagers decided not to do it, for the catechists were loved and valued for their religious work and for the instruction they had given to promote cooperatives. But such consciousness-raising was subversive in the military's view because it helped to awaken the Indian masses. The five catechists insisted the deed must be done. "It is better for us to die than for thousands to die."

> At 4:00 A.M., a weeping procession, led by the catechists, arrived at the cemetery. Graves were dug, the people formed a circle around the kneeling men, and relatives of the five drew their machetes. Many could not watch the scene; some fainted as the blades fell, and executioners' tears mingled with the blood of catechists. The bodies were wrapped in plastic and buried. The villagers returned home in silence.[25]

The third example concerns university priest-administrators and teachers, the six Jesuit Martyrs of San Salvador, brutally murdered on November 16, 1989. During the night, a group of uniformed Salvadoran army soldiers armed with M16 assault rifles, entered the Jesuit University of

---

25. Penny Lernoux, *People of God, the Struggle for World Catholicism* (New York: Viking Penguin Inc., 1989), 6. Also reported in Fernando Bermudez, *Death and Resurrection in Guatemala* (Maryknoll, NY: Orbis, 1986), 62-65.

Central America (UCA), went to the residence where six Jesuits were sleeping, pulled the Jesuits from their rooms, and proceeded to shoot them at close range. The university president, Ignacio Ellacuría, the academic vice-president and social psychologist Ignacio (Nacho) Martín-Baró, and the head of the university's Social Justice Institute, sociologist Segundo Montes, were deliberately shot in the head; the soldiers scooped their brains from their shattered skulls and placed them on the ground next to their blood-stained bodies. A crudely scribbled sign was left next to their bodies "See what happens to highbrows who upset people with dangerous ideas."

Why were the six Jesuits so brutally murdered?

Because in their scholarly writings and public addresses they repeatedly called for fundamental changes in the unjust social structures of El Salvador. They spoke openly and critically about the crimes of the military. According to Rivera y Damas, Archbishop of San Salvador, they were "keen analysts of the country's situation which exposed the social sin of injustice which needs to be remedied with profound changes. That, without doubt, was their sin. They were cut down by the blind hatred of those who want everything for themselves."[26] Their motivation is expressed in the strong words Ignacio Ellacuría once wrote: "Christians and all those who hate injustice are obligated to fight it with every ounce of their strength. They must work for a new world in which greed and selfishness will finally be overcome."

Evaluation of Liberation Theology Today

In the relatively short period since Medellin in 1968 and since Gustavo Gutiérrez published in 1971 *A Theology of Liberation*, liberation theology has proved a "well of hope" for the millions of oppressed poor of Latin America. Though some segments of the church in Latin America remain resistant to the message of liberation theology, the institutional church has officially expressed a "preferential option for the poor," and many dedicated religious and laity have committed themselves to work with and for the poor. Liberation theology has transformed the Latin American Church from a too-fatalistic, dormant, often superstitious Catholicism to a vibrant, dynamic, socially conscious church. Youth especially have been attracted to this church of the gospel and of action for the poor. No longer can religion be called the opiate of the people. Latin American liberation theology has also profoundly influenced black theology in the United States, African theology stressing African peoples' cultural heritage against the invasion of white western values, Asian theology dialoguing with the ancient oriental religions, and feminine theology

---

26. Thomas Rochford, "Blessed are They," *St. Louis Jesuit Bulletin* (April, 1990), 11.

worldwide challenging the plight of women. Moreover, liberation theology has challenged traditional Catholic theology as well.

> . . . it stands as the most dramatic expression of the "paradigm shift" brought about in post-conciliar theology. It offers a way of doing theology that originates, develops, and culminates in response to the destructive experiences that characterize the lives of the majority of human beings: oppression, injustice, hunger and persecution — life-threatening factors that are the result of social structures — become central concerns in the articulation of Christian responsibility in the modern world. And it is essentially a contextual theology . . . of developing a theological understanding through contact with the demands of particular social and historical situations.[27]

In his review of liberation theology from 1968-1988,[28] Jeffrey Klaiber of Lima, Peru, notes other accomplishments: religion has been rediscovered as a vital force in Latin American social and political life; "leftist circles" now regularly cite the Bible and papal social encyclicals; liberation theology has contributed to the democratization process throughout Latin America and served as an ecumenical bridge between social-minded Catholics and liberal Protestants in both the First and Third Worlds.

Theologians McGovern and Schubeck interviewed liberation theologians, social scientists, ethicists, and critics of liberation theology in their three-month study-tour of eight Latin American countries in 1988.[29] They reported "a new context for liberation theology that has led it into new directions without diminshing its fundamental 'option for the poor.'" With the demise of military rule in most countries, democratic governments make possible a new *praxis* or action by popular movements of the poor, whose goal has become participation in the democratic process. Social analysis has become more nuanced: Marxist analysis and the dependency theory are no longer prominent, though the *fact* of dependency still exists. A new understanding between liberation theologians and the Vatican has cleared the once-tense atmosphere. The growth of CEB's and the fact that liberation theologians began to work and live with the poor has led to appreciation of their popular religiosity and to learning from the poor and from their struggles to survive and shape their own destinies. Women liberation theologians have brought a new feminist perspective to liberation theology, and more explicit awareness of the special oppression suffered by Latin American women from the *machismo* still pervasive in Latin

---

27. Adrian Hastings, *Modern Catholicism*, 434.

28. Jeffrey Klaiber, "Prophets and Populists, Liberation Theology, 1968-1988," Catholic University, Lima, Peru.

29. Arthur McGovern and Thomas Schubeck, "Updating Liberation Theology," *America* 159 (July 16, 1988): 32-35, 47.

American society and from patriarchal structures; the most oppressed in society are poor women. Finally, liberation theology is moving into a more systematic theological integration, especially in spirituality, ethics, and doctrinal areas.

The authors found the new directions positive but admitted that "the political-social significance of liberation theology in Latin America . . . still remains small"; its force seems greatest in Brazil, thanks to the strong leadership of the bishops' conference there.

What is the future of liberation theology? The picture is ambiguous. It is possible, however, to discern three challenges.

John Paul II's call to a new evangelization challenges liberation theology to broaden its emphasis to ways of evangelizing the poor, the wealthy classes, and a secular culture that is no longer the traditional Catholic culture. The new evangelization is especially challenged by the explosive growth of the evangelical, pentecostal sects. Many poor are leaving the Catholic Church for these groups, which offer bibilical spirituality, community, personal discipline. Has the emphasis on liberation theology lessened the church's ability to speak to the *spiritual* needs of the poor? Has the comfortable lifestyle of some religious communities and bishops and the institutional interests of the church made the option for the poor ineffective?

A second challenge is how best to carry out the option for the poor in the new social and political situations of Latin America. With the fall of Communism, the failure of socialism, and the apparent global triumph of capitalism and a market economy, the "utopian ideal" of a modified socialism is no longer a viable alternative to liberal capitalism. Since the wealthy elites show no sign of conversion and the abuses of liberal capitalism weigh heaviest on the poor masses, how can liberation theology effect the transformation essential to lifting the poor masses? Violent revolution has been ruled out by all liberation theologians.

The recent promising study of the relationship between Catholic social thought (CST) and liberation theology (LT) provides a third challenge. A 1991 seminar in Rio de Janeiro[30] probed the principal areas of tension between CST and LT: ". . . the focus on solidarity and role of conflict; . . . alternatives to Marxist collectivism and liberal capitalism; the role of private property; and the option for the poor." One benefit was the insight which needs to be enriched by "serious dialogue with other cultures and the voices of women." The dialogue made clear that "the foundation of LT is the option for the poor, not Marxism." The seminar report concluded that "perhaps both CST and LT are being drawn into a deeper *kenosis* (the self-emptying of Jesus in his Incarnation and

---

30. Jim Hug, "CTS Seminar: Rio," *Center Focus* (December, 1991): 5-7.

Crucifixion), challenged to greater solidarity with the poor, invited into a new age beyond that which gave birth to both socialism and capitalism."

Summary

Liberation theology is the way of thinking that relates Christian faith to the situation of massive injustice and oppression in Latin America. It attempts to answer a basic question: how to be Christian in a world of destitution and inhumane conditions. The present reality of Latin America involves the oppressed poor, the powerful wealthy elite, the military, the Catholic Church, and the United States. The Catholic Church, in its 1968 Medellín meeting of all Latin American bishops, and later at Puebla in 1979 made a dramatic shift from its century-old alliance with the state and the wealthy class to a deliberate choice of working for and with the poor masses. The church thus accepted the need for social change, the goal of a Latin American society based on justice and human rights, and the methodology of social analysis, biblical reflection, and Christian action. A deeper understanding of liberation theology involves the full reality of the poor, the phenomenon of the base Christian communities, and the concepts of conscientization, structural sin, Christian *praxis*, and participatory democracy. Despite the charges of its critics, liberation theology is a *bona fide* theology, is not Marxist or Communist, does not advocate revolution or violence, was not condemned by the pope, and does not set up a peoples' church in opposition to bishops and pope. Owing in considerable part to the forces unleashed by liberation theology, Latin America has become a continent of martyrs for justice and love. A positive evaluation can be accorded liberation theology.

For Discussion

1. Do you think liberation theology can qualify as a true theology? Why or why not?

2. Does the objection that liberation theology is Marxist have validity? What of its use of dependency theory and class analysis?

3. Considering the determination of the wealthy elites and the military to remain in power, do you think social change and the transformation of Latin American society can occur peacefully? Or is revolution and violence necessary, as in Nicaragua by the Sandinistas in 1979?

4. Has liberation theology really accomplished that much to change Latin American society, to better the condition of the poor majority?

For Action

1. See the video of the movie, *Romero*, played by Raul Julia. Get to know this extraordinary man, Archbishop Oscar Romeo. Jon Sobrino's *Memories and Reflections* is beautifully written and most rewarding reading.

2. If you really want to understand liberation theology and the role of multinational corporations and the CIA in Latin America, read Penny Lernoux' classic *Cry of the People*.

3. Or try Mev Puleo's *The Struggle is One, Voices and Visions of Liberation*, about which Robert McAfee Brown said: "If I were to choose a single book by which to introduce North Americans to the real meaning of liberation theology, it would be this book." Ms. Puleo interviews 16 people — peasants, liberation theologians and bishops, who tell their eloquent and tragic stories.

4. Find out the role of the United States in the overthrow of President Arbenz in Guatemala in 1954. *Bitter Fruit: the Untold Story of the Coup in Guatemala* gives a complete account of this sordid venture. What role did bananas and "Communism" play?

5. Research the murder of the six Jesuits in El Salvador in 1989 and the role of the Salvadoran government and military and the U.S. Embassy in the cover-up.

Further Reading

Boff, Leonardo and Clodovis. *Introducing Liberation Theology*. Maryknoll, NY: Orbis, 1987.

Casaldáliga, Pedro. *I Believe in Justice and Hope*. Notre Dame, IN: Fides/Claretian, 1978.

Gutiérrez, Gustavo. *A Theology of Liberation*. Maryknoll, NY: Orbis, 1988. Revision of 1973 original.

Hooks, Margaret. *Guatemalan Women Speak*. Washington, DC: EPICA, 1993.

Kita, Bernice. *What Prize Awaits Us: Letters from Guatemala*. Maryknoll, NY: Orbis Books, 1988.

Lernoux, Penny. *Cry of the People*. Garden City, NY: Doubleday & Co., 1980.

McGovern, Arthur. *Liberation Theology and Its Critics*. Maryknoll, NY: Orbis Books, 1989.

Novak, Michael. *Will It Liberate? Questions about Liberation Theology*. New York: Paulist Press, 1986.

Puleo, Mev. *The Struggle is One, Voices and Visions of Liberation.* Albany, NY: State University of New York Press, 1994.

Schlesinger, Stephen and Kinzer, Stephen. *Bitter Fruit: the Untold Story of the Coup in Guatemala.* Garden City, NY: Doubleday, 1982.

Sobrino, Jon. *Archbishop Romero, Memories and Reflections.* Maryknoll, NY: Orbis Books, 1990.

Whitfield, Teresa. *Paying the Price: Ignacio Ellacuría and the Murdered Jesuits of El Salvador.* Philadelphia: Temple University Press, 1994.

CHAPTER 19

Unresolved Issues
and Present Tensions

The business of a Council always remains unfinished because of
the historicity, the pluralist nature, and the changing context of
human experience.[1]

"In essentials, unity; in nonessentials, freedom; in all things,
charity."   —Peter of Maiterland, 1616

Critical remarks can stem from an intense love of the Church . . .
Critique of the Church . . . can be highly constructive . . . a
prophetic inivitation to the Church's fuller self-realization under
the power of grace.[2]

Introduction

The Second Vatican Council left some important and complex issues
unresolved. Some were judged "premature." Others were left ambiguous because of their theological complexity and the need for compromise between
progressives and traditionalists in order to achieve near-unanimous votes.
Still others were so new and unprecedented that either sufficient time for a
more fully developed theology was lacking or further steps appeared too
novel and risky. Thus theologians speak of the "unfinished agenda" of Vatican II.[3] Both these unresolved issues and new issues rising with urgency

---

1. Adrian Hastings, ed. *Modern Catholicism, Vatican II, and After* (New York: Oxford University
Press, 1991), 221.
2. Francis Fiorenza and John Galvin, eds., *Systematic Theology, Roman Catholic Perspectives,
Vol I* (Minneapolis: Fortress Press, 1991), 5, from Chapter 6, "Church" by Michael Fahey.
3. L. Richard, D. Harrington, J. O'Malley, eds., *Vatican II The Unfinished Agenda: A Look to the
Future,* (New York/Mahwah: Paulist Press, 1987).

since the Council have caused tensions and divisions in the Catholic Church today.

The present divisions within the church are of genuine concern. Unity of belief, practice and worship is a paramount value going back to Jesus and St. Paul. In the church's long history, both popes and local bishops strove tirelessly to ensure this unity. However, unity is not uniformity. Differences of theology and ways of worshiping and living the Christian faith have always been present in the church, invariably leading to valuable new insights and necessary changes. For the church is a living organism in history; change and adaptation are signs of dynamic life. So the present tensions and divisions, though painful, are therefore not abnormal or catastrophic for the church.

As noted in the preface to this book, a major goal is "to present as faithfully as possible the complex Catholic Church *as it actually exists today.*" Since unresolved issues and painful tensions are part of the contemporary church in its pilgrim journey, these need to be acknowledged. Frank recognition of problems and tensions often contributes to the health and upbuilding of the church. In thus treating the following eight areas of church life, admittedly controversial and delicate, our intent is that of the Vatican Council itself, as stated in the opening sentence of its very first document, *The Constitution on the Sacred Liturgy*:

> It is the intention of this holy council to improve the standard of daily Christian living among Catholics; to adapt those structures which are subject to change so as better to meet the needs of our time; to encourage whatever can contribute to the union of all who believe in Christ; and to strengthen whatever serves to call all people into the embrace of the Church.[4]

◆

Preview: The Council left unresolved the practical working out of its principle of collegiality, the issues of celibacy for priests and contraception in married life, various questions concerning the exercise of authority in the church and dissent, and ecumenical aspects of the relationship between the Catholic Church and other churches. Other issues like the role of women in the church, the shift from the sacral to ministerial theology of the priesthood, the slow pace of ecumenism, polarization in the Catholic Church, and relations with the Holy See have become urgent issues since the Council. These issues have great practical consequences for the health and growth of the Catholic Church today.

◆

---

4. Norman Tanner, S.J., ed. *Decrees of the Ecumenical Councils,* (Washington, D.C.: Georgetown University Press, 1990), vol. 2, p. 20.

Collegiality

Its teaching on the collegiality of bishops was a major contribution of the Second Vatican Council. In an effort to complete the work of Vatican I and to balance an overemphasis on papal primacy, the Council sought to restore the proper relationship of bishops with their head, the successor of Peter, in episcopal service to the Church.[5]

The term collegiality, a new word in the church's vocabulary thanks to the Council, comes from the Latin *collegium*, a group, referring to the bishops of the world forming the "episcopal college." Collegiality refers primarily to the relationship between the Catholic bishops of the world and the bishop of Rome, the pope. But as an important ecclesial principle, collegiality applies to all levels of Church life: bishops among themselves, local bishop and his priests, parish pastor and his people.

The Council's classic treatment of episcopal collegiality is in *Lumen Gentium*, chapter 3, No.'s 22 and 23. The key statements are:

In virtue of his office as Vicar of Christ and pastor of the whole Church, the Roman Pontiff has full, supreme, universal power over the Church. (LG 22)

Together with its head, the Roman Pontiff, and never without this head, the episcopal order is the subject of supreme and full power over the universal Church. This power can be exercised only with the consent of the Roman Pontiff. (LG 22)

In speaking of the Second Vatican Council itself, Karl Rahner pinpoints the theoretical and practical problem involved:

The Council was, with and under the pope, the active subject of the highest plenary powers in the Church . . . But how can this highest plenary authority, borne by the pope "alone" *and* the Council, actually exist and be able to act in two subjects at least partially different? This has not really been theoretically clarified, nor is it apparent in practice what lasting and timely significance there is in the fact that the whole college of bishops is, with and under the pope, but really *with* the pope, the highest collegial leadership body in the Church.[6]

With the question of collegiality, we are at the heart of the leadership structure of the church: where does the ultimate authority/power reside? in the pope? in the bishops of the world? in both? How will this *be exercised in practice*? The Council strove to keep the authority of pope and bishops in a creative tension, while championing the ancient concept and practice of

5. J. Provost and Knut Wolf, eds., *Collegiality Put to the Test* (Philadelphia: Trinity Press International, 1990), vii.

6. Karl Rahner, "Towards a Fundamental Theological Interpretation of Vatican II," in *Vatican II, The Unfinished Agenda*, 20.

collegiality. But the resulting ambiguity and the Council's failure to deal with practical applications of papal and episcopal authority has resulted in major tension and problems in the church today. Four such tests of collegiality are the relationship between the local churches and the universal church, the consultative nature of the triennial Synod of Bishops, the process of appointing bishops, and the status of national conferences of bishops.

Local Churches and the Universal Church

Before Vatican II, Catholics tended to think first of belonging to a worldwide church centered in Rome with the pope as head and only secondarily, if at all, to a diocese and a bishop. People thus popularly viewed the Catholic Church as a corporation with the pope as "chief executive officer," Rome as the headquarters, and bishops as "branch managers" around the world and representatitives of the pope! Catholics found such universality attractive, a source of pride, the strength and uniqueness of their church — unchanging, eternal, monolithic.

By emphasizing the collegiality of bishops and the local or "particular" church, Vatican II changed this perspective. Joseph Komonchak termed it "a Copernican revolution· in ecclesiology . . . a reversal of a centuries-long process of institutional and administrative centralization and uniformity in almost all areas of church life."[7] The key passages are in the *Constitution on the Church.*

> The Church of Christ is truly present in all legitimate local congregations of the faithful which, united with their pastors, are themselves called churches in the New Testament. For in their own locality these are the new people called by God in the Holy Spirit. (LG 26)

> The individual bishop is the visible principle and foundation of unity in his particular church. . . . In and from such individual churches there comes into being the one and only Catholic Church. (LG 23)

The universal Catholic Church exists only by virtue of the local or particular churches. Thus the Catholic Church worldwide is understood as a **"communion of local churches."** Since the Council there has been a remarkable development in self-awareness of local churches, especially in the formerly colonial missionary countries of Latin America, Africa and

---

7. Joseph Komonchak, "The Local Realization of Church" in Alberigo, Jossua, Komonchak, eds., *The Reception of Vatican II* (Washington D.C.: The Catholic University of America Press, 1987), 78. In the early centuries of the church, local churches had much autonomy and diversity, with Rome being the foundation of communion and intervening only rarely to settle disputes. The centralizing trend accelerated in the 11th century, reaching its peak at Vatican I and right before Vatican II. With its emphasis on the local church, the Council is returning to an earlier, more traditional ecclesiology and practice.

Asia, whose bishops speak out confidently as pastors of their flocks and whose national bishops' conferences exert strong leadership.

The relationship between the local churches or dioceses headed by bishops and the universal church headed by the pope, aided by the curial congregations, is a current tension in the Roman Catholic Church. It takes the form of the center, the Holy See, exerting ever-greater control over the periphery, the local churches of the world and their bishops. Such centralizing of authority and power in Rome has many effects. It tends to undermine the collegial relationship that should exist between the bishops and the Holy See. It may severely limit the ability of local churches and national bishops' conferences to deal with the unique problems of their regions. It can inhibit creative pastoral response to the spiritual needs of local peoples in such areas as liturgy, evangelization, ministry of priests and laity. And it often restricts theological research and development of doctrine, thus reducing the credibility of the teaching office of the church.

English theologian Joseph Laishley, for example, spoke of "a growing devaluation of the local church in the interests of further building up the Roman curial structures as the administrative organ of a 'concrete' universal Church."[8] To illustrate the current tension between the universal church and local churches, he gave the painful example of Archbishop Raymond Hunthausen of Seattle, who was relieved of many of his duties as archbishop because of such alleged abuses as women teaching seminarians, allowing a gay Dignity Mass in the cathedral, the archbishop's anti-nuclear submarine demonstrations. It took a special committee of three American bishops to resolve collegially this unfortunate incident and restore the archbishop to his rightful place. This action of a curial official disciplining a local bishop compromises the right of a bishop to govern his church and poisons the relationship that should exist between a local church and Rome.

Synod of Bishops

At the request of the bishops of Vatican II, Pope Paul VI instituted the **Synod of Bishops** on September 15, 1965. The synod is a month-long meeting in Rome of over 200 bishops worldwide to discuss a previously chosen topic and give the pope input on the state of the church throughout the world. There have been nine ordinary synods, plus the two extraordinary synods, which were called to gauge the reception of Vatican II in and by the church.[9] These synods have in fact been a unique experience of

---

8. Joseph Laishley in Hastings, ed., *Modern Catholicism*, 224.

9. The first synod in 1967 dealt with five separate topics (canon law, "dangerous modern opinions," seminaries, mixed marriages, liturgy); the Extraordinary Synod in 1969, Collegiality; 1971, Justice in the World and Priestly Ministry; 1974, Evangelization; 1977, Catechesis; 1980, the Christian Family; 1983, Reconciliation and Penance; the Extraordinary Synod of 1985, A Celebration of Vatican II; 1987, Role of Laity in Church and World; 1990, the Formation of Priests; 1994, Consecrated Life.

collegiality in practice. For the bishops who represent all sections of the worldwide church express their concerns as equals in small language groups and in plenary sessions, thus experiencing their brotherly unity in the episcopal college. Moreover, the reports of some synods have been of much value and importance for the church, particularly the 1971 synod on social justice and the 1974 synod on evangelization, which resulted in Paul VI's remarkable apostolic exhortation *Evangelization in the Modern World.*

However, serious limitations for genuine collegial action by the Synods exist: the bishops do not decide the topic to be discussed; the assembled bishops have only a consultative, not legislative voice; frequently substantive suggestions for the good of local churches and the universal church are bypassed, and the final report in the form of an "apostolic exhortation" edited by curial officials and the pope sometimes omits topics discussed by the bishops and considered important to them. As long as the synods remain strictly consultative, they will not be fully collegial and will fall short of their potential to benefit the church as envisioned by Vatican II. This has led one commentator to term the collegiality of the synods of bishops "an unresolved problem."[10]

Archbishop Weakland of Milwaukee observed that "perhaps the greatest disappointment since Vatican Council II has been the breakdown of these structures [the Synods of Bishops and the local conferences of bishops] as vehicles of both unity and cultural diversity, communicating insights to the center from the local churches and from the center out to the local churches. The hope they engendered has, for the most part, not been realized."[11] The Archbishop suggests "Now is the time to rethink the aims of the synods and ask the basic question again: What should the synods be effecting for the Holy Father and for all the bishops, as the world-Church seeks to face the vital issues of our day? Can they become the Pope's sounding board and thus truly be effective sources of collegiality with and for him, in seeing all aspects of the world-Church today?[12]

The Appointment of Bishops

"Let a bishop not be imposed on the people whom they do not want." (Pope Celestine I)

---

10. See Jan Grootaers' "The Collegiality of the Synod of Bishops: An Unresolved Problem," 18-20, in Provost and Wolf, *Collegiality Put to the Test,* for an analysis of the 1969 and 1985 extraordinary synods. At both meetings, the request that synods have a deliberative competence was not accepted.

11. Archbishop Rembert Weakland, *Faith and the Human Enterprise, A Post-Vatican II Vision* (Maryknoll, New York: Orbis Books, 1992), 23. See pages 22-24 for his insightful discussion of the Synods of Bishops.

12. *Ibid.,* 24.

"He who has to preside over all must be elected by all . . . Let a person not be ordained against the wish of the Christians and whom they have not explicitly asked for." (Pope St. Leo the Great)

The debate on the question of the nomination and choice of bishops has been vigorous over the last decade. The Second Vatican Council did not deal directly with this question. However, its stress on the church as the people of God, on the laity's "right and even . . . duty to manifest to the sacred pastors their opinion on matters which pertain to the good of the Church" (LG 37), on the importance of the local church and the principles of participation and coresponsibility of all the faithful favor "the demand for the direct and active participation by clergy and laity . . . in the choice of the bishop."[13]

The problem concerning this issue in the church today is complex and delicate. The clergy and laity of a given diocese have no *official* voice in selecting their bishop. The papal nuncio in each country often has more say in the choice than the local diocese and the national conference of bishops. Thus, as in the celebrated cases of Holland in early 1970 and Cologne, Germany, and Salzburg, Austria in 1988, bishops have been chosen against the wishes of both local clergy and people, causing ill feeling and damaging the unity and pastoral effectiveness of the local church. Concerned Catholics today see a two-fold problem: an increasingly conservative episcopate throughout the world who, they fear, may be incapable of uniting Catholics and of dealing with today's urgent church issues; and the church being denied a core of innovative and pastorally sensitive bishops to lead the church into its third millennium.[14]

Collegial structures for nominating and choosing bishops has thus become a concern in the church today.

National Conferences of Bishops

Vatican II encouraged the formation of conferences of bishops in each country — or even internationally — as an exercise of collegiality for

---

13. Grootaers, "The Collegiality of the Synod of Bishops. . .," 100. "See Considerations on the Nomination of Bishops in Current Canon Law," 98-103.

14. Peter Hebblethwaite calls attention to criteria for choosing bishops according to a document/questionnaire to be filled in by those invited to evaluate candidates for bishop: #6. Orthodoxy: — convinced and faithful adherence to the teaching and magisterium of the church. In particular, the attitude of the candidate to the documents of the Holy See on the priestly office, the priestly ordination of women, marriage and the family, sexual ethics, especially the transmission of life according to the teaching of *Humanae Vitae* and of the apostolic instruction *Familiaris Consortio* . . . # 7 Discipline — fidelity and obedience to the Holy Father, the Apostolic See, the hierarchy, esteem and acceptance of priestly celibacy as it is presented by the church's magisterium . . . Hebblethwaite, "Secret Criteria set for bishops' appointments," *National Catholic Reporter*, 30, no. 14 (Feb. 4, 1994): 14.

better pastoral care of the local churches by bishops most knowledgeable of local needs:

> [the Council] considers it in the highest degree helpful everywhere that bishops belonging to the same nation or region form an association and meet together . . . so that by sharing their wisdom and experience and exchanging views they may jointly formulate a programme for the common good of the churches. (CD 37)

The *theological basis* for such conferences lies in the collegial nature of bishops and in the church as a communion of local churches. The Council, however, refrained from settling the currently controverted theological question on what precise way bishops' conferences participate in the collegiality of bishops in union with the pope, and consequently on whether they have teaching authority or not.

Examples of successful national bishops' conferences are the National Conference of Catholic Bishops in the United States (whose pastoral letters on a wide range of issues are praised as examples of collegial action) and the Brazilian National Bishops' Conference, praised by John Paul II in his talk to them at Forteleza, July 10, 1980 as a "characteristic expression and appropriate instrument of that collegiality" stressed by Vatican II. Examples of effective international episcopal conferences are South America's CELAM, which produced the influential Medellín and Puebla documents, the Council of the European Conferences of Bishops (CCEE), and the creative Federation of Asian Bishops' Conferences (FABC).

Recently Cardinal Ratzinger, head of the curia's Congregation for the Doctrine of the Faith, expressed the theological opinion that bishops' conferences have no teaching authority, only individual bishops, because they lack theological justification as not being in the true and proper sense collegial. This position was strongly attacked by theologians from many countries.[15] The cardinal raised legitimate questions. But to many, the operative issue appeared to be the Curia's fear that such conferences are a threat to its authority and control.[16] They see this opposition to bishops' conferences as a manifestation of the restoration mentality prevalent in the church today.

---

15. For a balanced treatment on this issue see Avery Dulles, *The Reshaping of Catholicism* (San Francisco: Harper and Row, 1988), 207-226, "The Teaching Authority of Bishops' Conferences" and Dulles "The Mandate to Teach," *America* 158 (March 19, 1988): 293-95. See also Ladislas Orsy, "Episcopal Conferences, Their Theological Standing and Their Doctrinal Authority," *America* 155 (November 8, 1986): 282-85. See also Weakland, *Faith and the Human Enterprise,* pp. 24-26. He sees conferences as central to today's world church and useful "for relating one sector of the church to others and of being truly a sounding board for the Holy Father."

16. "It was above all the threat of the emergence of a 'peoples church' [in Latin America] which motivated Cardinal Ratzinger's instruction on liberation theology and was an element in the imposition of a year's silence on [liberation theologian] Leonardo Boff." Joseph Laishley in Hastings, ed., *Modern Catholicism,* 222.

The recent action (October, 1994) of CDF in rescinding approval of the inclusive language translation of the *New Revised Standard Version (NRSV)* of the Bible for use in American and Canadian liturgical texts and catechetical instruction raised again questions about the authority of national conferences of bishops. The U.S. bishops had voted 195-24 in favor of the *NRSV* translation at their November 1991 meeting. The Canadian conference of bishops had likewise approved the text. The issue for CDF is the use of inclusive langauage. The American bishops in a November, 1990 statement, "Criteria for the Evaluation of Inclusive Translations of Scriptural Texts Proposed for Liturgical Use," had rejected exclusive language that "seems to exclude the equality and dignity of each person regardless of race, gender, creed, age or ability." Examples are the use of *man* when the meaning is clearly broader to include all men and women or the use of the masculine *he/him* referring to God. Bishop Donald Trautman, chair of the liturgy commission of NCCB, called inclusive language "a pastoral necessity, not only in the Scriptures, but in catechetics and liturgy. It is a necessity in our American idiom and culture today."[17] The larger issue is the right and pastoral responsibility of national bishops' conferences to make prudential decisions for the benefit of their own people. This incident is an example of the failure in collegiality as championed by Vatican II.

Conclusion. This issue of collegialty has immense *practical* ramifications in today's church: whether final decisions of great importance to the church are made by the pope alone (as in the case of the 1968 *Of Human Life*) or in collegial consultation with his brother bishops of the world; whether liturgical and missionary practices are judged by national conferences of bishops and individual bishops or by the curia exclusively; whether bishops should be disciplined or removed by curial congregations. Concerning relationships with other churches, a major ecumenical concern is whether union can occur with the Orthodox and Protestant churches without genuine collegial structures in the Catholic Church. Collegiality influences all levels of the church's life. It affects most of the major issues and tensions in today's church. If collegial living truly becomes the church practice of the future, it has the potential to help the church meet its enormous modern challenges and opportunities.

Celibacy and the Catholic Priesthood

Pope Paul VI ruled that the Council should not treat the complex question of priestly **celibacy**. However, it could not be avoided. Both Af-

---

17. Tom Roberts, "Vatican rescinds inclusive language approval," *National Catholic Reporter* 30 (Nov. 5, 1994): 4. See also "Catholics want solidarity with their bishops," *NCR* 30 (Nov. 11, 1994): 24.

rican and Asian bishops and most recently a Canadian bishop have requested permission from Rome to ordain married catechists in order to bring the sacraments to their people. In the Bishops' Synod of 1971, a large number of bishops spoke in favor of ordaining married men,[18] though the majority vote went against it. Yet Vatican II restored the ancient order of the permanent deaconate which has proved productive and popular in the United States where in 1993, 10,328 ordained permanent deacons, the vast majority married, serve the poor, preach homilies, baptize and witness marriages.

This issue involves many theological and practical questions. Theological arguments for celibacy are that the priest should image the celibate Christ; that sexual intercourse in some way is inconsistent with the sacral role of the priest; that celibacy symbolizes the "man set apart" for service of the divine. Practical questions have to do with the idea that celibacy enables the priest to serve God with an undivided heart and without the financial realities of supporting a family.

An increasing number of theologians no longer find these arguments convincing, nor see a necessary connection between priestly ministry and celibacy. Those who emphasize historical realism and the Spirit speaking through the signs of the times argue that Catholics have a right to the sacraments, especially the Eucharist, which is being denied them in the increasing number of priestless parishes in Europe and the United States, and in Latin American urban parishes of 50,000 to 100,000 persons, or in isolated mountain villages where a priest comes only several times a year.

Obviously there is a problem of major magnitude here. The official church declines to consider a change in what involves church discipline rather than doctrine; yet Catholics are being denied the Eucharist in a church that professes to be a sacramental church and which places the Eucharist at the center of its religious life. Maximos IV Saigh, Melchite Patriarch of Antioch, wrote to Paul VI at Vatican II: "In case of necessity the priesthood must not be sacrificed to celibacy, but celibacy to the priesthood."[19]

The celibacy question is highlighted by the worldwide departure of thousands of priests from the ministry in order to marry, and the reluctance of many young men to become priests because of the celibacy requirement in the western church. Moreover, a majority of Catholics in America and

---

18. "During the course of history, the Church has known how to proceed with prudence and courage for the restructuring of its ministerial ranks. . . . The necessity and possibility of ordaining as presidents of the Eucharist for the numerous communities the 'viri probate' present and operating within them should be studied more seriously. . . . There are no human forecasts that in the forthcoming generations there will arise sufficient authentic celibate vocations for pastoral service in many ecclesial communities which are in danger of falling into the situation of sects since they do not celebrate the Eucharist, the apex and source of ecclesial life." Bishop Valfredo Bernardo Tepe, O.F.M., of Ilheus, Brazil, as reported in *Osservatore Romano*.

19. Hastings, *Modern Catholicism*, 235.

Europe, according to various polls, now believe priests should be permitted to marry. A recent article "Are There Any More Priests Out There?" dramatically stated that "we Roman Catholics are in danger of losing the Eucharist which makes the church." The author insists that the urgent question to be asked today is not how to attract young men to become celibate priests but how can we continue to provide the Eucharist for future generations of Catholics. His bold recommendation is that the American bishops should tell Rome, "On this matter you are wrong," on the principle that local bishops share a "solicitude for all the churches" in the worldwide Catholic Church.[20] Since the needs of Catholics for the Eucharist and for priestly ministerial leadership continue to increase, it would seem that this urgent question of celibacy can no longer be avoided.

One avenue of approach that would provide for the needs of Catholics yet at the same time preserve celibacy as a gift to the church and a celibate priesthood as a powerful witness of sacrifice and service, is for the church to permit diocesan priests to marry, while retaining celibacy for priests in religious orders who already vow celibacy as part of their religious state.

The Catholic priesthood itself has become a topic of discussion since the conclusion of Vatican II. The issue is multifaceted: not only the rapid decline in the number of priests, but the new understanding of the nature of priesthood and the priest's role.

Some speak of the Catholic priesthood as being in a crisis. Statistics and various studies seem to bear this out. From 1964 to 1985, 48,351 priests left the active ministry worldwide. In the United States in 1968, there were 22,334 diocesan seminarians preparing for the priesthood; in 1978 9,560, and in 1988 4,981. In response to this trend, the U.S. bishops in 1988 approved a rite for laypersons to lead a communion service for the growing number of priestless parishes.

Yet the picture is ambiguous, according to various studies of priests themselves.

A 1988 study by U.S. bishops published in 1989 by their Committee on Priestly Life and Ministry admitted "a serious and substantial morale problem among priests." Factors mentioned were the following: many priests are overworked; they feel the official church is unwilling to face realistically the problem of the shortage of priests; priests are often caught in the middle between lay people anxious for change and "an official church more concerned with restoring discipline and centralizing authority." Other problems mentioned by the document include ". . . unclear role expectations, loneliness, the need for affirmation and issues related to sexuality — among them, psychosexual development, feminism, married clergy, optional celibacy and the role and place of homosexuality in minis-

---

20. William Shannon "Are There Any More Priests Out There?" *America* 165 (Oct. 12, 1991): 240-42.

try."[21] In addition to this morale problem is a poor public image which unfairly burdens the many good effective priests today.[22]

A more recent survey sponsored by the National Federation of Priest Councils in 1993 paints a brighter picture. While realistically recognizing problems mentioned above, the majority of priest respondents are happy in their priestly ministry: 90% say they would choose to be a priest again (70% definitely, 20% probably); 72% say they will definitely not leave the priesthood; 54% find life as a priest better than expected and another 36% as expected; only 14% say celibacy is a serious problem for them personally; 83% approve "strongly" or "somewhat" the job performance of the present pope and 72% of their own bishops.[23]

Rather than crisis, it seems more appropriate to view the priesthood as being in a state of transition. One factor is the disappearance of the immigrant church in which large numbers of Irish, Italian, German and Polish families established close-knit parishes. Their priests were esteemed and loved; families prayed for at least one son to become a priest. Priests clearly understood their role: to say mass in crowded churches, hear hundreds of confessions on Saturdays, give the sacraments, oversee a parochial school, do "parlor" counseling, run youth and other groups. Vocations were plentiful, seminaries full and priests enjoyed their long hours' work. It was a prestige vocation.

Now, with the growth of priestless parishes,[24] 2,180 worldwide in 1985, others took over parishes once led by priests: lay persons, 872 parishes; women religious 783; permanent deacons 212, religious brothers 77. New styles of priesthood began to be discussed: "a married priesthood, a non-stipendiary priesthood where priests would support themselves (and their families) by working in secular employment, women priests, and maybe even priests who would commit themselves for only a limited number of years to be engaged in active pastoral and sacramental work."[25]

Perhaps a major element of transition today is the shift in the theology of priesthood itself. "The sacral model of priesthood, presupposed in

---

21. For the above material, see Thomas Rausch, "Forming Priests for Tomorrow's Church: The Coming Synod," *America* 162 (Feb. 24, 1990): 168-69.

22. "Whether due to the perception of celibacy as weird in an age of sexual license, the exodus of large numbers of men in the late 1960s and early 1970s, the exaggerated publicity given to the rare cases of pedophilia, the association of the priesthood with the exclusion of women, the speculation about a large percentage of priests being gay, or just the general depiction of priests in films and television as naive, corrupt, or sex-starved, the image of the priest is just not the same as it used to be." Dennis Doyle, *The Church Emerging from Vatican II, A Popular Approach to Contemporary Catholicism* (Mystic CT: Twenty-Third Publications, 1992), 93.

23. Report is available from NFPC, 1337 W. Ohio St., Chicago, IL 60222. Priest-sociologist Andrew Greeley states "It is time for priests to realize that theirs is a satisfying and rewarding vocation." See Greeley "A Sea of Paradoxes: Two Surveys of Priests," *America* 171 (July 16, 1994): 6-10.

24. Hastings, *Modern Catholicism*, 252.

25. *Ibid.*, 253.

344 \ *Major Issues in Today's Church*

church teaching from the time of the Council of Florence (1439), has given way to a new understanding of priesthood as a particular kind of ministry and leadership."[26] In the sacral model of priesthood, the priest was understood as a "dispenser of mysteries," the one who had power to change bread and wine into the body and blood of Christ and to forgive sins; the priest was thus a sacred person, one set apart from the ordinary laity.

A "more critical and contemporary theology understands ordained priesthood [as consisting] of leadership in forming and nurturing the faith community, especially through a ministry of word and sacrament."[27] Theological bases are Vatican II's insight on church as the people of God and emphasis on the local church, on liturgical worship as the action of the entire Christian community, and on the Christian's vocation in and for the world. Accordingly, the priest's primary role is understood as one of leadership in creating and empowering a prophetic ministering Christian community. He thus "presides" — a new term — over the life of the community, especially through proclaiming God's word and presiding over the Eucharist.

This change in *emphasis* from sacral to ministerial priesthood has been a source of tension for many priests today, especially those trained in the sacral model, and for Catholics accustomed to putting their priest on a pedestal. It has also resulted in division in the seminary training of future priests: between the traditional approach stressing discipline, isolation from society, practices of piety in keeping with the sacral model, and the different approach of progressive seminaries that stress community life, openness to the world and its problems, and training in how effectively to serve and lead faith communities. A recently noted phenomenon of some seminaries is the increasing conservatism of seminarians who appear to desire a return to the sacral model.

Vatican II, especially in its *Decree on the Ministry and Life of Priests* (No.'s 4, 6, 9) and *Lumen Gentium* (28) recovered from the early church the ministerial role of the priest. The Counter-Reformation sacral model defined priest almost exclusively by the power to consecrate the Eucharist. Vatican II rooted the ministry of the priest in Jesus' ministry as prophet, priest and king, with primacy given to preaching the gospel. Vatican II thus closely linked the ministry of the priest to the community, to the word of God in Scripture, and to justice issues, in addition to dispensing sacraments and the Eucharist.

---

26. Rausch, "Forming Priests for Tomorrow's Church," 170.

27. *Ibid.* For this kind of leadership, a report of the East Asian Pastoral Institute on "Priests for the 21st Century" described the kind of priest needed: a loving person aware of his gifts and sinfulness; someone who recognizes the reality of change as an invitation rather than a threat; a disciple ready to listen and learn from any person and any experience; someone alive to the reality of society, to the challenges of biocide, poverty, injustice; a person who can accompany and guide people in their search for God in the everyday realities of their lives and who can lead the community in celebration of that reality and of God's presence in it. No small order!

This "new" theology of priesthood and vision of today's priest presents an exciting challenge to both older and younger priests and to young men considering the priesthood: to lead, animate and serve the Christian community in a new spirit of collaboration with lay Catholics and to nourish Catholics' hunger for deeper spirituality. What seems to be needed in this period of transition in the Catholic priesthood is sensitivity to the "signs of the times," openness to change, abundance of trust in the Holy Spirit guiding the church, and courage and faith to risk the new and untried.

Contraception in Marriage

Pope Paul VI decided that this issue likewise not be debated by the Council, but would be given for further study to the commission originally set up by John XXIII. In March 1965 this commission was made up of 34 lay men and women (doctors, scientists, professors, three married couples) and 21 priests, including moral theologians. The theologians voted 15 to 4 that contraception was not to be considered intrinsically evil. Six cardinals and nine bishops joined the commission in Spring 1966. After two months of meetings and hearing the testimony of moral theologians, doctors, scientists, university professors, married couples and several cardinals, the commission voted overwhelmingly, 64 to 4, to petition a change in the traditional teaching against contraception. The cardinals and bishops voted 9 to 3, with three abstentions, to draft a report which Pope Paul VI received in 1967.[28]

The majority report affirmed "that the morality of sexual acts between married people takes its meaning first of all and specifically from the ordering of their actions in a fruitful married life . . . It does not then depend upon the fecundity of each and every particular act."[29] The minority report drafted by the four dissenting commission members opposed any change in the official teaching based on the principle of a specific ordering of each generative act to procreation; contraception is thus morally evil based on the premise that certain acts are intrinsically evil and on the consistent claim of the church's leadership to make universally binding prohibitions of such acts.

Pope Paul VI accepted the minority report, promulgating it in the now famous *Of Human Life* letter July 25, 1968. Despite its profound and beautiful teaching on married love, few documents have so divided Catholics or damaged the teaching authority of the papal office and hurt the credibility of the church among Catholics and non-Catholics alike. That

---

28. For much of this material see Robert Kaiser, *The Politics of Sex and Religion : A Case History in the Development of Doctrine, 1962-1984* (Kansas City, MO: Leaven Press, 1985).

29. Hastings, *Modern Catholicism*, 235.

this teaching on individual contraceptive acts was not universally accepted by Catholics in Europe and North America posed at the time enormous conscience problems for Catholics concerned to be loyal to papal teaching. Likewise, many priests counseling in the confessional and even some bishops were torn between obedience to the church and their own convictions and the pastoral needs of their people. Six national bishops' conferences issued pastoral letters to guide their people in this conscience dilemma; the letters upheld papal teaching but stated that those married couples who practiced contraception were not to be considered bad Catholics.[30]

In his Sept. 29, 1980 speech in Rome at the Synod of Bishops meeting on the family, Archbishop John Quinn of San Francisco spoke of this "immense problem for the Church today" of its teaching on contraception. He stated that many persons of good will do not accept "the intrinsic evil of each and every use of contraception." This conviction is held by "theologians and pastors whose learning, faith, discretion and dedication to the Church are beyond doubt." He cited studies indicating that nearly 80% of U.S. Catholic married women use contraceptives and that only 29% of U.S. priests consider artificial contraception "intrinsically wrong." He concluded that such widespread opposition to the Church's teaching cannot be dismissed and "constitutes a profound theological and pastoral problem for the church." He therefore made three proposals: a new context for the teaching; a worldwide dialogue between the Vatican and moral theologians on the meaning of this widespread dissent; more care to the process by which papal documents are written and communicated to Catholics.[31] It should be noted that Archbishop Quinn did not call into question the teaching itself, as he expressly stated in a later press conference.

More recently Bishop Kenneth Untener of Saginaw, Michigan, has urged the church to begin an "honest and open discussion" of its teaching on birth control. He admitted that "since **Humanae Vitae** church teaching authority has been less credible in the eyes of very many people, including many Catholics." He called attention to a disturbing fact: "In the eyes of many the issue has shifted. It is no longer an honest evaluation of the

---

30. The six were Austria, Canada, Belgium, France, Holland, and Switzerland. The Belgium bishops: "Someone, however, who is competent in the matter under consideration and capable of forming a personal and well-founded judgment — which necessarily presupposes a sufficient amount of knowledge — may, after a serious examination before God, come to other conclusions on certain points. In such a case he has the right to follow his conviction provided that he remains sincerely disposed to continue his inquiry." The Scandinavian bishops: "No one should, therefore, on account of such divergent opinions alone, be regarded as an inferior Catholic." The Canadian bishops: "These Catholics should not be considered, or consider themselves, shut off from the body of the faithful." Quoted in Richard McCormick, *"Humanae Vitae 25 Years Later," America* 169 (July 17, 1993), 6-7.

31. Archbishop John Quinn, "New Context for Contraception Teaching," *Origins* 10 (Oct. 9, 1980): 263-67.

moral implications of artificial birth control. The issue is loyalty to church authority."[32]

Of Human Life has thus become painfully divisive within the Catholic Church. Some Catholics make acceptance of the encyclical the test of whether one is a loyal, obedient, and therefore good Catholic; others desire that John Paul II make it an infallible teaching. The question of infallibility, however, was settled when Pope Paul VI stated publicly that he did not intend *Humanae Vitae* to be infallible. Furthermore, the church has wisely never defined infallibly a moral question since a process of development of teaching on moral issues is a normal historical process in the church. A few examples are usury, slavery, and St. Augustine's teaching that only procreation could keep sexual intercourse from being sinful.

Once again, this issue involves many others: the traditional and revisionist approach to moral theology; the primacy of individual conscience; the relationship between married sexual love and procreation; the credibility of the church's opposition to abortion when it prohibits contraception; large families in the Third World, where parents cannot feed and give health care to babies born every year; and the larger question of overpopulation in poverty-stricken developing countries of the world.

Conscience, Dissent, and Church Authority

> [the] failure to reconcile what one might call the spirit of *Dignitatis Humanae* and *Gaudium et Spes* regarding human dignity and conscience with certain sections of *Lumen Gentium* set the stage for subsequent post-conciliar polarization among Catholics.[33]

The bishops at Vatican II spoke strongly about religious freedom, the dignity of each person, and the primacy and sacredness of one's conscience. The pertinent passages about conscience occur in the *Church in the Modern World (GS)* and the *Declaration on Religious Liberty (DH):*

> Deep within his conscience man discovers a law which he has not laid on himself but which he must obey. . . . His dignity lies in observing this law and by it he will be judged. His conscience is man's most secret core and his sanctuary. (GS 16)

> In all his activity a man is bound to follow his conscience faithfully. . . . It follows that he is not to be forced to act in a manner contrary to his conscience. . . . For, of its very nature, the exercise

---

32. Bishop Kenneth Untener, "*Humanae Vitae:* What Has It Done to Us?" *Commonweal* 120 (June 18, 1993): 13. The bishop said there is a wide perception that the encyclical is used as a loyalty test in the appointment of moral theologians and bishops. At the U.S. bishops'meeting in November 1990, he told the assembled bishops that their inability to discuss the widespread dissent from the church's official teaching made them appear to be a "dysfunctional family that is unable to talk openly about a problem that everyone knows is there."

33. Richard, *et al., The Unfinished Agenda,* 165.

of religion consists before all else in those internal, voluntary and free acts whereby man sets the course of his life directly toward God. (DH 3)

At the same time in emphasizing the authority of the hierarchy, *Lumen Gentium* seemed to rule out the possibility of conscience disagreement.

> In matters of faith and morals, the bishops speak in the name of Christ and the faithful are to accept their teaching and adhere to it with a religious assent of soul. This religious submission of will and of mind must be shown in a special way to the authentic teaching authority of the Roman Pontiff, even when he is not speaking *ex cathedra* [infallibly]. (LG 25)

Specifically in the matter of responsible disagreement, the Council, as Avery Dulles noted "did not squarely face the question about the rights and duties of the Catholic who is conscientiously convinced that the official church has erred on a given point."[34] Had the Council resolved the issue of conscience and dissent in relation to authoritative but fallible church teaching, much tension and division in the church today might have been avoided or at least minimized.

The topic of disagreement or dissent from the ordinary teaching office of the church constitutes one of the most critical tensions and divisions in the Catholic Church today. It involves a host of important issues: not only the primacy of the individual conscience and the authoritative teaching office of the church, but also the vocation and responsibility of Catholic professional theologians, the nature of genuine scholarship, the most appropriate exercise of church authority and its credibility today, the development of doctrine, the long-range good and health of the church. We must therefore give careful attention to this major issue in the church today.

There has always been disagreement with official church teaching and practice throughout the history of the church. In the past the church often dealt harshly with dissenters, too easily branding them as heretics. Yet from the vantage point of history we realize that such dissent often led to clarification and more complete teaching, to positive development of doctrine, to healthy progress.

The publication *Of Human Life* by Pope Paul VI in 1968 brought the question of dissent to the fore in the Catholic Church. Unfortunately, for some Catholics dissent became a test of one's loyalty to the Catholic Church, to the magisterium, and to the pope himself. And some Catholics used the term magisterium uncritically, without understanding how its teachings are formulated and how it functions in the life of the church. Yet the issue of dissent is particularly important in the relationship between

---

34. Avery Dulles, "Authority: the Divided Legacy," *Commonweal* 112 (July 12, 1985): 401.

theologians and the magisterium because it involves the necessary service of theological thought to the teaching office of bishops and pope.

What then are the fundamental issues concerning dissent?

We must first clarify terminology. The magisterium is the official authoritative teaching of pope and bishops; as such it can expect the Spirit's guidance and is to be respected by all Catholics, who should give it their moral assent. The *extraordinary* magisterium, rarely used, is the infallible teaching of pope or ecumenical council and is guaranteed freedom from error by the Holy Spirit. The *ordinary* magisterium is the normal, day-by-day non-infallible teaching of pope and bishops as part of their office. Dissent then is disagreement with the authentic teaching of this *ordinary* magisterium. Such dissent can be private or public. When *private* it is permissible if one follows a sincere, informed conscience; when *public* the CDF forbids Catholic theologians to dissent by writing or speaking in the public media.

The Case against Dissent, especially Public Dissent. Theologian Francis Buckley reminds us that the teaching of the ordinary magisterium provides "precious helps" in the formation of conscience and in shaping understanding about God and the world. For the church has been given by Christ the mandate to teach the faithful, with his promise of divine assistance; its ordinary exercise of this responsibility is essential to the church's mission and deserves respect and acceptance for the common good of the church. In 1990 Cardinal Ratzinger, head of the Congregation for the Doctrine of the Faith, issued a 28-page *Instruction on the Ecclesial Vocation of the Theologian* in which he analyzed the "problem of dissent" (No.'s 32-41), urged theologians to avoid public dissent, to show "love for the Church" and "respect for her divinely assisted magisterium," and to take care not to bring "spiritual harm" to the faithful.[35] He argued for "the right of the People of God to receive the message of the Church in its purity and integrity and not to be disturbed by a particular dangerous opinion."[36] Catholic theologians teach in the name of the church; therefore they have the responsibility of following the teaching of the church's ordinary magisterium.

Case for Dissent, even Public Dissent. History makes it clear today that some ordinary official church teaching in the past was incomplete and actually erroneous. Examples are "no salvation outside the church," denying freedom of religious practice to other churches and religions, the Galileo case concerning the position of the earth in the universe, usury, slavery, private property. Church teaching has "developed," change has occurred.

---

35. Cardinal Josef Ratzinger, "Instruction on the Ecclesial Vocation of the Theologian," *Origins* 20: No. 8 (July 5, 1990), 118-26. For an insightful response to this Instruction and the issue of dissent, see Richard McCormick and Richard McBrien, "Theology as a Public Responsibility," *America* 165 (Sept. 28, 1991): 184-89 and 203-06.

36. *Ibid.*, Ratzinger, 125, no. 37.

The precise vocation and responsibility of Catholic theologians is to serve the church by rigorous, scholarly search for truth.

> The task of the theologian is to analyze and reflect on the Tradition in order better to understand and explain its achievements and to explore its possibilities for future development. . . . The Tradition is best served by theologizing that presses every question to its limit, that can investigate every aspect of doctrine, that deals publicly with difficult challenges.[37]

Moral theologian Richard McCormick in his frank article, "The Search for Truth in the Catholic Context," calls attention to the fact that

> The church is a pilgrim church. It is *in via* (on the way). That means that its formulations of its moral convictions are also *in via*, never finished and always in need of improvement, updating and adjustment to changing circumstances. Not only are moral and doctrinal formulations the product of limited minds, with limited insight, concepts and language; they are historically conditioned by the circumstances in which they were drafted.[38]

Regarding public dissent by Catholic theologians, McCormick insists that since theology is a public enterprise, it must be done in public:

> [theology] is a reflection on the faith of the church, and therefore should flourish wherever that faith is found. Theological research examines, draws upon, challenges, deepens the faith of people — and therefore must interplay with, be available to, be tested by, make sense to those whose faith is involved. Briefly, since it is of the public, with the public, and for the public, it must be done in public.[39]

To answer the objection that public dissent scandalizes the simple faith of Catholics, McCormick insists that the "solution lies in education of Catholics" to history, to the role of bishops and theologians in the church, to the fact that "God writes straight with crooked lines," that is, that the magisterium is made up of fallible humans, a reality that puts limits to its teaching competence.[40]

In speaking of the church's teaching mission, Archbishop Weakland comments:

> Another misconception that must be avoided is to think of the laity in the Church today as uninformed or bewildered sheep. That laity is often better instructed than the pastors, and more zealous

---

37. April, 1988, Draft Proposal "Statement of the College Theology Society on Freedom of Public Dissent by Theologians," no.'s 4 and 5.

38. Richard McCormick, "The Search for Truth in the Catholic Context," *America* 155 (Nov. 8, 1986): 281.

39. *Ibid.*

40. *Ibid.*, 281.

as well. They are not so easily scandalized as some would assume. If they are scandalized, it is more often by unjust or unfair procedures than by theological error. We do a disservice to our lay people if we do not see them as mature, committed, intelligent, discerning adults.[41]

McCormick is convinced that "the problem of the Church is not dissent but how to use it constructively, how to learn from it, how to profit from it." He sees "the problem is to convince some Catholics that dissent is not a threat — unless they conceive the Church as an isolated fortress — but an invigorating contribution to continued life and growth." He states the issue as: "what must the Church do to insure that its teaching is the soundest reflection of the Gospel at a particular time? . . . If the Church is intolerant of dissent, is it not excluding a possible source of correction and improvement, as well as of error?"[42]

Author and professor of psychology, layperson Sidney Callahan, echoes this conviction: "The Church must work toward respecting loyal dissent and reverencing individual conscience. Catholics who in conscience dissent from church teachings may be wrong or they may be responding to what the Holy Spirit intends for the future of the Church."[43]

A significant aspect in this discussion on dissent is the existence among Catholics of what the *Constitution on the Church* called the "sense of faith." It is that religious sixth sense or supernatural instinct by which faithful Christians understand what is authentic or inauthentic, central or peripheral Christian belief and teaching.

> The body of the faithful as a whole . . . cannot err in matters of belief. Thanks to a supernatural sense of faith which characterizes the People as a whole, it manifests this unerring quality. . . . For by this sense of faith which is aroused and sustained by the Spirit of truth, God's people accepts not the word of men but the very Word of God. (LG 12)

This *sensus fidelium* or instinctive sense that believers have under the guidance of the Holy Spirit has received much attention by theologians since the Council, especially in the reception or nonreception of non-infallible teaching of the magisterium. Obviously, careful discernment of this "sense of the faithful" is needed; yet it cannot be overlooked in regard to dissent and the relationship between church authority and the sincere conscience of Catholics.

In the light of the above reflections, we can more readily appreciate the "Norms of Licit Theological Dissent"[44] issued by the U.S. bishops in

---

41. Weakland, *Faith and the Human Enterprise*, 148.
42. McCormick, "The Search for Truth . . ." 280.
43. Sidney Callahan, "Conscience Reconsidered," *America* 155 (Nov. 1, 1986): 251-53.
44. U.S. Bishops, *Human Life in Our Day* (Boston: Daughters of St. Paul, 1968), 26-27.

1968 in response to *Humanae Vitae* and the widespread dissent that followed.

> There exists in the church a lawful freedom of thought and also general norms of licit dissent. This is particularly true in the area of legitimate theological speculation and research. When conclusions reached by such professional theological work prompt a scholar to dissent from non-infallible received teaching, the norms of licit dissent come into play.
>
> The expression of theological dissent from the magisterium is in order only if the reasons are serious and well-founded, if the manner of dissent does not question or impugn the teaching authority of the church and is such as not to give scandal.
>
> Even responsible dissent does not excuse one from faithful presentation of the authentic doctrine of the church when one is performing a pastoral ministry in her name.

What then is the responsibility of Catholic professional theologians in their scholarly service to the church? And how are ordinary Catholics to react when they find themselves unable to agree with an official teaching of the church?

Both groups should respect the authority of the teaching office and its individual teachers. They should keep an open, humble mind, seeking to understand the Christian values of the teaching and the context in which it is made. At the same time, however, they must follow their own conscience when sincere and informed. Especially theologians, in faithfulness to their scholarship and service to the church, will at times feel compelled to dissent; when this happens, their dissent, even when by necessity public in today's age of communications, most benefits the church when based on solid scholarship, when moderate and expressed in such a way as to build up rather than tear down the church. Both truth and charity ought to prevail.

This issue of conscience, dissent, and authority is critically important to the Catholic Church today. It profoundly affects the lives of individual Catholics and the role of theologians, especially moral theologians. It has created polarization and division within the church, weakening the bond of love that should exist. Many do not experience the church as a sacrament of love and unity. Fear of dissent has caused church leaders to overstress in a defensive manner their own authority and Catholics' obligation to obedience. This tends to obscure deeper issues and reduce the credibility of the teaching office among educated Catholics. One result is to dissipate energy and distract the church from its mission of evangelization and sanctification. Another result is burdening the church's ecumenical outreach, making future union, if not impossible, at least much more difficult.

Catholics generally accept the authority of bishops and the pope and both value and want such authority. The crucial issue today is the way this authority is sometimes exercised.

The Role of Women in the Catholic Church

Women have always played a major role within the church. The "good nuns," through an astounding network of elementary and high schools, educated millions of Catholic youth in the United States as well as staffing hospitals and many other good works; married and single women have always been the most generous and visible in parishes in myriad ways. These great women served humbly, but had little or no say in the decisions that affected the church and indeed their own lives.

Inspired by the possibilities Vatican II offered and influenced by the feminist movement sweeping the country, Catholic feminism has become a force in the American church and beyond. Many Catholic women, both young and not so young, began to express concern and even anger that they had no part in church decision-making, were not treated as equals to men within the church, and that their gifts to enrich the church were not recognized in practice.

Thus competent, articulate Catholic women theologians and Scripture scholars produced in the past 20 years a near-deluge of books on a wide variety of feminist concerns. A sampling of some of the titles indicates the breadth and richness of topics treated. *In Memory of Her: A Feminist Theological Reconstruction of Christian Origins,* Elisabeth Schüssler Fiorenza; *Women-Church: Theology and Practice of Feminist Liturgical Communities,* Rosemary Radford Ruether; *Mother Church, What the Experience of Women is Teaching Her,* Sally Cuneen; *Beyond Anger, On Being a Feminist in the Church,* Sr. Carolyn Osiek; *Women and Sexuality,* Lisa Sowle Cahill; *New Catholic Women: A Contemporary Challenge to Traditional Religious Authority,* Mary Jo Weaver; *Women's Spirituality: Resources for Christian Development,* Joanne Conn, ed.; *Women, Ministry and the Church,* and *Job's Daughters: Women and Power,* Sr. Joan Chittister; *Women and the Word: the Gender of God in the New Testament and Women's Spirituality* and *Beyond Patching: Faith and Feminism in the Catholic Church,* Sandra Schneiders; *Transforming Grace: Christian Tradition and Women's Experience,* Anne Carr; *Woman to Woman, An Anthology of Women's Spiritualities,* Phyllis Zagano, ed.; *They Call Her Pastor, A New Role for Catholic Women,* Ruth Wallace.

The key to understanding the deep feelings of these Catholic feminists and indeed a central theme of the Catholic feminist movement is the perceived reality of *patriarchy* in the Catholic Church. Patriarchy in society is the institutionalization of male dominance over women, that is, men hold power in the important institutions of society, with women deprived of access to such power. In the Catholic Church, patriarchy is expressed in a male hierarchy holding all decision-making and power, of jurisdiction being tied to ordination, of exclusively male language in church documents and worship and in translations of Scripture.

Today's well-educated Catholic feminist women have become acutely aware of the long history of patriarchy in the Catholic Church and increasingly demand a more meaningful participation in the life of the church and a voice in decisions that affect them. To achieve these goals some women theologians call for "women church," women coming together in worship communities to pray, to analyze the oppression they experience, and to support each other in their liberation struggle. Theologian Anne Carr explains women church as the movement of various women's groups to join together in the search for ways of being church that are open to the experience of women.

Catholic feminist Scripture scholars and theologians see evidence of patriarchy in the Bible referring to God as male; as a corrective they point out the feminine qualities attributed to God in the Hebrew Scriptures and evidenced by Jesus in the Christian Scriptures. Their concern for this exclusive male language in the Scriptures and in Catholic worship has resulted in "inclusive" language translations of the Bible and deletion of exclusive language in the Mass and the sacraments.

However, Catholic feminists realize the ultimate example of patriarchy is the exclusion of women from ministerial roles in the church, specifically the priesthood. Only ordained persons have authority and power in the church. Thus women's ordination has become the focus of Catholic feminism.

The church's position on women's ordination is expressed in the "Declaration on the Admission of Women to the Ministerial Priesthood" (Latin title, *Inter Insigniores*) issued by the Congregation for the Doctrine of the Faith in 1977.[45] In carefully chosen language, the Declaration states "the Church, in fidelity to the example of the Lord, does not consider herself authorized to admit women to priestly ordination." This conviction is based on church practice, "an unbroken tradition throughout the history of the Church, universal in the East and in the West," which has a "normative character." The church thus does not see itself able to change a tradition going back to its origins. The document also offered supporting arguments from what is fitting (*ex convenientia*): "Jesus did not call any woman to be part of the Twelve"; the priest should image the male Christ since "in the exercise of his ministry . . . [he] represents Christ who acts through him"; priesthood is not a personal right nor does baptism confer a "personal title to public ministry in the Church."

---

45. "Vatican Declaration: Women in the Ministerial Priesthood," *Origins* 6, No. 33 (Feb. 3, 1977): 517-24 plus commentary 524-531.

Those who favor women's ordination do not see the force of these arguments: the emphasis on Jesus' priesthood is not his maleness but his common humanity; church tradition is not absolute and can be changed — in fact, there appears to be evidence of women having been ordained to the order of deacon; the International Biblical Commission mandated by Pope Paul VI to consider this question reported that there is nothing conclusive for or against women's ordination in the Christian Scriptures; Jesus would not have chosen women to be priests since Jewish society of Jesus' day would not have accepted women Apostle-priests. Advocates of women's ordination quote St. Paul's striking statement: "In Christ Jesus there is neither Jew nor Gentile, slave or free, male or female . . ." (Galatians 4:28) to show that serving Christ in the church transcends gender. They argue from experience that women have gifts and charisms to priestly ministry that would greatly enrich the church. Finally, women argue that their baptism into the Body of Christ gives them a legitimate right to serve the church as priests.

In a May 22, 1994 apostolic letter to all bishops of the Catholic Church titled "Priestly Ordination Reserved to Men Alone,"[46] Pope John Paul II sought to settle the question of women's ordination.

> Wherefore, in order that all doubt may be removed regarding a matter of great importance, a matter which pertains to the Church's divine constitution itself, in virtue of my ministry of confirming the brethren (cf. Lk 22:32) I declare that the Church has no authority whatsoever to confer priestly ordination on women and that this judgment is to be definitively held by all the Church's faithful.

The Holy Father clearly intends to close debate on priestly ordination for women and to rule out its possibility for the future. He stresses that this is not a matter of church discipline only but of doctrine concerning the nature of priesthood. Though not an infallible statement (despite language

---

46. See *Origins* 24 (June 9,1994): 50-58 for text of John Paul II's "Apostolic Letter on Ordination and Women," an interpretative text by the Vatican and comments by Americans Archbishop Keeler, Bishop Matthiesen, Cardinal Law, Archbishops Weakland and Buechlein, Cardinal Bernardin, and Bishop Hamelin, president of the Canadian Conference of Catholic Bishops. Archbishop Weakland's reflections are particularly thought-provoking in their pastoral sensitivity, frankness, and the theological questions they raise. He said "As a bishop I will have to ponder what the phrase 'this judgment is to be held definitively' means in terms of its demands on the faithful." In terms of "the pastoral problems I now will face in my archdiocese," he asks what effects this declaration will have on four groups: l. "so many women and men, especially younger women and vowed religious who still see this question as one of justice and equality"; 2. "on theologians who are still concerned about the theological underpinnings of the pope's teachings"; 3. "on those men and women for whom the issue of the way in which the church exercises its authority is already a problem"; 4. "on ecumenical dialogue . . . will this declaration mean that full communion is ruled out with all except the Orthodox churches . . . [which] may agree with the pope . . . but are usually shocked when the pope teaches the bishops and does not speak in union with them."

like "to be definitively held" and "in virtue of my ministry. . ."), it is meant to be a serious exercise of "the ordinary papal magisterium in a definitive way," according to a Vatican text on the pope's letter, and thus asks for an assent of faith by Catholics.

Recognizing that the concerns of Catholic women will not go away but are likely to become a source of greater tension, the United States bishops at their November 1994 meeting voted 228-10 to approve a remarkable statement "Toward Strengthening the Bonds of Peace, A Reflection on Women in the Church occasioned by Pope John Paul's Letter on Priestly Ordination."[47] It is a positive document aimed at addressing the concerns of American Catholic women and at utilizing their gifts to the fullest, short of priestly ordination. In stating that "we need to look at alternative ways in which women can exercise leadership in the church," the bishops pledged to "commit ourselves to enhancing the participation of women in every possible aspect of church life." They encouraged women "to pursue studies in Scripture, theology and canon law . . . that the church may benefit from their skills in these areas." In calling on the all-male leadership to reject authoritarian conduct, to use gender-neutral language in religious education materials and to guard against sexism in church teaching and practice, the bishops stated "We commit ourselves to make sure that our words and actions express our belief in the equality of all women and men."

The American bishops irenic statement is timely. Retired Bishop William McManus had warned: "Fewer and fewer women, I fear, will listen to a Church in which women have only a muted voice at the highest levels of decision-making. The Church is going to be heard most by those to whom it has listened." Milwaukee's Archbishop Weakland observed that "the Church's voice in society is muted by its inability to integrate women totally into its own life. Its preaching of the gospel will remain wounded . . . ."[48] A recent study by priest-sociologist Andrew Greeley indicated that over a million Catholic women have left the church in the United States over this issue. Psychologist Eugene Kennedy in a Feb. 4, 1985 *Time* magazine article had stated that "the major issue facing the Catholic Church in the U.S. is how it deals with women."

What can be done? A promising step is the bishops' call for a worldwide dialogue on women's "leadership in the church, equality of women and men and diversity of gifts." Such open discussion involving women themselves may at this period in the church best reflect the guidance of the Holy Spirit and discover God's will for the church.

---

47. "Strengthening the Bonds of Peace," *Origins* 24 (Dec. 1, 1994): 417-22.
48. Weakland, *Faith and the Human Enterprise*, 159.

The Current Slow Pace of Ecumenism

Despite impressive collaboration between churches and among individual Christians, despite the truly remarkable theological agreements achieved, and despite the warm relations and prayer that exist between various church leaders and members, the Christian churches remain far from achieving unity. There exists a discouragement, a frustration, a decreasing lack of enthusiasm, even a cynicism among those committed to ecumenism. Many fear that the *kairos* "moment of grace" after the Council has passed the churches by.

The current slow pace toward the Council's goal of "restoration of unity,"[49] especially between the Roman Catholic, Orthodox, Anglican and at least some mainline Protestant churches, is the source of considerable disappointment among both ecumenical theologians and Catholics deeply committed to overcoming the scandal of disunity.

There are, however, reasons to be hopeful: the strong commitment of the Holy Father John Paul II to ecumenism as manifested in his many inspiring statements and ecumenical gestures, the monumental activity of ecumenical theologians in the theological dialogues and the untiring work of the Pontifical Council for Promoting Christian Unity and its most recent document mandating a high priority for ecumenism,[50] the activity of diocesan ecumenical commissions, and of countless bishops, priests and Catholic laity.

Yet skepticism remains. The theological dialogues with Anglicans and Lutherans have already revealed substantial *faith* agreement on baptism, Eucharist and ordained ministry, though different theological explanations of that faith exist. Yet the Congregation for the Doctrine of the Faith, as evident from its 1991 response to the Final Report of the Anglican-Roman Catholic International Commission (ARCIC I), appears to demand almost total *theological* agreement expressed in Catholic terminology.[51] Some contend that with each theological agreement reached in the

---

49. Yet in fairness to the Council bishops, their *Decree on Ecumenism,* being such an unexpected break with the past by introducing new ecclesiological principles, could hardly resolve all the questions and possibilities the decree opened for the church.

50. *Directory for the Application of the Principles and Norms of Ecumenism* by Pontifical Council for Promoting Christian Unity (Boston: St. Paul Books & Media, 1993).

51. CDF waited 10 years to make its response to ARCIC I's Final Report. Its judgment is that "important differences regarding essential matters of Catholic doctrine" still remain so that "it is not yet possible to state that substantial agreement has been reached." Anglican Archbishop George Carey of Canterbury went to the heart of the issue when he noted: "Both communions were asked the same question: Are the agreements in the Final Report consonant with the *faith* of the RCC/Anglican Communion?" whereas the Vatican appeared to understand the question as asking: "Is the Final Report *identical* with the *teachings* of the Roman Catholic Church?" that is, the theological formulations rather than faith. (Emphasis added) See "Vatican Responds to ARCIC I Report," *Origins* 21 (Dec. 19, 1991): 441-47. The CDF response was criticized by Catholic commentators as misunderstanding both the dialogue process and specific statements and as misrepresenting some of the agreement language.

dialogues between the churches, the CDF "ups the ante," demanding even more agreement than actually exists among Catholics themselves. Thus, despite the language of communion as a model for future ecclesial unity, to many CDF appears to hold a "submit and return" to the Catholic Church as its model of union.

Other situations creating skepticism are the Catholic Church's inability to recognize the ordinations and ministries of at least Anglican and Lutheran churches and the church's negative position on eucharistic sharing or "intercommunion" as a *means* of fostering church union. In its directory on ecumenism issued shortly after Vatican II and reaffirmed in the 1993 revised Directory,[52] priority is given to the Eucharist as a *sign* of church unity which does not yet exist, thus limiting eucharistic sharing as a *means* of achieving unity to a few extraordinary cases under four conditions. In effect, this prohibits Protestants from sharing Catholic Eucharists. For their part, Catholics may not receive Protestant eucharists judged to be invalid, owing to the lack of the sacrament of orders and validly ordained ministers.

Another disheartening factor was Cardinal Ratzinger's negative appraisal of *Unity of the Churches, an Actual Possibility,* co-authored by theologians Karl Rahner and Heinrich Fries, who asked "whether a unity of faith and church could be achieved in the foreseeable future among the large Christian churches?" Their answer was affirmative if eight conditions were met, "which seem to us to be realizable in a relatively short time, if one perceives that this unity is such a radical obligation coming from Jesus that one has the courage to postpone a number of rather significant scruples."[53] Their conditions were formulated in eight theses, the first of which stated "The fundamental truths of Christianity, as they are expressed in Holy Scripture, in the Apostles' Creed, and in that of Nicaea and Constantinople are binding on all partner churches of the one Church to be," a condition already accepted by a large number of Christian churches.

In a recent interview, Rembert Weakland, chairperson of the U.S. Bishops' Committee on Ecumenical and Interreligious Affairs, admitted there is "every human reason for discouragment," but gave wise and hopeful counsel: "all of us, not just Roman Catholics, must continually remind ourselves that the [ecumenical] movement is not a human endeavor we can program. It is really a response to the Holy Spirit. The present slowdown is a graced opportunity for a deeper assessment. Where is the Spirit leading us and how are we responding?"[54]

---

52. *Directory for Application. . . of Ecumenism*, No.'s 129-132.
53. H. Fries and Karl Rahner, *Unity of the Churches, An Actual Possibility* (Philadelphia: Fortress Press and New York/Ramsey: Paulist Press, 1985), 7.
54. James Torrens, "Ecumenism, Slowing or Steady?" *America* 172 (Jan. 14, 1995): 13.

Polarization and Catholic Fundamentalism

Archbishop Rembert Weakland of Milwaukee, in an introduction to a book of essays on Vatican II and the church after the Council, describes the present painful situation of polarization in the Catholic Church:

> I have to admit that polarization is much more common than the willingness to work toward a common solution. Part of that polarization has come about through a return to a pre-Vatican Council II concept of a perfect Church, some claiming to already possess that Church or at least wanting to restore it. All of the humility [of the Council] in the approach to the world seems to be gone, and it is rare today that one hears anyone in authority talk, as Pope John XXIII did, of a Church that was constantly in need of reform.
>
> Polarization simply means that people no longer dialogue. . . . Polarization also leads to a certain amount of bitterness and can induce much rash judgment. . . . The whole Catholic tradition of both/and almost always ends up being either/or. That polarization makes life within the Church not only difficult, but at times almost totally unbearable . . . it leads only to discouragement and apathy. Loyalty and disloyalty become the politicized terms used . . .[55]

An ongoing source of tension today is this polarization between traditionalists and progressives in the Catholic Church. Both groups care deeply about the church but have different ecclesiologies and perceptions of what is best for the church in today's world. Both groups are needed in the church: traditionalists to preserve values, ideas and practices and the community's historical heritage; progressives to challenge the church to make necessary changes and meet contemporary needs. If the church is to be an attractive, credible sacrament of Christ's love and unity to the world today, Catholics will need to overcome as far as possible the negative aspects of this polarization.

A more extreme form of polarization that painfully wounds the church and causes great harm to Catholic unity is the contemporary phenomenon of Catholic fundamentalism. As one of the most divisive forces in the United States Catholic Church, it needs to be understood better. We are indebted to Patrick Arnold's analysis "The Rise of Catholic Fundamentalism."[56]

He terms Catholic **fundamentalism** "a religious disease that focusses on nonessential matters in Catholic belief." He describes it as "a product of cultural convulsion and always religiously divisive" which stresses

---

55. Rembert Weakland, "Introduction" in Pierre Hegy, ed., *The Church in the Nineties, Its Legacy, Its Future* (Collegeville, MN: Liturgical Press, 1993), xxii-xxiii.

56. Frank Arnold, "The Rise of Catholic Fundamentalism," *America* 156 (April 11, 1987): 297-302.

authority, is "obsessed with questions of individual salvation and sexual morality" and is made up of "frightened and hurt people who need healing like the rest of us."

Arnold lists five unhealthy characteristics of fundamentalism in all religions, making application to contemporary Catholic fundamentalism.

◆

Five Unhealthy Characteristics of Fundamentalism

1. "Fundamentalism is a reactionary movement that develops within cultures experiencing social crisis." Many Catholic fundamentalists insist the church has fallen prey to secular humanism, Marxism and atheism.

2. Fundamentalists' "fear and rage are directed, not primarily at the actual agents of secularization . . . but mainly at co-religionists." Targets of Catholic fundamentalist criticism and letter-writing to Rome, according to Arnold, have been "liberal" Seattle Archbishop Hunthausen, and Archbishop Rembert Weakland of Milwaukee, "disloyal" theologians who have dared dissent from papal teaching, and nuns who are involved in social justice causes and fail to wear their religious garb.

3. Fundamentalists tend to be captive to the "myth of the Golden Age" in an imaginary past.

   > Catholic fundamentalists seem content with a church that achieved its final, immutable form in the glorious decade before Vatican II. Supported by eternal truths formulated in the thought of Thomas Aquinas, confirmed in the unmistakable moral certitudes of the Baltimore catechism . . . this nostalgic church presents an alluring alternative to the blandness of contemporary Catholicism.

4. "Fundamentalists insist upon the absolute, infallible, inerrant and unambiguous authority of official religious texts." In the case of Catholic fundamentalists, Arnold indicates that this type of authority is not to be found in Scripture but in the official statements of the Roman magisterium, which is to be obeyed absolutely. However, the Catholic fundamentalist is selective: church teachings on "authority or sexual morality are given enormous weight," whereas church teaching on social questions such as poverty, a just wage, human rights, nuclear disarmament are often "dismissed as 'interference with politics.'"

5. "Fundamentalists in the 1980s are usually closely allied with right-wing or repressive political regimes in the hope of advancing theocratic principles." Catholic fundamentalists tended to side with U.S. policy financing Latin American military dictators because they were "fighting godless Communism," and tended to attack "liberals" who championed social justice, human rights, and liberation theology.

◆

Arnold's final critique of Catholic fundamentalism is "what it fails to discuss, promote, or preach."

> Neo-orthodox tracts rarely mention Jesus Christ or the kind of moral issues that evidently most concerned him: greed, religious hypocrisy or misuse of authority. For all their outcry against secularism, their writings are largely bereft of any spirituality. . . .

A significant example of Catholic fundamentalism in the United States is the phenomenon of Catholics United for the Faith (CUF). The founding statement of CUF proclaims: "We exist in order to be a rallying point, a point of unity, for the multitude of Catholics who have felt bewildered and blown about by the 1000 winds of false doctrine being constantly puffed out by a 1000 counterfeit teachers." We follow the analysis of Timothy Iglesias.[57]

Born in Washington, D.C., in 1968 to counteract the dissent by Catholic moral theologians against Pope Paul VI's encyclical *Of Human Life*, CUF is a financially influential group of 20,000 Catholics worldwide who profess total loyalty to the pope and the magisterium and who permit little or no pluralism or diversity within the church. Its obsession with orthodoxy is summarized in two words: truth and authority. Truth can be known with complete clarity and can be defined as such by proper authorities. Any concept of "loyal dissent" is totally rejected.

> CUF maintains that "dissent" and the questions raised by "dissenters" do not arise from intellectual rigor, ambiguity in key texts, sincerity, openness to one's experience or the struggle to evangelize faithfully in a wayward culture, but rather from a disordered mind or a disordered will. . . . CUF considers assent to *Humanae Vitae* to be a unique litmus test of one's orthodoxy and, thus, of belonging to the Church at all.

Regarding Vatican II, CUF accepts a conservative interpretation of the Council. "CUF's view of the renewal called for by Vatican II stresses an inner, personal and moral renewal . . . almost to an exclusion of an updating of the church in the modern world." Its ecclesiology or understanding of the church has set it in conflict with theologians, catechists, and bishops.

But it is CUF's tactics that have caused bitter division in the church and injury and injustice to good persons. CUF, along with *The Wanderer* newspaper,[58] wages letter-writing campaigns to curial officials in Rome

---

57. M. Timothy Iglesias, "CUF and Dissent, A Case Study in Religious Conservatism," *America* 156 (April 11, 1987): 303-07. A subhead reads: "Formed in reaction to a crisis of authority in the church, this international Catholic lay apostolate is neither as wicked and dangerous as some critics assume nor the angel of light it purports to be."

58. Typical of Catholic fundamentalists, CUF members, and *The Wanderer* readers, is the lead editorial by the paper's editor, A.J. Matt, Jr., urging a letter writing campaign to Rome on the occasion of the U.S. bishops' *ad limina* visit to the pope in 1988. He suggests areas to report on:

that have influenced the Vatican's investigation and subsequent disciplining of Seattle's Archbishop Hunthausen, in banning the popular catechism *Christ Among Us*, even though it had an *imprimatur* of many years' standing, and in CDF relieving Fr. Charles Curran of his teaching post at the Catholic University of America in Washington, D.C. CUF is perceived as maintaining a list of theologians and priests and even bishops that it suspects of "abuses" or unorthodoxy or disloyalty to the Holy See.

Iglesias concludes with an important distinction. Catholic *conservatism*, the "philosophy that values established, traditional ideas and practices, and seeks to preserve a given community's historical heritage," is a necessity in the modern church, provided it can "discern properly those aspects of the Tradition that are truly essential and those that are merely time-bound, antiquated relics."[59] Catholic *fundamentalism*, however, fails to do this and seriously harms and divides the church and severely impedes the genuine Vatican II renewal.

We close this topic of polarization in the Catholic Church today with an apt statement from an editorial in the *National Catholic Reporter*.

> A healthy Church generates charity. It exhibits concern, support, encouragement. It invites, embraces and forgives. An unhealthy Church generates division. It exhibits righteous judgment, arrogance, discouragement. It rejects, excludes, demeans.[60]

Relations with the Vatican[61]

A high-ranking bishop recently spoke of a delicate reality in the American Catholic Church and elsewhere: the growing disaffection for the Apostolic See on the part of large numbers of Catholics.[62] This attitude is

---

abuses in the liturgy; sound orthodox teaching in priests' homilies; solidly orthodox religious education or modernist opinion; public statements and policies of your bishop, etc. He gives five guidelines for reporting to Rome: 1. identify yourself and your diocese and bishop by name; 2. limit your comments to a few issues; 3. identify individuals by name, title, parish; 4. include supporting documentation; 5. type your report. A.J. Matt, Jr., "The State of the Church," *The Wanderer* 121 (Mar. 10, 1988). Matt apparently did not trust the U.S. bishops to give an accurate portrayal of the state of Catholicism in their dioceses!

59. Arnold, "Rise of Fundamentalism," 298.

60. Editorial, "Let Pope field Wanderer blooper," *National Catholic Reporter* (March 18, 1988).

61. In the strict sense the name "Vatican" refers to the geographic political city-state centered in Rome; however, we often use the term in its popular sense when the meaning intended is the Apostolic See that embraces the office of Peter and the curial congregations.

62. "As I travel around the country, I find a growing disaffection from Rome. . . . It takes on two forms. At times it is rather just an expression of indifference to what Rome says. People just do not find that it matters much to them. I find this attitude very pronounced in the academic circles but am always surprised to find it elsewhere as well at all cultural levels. In addition to this indifference, there is also a second group that shows much anger and some degree of animosity toward Rome. Such negativism toward any authority in any organization, if prolonged over a long period of time, is not healthy and should be worrisome. The Protestant Reformation would never

shown by increasing indifference to curial and even papal judgments and statements and anger at various policies. Honest recognition of this fact in today's church demand we treat this unfortunate reality with sympathetic frankness.

Examples of this disaffection are many. A recent poll indicated growing disagreement between the laity and church leaders on ethical issues, especially birth control, and a strong desire for more democratic procedures in the Catholic Church.[63] Many Catholics feel the official church is not listening to them and feel helpless in decisions over which they have no control. Especially alienated groups are women, gay persons, divorced and remarried, single parents. The people of Seattle, as well as knowledgeable Catholics, theologians, and others elsewhere were appalled and angered at CDF's treatment of Seattle's Archbishop Raymond Hunthausen.[64] (See section on collegiality earlier in this chapter.) The Vatican refusal to discuss urgent issues like a married priesthood and the equality of women in the church, including ordination, add to the loss of credibility by the Vatican among many contemporary Catholics. The Curia's recent rescinding of the gender-inclusive translation of the *New Revised Standard Version* of the Bible for liturgical and catechetical texts in Canada and the United States (see NCCB under "Collegiality" in this chapter) has caused considerable resentment. The executive board of the Catholic Biblical Association called the curial action "demeaning . . . treatment of the American hierarchy."[65]

A special situation causing tension is the perceived negative judgments about the American Catholic Church by the Vatican. A two-fold

---

have been possible if there had not been a separation of affection from Rome on the part of clergy and laity long before the event that broke the ties." Archbishop Rembert Weakland. "Inside NCR," *National Catholic Reporter* 31 (November 4, 1994): 2.

63. Reported in William D'Antonio, ed., *American Catholic Laity in a Changing Church* (Kansas City, MO: Sheed and Ward, 1989).

64. Archbishop Hunthausen's own statement on his meeting in Rome, Dec. 3, 1988, with Cardinals Ratzinger and Gantin. "The Apostolic visitation conducted by his Eminence James Cardinal Hickey . . . and its long aftermath, the appointment of Bishop Wuerl as auxiliary bishop with special faculties, and the appointment of Cardinal Bernardin, Cardinal O'Connor and Archbishop Quinn to serve as special apostolic commission have all combined to create a time of pain and severe tension for ourselves and the archdiocese of Seattle. . . . I regret that other ways were not found to address the issues of concern." From Dec. 7, 1988 News Release of the Catholic Archdiocese of Seattle.

65. "We are deeply concerned about the implications of this [Vatican] approach to something that impinges so directly on the pastoral efforts made by the American hierarchy. . . . Furthermore we consider demeaning the treatment of the American hierarchy in this matter. . . ." The board listed various grievances: "that no explanation was given for the action; that the action suggests that the U.S. bishops 'are not able to determine what is doctrinally sound and pastorally appropriate'; and that the 'action would nullify the collegiality and principle of subsidiarity guaranteed by Vatican II.'" "Catholics want solidarity with their bishops," *National Catholic Reporter* 30 (Nov. 11, 1994): 24.

cause is the Curia's apparent inability to understand and appreciate the American democratic way of life and the negative stream of letters from right-wing Catholic groups to curial officials about "aberrations" of the church in the United States.[66] During the 1989 meetings of a group of U.S. archbishops with curial officials to discuss the state of the church in the United States, Archbishop May of St. Louis explained American culture: "The United States is pluralistic; it enjoys total religious liberty; organized religion abounds in America; there is full freedom of thought, and the spirit of democracy runs strong." He indicated that authoritarianism is suspect in any area of learning and culture, and many Americans "consider the divine right of bishops as outmoded as the divine right of kings."[67] Pope John Paul II, who attended most of the meetings, admitted he had received wrong information about the American church.

Priests and even bishops have misgivings. Many priests disagree with the church's position on contraception in marriage and believe the church is not addressing the increasing problem of shortage of priests and declining vocations. Bishops, "unable to discuss openly the issues that most concern them or to make suggestions . . . are often reduced to placing on their agenda topics that will not get them into trouble with Rome. They must also spend their energies in damage control of offensive Roman statements sent to them by CDF justifying in certain cases discrimination on the basis of sexual orientation."[68]

This disaffection obviously is not a healthy situation and is a cause of sadness for all who love the church. Yet honesty and concern for the good of the church demand that substantive issues be honestly and respectfully raised.

What are the causes of this situation? Many knowledgable Catholics believe the underlying cause is the perceived attempt to centralize authority and power at the expense of local churches and their bishops and of the collegiality championed by Vatican II. As we have seen, the name for this attempt is the *restoration,* that complex effort to restore discipline throughout the church, especially over dissenting theologians; to insist on uniformity over unity-in-diversity, and to achieve absolute clarity of doctrine and teaching; and in some countries to restore an "integralist" philosophy in

---

66. In the News Release, Archbishop Hunthausen refers to such a group in the Seattle archdiocese. ". . . sad experience tells us that there will be continued mean-spirited criticism from a small cadre of people of anything and everything we do . . . they seem bent on undoing the fabric of unity that exists among sincere and conscientious believers within the Body of Christ. In our judgement their criticisms ought not to be given serious attention [by Rome] — certainly not without careful inquiry of the diocesan Bishop. Failure to do this can only help to erode the authority of the Bishop and the credibility of the Church's Magisterium."

67. Quoted by Thomas Reese. "Discussions in Rome," *America* 160 (March 25, 1989): 260.

68. Thomas Rausch, "Church, Hierarchy and Churches: Popular Catholic Misconceptions," *America* 167 (Dec. 5, 1992): 446.

which the church is favored by the state with special privileges and the church in turn supports and legitimizes the state.

A dramatic example of resistance to these centralizing and restoration tendencies is the "Cologne Declaration" by 163 theologians from Germany, Austria, Switzerland and the Netherlands on January 27, 1989. They felt compelled to protest, among other things, current curial practices in appointing bishops and disciplining qualified theologians. This is their opening statement:

◆

"Cologne Declaration"

A number of events in our Catholic church compel us to make the following public declaration.

We are deeply distressed by difficulties in three specific areas:

1. The Roman Curia is aggressively pursuing a strategy of unilaterally filling vacant episcopal sees around the world, without regard for the recommendations of the local church and without respect for their established rights.

2. All over the world, many qualified theologians, men and women, are being denied ecclesiastical permission to teach. This represents a serious and dangerous interference in the free exercise of scholarly research and teaching, and in the pursuit of theological understanding through dialogue, principles which Vatican II repeatedly emphasized. The power to withhold official permission to teach is being abused; it has become an instrument to discipline theologians.

3. There have been theologically questionable attempts to assert the pope's doctrinal and jurisdictional authority in an exaggerated form.

What we observe seems to indicate the following changes in the post-conciliar Church: a creeping extension of exaggerated hierarchical control; progressive undermining of the local churches, suppression of theological debate, and reduction in the role of the laity in the church; antagonism from above which heightens conflict in the church through means of disciplinary measures.

Because of our responsibility for the Christian faith; as an exercise of our ministry as teachers of theology; for the sake of our own consciences; and in solidarity with all Christian women and men who are scandalized by the latest developments in our church, or even despair of it, we cannot remain silent but consider this declaration a necessity.[69]

◆

---

69. "The Cologne Declaration" *Commonweal* 116 (Feb. 24, 1989): 102.

It is important in this unfortunate situation in the contemporary Catholic Church to keep perspective. In the long and complex history of the church there has always been tension between the papacy and individual countries, between the center and the periphery. In fact, church history could be read from the viewpoint of the papacy struggling for power and control in both the temporal and spiritual realms. Today, the issue is not one of legitimate papal authority, for this is not questioned, but of the best *exercise* of papal and curial authority, for the gospel of Christ and the kingdom of God. In the intense, often emotional debate on the best exercise of authority, it is essential to recognize the competency and love of the church by all involved. Cardinal Ratzinger, an excellent theologian, is convinced his approach as watchdog of orthodoxy is best for the church. The Holy Father, John Paul II, is highly intelligent, deeply spiritual, and totally committed to the church and to his office; he is following a policy he is convinced is necessary and good for the church today. Theologians are competent professionals firmly committed to serve the best interests of the church as they perceive them. Catholic laypersons are aware that the Spirit guides them to discern what is the essential faith of the church. For all, the Catholic presumption is to trust the Spirit's guidance of church leaders, especially the Holy Father. Perhaps today church leaders, theologians and faithful alike need in humility to admit they do not have all the answers.

A Concluding Reflection

These eight areas of unresolved issues and of tension and division in today's Catholic Church should be seen in the context of the Second Vatican Council: its emphasis on the church as *all the baptized,* including women, rather than the hierarchy alone, on the importance of the *local church and its bishop* as successor of the Apostles, on the pervasive principles of *collegiality* and **subsidiarity** that have influenced the relationship of local churches to the pope and curia. The Council's emphasis on our common baptism, on Jesus' prayer for unity so as to evangelize the world, and on the Spirit bringing salvation through other Christian churches has given urgency to Christian *ecumenism.* The Council's stress on religious freedom, on the primacy of one's conscience and on the Spirit guiding individual Christians made *dissent* possible and even necessary. The Council's fuller understanding of church history, of how teaching of doctrine develops and of the manner in which the church's magisterium operates has highlighted the important work of *theologians.* Thus dissent and a certain disaffection need not mean disloyalty; rather both often proceed from a deep concern and profound love for the church. As St. Augustine reminds us: "In essentials unity, in nonessentials freedom, but in all things charity."

Despite these real and painful tensions and divisions in the contemporary Catholic Church, it is both encouraging and important for a balanced understanding and appreciation of today's church to reflect on the many rich *values* and gifts the Vatican II Catholic Church offers its members and the world today. This forms the subject of our next chapter.

Summary

An ecumenical council such as Vatican II is the beginning of a long process whose work necessarily remains incomplete. On the one hand the Council or Pope Paul VI chose not to tackle or resolve certain issues; on the other such new theological principles and insights needed time to be absorbed and translated into the practical life of the church. Yet leaving important issues unresolved or ambiguous both during and after the Council has resulted in unfortunate tensions and divisions within the church, impeding the church's renewal and disappointing expectations raised by the Council. We considered eight such issues and areas of church life. Concern and love for the church demand they be acknowledged and addressed.

For Discussion

1. Discuss the pros and cons for a married priesthood in the Catholic Church. Consider the values of celibacy. Would permitting priests to marry solve the problem of priest shortage?

2. What is the ideal exercise of authority by the pope today? by bishops? Should *public* dissent by Catholic theologians be permitted today?

3. Is the slow pace of ecumenism today partially owing to the Catholic Church? Why or why not?

4. Do you think women should be ordained in the Catholic Church today? Why? Why not?

5. Is Catholic disaffection with the Vatican overstated? What is your attitude toward the Vatican? your knowledge of the Vatican?

6. Do you think the present divisions and tensions are seriously harmful to the Catholic Church today? What do you think *needs* to be done? *can* be done?

For Action

1. Research the Archbishop Hunthausen case. What were the issues? Did the Congregation for the Doctrine of the Faith handle this situation wisely and justly?

2. When did obligatory celibacy for priests begin in the Catholic Church? What were the reasons for it?

3. Research the papal commission of Paul VI on contraceptive use in marriage and the reaction to the publication *Of Human Life* by national conferences of bishops, by moral theologians, and by married Catholics.

4. Research the removal of Fr. Charles Curran from his teaching post at the Catholic University of America in Washington, D.C.

Further Reading

Arbuckle, Gerald. *Refounding the Church, Dissent for Leadership.* Maryknoll, NY: Orbis Press, 1993.

Bacik, James. *Tensions in the Church, Facing the Challenges, Seizing the Opportunities.* Kansas City: Sheed & Ward, 1993.

Dunn, Joseph. *The Rest of Us Catholics: The Loyal Opposition.* Springfield, IL: Templegate Publishers, 1994.

Kaufman, Philip. *Why You Can Disagree and Remain a Faithful Catholic.* New York: Crossroad, 1989.

Küng, Hans and Swidler, Leonard, eds. *The Church in Anguish, Has the Vatican Betrayed Vatican II?* San Francisco: Harper & Row, 1987.

Provost, J. and Wolf, Knut, eds. *Collegiality Put to the Test.* Philadelphia: Trinity Press International, 1990.

Part VI

Toward the
Third Millennium

CHAPTER 20

Values / Gifts
the Church Offers Today

Introduction

Each semester I ask my students to write down five values the Catholic Church offers its members and society as a whole. Here in no particular order is a sampling of some of their responses: a moral conscience to guide us; way to channel my faith in God; sanctuary from the world; God is alive in the church; diversity, not conformity; shows me how to love God; respect for justice; receive God's forgiveness; "somewhere" to form community; love of neighbor; to come to know and love Jesus; respect the earth we live on; its teaching on marriage; compassion; is family-oriented; it takes marriage seriously; to serve the poor; sense of belonging; the Eucharist; recognize the signs of the times; moderating influence on materialism; teaches, challenges, supports Catholics; promotes morality and personal responsibility among its members; challenges us to conversion; protects human life; reminds me that God loves me; a guide in sexual matters; a great teacher of values, and so forth. This list reveals to some degree how university students see the Catholic Church today and, though incomplete, does identify values and gifts the church in fact offers.

As the Catholic Church moves toward its third millennium, it is particularly appropriate to reflect on the extraordinary wealth of religious riches she brings to her third thousand years. After having frankly considered the unresolved issues, tensions and divisions in the contemporary church, with the consequent risk of caricaturing her actual reality, this chapter seeks to balance the picture by calling attention to the truly remarkable values and gifts the Catholic Church offers her members, other Christians and society at large today.

We have seen that the exalted vocation of the church is to be the sacrament of Christ on earth, that is, to mirror Christ himself and his gospel values to the world. As Christ is the *sacrament* or visible manifestation of God, so the church is called to manifest Christ by its life and actions to the human family. The church does this by the Christian values it continues to offer.

We have chosen those values particularly characteristic of the Catholic Church and in most cases unique to it. With the exception of the Sanctuary movement, we have omitted values characteristic of other Christian churches. Such are the Orthodox emphasis on the Holy Spirit, contemplation and sacraments; Protestants' loving reading of the Bible and their resulting biblical spirituality; the current concern for the environment and stewardship of the earth championed by the World Council of Churches; the presence of bishops in Orthodox churches and the Anglican communion, and much else.

Choosing values and limiting them to 20 is risky business! Worthy values and gifts have undoubtedly been omitted. Our goal is to highlight distinctive values with special contemporary significance. Most, it is true, are part of the rich tradition and heritage of Catholicism, though some are the direct result of the Second Vatican Council. Though many of the following topics have appeared in previous chapters, we now treat them from their aspect of unique religious values. These 20 values and gifts evidence the Spirit's presence and guidance of the Catholic Church and provide an encouraging picture of a dynamic, caring church that nourishes and serves its members and is aware of its larger responsibility to other Christians and for the world itself.

The following 20 values may conveniently be grouped under the five models or various ways of describing the nature and purpose of the church made famous by ecclesiologist Avery Dulles. (See chapter 4) This is not a rigid grouping, since some values also express other models: for example, Catholic Education also fits under "Communion"; Ecumenism and Human Rights under "Herald"; Human Life under "Service." All 20 values in various ways illustrate the church as "sacrament."

Values According to Various "Models" of Church	
As *Institution*	Vatican II (1) Petrine Ministry (2) Catholic Theology (12) *Nostra Aetate* (14)
As *Communion*	Catholic Spirituality (7) Devotions (8) Christian Ecumenism (9)
As *Sacrament*	Sacramental Life (3) Marriage in Christ (4) Integrity (19) Aesthetic Treasures (20)
As *Herald*	Religious Communities (5) Missionary Outreach (6) Social Teaching (10) Role of John Paul II (15) Human Life (17)
As *Servant*	Liberation Theology (11) Catholic Educational System (13) Human Rights (16) Refugees (18)

Twenty Values and Gifts of the Church

1. Totally Unexpected Event of Vatican II

To appreciate the great value that Vatican II is to Catholics, one has only to consider what it would be like today to attend only Latin masses, not to know and enjoy the Bible, to live in a highly triumphalist and clericalist and legalistic church, to be aloof and superior to Protestants and to risk sinning for attending a "false" Protestant service, to look down on Jews and Muslims, not to mention Hindus and Buddhists, as inferior religiously and whose salvation was extremely doubtful, to look to the pope and curia for the answer to every doctrinal, moral and disciplinary question, to be a church emphasizing law and regulations, not to trust one's own conscience in moral questions, the nonordained laity to consider themselves second-class citizens of the church, and so forth. Vatican II has given the Catholic Church an entirely new perspective!

2. The Petrine Ministry

Many Catholics hold that the greatest value in the Catholic Church is the office of Peter as rock of unity, held through two millennia by the popes. Despite the human limitations and sinfulness and in some periods of church history scandalous moral lives of individual popes, the papacy or office of Peter in the church has managed to keep intact the basic unity of the church in belief and morality, in worship and sacraments, in the members with each other through almost 2000 years, thanks to Jesus' promise to be with his church through his Spirit until the end of the world. The papacy is a Christ-given value that Catholics can never relinquish.

3. Sacramental Life

Catholicism is a sacramental, liturgical church. As community encounters with the risen Christ, as powerful sources of divine grace, often as intense religious experiences, and always as privileged moments of Catholic life, sacraments constitute an enormous value for Catholics worldwide.

The church goes to great length to provide sacraments for its members: urban parishes in virtually every country in the world offer multiple "Masses" each Sunday and at least one on weekdays; missionary priests spend hours, even days, via mule or jeep to visit isolated jungle or mountain villages to baptize infants, witness marriages, hear "confessions," and celebrate the Eucharist. Catholics themselves often make great effort to receive the sacraments. Besides the Eucharist, they especially value baptism and marriage as meaningful family events, the anointing of the sick for the peace it brings, and the sacrament of reconciliation for its healing and consoling power and the joy of forgiveness and the fresh start it gives. Sacramental practice is a unique value of Catholic life.

4. Marriage in Christ

In the increasing secularization of modern life, with its high divorce rate and loss of respect for permanent, faithful commitment in marriage, the Catholic Church provides its members and society at large a great value by witnessing the sacredness of marriage. Its theological teaching on a Christian sacramental marriage as marriage in Christ that mirrors the total self-giving and never-ending faithful love of Christ for his Christian people provides a powerful example and value to Catholic couples to love deeply, faithfully, and permanently till death. In an age of increasing promiscuity and diminishing ability to make and keep permanent commitments, the church's teaching and position on marriage constitutes a strong value for people today.

5. Religious Communities of Women and Men

The religious orders and congregations constitute an extraordinary value for the worldwide Catholic Church. They are a phenomenon unique to that church in their very existence, their ancient and modern origins, their presence in virtually every country in the world, their amazing variety, their astounding numbers, their extraordinary and heroic missionary achievements, their prodigious apostolic activities for building the kingdom of God on earth. Moreover, by their consecrated lives of poverty, chastity and obedience religious women and men witness Jesus Christ, and his gospel values, and our ultimate goal of eternal life with God in heaven to today's materialistic, pleasure and power-seeking society.

6. Extraordinary Missionary Outreach

The Catholic Church grew from a tiny band of Christians after Christ's Spirit took hold of the Apostles at Pentecost to one billion Catholics today, thanks to the heroic labors for almost 2000 years of missionaries filled with great love of God, with boundless courage and ingenuity, and with indefatigable zeal to bring Christ to the five continents.

We think of St. Paul and his strenuous journeys throughout Asia Minor to bring the Good News about Christ to the Gentiles; of St. Patrick, who converted Ireland in the 4th century and the monk, St. Augustine, who converted the warlike Anglo-Saxons in England in the 6th century; of the brothers Cyril and Methodius, who brought Christianity to the Slavs of Russia and the Ukraine in the 10th century; of Francis Xavier, the great Jesuit missionary to India and Japan, said to have baptized a half-million persons; of Mateo Ricci, scientist and astronomer in the Emperor's Court, who introduced Christianity to China in the 16th century; of the French Jesuit martyrs barbarously murdered by Iroquois and Mohawk Indians in Canada and New York State; of the intrepid Spanish and Portuguese religious order priests who evangelized the entire continent of South and Central America and Mexico and southwestern United States; of the European missionary priests who preached Christ throughout Africa in the past century.

Today, following in the footsteps of these great missionaries, priests and sisters, lay women and men, like Maryknoll missionary associates, and young women and men college graduates, like the Jesuit Volunteers, are working all over the world to bring the Christian message of love and justice to far-flung peoples. Such missionary spirit remains a treasured value of the church.

7. Rich Tradition of Catholic Spirituality

In its almost 2000-year tradition of spirituality, the Catholic Church offers its members and other Christians rich and valuable ways to approach God. Catholic spirituality is intensely personal: the awesome mystery of the triune God, the powerful Spirit active in the world and in each person, above all the very person of Jesus Christ, especially in his humanity. This personal quality is especially evident in Catholics' veneration of Jesus' mother, the Virgin Mary, and of Jesus' heroic imitators, the vast numbers of canonized saints. Catholic spirituality is nourished by the example and writings of the great saints and mystics; by a vast literature of biographies of holy women and men and treatises on spirituality; by the many types of retreats (Cursillo, Marriage Encounter, Teens Encounter Christ, and the world famous Spiritual Exercises of St. Ignatius). Both Catholics and other Christians are increasingly becoming aware of the extraordinary value found in the long tradition of Catholic spirituality.

8. Devotional Life

Over the centuries the Catholic faithful have developed a variety and richness of both individual and group religious prayers and practices, referred to as "devotions" to distinguish them from the official public worship of the church. Some devotions have become universal, like the Christmas crib fashioned by St. Francis of Assisi to make dramatically real the Christian belief in the Eternal Word taking on human flesh and being born of a human mother; others are regional, like Mexicans' and Hispanics' enthusiastic devotion to their dark-skinned Lady of Guadalupe; still others are local to cities as in Naples, Italy, where the citizens venerate the martyr St. Januarius, whose congealed blood liquefies in its vial on his feast day in September.

The most important devotions appropriately center first on Jesus Christ, then on his mother, the Virgin Mary, and on the saints. Catholics use sacred objects like the crucifix, relics of martyrs and saints, icons, holy water, statues and religious paintings and holy cards as helps to religious devotion. Properly understood and used, this wealth of popular devotions are valuable gifts that nourish the spiritual lives of Catholics and satisfy their human down-to-earth religious needs and desire for God.

9. Christian Ecumenism

Committing the Roman Catholic Church to ecumenism represents one of the most important success stories of Vatican II. The startling change from the church's negative, condemnatory approach toward other Christian churches to one of appreciation and friendship is a remarkable value both to Catholics and for our separated sisters and brothers. The resulting leadership role of the Catholic Church, particularly in the extensive theological dialogues between the churches, constitutes an enormous value in terms of mutual understanding, deepening personal friendships, and significant steps toward eventual union of the separated churches.

Some examples. Pope Paul VI and Orthodox Patriarch Athenagoras of Constantinople publicly embraced in Jerusalem and lifted the mutual excommunication of 1054 A.D.! Pope John Paul II participated in a moving prayer service at Canterbury Cathedral in England with Anglican Archbishop Runcie, during which they recommitted themselves to the full unity of both churches. American Lutheran Bishop Gormely has met with Pope John Paul II more than once. Some U.S. Catholic and Lutheran bishops make retreats together, praying for unity and sharing each others' spirituality. At the grassroots, as in the San Francisco Bay Area, the Lutheran-Anglican-Roman Catholic (LARC) clergy and lay group sponsor an annual retreat and quarterly supper theological lectures-dialogues and publish a quality newsletter.

10. Social Teaching

A slim booklet *Our Best Kept Secret, the Rich Heritage of Catholic Social Teaching* best expresses this unique value of the Catholic Church. For over 100 years, enlightened popes gradually developed a coherent teaching that proclaimed the dignity of each human person and his or her rights, and made practical applications to labor, fair wages, the gap between the rich and poor and even between rich and poor nations, and to liberal capitalism and socialism.

The popes' social teaching has resulted in the Catholic Church becoming a powerful force in the world for justice and peace and human rights and a formidable prophetic voice against injustice and crimes against human dignity. This teaching and commitment to social justice has won the admiration and respect of world leaders, intellectuals and concerned individuals, thus exercising much influence on the world stage. As such it has contributed to bettering the human family.

11. Liberation Theology

Misunderstood by many and condemned as Marxist by others, the new theology that burst on the world from Latin America just 25 years ago has become a most significant development within Catholicism today. Liberation theology has influenced Catholics — bishops, priests and religious, and laypersons — throughout the world, conscientizing them to the terrible centuries-long suffering and injustice in Latin America. It has given Christian hope to millions of indigenous peoples living in hopeless situations, creating in them a sense of solidarity and caring Christian love and inspiring countless acts of extraordinary courage and heroism. Liberation theology has thus awakened the slumbering Latin American church and made it a dynamic, esteemed, much-loved presence and force in the lives of the poor. Liberation theology is thus a dramatic, far-reaching value in the life of the church today.

12. *"Catholic Theology, Ever Old and Constantly New"*

A significant value for the Catholic Church and for other Christian churches as well is the rich theological tradition from St. Paul, St. Augustine, Cyprian, Athanasius, St. Anselm, Peter Lombard, St. Thomas Aquinas, Cardinal John Henry Newman to the modern theological giants: Protestants Paul Tillich and Karl Barth and Catholics Yves Congar, Karl Rahner, Edward Schillebeekx, Hans Urs von Balthasar, Avery Dulles and in moral theology Bernard Häring, Richard McCormick, Charles Curran.

The Second Vatican Council, in following a new direction in theology, has provided a unique value for the contemporary Catholic Church. The church has discovered a new freedom to challenge past rigidly held positions and to adapt ones more in keeping with human values and the needs of the modern world. The church can more easily acknowledge past inadequate theologizing, thus gaining credibility among educated Catholics and other Christians alike. The church is now in possession of theological principles to overcome the tragic divisions in Christianity and to restore unity among the separated Christian churches. The Catholic Church can thus move confidently into the 21st century more able to confront crucial issues within the church and to become a truly "catholic" or world church.

13. *Educational System*

A truly remarkable value of the Catholic Church has been its educational apostolate. The vast network of Catholic schools in the United States — elementary, secondary, college and university — is unmatched anywhere in the Catholic world. In 1991, 9,173 Catholic schools educated 3,278,894 students according to this breakdown: 7,517 elementary schools, 1,988,497 students; 1,421 high schools, 640,083 students; 235 colleges and universities, 650,314 students. In Latin America the system of *Fe y Allegria* (faith and happiness) schools educate 350,000 very poor young people who cannot afford the traditional Catholic schools. These schools are staffed by 12,000 teachers, with 150 different religious communities of sisters and priests being involved.

U.S. Catholic universities and colleges — after a period of acute financial struggle and an identity crisis as to what it meant to be a Catholic institution of higher education — have become outstanding educational institutions. The University of Notre Dame of South Bend, Indiana, comes immediately to mind. The Society of Jesus (Jesuits) operate the largest network of universities and colleges, 27 in all, in the United States, of which the most prestigious are Georgetown University, Fordham University in New York, Boston College, Marquette University in Milwaukee, Loyola University of Chicago, St. Louis University, and Creighton University in Omaha. The last three mentioned have quality medical schools. These institutions have formulated a strong Catholic identity and commitment, while at the same time promoting academic autonomy in the pursuit of truth and excellence. They respect pluralism of religious belief and value a diverse religious and ethnic student body.

Considering the financial difficulties facing private education, the Catholic educational system in the United States today must be counted as one of the most unique and dramatic values of the Catholic Church in the contemporary world.

14. New Appreciation of the Great World Religions

Vatican II's breakthrough document, *Declaration on the Relation of the Church to non-Christian Religions (Nostra Aetate)*, has proved to be an unexpected value in many ways. In taking a positive view toward Buddhism, Hinduism, Islam and Judaism and in recognizing that these ancient religions are in God's providence a way of salvation for millions of people in the human family, the church corrected a too narrow theology of God's salvific will for all peoples.

The Council urged Catholics to "acknowledge, preserve and encourage the spiritual and moral truths found among non-Christians," as well as "their social life and culture." It encouraged Catholics to enter "into discussion and collaboration with members of other religions" (NA 2). Presently the Catholic Church is engaged in serious theological dialogues with Buddhist, Hindu, Muslim and Jewish religious leaders and scholars. That these religions of the world respect and live in harmony with each other is critical for world peace today.

Moreover, it is important that Catholics as a small minority religion in the mid-East and Asia understand and appreciate their co-religionists and develop a theology of collaboration rather than proselytism. This is a demanding theological task for, as the Declaration cautions, the church ". . . is in duty bound . . . to proclaim . . . Christ who is the way, the truth and the life. In him . . . men find the fullness of their religious life" (NA 2). This reminder raises theological questions about Christ's role in salvation and the proper missionary outreach of the church.

Another distinctive value is the special section of the declaration devoted to the Jewish religion. It is responsible for the close relationships that have developed since the Council between Jews and Christians. The Council bishops took several strong positions:

* The Christian claim that Christ as Messiah "fulfills" the Old Testament does not imply the rejection of Israel by God. "God does not take back the gifts he bestowed or the choice he made," referring to his special covenant with the Jewish people (NA 4). So today it is more appropriate to refer to the Hebrew and Christian Scriptures than to the Old and New Testaments, as though the latter supplanted the former.

- Christians may not hold the Jewish people responsible for the death of Christ. This is very important since the taunt of "Christ-killer" accounted for Christians persecuting Jews through the centuries.

- The Council takes a strong stand against anti-Semitism: "She deplores all hatreds, persecutions, displays of anti-Semitism leveled at any time or from any source against the Jews" (NA 4).

- Finally, the bishops strongly condemn discrimination. "The Church reproves . . . any discrimination against people or any harassment on the basis of their race, color, condition in life or religion" (NA 5).

This declaration has assumed even greater importance today in the light of rising anti-Semitism in the United States and Europe, of anti-Arab feeling and the rise of Islamic fundamentalism, and of Hindu intolerance to other religions in India. As evidencing a new spirit in Catholicism, this brief document of Vatican II is of enormous value for Catholics, for other Christians, and for the human family itself.

15. Worldwide Role of Pope John Paul II

No other human leader today enjoys such respect as spokesperson for moral and religious values or receives so much media attention worldwide. John Paul II has become a powerful force for the poor of the world, for justice and human rights, and for peace through his encyclical letters and his many speeches in Rome and throughout the world. As head of both Vatican City and the worldwide Catholic Church, he receives world leaders for talks on world peace, justice, concern for poor nations, and the rights of the church. In his pastoral visits to over 100 nations, he has reached a worldwide audience of millions, especially in his Masses attended by vast crowds. His Mass celebrated in Manila in January 1995, for example, was attended by a throng estimated at over three million people. These pastoral visits make vivid in peoples' minds that the pope is in fact a Holy Father and visible symbol of unity for one billion Catholics. In his role as spiritual leader, he has often spoken and acted for Christian unity, as when he visited Canterbury Cathedral in England and prayed with the Anglican Archbishop for the union of these two great religious communions. To promote the broader ecumenism, John Paul II invited the leaders of the great world religions to Assisi in Italy, the birthplace of the gentle St. Francis, for a day of prayer for mutual understanding and collaboration.

In his role as world leader, John Paul II has often used his prestige to achieve peace and freedom. He mediated peace between Argentina and Chile over a longstanding border dispute. He has lectured military dictators on their responsibility for human rights and justice. He even received credit, along with Mikhail Gorbachev, in a *New York Times* op ed piece for the remarkable fall of the Berlin Wall and the freedom of Eastern

Europe. A Polish Jesuit verified this judgment with me in Krakow in 1990 by recounting how at a Mass attended by a million Poles, the pope encouraged them to realize their power when united. A year later, Solidarity was born. Eastern Europeans, he said, took hope from Poland and Solidarity and acted when the right moment came. Gorbachev himself, in his 1992 *La Stampa* article, stated that "everything that happened in Eastern Europe in these last few years would have been impossible without the presence of this pope."

Moreover, Pope John Paul II was chosen as *Time* magazine's "Man of the Year" for 1994. In its article "Empire of the Spirit," *Time* explained its choice: "In a time of moral confusion, John Paul II is resolute about his ideals and eager to impose them on a world that often differs with him. . . . His appearances generate an electricity unmatched by anyone else on earth. . . . When he talks, it is not only to his flock of nearly a billion; he expects the world to listen." *Time* noted that the pope's book *Crossing the Threshold of Hope* became an immediate best-seller in 12 countries!

People of all faiths or none thus recognize John Paul II's powerful religious and social role in the world today. As such, this first Polish pope has become a unique value both for the Catholic Church and for the human family.

16. Heroic Struggle for Human Rights

Today the Catholic Church is the acknowledged leader in the struggle for justice, for human rights and dignity, and for peace throughout the world. Pope John Paul II tirelessly and courageously champions the dignity of each human person, basic human rights, justice within and between nations, and the responsibilities of wealthy nations of the north to the poor, developing nations of the southern hemisphere. Latin American bishops at Medellín in 1968 and Puebla in 1979 spelled out in concrete terms the demands of justice and of human rights and committed themselves to a "preferential option for the poor." Liberation theologians and the thousands of base Christian communities strive mightily to overcome the continent's massive poverty, oppression and structural injustice.

The United States bishops' landmark letters on World Peace and Economic Justice raised a strong prophetic voice for the responsibilities and opportunity of the richest, most powerful nation of the world toward its own citizens and the poor nations of the world. The large number of martyrs for justice and human rights, led by Archbishop Oscar Romero, the scores of priests and sisters and more recently the six Jesuits of the University of Central America in San Salvador, and the countless lay Catholics (delegates of the Word, CEB leaders, catechists, union leaders, unlettered *campesinos*, university students) have witnessed with their lives to the church's commitment to justice and human rights.

In *Cry of the People*, Penny Lernoux describes the enormous price the Catholic Church has paid for its defense of the poor and their fundamental human rights. In a revealing Appendix covering the period 1964-1978 in Latin America, Table One names, country by country, murdered bishops, priests, religious and laity; Table Two gives the following total statistics: 314 threatened/defamed, 935 arrested, 73 tortured, 79 killed, 37 disappeared, 288 expelled; Table Three breaks down these statistics according to each country of South and Central America. The price paid by the church has climbed much higher during the period 1978 to the present, especially in Guatemala and El Salvador.

Such a heroic struggle for human rights constitutes another enormous value the church offers to its members and to the whole of humanity. It speaks loud and clear that God in his loving plan wills that every human live a decent life befitting his and her God-given dignity and enjoys all the rights coming from that dignity. This value constitutes a powerful affirmation of the church's commitment to building the kingdom of God on this earth as the work of Jesus himself.

17. Champion of Human Life

More than any organization or Christian church, the Catholic Church has consistently and courageously fought for the sacredness of human life in all its manifestations. In its early centuries the church founded the first hospitals to care for the sick and dying, established orphanages for the many foundlings and orphans of medieval Europe, condemned the crime of infanticide and abortion, and would not accept a soldier into the catechumenate because his job involved killing. Today the Catholic Church and evangelical Christians are in the forefront of the battle against abortion-on-demand in the United States. The church's conviction about the sacredness of human life is well-expressed in Joseph Cardinal Bernardin's "seamless garment" statement, that human life must be protected in all its manifestations from "the womb to the tomb."

Applications of the seamless garment image include the church's condemnation of abortion, of capital punishment, of all war, particularly nuclear war, and euthanasia. Allied to these is the church's concern and commitment to help the world's refugees, victims of hunger worldwide, the tragic victims of regional wars by oppressive governments, and malnourished and dying children.

Though the church's teaching and stand on these issues, especially abortion, is unpopular and strongly criticized, nonetheless the church provides an inestimable value to the conscience of the world by constantly reminding governments and individuals that each human life, no matter how poor or pitiable or handicapped, is sacred because personally created by God and of incalculable value. A tragic characteristic of the modern world is its callousness to human life: the senseless slaughter of millions of innocent people in wars of domination; genocide and ethnic cleansing; the neglect of countless children dying of hunger, malnutrition, lack of basic hygiene and health care; random "thrill killings" by total strangers; the 40 million abortions performed worldwide each year. That the church fights for the sacredness of each unique human life is a momentous value for humanity today and for its future.

18. Care for Refugees, "This Immense Human Tragedy"

The enormity of the human tragedy of refugees, humans like ourselves in their joys and sorrows, hopes and desires, paralyzes the mind. The response of the Catholic Church as well as other Christian churches to "this immense human tragedy" constitutes an extraordinary contemporary value for the human family and for the Christian Church itself.

The United Nations defines a refugee as one who flees his or her homeland for fear of persecution to a camp in a second country, while waiting to return home or resettlement in a third country. In 1985 the United Nations High Commissioner for Refugees reported 10,261,600 refugees worldwide; in 1988 the number had climbed to 14,256,600. Today it is estimated to be well over 20,000,000. The world knows the plight of the Vietnamese boat people; of the long-suffering Palestinians in refugee camps in Jordan, the Gaza strip, Lebanon, and the West Bank of Israel; of Cambodians in Thailand; of Afghans in Pakistan; and currently the tragic refugees fleeing Haiti and Bosnia-Herzogovina and Rwanda. Less-well-known are the estimated 5,000,000 refugees in Africa.

Statistics fail to tell the intensely human stories of refugees: of families forcibly separated; of children psychologically traumatized when forced to watch parents or older brothers and sisters beaten, abused and cruelly murdered; of the extreme hardships of crowded refugee camps; of the lives and careers uprooted and the consequent longing for home and a lost way of life; of hunger, destitution, disease, and death. In El Salvador a 13-year old girl "died of sadness" after seeing her mother and brother tortured and killed; a 11-year old boy found lying under the bullet-ridden bodies of his mother, grandmother and three older brothers asked a priest in his orphanage, "Padre Miguel, pray for me that I can forgive the soldiers who killed my mother and brothers."

The Catholic Church has called attention to the enormity of this human tragedy and the responsibility of the world community. Addressing the diplomatic corps in Tanzania, Pope John Paul II spoke of the "millions of our brothers and sisters [who] are homeless and in exile, deprived of dignity and hope." He reminded "the governments you represent that the situation cries out for urgent intervention . . . to help these people not only to survive, to feed themselves, to receive medical assistance and health care, but also to live useful and respectable lives and to maintain their hope of a better future for themselves and their children."

Catholic Charities, Caritas International, the Jesuit Refugee Service among others have provided heroic help to refugees worldwide; priests, nuns, lay women and men work and live in refugee camps all over the world as teachers, medics, counselors, food and clothing providers, and resettlement facilitators. Their presence is a living witness to the dignity of each human being regardless of race, religion, nationality; their heroic work is a dramatic witness of compassionate Christian love and of Jesus' invitation to love even the lowliest and the stranger in our midst.

In the United States a uniquely Christian, highly effective response to the human tragedy of 500,000 Guatemalan and El Salvadoran refugees fleeing government and military persecution is the now-famous Sanctuary Movement. How it began is an instructive story of Christian response to an ignored tragedy in our midst. In 1980 a coyote (person who smuggles refugees from Mexico into the United States for a fat fee) led 26 Salvadorans in family groups across the border near Nogales by night and deserted them in the Sonoran desert. Within days half of them — men, women and children — died a horrible death; the other half, surviving by drinking their own urine, struggled northward till spotted and helped by a rancher near Tucson. The survivors were brought to Tucson hospitals where Rev. John Fife, a Presbyterian pastor, heard their "incredible stories of terrorism, torture and death squads in their country."

He opened his southside Presbyterian church in Tucson as a place of sanctuary (refuge and protection) for the steady stream of Guatemalan and Salvadoran refugees. When on March 24, 1982 he publicly declared his church a sanctuary, the **Sanctuary Movement** was born. Protestant and Catholic churches in Tucson and then throughout the United States joined the movement, which soon extended from the Mexican border to Christian congregations in the northwest, midwest, and northeast. This network of church people has been likened to the "underground railroad" of the Civil War era, which helped slaves escape to freedom in northern states.

The Sanctuary Movement has helped thousands of refugees move from Tucson and other border cities to safety in sanctuary parishes in officially proclaimed sanctuary cities like Berkeley and San Francisco. During the 1980s, U.S. federal agents arrested and prosecuted Catholic priests and sisters, Protestant ministers and pastors, and committed Christians like rancher Jim Corbett, the founder of the modern underground railroad, for harboring and transporting illegal aliens. One such person sentenced to jail in 1984 was a young Methodist woman, Stacey Merkt, whose testimony at her trial witnesses to one Christian's response to "this immense human tragedy."

> I believe in a God of life and a God of love. . . . I am called to extend my hand to those in need — to these Salvadorans — but I am also called to work for justice so that I don't need to extend my hand. . . . I'm no martyr. . . . I am a woman with a heart and

mind. My faith commitment connects me to the people and to justice.

19. Integrity and Consistency

Though the Catholic Church has often been accused of rigidity and failure to be up-to-date, yet in her long history the church has exhibited an admirable tenacity and consistency in her doctrinal and moral teaching. She has taken very seriously her responsibility to pass on without distortion or compromise the Christian tradition received from Jesus and the Apostles and developed by the Church Fathers of the early centuries. Thanks to outstanding theologians in almost every century and to her vigilant magisterium, the Catholic Church has painstakingly developed a remarkably consistent formulation of the Christian faith.

In an age of moral relativism in which people are increasingly confused about basic principles and values, the church has stood firm, often at great cost, in proclaiming human dignity, justice, the inviolability of human life, and in safeguarding through respect and moderation the sacredness of sex and the high ideals of permanent faithful, fruitful Christian marriage and of chastity for the unmarried. Our world today would indeed be impoverished without the strong prophetic voice of the Catholic Church proclaiming the gospel of Jesus Christ and keeping before the human family high moral ideals.

20. Timeless Aesthetic Treasures

Throughout the centuries the Catholic Church has been a veritable treasure house of artistic masterpieces that constitute an incomparable value for humanity, both aesthetically and religiously. Soaring cathedrals with their hundreds of stone sculptures, colorful stained glass and dazzling mosaics; the profusion of religious paintings by Renaissance masters and more recent artists; the vast body of religious writings: novels, poems, spiritual treatises, biographies of saints and of great Christian men and women; exquisitely wrought chalices, monstrances, and crucifixes; richly brocaded priestly vestments; the realistic polychrome wood carved statues of Christ, Mary and the saints, especially in Spain and Latin America: all these quicken the heart and raise mind and emotions to God and to religious values.

We give examples of only a few such treasures.

Cathedrals: Notre Dame, Rheims, Amiens (France); York, Durham, Salisbury, Lincoln (England); St. Peters and Mary Major in Rome; the churches of Florence, Siena, Orvieto (Italy); of Toledo, Salamanca, Burgos (Spain).

Mosaics: in the 4th and 5th century churches of Ravenna, Italy; in the church of Monreale near Palermo, Sicily; St. Mark's Basilica, Venice.

Stained Glass: Chartres Cathedral outside Paris, La Sainte Chapelle, Paris (France); León (Spain).

Sculpture: the stone statues on the exterior of Chartres Cathedral (France); Michelangelo's marble Pietà and Moses in Rome and David in Florence (Italy); the thousands of life-size wood-carved painted Christs and Virgin Marys and saints throughout Europe and Latin America.

Painting: thousands of madonnas (Mary with child Jesus) of Renaissance Europe; rich Byzantine icons in Athens, Crete, Egypt; Michelangelo's incomparable Sistine Chapel ceiling and powerful Christ of the Last Judgment on the front wall; El Greco's dramatically elongated Christs and Mary and the Apostles; Giotto's giant frescos of the life of St. Francis of Assisi in the upper church in Assisi, Italy; the Book of Kells and many other spectacular illuminated Gospels and Scriptures and manuscripts.

Literature: St. Augustine's *City of God* and *Confessions*; Dante's *Divine Comedy*; Chaucer's *Canterbury Tales*; St. John of the Cross' *Dark Night of the Soul* and St. Teresa of Avila's *The Interior Castle*; Newman's *Apologia*; Bernanos' *Diary of a Country Priest*, and many others.

Museums: Vatican Museum in Rome; Louvre in Paris; the Prado in Madrid; Byzantine Icon Museum in Athens; Uffizi in Florence; many others throughout Europe and elsewhere containing religious masterpieces.

As repository of religious masterpieces of the human spirit, the Catholic Church has preserved and made available for humankind a powerful means of experiencing the divine. The human family is immeasurably enriched.

Further Reading

Dulles, Avery. *Models of the Church*. Garden City, NY: Image Books, 1987 (original 1974).

Golden, Renny and McConnell, Michael. *Sanctuary, the New Underground Railroad*. Maryknoll, NY: Orbis Books, 1986.

John Paul II. *Crossing the Threshold of Hope*. New York: Alfred A. Knopf, 1994.

"Man of the Year." *Time*. Dec. 26, 1994/Jan. 2, 1995, 53-80.

O'Malley, William. *Why Be Catholic?* New York: Crossroad, 1994.

The Church's Future:
Challenges and Opportunities

In the present situation, the unsearchable wisdom of Divine
Providence is leading us to a new reality which through our efforts and even beyond our expectations is moving toward the
fulfillment of the designs of God.   —Pope John XXIII

The words imaginative, collaborative, witnessing, confident will
guide us to the Third Millennium. . . . This pilgrim church of
San Francisco must be a church of hope and faith, of unity and
charity even in difficult times. . . . We should give thanks for
this present hour in our journey which mingles great promise
and bright hopes with severe challenges.[1]
                                   —Archbishop John Quinn

Does the Catholic Church have a future? Of course it does. But
the price of that future will be profound change. This process
has already begun. . . . Catholicism has emerged as one of the
most creative and positive forces in the world today. Vatican II
was the beginning.   —Paul Collins[2]

Introduction

We recalled in chapter 19 that a major goal of this book was to present the contemporary Catholic Church *as it actually exists today*. A

---

1. November 16, 1993 letter to Archdiocese.
2. Paul Collins. *Mixed Blessings: John Paul II and the Church of the Eighties* (Ringwald,
Australia: Penguin, 1986), 254.

prominent aspect of today's church is a growing sense among those who love the church deeply and are concerned for her well-being — informed adult Catholics, thoughtful young people, committed priests, sisters and bishops — that the Church is entering a dramatically new and different period in her long history and that change and a certain kind of conversion as agent of change is urgently needed today. A growing literature attest to this sense.

Indications are that the Catholic Church entering its third millennium will be a far different church in a number of ways. First, demographically it will no longer be a western, European Church. Of more than one billion Catholics by the year 2000, roughly two-thirds will live in Africa, Asia, Central and South America. Since the majority in these continents are poor, the Catholic Church will increasingly be a *church of the poor*. Second, it will be a *free church*, that is, Catholics will more and more make their own free conscience decisions to remain in the church or to leave it. Gone are the days when rigid rules, fear of hell, commands from authority and exhortations to obedience ensured members' allegiance. Only a church whose teachings and actions are credible will attract and maintain members. Such a church will need to reflect in its daily life values like democracy and freedom and justice that moderns esteem so highly.

Third, it will be a *spiritual church* that satisfies the deeply felt religious needs of its members, that nourishes them with the Word of God in the Bible, as well as with sacraments, that provides faith communities in which to find and experience God. Otherwise, its members will look elsewhere without guilt feelings. Fourth, it will be an *ecumenical church* since the Catholic Church's relation to other Christian churches will change as faith and theological agreement become ever more evident and the consequent scandal of separation in an increasingly secular world becomes more intolerable. Fifth, the third millennium will be the age of the laity and of lay ministry, profoundly altering present church structures and relationships. Thus it will more fully be a *church of the laity*. Finally, it will be a *church of young people*, at least in the Third World, where 42% of the population is under 15 years of age!

This new ecclesial situation presents great challenges to the Catholic Church in its third millennium. It likewise affords magnificent opportunities.

To meet these challenges and realize these opportunities, many Catholics today believe the Catholic Church must be able to change profoundly. Change means taking risks and moving into uncharted waters. Is the barque of Peter "up to it"? Will it have the will and the trust in the guiding Holy Spirit to risk a new course? Can it "let go" of "baggage" unessential to the gospel?

To achieve such change the Catholic Church, leaders and lay Catholics alike, are being called to undergo conversion — a two-fold movement of renouncing nonessentials and more fully embracing authentic gospel values. Every conversion involves major decision-making that translates into concrete deeds. Vatican II began this process of conversion in its opening to the world, its commitment to ecumenism, its emphasis on religious freedom and personal conscience, its liturgical renewal, its insistence on collegiality in all aspects of church life, and its admission that it needs ongoing reformation and that its teaching office is subordinate to the word of God in Scripture.

The Council thus set the church on a new *direction*, establishing the needed theological *principles* and opening up *possibilities* for development. Yet the forces of renewal unleashed at the Council, though far advanced, have not been sufficiently realized in specific actions; many sense that full renewal lags under the brake of the *restoration*. Moreover, new issues have arisen with an urgency demanding decisive action. Nothing short of carrying out more fully the renewal begun at Vatican II will suffice at this moment in the church's pilgrimage.

◆

Preview: We have chosen 12 topics as urgent areas of church decision-making. As such they are dramatic challenges. At the same time they offer unparalleled opportunities for the Catholic Church entering its third millennium. These topics draw on themes/issues/problems/tensions/values treated throughout this book. In a sense they recapitulate the preceding chapters. We shall treat these 12 challenges and opportunities in three groups: those internal to the Catholic Church, those involving other Christian churches, and that great challenge and opportunity calling particularly the Roman Catholic but other Christian churches as well.

◆

Challenges and Opportunities Within the Catholic Church

1. Become a Truly Global Church

Karl Rahner, one of the greatest theologians of this century and a major influence on the Second Vatican Council, made the dramatic claim that Vatican II was the beginning of a new historical epoch in the Catholic Church.[3] Like the 1st-century church's decision to move from being a Jewish church to becoming a Greco-Roman Gentile church, Vatican II took the initial steps to becoming a truly pluralistic, non-western, transcultural

---

3. Karl Rahner, "A Fundamental Theological Interpretation of Vatican II," in *Vatican II: The Unfinished Agenda, A Look to the Future,* Lucien Richard, ed. (New York/Mahwah: Paulist Press, 1987), 9-21 and Karl Rahner, "Perspectives for Pastoral Theology in the Future," *Theological Investigations, Vol. 22, Humane Society and the Church of Tomorrow* (New York: Crossroad, 1991), 106-119.

world church. In terms of Christian history, one could generalize that the first millennium belonged to eastern Christianity, where the first seven ecumenical councils were held, the second millennium to the western Roman Church, while the third millennium will feature the church of the southern hemisphere. Demographics show the shift: in 1900 only 23% of Catholics lived in Latin America, Africa, Asia and Oceania; in 1970 the figure rose to 51%, to 60% in 1985, and is projected to be 70% by the year 2000. Today local indigenous bishops number almost 95% in Asia and 75% in Africa. The Catholic Church is firmly planted in all six continents, a world church.

To become in fact an authentic world church, Rahner warns that the Catholic Church needs to deal with four major issues. One, the *renewal of the papacy* in the way the Petrine ministry is exercised today. The Petrine office of preserving unity in the church, he believes, must become to a greater degree the promoter and protector of diversity among the local and regional churches by giving them the necessary autonomy to develop their own spirituality and mission.

Two, true *collegial relationships* between the local bishops of the world and the pope. Receiving his authority from Christ rather than from the pope, each local bishop should be able to exercise his spiritual authority without interference from Roman curial congregations. Likewise, national episcopal conferences need to have real authority.

Three, genuine *participation of Catholic laypersons* in the ministry and mission of the church. In a true world church, Catholics must participate in decisions that affect their Christian lives, in a spirit of freedom and democracy.

Four, a world church must be an *open church* — to the world, to theological and cultural pluralism, to other Christian churches and to the great world religions. Otherwise it risks becoming a sect, defensive, and isolated. Rahner stresses that theologians must be encouraged in their scholarly research and be free from constant surveillance and disciplining by the curial offices.

The principle of pluralism and diversity-in-unity repeatedly stressed by Vatican II is the necessary basis of a church that is truly global. Its theological underpinning is the theology of church as communion of local churches; pre-Vatican II theology stressed the unity and singleness of the Roman Catholic Church, rarely referring to church in the plural. The principle of diversity-in-unity means that the local churches and their bishops be recognized and given the autonomy to make those decisions that meet their individual pastoral needs. "The Constitution on the Liturgy" accepted to some extent a liturgical pluralism. Theological pluralism was commended in the "Decree on Ecumenism," where a genuine diversity "even in the theological elaborations of revealed truth" (4) was recognized, and in the "Decree on Eastern Churches," where differing theological formulations are "often to be considered as complementary rather than conflicting" (17).

The teaching on the existence of a *hierarchy of truth* (UR 11) and John XXIII's assertion in his introductory speech to the Council that the substance of the faith can be expressed in different formulations confirm theological pluralism. The communion model for the future union of the Christian churches depends on the various churches maintaining their diversity while achieving a basic unity. Likewise, the success of evangelization and inculturation relies on the church respecting different cultures.

Despite the Council's positive approach to pluralism and diversity, the contemporary church finds difficulty in accepting the reality of pluralism in all aspects of its life. Adrian Hastings believes that "by the 1980s . . . the crucial ecclesiastical issue . . . had become the acceptability of diversity," whereas "the curial mind had never escaped from the conviction that unity required uniformity."[4]

To become a true global church is to recover and reinvigorate catholicity, that forgotten fourth mark of the church, which cannot be one, holy, or even apostolic unless it is truly *catholic*. The characteristics of a global church truly catholic are:

- a universal vision and way of thinking;

- an appreciation for diversity-in-unity that not only permits but encourages pluralism in theology, liturgy and ways of being Christian;

- a respect for other than western, Mediterranean cultures so that the gospel of Jesus can be truly "inculturated" in the thought patterns and worship of Africa, Asia, and Latin America;

- strong support for the local bishops of the world to make those urgent decisions necessary for the vigor and growth of their local churches;

- practical collegiality so that the bishops of the world, as in the triennial synod of bishops, share responsibility for decisions affecting their own churches as well as the universal church;

- the Catholic laity of the world be heard on the issues that most ultimately affect them;

- freedom and democratic procedures as a prominent characteristic of the world church.

Vatican II laid the basis for an emerging world church; the church now has the enormous challenge and opportunity to move confidently and with trust in the guidance of the Holy Spirit to achieve a genuine global church — *catholic, collegial, local, inculturated,* and *pluralistic.*

---

4. Adrian Hastings, *Modern Catholicism. Vatican II and After* (New York: Oxford University Press, 1991), 11.

2. Rise to the Challenge of the "New" Evangelization

In urging the *new* evangelization, John Paul II has issued what might become the most prominent challenge and opportunity for the Catholic Church and for individual Catholics in the 21st century. He sees "the dawning of a new missionary age . . . if all Christians . . . respond with generosity." He believes "God is preparing a great springtime for Christianity and one can already see its first signs."[5]

The Holy Father describes evangelization as "a clear proclamation that in Jesus Christ . . . salvation is offered to all as a gift of God's grace and mercy." As such, it has always existed in the church. But John Paul II's evangelization is startlingly new; it looks to the third millennium of Christianity in a totally new world order and embraces all continents, cultures, and groups of peoples. In the case of Latin America, first evangelized by Spanish and Portugese almost five centuries ago, he speaks of a reevangelization that forges a new culture open to the gospel message and promotes the social transformation of the continent.[6] He repeated the need to reevangelize formerly Christian First World countries, where large groups have lost a living sense of faith. He challenged Catholic lay persons to show how the Christian faith has a valid response to society's problems. His vision extended to whole new sections of modern life: inner cities, migrants, refugees, youth, the "new humanity" so dependent on the mass media.[7]

This new evangelization is indeed an enormous challenge. China, with its 1.3 billion people, may at some point in the first century of the third millennium be ripe for the gospel. India, with its teeming millions, already has a small but vigorous Christian presence. Europe and North America, with their large numbers of "baptized unbelievers," are in dire need of reevangelization. The bishops of Latin American in their Medellín and Puebla documents spoke at length of the grave need to evangelize not only the wealthy elites but the impoverished masses as well. In the United States, evangelization includes the unchurched, young people, and large numbers of inactive, alienated and angry Catholics.

To form and inspire such evangelizers is essential for the new evangelization to succeed. How will Catholics rise to meet this challenge, to seize this great opportunity? How will lay Catholics, so accustomed to letting their priests and sisters do evangelization, catch the spark that animates zealous evangelical and Pentecostal Christians? A veritable "conversion" will need to take place. Catholics must first become convinced that in their baptism and confirmation they are personally called by Christ

---

5. John Paul II, "Mission of the Redeemer," *Origins* 20, No. 34 (Jan. 31, 1991), 541-68.

6. John Paul II, "Toward the Fifth Centenary of New World Evangelization," *Origins* 20 (Sept. 6, 1990): 215, No. 28.

7. *Ibid.*, No. 37.

to share their Christian faith by proclaiming the good news about Jesus Christ. Pope John Paul II sketched the spirituality needed: a close personal relationship to the Lord and confidence in the Holy Spirit.

How is the new evangelization to be done?[8] Above all, today's evangelizers need to give people a personal experience of God as loving, caring, compassionate, intensely interested in them, eager to enter into a personal relationship with them; a personal experience of Jesus as good news who brings joy and peace, who desires to establish on earth his Father's reign of peace, justice, and mutual love; a personal experience of the Spirit who inflames human hearts and minds with powerful gifts. Evangelizers best do this by example. For today people are most effectively evangelized by Christ-centered, Christ-enthused, faith-filled Christians in the work place, recreation, schools, families. Large impersonal parishes may need to give way to small groups of Christians who radiate love and care for each other, who show compassion for the poor and sick and disadvantaged about them, and who share their joy in the risen Lord in their worship celebrations. This was the highly successful evangelization characteristic of Christians in the early centuries of the church.

In John Paul II giving "the highest priority to evangelization in the mission of the Church," theologian Avery Dulles sees "a remarkable shift in the Catholic tradition . . . the birth of a new Catholicism . . ."[9] The new evangelization is indeed an enormous challenge and rich opportunity for lay Catholics, as well as bishops, priests, and religious sisters and brothers.

3. Establish Fully Inculturated Local Churches

For the new evangelization to succeed, fully inculturated local churches are essential.

The principle of inculturation (see chapter 6) is now universally accepted throughout the Catholic Church. The issue today is its full practical application. Aylward Shorter, an African missionary of 25 years experience, states that "the Church does not appear ready to enter upon a consistent and comprehensive program of inculturation. This prospect is a cause of deep disappointment and misgiving to Third World Christians."[10] Full inculturation of the gospel and of the church is a highly complex challenge for today's church, especially in missionary areas among youthful local churches. It frequently demands moving into the unknown and taking risks. Prudent discernment is necessary. Such inculturation is an opportunity that may not be available indefinitely. The stakes are high: the Chris-

---

8. See *The Catholic World* 235 (July/August, 1992) issue, especially Patrick Brennan, "Strategies for an Evangelizing Parish" and Robert Hater, "Ten Distinctive Qualities of Catholic Evangelization."

9. Avery Dulles, "John Paul II and the New Evangelization," *America* 166 (Feb. 1, 1992), 70.

10. Aylward Shorter, *Toward a Theology of Inculturation* (London: Geoffrey Chapman, 1988), 270.

tian life of millions and the vast potential for evangelization of whole continents. Presently there are four areas of the world where inculturation is the key to successful evangelization.

China. A unique situation exists in China today. The one Catholic Church is split into the government-controlled Catholic Patriotic Association (CPA) and the underground church of bishops, priests and lay Catholics, many of whom spent 20 or more years in prison because of their heroic determination to remain in communion with the pope and who today refuse to accept CPA bishops and priests. With the easing of restrictions in the early 1980s under Deng Xiao Peng, the government refurnished Catholic churches and opened seminaries staffed by CPA bishops and priests. Catholic life is flourishing today in China: devout Catholic Chinese pack the CPA-controlled churches for five or more Sunday Masses, and large numbers of young men have begun studying for the priesthood. Underground priests risk celebrating private Masses in homes of underground Catholics. But the situation is ambiguous: CPA bishops are validly but "irregularly" consecrated, resulting in valid but unauthorized ordinations of priests. Many CPA bishops and priests pray for the Holy Father and long for formal communion with him, but are prohibited to do so by the Communist government officials who view the Vatican as a foreign political power bent on interfering with Chinese internal affairs.

The existence of such bishops, priests, and lay Catholics not in formal communion with the pope and thus not under his spiritual leadership and jurisdiction is a unique modern example of the church struggling to inculturate itself in a Communist society. It can learn from the tragic failure of inculturation in 16th-century China regarding the Chinese-rites experiment, led by the famous Mateo Ricci.

Ricci, an Italian Jesuit who arrived in China in 1583, sought to present Christianity as not incompatible with Chinese culture. He steeped himself in the ancient culture of China, authored over 20 works in Chinese, and used his expertise in astronomy, mathematics and the physical sciences to be accepted into the imperial court in Peking. He gave the traditional Chinese expression "Lord of Heaven" as the name for God and made the judgment that rites honoring the philosopher Confucius and people's ancestors (prostrations, burning incense, offering food at family members' graves) were not idolatrous practices. This inculturation of Chinese rites bore fruit: over 3000 Chinese were baptized by the time of Ricci's death in 1610; the church had been planted within Chinese culture and grew steadily.

But Ricci's attempt at inculturation was challenged by other missionaries in China, who wrote their misgivings to Rome. The subsequent "rites controversy" raged in China and Rome. Pope Clement XI's condemnation of the Chinese rites in 1704 precipitated the emperor's persecution of Catholics; the promising evangelization of China came to a tragic end.

Two hundred years later, Ricci's inculturation was vindicated: Pope Pius XI in 1935 approved the cult of Confucius as essentially nonreligious, and Pius XII in 1939 did the same for traditional Chinese funeral rites and the cult of ancestors.[11]

Africa. The continent where Christianity is growing fastest, Africa is another example of the critical need for inculturation. The Catholic Church must move from an "outdated theology of adaptation" (to use African bishops' strong words to describe the encounter of two cultures in which both are merely superficially changed) to a genuine inculturation in which a new creation results; or in the words of Pope Paul VI, "you must have an African Christianity."[12]

Aylward Shorter suggests areas where inculturation is needed in Africa. *Liturgy*: greater use of dance since "dancing normally accompanies song and all forms of ritual movement in African culture"; *Theology*: in 1974 the bishops of Africa and Madagascar called for "African theological research" and a theology "open to the aspirations of the people of Africa." *Pastoral*: The 1985 Synod of Bishops' report recognized that Africans "want a simpler Christianity integrated into all aspects of daily life, into the sufferings, joys, work, aspirations, fears and needs of the African." *Church law*: Africans object that "canon law is culturally western . . . intrinsically incapable of expressing the concerns of non-western cultures." Western insistence on celibacy for priests is not understood in African society that values family and children so highly.

Reasonable autonomy of local bishops and regional bishops' conferences: African bishops at the 1974 Synod on Evangelization unsuccessfully asked to ordain married catechists so that the burgeoning Catholic population would have the Eucharist and the increasing number of catechumens be instructed. In 1980 the bishops of Zaire asked for an "African Council" of all African bishops to realize integral evangelizing, to study the tasks of inculturation, and to deal with questions decisive for Christianity in Africa.[13] Their request was finally realized in 1994, but not as they had wanted. At the Vatican's insistence, the meeting was a synod held in Rome; the African bishops desired a decision-making *council* rather than a purely consultative *synod,* and the meeting to be held in their own continent of Africa. This action by Rome was seen by many as a failure in collegiality, in respect for the local church and regional bishops' conferences, and ineffective inculturation.[14]

---

11. *Ibid.,* 157-59.

12. *Ibid.,* 210.

13. *Ibid.,* 258.

14. A major reason for the Vatican's reluctance to encourage full inculturation in Africa is the concern to preserve in its integrity the gospel message and Catholic life and practice. An example is the centuries-old tribal custom of men with several wives, a practice that challenges Christian monogamous sacramental marriage. Yet a serious pastoral and cultural problem is

Asia. Christianity is a decided minority among the population of Asia, where the great ancient religious traditions of Hinduism and Buddhism provide meaning and salvation for tens of millions. Asian bishops through FABC (Federation of Asian Bishops' Conferences) and their theologians have a record of creative inculturation in the period since the Council, especially in the area of liturgical worship, appreciation for Eastern meditation and prayer, and interreligious dialogue. Indian rituals, customs, and prayer forms have been incorporated into the eucharistic liturgy in India. The recently-deceased Benedictine Bede Griffiths, through his ashram in southern India and his many writings, has brought a new appreciation of eastern prayer and asceticism to the West and shown how the western church needs to be enriched by the wisdom and religious life of the East. Catholic theologians, priests, and laity in Thailand, Sri Lanka, Korea and Japan make Buddhist retreats, receive spiritual guidance from Zen Buddhist masters, and gain knowledge and appreciation of the rich Buddhist heritage.

Latin America. Liberation theology is a dramatic form of inculturation in that Catholic theology and life have penetrated and transformed Latin American culture in the short period of 25 years. Another example is the acceptance of the popular religiosity of the indigenous peoples of Latin America. After decades of looking down on the "superstitious" practices of popular religiosity, the church has come to appreciate the importance and value of highly personal devotion to the saints, of religious processions, elaborate fiestas celebrating saints' feastdays, of whole villages during Holy Week dramatizing Jesus carrying his cross and his crucifixion, and of ostentatious devotion to the Virgin. In this newfound appreciation, the church has purified and elevated popular religiosity and herself been enriched.

Successful inculturation, according to Shorter, demands "a truly multi-cultural church . . . in which local solutions to pastoral problems and local formulations of doctrine and worship are favored . . . and priorities are decided locally."[15] Peter Schineller observes that "inculturation is a two-way street [in which] . . . the insights of Latin America on the role of the church in the work of justice, of the African church on the nature of celebration and on the healing power of the church, and of the Asian church on the mystery and transcendence of God" need to be accepted by the universal Catholic Church.[16] Its challenge today is to have the "courage to undertake true and radical inculturation. . . . The way forward de-

---

involved: becoming Catholic means choosing one wife and rejecting the others; the rejected wives become outcasts and unmarriageable. Is this just and Christian? Shorter believes another reason may be Rome's "fear of losing control [which] seems to be very real among members of the Catholic hierarchy." *Ibid.*, 252.

15. *Ibid.*, 259.

16. Peter Schineller, *A Handbook on Inculturation* (New York/Mahweh: Paulist Press, 1990), 120.

mands deep faith in the power of the gospel and in the rich tradition of the church . . . [and] in the presence of God already at work in new cultures and contexts."[17]

4. Empower Catholic Laypersons for Mission and Ministry

"Our well-trained laity represents the finest asset we have in the American church today and is the source of its strength and vitality." So writes Archbishop Rembert Weakland about the high educational level of Catholics today.[18] He believes the church of the year 2000 needs "ways of permitting the different gifts of all the faithful to find expression." He stressed that since "the fullness of the Holy Spirit dwells in the people of God" because of their baptism, bishops must listen to the Catholic laity and accept their role in the church.[19]

The archbishop's statements highlight a significant fact in the church today: Catholic laypersons represent an enormous pool of untapped, under-utilized talent and energy, generosity and leadership potential for the church in its mission to the world and its own members. For too long have the Catholic laity been accustomed to defer to priests and bishops. And perhaps too strenuously has the church stressed the separation between the ordained priesthood and the priesthood of all baptized Catholics.

Today, increasing numbers of Catholics, conscious that their baptism gives them responsibility for the church's mission, ask to participate more fully in the life of their church. Empowering Catholic laity, especially Catholic women at this moment in the church, means in practice that bishops and priests welcome lay Catholics as *co-partners* in the church's mission, asking their advice and insights, inspiring and motivating them to come forward, and creatively offering opportunities for mission and ministry both within the church and to the world.

To empower the laity for ministry *within* the church is much more than ordaining married deacons, training lectors and eucharistic ministers, creating parish councils, as valuable as these are. It involves church leaders listening to the Holy Spirit speaking through the Catholic faithful, finding ways to utilize their talents and gifts, giving them voice in the decisions that affect them, their mission, and their ministry. It also means learning from their experience of married love and family life and how they live their sexuality in today's world.

However, the role of the laity must not be restricted to *inner* church life. Pope John Paul II has cautioned against "clericalizing" the laity. He stresses that the sacraments of baptism and confirmation insert the Chris-

---

17. *Ibid.*, 121-22.
18. Rembert Weakland, "The Church in Worldly Affairs: Tensions between Laity and Clergy," *America* 155 (Oct. 18, 1986): 201.
19. *Ibid.*, 202.

tian into the full mission of the church to the world in the political, social, and economic orders. Empowering Catholic laypersons in their role of transforming the secular world means helping them escape the dichotomy of separating secular and religious life; it means inspiring them to become acquainted with the rich Catholic social teaching; it means supporting rather than criticizing Catholic elected officials in their difficult task of living gospel values in a pluralist, democratic society.

The Holy Spirit appears to be giving the Catholic Church today an unprecedented opportunity to empower its lay members to take leadership roles in the church's mission, both within the church and to the world.

5. Deepen Spirituality of Catholics

Various questionnaires and national polls are discovering a happy phenomenon in today's church: Catholic people are experiencing a need for deeper spirituality. Its cause appears to be the increasing complexity and uprootedness of modern life and the liturgical and biblical renewal of Vatican II. This desire for spirituality inspired by the Holy Spirit is an important challenge to Catholic pastors and a valuable opportunity for the church of the 21st century. Three areas provide special challenge and rich opportunity today.

The Parish. Is the Catholic Church in its parishes effectively meeting the religious needs of Catholics today? The answer would appear to be yes from the Notre Dame study of Catholic life in 1099 parishes since Vatican II.[20] The study, made during a five-year period from 1981 to 1986, found that among "core Catholics," those actively engaged in their parish, 85% say their parish does meet their spiritual needs.[21] They cite Sunday Mass, receiving Communion, and private prayer.[22] However, an overwhelming 90% felt the church "should stress personal spiritual relationship to Christ";[23] only 46% of the parishes offered "prayer/reflection groups."[24] Concerning homilies at Mass, core Catholics found them generally inspiring and interesting, but decidedly uninformative and unhelpful to growth in faith.[25]

This data seems to indicate that the deeper spiritual needs of Catholics need more attention: instruction and guidance in developing and growing in a prayer life; challenge and help to deepen one's relationship with God, to develop intimacy and friendship with Jesus, and to experience the

---

20. Jim Castelli and Joseph Gremillion, *The Emerging Parish: The Notre Dame Study of Catholic Life since Vatican II* (San Francisco: Harper & Row, 1987).

21. *Ibid.,* 58-59.

22. *Ibid.,* 160.

23. *Ibid.,* 37.

24. *Ibid.,* 61.

25. *Ibid.,* 134.

Holy Spirit active in daily life; more opportunities for prayer groups, spiritual direction, and retreats; in a word, spirituality — helping Catholics live a fuller spiritual life. Pastors might introduce Catholics to the exceedingly rich and largely unknown mystical tradition of the church, especially of women mystics. Clearly priests and deacons need to improve the quality and depth of their homilies and to develop skill in spiritual direction; they also need to improve pastoral care in the confessional and to make the celebration of the sacraments, especially the Eucharist, prayer experiences of the risen Christ and his Spirit. Catholics' desire for deeper spirituality may well point to a need that the gifts women bring to ministry be more available to Catholics. An encouraging development is the growing number of laypeople being trained as spiritual directors and retreat givers.

Faith Communities of Word and Sacrament. Despite the extraordinary achievements of the large urban parishes with their packed multiple Sunday masses, their elementary schools, the diversity of organizations and activities, there is a growing sense that 1000-2000 family parishes no longer sufficiently supply the religious needs of their members. A typical Sunday congregation reveals a preponderance of white heads; young people are conspicuously absent. Catholics, especially younger couples and Hispanic families, desire more community-oriented parishes.

> The parish many of us knew and loved is inadequate to meet the evangelical needs of believers in the future. . . . the paradigm for parish remains basically the same as it was for our grandparents . . . [which] simply is not as effective as it once was amid the social changes that our age has witnessed.[26]

Small Christian faith communities may be the providential answer of the future!

The base Christian communities (CEB's) of Latin America have provided examples of how the passive faith of millions has been dynamically transformed. Ten to fifteen families meet weekly to read, reflect on, and discuss the Bible, apply their insights to their real-life situations, and then to decide on concrete action. These CEB's, over 100,000 in Brazil alone, become a powerful Christian force in the lives of their members; they have revitalized Catholic life in Latin America.

These small faith communities manifest the following characteristics:

- The members are formed and inspired by God's word in the Bible.
- The risen Christ and His Spirit become real in the community.
- Celebration of the Eucharist becomes the life of the community.

---

26. See Michael Leach, "The Last Catholics in America: A Time to Recapture the 'Chosen Things,'" *America* 165 (Nov. 30, 1991): 412.

- The members' faith is purified and deepened and their Christian hope becomes a powerful force, even in humanly hopeless situations.
- The members take responsibility and care for each other in Christian solidarity and love.
- The community is person-oriented and loving.
- Leadership, generally lay, rises from the community itself.
- It is open to all: saint and sinner, old and young, male and female.

Such faith communities have the potential to change the church profoundly. Moral theologian Bernard Häring made startling predictions[27] about the church of the first century of the third millennium. He foresees that "all believing communities, even those that are tiny and remote . . . will gather every Sunday around the altar of the Eucharist" because "their Christian birthright . . . [is to] have a recognized right to a eucharistic minister of the altar from their midst": that is, women and married men chosen from the community to be its priests. Such communities will develop a biblical spirituality; and who can predict the fruits the word of God can effect? Nominal Catholics will be converted into Spirit-filled Christians and become a powerful force for the new evangelization. Catholic laity will truly become the people of God as their special gifts and charisms are recognized and exercised. A new relationship between lay Catholics and their priests and local bishops will result, to the benefit of both groups.

Though it would be rash to rush to restructure the existing large and often successful parishes, still "the signs of the times" challenge the Catholic Church to develop small faith communities centered around the Scriptures and the Eucharist. A magnificent opportunity awaits the church to infuse new life into its members, to become a more gospel-centered and missionary church, and to utilize the gifts of all the people of God under the inspiration of the Holy Spirit. Such small, personalized faith communities may be the single most effective way for the church to staunch the flow of poverty-stricken Catholics in Latin America into evangelical Pentecostal groups, to minister more effectively to Hispanic Catholics in the United States, and to reclaim the large number of under-30 inactive Catholics.

The Third Rite of Reconciliation. It is no secret that since Vatican II, Catholics in very large numbers have stopped "going to confession." It is not uncommon to meet young people who haven't received the sacrament since the time of their first communion. This is a great loss for Catholics, young and old, who need to acknowledge their sinfulness and to experience God's

---

27. Bernard Haring, "The Church I Want," *The Tablet* 244 (July 28, 1990): 94.

loving forgiveness. Clearly, reconciliation with God and others is central to Jesus' gospel message.

Instead of deploring this situation, the church, many pastors think, should admit that its discipline of private confession is not successful in attracting Catholics today. But all is not lost. The church has provided a third way of using the ritual of reconciliation: communal reconciliation service with general absolution. By broadening the conditions for using this third rite, the church has a unique and wonderful opportunity to make the sacrament of reconciliation once again a normal and popular part of parish life that deepens the spiritual lives of Catholics.

Many believe today that the church needs to offer this third rite without attaching conditions of grave necessity for its use. Bishop Carroll Dozier of Memphis, Tennessee, decided to do just that in 1976. He issued a "Call to Reconciliation" to inactive Catholics, our "absent brothers and sisters," utilizing the provision for general absolution as "an extended hand to those alienated from the Catholic community." The careful six-month educational preparation included an adult education packet sent to each parish on the theology of reconciliation, a series of three sermons preached in each parish of the diocese on the theology of the "call," and a day of eucharistic adoration in every parish to pray for success. The call soon developed into an invitation to all Catholics in the diocese to take seriously the gospel imperative of reconciliation.

The result was startling. On two Sundays in Advent, more than 13,000 Catholics, over one-quarter of the Memphis diocese, responded to the call to celebrate the Lord's forgiveness. One Memphis priest wrote that "in my priesthood of nine years, I have never experienced any diocesan program that has created such a spirit of prayer, of unity among believers, of hope for the future of the church."[28]

Monthly communal reconciliation services with general absolution is a promising opportunity for the church to restore the sacrament of reconciliation to Catholic life and to revitalize whole parishes. The result: Catholics gain a more profound sense of sin, experience deep sorrow and repentance for offending God and others, and overcome their distaste and fear of confession. Their experience of God's loving forgiveness and of their consequent peace and joy invariably causes them to begin again the practice of private profession.

6. Strengthen the Church's Commitment to Justice throughout the World

Inspired by the Council's opening to the world and by John Paul II's passionate commitment to justice and human rights, the church everywhere

---

28. Albert Kirk, "Reconciliation in Memphis: A Diocese Prepared," *America* 136 (Feb 19, 1977): 146-48.

has become the major spokesman and fighter for the rights of every human person, especially the poor, the oppressed, and the most disadvantaged. Building on this modern achievement, the Catholic Church now has the challenge and opportunity to be even more the prophetic moral conscience of the world; to become the effective voice of the increasingly poor under-developed nations of the world; to conscientize and prod the rich nations of the North to moderate capitalist abuses and face their global responsibility to the poor South in terms of sustainable development, environmental protection, debt remission, and slowing the depletion of their national resources as the pope has done in his recent social encyclicals and in his public utterances; and to deal realistically with overpopulation in developing countries that too often contributes to destruction of the land, periodic starvation, and immense human suffering.

The following are concrete steps the Catholic Church could now take.

First and most fundamentally important is the opportunity to repudiate once and for all the mentality of an "established" church, that is, the mind-set that promotes holding a privileged position in a country by which the church's interests are protected by the government so that the church may maintain an influential role in morality, education, and politics. Such a church compromises preaching the gospel and living gospel values and is rarely a prophetic church.

Second, the Catholic Church, leaders and faithful alike, are challenged by events and by prophetic voices within the church to make positive applications of the church's preferential option for the poor of the world. Pope John Paul II's many public statements are eloquent and forceful about the plight of the poor of the world and of poor nations; but attitudes and actions of some curial officials, some papal nuncios, some bishops and priests and many affluent Catholics negate these strong statements. Liberation theologians remind us that one cannot be truly committed to the poor without personally living a simple life, or better yet, actually living and working with the poor. In this age of massive poverty and oppression, when the church itself is rapidly becoming a church comprised of poor people, the Catholic Church has an opportunity to give a powerful witness of poverty and a simple lifestyle, in imitation of the poor Christ to the rich nations of the world. Such witness is a vivid example of Christian love.

A third challenge and opportunity is for the church to support its courageous and prophetic local bishops, religious, and priests in their struggle, often to death, for justice for the poor and oppressed of the world. One thinks of the heroic struggle of Bishop Pedro Casaldáliga in Brazil's Mato Grosso area, with wealthy landowners who have murdered many of his Indian people and who have often threatened him. One remembers the murdered Archbishop Romero, "the voice of those who have no voice" in El Salvador, and the attacks he suffered from some Vatican officials, from his own bishops, and from the wealthy elite in his country. A more recent example is Mexican Bishop Samuel Ruiz Garcia of San Cristóbal de las Casas, who has been undermined by the papal nuncio in Mexico because of his strong support for the rights of his impoverished Indians of Chiapas. The church has an unprecedented opportunity today to give unequivocal support to those bishops, priests and lay Catholics who are living examples of justice and Christian love in their day-by-day actions.

Fourth, today's world provides the church with opportunities to take specific actions for justice and peace that speak powerfully to the world: to collaborate on an equal basis with other Christian churches and the world religions in works of justice, as Pope John Paul II has repeatedly encouraged; to encourage a more simple and poor lifestyle for some bishops and papal nuncios, especially in underdeveloped countries; to move forward the process of canonization of Archbishop Oscar Romero, the martyr of justice and Christian love, whom the poor *campesinos* of Central America have already spontaneously proclaimed a saint in the fashion of the early centuries, before the church set down the norms and stages of canonization.

To canonize Archbishop Romero is to make a strong statement about the priorities of the church, and would give great consolation and hope to the masses of the poor and oppressed of Latin America and of the world and to those bishops, priests, religious women and lay leaders so heroically committed to them. St. Oscar Romero and Companions! What a tribute to a shepherd who gave his life for his flock and for the thousands of priests, nuns, delegates of the Word, *campesinos,* and indigenous peoples likewise murdered for their commitment to justice and Christian love!

A final challenge and opportunity is more subtle and difficult: to educate Catholics to the social teaching of the church and to inspire affluent Catholics to become committed in practical ways to the works of justice, in order to alleviate the terrible consequences of structural injustice and the increasing imbalance between the wealthy and poor of the world. Pope John Paul II has spoken in strong terms about consumerism and amassing unneeded luxuries when over half of humanity lacks the barest necessities for human life. He reminds us that the goods of this earth are meant for all who have a right to them in justice. The question is not therefore whether the affluent are entitled to enjoy the fruits of their talents and honest hard work, because they are. Rather the urgent question today is: What is enough? When do luxuries and status symbols become extravagant and unjust in a world of massive poverty, hunger, disease, homelessness? Were a new consciousness to take hold in the world, were even a small percentage of the affluent deliberately to scale back their luxuries in order to give the differential to the desperately poor, much poverty and disease and hunger could be overcome and the suffering and early deaths of children avoided. The difference between a Mercedes Benz and a Ford!

For the Catholic Church, laity and leaders, to enter fully into the struggle for justice and peace will demand conversion on all levels. The challenge is indeed great; the opportunity even greater.

7. Support Theologians in Their Ecclesial Vocation

A characteristic of today's church is the publicity given to the relationship between Catholic theologians and the teaching authority of the church, particularly as regulated by the Congregation for the Doctrine of the Faith (CDF).

Thus support — or lack of it — for theologians, especially moral theologians, is a pressing issue in the Catholic Church today. It involves a host of other issues: the indispensable role of theologians and the necessity of quality theological scholarship; the important role of the church's magisterium; past and present practices of the curia's CDF; the credibility of the church to its own members and to other Christians.

The role and responsibility of theologians in their ecclesial vocation in service to the church is to explain and synthesize through painstaking research, the truths of revelation and the Christian faith in the context of modern events and the expansion of knowledge. For this theologians need a certain autonomy and trust from the official magisterium and CDF. For its part, the responsibility of the magisterium is to hand on to succeeding generations the Christian faith without error and to encourage theological scholarship and the development of doctrine. Both theologians and the teaching office are painfully aware that poor, inadequate, rigid theology has in the past invited heresy and schism and the departure of scores from the church.

"To create a climate of reduced tension in the church," Cardinal Ratzinger, head of CDF, published in 1990 a carefully worded "Instruction on the Ecclesial Vocation of the Theologian,"[29] in which he described the role of theologians, the mission of the magisterium and the cooperation that should exist between the two.

> [The theologians'] role is to pursue . . . an ever deeper understanding of the word of God found in the inspired Scriptures and handed on by the living tradition of the church. (6)

> The magisterium has the mission to set forth the Gospel's teaching, guard its integrity and thereby protect the faith of the people of God. In order to fulfill this duty, it can at times be led to take

---

29. See *Origins* 20 (July 5, 1990): 117-26 for the 80,000-word text. Ladislas Orsy presented a brief analysis "Magisterium and Theologians, A Vatican Document," *America* 163 (July 21, 1990): 30-32.

serious measures as, for example, when it withdraws from a theologian who departs from the doctrine of the faith the canonical mission or the teaching mandate it had given him or declares that some writings do not conform to this doctrine. (37)

Regrettably, in its zeal to protect orthodox doctrine, the Catholic Church has too often been guilty of repressive and cruel measures. Aside from the **Inquisition** and periodic "witch hunts for heretics," the church's reaction to its perception of "**modernism**" in the past century was immensely damaging, setting back theological research, greatly impoverishing the church and unjustly ruining the careers of scholar-theologians loyal to the church.

In the first decade of the [twentieth] century, during the pontificate of Pope Pius X, seminaries were closed, theological periodicals were suppressed, a network of 'informers' in each diocese was organized, oaths [of orthodoxy] were repeatedly taken, intellectually rigid bishops were appointed, and fear and distrust were everywhere. . . . The theological suppression . . . and the fears it instilled resulted in a total lack of theological creativity in the United States for half a century . . . [and] left us unprepared for the dramatic changes of the sixties.[30]

Moreover, in the period before Vatican II, theologians like Yves Congar, Jean Daniélou, Henri de Lubac, and John Courtney Murray were forbidden to teach and publish. Fortunately, they became advisors to bishops at Vatican II and architects of Council documents. Likewise, European Scripture scholars were vindicated by Vatican II's positive pronouncements on biblical exegesis and the historical-critical methodology. Since the Council, CDF has disciplined various theologians worldwide, removing in some cases their mandate to teach in Catholic institutions.

The U.S. bishops in June 1989 approved a positive set of guidelines titled "Doctrinal Responsibilities: Approaches to Promoting Cooperation and Resolving Misunderstandings between Bishops and Theologians."[31]

Authoritative teaching and theological inquiry are distinct but inseparable tasks. For this reason, bishops and theologians need to cooperate with one another in accordance with their respective responsibilities. . . . This cooperation is intended to realize the ideals of mutual encouragement, support and assistance . . . as well as to promote the efficacy of the episcopal office, the soundness of theological scholarship and that unity without which the church's mission in the world becomes weak and diffuse.

---

30. Archbishop Rembert Weakland, "The Price of Orthodoxy II," *The Milwaukee Catholic Herald* (Sept. 18, 1986): 3.

31. U.S. Bishops, "Doctrinal Responsibilities," *Origins* 19, No. 7 (June 29, 1989): 97-110.

Thus the health, progress, and credibility of the church is involved in the positive collaboration of magisterium and theologians. For a *healthy* church does not instill fear and punish theologians devoted to their profession and to the church they love, thus limiting their necessary theological contribution. The church, inextricably involved in the historical world, makes *progress* only if her best minds confront new problems and challenges. As Archbishop Weakland remarks, "Repeating old formulas does not answer new problems; they demand new thinking in the light of held truths . . . the glory of the Catholic Church, as distinct from fundamentalism, has been its willingness . . . to accept truth wherever it comes from and to integrate it with revealed truth. . . ."[32] The *credibility* of the church, both to its own members and to other Christians, as well as people in general, is severely damaged by rigid orthodoxy, authoritarian measures, suppression of theological thought and silencing of theologians. A death blow is dealt to theological scholarship and Christian ecumenism.

In this sensitive area in today's church, a delicate balance is needed. The church must safeguard the integrity of its teaching on matters of faith and morality, for it cannot afford the doctrinal uncertainty and ambiguity found in some churches. Yet, it equally cannot afford to inhibit freedom of theological scholarship, theological pluralism, and responsible disagreement that often leads to legitimate development of doctrine. The Catholic Church has a critical opportunity today in relation to the theological enterprise to witness to its own scholars, to other churches in ecumenical partnership, and to the world at large that it is indeed an open, searching church, unafraid of freedom and truth.

Perhaps the wise, optimistic advice of John XXIII from his address to the bishops that opened the Second Vatican Council is appropriate here:

> Often errors vanish as quickly as they rise, like fog before the sun. The church has always opposed these errors. Frequently she has condemned them with the greatest severity. Nowadays, however, the spouse of Christ prefers to make use of the medicine of mercy rather than that of severity. She considers that she meets the needs of the present day by demonstrating the validity of her teaching rather than by condemnations.[33]

8. Support Development in Sexual Morality

A reality in the Catholic Church today is the widespread disagreement among Catholics concerning the church's teaching in the area of sex. Rank-and-file Catholics, both young people and married couples, challenge the church to develop a theology of human sexuality that is congruent with their life experience. Many young people cannot accept that pre-marital

---

32. Weakland, "Price of Orthodoxy I" (Sept. 11, 1986): 3.

33. Walter Abbot, ed., *The Documents of Vatican II* (New York: The America Press, 1966), 716.

sex in a genuinely committed relationship leading to marriage is seriously sinful. Archbishop John Quinn observed at the 1980 Bishops' Synod that the church's teaching on contraception in marriage "is not working." Educated Catholics and non-Catholics alike, concerned about the exploding world population, particularly in poverty-stricken countries that suffer from chronic hunger, malnutrition, brain-damaged children, and actual starvation, find the church's stand unrealistic. They believe that if contraception were not condemned as an intrinsically evil action in all circumstances, the church's teaching on abortion would become more convincing and accepted. Many Catholics today express the opinion that the church would be wise to keep official pronouncements and condemnations in sexual matters to a minimum.

In her long familiarity with human nature, the Catholic Church knows well the explosive power of sex that needs restraint and control. The church has the right and responsibility to teach concerning morality. The challenge, however, is for the church to teach well, relying on the expertise and responsibility of her competent moral theologians. Thus an urgent two-fold challenge for the church today is to *listen* to the lived experience of her members, married and single, straight and gay, and to *support* her moral theologians in their difficult task. Today's well-educated Catholics too often perceive the church as excessively negative, inflexible and authoritarian in the area of sexual morality. Thus, as the church moves into its third millennium, it has a crucially important responsibility and opportunity to develop a sexual morality that is understandable, positive, and helpful to people in their daily lives. The pastoral care of its members, as well as the credibility of its teaching office, are at stake.

Challenges and Opportunities with Other Christian Churches

9. Break Today's Ecumenical Impasse

Despite the extraordinary progress of the theological dialogues between the separated Christian churches and their exciting discoveries of substantial faith agreement, both Catholic and Protestant ecumenists recognize the ecumenical impasse today. There is a growing malaise and frustration, after the optimism and excitement following the Council and during the 70s. Now one hears expressions like "ecumenism is dead," "union is impossible."

In this situation many ecumenists believe that the Catholic Church holds the key to breaking the current ecumenical impasse. As the oldest (along with the Orthodox) and the largest and most influential church, its ability to restore the broken unity of the Christian Church is perhaps the greatest. In its claim to be the fullest expression of Christ's Church, it can be said to bear a large share of responsibility to answer Jesus' prayer for unity. As establishing requirements for other churches to enter into full communion with itself, the Catholic Church has the opportunity to accept the existing faith and ecclesial realities other churches possess as sufficient for at least some immediate steps toward union.

In his article, "The Conversion of the Churches: Conditions for Unity,"[34] canonist and theologian Ladislas Orsy has formulated seven obstacles to church union which he believes the Catholic Church represents for other churches and which accordingly call for institutional conversion. These obstacles are expressed in seven statements that conclude the sentence beginning:

"Ecclesial union is impossible as long as . . ."

. . . the Church of Christ is conceived as existing exclusively in one given community or denomination.

. . . apostolic succession is seen as an "unbroken line of episcopal ordinations from the Apostles to the bishops today" and therefore is accepted as the *only* criterion of valid ordinations and sacraments.

. . . theological and ecclesial pluralism and the principle of unity in diversity are denied.

. . . the Roman curia seeks to exercise total centralized control over the whole church, especially local bishops and their churches.

. . . the papal office remains unrenewed according to the Gospel of Jesus.

. . . the Vatican refuses to recognize at least Anglican and Lutheran ordinations and sacraments and to promote eucharistic sharing.

. . . synodical and conciliar models of church are denied in practice."

If the preceding statements are recognized as constituting intractable obstacles to healing the broken unity of the Church of Christ today, then Orsy's two questions pinpoint the challenge and opportunity facing the Catholic Church today: "How can our Church, the Roman Catholic Church, contribute to the healing of the Church of Christ through the process of institutional conversion? How can it enter into a *kenosis*, an emptying of itself for the sake of others?"[35]

What specific steps then could/should the Catholic Church take today to grasp this opportunity to heal the body of Christ? The following steps provide promising potential for future church union and at the same time

---

34. Ladislas Orsy, "The Conversion of the Churches: Condition for Unity, A Roman Catholic Perspective," *America* 166 (May 30, 1992): 479-87. This article was inspired by the remarkable work of the *Groupe des Dombes,* an independent group of Catholics and Protestants in France who issued a challenge to the divided churches: "to recognize that their identity is grounded in a continual conversion — without which their unity can never be realized." Groupe des Dombes, *For the Conversion of the Churches* (Geneva: WCC Publications, 1993).

35. *Ibid.,* 481.

seem theologically possible for the Catholic Church today. Each deserve brief comment.

- Recognize two facts about *apostolic succession*: that an *unbroken* line of episcopal ordinations back to the Apostles does not exist, either as "unbroken" in history or as traceable to one or more of the 12 Apostles (see Chapter 10, issue 2); that the original meaning of apostolic succession, as BEM emphasized, stressed the handing on of the apostolic *faith* guaranteed by a given bishop, able to trace his ordination to an apostolic church rather than to an individual Apostle (see Chapter 10, issue 4). Accordingly, if Anglican and Protestant churches have in fact substantially maintained today the *apostolic faith*, then a theological case may be made that they are within the apostolic succession and thus *capable* of possessing valid ordinations (even though apostolicity in teaching and faith is not of itself sufficient to constitute the *sacramentality of ministry*).

- Recognize *Protestant ministry* as bringing the means of salvation to its members. (UR 3) Though the Council did not attribute real church status to Protestant churches, rather referring to them as "ecclesial communities," still a theological case can be made for their real ministry and orders on the basis that they do bring God's grace and salvation to their members. Moreover, one cannot assert with certainty that the Holy Spirit denies sacramental efficacy/validity to responsible ecclesial bodies.

- Permit and promote *eucharistic sharing* between those churches that have genuine eucharistic faith, even if the theological explanation (transubstantiation) and practices (reservation of the species) differ. Vatican II did recognize that eucharistic sharing as means to future union of the churches is to be recommended, though under limited conditions. Eucharistic sharing is a significant grassroots experience of unity in Christ. As a result, the laity and many priests might be inspired to become ecumenically active, providing a needed groundswell toward ecclesial union. On the other hand, ecumenists recognize that eucharistic sharing might simply produce indifference toward further necessary steps toward union.

- Renew the functioning of the *papal office* according to gospel values of service and love. Lutheran theologians stated they could accept the papal office in a future united church of Lutherans and Catholics, "provided the pope renew himself according to the Gospel." Protestants and Orthodox will not be attracted to union with Rome until the papal office uses its authority in a more collegial way and becomes a protector and promoter of diversity-in-unity. In terms of union with the Orthodox, the Catholic Church might explore a return to the practice of the first three centuries, when the five patriarchs of Jerusalem, Antioch, Alexandria,

Constantinople, and Rome were in communion with each other, without one dominating the others in jurisdiction. The Orthodox do accord a primacy of honor to the pope, but cannot recognize a primacy of universal jurisdiction.

• Explore and offer to Protestant churches the *"uniate" model* that exists between Eastern Catholic churches and the Roman Catholic. In this model Anglicans, Lutherans, Methodists and others would be in communion with the bishop of Rome as successor of Peter but would retain their own bishops and priests/ministers, their own theological and spirituality traditions, their own worship, and their own discipline including married pastors and women priests. In a sermon preached at St. Mary's Church, Cambridge, on July 18, 1970, Cardinal Willebrands, head of the Vatican Curia's Secretariate for Promoting Christian Unity, went beyond the uniate model in speaking of "a plurality of *typoi* within the communion of the one and only Church of Christ."

> Where there is a long coherent tradition, commanding men's loyalty, creating and sustaining a harmonious and organic whole of complementary elements [characteristic theological method and approach, characteristic liturgical expression], each of which supports and strengthens the other, you have the reality of a *typos*. . . . The life of the Church needs a variety of *typoi* which would manifest the full Catholic and apostolic character of the one and holy Church.[36]

• Realize in concrete practice Vatican II's understanding of the Church of Christ as a *communion of local churches*. Essential to this model is the genuine though not exclusive autonomy of local bishops and their local churches. By reversing the current trend to centralize power and decision-making in the Roman curia, a serious obstacle to other churches coming into communion with the Roman Catholic Church will be lessened.

• Recognize the *validity of Anglican Orders*. When King Henry VIII severed communion with the pope in the 16th century, the bishops of England were validly ordained in the apostolic succession; they thus ordained other bishops and priests, who accordingly celebrated valid Eucharists. As the Church of England became more Protestant, Catholics argued that in the 18th century, for various complex reasons, the Anglican Church lost valid orders. The commission created by Pope Leo XIII in 1896 to study the question of "Anglican Orders" voted 5 to 4, after extensive historical research, against their validity. The subsequent document stated that Anglican orders are "absolutely null and void."

---

36. Barry Till, *The Churches Search for Unity*. (Baltimore: Penguin Books, 1972): 437-38.

In the totally new ecumenical reality today, thanks to the theological dialogues between Anglicans and Catholics and owing to new scholarly research, both Anglican and Catholic theologians desire that the issue be reopened and that, on the basis of new evidence, Anglican ordinations be recognized as valid. Anglican bishops and priests would thus enjoy the same status as Orthodox bishops and priests. To recognize Anglican ordinations and their bishops would constitute a giant step toward the expressed goal of organic unity between the Anglican and Roman Catholic churches. However, the Holy See holds that the time is not yet "opportune," especially in light of some churches in the Anglican Communion ordaining women.

What seems to be needed today are bold, concrete, practical steps toward union that will break the ecumenical impasse. The above seven points may provide such steps; they constitute a remarkable challenge to the Catholic Church and an opportunity uniquely open to it.

10. Meet the Challenge of Fundamentalist and Evangelical, Pentecostal Churches

An unusual and serious challenge in the latter part of the 20th century facing the Roman Catholic Church — and mainline Protestant churches as well — is the rapid growth of fundamentalist and evangelical Pentecostal churches in Catholic Latin America and among Hispanic Catholics in the United States. Some statistics show the extent of the challenge. An estimated 500,000 Catholics in Brazil and between 60,000-100,000 Hispanics in the United States leave the Catholic Church each year to join Pentecostal or fundamentalist congregations. By the year 2000, at current growth rate, Brazil will have 35 million Pentecostals. According to David Stoll, *Is Latin America Turning Protestant?*, the 400 groups planting evangelical Pentecostal churches in Guatemala "might make it the first predominantly evangelical country in Latin America." Though Mormons are not strictly Pentecostal, their membership in Latin America has tripled in the last decades to one million. Thus Brazil's Catholic Bishop Bonaventura Kloppenburg stated that Latin America is becoming Protestant more rapidly than Europe did in the 16th-century Protestant Reformation!

To respond to this challenge, the Vatican published on May 4, 1986, a well-researched, irenic report "Sects, Cults and New Religious Movements."[37] After an objective analysis of nine reasons for their success in attracting Catholics, the report made this remarkable judgment:

---

37. "Vatican Report on Sects, Cults and New Religious Movements," *Origins* 16, No. 1 (May 22, 1986): 1-10.

> . . . if we are true to our own beliefs and principles in respect for
> the human person, respect for religious freedom, faith in the action
> of the Spirit working in unfathomable ways for the accomplish-
> ment of God's loving will for all humankind, for each individual
> man, woman and child, we cannot simply be satisfied with con-
> demning and combating the sects . . . The "challenge" of the new
> religious movements is to stimulate our own renewal for a greater
> pastoral efficacy.[38]

The report then outlined six practical "positive pastoral approaches" so that
"the challenge of the sects" may be "a useful stimulus for spiritual and
ecclesial renewal."[39]

Before considering these pastoral approaches, it is necessary to clarify terms. *Evangelical* is the broadest term: evangelicals seek to convert
the world to Christ by preaching the gospel (*evangelium*); they stress the
subjective experience of personal salvation and of being "born again"
through personal conversion to Christ. **Fundamentalism** is narrower in
scope, insisting on a few clearly defined fundamental beliefs. **Pentecostalism** is both evangelical and sometimes fundamentalist, but particularly emphasizes the Holy Spirit, healings, prophecy, joyful praise of God.

◆

The Main Tenets of *Fundamentalism*

- *Literal interpretation* of the Bible as the literal word of God.

- *Absolute inerrancy* of the Bible; since it cannot err, the Bible has the
  answer for everything. Fundamentalists use texts from the Bible uncritically to prove certain positions.

- *Apocalyptic view of history,* that is, the end of the world is coming
  soon, along with God's harsh judgment of sinners. Allied to this is *pre-
  millennarianism*, that is, the world will suffer a great cataclysm,
  followed by Jesus' return and a 1000-year period of peace. The "rap-
  ture" will occur during the cataclysm in which Jesus will "seize" the
  good people, thus saving them from the catastrophe that awaits sinners.

- *Unity of church and state* so that government can force fundamentalist
  views of God and religion on everyone, thus Christianizing a sinful
  world. For this end, the Religious Right was formed by Pat Robertson
  and others to use politics to Christianize America.

- The *great enemies* are secular humanism, atheism and communism.

◆

---

38. *Ibid.*, 8.
39. *Ibid.*,

Today in the United States, evangelical and fundamentalist religion is taught in hundreds of small bible colleges and some universities, like Oral Roberts University in Tulsa. It is promoted over a large network of TV and radio stations by TV evangelists like Pat Robertson, Jimmy Swaggart, Oral Roberts, Jerry Falwell and the recently deposed Jim Bakker, whose programs reach vast audiences and rake in millions of dollars from their impassioned preaching.

The most active and visible *Pentecostal churches* in Latin America and among U.S. Hispanics are the Assemblies of God, the Church of God, Seventh-Day Adventists, and scores of nondenominational evangelical groups. They preach a simple, uncomplicated religion: believe "in Christ," read the Bible and you will be saved. Pentecostals offer small, intimate communities of worship and support. They promise absolute certitude of belief and thus a sense of security in a complex world. Their ministers are extremely zealous and confident; their goal is to convert the world to Christ. They bring highly developed organizational skills in the use of radio, TV, mass mailings and sophisticated sales techniques, and are backed by enormous funds from the United States. They often give food and clothing to destitute Indians and sometimes build homes for them. They capitalize on the failure of the Catholic Church to provide the experience of God and Jesus and the Bible in supportive Christian communities.

How should Catholics react to the challenge of evangelical Pentecostal churches and their remarkable growth? From one viewpoint, their success can be a cause of rejoicing in that "converted" Catholics come to know and love the Bible, experience joyful worship and warm support in small groups of Christians, choose Jesus as their personal savior to whom they commit their lives, and turn from alcoholism, drugs and adultery.

From another viewpoint, Catholics who join evangelical or Pentecostal churches too often receive a diminished Christianity, a false understanding of the Bible through literal interpretation of individual texts, become alienated from their centuries-old Catholic culture, and are denied the full richness of Catholic faith and life. Unfortunately, more than a few evangelical and Pentecostal missionaries use unchristian methods of gaining converts: they unjustly criticize Catholic "idolatrous worship" of Mary, the "superstition" of the Mass, and the role of the pope in the Church. By claiming exclusively to have the truth, they implant a closed mentality in their converts. A special problem in some Latin American countries has been the cozy relationship between Pentecostal missionaries and military dictatorships; since most evangelicals and Pentecostals steer clear of social justice issues and action, they have been favored with privileges, protection, and financial backing by local military governments.[40]

---

40. The Rios Mont dictatorship in Guatemala, between March 1982 and August 1983, was one of the worst examples of cooperation between evangelical, Pentecostal missionaries and a terrorist regime.

To meet this formidable evangelical Pentecostal challenge, the Vatican document proposes six areas of action for the Catholic Church:[41]

- Rethink the traditional parish-community system; create "caring communities of lively faith, love (warmth, acceptance, understanding, reconciliation, fellowship) and hope."[42]

- Provide "ongoing formation . . . evangelization, catechesis, education, and ongoing education in the faith — biblical, theological, ecumenical."

- A personal, holistic approach: "discovering Christ personally through prayer and dedication."

- Inculturation: "a simpler Christianity integrated into all aspects of daily life."

- Prayer and worship: greater sense of communal celebration; rediscovery of the word of God.

- Laypersons exercise true leadership and a diversified ministry.

If implemented, these well-chosen goals will help. But do they go far enough? James McCrea believes "radical restructuring of community, ministry, worship and evangelization" is needed. Otherwise "Catholicism, as it exists [in Latin America], seems doomed to move ponderously, self-protectively and painfully ineffectively, while Protestantism in its more spirited forms sweeps through the barrios and the middle-class suburbs."[43]

The missionary zeal and success of the evangelical, fundamentalist, and Pentecostal churches today emphasize the urgent need for the Catholic Church to move swiftly and creatively: to form supportive Christian communities with participative worship and genuine prayer; to increase without delay the number of priests, which means ordaining married persons; to inspire and train enthusiastic, Christ-committed lay evangelizers; to continue the preferential option for the poor and support for liberation theology. This constitutes an enormous challenge as well as opportunity for the Catholic Church in Latin America and among U.S. Hispanics in the next decades.

11. Call "A Genuinely Universal Council"

In 1970 Lukas Vischer, then director of the World Council of Churches' Faith and Order department, proposed to the Christian world "a genuinely universal Council" that might speak for all Christians.[44] Since

41. "Vatican Report on Sects, Cults. . .," 7-8.

42. Where the base Christian communities flourish in Latin America or supportive Christian parish communities with vibrant liturgies exist among Hispanics in the United States, Pentecostals are unable to attract Catholic converts.

43. James McCrea, *America* 164 (Feb. 16, 1991): 189.

44. Lukas Vischer, "A Genuinely Universal Council," *The Ecumenical Review* 22, No 2 (April, 1970): 97-106.

then there have been calls for a Vatican III or a Jerusalem II or simply the Eighth Ecumenical Council for, as Pope Paul VI acknowledged, only the first seven Councils were truly ecumenical as including all of Christianity, both the East or Orthodoxy and the West or Roman Catholicism; subsequent Councils Paul VI termed synods of the western Roman Catholic Church!

Technically, this Council would be called by the pope, since only he, as the successor of Peter, could legitimately and authoritatively summon a Council. Yet, for historical, theological and ecumenical appropriateness, the Orthodox patriarch of Constantinople could be a co-summoner. They would invite all eastern patriarchs, Catholic bishops, and their Protestant counterparts. Those churches in theological dialogue with each other would most conveniently be invited: Anglican, Baptist, Catholic, Disciples of Christ, Lutheran, Methodist, the Orthodox, Pentecostals, Presbyterian or Reformed.

The Council's purpose might aptly be the goals John XXIII set for Vatican II: the reunion of the separated Christian churches, their renewal according to the gospel, common action toward dealing with the great problems of the human family, plus collaboration in evangelization. As the Spirit moved the bishops at Vatican II in unexpected ways, so might Christ's Spirit lead the still-separated churches toward full communion. They would surely experience their united power to deal with humanity's massive problems: hunger, war, refugees, secularism, systemic injustice, environmental destruction, racism and sexism. One result might be a new vitality for each of the churches as they experience the new Pentecost John XXIII prayed Vatican II would bring about.

In a genuinely ecumenical council, Vischer cautions that the churches need to come together as equal partners in dialogue and prayer. It is imperative that each be a part of the decision-making process whose vote is counted. This will demand a genuine conversion on the part of all the churches: a strong sense of being one in Christ, a real trust in each other and in the Spirit's guidance, and ultimately a *kenosis* or self-emptying.

For such a Council to happen, Vischer insists that the churches must first have fellowship with each other. He suggests four conditions that must be present for this fellowship to exist: the churches must be truly reconciled to one another; they must be able to celebrate Eucharist together; they must possess a sense of universal solidarity, aware that in Christ they belong together as one and are responsible for each other; and they must overcome the racial, national and gender barriers that divide people and keep them from being a universal family. Vischer warns that presently the churches are marked by structures primarily intended to preserve their own identity; these must be replaced by "structures of change" and by focusing on the future rather than on past differences.

Would the separated churches agree to such a Council? Would the Orthodox and Roman Catholics? For the Catholic Church to accept other churches as "equal partners in dialogue" would mean recognizing they had the same doctrinal teaching authority as bishops in the Catholic Church. Likewise, to be "part of the decision-making process" would also pose a major problem in disciplinary and moral questions held strongly by the Catholic Church. Thus, the obstacles are great, the difficulties many. Yet the separate existence and activity of the Christian churches becomes increasingly incomprehensible and contradictory in the world today. Failure to act together will make the churches more and more irrelevant and continue to limit their "evangelization of the nations." A genuinely ecumenical council may well deserve a chance: it is a creative challenge and opportunity for Christianity today.

The Ultimate Challenge and Opportunity Today

12. Achieve Individual and Institutional Conversion

To accomplish the previous 11 challenges and opportunities for the church approaching its third millennium, the Catholic Church, members and leaders alike, and indeed all Christian churches need to undergo a profound conversion, that is, a radical change in accustomed ways of thinking and acting.

The call to conversion was at the heart of Jesus' teaching. He challenged his hearers to "love God with all your heart, with all your soul and with all your strength, with all your mind, and your neighbor as yourself (Luke 10:27). Jesus' first recorded words in Mark's Gospel are "the reign of God is at hand. Repent. . .," that is, reform your lives, be converted. His famous beatitudes show his deepest values: "Blest are the poor in spirit . . . the lowly . . . they who hunger and thirst for justice . . . who show mercy . . . the single-hearted . . . the peacemakers" (Mt. 5:3-10).

The renewal of the Catholic Church begun at Vatican II was essentially a two-fold call to conversion: for *Catholics* to live their Christian life at a deeper level, to develop a biblical and eucharistic spirituality, to think and act ecumenically, to become evangelizers proclaiming the good news of Christ, to claim their vocation to establish God's kingdom in this world; for the *official church* to renew its structures, to develop collegiality at all levels of its life, to restore the broken unity of Christ's Church, to move into the world as a prophetic voice for justice and peace, to respect the equal dignity of all its members, to promote religious freedom, to dialogue with the great world religions, in a word, to be the sacrament of Christ on this earth by mirroring the risen Christ and his values.

Though conversion always involves one's relationship to God and to Jesus Christ, in today's world where greed and gross selfishness oppress and kill others on a massive scale, conversion takes the form of concern for our fellow sisters and brothers and for deeds of love. The heart of Christianity is practical love for others, especially those in most need. The world needs more than ever today to hear and act upon Jesus' parable of the Good Samaritan who, moved with compassion, took care of the man beaten and robbed by thieves and left to lie on the roadside. Jesus' parable is meant to answer the question, "Who is my neighbor?" Whoever is in need is my neighbor (Luke 10:20-38)!

Following the spirit of Vatican II's *Gaudium et Spes*, conversion today necessarily demands linking Christian faith to works of justice. This means turning from systemic injustice to social justice, from materialism to spiritual values, from consumerism and waste to care for the world's limited resources, from narrow nationalism to global vision, from militarism to peacemaking, from selfish amassing of wealth to sharing with the world's poor and dispossessed. Members of the Jesuit order express this linkage of faith with justice in a phrase that has become their special mission today: "the faith that does justice." Their much-loved recent Fr. General, Pedro Arrupe, capsulized this spirit in the phrase "men for others." The challenge to be persons for others by doing the works of justice in order to become a force for changing the world is especially addressed to youth today. Young people are beginning to respond to this call. For they recognize the contradiction between calling themselves Christian and remaining unconcerned, even comfortable, in the face of the hunger and starvation, the massive injustice and poverty and violence suffered by millions today.

Church leaders are not exempt from Jesus' call to conversion. Such conversion means repudiating the last vestiges of "triumphalism, clericalism, and legalism" in their exercise of authority. It means following Jesus' example of washing his disciples' feet at the Last Supper through humble service rather than domination and control. It means listening carefully to the Spirit speaking through the people of God in the local churches of the world and in the signs of the times. It means carrying out resolutely, not selectively, the renewal of the Second Vatican Council. It means being able to admit the church's failures and mistakes. Ultimately, it means humble trust in the risen Christ and his Spirit present in and guiding the church.

Institutional Conversion

Institutional aspects of the church refer to its visible structures of government (papacy, bishops, curial offices, canon law), of worship (liturgical rites, sacraments), of belief (creeds, teaching office), of Scripture (Gospels and Letters, Biblical Commission), of missionary outreach (evangelization and inculturation). Institutional conversion in these areas means giving priority to Jesus' gospel values and the urgent pastoral needs of the faithful over preserving nonessential institutional interests. It involves the willingness to sacrifice or modify historically-conditioned structures and policies which rose to meet specific needs or simply reflected secular models and the prevailing culture and are not essential to the church's nature or its mission. When such structures no longer serve the primary mission of the church or fall prey to abuse, the need for institutional conversion becomes apparent.

Institutional conversion may also involve creating new church structures or modifying existing ones. Some examples frequently mentioned today are: structures of accountability and due process (legislative, executive and judicial "branches" are presently identical in the church!); structures of collegial relationships and democratic procedures at all levels of the church's life; synodical structures that are truly deliberative rather than merely advisory (particularly the triennial synod of bishops).

In this context, canonist-theologian Ladislas Orsy observed that "the intense movement of conversion at Vatican II . . . slowed down considerably" after the Council in the needed "transformation of centuries-old structures."[45] He proposed specific areas of institutional conversion:

- Granting the laity "a greater share in the operations of the church."

- Granting a more effective role to women in the church. "The need for an institutional conversion is there for all to see."

- Give a more effective role to the episcopal college: "a real but unfinished movement of conversion in the Roman Catholic Church."

- The Petrine ministry become a "a promoter of diversity": "to promote legitimate differences, to let local churches blossom, to be restrained in the use of power . . . would be a strong protection against an excessive centralization that the Council certainly wanted to avoid."

- Safeguard the "legitimate autonomy of bishops."

He stressed that institutional conversion concerns the way church leadership operates and how its decisions affect its own members, as well as other churches.

The 1990 "Call for Reform" by 4505 Catholics — predominantly lay women and men, but including priests and sisters — appealed "to the institutional church to reform and renew its structures." Their contention was that "today's church is crippled by its failure to address fundamental justice issues within its own institutional structures. It thus becomes a stumbling block to its own members and to society."

◆

The 1990 "Call for Reform" Catholics cited *eleven areas of reform*: women in ministry and decision-making; priesthood open to women, married men, and resigned priests; teaching on human sexuality; selection of local bishops; new forms of liturgy, language and leadership; open dialogue, aca-

---

45. Orsy, "The Conversion of the Churches," 482.

demic freedom, and due process; financial openness; meaningful movement toward reuniting the Christian churches; affirmation of the collegial and collaborative leadership style of the National Conference of Catholic Bishops; a voice in decisions to close parishes and schools; youth alienated by a church they view as authoritarian and hypocritical.

◆

Several of their statements underline urgent unaddressed needs in today's church:

> We see many Catholics deprived of the *church's sacramental life* because of the declining number of priests. In particular we see Catholics denied regular access to the Eucharist, the center of our worship and spiritual life. We call upon the church to discard the medieval discipline of mandatory priestly celibacy and to open the priesthood to women and married men, including resigned priests, so that the Eucharist may continue to be the center of the spiritual life of all Catholics.

> We see the pope and the Roman curia *selecting bishops* throughout the world without input from local churches. . . . We claim our responsibility as committed laity, religious, and clergy to participate in the selection of local bishops, a time-honored tradition in the church.

> We see very few instances where the people of God are allowed by church authorities to *participate in decisions* that affect their lives. . . . We call for extensive consultation with the Catholic people in developing church teaching on human sexuality.

> We see *women* experiencing oppression . . . and inequality. . . . We call upon church officials to incorporate women at all levels of minstry and decision-making.

> We see many *young adults* and children of Catholic families who are reluctant to affiliate with a church they view as authoritarian and hypocritical. We call for a fundamental change so that young people will see and hear God living in and through the church as a participatory community of believers who practice what they preach. (emphases added)[46]

Clearly the Catholic Church is being challenged to institutional conversion by its own members today. Martin Luther and the Protestant Reformers saw the urgent need for institutional reform of the 16th-century Catholic Church. In recognizing the sinful aspect of the church, the Second Vatican Council acknowledged the need for ongoing reformation and con-

---

46. "A call for Reform in the Catholic Church: A Pastoral Letter from 4505 Catholics Concerned about Fundamental Renewal in our Church" appeared in the Feb. 28, 1990 *New York Times* on pages A14 and A15. Copy of the "Call" is available from: Call for Church Reform, Call to Action, 3900 N. Lawndale, Chicago, IL 60618.

version. Increasing numbers of concerned and deeply committed Catholics call for further renewal and institutional conversion. Though these Catholics are sometimes branded as overly negative, naive in their demands, and disloyal, this groundswell of voices needs to be heard.

If *individual Catholics* become truly converted to the gospel values of Jesus and if the *official church* achieves institutional conversion, the great challenges and opportunities before the Catholic Church in the first century of its third millennium can be accomplished. The Spirit appears to be moving the church and society along new paths with new vision; should the church fail to move with the Spirit, it risks losing more members and becoming increasingly irrelevant. But if it can muster the will and trust in the guiding Spirit to embark on new decisions and daring initiatives, the Catholic Church may be poised for a dramatic take-off into a new and rich future for the kingdom of God!

Summary

The Catholic Church that begins its third millennium of life will be a vastly different church than we have known in at least six ways. It faces crucial challenges that are simultaneously promising opportunities for growth. To meet these challenges and opportunities, dramatic change must occur, which involves risk and trust in the guiding Spirit. Only a profound conversion of both members and leaders will be equal to the task. The 12 topics in this final chapter, which recapitulate major themes throughout the preceding chapters, attempt to identify and explain the most visible and urgent challenges and opportunities before the Catholic Church as it enters its 21st century.

For Discussion

1. How would you arrange these 12 topics in order of importance? Why do you put them in this particular order?

2. Of these 12, which three do you think provide the most promising opportunities for the Catholic Church today in terms of their being able to be accomplished?

3. How far do you think inculturation of the Christian message and life can and should go in Africa? in China? in the United States?

4. Where do Catholics most need conversion? Is the case for the institutional conversion of the Catholic Church overstated? Give specific reasons.

5. Do you think the Catholic Church has a bright future? Why? Why not?

For Action

1. Talk to an Assembly of God or Church of God member or minister about their converting Hispanic Catholics.

2. Find out from a Catholic who has made a Cursillo what difference it has made in his or her life.

3. Find out why the Vatican Commission called Anglican Orders "absolutely null and void." Was it justified?

4. Read up on the amazing Chinese Rites controversy. Form an opinion. Does it have any lesson for today's church?

5. Choose one of the 12 topics that interests you most and develop it further in the context of today's church and world.

Further Reading

Bühlmann, Walbert. *The Coming of the Third Church, an Analysis of the Present and Future of the Church.* Maryknoll, NY: Orbis Books, 1978.

Flannery, Edward. *The Anguish of the Jews: Twenty-three Centuries of Anti-Semitism.* New York: Macmillan, 1965.

Greeley, Andrew. *The Catholic Myth, the Behavior and Beliefs of American Catholics.* New York: Macmillan Publishing Co., 1990.

Griffiths, Bede. *The Marriage of East and West.* London: Wm. Collins Sons & Co. Ltd, 1982.

Group des Dombes. *For the Conversion of the Churches.* Geneva: WCC Publications, 1993.

Hegy, Pierre, ed. *The Church in the Nineties, Its Legacy, Its Future.* Collegeville, MN: The Liturgical Press, 1993.

Hughes, John Jay. *Absolutely Null & Utterly Void: An Account of the 1896 Papal Condemnation of Anglican Orders.* Washington, DC: Corpus Books, 1968.

Lernoux, Penny. *People of God, the Struggle for World Catholicism.* New York: Viking Penguin, 1989.

McBrien, Richard. *Report on the Church, Catholicism after Vatican II.* San Francisco: Harper, 1992.

Neuhaus, Richard. *The Catholic Moment. The Paradox of the Church in the Postmodern World.* San Francisco: Harper & Row, 1987.

Pennington, M. Basil. *Vatican II, We've Just Begun.* New York: Crossroad, 1994.

Provost, James and Wolf, Knut. *Collegiality Put to the Test.* Philadelphia: Trinity Press, 1990.

Rausch, Thomas. *Authority and Leadership in the Church. Past Directions and Future Possibilities.* Wilmington, DE: Michael Glazier, 1989.

Sanks, T. Howland. *Salt, Leaven and Light, The Community Called Church.* New York: Crossroad, 1992.

Tavard, George. *A Review of Anglican Orders, the Problem and the Solution.* Collegeville, MN: The Liturgical Press, 1990.

Walsh, John. *Evangelization and Justice, New Insights for Christian Ministry.* Maryknoll, NY: Orbis Books, 1982.

See Further Reading in chapter 6 for important books on inculturation by Hillman, Schineller, Shorter.

Bright Future?

Introduction

The Catholic Church is at a crossroads today!

Can the Catholic Church move ahead resolutely with the renewal begun by the Council? Can it apply the theological principles already in place to its practical life? Can it couragously confront crucial decisions no longer to be ignored? Can it create structures that make change possible? Can it respond to the ever-larger numbers of the faithful who seek a hearing and a voice in decisions affecting their lives?

For Vatican II is still happening; its work remains unfinished. Today's Vatican II church is a church in painful transition: from an authoritarian to more collegial church; from clericalized to pilgrim-people-of-God church; from Rome-centered to local church; from integralist to servant church; from triumphalist to ecumenically sensitive church; from Europeanized to global church; from a church wary of freedom to one unafraid of democratic procedures; from a church still somewhat suspicious of the secular world to one open to embracing the Spirit's action in human affairs.

This transition-church is faced with difficult decisions. Should priestly celibacy be maintained when millions of Catholics are denied the Eucharist and idealistic young men are forced to choose between marriage and a celibate priesthood? Can women be given a genuine role in church ministry and leadership? In the light of faith and theological agreements already achieved, what steps can the Catholic Church take to restore the broken unity of Christ's Church? What structures need be established to make the principles of collegiality and subsidiarity operative throughout the church? What development in sexual morality is possible today?

Is the Catholic Church in crisis today? out of control? in danger of schism?

Many good people think so. They point to tragic scandals exploited by the media, to polarization within the church, to tension between the Holy See and the church's most educated and committed Catholics, to widespread dissent from magisterial teaching, to the startling decline in vocations to the priesthood and the religious life, to confusion on sexual morality, to the departure of youth from the church, and so forth. The answer of restorationist Catholics to this perceived crisis is to restore discipline and clarity of teaching.

Many others disagree with this crisis-restoration view. They point to the vitality of the Catholic Church today. Its Vatican II renewal is far advanced, firmly entrenched in Catholic consciousness in the remarkably short period of 30 years. Catholics are experiencing a deepening of spirituality based on the riches of the Scriptures and of the eucharistic liturgy. They manifest increasing social consciousness and a growing concern for justice and human needs, thanks in great part to the strong leadership of John Paul II and of socially committed bishops. They have become ecumenically-minded, breaking down stereotypes and barriers between Christians. Lay Catholics in large numbers are exercising valuable ministry within the church and to the world. The Catholic Church itself is becoming a church of and for the poor and a church of martyrs for justice and Christian love.

This book has endeavored to present the contemporary church as it actually exists today: renewed by Vatican II, rich in sacramental-liturgical life, alive with a thirst for justice and human rights, in the forefront of the ecumenical movement, unafraid to be countercultural in modern life, assuming its role as spokesperson for human values and rights, increasingly the sacrament of Jesus Christ to its members and the world; yet a church wracked by inner tensions and divisions, burdened by its own limitations and sinfulness and continuing need for renewal/conversion, at times rigid and insensitive to the religious needs of its members, resistant to change, too often jealous of its institutional prerogatives, authoritarian and overly insistent on obedience.

What, then, might the Catholic Church be in the future?

As we have seen, it will be a far different church in the 21st century. Its center of gravity will have shifted from Europe and the West to Africa, Latin America and perhaps Asia. The majority of its members will be poor and young. They will remain in the church only if that church meets their religious needs and reflects values like freedom, democracy, justice. It will be a church of the laity who will assume ever-greater responsibility for the mission and ministry of their church as they demand a voice in decisions affecting them. It will be a prophetic church encountering growing opposition from the dominant culture, especially in the United States, where its bishops "remain unshakable supporters of Catholic social teaching . . . as it affects the poor, the oppressed, the immigrant, . . . the bishops are not willing to compromise."[1]

Challenges abound. Will the scandal of divided Christianity become so intolerable that the Roman Catholic, Orthodox, Anglican and mainline Protestant churches take determined action to achieve a form of union respectful of each other's gifts and uniqueness? Will collegial relationships at all levels become the normal life of the Catholic Church? Will the papacy develop in its exercise of authority to ensure unity while protecting diversity? Will responsible pluralism become a mark of the church? Will affluent Catholics, especially those whose decisions effect the lives of so many, live Gospel spirituality?

Does the Catholic Church, then, have a bright future?

Despite apparently overwhelming problems and seemingly unresolvable internal divisions, the Catholic Church is in fact well-equipped to enter the 21st century. It possesses well-educated, committed lay Catholics ready to exercise their ministry in world and church; heroic Third-World Christians suffering and dying for justice and Christian love; intelligent, dedicated pastoral bishops exercising strong leadership; competent, holy recent popes, like John XXIII and Paul VI and today John Paul II, who have positioned the church for dramatic advance of God's kingdom. It is a church progressively being purified through acknowledging its sinfulness and limitations and need for total reliance on its Lord and his guiding Spirit. It is a church of holiness, of saints and martyrs aplenty.

There is thus reason to foresee a bright future for the Catholic Church entering its third millennium. For the renewal unleashed by the Second Vatican Council, with its new vision and direction for the church, is irreversible despite setbacks and pockets of opposition. Even when presenting—by necessity—the present contemporary church with its warts, its problems and tensions as well as its many virtues, values and gifts, a pervading spirit throughout this book has been, I hope, one of Christian optimism. For tensions and problems are signs of life in a living organism and inevitable in a church acknowledged by the Council to be sinful and in need of continuing reformation; indeed, these can be lifegiving, challenging the church to change and to grow.

---

1. *National Catholic Reporter* 31 (Dec. 2, 1994): 36.

There is much reason for optimism.

With remarkable vision, global perspective and historical sense, Pope John Paul II in an apostolic letter released November 14, 1994, "As the Third Millennium Draws Near,"[2] announced a worldwide celebration for the jubilee year 2000. The jubilee "is meant to be a great prayer of thanksgiving, especially for the gift of the incarnation of the Son of God and of the redemption which he accomplished." (#32) The Holy Father plans simultaneous celebrations in the Holy Land, in Rome, and in the local churches (dioceses) of the world. Stressing the "ecumenical and universal character of the Jubilee Year," the pope hopes for a meeting of all Christians and invites representatives of the great world religions to participate "so that we can celebrate the Great Jubilee, if not completely united, at least much closer to overcoming the divisions of the second millennium." (#34) He calls for "an examination of conscience" within the Catholic Church, acknowledging that church members have in the past been intolerant and even violent and that truth cannot be imposed on people.

He proposes a three-year period of spiritual preparation and theological reflection: 1997 on Jesus Christ and faith, 1998 on the Holy Spirit and hope, and 1999 on God the Father and charity. John Paul II stressed "a renewed commitment . . . [to] the teachings of Vatican II (# 20) and suggested specific means of church renewal: continent-wide synods for Asia, Oceania and North America; recognition of heroic holiness of married couples through canonization; the call for Christians to practice justice and "raise their voice on behalf of the poor of the world." (# 51) This Jubilee Year celebration of the third millennium of Christianity carries promise for the renewal of the Catholic Church, the spiritual growth of Christians, and progress of God's kingdom.

A former Lutheran pastor and theologian who recently became a Catholic has devoted a book to *The Catholic Moment,* in which he argues that John Paul II's papacy has strengthened the movement toward Christian unity and made the church an effective voice in the world.[3] Historian Jay Dolan refers to a new spirit alive in the American Catholic Church so that "the twenty-first century belongs to it!"[4] Above all, the Holy Spirit John XXIII prayed to come on the Catholic Church in a new Pentecost at the Council is today guiding the church, leaders and members alike, bringing us to a future yet unknown but, we may confidently hope, rich in promise.

---

2. John Paul II, "As the Third Millennium Draws Near: Apostolic Letter for the Jubilee of the Year 2000," *Origins* 24: No. 24 (Nov. 24, 1994): 401-16.

3. Richard Neuhaus. *The Catholic Moment: the Paradox of the Church in the Postmodern World* (San Francisco: Harper & Row, 1987).

4. Jay Dolan, *The American Catholic Experience: A History from Colonial Times to the Present* (New York: Doubleday, 1985).

One thing seems certain: the next decades in the church's life will be difficult, full of challenges and opportunities, and very exciting!

I conclude with the optimistic words of two church leaders. England's Cardinal Basil Hume told the Louvain, Belgium, theology faculty in March 1989:

> The church in our day is undergoing the most profound, far-reaching and positive renewal since the time of the Counter-Reformation. Some see only death. Others already discern resurrection. To the new world being created around us, the renewed church, the Easter people, brings a message of life and hope.

Archbishop John Quinn addressed the priests and deacons of the church of San Francisco, June 14, 1993:

> The archdiocese is a microcosm of the new world in which the new church is struggling to be born. We cannot be content with the ways of the past. We have new challenges and we must be imaginative in meeting them; we must not be afraid to take risks. We must have vision, daring and more than a dash of courage.

Glossary

These glossary entries (followed by the chapter in which they first appear) are printed in bold in their first appearance in the text. The following references were helpful in composing the explanation given below: Gerald O'Collins and Edward Farragia, *A Concise Dictionary of Theology* (New York/Mahwah, NJ: Paulist Press, 1991); John Hardon, *Modern Catholic Dictionary*, (Garden City, NY: Doubleday, 1980).

Acts of the Apostles 6: The 28-chapter account attributed to the evangelist Luke of the church's origin and growth from Jesus' Resurrection to Paul's imprisonment in Rome. Peter and the Jerusalem community dominate the first half; Paul's mission to the Gentiles in his travels throughout Asia Minor founding churches compose the second half.

Advent 5: Four-week period of preparation for Christmas which begins the liturgical year.

***Anamnesis* 14** (Greek, remembrance): Recalling Christ's passion, death, resurrection. Refers to Christ's command repeated in the Eucharist "Do this in memory of me" (1Cor 11:24-25; Luke 22:19). In the Anglican-Roman Catholic International Dialogue, this ancient concept enabled the two churches' theologians to reach agreement on the Eucharist as sacrificial meal.

Anglican communion 1: Various national churches which arose from the English Reformation of Henry VIII in the 16th century and which recognize the honorary leadership of the Archbishop of Canterbury.

Annulment 15: Official declaration, after thorough investigation by a church court, that a marriage did not in fact exist because of a preexisting impediment to a valid sacramental marriage.

Apparitions, Marian 7: Appearances of the Blessed Virgin Mary, generally to children, who communicates messages urging prayer and penance

428

for the salvation of the world. The church is very slow to approve these alleged appearances; the best-known approved apparitions are Guadalupe, Lourdes, Fatima.

Apostolic See 11 (Latin, *sedes* or seat): The governing and spiritual authority of the pope over the Catholic Church, symbolized by his chair (seat, throne) as bishop of Rome. Another term is Holy See. Both terms include the various offices of the curia that assist the pope in church government.

Apostolic succession 10: The office given by Christ to the 12 Apostles continues in the church today in properly ordained bishops. In a broader sense, the unbroken continuity in essential belief and practice between the church today and the church Christ founded on the Apostles; this continuity is expressed in bishops being the successors of the Apostles.

Audience 11 (a hearing): Meeting of small or large groups to see and "hear" the pope. His weekly Wednesday "audience" is held during winter in the Paul VI Audience Hall before 6000-7000 people and in summer outside in St. Peter's Square for much larger crowds; the pope gives a prepared talk, welcomes pilgrims from various countries, and touches outstretched hands as he makes his way down the aisle entering and leaving.

Autocephalous 8 (Greek, "having its own head"): Term used for eastern and oriental Orthodox churches governed by their own synods and in communion with each other.

Baptist 1: Numerous evangelical churches that trace their origin to the 17th century, when they broke with the Anglican Church of England. Only believers who make a conscious profession of faith in Christ are baptized. Each local congregation is relatively autonomous.

Biblical criticism 2: The scientific study and analysis of the human elements in the writing of the Bible. Called the historical-critical method, it includes textual, historical, form, tradition, redaction and literary criticism. It does not deny the divine inspiration of the Scriptures as the inspired word of God.

Canonization 7 (Greek, canon or list): Church's solemn declaration that a person, now dead, had achieved heroic holiness, is among the saints in heaven thus able to be publicly invoked by prayers, and is worthy of imitation. Canonization adds a person to the list of Saints.

Carmelites 12: The contemplative Discalced (shoeless) Carmelites, founded by St. Teresa of Avila in 1563, live enclosed lives of poverty, abstinence from meat, prayer and manual labor. The Carmelite order for men was founded in the 12th century, taking its name from Mt. Carmel in Palestine.

Catechumenate 13: The lengthy period of preparation for baptism in the early church, culminating in the scrutinies and prayers of healing on the 3rd, 4th and 5th Sundays of Lent and the actual baptism during the Easter Vigil. **Catechumens** were those preparing for baptism. Vatican II restored this practice in the Rite of Christian Initiation for Adults (RCIA).

Catholic Substance 1: Protestant theologian Paul Tillich's term to indicate the given essence of Christianity — origin in Christ, historical continuity, Scriptures, creeds, tradition including councils, church order and so forth maintained in the Catholic Church. Its necessary complement, according to Tillich, is the Protestant principle of returning to early Christian sources, relativizing claims to absolute authority and constant questioning, reforming, renewing "the given" of the Catholic substance.

Celibacy 19: The renunciation of marriage. In the Latin tradition of the Roman Catholic Church, celibacy is required of candidates for the priesthood; permanent deacons are not permitted to marry after their ordination. Eastern Catholics have a married clergy. Orthodox priests and deacons are generally married, but bishops must be celibate.

Charism, 12 (Greek, gift or talent): St. Paul's term for special gifts given Christians by the Holy Spirit. The **charismatic renewal** (7) is a movement within the Catholic Church since Vatican II of persons (**charismatics**) who experience the gifts of the Holy Spirit, especially joy in prayer and sometimes healing and speaking in tongues.

Collegiality 2: Responsibility for the whole church shared by the bishops in communion among themselves and with the head of the college of bishops, the pope. Collegiality is most fully exercised in an ecumenical council, but also through episcopal conferences and synods of bishops. It was a major emphasis of Vatican II.

Communion (together with): Multiple usage in this book: to express how the Catholic Church is united worldwide through bishops and their people being "**in communion with**" (10) the successor of Peter, the pope (Vatican II thus described the worldwide church as a **communion of local churches** (19); to describe the Council's favored **communion model** (8) of future church union — churches reestablishing communion with each other and the bishop of Rome; the **communion of saints** (4) is the spiritual union between Christ and all Christians, whether already in heaven (or purgatory) or still living on earth.

Concordat 11: Formal agreement between the Vatican state and various nations to protect the spiritual and temporal interests of the Catholic Church and the rights of its members in those countries.

Conscience 16: The ability to judge and choose a course of action in accordance with the law God has "written" in every human person (Rom 2:12-16).

Conscientization 18 (raising awareness): The effort in liberation theology to cause native peoples, oppressed for centuries, to realize their human and Christian dignity and rights and the causes of their oppression in order to rise above their condition and fashion their own destiny.

Contemplation 6: Form of silent prayer in which the mind and imagination are less active and the person "contemplates" or looks at and rests in the love of God and the divine mysteries.

Conversion 16: Complete change of heart or turning away from sin, selfishness, attachment to worldly values toward God, spiritual values, and living for God and others. Biblical word is *metanoia* (Greek, change of mind).

Counter-Reformation 2: Movement of Catholic reform that began in reaction to the Protestant Reformation, was legislated for in the Council of Trent (1545-63), and carried out in succeeding centuries, especially in Europe.

Covenant 4: Special formal friendship-love agreement or compact between God and the Jewish people; between Jesus and Christians through his blood on the cross; between a Christian man and woman in a sacramental marriage.

Curia, Vatican or Roman 2: The large organization in Rome of administrative and judicial offices, especially the nine curial congregations, that help the pope govern and lead the universal Catholic Church.

Devotio Moderna 7: A spiritual movement in Belgium and Holland in the 14th century that stressed the practice of simple piety, asceticism and the imitation of Christ; by meditating on his sacred humanity one contemplates his divinity and attains union with God that liberates the soul. Founded by Gerard Groote (1340-84), its finest example is Thomas à Kempis, whose much-read *Imitation of Christ* focused on the interior life and the Eucharist, on separation from the world and inner conversion.

Devotions 7: Nonliturgical prayers and practices (way of the cross, rosary, novenas, vigil lights, home altars, etc.) that nourish Catholics' spiritual lives and deepen their faith and love of God.

Dialogues, theological 8: Scholarly discussions between theologians from the divided Christian churches to clarify differences, discover common faith, and reach theological agreement where possible. Vatican II encouraged Catholics to dialogue also with members of non-Christian religions (interreligious dialogue) and with the world at large.

Dissent 17: Disagreement with official noninfallible teaching of the church. /
Private dissent as a conscience matter is permissible; the tension today
concerns public dissent. Dissent has played a major role in both the
development of doctrine and change in church discipline throughout
the centuries.

Doctrine 1: Official church teaching in its many forms. Not to be confused
with dogma, a divinely-revealed truth proclaimed infallibly by the
church and binding permanently on all Catholics. **Development of
doctrine** (1) is growth in the church's understanding of the truths of
divine revelation since the age of the Apostles. The substantial truth
of the revealed mystery remains unchanged; but with the help of the
Holy Spirit the church deepens its grasp and appreciation of what the
truth means and how it affects life in different historical circumstances. New developments cannot contradict the original revealed
"deposit of faith." Theologians are indispensable in the development
of doctrine.

Dulles, Avery 1: Jesuit theologian recognized as perhaps the leading
American ecclesiologist, owing to his broad scholarship, balance, and
clear writing. Convert to the Catholic faith and son of former Secretary of State John Foster Dulles.

Ecclesiology 1 (Greek, study of the church): The branch of theology that
reflects on the origin, nature, distinguishing characteristics and mission of the church. Vatican II was the "council of the church," the
first to deal exclusively with the church. Since the church shares in
the mystery of God, no single ecclesiology can exhaust the meaning
of the church. Different ecclesiologies exist: the New Testament presents various images for the church; through the centuries different
aspects of the church were emphasized; today the hierarchical, people
of God and body of Christ emphases are prominent.

Economia 15 (Greek, house management): In eastern Orthodox theology,
economy refers to the church applying God's understanding mercy to
human weakness to help its members live the Christian life in conflicting and difficult situations of human life.

Encyclical 9 (Greek, circular letter): A bishop's letter intended for wide
circulation. Since the 18th century, a letter addressed by the pope to
the whole Catholic Church; such papal encyclicals are not infallible
but are authoritative statements of the ordinary magisterium.

Enlightenment, Age of 1: Movement starting in 17th-century Europe that
resisted authority and tradition, defended freedom and human rights,
stressed empirical methods in scientific research and the use of reason.
Many of its followers rejected divine revelation and miracles, strongly
opposed Christianity, and supported biblical criticism.

Episcopacy 10 (Greek, overseer, hence bishop): Church government by bishops. The world's bishops make up the **episcopate** (10); as **episcopal college** (10) they are successors of the apostolic college. An **episcopal conference** (10) is the organization of bishops in a nation or region to help them form policy, issue directives and guidelines, and handle internal church affairs as well as to lobby governments to influence laws.

Euthanasia 17 (Greek, mercy killing): Use of direct, intentional means to bring about a suffering person's death or the failure to use reasonable ordinary means to keep a person alive.

Evangelicals 1 (Greek, good news or gospel): Term for Protestant Christians who stress justification by faith and the supreme authority of the Bible.

Evangelization 2: The proclamation to all peoples (Matt. 28:19-20) and to all cultures the good news about Jesus Christ to bring about the assent of faith.

Excommunication 8 (Latin, exclusion from communion): Church penalty for specific serious moral acts or faith denial that excludes from receiving the sacraments and being part of the church community.

Faith and Order 8: Unit within the World Council of Churches in Geneva, Switzerland, devoted to studying theological problems dealing with faith belief and church ordinations in order to achieve the unity of the separated Christian churches. It organized world ecumenical assemblies at Lausanne (1927), Edinburgh (1937), Lund (1952), Montreal (1963), and Santiago de Compostella (1993).

Fatalism 18: The belief that poverty and oppressed conditions were God's will, and therefore to be accepted as a cross in life in the hope of a better eternal life. Liberation theology seeks to destroy this attitude.

Fathers of the Church 7: Title given to the great Christian thinkers and writers (mostly bishops), beginning with St. Clement of Rome (d. 97 AD) and ending in the west with St. Isidore of Seville (d. 636) and in the east with St. John of Damascus (d. 749). Because of their outstanding teaching and holiness, their unanimous consent became a norm of orthodox doctrine in theological controversies.

Fundamental option 16 (basic choice): The radical orientation of one's life toward or away from God by a personal, serious decision that determines one's essential moral and religious life situation for good or evil. A person's destiny is determined by this basic choice rather than by individual actions. This theory developed in reaction to a legalism that considered moral actions in isolation from the whole context of one's life and personal growth.

Fundamentalism 19: Movement in 20th-century Protestantism, especially in the U.S., which interprets the Bible without considering its historical formation, literary forms and original meaning — thus opposing the historical-critical method of biblical criticism.

Gentile 3: Term for non-Jews. St. Paul, through his missionary journeys throughout the Mediterranean world, is known as the Apostle to the Gentiles.

Glossolalia 7 (Greek, speaking in tongues): A gift of the Holy Spirit by which persons speak in unintelligible words or in foreign languages. The early Christians in the time of St. Paul spoke in tongues; today's charismatics often do the same. Individuals gifted with prophetic inspiration are sometimes able to interpret these utterances to others.

Gregorian chant 5: The music of the Latin rite attributed to Pope Gregory I (ca. 540-604) and characterized by austere beauty and discipline that creates an atmosphere of prayer. Also called plainsong or plain chant.

Gustavo Gutiérrez 18: Peruvian priest-scholar who launched liberation theology with his book, *A Theology of Liberation,* in 1971. Though he continues to publish and lecture, his chosen work is with the poor as pastor in Lima.

Heresy 2: A false teaching which denies an essential doctrine of the Catholic faith. A **heretic** is a baptized person who deliberately and persistently denies orthodox doctrines of faith.

Hermeneutics 1 (Greek, interpretation): The theory and practice of understanding and interpreting biblical texts using the historical-critical method of biblical criticism. By extension, the scientific theological interpretation of church documents.

Hierarchy 10 (Latin, holy authority or order): The ordained ministers in the church, bishops, priests and deacons. By reason of jurisdiction, the hierarchy is made up of pope and bishops. Thus in popular usage the term refers to the pope and bishops. The concept of a hierarchy of bishops-priests-deacons deriving their authority from the sacrament of orders and not from the consent of the people distinguishes the Roman Catholic and Orthodox tradition from Protestant churches.

Hierarchy of truths 8: The principle enunciated by Vatican II (UR 11) for interpreting the truths of faith by their nearness to the central mystery of faith: the revelation of the Trinity; the Incarnation of the Son; the divinity of Jesus and his saving death and resurrection; and the role of the Holy Spirit. Such "classifying" of truths according to their relative importance can eliminate false emphases and facilitate ecumenical dialogue.

Holy Office 2: Name formerly given to the present curial Congregation for the Doctrine of the Faith, also formerly called the Inquisition.

Holy Spirit 1: The third person of the Trinity, adored and glorified together with the Father and the Son as one in nature and equal in personal dignity with the Father and Son. The work of sanctification is attributed to the Spirit through the Spirit's many gifts. The Spirit came upon the Apostles on Pentecost Sunday to begin the church.

Holy Week 5: The most solemn and important week in the church's liturgical year that celebrates Jesus' saving death and resurrection. It begins with the blessing and procession with palms on Palm Sunday, recalls Jesus' institution of the Eucharist on Holy Thursday and his passion and death on Good Friday, and culminates in the Easter Vigil on Holy Saturday night. In the eastern churches it is known as "The Week of Salvation" or "The Great Week" by the Greek Orthodox.

Humanae Vitae 19 (Of Human Life): The encyclical by Pope Paul VI in 1968 that condemned artificial means of birth control.

Icon 7 (Greek, image): A sacred image painted on wood or formed by a mosaic, highly revered by the Orthodox and eastern churches. Icons of Christ, Mary, angels and the saints present them symbolically rather than realistically. Icons are noted for brilliant colors and spiritual quality and often are valuable works of art.

Incarnation 1 (Latin, enfleshing): The event of the eternal Son of God, while remaining fully divine, becoming truly and fully human in Jesus of Nazareth who had a human body and soul.

Inculturation 2: Contemporary term to express how the Christian message and life take shape in the various cultures and peoples of the world.

Indigenous 18: Refers to peoples originally native to a country, as the Mayans in Guatemala, native Americans in the United States. "Indians" as a term for indigenous peoples is inaccurate and resented by them as too often a debasing title.

Indissoluble 15: Not able to be broken or put aside, in reference to the bond of a sacramental marriage that has satisfied all requirements for validity and been consummated sexually.

Inquisition 21 (Latin, investigation): A special church tribunal set up by Pope Innocent III (d. 1216) for tracking down, examining and punishing heretics perceived as a threat to the social order as well as the faith of Catholics. In 1479 Ferdinand and Isabella introduced the feared Spanish Inquisition against relapsed converts from Judaism and Islam; those found guilty were handed over to the state for punishment.

Institutionalized violence 18: The moral and physical suffering done to oppressed peoples when the very institutions of society — health care, education, legal system, police and military, etc. — far from helping, are deliberately used to oppress poor indigenous peoples in order to keep them in subjection. Liberation theologians call it structural sin.

Jurisdiction 10 (Latin, judgment on what is lawful): The right and duty (legal authority) the pope and bishops possess to govern the church. In practice, bishops get jurisdiction in some matters from the pope, priests from their bishops. Vatican I stated that the pope has full jurisdiction over the whole church.

Kairos 8 (Greek, "right time"): Based on the original meaning of God's special interventions at key points in historical time, a popular meaning today is a specially favored time to accomplish important actions or changes in the church that may not occur again.

Kingdom of God 6: The reign or rule of God in the world at large, especially in the minds and hearts of people. As a *process* of establishing respect-love-obedience for God and justice-love-peace in human affairs, it is called the reign of God; as the *future goal* of this effort, it is often referred to as the eschatological or perfect kingdom of God at the end of the world. Jesus' and the church's main mission is to establish and work for the reign and kingdom of God; the church, however, is not to be identified with God's kingdom, which can and does exist outside the church and its members.

Koinonia 8 (Greek, "fellowship," "communion"): Rich ecclesial term used by St. Paul in the early church to refer to the bond of love with Christ and among Christians and between Paul's various churches. Popular term today to express the union which already exists and should further exist between Christians and their separated churches.

Laity 4 (Greek, *laos* or people): The faithful who have been fully incorporated into the church through baptism, confirmation and Eucharist but who have not received holy orders and become clerics. Vatican II sought to restore laypersons in the church to their proper importance and rights.

Lent 5: The 40-day period beginning with Ash Wednesday of prayer, fasting, almsgiving, penance and conversion to prepare Christians for Easter, the greatest feast of the liturgical year. In the early church Lent was the special time for catechumens to prepare for baptism.

Liberation Theology 1: A largely Latin-American movement inspired by the massive poverty, injustice and marginalization of the majority of Latin Americans and by a reading of the Bible in terms of God's concern for justice and care for the poor and Jesus' proclamation of God's kingdom on earth; its goal is the liberation of the poor and oppressed.

Liturgy 2 (Greek, "public service"): Official community worship, especially the eucharistic liturgy or Mass. The liturgical movement, which began in the late 19th century in France pioneered by Benedictine scholars and liturgists, encouraged all members to participate fully in church worship and make the Eucharist the center of community life. The renewed Mass after Vatican II is made up of two parts: the **liturgy of the word** (14) focusing on three Scripture readings and homily and the **liturgy of the Eucharist** (14) highlighting Jesus' words of institution over bread and wine and the peoples' participating in the sacrificial meal at the holy communion. The **liturgical year** (5) is the church's calendar of Masses celebrating the major events in Christ's life, Mary's role in salvation, and saints' feast days.

Local church 2: The Christian community in union with its bishop, hence the geographical "diocese" made up of one bishop (the Ordinary), his priests and deacons and the baptized believing lay members. The universal or worldwide church presided over by the pope as center of unity is, in Vatican II's term, a "communion of local churches." Vatican II restored the importance of the local church and its bishop.

Lutheran 1: Those churches that follow the basic teachings of Martin Luther, the initiator of the German Reformation: *sola fides* or justification by faith alone, not by good works; *sola gratia* or justification through God's grace alone; and *sola Scriptura* or the Bible, not human traditions, as the only authoritative rule of faith. Lutherans emphasize Christ's cross and human bondage to sin.

Magisterium 1 (Latin, "office of teacher"): The official teaching office of the Catholic Church, composed of the pope as successor of Peter and all the bishops as successors of the 12 Apostles. The *ordinary*, day-by-day, noninfallible magisterium is exercised by the pope and by individual bishops; the *extraordinary* magisterium is exercised when the pope or all bishops, whether in an ecumenical council or scattered around the world, "define" or proclaim a revealed truth to be believed absolutely. In the Middle Ages, theologians and theological faculties exercised a certain kind of magisterium. Despite today's tension between theologians and some bishops, theologians and Scripture scholars are an essential aid to the church's teaching office.

Martyr 1 (Greek, "witness"): A person who witnesses Christ through freely offered suffering and death rather than deny faith in Christ and the truths of the Christian faith. Martyrdom is the supreme act of love. The church liturgical calendar is full of saint-martyrs.

Mass 5 (perhaps from the Latin *Ite missa est,* Go, the mass is ended): Popular term before Vatican II for the full eucharistic liturgy. The terms Eucharist or "THE liturgy" are supplanting "Mass" since Vatican II.

Methodist 1: The churches that follow John and Charles Wesley, who sought to renew the Church of England in the 1700s. From their revival movement was born Methodist worship and a later separate church. Methodists stress evangelism, priesthood of all the faithful and social action; they tend to prefer a religion of the heart over rigid and rationalist teaching.

Millenarianism 21 (Latin, "thousand"): The belief based on an interpretation of the book of Revelation that Christ will reign on earth for a thousand years with his saints until the final defeat of Satan and a definitive entry into glory.

Ministry 4 (Latin, service): Sharing in Christ's mission and roles as prophet, priest and king by all Christians through their baptism and confirmation and by the clergy in a special way through the sacrament of orders. Since Vatican II, the ministry of the laity has been stressed, resulting in a proliferation of lay ministries.

Modernism 21: An umbrella term for a complex Catholic theological movement in the late 1800s and early 1900s in Europe to proclaim the Catholic faith so as to be understandable and acceptable to people of that period. Modernist theologians supported modern progress in science and philosophy, biblical criticism, historical development in Christianity. Some erred in appearing to make religion a matter of personal or collective religious experience and to deny objective revelation from God. They were strongly condemned by Pius X. Vatican II vindicated most of the concerns and theological insights of the modernists.

Monasticism 7 (Greek, "life alone"): Movement in the Catholic Church begun by ascetics in the deserts of Egypt, Palestine and Syria and standardized by St. Benedict and his rule of life in the 6th century Italy, whereby devout Christians answered Christ's call to perfection by giving themselves through poverty, celibacy and obedience to a community life of prayer, common worship and service of others. They came to be known as monks and were an extraordinary presence and influence in Christianizing Europe.

Moral theology 17: That branch of theology which studies God's revelation in the Scriptures and church teaching, in philosophic reasoning and human experience, and in various sciences to show how Christians ought to live and to determine the rightness or wrongness of human action. **Moral theologians** (17) are professionally trained to practice moral theology for the benefit of the church.

Moral Norms 17: Standards, guidelines, criteria that point to what is good and to be done in human behavior, thus helping persons make moral decisions. Moralists distinguish two kinds: *formal* or *general* norms like "do good and avoid evil, don't lie or murder" which are absolute, binding at all times; *material* norms that deal with specific particular actions like "speak the truth, don't take human life" are not absolutes but allow exceptions as, for example, speaking a falsehood to save another's life or killing in self-defense and in a just war. **Moral absolutes** (17) are considered by traditionalist moral theologians to bind at all times, without exception, and are called intrinsically evil acts.

Mysticism 7: A special, deep experience of union with and knowledge of God freely given as gift by God. Mystical experiences are often accompanied by ecstasy, visions and other phenomena. Genuine **mystics** (7) are dedicated to prayer, sensitive to God's presence in their lives, and show great love of God and other people.

Natural law 17: The universal, moral law given by God in the very act of creating human beings and able to be known by human reason. Or simply put, God's plan or will for humans "written" into the physical and human natures God created. The Catholic Church has for many centuries followed natural law philosophy in its moral judgments. Moral theologians before, and especially since Vatican II, have criticized a narrow, rigid understanding of the natural law, developing a more nuanced, complete explanation.

Nicene-Constantinopolitan Creed 1: The creed or statement of Christian belief about God, the divinity and nature of the eternal Son and Jesus, and the Holy Spirit. It was formulated at the first ecumenical council at Nicaea (modern Turkey) in 325 and completed at the second council at Constantinople (current Istanbul) in 381. This creed is accepted by all Christians and recited every Sunday at Catholic Eucharists.

Nuncio 2 (Latin, messenger): The pope's representative in a country that has diplomatic relations with the Vatican. The nuncio has the status of ambassador, representing the Vatican state. He is always a bishop. In a country not having diplomatic relations with the Vatican, the pope's representative is called an apostolic delegate, as was the case in the United States until recently.

Ordinary 10: The bishop of a diocese (local ordinary) who has jurisdiction and chief responsibility for his local church. In larger dioceses or archdioceses, the Ordinary is aided by "auxiliary" bishops who do not exercise jurisdiction over the diocese.

Orthodox 1 (Greek, "right belief"): Those eastern churches, generally national churches like the Greek Orthodox (8) and **Russian Orthodox** (1), ruled by a patriarch, which are not in communion with the bishop of Rome as a result of the schism or break finalized in 1054 between the eastern and western portions of Christianity.

Parish 4 (Greek, "neighborhood"): Catholic people living within a specific area of the diocese with their own priest as pastor and their own church building, generally named after a saint or title of Christ or Mary (Sacred Heart parish, St. Anselm, Holy Redeemer, Star of the Sea — the titles are ingenious in their variety).

Patriarch 8 (Greek, "father who rules"): Since the 6th century, the title given to the bishops of Rome, Constantinople, Alexandria, Antioch and Jerusalem, each of whom exercised wide authority within their own area. A title of the pope today is patriarch of the western church. Ecumenical patriarch is the title of the patriarch of Constantinople. Patriarch is the usual title of that bishop with major authority in Orthodox churches today who heads a **patriarchate** (8) made up of Orthodox Christians in a given country or area.

Patriarchy 7: The mentality and institutionalization of male dominance over women in society and in the church, with men holding power and denying it to women. In the Catholic Church today, women complain they are excluded from decision-making that affects their lives, the major exclusion being ordination to the priesthood.

St. Paul 1: A Jewish pharisee who severely persecuted Christians until converted on the road to Damascus by a vision of the risen Christ. This changed his life; he became the great Apostle to the Gentiles through indefatigably preaching the risen Christ and founding churches all over Asia Minor. His letters to these churches contain profound theology centered on the resurrection of the crucified Jesus.

Pentecost 2: Originally a major Jewish feast, the Christian feast of Pentecost recalls the day the Holy Spirit descended on Jesus' disciples, Peter preached to the people, and 3,000 accepted his message and were baptized, thus beginning the Christian Church. **Pentecostal** (1) churches stress baptism in the Spirit, special gifts like healing and prophecy, and convert-making through aggressive preaching and missionary programs, especially in Latin America.

Pontiff, the Roman 11 (Latin, "bridge builder"): A title of the pope from *Pontifex*, the title given the priestly caste of the Roman empire as mediator between the gods and the Roman populace. Thus pontiff indicates the pope's pastoral and teaching authority.

Popular religiosity 7: Very personal devotion to saints, Mary and the suffering Christ, expressed in elaborate feastday celebrations, processions, acting out the suffering and death of Jesus by whole villages on Good Friday, etc. Because "pagan" elements and superstition were intermixed, the church had criticized this popular religion; now it is appreciated and respected as nourishing the faith life of people oppressed for centuries and as helping them cope with their hardships and suffering.

Primacy (Latin "the first place") **of honor and jurisdiction** 11: The office of the leading bishop or *primate* in a church and the respect due his rank. The pope is considered by Orthodox and a growing number of Anglicans and some Protestants as the first bishop of the world in terms of *honor* because the Apostle Peter was martyred in Rome.

Only Catholics recognize the bishop of Rome's preeminent *jurisdiction* or spiritual and teaching authority over the whole church.

Purgatory 7 (Latin, "purification"): A process of purification for those who die in God's friendship and are thus assured of heaven but who need to be purified from the effects of personal sin and to grow spiritually before enjoying the presence of God in heaven. Scripture does not "prove" the existence of purgatory; but the ancient tradition of the church indicates that Christians prayed and offered the Eucharist for their dead loved ones since the 2nd and 3rd centuries. Martin Luther rejected the value of indulgences for the dead and the existence of purgatory. Vatican II briefly endorsed Catholic teaching on purgatory made by the councils of Florence (1438-45) and Trent (1545-63).

RCIA 4 (Rite of Christian Initiation of Adults): Based on the ancient catechumenate, this ritual introduced after Vatican II in 1972 is a year-long course preparing adults for baptism and entrance into the Catholic Church. They receive the sacraments of Christian initiation — baptism, confirmation and first Eucharist — at the Easter Vigil Mass.

Reception 17: Technical term denoting the process by which official church teachings and decisions are accepted, assimilated and interpreted by the whole church.

Reformation 1: Though the cry for "reform in head and members" existed in the church at least since the Council of Vienne (1311-12), Reformation popularly refers to the Protestant reform begun by Martin Luther and carried on by John Calvin, Ulrich Zwingli and others in the first part of the 16th century. Vatican II acknowledged the need for "continued reformation" in the Catholic Church (UR 6).

Reformed 1: Term applied to Christians following the teachings of John Calvin in Geneva, Holland and France and John Knox in Scotland. In the United States, Presbyterians and the United Churches of Christ formed from various Congregational churches are in the Calvinist-Reformed tradition.

The Restoration 1: Term used by Cardinal Ratzinger, head of the curial Congregation for the Doctrine of the Faith, to describe the current effort in the Catholic Church to restore traditional values, teachings and discipline alleged to have been lost or distorted since the Second Vatican Council.

Resurrection 1 (Latin, "rising," "being raised"): Not a mere return to earthly life but the passage of Jesus through death to his transformed glorified life. Jesus' resurrection guarantees the resurrection of human beings as the creed states ("resurrection of the body"). The Resurrection is the central truth of Christianity and was the heart of the Apostles' early preaching of the good news.

Revelation 2 (Latin, "taking away the veil"): God's self-communication through creation, historical events, prophets, and especially Jesus Christ in his life, death, resurrection and sending of the Spirit. Thanks to Vatican II, theology understands that God's revelation is ongoing today.

Rubric 2 (Latin, "red"): Directives printed in red alongside the main text in black that guide bishops, priests and deacons while celebrating Mass, administering sacraments and preaching. Because of overemphasis on external actions and minute practices, rubricism came to be looked down on as distracting from the deeper meaning of liturgy.

Sacrament 3: Any visible sign of God's invisible presence and action. The **sacraments** (5) of the church are ritual signs through which the church manifests its faith and gives the grace of Christ present in the church and in the signs themselves. Catholics, Orthodox and Anglicans accept seven sacraments; Protestants generally accept only baptism and the Lord's Supper.

Sanctuary Movement 20: Cooperative effort of Christians and some Jews to secure safety and a new life in the United States for Central Americans fleeing persecution and injustice in their own countries.

Scriptures 1: The sacred writings inspired by God and expressing the Jewish and Christian faith in a way that is normative for all time. Other terms are the Bible, the Old and New Testaments. Today, Hebrew and Christian Scriptures is the more appropriate designation.

Sensus fidei or *sensus fidelium* 3 (sense of faith or of the faithful): That instinctive sense in matters of the Christian faith possessed by the whole body of Christian believers guided by the Holy Spirit. Cardinal John Henry Newman (1801-90) developed this theological concept. Since Vatican II, theologians have called attention to the importance of the agreement of the faithful rising from their sense of what constitutes Christian faith and practice.

Jon Sobrino 18: Prominent liberation theologian who teaches theology at the Jesuit Central American University in El Salvador. An extensive writer, his best known works are *Christology at the Crossroads, The True Church and the Poor, Jesus in Latin America, Spirituality of Liberation, Archbishop Romero, Memories and Reflections.*

Social Teaching 9: Comprehensive body of teaching, beginning with Pope Leo XIII in 1891, concerning the rights and obligations of different members of society in their relationship to the common good, both national and international. **Social justice** (9) deals with the basic rights and corresponding obligations of individuals in society.

Spirituality 7: Systematic practice of and reflection on a prayerful, devout and disciplined Christian life. Schools or styles of spirituality have often followed the charisms of various religious orders and their founders.

Subsidiarity 19 (Latin, "assistance"): A principle of Catholic social teaching that decisions and activities should be made and done at the lowest possible level. In social and civil life and in the church since Vatican II, this means that central organs of authority should not intervene at the local level which often acts equally as well or better than the higher level.

Syllabus of Errors 2: A list of 80 errors attached to Pope Pius IX's encyclical *Quanta Cura* in 1864 and expressed in propositions that are strongly condemned.

Synod 2 (Greek, "council"): An official meeting of bishops and other church leaders to determine matters of church doctrine, discipline and worship. These meetings can occur at the international, regional, national or diocesan level. The **Synod of Bishops** (14), mandated by Vatican II, meets every three years in Rome to advise the pope in matters of doctrine, discipline, morality and worship.

Taizé 11: An ecumenical religious community founded by Protestant Brother Roger Schutz, near a town of the same name in France, to pray and work for the union of the separated Christian churches through the example of various Christians living in community. Thousands of young people from all over the world flock to the monastery, live in tents, pray in the massive church of the Resurrection, share idealism and discuss how to change the world. Taizé monks conduct popular, distinctive Taizé prayer sessions in the United States and elsewhere.

Tiara, papal 11: Large "beehive" headdress with which popes were "crowned" and which they wore on solemn nonliturgical functions. Pope Paul VI sold his tiara and gave the money to the poor. Pope John Paul I refused to have a "coronation" ceremony. The tiara has fallen into disuse!

Tradition 1 (Latin, "transmission" or "handing on"): The *process* by which Catholic teaching and life are passed on to succeeding generations; with a capital "T," the *content* of what has been passed on ("church in her doctrine life and worship," DVS). It is distinct from traditions (plural, with small "t") which are various practices which have developed over the centuries in different places and times.

Trappists 12: Popular name for Cistercian monks forming a contemplative religious group of men who stress prayer, physical work and penance. Thomas Merton, author of the best-seller *Seven Storey Mountain* and many books on contemplation and prayer, was the best known American Trappist.

Council of Trent 2 (1545-63): The 19th ecumenical council held in the northern Italian city of Trent to meet the grave need for reform in the Catholic Church and respond to the Protestant Reformation. It met for three periods, clarified church doctrine and renewed discipline. Its comprehensive decrees initiated the Catholic Counter-Reformation and resulted in a remarkable revitalization of Catholic life in succeeding centuries.

Ultramontanism 11 (Latin, "beyond the mountains"): A negative term applied to European Catholics after the French Revolution who exaggerated papal authority and looked for all solutions "beyond the Alps" to the authority of Rome. The ultramontane movement culminated in the definition of papal infallibility at Vatican I in 1870.

Uniates 8: The name given to Eastern Rite Christian churches that reestablished communion with the pope to become Eastern Rite Catholics. The Orthodox consider uniate eastern churches the result of unfair Catholic proselytism — **uniatism** (11) —and thus a stumbling block to union of Orthodox and Catholics. However, the uniate model is proposed as a way of reuniting Protestant churches which could, for example, while retaining their own individuality become Anglican or Lutheran rites in communion with Rome.

Universal church 2: Emphasis on the worldwide Catholic Church and its central authority in the pope and in its organizational structures in Vatican City. The post-Vatican II Catholic Church is experiencing difficulty in balancing emphases between the universal church and the local churches of the Catholic world.

Validity 10 (Latin, "efficacious"): A legal term signifying that the Catholic Church officially recognizes the effects of a certain action; it describes the conditions for an action (a sacrament) to be efficacious or really existing, as a valid sacramental marriage. An invalid act or sacrament may have consequences that the Church does not officially recognize. Validity has special ecumenical significance in evaluating Anglican Orders and Protestant sacraments, ministers and ministries.

World Council of Churches 8: An international fellowship of Orthodox, Anglican and Protestant churches based in Geneva, Switzerland, whose goal is to call the churches to visible unity in one faith and in one eucharistic sharing. Though not a member, the Roman Catholic Church has close contacts through a Joint Working Group and theologians as full-time members of WCC's Faith and Order Commission.

Bibliography

This list both includes and supplements the books suggested for Further Reading at the end of each chapter. Books are arranged according to areas of interest, roughly corresponding to the various Parts of this book. Periodical literature is not included here but is referenced in the footnotes.

Vatican II: Evaluation and Reception (Part I and throughout book)

Abbott, Walter. *The Documents of Vatican II*. New York: Guild Press, 1966.

Alberigo, Giuseppe, Jean Pierre Jossua, Joseph Komonchak, eds. *The Reception of Vatican II*. Washington, DC : The Catholic University of America Press, 1987.

Hastings, Adrian. *Modern Catholics: Vatican II and After*. New York: Oxford University Press, 1991.

Hebblethwaite, Peter. *The Runaway Church: Postconciliar Growth or Decline*. New York: Seabury, 1975.

_____ *Synod Extraordinary: The Inside Story of the Rome Synod*. Garden City, NY: Doubleday, 1986.

Küng, Hans and Leonard Swidler, eds. *The Church in Anguish: Has the Vatican Betrayed Vatican II?* San Francisco: Harper & Row, 1987.

Latourelle, René, ed. *Vatican II: Assessment and Perspectives*, 2 vols. Mahwah, NJ: Paulist Press, 1988.

McBrien, Richard. *Report on the Church, Catholicism after Vatican II*. San Francisco: Harper & Row, 1992.

Novak, Michael. *The Open Church: Vatican II, Act II.* New York: Macmillan, 1964.

O'Connell, Timothy, ed. *Vatican II and Its Documents, an American Re-appraisal.* Washington, DC: Michael Glazier, 1986.

O'Malley, John. *Tradition and Transition: Historical Perspectives on Vatican II*, Wilmington, DE: Michael Glazier, 1988.

Ratzinger, Cardinal Josef. *Theological Highlights of Vatican II.* New York: Paulist Press, 1966.

Rynne, Xavier. *John Paul's Extraordinary Synod. A Collegial Achievement.* Wilmington, DE: Michael Glazier, 1986.

Schillebeeckx, Edward. *The Real Achievement of Vatican II.* New York: Herder & Herder, 1992.

Stacpoole, Alberic, ed. *Vatican II: By Those Who Were There.* London: Geoffrey Chapman, 1986.

Van Beeck, Franz. *Catholic Identity after Vatican II.* Chicago: Loyola University Press, 1985.

Vorgrimler, Herbert, ed. *Commentary on the Documents of Vatican II*, 5 vols. New York: Herder & Herder, 1967-69.

Weltgen, Ralph. *The Rhine Flows into the Tiber.* New York: Hawthorne Books, 1967.

Ecclesiology (Parts I and III)

General:

Arbuckle, Gerald. *Out of Chaos: Refounding Religious Congregations.* Mahwah, NJ: Paulist Press, 1988.

Boff, Leonardo. *Ecclesiogenesis.* Maryknoll, NY: Orbis Books, 1986.

Bokenkotter, Thomas. *A Concise History of the Catholic Church.* Garden City, NY: Doubleday, 1977.

_____ *Essential Catholicism.* Garden City, NY: Image Books, 1986.

Catechism of the Catholic Church. Washington: United States Catholic Conference, 1994.

Chittister, Joan. *Winds of Change: Women Challenge the Church.* Kansas City: Sheed & Ward, 1986.

Cunningham, Lawrence. *The Catholic Heritage.* New York: Crossroad, 1985.

Dwyer, John. *Church History, Twenty Centuries of Catholic Christianity.* New York: Paulist Press, 1985.

Dulles, Avery. *Models of the Church.* Garden City, NY: Image Books, 1987.

_____ *The Reshaping of Catholicism: Current Challenges in the Theology of the Church.* San Francisco: Harper & Row, 1988.

_____ *The Resilient Church: The Necessity and Limits of Adaptation.* Garden City, NY: Doubleday, 1977.

Gelpi, Donald. *Pentecostalism: A Theological Viewpoint.* New York: Paulist Press, 1971.

Greeley, Andrew. *The Catholic Experience.* Chicago: University of Chicago Press, 1956.

_____ *The Catholic Myth: The Behavior and Beliefs of American Catholics.* New York: Scribner, 1990.

Johnson, Paul. *A History of Christianity.* New York: Atheneum, 1985.

Kaspar, Walter. *Theology of the Church.* New York: Crossroad, 1989.

Kennedy, Eugene. *Tomorrow's Catholics, Yesterday's Church.* San Francisco: Harper & Row, 1988.

Kloppenburg, Bonaventure. *The Ecclesiology of Vatican II.* Chicago: Franciscan Herald Press, 1974.

Kress, Robert. *The Church: Communion, Sacrament, Communication.* Mahwah, NJ: Paulist Press, 1985.

Küng, Hans. *The Church.* Garden City, NY: Orbis Books, 1986.

Larentin, René. *Catholic Pentecostalism.* Garden City, NY: Image Books, 1978.

Lernoux, Penny. *Hearts on Fire.* Maryknoll, NY: Orbis Books, 1992.

McBrien, Richard. *Catholicism,* (revised, updated edition). San Francisco: Harper, 1993.

Murray, John Courtney. *Religious Liberty: An End and a Beginning.* New York: Macmillan, 1966.

Powell, John. *The Mystery of the Church.* New York: Bruce Publishing, 1967.

Ratzinger, Joseph. *The Ratzinger Report: An Exclusive Interview on the State of the Church.* San Francisco: Ignatius Press, 1985.

Sanks, T. Howland. *Salt, Leaven, and Light: The Community Called Church.* New York: Crossroad, 1992.

Schillebeeckx, Edward. *Church: The Human Story of God.* New York: Crossroad, 1990.

Sullivan, Francis. *The Church We Believe In.* Mahwah, NJ: Paulist Press, 1988.

Tavard, George. *The Church, Community of Salvation: An Ecumencial Ecclesiology.* Collegeville, MN: The Liturgical Press, 1992.

Ware, Ann. *Midwives of the Future: American Sisters Tell Their Story.* Kansas City, MO: Leaven Press, 1985.

Church Leadership

Brockman, James. *Romero, A Life.* Maryknoll, NY: Orbis Books, 1989.

Brown, Raymond, Karl Donfried, and John Reuman, eds. *Peter in the New Testament.* Minneapolis: Augsburg Publishing House, 1973.

Brown, Raymond. *Priest and Bishop: Biblical Reflections.* New York: Paulist Press, 1990.

Empie, Paul and T. Murphy, eds. *Papal Primacy and the Universal Church.* Minneapolis: Augsburg Publishing House, 1974.

Granfield, Patrick. *The Limits of the Papacy.* New York: Crossroad, 1987.

Hebblethwaite, Peter. *In the Vatican.* Bethesda, MD: Adler & Adler, 1986.

_____ *Pope John XXIII, Shepherd of the Modern World.* Garden City, NY: Doubleday, 1985.

_____ *Paul VI, the First Modern Pope.* New York: Paulist Press, 1993.

_____ *The Year of the Three Popes.* Cleveland, OH: Collins, 1978.

Kerrison, Raymond. *Bishop Walsh of Maryknoll.* New York: Putnam, 1962.

Reese, Thomas. *Archbishop: Inside the Power Structure of the American Catholic Church.* San Francisco: Harper & Row, 1989.

_____ *A Flock of Shepherds.* Kansas City: Sheed & Ward, 1993.

Sobrino, Jon. *Archbishop Romero: Memories and Reflections.* Maryknoll, NY: Orbis Books, 1990.

Tang, Dominic. *How Inscrutable His Ways! Memoirs 1951-1981.* Hong Kong: Caritas Printing Centre, 1991, 2nd edition.

Tillard, J. *The Bishop of Rome.* Wilmington, DE: Michael Glazier, 1983.

Wilkes, Paul. *The Education of an Archbishop: Travels with Rembert Weakland.* Maryknoll, NY: Orbis Books, 1993.

Lay Ministry

Bausch, William. *Tradition, Tensions, Transitions in Ministry.* Mystic CT: Twenty-Third Publications, 1982.

Brennan, Patrick. *Re-Imagining the Parish: Base Communities, Adulthood and Family Consciousness.* New York: Crossroad, 1990.

Dolan, Jay, ed. *Transforming Parish Ministry: The Changing Roles of Catholic Clergy, Laity and Women Religious.* New York: Crossroad, 1990.

Hater, Robert. *The Ministry Explosion: A New Awareness of Every Christian's Call to Minister.* Dubuque, IA: William C. Brown, 1979.

John Paul II. *Vocation and Mission of Lay Faithful in the Church and in the World.* Washington, DC: United States Catholic Conference, 1989.

Lawler, Michael. *A Theology of Ministry.* Kansas City, MO: Sheed & Ward, 1990.

Osborne, Kenan. *Ministry: Lay Ministry in the Roman Catholic Church.* New York: Paulist Press, 1993.

Walsh, John. *Evangelization and Justice, New Insights for Christian Ministry.* Maryknoll, NY: Orbis Books, 1982.

Church's Mission (Part II)

Evangelization

Hater, Michael. *News That Is Good: Evangelization for Catholics.* Notre Dame, IN: Ave Maria Press, 1990.

Hillman, Eugene. *Toward an African Christianity, Inculturation Applied.* New York/Mahwah: Paulist Press, 1993.

_____ *Many Paths: A Catholic Approach to Religious Pluralism.* New York: Orbis Books, 1989.

Luzbetak, Louis. *The Church and Cultures: New Perspectives in Missiological Anthropology.* Maryknoll, NY: Orbis Books, 1988.

Pope Paul VI, "Evangelization in the Modern World," in *The Pope Speaks, The Church Documents Quarterly* 21 (#1, 1976): 4-51.

Schineller, Peter. *A Handbook on Inculturation.* New York/Mahwah: Paulist Press, 1990.

Shorter, Aylward. *Toward a Theology of Inculturation.* London: Geoffrey Chapman, 1988.

United States Catholic Bishops, *Heritage and Hope, Evangelization in the United States.* Washington, DC: U.S. Catholic Conference, 1991.

Spirituality

Au, Wilkie. *By Way of the Heart: Towards a Holistic Christian Spirituality.* Mahwah, NJ: Paulist Press, 1989.

Barry, William. *Spiritual Direction & the Encounter with God.* New York/Mahwah, NJ: Paulist Press, 1992.

_____ and William Connolly. *The Practice of Spiritual Direction.* New York: Seabury Press, 1982.

Conn, Joan. *Spirituality and Personal Maturity.* Mahwah, NJ: Paulist Press, 1989.

Cunningham, Lawrence, *The Meaning of Saints.* San Francisco: Harper & Row, 1980.

Eagan, John. *Traveler Toward the Dawn, The Spiritual Journey of John Eagan, S.J.* Chicago: Loyola University Press, 1990.

Egan, Harvey. *What Are They Saying About Mysticism?* New York: Paulist Press, 1982.

Flendors, Carol Lee. *Enduring Grace: Living Portraits of Seven Women Mystics.* San Francisco: Harper, 1990.

Lappin, Peter. *First Lady of the World: A Popular History of Marian Devotion.* New York: Don Bosco, 1988.

Merton, Thomas. *New Seeds of Contemplation.* Norfolk, CT: New Directions, 1961.

Nouwen, Henri. *Making All Things New: An Invitation to the Spiritual Life.* San Francisco: Harper & Row, 1981.

Reuther, Rosemary. *Mary in the Feminine Face of the Church.* Philadelphia: Westminster Press, 1977.

Rohr, Richard. *Near Occasions of Grace.* Maryknoll, NY: Orbis, 1993.

Ecumenism

Baptism, Eucharist and Ministry. Geneva, Switzerland: World Council of Churches, 1982.

Baptism, Eucharist & Ministry 1982-1990, Report on the Process and Responses. Geneva: WCC Publications, 1990.

Congar, Yves. *Diversity and Communion.* Mystic, CT: Twenty-Third Publications, 1985.

Cullman, Oscar. *Unity Through Diversity.* Philadelphia: Fortress Press, 1988.

Dessaux, Jacques. *Twenty Centuries of Ecumenism.* New York/Ramsey, NJ: Paulist Press, 1984.

The Final Report, Anglican-Roman Catholic International Commission. Washington, DC: U.S. Catholic Conference, 1982.

Fries, H. and Karl Rahner, *Unity of the Churches, an Actual Possibility.* Philadelphia: Fortress Press, 1985.

Hughes, John Jay. *Absolutely Null and Void: An Account of the 1896 Papal Condemnation of Anglican Orders.* Washington, DC: Corpus Books, 1968.

Kilcourse, George. *Double Belonging, Interchurch Families and Christian Unity.* New York/Mahwah, NJ: Paulist Press, 1992.

Kilmartin, Edward. *Toward Reunion: The Orthodox and Roman Catholic Churches.* New York: Paulist Press, 1979.

Kinnamon, Michael. *Truth and Community: Diversity and Its Limits in the Ecumenical Movement.* Grand Rapids, MI: Wm. Eerdmans Publishing, 1988.

Lawler, Michael. *Ecumenical Marriage and Remarriage: Gifts and Challenges to the Churches.* Mystic, CT: Twenty-Third Publications, 1990.

Macquarrie, John. *Christian Unity and Christian Diversity.* London: SCM Press Ltd., 1975.

Tavard, George. *A Review of Anglican Orders, The Problem and the Solution.* Collegeville, MN: The Liturgical Press, 1990.

Thurian, Max, ed. *Churches Respond to BEM.* Geneva: World Council of Churches, 1986- . 6 vols. to date.

Ware, Timothy. *The Orthodox Church.* New York: Penguin Books, 1983.

Social Teaching

Coleman, John, ed. *One Hundred Years of Catholic Social Thought.* Maryknoll, NY: Orbis Books, 1991.

Dorr, Donal. *The Social Justice Agenda: Justice, Ecology, Power and the Church,* Maryknoll, NY: Orbis Books, 1991.

_____ *Option for the Poor: A Hundred Years of Vatican Social Teaching.* Maryknoll, NY: Orbis Books, 1983.

Henriot, Peter, ed. *Catholic Social Teaching.* New York: Orbis Books, 1988.

John Paul II. *Centesimus Annus (On the Hundredth Anniversary of Rerum Novarum).* Washington, DC: U.S. Catholic Conference, 1991.

_____ *Laborem Exercens (On Human Work).* Washington, DC: U.S. Catholic Conference, 1981.

_____ *Sollicitudo Rei Socialis (On Social Concern).* Washington, DC: U.S. Catholic Conference, 1988.

Lappe, Francis, and Joseph Collins. *World Hunger: Twelve Myths.* New York: Grove Press, 1986.

Paul VI. *Populorum Progressio (The Development of Peoples).* Washington, DC: U.S. Catholic Conference, 1967.

Schultheis, Michael. *Our Best Kept Secret, the Rich Heritage of Catholic Social Teaching.* Washington, DC: Center for Concern, 1985.

Sobrino, Jon, and Juan Pico. *Theology of Christian Solidarity.* Maryknoll, NY: Orbis Books, 1985.

U.S. Catholic Bishops. *The Challenge of Peace.* Washington, DC: U.S. Catholic conference, 1983.

_____ *Economic Justice for All.* Washington, DC: U.S. Catholic Conference, 1986.

Walsh, Michael, and Brian Davies. *Proclaiming Justice and Peace: Papal Documents from Rerum Novarum through Centesimus Annus.* Mystic, CT: Twenty-Third Publications, 1991.

Sacraments and Liturgy (Part IV)

Bausch, William. *A New Look at Sacraments.* Mystic, CT: Twenty-Third Publications, 1983.

Brunsman, Barry. *New Hope for Divorced Catholics: A Concerned Pastor Offers Alternatives to Annulment.* San Francisco: Harper & Row, 1985.

Coleman, Gerald. *Divorce and Remarriage in the Catholic Church.* New York: Paulist Press, 1988.

Cooke, Bernard. *Sacraments and Sacramentality.* Mystic, CT: Twenty-Third Publications, 1983.

Guzie, Tad. *The Book of Sacramental Basics.* New York: Paulist Press, 1981.

_____ *Jesus and the Eucharist.* New York: Paulist Press, 1974.

Hart, Kathleen and Thomas Hart. *The First Two Years of Marriage: Foundation for Life Together.* New York: Paulist Press, 1983.

Hellwig, Monica. *The Meaning of Sacraments.* Dayton: Pflaum-Standard, 1972.

_____ *The Eucharist and the Hunger of the World.* New York: Paulist Press, 1976.

Kavanagh, Aiden. *The Shape of Baptism: The Rite of Christian Initiation.* New York: Pueblo Publishing Co., 1978.

Kiefer, Robert. *Blessed and Broken: An Exploration of the Contemporary Experience of God in Eucharistic Celebration.* Wilmington, DE: Michael Glazier, 1982.

Lawler, Michael. *Secular Marriage, Christian Sacrament.* Mystic, CT: Twenty-Third Publications, 1985.

_____ *Symbol and Sacrament: A Contemporary Sacramental Theology.* New York/Mahwah: Paulist Press, 1987.

Martos, Joseph. *The Catholic Sacraments.* Wilmington, DE: Michael Glazier, 1983.

Mitchell, Leonel. *The Meaning of Ritual.* New York: Paulist Press, 1977.

Osborne, Kenan. *The Christian Sacraments of Initiation: Baptism, Confirmation, Eucharist.* New York/Mahwah, NJ: Paulist Press, 1987.

_____ *Sacramental Theology, A General Introduction.* New York: Paulist Press, 1988.

Reilly, Challon, and William Roberts. *Partners in Intimacy: Living Christian Marriage Today.* New York: Paulist Press, 1988.

Reilly, Christopher. *Making Your Marriage Work, Growing in Love after Living in Love.* Mystic, CT: Twenty-Third Publications, 1989.

Roberts, William. *Marriage, Sacrament of Hope and Challenge.* Cincinnati: St. Anthony Messenger Press, 1988.

Searle, Mark. *Christening, the Making of Christians.* Essex, Great Britain: Devin Mayhew Ltd., 1977.

Thomas, David. *Christian Marriage, A Journey Together.* Wilmington, DE: Michael Glazier, 1983.

Young, James. *Divorcing, Believing, Belonging.* New York: Paulist Press, 1984.

Current Issues (Part V)

Morality

Avvento, Gennaro. *Sexuality, A Christian View: Toward Formation of Mature Values.* Mystic, CT: Twenty-Third Publications, 1982.

Curran, Charles. *The Living Tradition of Catholic Moral Theology.* Notre Dame, IN: University of Notre Dame Press, 1992.

Dominion, Jack, and Hugh Montefiore. *God, Sex and Love.* Philadelphia: Trinity Press International, 1989.

Dwyer, John. *Human Sexuality: A Christian View.* Kansas City, MO: Sheed & Ward, 1987.

Genovesi, Vincent. *In Pursuit of Love, Catholic Morality and Human Sexuality.* Wilmington, DE: Michael Glazier, 1987.

Gula, Richard. *What Are They Saying about Moral Norms?* New York: Paulist Press, 1982.

_____ *Reason Informed by Faith, Foundations of Catholic Morality.* New York: Paulist Press, 1989.

Hanigan, James. *As I Have Loved You: the Challenge of Christian Ethics.* Mahwah, NJ: Paulist Press, 1986.

_____ and Richard McCormick. *Readings in Moral Theology, No. 8: Dialogue About Catholic Sexual Teaching.* New York/Mahwah: Paulist Press, 1993.

_____ *Homosexuality: The Test Case for Christian Social Ethics.* New York: Paulist Press, 1988.

_____ *What Are They Saying about Sexual Morality?* New York: Paulist Press, 1982.

Keane, Philip. *Sexual Morality, A Catholic Perspective.* New York: Paulist Press, 1977.

MacNamara, Vincent. *Love, Law and Christian Life: Basic Attitudes of Christian Morality.* Wilmington, DE: Michael Glazier, 1988.

Mahoney, John. *The Making of Moral Theology.* New York: Clarendon Press, 1990.

May, William. *Introduction to Moral Theology.* Huntington, IN: Our Sunday Visitor, 1994.

O'Connell, Timothy. *Principles for a Catholic Morality.* San Francisco: Harper, 1990.

U.S. Bishops. *Human Sexuality: A Catholic Perspective for Education and Lifelong Learning.* Washington, DC: U.S. Catholic Conference, 1990.

Liberation Theology

Alvarado, Elvia, and Medea Benjamin, ed. *Don't Be Afraid, Gringo, A Honduran Woman Speaks from the Heart.* San Francisco: Institute for Food and Development Policy, 1987.

Berryman, Philip. *Liberation Theology.* Oak Park, IL: Meyer-Stone Books, 1987.

Boff, Leonardo. *Church, Charism and Power.* New York: Crossroad, 1985.

_____ and Clodovis. *Introducing Liberation Theology.* Maryknoll, NY: Orbis, 1987.

Casaldáliga, Pedro. *I Believe in Justice and Hope.* Notre Dame, IN. Fides/Claretian, 1978.

Eagleson, John and Philip Scharper, eds. *Puebla and Beyond.* New York: Orbis, 1979.

Ellis, Marc, and Otto Maduro, eds. *Expanding the View: Gustavo Gutierrez and the Future of Liberation Theology.* Maryknoll, NY: Orbis, 1990.

Ferm, Deane. *Profiles in Liberation: Portraits of Third World Theologians.* Mystic, CT: Twenty-Third Publications, 1988.

_____ *Third World Liberation Theologies: An Introductory Survey.* New York: Orbis, 1986.

Ford, John, and ·Darlis Swan. *Twelve Tales Untold: A Study Guide for Ecumenical Reception.* Grand Rapids, MI: William Eerdmans Publishing Co., 1993.

Gutiérrez, Gustavo. *A Theology of Liberation.* Maryknoll, NY: Orbis, 1990.

Hennelly, Alfred, ed. *Santo Domingo and Beyond.* Maryknoll, NY: Orbis, 1993.

Hennelly, Alfred. *Santo Domingo and Beyond.* Maryknoll, NY: Orbis, 1993.

Hooks, Margaret. *Guatemalan Women Speak.* Washington, DC: EPICA, 1993.

Kita, Bernice. *What Prize Awaits Us: Letters from Guatemala.* Maryknoll, NY: Orbis, 1988.

Lernoux, Penny. *Cry of the People.* Garden City, NY: Doubleday, 1980.

MacEoin, Gary, and Nevita Riley. *Puebla: A Church Being Born.* New York: Paulist Press, 1980.

McGovern, Arthur. *Liberation Theology and Its Critics.* Maryknoll, NY: Orbis, 1989.

Medellín Conference of Latin American Bishops. *The Church in the Present-Day Transformation of Latin America in the Light of the Council.* Washington, DC: U.S. Catholic Conference, 1973.

Novak, Michael. *Will It Liberate? Questions about Liberation Theology.* Mahwah, NJ: Paulist Press, 1986.

Segundo, Juan. *Theology and the Church: A Response to Cardinal Ratzinger and a Warning to the Whole Church.* Minneapolis: Winston Press, 1985.

Sigmund, Paul. *Liberation Theology at the Crossroads: Democracy or Revolution?* New York: Oxford University Press, 1990.

Whitfield, Teresa. *Paying the Price: Ignacio Ellacuría and the Murdered Jesuits of El Salvador.* Philadelphia: Temple University Press, 1994.

Other Issues

Arbuckle, Gerald. *Refounding the Church, Dissent for Leadership.* Maryknoll, NY: Orbis, 1993.

Briggs, Kenneth. *Holy Siege, The Year That Shook Catholic America.* San Francisco: Harper, 1992.

Brown, Raymond. *Biblical Reflections on Crises Facing the Church.* New York: Paulist Press, 1975.

Carr, Anne. *Transforming Grace: Christian Tradition and Women's Experience.* San Francisco: Harper & Row, 1988.

Congregation for the Doctrine of the Faith. "Inter Insigniores." in *Vatican II: More Post-Conciliar Documents.* ed. by Austin Flannery. Collegeville, MN: The Liturgical Press, 1982.

Cooke, Bernard, ed. *The Papacy and the Church in the United States.* New York: Paulist Press, 1989.

Cox, Harvey. *The Silencing of Leonardo Boff: The Vatican and Future of World Christianity.* Oak Park, IL: Meyer-Stone, 1988.

Curran, Charles. *Faithful Dissent.* Kansas City, MO: Sheed & Ward, 1986.

_____ *Issues in Sexual and Medical Ethics.* Notre Dame, IN: University of Notre Dame Press, 1978.

_____ *Toward an American Catholic Moral Theology.* Notre Dame, IN: University of Notre Dame Press, 1987.

_____ and Richard McCormick, eds. *Readings in Moral Theology No. 6: Dissent in the Church.* New York/Mahwah: Paulist Press, 1988.

Dulles, Avery. *A Church to Believe In: Discipleship and the Dynamics of Freedom.* New York: Crossroad, 1982.

Hoge, Dean. *The Future of Catholic Leadership: Responses to the Priest Shortage.* Kansas City, MO: Sheed & Ward, 1987.

Kelleher, Stephen. *Divorce and Remarriage for Catholics?* New York: Doubleday, 1973.

May, William, ed. *Vatican Authority and American Catholic Dissent: The Curran Case and Its Consequences.* New York: Crossroad, 1987.

Osborne, Kenan. *Priesthood: A History of Ordained Ministry in the Roman Catholic Church.* Mahwah, NJ: Paulist Press, 1988.

Parent, Remi. *A Church of the Baptized: Overcoming the Tension between the Clergy and the Laity.* Mahwah, NJ: Paulist Press, 1989.

Provost, James, and Knut Wolf. *Collegiality Put to the Test.* Philadelphia: Trinity Press, 1990.

Reuther, Rosemary. *Women-Church: Theology and Practice of Feminist Liturgical Communities.* San Francisco: Harper & Row, 1985.

Schoenherr, R. and Young, L. *Full Pews and Empty Altars: Demographics of the Priest Shortage in U.S. Catholic Dioceses.* Madison: University of Wisconsin Press, 1993.

Sullivan, Francis. *Magisterium.* Mahwah, NJ: Paulist Press, 1983.

Swidler, Leonard and Arlene Swidler, eds. *Women Priests: A Catholic Commentary on the Vatican Declaration.* New York: Paulist Press, 1977.

Támez, Elsa, ed. *Through Her Eyes, Women's Theology from Latin America.* Maryknoll, NY: Orbis, 1989.

U.S. Bishops. *Partners in the Mystery of Redemption: A Pastoral Response to Women's Concerns for Church and Society.* Washington, DC: U.S. Catholic Conference, 1988.

Wallace, Ruth. *They Call Her Pastor: A New Role for Catholic Women.* Albany: State University of New York Press, 1992.

Future Church (Part VI)

Bühlmann, Walbert. *The Coming of the Third Church, An Analysis of the Present and Future of the Church.* Maryknoll, NY: Orbis, 1978.

_____ *The Church of the Future: A Model for the Year 2001.* Maryknoll, NY: Orbis, 1986.

Donovan, Vincent. *Christianity Rediscovered.* Maryknoll, NY: Orbis, 1982.

_____ *The Church in the Midst of Creation.* Maryknoll, NY: Orbis, 1989.

Dunn, Joseph. *The Rest of Us Catholics: The Loyal Opposition.* Springfield, IL: Templegate Publishers, 1993.

Flannery, Edward. *The Anguish of the Jews: Twenty-Three Centuries of Anti-Semitism.* New York: Macmillan, 1965.

Gallup, George and Jim Cassidy. *The American Catholic People: Their Beliefs, Practices and Values.* Garden City, NY: Doubleday, 1987.

Greeley, Andrew, and Mary Durken. *How to Save the Catholic Church.* New York: Viking Press, 1984.

Griffiths, Bede. *The Marriage of East and West.* London: Fount Paperbacks, 1983.

Häring, Bernard. *My Witness for the Church.* New York: Paulist Press, 1992.

Hegy, Pierre, ed. *The Church in the Nineties, Its Legacy, Its Future.* Collegeville, MN: The Liturgical Press, 1993.

Knitter, Paul. *No Other Name? A Critical Survey of Christian Attitudes toward the World Religions.* Maryknoll, NY: Orbis, 1985.

Leddy, Mary, Bishop Remi De Roo and Douglas Roche. *In the Eye of the Catholic Storm: The Church Since Vatican II.* San Francisco: Harper, 1992.

Lernoux, Penny. *People of God, the Struggle for World Catholicism.* New York: Viking Penguin, 1989.

Lindbeck, George. *The Future of Roman Catholic Theology.* Philadelphia: Fortress Press, 1970.

Metz, Johann. *The Emergent Church: The Future of Christianity in a Post-Bourgeois World.* New York: Crossroad, 1980.

Neuhaus, Richard. *The Catholic Moment. The Paradox of the Church in the Postmodern World.* San Francisco: Harper & Row, 1987.

O'Malley, William. *Why Be Catholic?* New York: Crossroads, 1994.

Panikkar, Raymundo. *The Intra-Religious Dialogue.* Mahwah, NJ:Paulist Press, 1978.

Pawlikowski, John. *What Are They Saying about Christian-Jewish Relations?* New York: Paulist Press, 1980.

Rausch, Thomas. *Authority and Leadership in the Church. Past Directions and Future Possibilities.* Wilmington, DE: Michael Glazier, 1989.

Walsh, Michael. *Opus Dei: An Investigation into the Secret Society Struggling for Power Within the Roman Catholic Church.* San Francisco: Harper, 1992.

Periodicals and Magazines and Newspapers

(The brief comments are written by the publication in question)

1. *America*, the National Catholic Weekly. Award-winning journal of opinion published by Jesuits. Features crisp editorials and incisive articles on current events and contemporary theology.

2. *Commonweal.* Bi-weekly opinion magazine of liberal Catholics published by laypersons. A review of public affairs, religion, literature, the arts. Features widest diversity of views.

3. *Desert Call.* Fosters contemplation for everyone who refuses to be casual about God. Is earthy and mystical, critical and creative, Catholic and ecumenical, traditional and visionary, prophetic and practical. Quarterly.

4. *The Family* - A Catholic Perspective. Stories and articles that address issues facing today's families. Helps parents nurture their families' unique Catholic culture. Monthly.

5. *Lay Witness.* Monthly newsletter of Catholics United for the Faith. Has earned a reputation as "racing form" for Vatican watchers.

6. *The Other Side.* The liveliest, most creative periodical available on issues of peace, justice and Christian faith. Bimonthly.

7. *New Oxford Review.* Will knock your socks off. Defies ideological pigeonholing. Intellectuals engaging the secular. Uncompromisingly Catholic but ecumenical. Monthly.

8. *St. Anthony Messenger.* Colorful, inspiring reading for the modern Catholic whose belief is steeped in a rich, abiding tradition. Always current and readable and on target with topics Catholics want and need to know more about. Monthly.

9. *Theology Digest.* Condensations of significant articles from 400 foreign-language and some English journals. Quarterly.

10. *The Catholic World.* Published by Paulist Fathers. Each issue focuses on one topic, addressing moral and religious questions asked by people today. Bi-monthly.

11. *The Catholic World Report.* International news monthly for anyone seeking to keep informed. Editorial offices close to the Vatican and worldwide reporters offer balanced presentation of world events and the most complete and insightful coverage of the church in Rome and abroad.

12. *U.S. Catholic.* For everyday Catholics who want to talk about real issues facing them in their everyday lives. Carries on a continuing conversation with its readers. Monthly.

Catholic Newspapers. (Descriptions of first four by Lutheran theologian Martin Marty in *Religion Watch*, July/August 1987.)

1. *National Catholic Reporter.* Progressive, specializes in controversies other Catholic publications might not handle. Often dissents from the Vatican on issues. Extensive coverage of peace and justice issues. Weekly.

2. *National Catholic Register.* Moderately conservative. Stresses in-depth and nonconfrontational reporting on social issues and positive developments in the church. Features developments in the European and Latin American churches. Weekly.

3. *Our Sunday Visitor.* Mainstream moderate. Supports Vatican teachings but does not attack dissenters on Vatican II changes. Fair and wide-ranging church coverage. Weekly.

4. *The Wanderer.* Militantly conservative. Convinced that most U.S. bishops are soft on liberalism and going in opposite direction from the Vatican. Frequently attacks church leaders. Weekly.

5. *L'Osservatore Romano.* Reports news of the Apostolic See with emphasis on the pope's activities and speeches. Weekly English edition available Via del Pelegrino, 00120 Vatican City, Europe.

Documentary Sources: The best is *Origins* (biweekly). *The Pope Speaks* is also helpful. For statements and letters by the U.S. bishops and the more important papal encyclicals, the United States Catholic Conference office of publishing services in Washington, D.C. is outstanding.

Index

Spiritual Exercises (Ignatius of Loyola), 222-23, 225
spirituality, 112, 375-76, 398-401; Anglican, 116-17; biblical, 123; Catholic, 118-22; creation, 129; ecumenical, 123; feminist, 128; liturgical, 123; lay, 122; Lutheran, 117; Orthodox, 116; "spirit," 124; Vatican II, 122
The Splendor of the Truth (Pope John Paul II), 294-98
Statement on Capital Punishment (NCCA), 306-7
Stephen, St., 120
Stoll, David, 411
Stroessner, 313
subsidiarity, 167, 366
succession, apostolic, 155, 186, 409; of ordination or apostolic teaching, 194-95
Suenens, Josef, Cardinal, 26, 127
superstition, 121
Swaggart, Jimmy, 413
Syllabus of Errors, 35
synod of bishops, 41-43, 336-37

Taizé, 206
Tang, Dominic, Archbishop, 184, 189
Tauler, 115
Teilhard de Chardin, Pierre, 225
Teresa of Avila, 102, 104, 115, 386
Teresa, Mother, 49, 71. 220, 227
Thérèse of Lisieux, St., 102, 115
terna, 193
theology, 8; "signs of the times," 162; kingdom of God, 163-64
A Theology of Liberation (Gutiérrez), 326
They Call Her Pastor (Wallace), 353
Thomas More, St., 102, 120
Tillich, Paul, 378
tradition, 10, 34
Transforming Grace (Carr), 353
Trautman, Donald, Bishop, 340
Trent, Council of, 21, 223, 277
Trujillo, Alfonso, Archbishop, 318
Tutu, Desmond, Archbishop, 156

Uniates, 154, 213, 410
Unitatis Redintegratio, 32-33, 132-33
unity, 333
Unity of the Churches (Rahner and Fries), 358
Untener, Kenneth, Bishop, 346
ultramontanism, 212

Vatican, 207-8
In the Vatican (Hebblethwaite), 202
Vatican I, 21, 29, 185, 214
Vatican II, 12-15, 19-28, 43-44, 214, 372
Vincent de Paul, St., 120
Vischer, Lukas, 414-15
Voltaire, 223

Waldensians, 221
Wallace, Ruth, 353
Walsh, Archbishop, 184
The Wanderer, 361
war, 307-8
Weakland, Rembert, Archbishop, 14, 337, 350, 356, 358, 359-60, 397, 406
Weaver, Mary Jo, 353
Wesley, John and Charles, 117, 136
Willebrands, Cardinal, 410
Woman to Woman (Zagano), 353
Women-Church (Ruether), 353
Women, Ministry, and the Church (Chittister), 353
Women and Sexuality (Cahill), 353
Women and the Word (Schneiders), 353
Women's Spirituality (Conn), 353
word of God, 102
World Council of Churches (WCC), 133, 139-40, 152, 157, 243
Wyczinski, Archbishop, 184

Zagano, Phyllis, 353